A HISTORY OF
MATRIMONIAL INSTITUTIONS

A HISTORY OF
Matrimonial Institutions

CHIEFLY IN ENGLAND AND THE UNITED STATES WITH AN INTRO-
DUCTORY ANALYSIS OF THE LITERATURE AND THE
THEORIES OF PRIMITIVE MARRIAGE
AND THE FAMILY

BY

GEORGE ELLIOTT HOWARD Ph.D.

PROFESSORIAL LECTURER IN THE UNIVERSITY OF CHICAGO AUTHOR OF "LOCAL
CONSTITUTIONAL HISTORY OF THE UNITED STATES"

VOLUME TWO

CHICAGO
THE UNIVERSITY OF CHICAGO PRESS
CALLAGHAN & COMPANY

LONDON
T. FISHER UNWIN, PATERNOSTER SQUARE
1904

CC

Copyright 1904
The University of Chicago

Entered at Stationers' Hall

May, 1904

TO

Alice Frost Howard

HER HUSBAND DEDICATES THIS BOOK IN
GRATEFUL RECOGNITION OF HER
AID IN MAKING IT

ANALYTICAL TABLE OF CONTENTS

VOLUME ONE

PART I

ANALYSIS OF THE LITERATURE AND THE THEORIES OF PRIMITIVE MATRIMONIAL INSTITUTIONS

xi

PART III

MATRIMONIAL INSTITUTIONS IN THE UNITED STATES

VOLUME THREE

PART III — *Continued*

PART II
MATRIMONIAL INSTITUTIONS IN ENGLAND
Continued

CHAPTER XI

HISTORY OF SEPARATION AND DIVORCE UNDER ENGLISH AND ECCLESIASTICAL LAW

[BIBLIOGRAPHICAL NOTE XI.—For divorce among the Athenians Meier and Schömann's *Der attische Process* (Berlin, 1883–87) is important. Assistance has also been given by Hruza, *Ehebegründung nach att. Rechte* (Leipzig, 1892); *idem, Polygamie und Pellikat* (Leipzig, 1894); and Müller and Bauer, "Die griech. Privat- und Kriegsalterthümer" (1893), in Müller's *Handbuch*. The Hebrew law on the subject is well treated by Mielziner, *The Jewish Law of Marriage and Divorce* (Cincinnati, 1884); and especially by Amram, in his excellent *Jewish Law of Divorce* (Philadelphia, 1896). In his "Divorce on Condition," in the *Green Bag*, III, August, 1891, the last-named writer has described a curious device for escaping marriage with a brother-in-law and employed also in cases of long absence. Besides the works of Stubbe, Duschak, Döllinger, and Lichtschein, elsewhere noticed, see Selden, *Uxor ebraica* (Frankfort, 1673), or the same in his *Opera*, II (London, 1726); Fraenkel, *Grundlinien des mosaisch-talmud. Eherechts* (Breslau, 1860); Saalschuetz, *Das mosaische Recht* (2d ed., Berlin, 1853); and Meyer, *Die Rechte der Israeliten, Athener, und Römer* (Leipzig, 1862–66).

The leading work on Roman divorce is Wächter's *Ueber die Ehescheidungen* (Stuttgart, 1821). There is also a good account in the seventh and eighth chapters of Hasse's *Das Gütterrecht der Ehegatten nach röm. Recht* (Berlin, 1824). Savigny has an article on "Die erste Ehescheidung in Rom," in *Abhandlungen der könig. Akad. der Wiss. in Berlin, 1814–16* (Berlin, 1818). Very important also is Rein, *Das röm. Privatrecht* (Leipzig, 1836); and on divorce in connection with the alleged depravation of morals at the close of the republic there is a fine passage in Lecky, *European Morals* (3d ed., New York, 1881). The subject is treated by Marche, *Historia juris civilis de divortiis* (Leipzig, 1764); Langeron, *Du divorce en droit romain* (Paris, 1857); Morael, *Droit romain: du divorce* (Paris, 1888); and Combier, *Du divorce en droit romain* (Paris, 1880). Esmein, *Mélanges* (Paris, 1886), has a chapter dealing in part with Roman divorce; and in the same volume may be found the best existing treatment of adultery in connection with the *Lex Julia de adulteriis*. With other matter this law is also considered by Gessert, *Ad leg. Jul. de adult. coerc.* (Würtem-

3

berg, 1795); Haupt, *De poena adulterii ex leg. Jul.* (Leipzig, 1797);
Jörs, *Die Ehegesetze des Augustus* (Marburg, 1894); and Bennecke in
his able monograph *Die strafrechtliche Lehre vom Ehebruch* (Marburg,
1884), bringing the general history of his subject down to the middle
of the fifteenth century. In this connection have likewise been of
service Sohm's *Institutes* and the works of Fustel de Coulanges,
Hölder, Rossbach, Karlowa, Unger, Maine, Marquardt, and Zhishman
elsewhere described. The ground of the chapter is mainly covered by
Woolsey, *Divorce and Divorce Legislation* (2d ed., New York, 1882);
and Glasson, *Le mariage civil et le divorce* (2d ed., Paris, 1880); as also
by the general works of Popp, *Ehescheidung* (Amberg and Sulzbach,
1800); Tissot, *Le mariage, la séparation et le divorce* (Paris, 1868);
Thwing, *The Family* (Boston, 1887); Gide, *La femme* (2d ed., Paris,
1885); Scheurl, *Das gemeine deutsche Eherecht* (Erlangen, 1882); and
there is a concise historical account by Friedericus, *De divortio
meditationes* (Leipzig, 1842).

For the origin and early development of the Christian doctrine,
besides the Scriptures, the principle sources are, of course, the writings of the Fathers and the provisions of the first ecclesiastical
councils. The most important monograph is Geffcken's *Zur Geschichte
der Ehescheidung vor Gratian* (Leipzig, 1894). The subject is treated
in Moy, *Das Eherecht der Christen* (Regensburg, 1833). There is a
good account by Loening, *Geschichte des deutschen Kirchenrechts*
(Strassburg, 1878); and another by Meyrick in his article "Marriage,"
in the second volume of the *Dict. of Christ. Antiquities*. The rigid
theological point of view is taken by Watkins, *Holy Matrimony*
(London, 1895); and Luckock, *History of Marriage* (London, 1894).
Among similar works, mainly controversial, may be consulted Ap
Richard, *Marriage and Divorce* (London, 1888); Caverno, *Treatise on
Divorce* (Madison, 1889); Hovey, *The Scriptural Law of Divorce*
(Philadelphia, 1866), Greve, *Die Ehescheidung nach der Lehre des
Neuen Testamentes* (Leipzig, 1873); and the anonymous *Ueber den
einzig wahren Ehescheidungsgrund in der christ. Kirche* (Bayreuth,
1838). Standard Catholic treatises are Cigoi,*Die Unauflösbarkeit der
christ. Ehe* (Paderborn, 1895); Didon, *Indissolubilité et divorce* (4th
ed., Paris, 1880); or the German translation of the same by Schneider
(Regensburg, 1893) ; Roskovány, *De matrimonio in eccle. cath.*
(Augustae Vindelicorum, 1837); Scheicher-Binder, *Praktisches Hand-
buch des kath. Eherechts* (4th ed., Freiburg, 1891); and especially
Perrone, *De matrimonio christ.* (Leodii, 1861). Pompen has a special
Tractatus de dispensationibus et de revalidatione mat. (2d ed.,
Amsterdam, 1897).

On Germanic law and custom see Tacitus's *Germania;* the *Monu-
menta Germaniae Historica;* and the collections of Thorpe, Schmid,

and Liebermann. Heussler's *Institutionen,* Weinhold's *Deutsche Frauen,* Grimm's *Rechtsalterthümer,* Brunner's *Rechtsgeschichte,* and the similar works of Schroeder, Zoepfl, and Walter have all been consulted. The penitentials, containing evidence of compromise between Teutonic usage and the strict dogmas of the church, may be found in Thorpe, *Ancient Laws;* Haddan and Stubbs, *Councils;* Wasserschleben, *Bussordnungen* (Halle, 1851); and Schmitz, *Bussbücher* (Mayence, 1883). These have largely superseded the older works of Kuntsmann, *Die lateinischen Poenitentialbücher der Angelsachsen* (Mayence, 1844); and Hildebrand, *Untersuchungen über die germ. Poenitentialbücher* (Würzburg, 1851). The penitentials are analyzed by Bennecke, Esmein, and Freisen; also by Hinschius, "Das Ehescheidungsrecht nach den angelsäch. und frank. Bussordnungen," in *Zeitschrift für deutsches Recht,* XX; and Rosenthal, *Die Rechtsfolgen des Ehebruchs nach kan. und deutsch. Recht* (Würzburg, 1880). In this connection may also be read Heller, *Ueber die Strafe des Ehebruchs* (Ulm, 1773); Wächter, *Abhandlungen aus dem Strafrechte* (Leipzig, 1835), I, dealing with *Entführung* and *Nothzucht;* Wilda, *Strafrecht* (Halle, 1842); and Pollen, *Fatal Consequences of Adultery* (London, 1772), giving literary and other curiosities of the subject. A useful book is Boehmer's *Ueber die Ehegesetze im Zeitalter Karls des Grossen* (Göttingen, 1826), discussing the inconsistency of temporal and ecclesiastical legislation regarding divorce; as is also Sdralek's *Hinkmars Gutachten über die Ehescheidung des Königs Lothar II.* (Freiburg, 1881).

Primary sources for the settlement of the canon law on the subject of divorce are the *Decretum* of Gratian and the other materials comprised in Richter-Friedberg's *Corpus juris canonici.* For England Johnson's *Canons* and Godolphin's *Repartorium canonicum* (3d ed., London, 1687) are serviceable. The state of the law in the age of the decretalists may be learned from Wunderlich's edition of Tancred's *Summa de matrimonio* (Göttingen, 1841); and for its historical development the great works of Esmein and Freisen, elsewhere mentioned, are indispensable. Schulte's *Lehrbuch* and the *Lehrbuch* of Friedberg cover the subject. In connection with the rise of the jurisdiction of the church should be read Sohm, "Die geist. Gerichtsbarkeit im frank. Reich," in *ZKR.,* IX (Tübingen, 1870). For the matrimonial experiences of Margaret of Scotland, illustrating the facility of divorce by indirect methods under the canon law, see Tait's article in the *Dict. of Nat. Biog.,* XXXVI; and similar material in the *Reports of the Historical Manuscripts Commission.* For the literature relating to the Council of Trent consult Bibliographical Note VII.

The foundation of the Protestant doctrine of divorce was laid by Martin Luther. His writings on the subject may, of course, be found in his collected works mentioned in Bibliographical Note IX; or in the source-book of Strampff, *Luther: Ueber die Ehe* (Berlin, 1857); while the more important papers are reprinted in Vol. II of the *Kleinere Schriften Dr. Martin Luthers: von Ehe- und Klostersachen* (Bielefeld and Leipzig, 1877). An earlier book of a somewhat similar character is Froböse's *Dr. Martin Luther's ernste, kräftige Worte über Ehe und eheliche Verhältnisse* (Hanover, 1825). In the sixteenth century Luther's relatively conservative teaching regarding the scriptural grounds of divorce is adopted in the main by the theologians Brenz, *Wie yn Ehesachen . . . . zu Handeln* (1530); Bugenhagen, *Von Ehebruch und Weglaufen* (1539); also in the collections of Sarcerius, below mentioned; Chemnitz, *Examen concilii tridentini* (Frankfort, 1615); Beza, *Tractatio de repudiis et divortiis* (Geneva, 1569); the jurists Kling, *Matrimonialium causarum tractatus* (1st ed., Frankfort, 1553; 3d ed., here cited, 1577), being a reprint of the title "De nuptiis" of his *Enarrationes in Institutiones* (1542); Beust, *Tractatus de jure connubiorum* (3d ed., Leipzig, 1592); *idem, Tractatus de sponsalibus et matrimoniis* (Wittenberg, 1586); Schneidewin, *Commentarius in Institutiones* (1st ed., Wittenberg, 1571); and *idem, De nuptiis* (Jena, 1585), being a part of the earlier work published by the heirs after the author's death. In the seventeenth century the more stringent tendency is represented by the theologians Bidembach, *De causis matrimonialibus tractatus* (Frankfort, 1608); Mentzer, *De conjugio tractatus* (Wittenberg, 1612); and by the jurists Cypräus, *De connubiorum jure* (Frankfort, 1605); Nicolai, *Tractatus de repudiis et divortiis* (Dresden, 1685); and Brouwer, *De jure connubiorum* (Amsterdam, 1665), whose book has the distinction of being placed on the *Index*. On the other hand, in the age of Luther a more liberal direction is taken by Erasmus, *Annat. in Nov. Testam.* (Basel, 1515); whose influence, according to Richter, is felt by Zwingli, "Ordnung wie zu Zürich . . . . über eelich sachen gericht soll werden" (1525): in Richter, *Kirchordnungen*, I, 21, 22; and his "Commentary on Matthew xix, 9," in Richter, *Beiträge*, 7; and by Zwingli's disciple Bullinger, *Der christlich Ehestand* (1579). The laxer tendency is also represented by Lambert of Avignon, *De sacro conjugio* (Strasburg, 1524); Melanchthon, "De conjugio" (1551), in *Opera*, I (Erlangen, 1828); Bucer, whose work is mentioned in connection with the English Reformation; the jurist Monner, *Tract. de matrimonio et clandestinis conjugiis* (Jena, 1561); and in the seventeenth century especially by Hülsemann, *Extensio breviarii theologici* (3d ed., Leipzig, 1655); and the jurist Forster, *De nuptiis* (Wittenberg, 1617). The more essential parts of the works of Luther, Brenz, Bugenhagen, Bullinger, and Melanchthon may also be found in that remarkable treasury of materials gathered by Sarcerius, *Ein Buch vom heiligen Ehestande* (1553); enlarged under title *Corpus juris matrimonialis* (Frankfort, 1569).

Heading the modern literature is Richter's able *Beiträge zur Geschichte des Ehescheidungsrechts in der evang. Kirche* (Berlin, 1858), which has the special merit of first classifying the post-Reformation writers on divorce according to their more rigid or more liberal tendencies. The subject is also treated with the usual precision and thoroughness in his *Lehrbuch des kath. und evang. Kirchenrechts* (8th ed., Leipzig, 1886). Important likewise are Strippelmann, *Das Ehescheidungsrecht* (Cassel, 1854); Goeschen, "Ehe," in Herzog's *Encyclopaedie*, III, 666–707 (Stuttgart and Hamburg, 1855); Hauber, "Ehescheidung im Reformations-Jahrhundert," in *Jahrbücher für deutsche Theologie* (1857), II; Hubrich, *Das Recht der Ehescheidung* (Berlin, 1891); Buchka, *Das mecklenburgische Ehescheidungsrecht* (Wismar, 1885); Gräbner, *Ueber Desertion und Quasidesertion* (Colberg, 1882); and Friedberg, "Beiträge zur Geschichte des brand.-preuss. Eherechts," in *ZKR.*, VIII (Tübingen, 1886–87). Weydmann, *Luther* (Hamburg and Gotha, 1850), has two chapters on Luther's views and his matrimonial life. The second and third parts of Vol. III of Schulte's *Geschichte der Quellen und Litteratur des can. Rechts* (Stuttgart, 1880) provide a mass of valuable biographical and bibliographical material for the whole post-Reformation period.

Richter's well-edited and now exceedingly scarce *Kirchenordnungen des sechszehnten Jahrhunderts* (Weimar, 1846) contains the legislation of the Evangelical churches on marriage and divorce. Especially important for the seventeenth century is the very rare *Des Herzogthums Wirtemberg erneuerte Ehe- und Ehe-Gerichts-Ordnung* (Stuttgart, 1687), marking the beginning of a more liberal treatment of the divorce problem. The ecclesiastical ordinances are analyzed by Goeschen, *Doctrina de matrimonio* (Halle, 1848); and by Dietrich, *Evangelisches Ehescheidungsrecht* (Erlangen, 1892). Original divorce decrees and opinions are collected in Bruckner's *Decisiones juris matrimonialis*, II (Gotha, 1724); and several cases are published by Schleusner, "Anfänge des protest. Eherechts," in *ZKG.*, XIII (Gotha, 1892). The best monographs on the evolution of jurisdiction and process in such causes, aside from the work of Dietrich just mentioned, are Geffcken, "Zur ältesten Geschichte und ehegericht. Praxis des Leipzig. Konsist.," in *ZKR.*, 3. Folge, IV (Freiburg and Leipzig, 1894); Hinschius, "Beiträge zur Geschichte des Desertionsprocesses," *ibid.*, II (Berlin, 1862); and especially Stölzel, *Ueber das landesherrliche Ehescheidungsrecht* (Berlin, 1891), the first part of which having already appeared in *ZKR.*, XVIII (Freiburg and Tübingen, 1883). Stölzel holds that the authority of the chief magistrate to grant divorce is originally a right of episcopal dispensation, and that his authority is not superseded by the imperial law of 1875. On the controversy growing out of this dual question see Meurer, *Das landesherrliche Ehe-*

scheidungsrecht (Freiburg, 1891); and compare Scheurl, " Die Ablösung des Eherechts von dem Kirchenrecht," in *ZKR.*, XIII (Tübingen, 1876); Buchka, " Das Eheschliessungsrecht," *ibid.*, XVI; Sicherer, *Personnenstand und Eheschliessung* (Erlangen, 1879); the two dissertations of Wasserschleben, each entitled *Das Ehescheidungsrecht kraft landesh. Machtvollkommenheit* (Giessen, 1877; Berlin, 1880); and Hinschius, *Das Reichsgesetz* (3d ed., 1890). On the rise of the early consistorial courts see especially Mejer, "Anfänge des Wittenberger Consistoriums," in *ZKR.*, XIII (Tübingen, 1876); *idem*, " Zur Geschichte des ältesten protest. Eherechts," *ibid.*, XVI (Tübingen, 1881); both articles being reprinted with other matter in his *Zum Kirchenrecht des Reformationsjahrhunderts* (Hanover, 1891).

Since the Reformation the questions of the proper grounds of divorce and of the remarriage of divorced persons have given rise to perennial discussion. Among the many writings so produced may be mentioned Gerlach, *Kirchenrechtliche Untersuchung* (Erlangen, 1839); Savigny, "Darstellung der in den preuss. Gesetzen über die Ehescheidung unternommenen Reform," in *Vermischte Schriften*, V (Berlin, 1850); Müller, *Ueber Ehescheidung und Wiederverehlichung geschiedener Gatten* (Berlin, 1855); Hundrich, *Ueber Ehen und Scheidungen* (Breslau, 1855); Seidler, *Beiträge zur Reform der preuss. Gesetzgebung* (Nordhausen, 1861); Hoyer, *Die Ehescheidungsfrage* (Berlin, 1859); Scheurl, *Zur praktischen Lösung der Ehescheidungsfrage* (Nürnberg, 1861); Harless, *Die Ehescheidungsfrage* (Stuttgart, 1861); Bräunig, *Das Recht der Ehescheidung* (Zwickau, 1861); Huschke, *Was lehrt Gottes Wort über die Ehescheidung?* (Leipzig and Dresden, 1860); *idem, Beleuchtung der Einwürfe gegen meine Schrift* (Leipzig and Dresden, 1861). Among the many Latin dissertations on the subject are Majer, *De separatione cohabitationis* (Tübingen, 1675); Eckstein, *De divortio ex causa desertionis* (Tübingen, 1675); Wagner, *De divortio, et convictus conjugalis separatione* (Magdeburg, 1723); Memminger, *De divortio propter insidias vitae structas* (Halle, 1738); Struvvius, *De jure divortiorum* (Jena, 1735); Seiff, *De divortio totali* (Giessen, 1740); Mossheim, *De divortio* (Jena, 1737, 1773); Scopp, *Tractatus, de jure divortiorum* (Frankfort and Leipzig, 1756); Wunderlich, *De separatione a thoro et mensa* (Jena, 1774); and especially the *Controversiae circa jura divortiorum* (2d ed., Halle, 1729), being a reprint of tracts of Kayser, Lange, and Michaelis. For the more recent development of the law in German lands see Schilling, *Der Ehescheidungsprocess in den sächsischen Gerichten* (Leipzig, 1831); *Ehegerichts-Ordnung für den Kanton Basel-Stadtheil* (Basel, 1857); Lauenstein, *Hannoverisches Eherecht und Process-Verfahren* (Hanover, 1869); Peters, *Die Ehescheidung* (Berlin, 1881); Wasserschleben, *Das Ehescheidungsrecht* (Berlin, 1887); Hergenhahn, *Das Eheschliessungs- und Ehescheidungs-Recht* (Hanover, 1890–

93); Ney, *Das Kirchenrecht* (Berlin, 1895); Part II of Lehr, *Le mariage, le divorce, et la séparation* (Paris, 1899); Erles, *Ehescheidungsrecht und Ehescheidungsprozess* (2d ed., Berlin, 1900); and Dedekind, *Das protest. Ehescheidungsrecht und Verwandtes* (Braunschweig, 1872), containing decisions extending over many years with full bibliographical citations.

Of primary importance for the Reformation in England are the writings of Becon, Hooper, Tyndale, and Whitgift, all, with the *Original Letters*, comprised in the publications of the Parker Society and described in Bibliographical Note IX. The radical doctrines of Bucer's *De regno Christi* (1557) were supported by Milton, who published an English version under title of "The Judgment of Martin Bucer," in *Prose Works*, III. Pocock's *Records of the Reformation: The Divorce, 1527–1533* (Oxford, 1870), has placed within easy reach a fine collection of original materials relating to Henry VIII.'s famous cause; and Huth, *The Marriage of Near Kin* (2d ed., London, 1887), has provided a bibliography of the extensive literature to which it has given rise. For the whole period Burnet's *History of the Reformation* (London, 1850) is of service. The state of public sentiment is reflected in Raynold's *Defence of the Judgment of the Reformed Churches* (1609, 1610); the opposing work of Bunny, *Of Divorce for Adultery, And Marrying againe: that there is no sufficient warrant so to do* (Oxford, 1610; prepared for publication in 1595); and the curious *Lawes Resolutions of Womens Rights* (London, 1632). The corruption and injustice often attending the proceedings of the old spiritual courts in actions for annulment of wedlock are revealed in Archbishop Abbot's *The Case of Impotency As Debated in England, In that Remarkable Tryal An. 1613, between Robert, Earl of Essex, and the Lady Frances Howard* (London, 1715), in which King James I. appears in the rôle of pander to the lust of his guilty favorite. The publication of this book, a century after it was written, appears to have been suggested by the similar *Pleadings for the Marquis de Gesvres against the Marchioness* (London, 1714). In this connection may also be mentioned as illustrative material the *Cases of Divorce for Several Causes* (London, 1715); and the *Crim. Con. Actions and Trials and other Legal Proceedings relating to Marriage before the passing of the present Divorce Act* (London, n. d.). With these may be compared the modern case *Ehescheidungs-Process Colin-Campbell* (London, 1886). For the Stuart period have also been used Barrington, *Observations Upon the Statutes* (2d ed., London, 1766); Hale, *History of the Pleas of the Crown* (London, 1800); Coke, *Reports* (London, 1826); his *Institutes;* and the *Reports* of Croke, Kelyng, and Marche.

Milton's "Doctrine and Discipline of Divorce," "Tetrachordon," and "Colasterion" may be found in Vols. III and IV of his *Prose*

Works (London, 1889–90). The only special work on parliamentary divorce is that contained in Macqueen's *Practical Treatise on the Appellate Jurisdiction of the House of Lords and Privy Council* (London, 1842). There are a number of papers relating to the early cases in the *Reports of the Historical Manuscripts Commission.* Morgan, *Marriage, Adultery, and Divorce* (Oxford, 1826), has a long account; and the Lord Roos suit gave rise to *The Case of Divorce and Re-Marriage* (London, 1673). The proceedings in the Northampton case may be found in Howell's *State Trials*, XII.

The *Statutes at Large* and Hansard's *Parliamentary Debates* are, of course, in frequent requisition. For the reform of the laws relating to affinity and divorce important sources are the "First Report of the Commissioners" (affinity), in *Brit. Documents, 1847–8*, XXVIII (London, 1848); "First Report of the Commissioners" (divorce), *ibid., 1852–3*, XL (London, 1853); "Evidence before the Select Committee of the House of Lords, 1844" (divorce), reprinted *ibid.; A Return giving an Outline of Marriage Laws, and the State of the Law of Divorce*, in three parts (London, 1894); *Return of the Number of Divorces*, Part I, "Foreign Countries;" Part II, "Brit. Colonies" (London, 1895–96); and the *Report of the Upper House of the Convocation of Canterbury, 1885* (divorce).

The development of a liberal sentiment in contemporary literature may be traced in *A Treatise Concerning Adultery and Divorce* (London, 1700); *Two Cases: The First of Adultery and Divorce* (London, 1702); the anonymous *Essay upon Divorcement* (London, 1715), replying to Milton; Salmon, *A Critical Essay Concerning Marriage* (London, 1824), accepting Milton's views; *Cri d'une honnête femme qui réclame le divorce* (London, 1770); *Observations on the Marriage Laws particularly in reference to the Case of Desertion* (London, 1815); and *Plea for an Alteration of the Divorce Laws* (London, 1831). With these writers may be compared Ireland, *Nuptiae sacrae* (London, 1801, 1821, 1830), opposing Bishop Horsley's argument that in case of divorce the Scriptures directly prohibit the marriage of the adulterer with the adulteress; Tebbs, *Essay on the Scripture Doctrines of Adultery and Divorce* (London, 1822), too harshly accused of plagiarism by the author of the preceding book; Keble, *Sequel of the Argument against immediately repealing the Laws which treat the Nuptial Bond as indissoluble* (Oxford, 1857), opposing the proposed divorce law; and Browne, *The Marriage of Divorced Persons in Church* (London and New York, 1896), taking a reactionary position.

Important for the chapter are Glasson, *Histoire du droit et des institutions . . . . de l'Angleterre* (Paris, 1882–83); Cleveland, *Woman under the English Law* (London, 1896); Barclay, *La femme anglaise* (Paris, 1896); Lehr, *Le mariage, le divorce, et la séparation* (Paris,

1899); Lecky, *Democracy and Liberty* (New York, 1896); Neubauer, "Ehescheidung im Auslande," in *ZVR.*, VII (Stuttgart, 1887); Swinderen, "Ueber das Gütterrecht der Ehefrau in England," *ibid.*, V (Stuttgart, 1884); Hirschfeld, "The Law of Divorce in England and in Germany," in *Law Quarterly Review*, XIII, October (London, 1897); Montmorency, "The Changing Status of a Married Woman," *ibid.*, April (London, 1897); and the able article "Divorce," in *Law Review* (English), I (London, 1845). The absurd conflicts of English and Scottish law, as illustrated especially by Lolley's case, are discussed in Brougham's "Discourse on the Law of Marriage, Divorce, and Legitimacy" (1835) and his "Speech on the Scotch Marriage and Divorce Bills" (1835), both in *Speeches*, III (London, 1838); Fraser, *Conflict of the Laws in Case of Divorce* (Edinburgh, 1860); and Fergusson, *Reports of Some Decisions* (Edinburgh, 1817); while the proceedings in divorce under the old law are treated by Poynter, *Doctrine and Practice of the Ecclesiastical Courts in Doctors Commons* (London, 1822). Besides the technical treatises of Bishop, Geary, Ernst, and Hammick may be consulted Spence, *Equitable Jurisdiction* (Philadelphia, 1846); Baker, *Husband and Wife and the Married Women's Property Act, 1882* (London, 1882); Barrett-Leonard, *The Position in Law of Woman* (London, 1883); Shelford, *Marriage and Divorce* (London, 1841); Browne, *Divorce and Alimony* (Philadelphia, 1890); Browning, *Practice and Procedure of the Court for Divorce* (London, 1862); *idem*, *Exposition of the Laws of Marriage and Divorce* (London, 1872); and Harrison, *Probate and Divorce* (4th ed., London, 1891). Among the works elsewhere described from which aid has been derived are those of Bracton, Blackstone, Reeves, Burn, Jeaffreson, Lingard, Wharton, Pollock and Maitland, and Haggard, *Reports of Cases in the Consistory Court of London* (London, 1822).

For the literature relating to marriage with a deceased wife's sister and other kindred see a footnote below and the elaborate bibliography by Huth in the work already mentioned.]

I. THE EARLY CHRISTIAN DOCTRINE AND THE THEORY OF THE CANON LAW

a) Historical elements of the Christian teaching.—According to the spirit of the earliest Christian teaching divorce, properly so called, is strongly condemned, though by a strict interpretation of its letter it may not be entirely forbidden. Between the first assertion of the new doctrine and the final triumph of the canonical theory of absolute indissolubility of the marriage bond intervenes a struggle of twelve hundred years, whose more salient features may now be sketched in rapid outline.

To understand the influences which aided in molding the conceptions of the founders of the Christian church relative to marriage and divorce, one must first of all notice the legal and social environment.   By each of the three systems of law with which originally the Christians were most acquainted marriage was treated as a private or lay contract, and its dissolution was therefore freely allowed.   Among the early Greeks, at any rate in the Homeric age, divorce is thought, on slender evidence, to have been entirely unknown,[1] although the practice arose later.   By the Athenian law, which probably was not entirely supplanted by the Roman until 212 A.D.,[2] it was freely granted to either spouse.   The benefit inured, however, mainly to the husband, since to begin proceedings for a divorce the wife was required to present in person to the archon a written statement of her desire; and this, in a society where popular sentiment relegated woman to a seclusion truly oriental, it was in practice exceedingly hard to do.[3]

By the Jewish law, as it still existed at the dawn of the present era, divorce was the one-sided privilege of the man.[4]

[1] HOMER, *Odyssey*, x, 58; xxii, 38.   *Cf.* MEIER-SCHÖMANN, *Der attische Process*, II, 510; GEFFCKEN, *Ehescheidung vor Gratian*, 12; GLASSON, *Le mariage civil et le divorce*, 151; HRUZA, *Polygamie und Pellikat*, 64 n. 7.

[2] GEFFCKEN, *op. cit.*, 15.

[3] Thus Alcibiades "collected a band of men and dragged" his wife Hipparete from the archon, when she attempted to get a divorce on account of his licentiousness: WOOLSEY, *Divorce and Divorce Legislation*, 31.   *Cf.* GEFFCKEN, *op. cit.*, 12, 13; and in general on the Grecian law of divorce see MEIER-SCHÖMANN, *Der attische Process*, II, 510–13; MÜLLER, *Handbuch der Alterthumswissenschaft;* MÜLLER AND BAUER'S *Die griech. Privat- und Kriegsalterthümer* (1893), 152; POPP, *Ehescheidung*, 12–18; TISSOT, *Le mariage*, 53 ff.; GLASSON, *Mariage civil et le divorce*, 151–53; WOOLSEY, *op. cit.*, 25–34.   The unfavorable position of the Athenian woman is discussed by HRUZA, *Die Ehebegründung nach attischem Rechte*, 21, 22; GIDE, *La femme*, 63 ff., 74 ff.; COMBIER, *Du divorce*, 17 ff.; TEBBS, *Essay*, 44 ff.

[4] On Jewish divorce in general see STUBBE, *Die Ehe im alten Testament*, 31, 32; FRAENKEL, *Grundlinien des mosaisch-talmud. Eherechts*, 42 ff.; MEYER, *Die Rechte der Israeliten, Athener und Römer*, II, 370 ff.; DUSCHAK, *Das mosaisch-talmud. Eherecht*, 83 ff.; MICHAELIS, *Ehegesetzen Mosis*, 358, 359; LICHTSCHEIN, *Die Ehe nach mosaisch-talmud. Auffassung*, 85 ff.; MIELZINER, *The Jewish Law of Divorce*, 115 ff.; STRIPPEL-

At most there was only a faint trace of the woman's later right, sanctioned by the Talmud, of demanding a separation.[1] Legally, for the slightest reason, as the school of Hillel justly maintained, the husband could put away the wife by simply handing her a "get" or bill of divorce.[2] By the written law only in two cases, for grave misconduct, was he deprived of this power;[3] though in practice there were several ameliorating conditions which tended to put a check upon arbitrary action.   Thus, while divorce was a private trans-action, certain formalities had to be observed in connection with the "get" which secured the restraining influence of publicity;[4] and in case the wife was unjustly repudiated the

MANN, *Ehescheidungsrecht*, 8 ff.; TISSOT, *Le mariage*, 44 ff.; POPP, *Ehescheidung*, 37 ff.; GLASSON, *Le mariage civil et le divorce*, 145-50; TEBBS, *Essay*, 8 ff.; GIDE, *La femme*, 56 ff.; COMBIER, *Du divorce*, 20 ff.; WOOLSEY, *Divorce and Divorce Legislation*, 10-34; THWING, *The Family*, 40-44; GEFFCKEN, *Ehescheidung vor Gratian*, 14, 16; and espe-cially the admirable book of AMRAM, *The Jewish Law of Divorce*, 22 ff. Among con-troversial works see LUCKOCK, *History of Marriage*, 16 ff.; AP RICHARD, *Marriage and Divorce*, 54 ff., 62-72; BROWNE, *Marriage of Divorced Persons in Church*, 5 ff.

[1] Exod. 21:7-11; as interpreted by AMRAM, *The Jewish Law of Divorce*, 55 ff.; MILTON'S *Prose Works*, III, 185 ff., 322 ff.

[2] "When a man hath taken a wife, and married her, and it come to pass that she find no favour in his eyes, because he hath found some uncleanness in her; then let him write her a bill of divorcement, and give it in her hand, and send her out of his house. And when she is departed out of his house, she may go and be another man's wife."—Deut. 24:1, 2. The Hebrew *Ervath Dabar*, here translated "uncleanness," literally "the nakedness of the matter," or "something unseemly," are the doubtful words. The school of Hillel, or the "broad constructionists of the Bible," held "that the husband need not assign any reason whatever for his divorce, and that he may, for instance, if he please, divorce his wife for spoiling his food." On the other hand, the school of Shammai, or the "strict constructionists," held that sexual immorality was the only scriptural ground of divorce: AMRAM, *op. cit.*, 32 ff. Some writers who accept the view of the school of Shammai for the ancient law admit that, in conse-quence of moral degeneration, the broad constructionists were right for the days of Christ: see DUSCHAK, *op. cit.*, 83 ff.; LICHTSCHEIN, *op. cit.*, 86; MIELZINER, *op. cit.*, 118-20. *Cf.* GEFFCKEN, *op. cit.*, 74; WOOLSEY, *op. cit.*, 15 ff.; TISSOT, *op. cit.*, 49; TEBBS, *op. cit.*, 28-30.

[3] Deut. 22:13-19, 28, 29: The case of the ravisher and that of the husband who falsely accuses the wife of ante-nuptial incontinence; in the latter instance he is not to "put her away all his days," which might be a trifle hard on the woman, unless indeed custom allowed her the right to free herself. See AMRAM, *op. cit.*, 41 ff. By the Mishnah or oral law other restrictions are gradually imposed: *ibid.*, 45.

[4] Before the compilation of the Mishnah the form of the get "was not yet strictly fixed, it only having been required to contain, besides the date and the names of the parties, the words 'Thou art now free for any man.'" But later custom required a more elaborate form and the "presence of at least ten persons."—MIELZINER, *The*

dower, representing the ancient *mohar*, or purchase price of the bride, had to be paid to her from the husband's property.[1] Moreover, some of the limitations of the husband's despotic power recognized by the Mishnah or oral law may already have been in force; and the highest ethical sentiment among the Jews had long been decidedly against too great freedom of divorce. It was the rabbi's duty as much as possible to discourage it and to effect reconciliations between husband and wife.[2]

Negatively, however, it was the later law of Rome which had most to do with shaping the ideas of the Christian Fathers relative to the nature of marriage and the doctrine of divorce.[3] By each of the three ancient forms of marriage the wife came or might come under the power of the husband, *in manu viri*. In the family she was legally regarded as being in a daughter's place, *in loco filiae;*[4] and in each

Jewish Law of Marriage and Divorce, 128. Eventually the procedure in ordering, writing, and delivering the bill of divorce became complex, and it took place before a rabbi specially skilled in the law, who thus had opportunity to check hasty or unjust action through his advice or by refusing to deliver the document: see SAAL-SCHUETZ, *Das mosaische Recht*, 801; MIELZINER, *op. cit.*, 116 ff.; DUSCHAK, *Das mosaisch-talmud. Eherecht*, 95 ff.; especially LICHTSCHEIN, *Die Ehe nach mosaisch-talmud. Auffassung*, 94 ff.; and AMRAM, *op. cit.*, 132-204, both giving full details as to the "get." For the form of the "get" see MEYRICK, "Marriage," *Dict. Christ. Ant.*, II, 1111; AMRAM, *op. cit.*, 157; LICHTSCHEIN, *op. cit.*, 136; DUSCHAK, *op. cit.*, 143, 144; MIELZINER, *op. cit.*, 129; SELDEN, *Uxor ebraica*, III, 24: in *Opera*, IV, 797.

[1] For full details see AMRAM, *op. cit.*, 47, 48, 111-31; MIELZINER, *op. cit.*, 85-89; STUBBE, *Die Ehe*, 20, 21.

[2] AMRAM, *op. cit.*, 25, 45, 78 ff.; LICHTSCHEIN, *op. cit.*, 87 ff.

[3] In general, on the Roman law of divorce, see ESMEIN, *Mélanges*, 17 ff.; SOHM, *Institutes*, 381-84, 341; PUCHTA, *Institutionen*, II, 403; WÄCHTER, *Ehescheidungen bei den Römern*, 19 ff., 62 ff.; GLASSON, *Le mariage civil et le divorce*, 173 ff.; REIN, *Das Privatrecht und der Civilprozess der Römer* (Leipzig, 1858), 445 ff., giving a bibliography of the older literature; POPP, *Ehescheidung*, 18 ff.; TISSOT, *Le mariage*, 56 ff.; BENNECKE, *Ehebruch*, 2 ff.; COMBIER, *Du divorce*, 29 ff.; TEBBS, *Essay*, 55 ff.; ZHISHMAN, *Das Eherecht der orient. Kirche*, 4 ff.; WOOLSEY, *Divorce and Divorce Legislation*, 34-49; GEFFCKEN, *Ehescheidung vor Gratian*, 9-12; STRIPPELMANN, *Ehescheidungsrecht*, 31 ff.

[4] By *confarreatio* and *coemptio* the man acquired the *manus* at the nuptials; but by the *usus*, or the form through which transition was made from the strict to the free marriage, he seems to have gained it only by a year's prescription: when the woman neglected her privilege of *trinoctium*. In the meantime, before the *manus* was acquired, it is a question whether the woman was legally *uxor* or merely *uxoris loco*: KARLOWA, *Die Formen der röm. Ehe*, 68 ff.; ROSSBACH, *Die röm. Ehe*, 156 ff.,

case divorce was solely the husband's prerogative.[1] But by the beginning of our era all these older and stricter forms, with their consequent one-sided right of separation, had been practically superseded by free contract in which the husband and wife were placed on an equal footing.[2] By this form marriage became a simple private agreement. The wife did not pass under the *manu* of the husband. She retained full control of her property, being in this regard, as it were, temporarily deposited at her husband's side;[3] while divorce became a formless private transaction to which the woman was as freely entitled as was the man.[4]

243 ff.; SEHLING, *Die Unterscheidung der Verlöbnisse im kanon. Recht*, 5; SOHM, *Institutes*, 263; GLASSON, *Le mariage civil et le divorce*, 161, 174; HÖLDER, *Die röm. Ehe*, 8 ff.; GEFFCKEN, *Ehescheidung vor Gratian*, 10 n. 4, who cites other authorities; WÄCHTER, *Ehescheidungen bei den Römern*, 28 ff.

[1] Whether the *confarreatio* or sacramental marriage was originally indissoluble even for the man is uncertain; but later it could be dissolved by *diffareatio:* GEFFCKEN, *Ehescheidung vor Gratian*, 11; SOHM, *Institutes*, 381; FUSTEL DE COU-LANGES, *Ancient City*, 60; THWING, *The Family*, 37; GLASSON, *Le mariage civil et le divorce*, 174, 179; ROSSBACH, *Die röm. Ehe*, 128 ff.; and ESMEIN, *Mélanges*, 17 ff., who believes at first *confarreatio* was indissoluble. The *coemptio*, or sale-marriage, was dissolved by remancipation, but only in a family council including the wife's relatives; but whether the *usus* was dissolved in the same way or by prescription we are not informed: GEFFCKEN, *op. cit.*, 11; ROSSBACH, *op. cit.*, 131; WOOLSEY, *Divorce and Divorce Legislation*, 37, 38; REIN, *Privatrecht*, 456; KUNTZE, *Institutionen* (Leipzig, 1869), I, § 776. For the very restricted legal grounds of divorce under the sacramental marriage see UNGER, *Die Ehe*, 71; and in general compare WÄCHTER, *Ehescheidungen*, 62 ff., 94 ff.

[2] After the second Carthaginian war free marriage, or *matrimonium sine conventione in manum mariti*, until that time regarded only as *matrimonium juris gentium*, was accepted as *matrimonium iustum* for plebeians as well as patricians; and it rapidly became the only form observed among the Romans, except that *confarreatio* was preserved for the *flamines;* while the *usus*, though not entirely abolished, was deprived of real significance by a *senatus consultum* under Tiberius which abrogated the effects of *manus* in the domain of private law: GEFFCKEN, *op. cit.*, 11, 12; *ap.* TACITUS, *Annales*, IV, 16; ZHISHMAN, *Das Eherecht der orient. Kirche*, 5. On free marriage see WÄCHTER, *op. cit.*, 77 ff., 95 ff.; ROSSBACH, *op. cit.*, 42-62, 182 ff., 242; KARLOWA, *Die Formen der röm. Ehe*, 79 ff.; ESMEIN, *Le mariage en droit canonique*, II, 46; SOHM, *Institutes*, 263, 267, 268; UNGER, *Die Ehe*, 72 ff.

[3] MAINE, *Ancient Law*, 150.

[4] Freedom of divorce in *matrimonium sine manu* reacted upon the *manus* marriages to the extent that the causes of dissolution were increased in number. "The famous divorce of Sp. Carvilius Ruga [*ca.* 520 A. U. C.] is not only the first Roman divorce in general, but also the first dissolution of a *manus* marriage in which no fault but merely a *vitium corporis* of the woman was assigned" as ground of action.— GEFFCKEN, *op. cit.*, 12. But it is very doubtful whether this is really the first divorce among the Romans: WÄCHTER, *op. cit.*, 82 ff.; COMBIER, *Du divorce*, 42 ff.

No intervention of court or magistrate was essential. So
far, indeed, was carried the theory of absolute liberty of
either spouse to dissolve the contract that, according to
Cicero, the jurists in one case were in doubt whether a
divorce did not legally arise *ipso facto* through the consummation of a second marriage by one of the parties during
the lifetime of the other.[1] Augustus, however, introduced
an important change in the interest of publicity, requiring
the party wishing a divorce to declare to the other his purpose in the presence of seven witnesses, who must be Roman
citizens of full age; otherwise the divorce to be null and
void.[2] But there was no intention through this condition of
establishing the jurisdiction of the state in the matter of
divorce, which remained, as before, a private legal act of the
interested persons. "Still less was it the purpose of the
state to put any material restriction upon the freedom of
divorce."[3] To this liberty there was but one exception.
The freedwoman might not repudiate her patron, her former
master, who had taken her in marriage.[4] In all other cases
the divorce, however arbitrary or unjust, was legally effective. There was no action for the restitution of conjugal

---

The time is uncertain. According to Dionysius, the divorce occurred in 520 A. U. C.;
while AULUS GELLIUS, *Noctes atticae*, IV, 3, §2, xvii, 21, gives confusingly 519 and
523 as the date. Compare WÄCHTER, *op. cit.*, 78 ff.; SAVIGNY, "Ueber die erste.
Ehescheidung in Rom," *Abhand. d. k. Akad. d. Wis. in Berlin*, 1814–16 (Berlin, 1818);
REIN, *Privatrecht*, 450 ff.; KARLOWA, *Rechtsgeschichte*, 188; GLASSON, *Le mariage
civil et le divorce*, 175; WOOLSEY, *Divorce*, 39; THWING, *The Family*, 36; POPP, *Ehescheidung*, 22; LANGERON, *Du divorce*, 17.

[1] CICERO, *De orat.*, I, 40, 56: GEFFCKEN, *op. cit.*, 12.

[2] By the *Lex Julia de adulteriis* of ca. 18 B. C.: GEFFCKEN, *op. cit.*, 15; JÖRS, *Die
Ehegesetze des Augustus*, 36–39. For the best analysis of the *Lex Julia*, with an
account of the preceding history, see ESMEIN, *Mélanges*, 71–169; and compare BEN-
NECKE, *Ehebruch*, 2–6.

[3] GEFFCKEN, *op. cit.*, 15.

[4] By the *Lex Julia et Papia Poppaea* of 9 B. C.; but even this restriction was
narrowed in various ways: GEFFCKEN, *op. cit.*, 15; WÄCHTER, *op. cit.*, 143 ff. It
should be noted, however, that the husband was compelled to put away a wife
guilty of adultery. On this law see JÖRS, *Die Ehegetze des Augustus*, 49 ff.; COMBIER,
Du divorce, 55.

rights; though the responsible party might in certain cases suffer pecuniary damage.[1]

What were the moral and social results of this excessive freedom of divorce? To many the answer seems easy enough; for during the later republic and the early empire the laxity of the nuptial bond became a notorious scandal. At the capital, and especially in the imperial circle, wives as well as husbands gave free rein to their licentious passions. Marriage became unpopular. A recent historian even declares that "almost always" it was ended by divorce.[2] Already in the age of the Gracchi, Metellus the Macedonian cynically exclaimed: "Romans, if we could get along without wives, assuredly none of us would accept so grievous a burden; but since nature has ordained that one cannot live easily with them, nor live without them, let us sacrifice the happiness of our short life to the perpetuity of our nation."[3] Later even the most distinguished and reputable men, as if in mockery of wedlock, put away their wives on purely selfish or absurdly trivial grounds.[4] To believe the exag-

[1] "Scheidung zufolge friedlicher Übereinkunft (*divortium consensu*) sowie einseitige Scheidung aus einem rechtmässigen Grunde, ohne dass eine Verschuldung des entlassenen Gatten vorlag (*divortium bona gratia*), war durchaus erlaubt und hatte für keinen der sich Trennenden nachteilige Konsequenzen, bei willkürlicher Scheidung (*repudium iniustum*) traf ihren Urheber, bei der durch Schuld des einen Teils, namentlich durch Ehebruch veranlassten Scheidung den Schuldigen Nachteil an Geld und Gut."— GEFFCKEN, *op. cit.*, 15, 16; *ap.* ULPIAN, VI, 13. See REIN, *Das Privatrecht*, 433 ff. Forfeiture of property rights for adultery was prescribed by the *Lex Julia de adulteriis:* ESMEIN, *Mélanges*, 114; UNGER, *Die Ehe*, 86; GLASSON, *Le mariage civil et le divorce*, 178, 179. On the legislation of Augustus compare WOOLSEY, *Divorce*, 47, 49, 88, 89, 92-94; and JÖRS, *Die Ehegesetze des Augustus.*

[2] GLASSON, *op. cit.*, 176, 178. Poisoning became a frequent substitute for divorce, especially where marriage by *confarreatio* had been contracted: *ibid.*, 177; WOOLSEY, *op. cit.*, 42, 43.

[3] AULUS GELLIUS, *Noctes atticae*, I, 6.

[4] "We find Cicero repudiating his wife Terentia, because he desired a new dowry; Augustus compelling the husband of Livia to repudiate her when she was already pregnant, that he might marry her himself; Cato ceding his wife, with the consent of her father, to his friend Hortensius, and resuming her after his death; Mæcenas continually changing his wife; Sempronius Sophus repudiating his wife, because she had once been to the public games without his knowledge; Paulus Æmilius taking the same step without assigning any reason, and defending himself by saying, 'My shoes are new and well made, but no one knows where they pinch

gerations of the satirists, one changed his partner almost as often as the cut of his garment.[1] "Seneca denounced this evil with especial vehemence, declaring that divorce in Rome no longer brought with it any shame, and there were women who reckoned their years rather by their husbands than by the consuls."[2] Nevertheless, the abuse was more a result than a cause of the gradual decline of Roman morals during the two centuries following the conquest of Carthage.[3] Doubtless, the state in neglecting to exercise a proper jurisdiction in this field had abrogated a function important for her own stability. Proper restraints would have lessened the evil. But the character of the law was very far from being its sole, or even its primary, cause. "In a purer state of public opinion," well observes Lecky, "a very wide latitude of divorce might probably have been allowed to both parties, without any serious consequences. The right of repudiation which the husband had always possessed was, as we have seen, in the Republic never or very rarely exercised. Of those who scandalised good men by the rapid recurrence of their marriages, probably most, if marriage had been indissoluble, would have refrained from entering into it. . . . . A vast wave of corruption had flowed in upon Rome, and under any system of law it would

---

me.' . . . . Christians and Pagans echoed the same complaint. According to Tertullian 'divorce is the fruit of marriage.' Martial speaks of a woman who had already arrived at her tenth husband; Juvenal, of a woman having eight husbands in five years. But the most extraordinary recorded instance of this kind is related by St. Jerome, who assures us that there existed at Rome a wife who was married to her twenty-third husband, she herself being his twenty-first wife."—LECKY, *Hist. of European Morals*, II, 306, 307, who cites the authorities in the margin. For other illustrations see WOOLSEY, *op. cit.*, 39–49; THWING, *The Family*, 36 ff.

[1] The evidence of the satirists, jurisconsults, and other writers regarding the abuses of divorce, with full citation, is collected by MARQUARDT, *Das Privatleben der Römer*, I, 66–80; and GLASSON, *op. cit.*, 175 ff. See, for example, JUVENAL, *Sat.*, XI, 229; VI, 230; PLAUTUS, *Mercat.*, 805; QUINTILIAN, V, 11, 35.

[2] LECKY, *Hist. of European Morals*, II, 307. *Cf.* SENECA, *De Benef.*, III, 16; also PLUTARCH, *Lives* (London, 1890), 526, 531, 532 (Cato of Utica).

[3] On the depravation of Roman society see UNGER, *Die Ehe*, 80 ff.; COMBIER, *Du divorce*, 51 ff.; POPP, *Ehescheidung*, 23 ff.

have penetrated into domestic life. Laws prohibiting all divorce have never secured the purity of married life in ages of great corruption, nor did the latitude which was accorded in imperial Rome prevent the existence of a very large amount of female virtue."[1] Nor, it may be added, does it appear that the family life of the people at large, notably that of the middle classes in the provinces, was seriously tainted by the social corruption of the capital, where all the causes of moral degeneration were especially active.

It is, however, not surprising that the founders of the Christian church should have regarded the laxity of the marriage bond as a sign, if not the primary cause, of the degradation of Roman society. From the beginning an earnest effort is made so far as possible to restrict the liberty of separation and to prohibit the persons separated on proper grounds from contracting further marriage. The various passages of the New Testament relating to the subject are disjointed and confusing in their details.[2] Many vital questions are either completely ignored or left in such obscurity as to open the way for wide divergence of doctrine and the bitter controversies of future ages, especially those of the Reformation period. According to the fundamental teaching of Jesus, as reported by Matthew, the

[1] Lecky, op. cit., II, 307, 308.

[2] The principal passages are Matt. 5:31, 32; 19:3-12; Mark 10:2-12; Luke 16:18; 1 Cor. 7:10-16; Rom. 7:2, 3.

In general, on the interpretation of these passages, consult Geffcken, Ehescheidung, 16 ff.; Esmein, Le mariage en droit canonique, II, 48 ff.; Freisen, Geschichte des can. Eherechts, 769, 770; Friedberg, Lehrbuch, 337 ff.; Loening, Geschichte d. deutschen Kirchenrechts, II, 606; Perrone, De mat. Chr., III, 147-219; Roskovány, De mat. in ecc. cath., II, 61-187; Meyrick, in Dict. Christ. Ant., II, 1110; Zhishman, Das Eherecht der orient. Kirche, 96 ff., 734; Gide, La femme, 169 ff.; Thwing, The Family, 45 ff.; Woolsey, Divorce, 50-85; Popp, Ehescheidung, 51 ff.; Tebbs, Essay, 74 ff.; Strippelmann, Ehescheidungsrecht, 11 ff.; especially Milton, "Doctrine and Discipline of Divorce," Prose Works, III, 180 ff.; idem, "Tetrachordon," ibid., 322 ff.; Mentzer, De conjugio, 190 ff.; Sarcerius, Vom heil. Ehestande, 161 ff.; and Bucer, in Milton's Prose Works, III, 296, passim. Partisan writers are Hovey, The Scriptural Law of Divorce; Caverno, Divorce, 29 ff.; Ap Richard, Marriage and Divorce, 77-112; Luckock, Hist. of Marriage, 44-79; Browne, Marriage of Divorced Persons in Church, 27 ff.

husband is forbidden to put away the wife except for unfaithfulness.[1] Divinely created as male and female, "they
twain shall be one flesh;" and "what therefore God hath
joined together, let not man put asunder."[2] Whether for
the same reason the woman may put away the man, or
whether either the innocent or the guilty party may contract a second marriage, we are here not expressly informed.
Inferences may, of course, be drawn by assuming that Jesus
had the principles of the Jewish law in mind; but this
mode of procedure is scarcely satisfying.[3] Nor do the other
sacred writers throw any clear light on these important
questions. Rather do they deepen the obscurity; for both
Mark and Luke appear absolutely to prohibit divorce, not
expressly admitting even the one ground of separation

[1] On the use here of the generic term *porneia* (fornication), instead of the specific
moicheia (adultery), see MILTON, "Tetrachordon," *Prose Works*, III, 394 ff.; also the
labored argument of WOOLSEY, *Divorce*, 60-70; ZHISHMAN, *Das Eherecht der orient.
Kirche*, 578 ff.; MEYRICK, in *Dict. Christ. Ant.*, II, 1110; GRAY, *Husband and Wife*,
95, 104 ff.; LUCKOCK, *Hist. of Marriage*, 56, 57; AP RICHARD, *Marriage and Divorce*,
80; SELDEN, *Uxor ebraica*, III, 23, 27.

The scope of *porneia* is of historical importance; for some of the early Fathers
and some of the leaders of the Reformation by giving it an allegorical meaning
sought to multiply the scriptural grounds of divorce. *Cf.* FREISEN, *Geschichte des
can. Eherechts*, 770; also MILTON, in *Prose Works*, III, 255 ff., 394 ff. In general read
the elaborate essay of MORGAN, *Marriage, Adultery, and Divorce*, II, 394-550, on
porneia.

[2] Matt. 19:4-6; *cf.* 5:31, 32, and Mark 10:6-9. This doctrine is laid down in reply
to the Pharisees who "tempting him" ask: "Is it lawful for a man to put away
his wife for every cause?"—doubtless having in mind the teaching of the school of
Hillel. When Jesus declares that "what therefore God hath joined together, let not
man put asunder," they further demand: "Why did Moses then command to give a
writing of divorcement, and to put her away?" To which "he saith unto them,
Moses because of the hardness of your hearts suffered you to put away your wives:
but from the beginning it was not so." Thus, it may be suggested, Jesus admits that
legally the followers of Hillel—the "broad constructionists"—are right in their
interpretation; while morally he sides with the school of Shammai. See n. 2,
p. 13, above. *Cf.* however, the specious assertions of WOOLSEY, *Divorce*, 58.

[3] By the Jewish law, of course, the woman had no right to divorce her husband
for any cause; the man putting away his wife could take other wives; and the
woman divorced for adultery—the only cause of separation contemplated by Jesus
—was stoned to death. *Cf.* GEFFCKEN, *Ehescheidung*, 17; and WOOLSEY, *op. cit.*,
59 ff., 70 ff., who holds that the words of Jesus apply to the wife equally with the
man, and that the innocent, though not the guilty, party may marry again, sustaining his position, as he fancies, by reference to Paul in 1 Cor., chap. 7. For a fair
sample of theological special pleading see BROWNE, *Marriage of Divorced Persons
in Church*, 30 ff.

granted on the authority of Matthew.   Moreover, Mark sets
up a new stumbling-block.   In the presence of the Pharisees, who sought to tempt him, Jesus is made to put aside
as morally wrong and born of hardness of heart the harsh
freedom of divorce secured to the man alone by the Mosaic
code; while "in the house" he tells his disciples that "whosoever shall put away his wife, and marry another, com-
mitteth adultery against her," and "if a woman shall put
away her husband, and be married to another, she commit-
teth adultery;" so leaving us in doubt whether legal separation *without* the privilege of a further marriage is sanctioned
—in effect thus anticipating the later distinction between
divorce *quoad thorum* and *quoad vinculum;* or, if such
separation be sanctioned, whether, in sharp contrast to the
spirit of Jewish law, the wife is placed on a level with the
husband in this regard.

The utterances of Paul on this subject,[1] as on all questions connected with marriage and the family, are of the
highest importance in view of their historical consequences.
Referring directly to the teaching of Jesus, he first seemingly denies the right of divorce to either party.   With
Mark and Luke he omits the exception mentioned by
Matthew; and with Mark he expressly forbids the wife to
"depart from her husband," adding, however, the inconse-
quent and bewildering command, "if she depart, let her
remain unmarried, or be reconciled to her husband."   Here
apparently, where both persons are believers, separation *a
mensa et thoro* is approved.   Whether in such case this is
the only Christian form of divorce allowed either party,
however grave the cause of separation;[2] or whether his rule

---

[1] 1 Cor. 7:8-16.

[2] The Catholic doctrine as finally settled. WOOLSEY, assuming that this is a
case of separation of two "believers" for some "dissension" or other cause less than
adultery (which he holds allows a second marriage), says, "we have here an actual
separation *a mensa et toro* without a separation *a vinculo matrimonii*. This third
state between absolute divorce and full marriage union has then the sanction of the

applies to the woman only, and then merely when some
lesser ground of action exists, the Apostle to the Gentiles
fails entirely to place beyond the field of debate.

Thus far Paul has spoken professedly on the authority of
"the Lord." Next he contemplates the case of an existing
union between a Christian and an unbeliever; and on his
own judgment he admits a new ground of separation. "But
to the rest speak I, not the Lord." The Christian may not
put away or abandon his spouse on account of difference in
religious faith. "For the unbelieving husband is sanctified
by the wife, and the unbelieving wife is sanctified by the
husband: else were your children unclean; but now are they
holy. But if the unbelieving depart, let him depart. A
brother or a sister is not under bondage in such cases."[1]
Again, through this last remark, the seeds of dissension are
planted; for it is not clear whether the "bondage" from
which the brother or sister is freed is that of the existing
marriage or the irksome necessity of perpetual single life
after separation.

Upon these Bible passages, often vague and puzzling in
the extreme,[2] was eventually erected the whole doctrine of
the mediæval church relating to divorce. It is not surprising that harmony was reached only after many centuries of
struggle. With the exact processes of argument by which
ingenious theologians have in all ages sought to reconcile
or interpret the scriptural teaching we are here but little
concerned. At present we are mainly interested in the

Apostle — not of course as something desirable, but probably as a kind of barricade
against divorce and a defense of the Saviour's commandment. It may be introduced
therefore into the law of Christian lands."— *Divorce*, 73, 74.

[1] 1 Cor. 7:12-16.

[2] Thus AUGUSTINE (*De adult. conjug.*) confesses the extreme difficulty of reconciling the scriptural texts relating to divorce and second marriage: "His ita pro
meo modulo pertractatis atque discussis quaestionem tamen de conjugiis obscuris-
simam et implicatissimam esse, non nescio." On this FREISEN (*Geschichte des can.
Eherechts*, 772, 773) remarks, "es wird ihm hierin gewiss jeder zustimmen, der die
Worte der hl. Schrift durchliest."

general results of thought as they find expression in the law and practice of the church previous to the Reformation. The subject presents four phases or aspects of development, each of which will be briefly considered: the views of the early Fathers; the legislation of the Christian emperors; the compromise with Germanic custom; and the final settlement of doctrine in the canon law.

b) Views of the early Fathers.—During the first four centuries of our era the so-called "strict" construction of the utterances of Jesus and Paul relating to the twofold question of separation and second marriage was formulated by the Fathers of the church; and the principles then agreed upon were in the end, after an intervening period of vacillation and compromise, to be accepted and elaborated into a complete system of law by the canonists. The literature of this early debate may be regarded as reaching from the Pastor of Hermas, a writer in the first half of the second century, highly respected in Christian antiquity,[1] to Augustine, late in the fourth century (died 430), who towers above all the other Fathers in his influence for good or evil in the history of European thought. At first the Pauline interdict of further marriage after separation receives more attention perhaps than the question of divorce itself, with its assigned cause as laid down by Jesus; for it is strongly urged that the chief evil of a too lax divorce system, such as the

[1] GEFFCKEN, *Ehescheidung*, 18–20. In general on the views of the early Fathers see also FREISEN, *Geschichte des can. Eherechts*, 770 ff.; ESMEIN, *Le mariage en droit canonique*, II, 48–55; MEYRICK, in *Dict. Christ. Ant.*, II, 1110; WOOLSEY, *Divorce*, 86 ff., 107 ff.; POPP, *Ehescheidung*, 54 ff.; GREVE, *Ehescheidung*, 190 ff.; *Observations on Mar. Laws*, 330 ff.; MOY, *Eherecht der Christen*, 10–45; ZHISHMAN, *Das Eherecht der orient. Kirche*, 99–102; LUCKOCK, *Hist. of Marriage*, 80–153; TEBBS, *Essay*, 125 ff.; MILTON, "Tetrachordon," *Prose Works*, III, 414 ff.; BURNET, *Hist. of the Reformation*, I, 26–133, 330 ff., who discusses Henry VIII.'s divorce from Queen Katherine and summarizes the results of Cranmer's examination of the Fathers and early canons in connection with the Northampton case. Burnet's summary is also given by GEARY, *Marriage and Family Relations*, 577, 578.

For the Roman Catholic view see particularly CIGOI, *Unauflösbarkeit der ch. Ehe*, 1 ff.; ROSKOVÁNY, *De mat. in ecc. cath.*, II, 1 ff., 187 ff., 198 ff.; PERRONE, *De mat. christ.*, III, 221 ff.

Roman, is the facility of second marriage regardless of the guilt or innocence of the parties.[1] Setting aside for the present the case of the Christian whose unbelieving spouse voluntarily departs—the *casus apostoli* or *privilegium Paulinum*, as it is later styled by the canonists[2]—nearly all are agreed that divorce is forbidden except for the one cause mentioned by Matthew. There is, however, a divergence of view in two important particulars. On the one hand, certain writers, such as Tertullian and pseudo-Ambrose, following the principle of the Jewish law, admit this ground of repudiation to the advantage of the man, but not to that of the woman; while others, like Epiphanius, maintain the equal right of the sexes in this regard. On the other hand, in a few instances the word "adultery"[3] is accepted in an allegorical or spiritual sense, thus greatly widening the field of divorce. In this way, for example, Hermas, Hieronymus, and, for a time, Augustine anticipate the mode of interpretation adopted by some of the Reformation Fathers, admitting idolatry, apostasy, and covetousness, equally with carnal transgression, as proper grounds of separation.[4]

The case is similar with respect to second marriage. Apparently there is a strong tendency from the beginning to treat marriage as indissoluble, but, "intentionally or unintentionally," the utterances of the Fathers on this vital question are unclear. Frequently they content themselves, as Geffcken observes, with a "paraphrase of the scriptural

[1] *Cf.* GEFFCKEN, *op. cit.*, 18.

[2] ESMEIN, *op. cit.*, I, 220 ff.; II, 268 ff.

[3] Or "fornication," the *porneia* of Matthew.

[4] *Cf.* the sources cited by FREISEN, *Geschichte des can. Eherechts*, 770; MEYRICK, in *Dict. Christ. Ant.*, II, 1110. This view is taken by AUGUSTINE, *De serm. dom. in monte*, c. xvi; but he doubts its correctness in the "Retractions;" MEYRICK, *loc. cit.* Tertullian shows also that mishandling and insult, as well as adultery, are considered sufficient grounds of separation: GEFFCKEN, *Ehescheidung*, 20, 21. See however, PERRONE, *De mat. christ.*, III, 231 ff.

texts relating to the matter."[1]   Seemingly, according to the common or prevailing opinion, neither party whether innocent or guilty is allowed to form a new marriage during the lifetime of the other; but there is on this point a great lack of precision.[2] Tertullian, after yielding to Montanism, even goes so far as to reject all second marriage as un-Christian; and the same position is taken by Minutius Felix.[3] There are, however, less rigid constructions. By some Fathers the right of remarriage is conceded to the man repudiating a guilty wife, while they deny it to the woman under like conditions. Others, actuated by a livelier sense of justice, like Epiphanius, concede it to both consorts alike; but these opinions are rejected by the majority.[4] More and more, in theory if not always in practice, the antagonism of the church to the second marriage of a divorced man or woman becomes apparent as we approach the close of the period under consideration. This is proved even by the action of the provincial assemblies. Thus the Spanish Council of Elvira of the year 306 decrees that the woman who puts away a guilty husband and marries another shall be excom-

[1] GEFFCKEN, op. cit., 21. Cf. FREISEN, op. cit., 770, who says: "Man hatte, wie es scheint, hier eine Scheu sich durchaus klar zu erklären. Sicher ist jedoch das eine, dass sich keine Stelle findet, welche die Wiederverheiratung in solchem Falle [adultery] als schriftgemäss verteidigt hätte. Vielleicht wurden die Kirchenväter bei ihrer Ansicht von der alten Anschauung geleitet, nach welcher die zweite Ehe in jener Zeit überhaupt gemissbilligt, als honesta fornicatio, angesehen wurde."

[2] Thus the strict view is taken by Justin Martyr, Clement of Alexandria, Tertullian, and Cyprian. They all declare, says FREISEN, that "whoever marries a divorced person commits adultery;" but he adds, "Dass dieser Ehebruch auch dann statthabe, wenn die erste Ehe wegen Ehebruch geschieden, sagt meines Erachtens keiner der genannten Kirchenväter, ebenso wenig wie sie sagen, dass in solchem Falle die Wiederverheiratung erlaubt sei."— Op. cit., 770, 771. Cf. LOENING, op. cit., 607; who is criticised by GEFFCKEN, op. cit., 19 n. 1; also ESMEIN, op. cit., II, 49 ff.; PERRONE, op. cit., III, 243 ff.; WOOLSEY, op. cit., 109, 110; ZHISHMAN, op. cit., 101.

[3] TERTULLIAN, "On Monogamy," in DONALDSON'S Ante-Nicene Fathers, IV, 66, 67. See also GEFFCKEN, op. cit., 19–21.

[4] ESMEIN, op. cit., II, 51. CHRYSOSTOM (De libello repudii, c. iii), Asterius of Amasea, Theodoret, and Hilarius of Poitiers all appear to hold that marriage is absolutely dissolved by adultery, from which the right of second marriage for both parties logically follows: ibid., II, 50, 51; ZHISHMAN, op. cit., 101, 102; GEFFCKEN, op. cit., 31.

municated; and, save in case of mortal sickness, she shall not be admitted again to communion until after her first husband's death. If, however, she have left her husband without cause and contracted another marriage, she shall not be admitted to communion even on the death-bed; but nothing is said concerning a dissolution of the later marriage.[1] Similar in spirit are the canons of the Council of Arles held in the year 314. The general principle of the indissolubility of the matrimonial relation is positively asserted,[2] but in connection with a concession which illustrates the practical difficulty of consistently enforcing the new doctrine in all parts of the Roman world. The youthful husband[3] who puts away a guilty wife is to be "advised" not to marry again during her lifetime; thus dealing far more gently with the man than did the Council of Elvira with the woman for the same offense.[4]

Finally, with Augustine, the strict doctrine of the early church takes a definite form, to which the masters of later times look back as to an authoritative canon of interpretation. He gave to the theory of indissolubility, declares Esmein, a "basis solid, in a measure scientific. He gave it a con-

---

[1] FREISEN, *op. cit.*, 771. *Cf.* also GREVE, *Ehescheidung*, 195, 208 ff. (second marriage in general); CIGOI, *Unauflösbarkeit*, 23 ff.; GEFFCKEN, *op. cit.*, 22; LOENING, *op. cit.*, II, 608.

[2] The rubric of Canon 10 of the council runs: "Ut is, cujus uxor adulteravit, aliam illa vivente non accipiat."—FREISEN, *op. cit.*, 771.

[3] The canon itself provides: "De his, qui conjuges suas in adulterio deprehendunt, et iidem sunt adolescentes fideles et prohibentur nubere, placuit, ut, in quantum possit, consilium iis detur, ne viventibus uxoribus suis licet adulteris alias accipiant."

[4] This disparity is variously explained. FREISEN, *op. cit.*, 771, sees here the influence of the Roman law (c. 1, *Cod. ad leg. Jul.* [ix-9]), which he alleges judges the man more leniently than the woman; but GEFFCKEN, *op. cit.*, 22, 23, explains it more reasonably as the result of a difference of local practice, since such a discrimination between man and woman "the church had thus far zealously opposed;" and, besides, he insists that the passage from the code is not in point. It should be remembered, also, that some of the early Fathers, as we have seen, followed the illiberal principles of the Mosaic law discriminating against the woman; this prejudice may have prevailed at the Council of Arles. On these councils see also ESMEIN, *op. cit.*, II, 55, 56; LOENING, *op. cit.*, II, 609 ff.

sistency forced from the sacrament of marriage. He set aside at one stroke all the causes of divorce admitted by the secular law: sickness, captivity, or prolonged absence. He was, one may say, the artisan who gave the final touch to the theory of indissolubility."[1] According to Augustine, adultery is the only scriptural ground of separation; but even this does not dissolve the nuptial bond. Moreover, those who, following the letter of Matthew's text, would for this offense allow the man, but not the woman, the right of repudiation, he "justly reproaches with violating one of the great principles of Christian law—the equality of the wedded pair."[2] Similar views are held by Hieronymus, Ambrose, Jerome, Chrysostom, and other contemporaries of Augustine;[3] and it is probably due to his influence mainly that in 407 the strict theory of indissolubility was proclaimed by the Council of Carthage;[4] as already in 405 it had been accepted in a decree of Pope Innocent I. addressed to the bishop of Toulouse.[5]

In practical life the strict theory of the Fathers came very far short of realization. Hermas, who strongly favors the rigid view, allows the man to marry again whose wife

[1] ESMEIN, op. cit., II, 53. "Mais c'est vraiment dans saint Augustin que l'on voit établie pour la première fois une relation logique et nécessaire entre le sacrement et l'indissolubilité."—Ibid., I, 65. Cf. WOOLSEY, op. cit., 110; ZHISHMAN, op. cit., 124.

[2] ESMEIN, op. cit., II, 51, 52, who collects the important passages from AUGUSTINE's De adult. conjug., and his other works. Cf. FREISEN, op. cit., 772–74; WOOLSEY, op. cit., 69, 110–12.

[3] FREISEN, op. cit., 772–74; WOOLSEY, op. cit., 112 (Jerome). See CHRYSOSTOM, Homilia, XIX, in 1 Cor., chap. 7, as opposed to his De libello repudii, c. iii, already cited. HIERONYMUS, Epist. 77 ad Oceanum de morte Fabiolae, c. 3, thus expresses the doctrine of equality of the sexes: "Apud nos, quod non licet feminis, atque non licet viris." Such also is the view of Lactantius: WOOLSEY, op. cit., 116.

[4] "Placuit, ut secundum evangelicam et apostolicam disciplinam neque dimissus ab uxore, neque dimissa a marito alteri conjungantur, sed ita permaneant, aut sibimet reconcilientur. Quod si contempserint ad poenitentiam redigantur": contained in Decret. Grat., c. 5 C. 32 qu. 7. Cf. FREISEN, op. cit., 774; ESMEIN, op. cit., II, 56, 57.

[5] FREISEN, op. cit., 774, 775; ESMEIN, op. cit., II, 59.

sins a second time after once being reconciled.[1]   Basil goes
farther, declaring that the husband abandoned by his wife
is worthy of pardon, and that the woman who then marries
him is not condemned.[2]   Even Jerome excuses Fabiola, a
young Christian woman of high position who had repudiated
a licentious husband and contracted a new marriage, saying,
"if she is blamed because when her husband was divorced
she did not remain unmarried, I will readily admit her
fault, while I admit her necessity."[3]   Origen shows that
some rulers of the church in such a case permit a woman to
marry again while the first husband is living;[4] and Augustine confesses that the women who abstain from remarriage
after divorce are extremely few.[5]

   c) *The legislation of the Christian emperors.*—Where
the most severe teachers of the early church, and even the
ecclesiastical councils themselves, as we have seen, were
thus led to temporize, it is not surprising that an enlightened secular policy should be compelled to take intermediate
ground.   The legislation of the first Christian emperors
goes far beyond the narrow limits which Tertullian, Clement, or Augustine would have drawn.   For centuries, through

---

[1] " Verily, if her husband do not take her back, he sins, and allows himself to
commit a great sin; he ought to take back the sinning woman who has repented; but
ought not to do this often.   For there is one repentance for the servants of God."
—HERMAS, Lib. II, mandat. iv, c. 1; WOOLSEY'S translation, *Divorce*, 108.   Thus
Hermas understands Paul in 1 Cor. 7:11 to refer to adultery as the cause of separation.   *Cf.* GEFFCKEN, *op. cit.*, 18, 19; FREISEN, *op. cit.*, 770: WOOLSEY, *op. cit.*, 107-9.

[2] BASILIUS, *Epist. ad Amphiloch.*, c. 9: " Quare quae reliquit, est adultera, si ad
alium virum accessit, qui autem relictus est, dignus est venia et, quae una cum eo
habitat, non condemnatur."   *Cf.* FREISEN, *op. cit.*, 772; GEFFCKEN, *op. cit.*, 30;
ESMEIN, *op. cit.*, II, 55; PERRONE, *op. cit.*, III, 263.   EPIPHANIUS (*Penarion*, lib. 59,
c. 4) takes a similar position; FREISEN, *op. cit.*, 772.

[3] JEROME, *Ad Oceanum*, cc. iii, iv.   *Cf.* WOOLSEY, *op. cit.*, 112, 113; ESMEIN, *op.
cit.*, II, 55.

[4] ORIGINES, *Comment. in Matt.*, tom. xiv, no. 23.   He declares this practice to
be against the Scriptures; but still he is not inclined to judge severely, as it has
been adopted to avoid worse evils.   *Cf.* FREISEN, *op. cit.*, 771; ESMEIN, *op. cit.*, II, 54.

[5] AUGUSTINE, *De conjug. adult.*, II, 17.   See FREISEN, *op. cit.*, 772.   Augustine
also admits that the man who contracts a new marriage after putting away a guilty
wife commits merely a venial sin: *De fide et operibus*, c. xix; ESMEIN, *op. cit.*, II, 53;
WOOLSEY, *op. cit.*, 115.

every change in the statutes, the Roman principles of one-sided divorce and divorce by mutual consent were maintained, though it was precisely these principles against which primitive Christianity took its firmest stand. "It was a maxim of Roman law far down beyond the time when the emperors became Christian, that no obstacle ought to be put in the way of a dissolution of marriage caused by the free consent of the partners, liberty of marrying again being in this case equally unrestricted. The lawyer Paulus says, that it has been thought improper that marriages, whether already contracted or about to take place, should be secured by the force of penalty (*poenae vinculo obstringi*), that is that two parties ought not to be forced by fear of penalty either to enter into a state of wedlock to which they were pledged, or to keep up such a state if they were agreed to the contrary. And it was laid down that marriage was so free, according to ancient opinion, that even agreements between the parties not to separate from one another could have no validity (*pacta ne liceret divertere non valere*)."[1] One-sided divorce was equally free, except in the cases and under the conditions fixed by Augustus,[2] "saving that here, if the woman had caused the divorce by her conduct, a large share of her dower was withheld from her, and if the man had caused it, he might be liable to pay over the whole of the dower, and that within a short term. The parties were subjected until the time of Justinian to a *judicium morum*, which might be instituted on a complaint of either consort. The fear, then, of losing a portion or the whole of the dower, and the dread of a loss of reputation, when the conduct of the parties in their married life should be investigated, seem

---

[1] Woolsey, *op. cit.*, 92, 93: Paulus, in *Dig.*, XLV, 1, 134; *Cod.*, viii, 39, 1, 2, de inutil. stip.

[2] The requirement of seven witnesses; the case of the freedwoman marrying her patron; and the obligation of the husband, under penalty, to put away a guilty wife: see above, p. 16.

to have been the only inducements to prevent one-sided divorces. But what if no misconduct could be alleged on the part of the man, what if he dismissed his wife to marry a richer woman, the law in this case had no restraining power. And where the wife brought no dower, as might happen in the lower classes, there could be no operation of the law at all."[1]

Accordingly, the legislation of the early Christian emperors shows no radical departure from the principles of the existing civil law. Divorce *ex consensu* was not prohibited until Justinian, who decreed that only when both partners are about to enter the cloister shall a separation by mutual agreement be permitted.[2] But this prohibition was short-lived; for in consequence of it the number of suits growing out of "poisoning or other attempts upon life among married people increased in so frightful a manner"[3] that the provision was abrogated by Justin II., the immediate successor of Justinian.[4] On the other hand, the efforts of Constantine and later rulers are directed mainly toward checking the evils of one-sided divorce. This is done chiefly through restricting the number of legal grounds of separation and sharpening the penalties for their disregard. Thus in 331 Constantine ordains that trifling causes (*exquisitae causae*) shall no longer suffice for a *repudium justum* or legal divorce at the will of one party. The woman may put away her husband only when he is a murderer, poisoner, or violator of sepulchers; and the man is allowed to repudiate his wife only when she is guilty of poisoning, procuring, or adultery. If the divorce takes place for any other reason, the woman so violating the statute shall forfeit all claim to restitution of dower and suffer transportation to an island;

1 WOOLSEY, *op. cit.*, 94. *Cf.* on the survival of the principles of Roman law, GEFFCKEN, *op. cit.*, 24, 25.

2 *Nov.*, 117, c. 10. 3 GEFFCKEN, *op. cit.*, 25.

4 *Nov.*, 140; *cf.* GEFFCKEN, *loc. cit.*

while the man in like case must at once surrender the entire
dos, being prohibited also from contracting another marriage.[1] "Still further, if he thus married, his repudiated
wife 'could invade his house,' as the law expresses it, and
acquire possession of the entire dower of her successor."[2]
It should be noted, however, that the Roman principle of
divorce *bona gratia*, or one-sided separation for a legal
cause not implying any guilt or offense, was still retained.[3]

In 363 Julian repealed the divorce law of Constantine;[4]
but the principle of restricting the grounds of arbitrary
repudiation was again adopted in 421 by Honorius and Con-
stantius; though, like Julian, they allowed arbitrary separation for lesser faults, with retention of some portion of the
dower.[5] Theodosius II., in 439, abrogating previous legislation, restored the law of the early empire; but "after ten
years of experiment, in which divorces had alarmingly increased, gave out another law,[6] which laid down the causes
for which one party might lawfully separate from the other.
The woman was authorized to do this if the man had been
guilty of certain crimes, among which are murder, poisoning,
plotting against the government, fraud, and various sorts of

[1] GEFFCKEN, *op. cit.*, 25: *L. I. C. Theod. de repud.*, 3, 16. *Cf.* also WOOLSEY, *op. cit.*, 96, 97. On the legislation of Constantine and his successors see WÄCHTER, *Ehescheidungen*, 201 ff., 259 ff.; GLASSON, *Le mariage civil et le divorce*, 203 ff.; ESMEIN, *Mélanges*, 157 ff.; LUCKOCK, *Hist. of Marriage*, 112 ff.; COMBIER, *Du divorce*, 81 ff.; TISSOT, *Le mariage*, 88 ff.; TEBBS, *Essay*, 139 ff.; BENNECKE, *Ehebruch*, 16 ff.; HENNET, *Du divorce*, 25 ff.; POPP, *Ehescheidung*, 62 ff.

[2] WOOLSEY, *op. cit.*, 97; WÄCHTER, *op. cit.*, 207 ff.

[3] Constantine allowed the wife the right of divorce whose husband had been four years absent in the army without sending her word. Justinian first raised the period of waiting to ten years, and then entirely abolished divorce for this cause. "Dagegen blieb die Scheidungsbefugniss bestehen für den Fall der Impotenz, wobei jedoch nach Justinians Bestimmung eine Probezeit von zwei, später von drei Jahren eingehalten werden sollte." A vow of chastity or imprisonment was also counted a legal ground of separation by Justinian: GEFFCKEN, *op. cit.*, 27. *Cf.* also GLASSON, *Le mariage civil et le divorce*, 205, who appears to confuse divorce *ex consensu* and *bona gratia*.

[4] *L. 2, C. Theod. de dotib.* 3, 13. *Cf.* GEFFCKEN, *op. cit.*, 25; WÄCHTER, *op. cit.*, 202, 213.

[5] *L. 2, C. Theod. de repud.*, 3, 16. *Cf.* WÄCHTER, *op. cit.*, 215, 216.

[6] *L. 8, C. de repud.*, 5, 17.

robbery, cruelty toward or attempts on the life of his wife, intimacy with prostitutes, and adultery. The causes for which a man could without penalty put away his wife were for the most part of the same description with those just mentioned. But peculiar to her are the offenses of passing the night out of his house, or visiting the theatre, circus, or other public place against his will."[1]   If the divorce occurs for any reason other than those mentioned in the statute, the penalty for either person is loss or surrender of the dower and the ante-nuptial gift; while in addition the woman, under penalty of "infamy," is prohibited from marrying again within five years.[2] This is a severe discrimination against the wife; but in one important matter, it will be noted, the law of Theodosius is strikingly impartial; for separation is permitted on account of adultery of the man as well as for that of the woman. In this regard the measure is far more liberal than the earlier Roman law, according to which adultery is not a crime which a husband can commit against his wife.[3] Moreover, while this offense is not always mentioned in the constitutions of the Christian emperors as legal ground for divorcing the husband, it is punished with extreme rigor. Sometimes both offenders are condemned to death. Sometimes a discrimination is made, the woman usually suffering the harsher penalty.[4]

[1] WOOLSEY, *op. cit.*, 98, 99; *cf.* GEFFCKEN, *op. cit.*, 25, 26. The woman is allowed fourteen causes of divorce and the man but six; but in effect they are nearly equivalent, except as indicated: see WÄCHTER, *op. cit.*, 216 ff.

[2] See the summary of the act in GEFFCKEN, *op. cit.*, 25, 26; and WÄCHTER, *op. cit.*, 218-20.

[3] L. 34, § 1, *Dig.*, XLVIII, 5, *ad. leg. Jul.*: L. 101, *Dig. de v. sign.* "It may need to be said that only a crime to which a married woman was a party could be called *adulterium*. The Romans held that the *jus tori* pertained to the husband. He could not commit this crime against his wife." — WOOLSEY, *op. cit.*, 90, note. *Cf.* FREISEN, *Geschichte des can. Eherechts*, 617.

[4] "Constantine the Great imposed death with confiscation of goods on the *adulterer*. His sons punished the adulteress with burning and took away from her paramour the privilege of appeal, but this seems to have been only a case of extraordinary and temporary legislation. Under Valentinian the guilty woman was again sentenced to death. Justinian's legislation shut up the woman in a cloister, making it

The legislation of Justinian, except in abolishing divorce by common consent, does not differ essentially in principle or detail from that of Theodosius II. The causes assigned for a reasonable divorce (*ex rationabili causa*) are much the same as in the former law. For disregard of the statute the woman loses her dower and is condemned to lifelong imprisonment in a cloister; while the man forfeits the nuptial gift (*donatio propter nuptias*), and besides must pay a fine equal to one-third of that donation.[1]

Thus it appears that during the two centuries between Constantine and Justinian the legislation of the state relative to the vital question of divorce is practically untouched by the influence of Christianity. Informal divorce *bona gratia*[2] and divorce by mutual consent, both contrary to Christian teaching, are freely allowed. The principle of further marriage after separation is fully maintained for the innocent party, and usually under restrictions for the guilty person as well. The causes of legal divorce are, indeed, limited and the penalties for unjust repudiation made more severe; but the strict principle of indissolubility of the marriage bond, as already conceived by Augustine and his contemporaries, is completely ignored.[3]

d) The compromise with German custom.—Far more important in its results is the contact of the Christian doctrine with Germanic customs and ideas. To the newly converted nations of Teutonic stock came the western empire as a proper

illegal for her husband to take her back within two years. If the parties were not reconciled at the end of this term the marriage was dissolved, and the woman's imprisonment in the cloister was perpetual. As for the offending man, he was visited with death, but not with confiscation of goods, if he had near relatives in the direct line."—WOOLSEY, *op. cit.*, 91, 92; REIN, *Criminalrecht*, 848–52; *Nov.*, 134, § 10. In general, on the development of the law relating to adultery, see FREISEN, *op. cit.*, 615–35, 830 ff.; ESMEIN, *Le mariage en droit canonique*, I, 102, 103, 111, 384–90; II, 61, 62, 90 ff., 125, 296 ff.; *idem, Mélanges*, 157 ff.; BENNECKE, *Ehebruch*, 13–33.

[1] *Nov.*, 117, cc. 8, 9. *Cf.* GEFFCKEN, *op. cit.*, 26, 27; WOOLSEY, *Divorce*, 99, 100; WÄCHTER, *op. cit.*, 206, 207, 222 ff.

[2] On divorce *bona gratia* see WÄCHTER, *op. cit.*, 224 ff.

[3] *Cf.* the conclusions of GEFFCKEN, *op. cit.*, 28, 29; WOOLSEY, *op. cit.*, 101.

heritage. It would be their task to make the history of the future; to construct a new civilization by blending the best elements of their own culture with the maturer results of Roman experience. But this could be accomplished only through ages of struggle and compromise; through a slow and painful process of amalgamation in religion, language, and jurisprudence. For the Germans were relatively young in social progress. In law and institutions at the time of conversion they stood about where the Romans were when Roman legendary history begins. With respect to the customs of marriage and divorce they stood even lower; for the earliest collections of folk-laws, some of which were made after the acceptance of Christianity, disclose marriage as a real contract of sale through which the wife in theory, and no doubt often in practice, becomes the husband's chattel. With regard to the primitive law of divorce there is scarcely any direct information. But it seems probable that originally the right of repudiation was the sole privilege of the man, though in practice the arbitrary use of his power must have been restrained by dread of the blood-feud and the fear of pecuniary sacrifice.[1] In the historical period, however, and long after the conversion divorce by mutual agreement seems to have prevailed very widely among the Germanic peoples; but with the exception of the *Lex romana Burgundionum*, it does not appear to be sanctioned in the folk-laws until the seventh[2] century, which fact has led to

---

[1] GEFFCKEN, *op. cit.*, 33, 34, 43, 44. With this view JEAFFRESON, *Brides and Bridals*, II, 295, 296, agrees: The Anglo-Saxon wife, he says, could be repudiated at will by her "master." But many writers hold that divorce by mutual consent is recognized in the ancient Teutonic law. Thus HEUSLER, *Institutionen*, II, 291, 292, declares that there was absolute liberty of separation by agreement, and that one-sided divorce (by *Kündigung*) was very restricted. A similar opinion is held by ZOEPFL, *Deutsche Rechtsg.*, III, 37, 38; POLLOCK AND MAITLAND, *Hist. of English Law*, II, 390; GLASSON, *Le mariage civil et le divorce*, 185 ff., 195; FREISEN, *Geschichte des can. Eherechts*, 779-81; LOENING, *Geschichte des deut. Kirchenrechts*, II, 617; SCHROEDER, *Rechtsgeschichte*, I, 174. In general, *cf.* BRUNNER, *Rechtsgeschichte*, 302 ff.; WEINHOLD, *Deutsche Frauen*, II, 43 ff.; GRIMM, *Rechtsalt.*, 454; WALTER, *Deutsche Rechtsgeschichte*, I, 134-36; GLASSON, *Histoire du droit et des inst. de l'Angleterre*, I, 119, 120.

[2] For examples among Franks and Alamanni see MEYRICK, in *Dict. Christ. Ant.*, II, 1111.

the conjecture that this form of separation, "originally alien to the German legal consciousness," was gradually adopted under Roman influence.[1] The folk-laws show that, side by side with divorce by free consent of the parties, the husband still possessed the right to put away his wife for certain specified crimes;[2] or, indeed, without assigning any cause whatever, though in that case he might suffer serious disadvantage with respect to property.[3]

Another principle of the ancient German law it is necessary to mention in order to obtain a starting-point for the measure of Christian influence. Originally, according to Wilda,[4] by the strict legal theory adultery is not a crime which a man can commit against his wife. He may be punished: indeed very generally in the folk-laws both the guilty persons may be slain when surprised by the aggrieved; but if he be punished "it is not for unfaithfulness to his wife, but for violating the rights of another husband."[5] On the

[1] GEFFCKEN, op. cit., 34, 43, 44. "Das erste Volksrecht, welches die freiwillige Scheidung ganz analog dem römischen *divortium communi consensu* gestattet, ist der seiner Entstehung nach in die erste Hälfte des 7. Jahrhunderts fallende *pactus Alamannorum.*"—*Ibid.*, 44. The first formulary (*libellum* or *libellus repudii*) for a divorce by mutual consent in the folk-laws appears in the *formulae Andegavenses*, a collection made in the last quarter of the same century: *ibid.*, 44; also BRUNNER, *Rechtsgeschichte,* 403, 404; FREISEN, op. cit., 778, 779. The following formulary for such a divorce is taken from Marculf (II, 30) by GLASSON, *op. cit.*,186, though it may have been intended for the Roman population living on Frankish territory: "Idcirco dum et inter illo et conjuge sua . . . . discordia regnat . . . . placuit utriusque voluntas ut se a consortio separare deberent. . . . . Propterea has epistolas inter se uno tenore conscriptas fieri et adfirmare decreverunt, ut unusquisque ex ipsis, sive ad servitium Dei in monasterio aut ad copulam matrimonii se sociare voluerit, licentiam habeat."

[2] *Lex Visig.*, III, 6, c. 2 (adultery); *Lex Burgund.*, 34, 3 (*adultera, maleficia, sepulcrorum violatrix*): FREISEN, op. cit., 779.

[3] *Pact. Alam.*, III, 3; *Lex Bajuw.*, VII, 14; *Lex Burg.*, tit. 34, c. 2; *Lex Vis.*, III, 6, c. 2; FREISEN, op. cit., 779.

[4] WILDA, *Strafrecht*, 821 ff. *Cf.* WALTER, *Deutsche Rechtsgeschichte*, II, 398 ff.; GLASSON, *Hist. du droit*, I, 120.

[5] GEFFCKEN, op. cit., 33. The following provision of the old English law illustrates this principle in all its harsh reality: "If a freeman lie with a freeman's wife, let him pay for it with his wer-geld, and provide another wife with his own money, and bring her to the other." Here doubtless the guilty woman had been slain: *Laws of Æthelberht*, 31: HADDAN AND STUBBS, *Councils*, III, 45. For the same offense with an "esne's" wife, sec. 85 of the same laws requires a man to "make two-fold bot": *ibid.*, III, 50. *Cf.* also secs. 10, 11: *ibid.*, III, 43; CLEVELAND, *Woman under the English Law*, 9, 51 ff. (adultery and divorce).

other hand, for similar misconduct the woman is put to
death. So "in Saxony, where the old heathen ideas survived until the forcible conversion under Charles the Great,
as Boniface reports, the adulteress, stripped to the girdle, was
driven out of her husband's house and whipped through the
streets of the village until she died."[1]

To analyze the secular laws or ecclesiastical canons
relating to divorce, as they were slowly developed on Germanic territory after the conversion, is not an easy task ; for
they reveal a striving to harmonize in various ways the often
irreconcilable elements of Roman, Teutonic, and Christian
ideas. In the first place, the imperial legislation remained
in force for the Roman population, though in the compilations made under the barbarian kings various changes are
made to satisfy new and complex relations.[2] Next, the German folk-laws show in many ways the evidences of compromise with Christian doctrine under the exigencies of
practical life.[3] National sentiment will not suffer the absolute interdict of further marriage after separation; but the
penalties for unjust action may be made so severe as to prepare the way for the strict theory of the church. In the
Burgundian code, for example, the man who puts away his
wife for any cause other than those named in the statute
must surrender to her his house and all his possessions;

---

[1] GEFFCKEN, *op. cit.*, 33. *Cf.* in general TACITUS, *Germania*, c. 19; GRIMM,
Rechtsalt., 451; FREISEN, *Geschichte des can. Eherechts*, 779; WEINHOLD, *Deutsche
Frauen*, II, 25–27, who shows that the guilty woman's paramour might lawfully be
slain by the husband when seized in the act.

For discussion of the customs of the early Germans regarding the punishment
of adultery and summaries of the provisions of the folk-laws, the capitularies, and
later legislation on the subject see ROSENTHAL, *Rechtsfolgen des Ehebruchs*, 40 ff.;
and BENNECKE, *Die strafrechtliche Lehre vom Ehebruch*, 82 ff. Of some service is
HELLER, *Ueber die Strafe des Ehebruchs*, 17 ff., *passim*.

[2] On the *Lex romana Burgundionum*, the *Lex romana Visigothorum*, and the
Lex romana curiensis, see FREISEN, *op. cit.*, 776–78. *Cf.* also GEFFCKEN, *op. cit.*, 42,
43. The folk-laws are clearly reviewed by MEYRICK in *Dict. Christ. Ant.*, II, 1111.

[3] BOEHMER, *Ehegesetze im Zeitalter Karls des Grossen*, 89 ff., summarizes the provisions of the folk-laws and capitularies regarding divorce, enumerating twelve
different causes of separation, some of them being properly grounds of nullity.

whereas in the West Gothic Interpretation of the Theodosian code the chapter on which this provision is modeled prescribes a similar penalty, not for the illegal divorce itself, but for contracting a second marriage after the unjust repudiation of the first wife.[1] Accordingly, in these laws one-sided divorce on the part of the husband is not entirely taken away; but the grounds on which he may act are more or less restricted in harmony with the scriptural rules; and the wife is herself given a rudimentary right of one-sided repudiation when the husband is guilty of very grave crimes. In the law of the West Goths, for instance, where Christian influence is more marked than in any of the other codes before the close of the eighth century,[2] the right of the man to put away his wife is restricted to the one cause mentioned by Matthew; while for two scandalous wrongs the woman may repudiate the husband and contract another marriage if she likes.[3] On the other hand, the ancient rule that a man cannot be guilty of adultery against his wife yields very slightly to the Christian principle of equality of the sexes with respect to the punishment of carnal sins. Gen-

[1] See GEFFCKEN's interesting discussion of tit. 34, c. 4, *Lex Burgundionum*, in *Ehescheidung*, 35-38. He shows, following LOENING, *Geschichte des deut. Kirchenrechts*, II, 619, note, that the clause in question is of later origin than the rest of tit. 34, probably under Christian influence. *Cf.* GLASSON, *Le mariage civil et le divorce*, 187, 188. For the text see SALIS'S edition of the Burgundian laws in *Mon. Germ. hist.: Legum*, sec. i, tom. ii, p. 68; and compare sec. xxiv, "De mulieribus Burgundiis ad secundas aut tertias nuptias transeuntibus," *ibid.*, pp. 61-63; and sec. lxviii, "De adulteriis," *ibid.*, p. 95.

[2] The *Lex Bajuwariorum*, near the end of the eighth century, likewise admits divorce only for the one cause: GEFFCKEN, *op. cit.*, 46.

[3] *Lex Visig.*, lib. iii, tit. iv, c. 3; tit. v, c. 5; tit. vi, c. 2. For sodomy or for forcing her to adultery, the wife may put away the husband and marry again. *Cf.* GEFFCKEN, *op. cit.*, 38-40; GLASSON, *op. cit.*, 187. There is a similar provision in the Longobard code: GEFFCKEN, *op. cit.*, 41. As a general rule, the woman is not allowed one-sided divorce; indeed, for attempting such a separation, the *Lex Burgund.*, tit. xxxiv, c. 1, prescribes the death penalty: *cf.* FREISEN, *op. cit.*, 780, who holds that the woman cannot by German law have the right of one-sided divorce, because she cannot dissolve the *mund* which belongs solely to the man; and he contends against Sohm, Schroeder, and Loening that when the woman, as in exceptional cases cited, has the right of separating, it is not she who dissolves the marriage, but the law indirectly by depriving the man of the *mund*.

erally, according to the harsh sanction of the ancient law, the guilty woman as well as her paramour may be slain by the aggrieved.[1] In theory, as Geffcken insists, a husband in similar case is still merely responsible for violating the rights of another man; the only concessions to the Christian teaching being a tendency to check concubinage and the privilege of the woman, already mentioned, of repudiating her husband for certain offenses, among which, it may be noted, intimacy with other women is not found.[2]

Such are the salient features of secular legislation on German territory following the migration and settlement of the new nations. Let us now look at the question from the opposite point of view—that of the decrees and practice of the church itself. For more than three hundred years after the strict theory of Augustine had been proclaimed by the Council of Carthage and by Innocent I. in the beginning of the fifth century, there is more or less wavering on the part of ecclesiastical authorities. In general, it may be said there is a tendency to uphold the rigid doctrine of indissolubility; but the evidences of compromise with popular sentiment are by no means wanting. Almost always in the papal letters divorce with remarriage is absolutely forbidden.[3] Yet in 726 Gregory II., in a letter addressed to St. Boniface, permits a man to contract a new marriage because his wife by reason of infirmity is unable to perform her conjugal duty; and this opinion has proved a sore puzzle to

[1] So by the Burgundian, West Gothic, and Longobard laws: GEFFCKEN, op. cit., 35, 39, 41.

[2] C. 6 of the laws of the Longobard Grimoald appended to the *Edictus Rothari* in 668, after acceptance of orthodox Catholicism, permits the wife not guilty of a *culpa legitima* to leave the husband who keeps permanently in the house a concubine whom he prefers to the wife. It may be noted that occasional fornication is not mentioned; and that c. 8 of the law assumes as a rule that there will be a reconciliation: GEFFCKEN, op. cit., 41, 42. *Cf.* FREISEN, op. cit., 780, who holds that, according to c. 8 of the *Lex Grimoald.*, bigamy does not allow the wife a divorce.

[3] ESMEIN, *Le mariage en droit canonique*, II, 59; FREISEN, op. cit., 782; LUCKOCK, *Hist. of Marriage*, 154–72.

canonists and theologians, for it is utterly inconsistent with
an earlier decision of the same pontiff.[1] A similar inconsistency exists in the conciliar decrees. The doctrine of
indissolubility is rigidly enforced by the Council of Angers
in 453; the two Councils of Orleans in 533; the Council of
Nantes in 658; that of Friuli in 796; and generally by
those of the ninth century.[2] On the other hand, several
decrees are much more tolerant. In 465 the Council of
Vannes "expressly exempts from anathema those men who
marry again after putting away their wives for adultery
proved;"[3] and, still more liberal, the Council of Agde, 505,
while expressly allowing more than one cause of separation
a vinculo, threatens with excommunication only those who
repudiate their wives for the sake of remarriage without
"establishing in advance before the bishops of the province
the causes of their divorce."[4]

At the time of the conversion the old English laws on
this subject were probably much the same in character as
those of their Teutonic kinsmen across the channel. From
the code of Æthelberht it may perhaps be inferred that
divorce is allowed at the will of either spouse. Apparently
in all cases of arbitrary separation the responsible party
suffers a severe penalty. The man loses all claim to repay-
ment of the purchase price of the wife; while the woman or
her guardian has to restore the same to the husband or his
family.[5] The penitentials, as will presently be seen, afford

---

[1] On Gregory's two decisions see ESMEIN, *op. cit.*, II, 59, 60; and FREISEN, *op.
cit.*, 331 ff., 782, who tries to explain away the contradiction, claiming that here is a
case of declaring a marriage void *ab initio*. *Cf.* PERRONE, *De mat. christ.*, III, 332 ff.;
LOENING, *Geschichte des deut. Kirchenrechts*, II, 623.

[2] ESMEIN, *op. cit.*, II, 57, 58.

[3] *Ibid.*, 57; FREISEN, *op. cit.*, 781.

[4] *Decret. Grat.*, c. 1 C. 33 qu. 2. *Cf.* FREISEN, *op. cit.*, 781; ESMEIN, *op. cit.*, II, 57.

[5] The statements of the text are probably sustained by *Æthelberht*, 31, 77-83: in
HADDAN AND STUBBS, *Councils*, III, 45, 49; THORPE, *Anc. Laws*, I, 11, 33, taking into
account the usual effects of wife-purchase. *Cf.* however, JEAFFRESON, *Brides and
Bridals*, II, 294-98, who holds that among the pagan Britons and Anglo-Saxons

abundant evidence that in practice the spirit of ancient
custom yielded but stubbornly to ecclesiastical influence.
But, so far as it could be done by legislation, the century
following the conversion of Kent saw the strict doctrine of
the Roman see established in the daughter-church of England.   At the Council of Hertford in 673 it is decreed that
divorce shall not be permitted except on the ground assigned
by the "holy evangel;" but should a man "put away the
wife united to him in lawful wedlock, if he wish to be
rightly a Christian, let him not be joined to another, but
remain as he is or else be reconciled to his wife."[1]   After
nearly two centuries, during which the records are silent on
this subject, the same rule is laid down in the so-called *Law
of the Northumbrian Priests*, by which anathema is invoked
on one in holy orders who shall "forsake a woman and take
another;" while the layman guilty of the same offense shall
want "God's mercy, unless he make bot;" everyone being
required to "lawfully keep his wife, as long as she lives,
unless . . . . they both choose, with the bishop's consent,
to separate, and will thenceforth observe chastity."[2]   From
this time onward, as clearly shown by the canons of Dun-
stan,[3] those issued under Æthelred at the Council of Eanham
(*ca.* 1009),[4] and later decrees, the theory of indissolubility

divorce may be described as "simple repudiation of wives at the will of their
masters." In the tenth century, he adds, Howell Dha, sovereign of Wales, "decreed
that a husband might righteously eject from his home the wife who had given a
single kiss to any man but himself." See also GLASSON, *Le mariage et le divorce*,
195, whose references to the laws of Æthelberht do not seem to warrant all his conclusions; also his *Histoire du droit*, I, 120; and POLLOCK AND MAITLAND, *Hist. of Eng.
Law*, II, 390. In general see ROSENTHAL, *Rechtsfolgen des Ehebruchs*, 55 ff.

[1] HADDAN AND STUBBS, *op. cit.*, III, 118. ESMEIN, *op. cit.*, II, 57, regards the
last clause as merely advising the man not to marry again; and FREISEN, *op. cit.*,
782, thinks it not quite certain that it applies to the case of separation for adultery.
Cf. also LUCKOCK, *Hist. of Marriage*, 167-69; and CIGOI, *Unauflös. der ch. Ehe*, 79.

[2] *Law of Northumbrian Priests*, secs. 35, 64, 65: THORPE, *Anc. Laws*, II, 296, 300.
Cf. LUCKOCK, *op. cit.*, 170, 171; JOHNSON, *Canons*, I, 950, 35, 54.

[3] JOHNSON, *op. cit.*, I, 963, 27.

[4] *Ibid.*, 1009, 8.

was unswervingly accepted by the English church under sanction of the temporal power.[1]

Already in the Carolingian empire, through co-operation of the secular authority, the teachings of Augustine had gained a similar triumph. The ecclesiastical capitularies of the Frankish kings, from the ascendency of the house of Charles Martel to the consolidation of the state under Charles the Great, are of especial interest in this connection, for they prepare the way for the synthetic work of the canonists. During the dark period of the Merovingian line any attempt through legislation to deal seriously with divorce or any similar social or moral problem could scarcely arise; for it would have meant some restriction of the prevailing licentiousness, to which all classes were committed. Civil rulers were steeped in debauchery. The church was apathetic and corrupt. "With the advent of the Carolingian major domus, the level of morality begins to rise."[2] Already

---

[1] The ecclesiastical laws of Howell the Good of Wales (928) show more clearly, perhaps, than is done anywhere else the way in which the church was often constrained to put up with barbarian custom. One-sided divorce with remarriage is allowed each party, under penalty for repudiation without legal cause. If the husband desert the wife within seven years, he must pay her the dower (*agweddi*), the maiden-fee (*cowyll*), and the maiden-dues (*gobyr*) for the lord. "If after seven years, he leave her; let all be shared between them, unless privilege should give precedence to the husband: two parts of the children go to the husband, and the third to the mother. The eldest and the youngest go to the father." "A man is free to forsake his wife, if she notoriously attach herself to another man; and she is to obtain nothing of her right excepting the three things [cowyll, argyvren (paraphernalia), wyneb-werth (fine for husband's fornication)] which are not to be taken from a woman, and the seducer is to pay to the lawful husband his saraad," or injury fine. "If a man deserts his wife unlawfully and takes another; the rejected wife is to remain in her house until the end of the ninth day; and then, if she be suffered to depart entirely from her husband, everything belonging to her is to go in the first place out of the house; and then she is to go last out of the house, after all her property; after that, on bringing the other into the house, he is to give dilysdawd (assurance) to the first wife; because no man, by law, is to have two wives." "Whoever shall leave his wife, and shall repent leaving her, she having been given to another husband; if the first husband overtake her with one foot in the bed and the other out; the first husband by law is to have her." "For three causes, if a woman desert her husband, she is not to lose her dower: for leprosy; want of connection; and bad breath."— Haddan and Stubbs, *Councils*, I, 246-51.

[2] Geffcken, *op. cit.*, 45, who gives, 44-46, 52-55, an interesting discussion of the reasons for the absence of divorce regulations during the Merovingian era.

in 744, at the Synod of Soissons, a royal capitulary clearly
forbids divorce to each spouse, except that a husband may
put away a guilty wife on the scriptural ground; but in that
case whether the innocent person may contract a new marriage we are not informed.[1] This attempt to enforce the
rigid doctrine of the ancient church seems to have been
premature; for a few years later, at the synods of Verberie
(753) and Compiègne (757), rules much more tolerant are
proclaimed.[2] These capitularies possess more than usual
historical interest in view of their "profound and durable
influence" on the final settlement of the law by Gratian and
his successors.[3] Several grounds of divorce with remarriage
are admitted. According to the decree of Verberie, the
man whose wife plots against his life may put her away and
take another spouse; but the divorced woman may not
remarry. So also, by the same decree, the man may form
a new marriage, if his wife through love of her parents or
some selfish interest refuses to accompany him when he
flees from danger or is constrained to follow his lord into
another duchy or province. In this case, the woman must
remain unmarried while her husband lives.[4] Again, the
Synod of Verberie provides that if either person in course
of the wedded life shall fall into slavery, the one remaining
free is at liberty to marry again when he likes. "A single
exception is admitted which throws a sombre light on the

[1] ESMEIN, *op. cit.*, II, 58, 64; GEFFCKEN, *op. cit.*, 55.

[2] The dates are uncertain. In general, on these synods see FREISEN, *op. cit.*,
782–84; GEFFCKEN, *op. cit.*, 55–57; and especially ESMEIN, *op. cit.*, II, 64–69; who gives
a clear summary of their decrees. *Cf.* PERRONE, *De mat. christ.*, III, 332, 338 ff.

[3] ESMEIN, *op. cit.*, II, 69.

[4] C. ix of the decree runs: "Si quis necessitate inevitabili cogente in alium
ducatum seu provinciam fugerit, aut seniorem suum, cui fidem mentiri non poterit,
secutus fuerit, et uxor ejus, cum valet et potest, amore parentum aut rebus suis,
eum sequi noluerit, ipsa omni tempore, quamdiu vir ejus, quem secuta non fuerit,
vivet, semper innupta permaneat. Nam ille vir ejus . . . . si se abstinere non potest,
aliam uxorem cum poenitentia potest accipere." *Cf.* ESMEIN, *op. cit.*, II, 66, note.
In contrast with this decision, the Synod of Compiègne forbids both parties to
remarry when the husband abandons his wife in order to escape private vengeance:
ibid., 66.

society of that epoch: if a spouse under pressure of misery
has sold himself as a slave, the partner remaining free, who
has shared the bread thus gained and whom the sale has
saved from hunger, is not entitled to a divorce."[1]

Even more striking is the decree of Compiègne regarding
the effect of religious vows. When by agreement either
partner enters the cloister, the spouse remaining in the world
has the right of remarriage. To this decision, so sharply in
contrast with the mature doctrine of the canon law, it is
significant that a papal delegate to the synod, Bishop George
of Ostia, gave his consent. The severer and more orthodox
principle had been followed by the Synod of Verberie, which
prohibits the man from remarriage when he suffers his wife
to take the veil.[2] Both decrees permit separation on various
other grounds, such as error of condition and certain degrees
of affinity, which, under the dangerous guise of nullity,
"constitute veritable exceptions to the rule" that the nuptial
tie cannot be dissolved.[3]

Finally there is a singular omission which has called
forth an instructive comment from a modern scholar. "It
is remarkable that neither of these decrees mentions adultery as a cause of divorce. This is so without doubt because
the capitulary of Soissons already gave that quality to the sin
of the woman who alone was considered. Besides, in that
rude society, this cause of divorce in most cases was probably
superfluous. The deceived husband had no need to invoke
it. Not merely when he surprised his wife *flagrante delicto*,
but also when he had grave suspicion against her, did he

---

[1] ESMEIN, *op. cit.*, II, 68; I, 325: *ap. c. vi*, decree of Verberie. *Cf.* also FREISEN,
op. cit., 788; and CIGOI, *Unauflös. der ch. Ehe.*, 74, who regards this synod more as an
imperial diet than an ecclesiastical assembly, and so excuses its action. *Cf.* HEFELE,
Konzilien-Geschichte, III, 537.

[2] ESMEIN, *op. cit.*, II, 65.

[3] These decrees are for the most part included in the collection of Gratian;
"mais il se fera tout un travail pour les mettre d'accord avec la règle triomphante
de l'indissolubilité; elles contribueront néanmoins à introduire, dissimulées sous la
forme de nullités, de véritables exceptions à cette règle."—ESMEIN, *op. cit.*, II, 69.

take justice into his own hands, killing the guilty woman; and the deed probably went unpunished. In this regard the church appears to have shown ample indulgence. No doubt she entirely forbade a new marriage to the spouse who slew a partner; but that was never more than a prohibitive impediment for which dispensation was granted with sufficient ease. Here a means was admitted by law and custom for evading the rule of indissolubility of the conjugal bond. St. Augustine had already contemplated it; and various passages of Hincmar of Rheims show clearly that more than one husband had recourse to it in his time."[1]

It is strange that so wide a relaxation of the principle accepted by the early church, in part under the sanction of Rome itself, should have preceded by so few years its complete triumph in the capitularies of Charles the Great. From 774 onward, with slight wavering, the rigid doctrine is maintained both by imperial and papal authority; as likewise it is expounded in the canonical literature of Gratian's predecessors, notably by Benedict Levita and Hincmar of Rheims.[2]

But there is other testimony of a most convincing nature that the practice of the church could not keep pace with her theory. It is afforded by the penitentials. These are private manuals designed for the practical guidance of priests in their daily ministrations, one of the oldest and most interesting of which is that bearing the name of Theodore of Tarsus,[3] the reorganizer of the English church and president

[1] *Ibid.*, 66, 67.

[2] *Cf.* GEFFCKEN, *Ehescheidung*, 57-62; FREISEN, *Geschichte des can. Eherechts*, 792 ff.

[3] The *Poenitentiale Theodori* is contained in HADDAN AND STUBBS, *Councils*, III, 173-213; also that of Ecgberht, *ibid.*, III, 413-31. Versions of these may be found in THORPE, *Ancient Laws*, II, 1 ff., 129 ff.; also with many others in WASSERSCHLEBEN, *Bussordnungen;* and in SCHMITZ, *Bussbücher*, 510 ff., 565 ff., who, contrary to the generally accepted view, traces (3 ff.) all the penitentials to Roman models. In general, see GEFFCKEN, *op. cit.*, 61-67; FREISEN, *op. cit.*, 785-92; ESMEIN, *op. cit.*, II, 60-64: PERRONE, *De mat. christ.*, III, 374 ff.; HINSCHIUS, "Das Ehescheidungsrecht nach den angelsächsischen und fränkischen Bussordnungen," *Zeitsch. für deut. Recht*, XX, 66 ff.; ROSENTHAL, *Rechtsfolgen des Ehebruchs*, 2 ff.; and especially BENNECKE, *Ehebruch*, 34 ff. LUCKOCK, *Hist. of Marriage*, 165-67, tries, of course, to take away the authenticity of THEODORE'S Penitential.

of the Council of Hertford, where the orthodox rule relating to divorce was proclaimed. On this penitential and the somewhat older one of the Irish Columban the earlier Frankish penitentials are modeled, sometimes with literal exactness. Divorce with remarriage is allowed to one or both persons on various grounds. In case of adultery a discrimination is made in favor of the husband. He is given the right of repudiating the guilty woman; and, in case it be a dissolution of the first marriage, he may take a new spouse without delay. Even the divorced woman may remarry after a penance of five years. For the like sin, however, the wife is forbidden to send the husband away, except to enter a monastery.[1]

Again, for malicious desertion on the part of the wife, the man may contract a new marriage after five years, if the bishop gives his consent;[2] and a woman whose husband loses his liberty for crime committed has the right to wed another man after a single year, if it be the first marriage which is thus dissolved.[3] Remarriage is allowed either spouse when the other is made captive in war;[4] and in case of conversion each spouse has the right of one-sided divorce, if the other

[1] *Poenitentiale Theod.*, II, xii, 5, 6: HADDAN AND STUBBS, *Councils*, III, 199: *cf.* THORPE, *Anc. Laws*, II, 17. For similar provisions, see *Poenitentiale XXXV Capitulorum*, c. 9, §1: WASSERSCHLEBEN, *Bussordnungen*, 511; and the *Excerptiones Ecgberti*, c. 121: THORPE, *op. cit.*, II, 114, 115.

[2] "Si mulier discesserit a viro suo despiciens eum, nolens revertere et reconciliari vero, post v. annos cum consensu Episcopi aliam accipere licebit uxorem."—*Poenit. Theod.*, II, xii, 19: HADDAN AND STUBBS, *op. cit.*, III, 200. The *Poenit. Merseburgense*, c. 104: WASSERSCHLEBEN, *op. cit.*, 402, seems to allow the man in such case to marry after one year: "Si mulier a viro discesserit et iterum reversa fuerit, suscipiat eam sine dote et ipsa ann. I poeniteat in p. e. a., similiter et ille, si aliam duxerit."— HINSCHIUS, *Das Ehescheidungsrecht*, 80; but GEFFCKEN thinks the second wife must be sent away when the first wife returns, the man doing penance: *Ehescheidung*, 63, 64. *Cf.* similar provisions in *Poenit. Cummeani*, c. 3, §31, *Poenit. XXXV Cap.*, c. 9, §2: WASSERSCHLEBEN, *op. cit.*, 474, 511; and *Poenit. Theod.*, I, xiv, 13: HADDAN AND STUBBS, *op. cit.*, III, 188.

[3] *Poenit. Theod.*, II, xii, 8: HADDAN AND STUBBS, *op. cit.*, III, 199.

[4] In that case, "licet aliam accipere; melius est sic facere quam fornicationes": *Poenit. Theod.*, II, xii, 23: HADDAN AND STUBBS, *op. cit.*, III, 200, 201; *cf.* THORPE, *op. cit.*, II, 19.

remains in paganism.[1] Several other grounds of repudiation
are recognized, as, for instance, when anyone has ignorantly
married a person of servile condition;[2] or when a husband
or wife is raised in rank and the consort remains in servitude.[3] But perhaps the most striking proof that in practice
the church was obliged to compromise with popular sentiment is the repeated recognition of divorce by mutual
consent.[4]

Such laxity seems to have marked the practice of the
Frankish, and probably also that of the Anglo-Saxon, church
during a period of a hundred and fifty years (650–800).
With the beginning of the ninth century, however, a turning-
point is reached. More stringent rules are prescribed by the
councils; and new penitentials are prepared under ecclesiastical authority much more in harmony with the teachings
of Rome. But even now, seemingly, the clergy shrank from
the attempt fully to carry out the reactionary discipline. As
a result a third class of manuals for a time appeared, occupy-
ing medial ground, and better fitted to satisfy the needs of
populations not yet entirely able to give up the liberty which
their ancient laws secured.[5]

---

[1] *Poenit. Theod.*, II, xii, 17, 18: HADDAN AND STUBBS, *op. cit.*, III, 200.

[2] *Poenit. Theod.*, II, xii, 32, xiii, 5: HADDAN AND STUBBS, *op. cit.*, III, 201, 202;
cf. ESMEIN, *Le mariage en droit canonique*, II, 64.

[3] *Poenit. Theod.*, II, xiii, 4: HADDAN AND STUBBS, *op. cit.*, III, 202.
These provisions (notes 4 and 5) are similar to those of the synods of Verberie
and Compiègne relating to *error conditionis* and loss of freedom. See p. 42, above;
and ESMEIN, *op. cit.*, I, 325; II, 68.

[4] "Legitimum conjugium non licet frangi sine consensu amborum."—*Poenit.
Theod.*, II, xii, 7: HADDAN AND STUBBS, *op. cit.*, III, 199. *Cf. Poenit. Mers.*, c. 123,
Poenit. XXXV Cap., c. 9, §1: WASSERSCHLEBEN, *Bussordnungen*, 403, 511. Sometimes in such case remarriage is forbidden: *Judicium Clementis*, §15: WASSER-
SCHLEBEN, *op. cit.*, 435. *Cf.* ESMEIN *op. cit.*, II, 61; GEFFCKEN, *op. cit.*, 64; GLASSON,
op. cit., I, 130, who favors the view of the text; but FREISEN, *op. cit.*, 779, 780, thinks
that §7 of *Poenit. Theod.* is supplemented by §12, which forbids separation on
account of infirmity or even to enter religion *cum consensu amborum*. This view
may be favored by *Excerptiones Ecgberti*, c. 120, 121: THORPE, *op. cit.*, II, 114, 115.

[5] For an illustration see the *Poenit. pseudo-Theod.*, c. iv (19), §24, in WASSER-
SCHLEBEN, *op. cit.*, 582. The best account of the three classes of penitentials is that
of GEFFCKEN, *op. cit.*, 62–65, which is here followed. See also ESMEIN, *op. cit.*, II, 60;
BENNECKE, *Ehebruch*, 54 ff.

e) Final settlement of the Christian doctrine in the canon law.—From the age of Charles the Great the ultimate triumph of the strict ecclesiastical theory of divorce was entirely assured. But there yet remained a twofold task which it would still require centuries to accomplish. On the one hand, the discordant utterances of the Fathers, the popes, and the councils had to be harmonized or explained away; while, at the same time, the results thus gained had to be exactly formulated and wrought into the intricate system of matrimonial jurisprudence. This was the work reserved for the canonists, and especially for the two great "masters," Gratian and Peter Lombard. On the other hand, the practice of the church must be made more thoroughly to coincide with her theory. A means must be found by which the people could be constrained, so far indeed as that was ever to be realized, to accept the canon law as a guide in the affairs of actual life. This end the church was destined to win by gaining exclusive control of divorce procedure as a part of her general competence in matrimonial causes.

Under the Roman law, as also by that of the Jews, divorce was a private transaction. The intention of the person repudiating his spouse was declared orally[1] before seven witnesses. The state might, indeed, punish the crimes causing the separation or enforce the penalties for unjust action, thus incidentally passing on the legality of the divorce itself; but if the proper forms were observed, the private divorce, whether one-sided or by mutual consent, was valid, and the state gave no action either for enforcing the separation or for the restitution of conjugal life.[2]

The same principle obtains among the German nations after the conversion. Divorce is a private act, and there is

---

[1] During the empire a written form, the *libellus repudii*, or letter of divorce, came into use; but the delivery of the *libellus* was not essential to the divorce: GEFFCKEN, *op. cit.*, 27: *ap.* SCHLESINGER, in *Zeitschrift für Rechtsgeschichte*, V (1866), 203 ff.

[2] GEFFCKEN, *op. cit.*, 26, 27; ESMEIN, *op. cit.*, II, 89.

no proper divorce process in the temporal courts. Separation by free consent is usually effected merely through exchange of duplicate copies of a written agreement, or *libellus repudii;*[1] and if sometimes the intention of the parties must be declared before judicial authority, it does not follow that there is any examination of the grounds of action or any judgment admitting or refusing the separation. The "function of the court can have only the purpose of establishing the formal correctness of the act of self-divorce."[2] In the case of one-sided divorce the same general rule prevails. There may be judicial action; but it is an action to punish the crime of the guilty person or to enforce the penalty for unjust repudiation. "The form of one-sided divorce in the Teutonic folk-laws rests upon the same fundamental principles as that of the *leges Romanae.* Self-divorce is in equal degree true Roman and true German. In each case justifiable separation may be preceded by a penal action to determine the guilt of the accused. In each case, moreover, it is not the divorce which the sentence directly decrees, but its justification. It still rests with the aggrieved spouse whether he will make use of his right of separation, or whether he will allow a reconciliation to take place."[3]

The church was ambitious to take the matter of divorce procedure entirely into her own hands; to establish a real jurisdiction which would enable her effectually to forbid separation except on the grounds which she herself approved, and to compel the restitution of married life when separation

[1] The *libellus* was copied from the Roman model. For an example, see above p. 35, note.

[2] GEFFCKEN, *op. cit.,* 47, referring to the *formulae salicae Merkelianae,* where the intention of the parties must be personally announced " an Gerichtsstätte vor dem Grafen und der Gerichtsgemeinde." His view, he declares, is intermediate between that of LOENING, *Geschichte des deut. Kirchenrechts,* II, 627 n. 1, who regards the count and judicial community as mere witnesses of the transaction (*Solennitätszeugen*); and that of SOHM, *Trauung und Verlobung,* 7, who sees here a judicial sentence.

[3] GEFFCKEN, *op. cit.,* 48, 49.

occurred for any other cause.[1]   It was long before this am-
bition was realized.   The council of Agde as early as the
year 505 did indeed declare, in effect, that, besides the penal
sentence of the temporal court, a recognition of the grounds
of divorce by the ecclesiastical authority shall be required
for a separation; and whoever puts away his wife without
first satisfying these conditions shall be excommunicated.[2]
To this decree, so emphatic in its demands, the origin of
spiritual jurisdiction in divorce questions is commonly traced;[3]
but this seems far from being the truth.   The decree must
rather be accepted as an early but "isolated" expression of
an ideal toward which the church for ages was striving; and
as such it became of more and more importance as the great
doctors of the canon law found themselves in a position to
give it meaning.[4]

Even during the Carolingian era theoretically the state
still maintained the old position.   The judgment in a penal
action neither nullified nor enforced self-divorce.   In reality,

[1] The church sought through excommunication and her system of penance to
enforce her rules regarding divorce. Her relation to the state in this regard is thus
forcibly described by GEFFCKEN, op. cit., 51: "Da jedoch eine aufrichtige Busse in
unserem Falle sinngemäss nur möglich ist, wenn die ungerechtfertigte Scheidung
rückgängig gemacht wird, so operiert die Kirche hier mit einer lex plus quam perfecta, d. h. einem Gesetz, das die Zuwiderhandlung bestraft und gleichzeitig für
nichtig erklärt, während dem weltlichen Richter nur eine lex minus quam perfecta
zu Gebote steht, er also nur die Übertretung bestrafen, nicht aber den durch sie her-
beigeführten Zustand redressieren kann. In dieser Sachlage ist die Erklärung der
ganzen Geschichte des christlichen Ehescheidungsrechtes bis zum endgültigen Siege
der kirchlichen Doktrin enthalten."

[2] C. 25, Council of Agde reads: "Saeculares, qui coniugale consortium nulla
graviori culpa dimittunt vel etiam dimiserunt et nullas causas discidii probabiliter
proponentes propterea sua matrimonia dimittunt, ut aut illicita aut aliena praesu-
mant, si antequam apud episcopos comprovinciales discidii causas dixerint et prius-
quam iudicio damnentur, uxores suas abiecerint, a communione ecclesiae et sancto
populi coetu pro eo, quod fidem et coniugia maculant, excludentur." Cf. GEFFCKEN,
op. cit., 50; FREISEN, op. cit., 781.

[3] It is preferably cited by Hincmar of Rheims in his decree concerning the divorce of Lothar and Teutberge; and since Regino of Prüm it belongs to the standing
armor of the canonists, until it receives its immortalization in the decree of Gratian
(c. 33, qu. 2, c. 1): GEFFCKEN, op. cit., 52, note.

[4] GEFFCKEN, op. cit., 52. Cf. on this decree and its use by the canonists ESMEIN,
op. cit., II, 89, notes.

however, the power of the church in this field was vastly increased at the expense of the state.[1] For the state then undertook as never before to enforce the discipline through which hitherto the church had striven in vain to realize her doctrine.[2] Backed by the state, the church thereafter had the power to compel a restitution of conjugal life when a divorce was attempted against her will—a power which the secular judge had never possessed. Accordingly, "the temporal divorce jurisdiction of the Frankish empire, so far indeed as one is justified in speaking of such a jurisdiction, was not abolished by a legislative act; but it gradually perished through the contradiction to its own laws in which the state of the Carolings involved itself when it made the unqualified support of the disciplinary jurisdiction of the church one of its cardinal principles of government."[3] Already by the beginning of the tenth century this process

[1] "Wenn trotzdem die Zeit der Karolinger als diejenige Epoche zu bezeichnen ist, in welcher die Kirche den ihren endgültigen Sieg im Kampfe um das Ehescheidungsrecht besiegelnden Fortschritt machte, so wird dieser Fortschritt weniger auf dem Gebiete des materiellen Rechtes als auf demjenigen des Ehescheidungsverfahrens gesucht werden müssen."—GEFFCKEN, op. cit., 68.

Geffcken criticises SDRALEK, *Hincmars Gutachten über die Ehescheidung des Königs Lothar II.*, 108 ff., who holds that the Frankish civil court has full authority to decree divorces. According to SOHM, "Die geistliche Gerichtbarkeit im fränk. Reich," *ZKR.*, IX, 218, 242 ff., the Frankish matrimonial law is "temporal law, and receives its development through temporal custom and legislation." The canons are statutes for the spiritual and not for the temporal law; and only through the public lawgiver do they have any effect upon the legal principles governing marriage. "By virtue of public law marriage is subordinate to the state and not to the church." The spiritual law is no law for the temporal court; and in matrimonial causes the spiritual court is no court according to public law. There exists, in fact, in the Frankish empire no spiritual jurisdiction in the sense of public law. With this view GEFFCKEN, op. cit., 68 n. 3, agrees; while rejecting as inconsistent therewith SOHM's later statement in *ZKR.*, XVII, 179, that the judgment of the temporal as well as that of the spiritual court was necessary for a divorce. Compare BOEHMER, *Ehegesetze im Zeitalter Karls des Grossen*, 108–16, who explains the contradictory enactments of the period as the result of the two systems of jurisprudence—the temporal and the spiritual.

[2] See the remarkable capitulary of Lothar I., 825. For the correction of all sins and crimes (*quibuslibet culpis atque criminibus*) the count is associated with the bishop. When excommunication fails to correct the offender, "*a comite vinculis constringatur*": quoted by GEFFCKEN, op. cit., 72; cf. ESMEIN, op. cit., I, 13, 14.

[3] GEFFCKEN, op. cit., 74.

was practically complete.[1] In German lands the diocesan court of the bishop had become the ordinary tribunal for divorce causes; and for annulment of the uncanonical separation an exact formula, the oath of reconciliation, had been devised.[2]

A powerful instrument was thus provided for the development and enforcement of a complete system of divorce jurisprudence. Little by little the canonists, in tedious succession from Hincmar of Rheims to the decretalist Tancred,[3] brought order out of confusion and agreement out of contradiction. Through special pleading and violent assumption, unscrupulous twisting and suppressing of texts, earnest argument and childish allegory, the law of divorce was gradually brought into some degree of harmony with the sacramental theory of marriage.[4] The middle of the tenth

[1] See GEFFCKEN's argument based on the *Libri duo de synodalibus causis et disciplinis ecclesiasticis* of Regino, abbot of Prüm (883-915): *op. cit.*, 77-79. In England under King Cnut the bishop already appears to have had jurisdiction in divorce cases, although not until more than a century later was the matrimonial jurisdiction of the English ecclesiastical courts fully established: POLLOCK AND MAITLAND, *Hist. of Eng. Law*, II, 364, 365.

[2] The following is the form of the *iuramentum de reconciliatione coniugatorum* taken by GEFFCKEN (*op. cit.*, 79) from cc. 241, 242, of REGINO's book: The man shall swear: "Ab isto die in antea istam tuam coniugem, nomine illam, quam iniuste dimiseras, ita tenebis, sicut per rectum maritus suam debet habere coniugem in dilectione et debita disciplina, nec eam per ullum malum ingenium a te separabis, nec ea vivente aliam accipies. Sic te Deus adiuvet." The oath of the woman runs: "A modo in antea istum tuum maritum, quem iniuste dimiseras, ita tenebis et amplexaberis, et ei in servitio, in amore et in timore ita eris subiecta et obediens, sicut per rectum uxor suo debet subiecta esse marito, nec unquam ab eo te separabis, nec illo vivente alteri viro te sociabis in coniugio aut adulterio. Sic te Deus adiuvet."

[3] See WUNDERLICH's excellent edition of *Tancredi summa de matrimonio*, especially 16 ff., on the impediments, and 70 ff., on causes of separation.

[4] Thus, for example, Gratian accounts for the liberty of divorce and remarriage accorded in the letter of Gregory II. (confusing him with Gregory I.) by assuming that it was in consequence of a papal dispensation in favor of the English (*Decret. Grat., dictum* to c. 18, C. XXXII, qu. 7), although elsewhere he more sensibly rejects Gregory's action as unorthodox. Peter Lombard makes no mention of Gregory's letter and with Gratian rejects as false the passage of pseudo-Ambrose allowing separation and remarriage for adultery (ESMEIN, *op. cit.*, II, 76); while others get out of the difficulty through the gratuitous assumption that pseudo-Ambrose refers, not to simple adultery, but to a case of incest committed by a woman with a relative of her husband, *affinitas superveniens*. Gratian will not accept this explanation, on

century saw the task virtually accomplished at the hands of Gratian and Peter Lombard,[1] the master-builders of the canon law;[2] although their teachings are still "on the surface obscured by reminiscences" of earlier theories, and after them the Decretals show certain aberrations from the strict doctrine, like "sporadic cases after a great epidemic."[3]

Theoretically, as commonly stated, divorce proper is entirely eliminated from the mature law of the western church; but inconsistently the name "divorce" is retained as a rubric in the collections of canons; and it is used in two

the ground that, according to the theory of *affinitas superveniens*, husband and wife are treated alike. Yet, with delicious inconsequence, he proceeds to explain why pseudo-Ambrose had given the man alone the right to remarry in case of the wife's adultery, without granting the woman the reciprocal privilege. In the text of Ambrose, he says, the words *vir* and *mulier* are not employed in their proper sense, but figuratively. Each is used for man irrespective of sex. *Vir* is from *virtus*, and means man as a strong being resisting temptation; *mulier* is from *mollities* (softness), and it is used to denote the weak-minded man guilty of sin (*Dec. Grat., dictum* to c. 18, C. XXXII, qu. 7. *Cf.* ESMEIN, *op. cit.*, II, 76; FREISEN, *op. cit.*, 582, 805). Ivo of Chartres, bent on sustaining the rigid theory of indissolubility, cites cc. 5 and 9 of the decree of Verberie in its favor, deliberately suppressing the clauses allowing the man to remarry (see his *Decretum*, X, 169; VIII, 189; also his *Panormia*, VI, 91: GEFFCKEN, *op. cit.*, 82); and Gratian, by adopting Ivo's text for c. 9 instead of the original, gets around a similar difficulty (FREISEN, *op. cit.*, 803). Celestin III. and Urban III. allowed the faithful spouse divorce and remarriage when the other becomes an infidel or a heretic; but the later canonists evaded this authority by claiming that these popes spoke merely as "simple doctors" (ESMEIN, *op. cit.*, II, 80).

On the wide use of "metaphor" in the history of the church see LECKY, *Democracy and Liberty*, II, 217; and especially his *Hist. of European Morals*, II, 326, 327, 356–58.

[1] For once at least we can almost pardon Milton for using strong language. SELDEN's work, *Of the Law of Nature and of Nations*, he holds more useful than anything which "pontifical clerks have doted on, ever since that unfortunate mother famously sinned thrice, and died impenitent of her bringing into the world those two misbegotten infants, and for ever infants, Lombard and Gratian, him the compiler of canon iniquity, the other the Tubalcain of scholastic sophistry, whose overspreading barbarism hath not only infused their own bastardy upon the fruitfullest part of human learning, not only dissipated and dejected the clear light of nature in us, and of nations, but hath tainted also the fountains of divine doctrine, and rendered the pure and solid law of God unbeneficial to us by their calumnious dunceries."—"Doctrine and Discipline of Divorce," *Prose Works*, III, 269.

[2] *Cf.* especially *Decretum Gratiani*, cc. 1–24, *causa* xxxii, qu. 7: RICHTER-FRIEDBERG, *Corpus Juris Can.*, I; PETER LOMBARD, *Sententiae*, IV, D. xxvii ff.

[3] ESMEIN, *op. cit.*, II, 79, 80. The early canonists are discussed by GEFFCKEN, *op. cit.*, 58–62, 75–82; CIGOI, *Unauflösbarkeit*, 93 ff.; but for the most minute examination of them all see FREISEN, *op. cit.*, 793–847; also the very clear account of ESMEIN, *op. cit.*, II, 71 ff. On the formation of the canon law see TISSOT, *Le mariage*, 111 ff.

senses, neither of which corresponds with its ancient and proper meaning as a complete dissolution of the bond of true wedlock. First, the term *divortium a vinculo matrimonii* is commonly employed to designate, not the dissolution of a lawful union, but the judicial declaration of nullity of a spurious marriage which on account of some impediment is void, or at least voidable, from the beginning. Secondly, the term *divortium a mensa et thoro* means a judicial separation of husband and wife which does not touch the marriage tie. In each case, therefore, the use of the word "divorce" is loose and very misleading.[1]

As finally settled, the canon law permits a separation from bed and board on three grounds. First is adultery. For this offense the woman as well as the man is given an action for divorce, which, however, may be defeated by pleading various exceptions, such as the like guilt of the accusing party.[2] The second cause is "spiritual adultery,"[3] being historically an enlargement of the first cause through allegorical interpretation. Originally under this head separation was allowed for various offenses;[4] but in the end it is restricted to the heresy or apostasy of one of the persons, and perhaps to the case of one spouse compelling the other to commit a wrong,[5] although on this point the authorities

---

[1] ESMEIN, *op. cit.*, II, 73, 85–89, who gives a brief account of the evolution of the uses of the term *divortium*. Originally, among the canonists, there was but one kind of *divorce*, *i. e.*, any judicial separation between man and wife, whether or not with the right to remarry. This led to confusion; and so the distinction between divorce *a vinculo* or *quoad vinculum* and *a mensa et toro* or *quoad mensam et torum* was differentiated. Beginning with Bernard of Pavia, the first compiler of the Decretals, the term *divortium* appears regularly as a rubric in the later collections of the canon law.

[2] For the exceptions see ESMEIN, *op. cit.*, II, 91, 92; FREISEN, *op. cit.*, 833–36; SCHEURL, *Das gem. deut. Eherecht*, 288, 289.

[3] More exactly speaking *fornicatio spiritualis* "as opposed to *fornicatio carnalis*," the first cause mentioned.

[4] Crimes against nature, idolatry, etc.: ESMEIN, *op. cit.*, II, 90 n. 1.

[5] Such as forcing a spouse to idolatry or to some heinous crime. This case is regarded as an enlargement of the conception of *fornicatio spiritualis*: ESMEIN, *op. cit.*, II, 90 n. 4, 92 nn. 8, 9. *Cf.* FREISEN. *op. cit.*, 836.

are by no means agreed.   A third cause for which separation may be demanded is cruelty committed by one partner
against the other.   Whether in this case blows alone will
suffice, especially as concerns the woman, is not settled by
the laws; but the "dominant opinion inclines to leave the
determination of this point to the discretion of the judge."[1]

It thus appears that theological subtlety, partly under
stress of the needs of actual life, has found a way to pass
far beyond the limits which any reasonable interpretation
of the scriptural precepts will permit.   In dealing with the
question of divorce *a vinculo* an inconsistency even greater
is shown, and the results are far more disastrous; for the
door is thereby opened for manifold hardships and corruption.   In the first place, two exceptions to the rule that a
genuine marriage cannot be dissolved are sanctioned by the
law and practice of the Church.   The *privilegium Paulinum*
is thus freely admitted.[2]   If the Christian convert is abandoned by his infidel spouse, he is allowed to contract a new
marriage.   Only by an ingenious assumption can this liberty
be harmonized with the prevailing dogma.   The case is no
exception, we are told, for it is the infidel, not the believer,
who dissolves the marriage; and the rule of the church does
not apply when the unbeliever "renounces his right" to
maintain that relation, in order to "make use of his own
heathen law."[3]   In England, where the canon law of

---

[1] ESMEIN, *op. cit.*, II, 93, 94. Earlier divorce *a mensa et thoro* was not granted
on this ground unless there was real danger to the life of one of the parties; but at
last it was decided that *nimia saevitia* would suffice, but the term is not defined:
idem, loc. cit. In general on this species of divorce see FREISEN, *op. cit.*, 830–47;
GEARY, *Marriage and Family Relations*, 238, 239, 350; SCHEURL, *Das gem. deut.
Eherecht*, 286–91.

[2] *Decret. Grat.*, II, *caus.* xviii, qu. 2, C. 2; and *Decretals* IV, 19, *de divortiis*, c. 7:
see RICHTER-FRIEDBERG, *Corpus juris can.*, I.

[3] This is FREISEN'S argument, *op. cit.*, 825–27, 817 ff. See also SCHEURL, *Das gem.
deut. Eherecht*, 276–78. The canon law maintains the validity of a marriage between
two infidels contracted before conversion. According to PETER LOMBARD, the believer
may, indeed, put away his unconverted consort, but may not remarry. Only when
the infidel is the active party, the Christian being the passive, is the latter released

divorce was in full force, the *casus apostoli* had a practical application to the advantage of the faithful in their dealings with the Jews. "In 1234 a Jewish widow was refused her dower on the ground that her husband had been converted and that she had refused to adhere to him and be converted with him. An Essex jury even doubted whether if two Jews married under the 'Lex Judaica' but afterwards turned to the 'Lex Christiana' and then had a son, that son could be legitimate;"[1] but this finding is not in harmony with the teaching of the canon law. Moreover, in modern times, with the spread of Catholic missions into many new lands, this privilege has been of increasing importance.[2]

By the second exception the church found herself entangled in the subtle theory accepted after Peter Lombard that a contract *de praesenti* constitutes a valid marriage whether followed by actual wedded life or not.[3] The mature doctrine of the canon law, which is still obeyed by the Roman church, permits the unconsummate marriage *de praesenti* to be dissolved through papal dispensation or *ipso facto* by taking holy orders.[4] Here in effect the older

---

from the marriage bond: *Sententiae, IV.*, D. 39, § G; FREISEN, *op. cit.*, 814. This privilege is much discussed in modern theological literature: see the references in FREISEN, *op. cit.*, 826 n. 27. In general compare WOOLSEY, *Divorce*, 74 ff., 125; ESMEIN, *op. cit.*, I, 220–32; II, 268 ff., 307; SCHEURL, *op. cit.*, 276, 277.

[1] POLLOCK AND MAITLAND, *Hist. of Eng. Law*, II, 391, 392: citing for the first case TOVEY, *Anglia Judaica*, 84; *Co. Lit.*, 31*b*, 32*a*; and for the second, *Calend. Geneal.*, II, 563.

[2] So in India: POLLOCK AND MAITLAND, *op. cit.*, II, 391 n. 2: citing Maine's speech on the "Remarriage of Native Converts," in *Memoir and Speeches and Minutes* (London, 1892), 130. *Cf.* especially ESMEIN, *op. cit.*, II, 268 ff., who discusses some of the "curious problems" growing out of this rule.

[3] For the evils arising in clandestine marriage *de praesenti*, the complexity of the law of forbidden degrees, and the conflicting jurisdiction of the temporal and spiritual courts, see chap. viii above.

[4] FREISEN, *op. cit.*, 826 ff., 212 ff., shows that the *dispensatio summi pontificis a matrimonio rato nondum consummato* originated with the reforms of Alexander III.; and argues rightly that these two kinds of dissolution — dispensation and orders — are in harmony with the rule of indissolubility according to the doctrine of Gratian, but not according to the existing theory. Thus, of the old eight causes which were

theory of Gratian, that only the consummate marriage is a real
marriage, is adopted for a practical end, although it is absolutely irreconcilable with the still accepted orthodox theory
of Lombard, whose enforcement in the ecclesiastical courts
has been the cause of so much evil in western Christendom.[1]

Taking the church's own definition of marriage, it seems,
after all, that divorce *a vinculo* did not in reality quite dis-
appear from the canon law.   It would be a serious error to
imagine that the opportunity for escaping entirely from the
bonds of undesirable wedlock was restricted to the contract
de praesenti not followed by actual conjugal life, which in
direct violation of her own theory the church was constrained
to treat as an imperfect marriage.   To all intents and purposes, when judged from a rational modern standpoint, the
decree of nullity was a divorce proper.   Practically speaking, it cannot be doubted that there existed a very wide
liberty of divorce in the Middle Ages, though it existed
mainly for those who were able to pay the ecclesiastical
judge for finding a way through the tortuous maze of forbidden degrees.[2]   In a divorce procedure masquerading
under the guise of an action for nullifying spurious marriages
lurked the germs of perjury and fraud.   When both persons
were willing to separate, the matter must have been easy
enough by collusion; and when one consort was tired of the
other, the ecclesiastical court for money would be able

---

sufficient of themselves to dissolve *matrimonium initiatum* — identical with the later
sponsalia de praesenti — holy orders alone remains; the papal dispensation has
taken the place of the other seven: *ibid.*, 827, 829; *cf.* on these exceptions SCHEURL,
Das. gem. deut. Eherecht, 278-86.

[1] See chaps. vii and viii, above.

[2] JEAFFRESON, *Brides and Bridals*, II, 299 ff., conjectures that during the Middle
Ages there must have been many irregular self-divorces; and he cites the famous
case of William Paynel and Margaret his wife who, in 1302, "petitioned the king for
the dower that was due to her as widow of her first husband John de Camoys," who
with her consent had "openly and before witnesses 'given, granted, released, and
quit-claimed' the said Margaret to 'her chivalric knight,'" the said William.   The
court refused the dower on the ground of desertion and adultery.   *Cf.* on this case
POLLOCK AND MAITLAND, *Hist. of Eng. Law*, II, 393, 394.

to find good reasons for effecting his release.[1] "Spouses who had quarreled began to investigate their pedigrees and were unlucky if they could discover no *impedimentum dirimens*" or cause which would have prevented the contraction of a valid marriage.[2] "The canons prescribing the prohibited degrees of relationship were marvels of ingenuity. Spiritual relationships, those gained in baptism, were recognized no less than natural relationships, and equally with them served as barriers to legal marriage. Marriage was prohibited within seven[3] degrees of relationship and affinity; and none but the astutest students of the law were able to unravel so complicated a system. The annulling of marriages, which had been contracted within the prohibited degrees, became a flourishing business of the Church. No exercise of its power yielded more money, or caused more scandal. So tangled was the casuistry respecting marriage, at the beginning of the sixteenth century, that it might be said that, for a sufficient consideration, a canonical flaw could be found in almost any marriage."[4]

The marvelous resources of the church in the binding and unbinding of wedlock are strikingly exhibited in the matrimonial adventures of Margaret Tudor, daughter of Henry VII. To enable her to marry King James IV. of Scotland a papal dispensation was requisite, as they were related within the fourth degree. After he was slain at the battle of Flodden (1513), Margaret espoused Archibald Douglas, sixth earl of Angus; and from him in 1527 she obtained by papal authority a divorce "on the desperate

---

[1] JEAFFRESON, *op. cit.*, II, 306-9.

[2] POLLOCK AND MAITLAND, *op. cit.*, II, 391 n. 1. Read the interesting remarks of LECKY, *Democracy and Liberty*, II, 193-96, who cites, as illustrative of the policy of the Roman church, the divorce case of Napoleon and Josephine. See also *Law Review* (English), I, 353-56.

[3] Before Innocent III., 1215, who reduced the number to four: WOOLSEY, *Divorce*, 121.

[4] THWING, *The Family*, 83. *Cf.* WOOLSEY, *op. cit.*, 118 ff.

plea first brought forward in 1525, that James IV. had lived
for three years after Flodden," and so was alive at the
time of her second nuptials.[1] Her next experiment in the
spiritual courts was less successful. In vain she tried to rid
herself of her third consort, Henry Stuart, on the pretext
that her previous cohabitation with her husband's fourth
cousin, the earl of Angus, had created a bar to their marriage through affinity.[2]

Long before this, in the days of Edward II., a satirist
describes the "prodigious traffic" in divorces. Any husband having "selver among the clerkes to send" could rid
himself of his wife by "bringing her to the constery" or
consistory court, with two false witnesses to support his
declarations.[3] A case is mentioned by Coke "in which a

[1] It is interesting to find Wolsey writing in Henry VIII.'s name "to remind her
of the 'divine ordinance of inseparable matrimony first instituted in paradise,' protesting against 'the shameless sentence sent from Rome'": TAIT, in *Dict. of Nat.
Biog.*, XXXVI, 155.

[2] Henry Stuart (Stewart) was made Lord Methven by Margaret's son, James V.
She "attempted to get rid of that nobleman by a sentence of the ecclesiastical
court, on the ground that before the marriage she had been (as the record expresses
it) *carnaliter cognita* by her husband's fourth cousin, the earl of Angus."—RIDDELL,
Scots' Peerage Law, 187; *Law Review*, I, 354. On Margaret's marriages and divorces
compare THWING, *The Family*, 83; WOOLSEY, *Divorce*, 169, who says she "got from
Rome a separation from her second husband, the Earl of Angus, on the pretext
of a pre-contract between him and another lady;" and especially the very accurate
account of TAIT, in *Dict. of Nat. Biog.*, XXXVI, 150-57.

[3] JEAFFRESON, *Brides and Bridals*, II, 310, who quotes the following verses
entitled "A Poem on the Times of Edward II." from the *Percy Society Publication:*

> "If a man have a wyf,
> And he love her nowt,
> Bring her to the constery,
> There trewth schuld be wrowt.
> Bring twei fals wytnes with hym,
> And hymself the thrydde,
> And he shall be deperted,
> As fair as he wold bydde,
>   From his wyf;
> He schal be maynteyned fulle well
>   To lede a sory lyf.
>
> "When he is deperted
> From hys trew spowse,
> Take hys neyghboures wyf
> And bryng her to howse,
> Yif he have selver
> Among the clerkes to send,
> He may have hir to hys wyf
> To hys life's end,
>   With onskylle,
> Thei that so fair with falseness dele
>   Godde's corse on her bille."

marriage was pronounced null because the husband had stood god-father to the cousin of his wife."[1]   Before the Reformation the voidance of alleged false wedlock on the ground of pre-contract or forbidden degrees of affinity, spiritual relationship, consanguinity, or on some other canonical pretext, had become an intolerable scandal.   "Marriages have been brought into such an uncertainty thereby," complains a statute of Henry VIII., "that no marriage could be so surely knit or bounden but it should lie in either of the parties' power . . . . to prove a pre-contract, a kindred and alliance, or a carnal knowledge to defeat the same."[2]

Nevertheless, the Council of Trent introduced no essential change in the divorce law of the Catholic church.[3]   A vain attempt was made to remedy the evils arising in the confusion of terms.[4]   Anathema was pronounced against

[1] LECKY, *Democracy and Liberty*, II, 194.   For other examples see HUTH, *Marriage of Near Kin*, 118-20.

[2] 32 H. VIII., c. 38: *Statutes at Large* (London, 1763), II, 298.
The facility with which dispensations could be secured is illustrated by a Scotch case in 1426-28.   On April 11, 1426, Pope Martin V. granted a dispensation to Alexander of Hume and Marion of Lander to marry, though of double fourth degree of consanguinity.   Curiously enough, perhaps because this dispensation had not yet been received, on Oct. 6, 1427, Hume appeared before the rector sitting as judge and proposed that his marriage could not stand of right because of consanguinity.   The marriage was therefore pronounced null and void, and the parties were given license to marry whom they pleased.   On the fourth day of the following January Hume and his former wife presented a petition to the papal see, announcing that, aware of their consanguinity, they had contracted marriage *per verba de praesenti* and begotten children; that when their ordinary heard of the consanguinity he rightly celebrated a divorce, which they obeyed; but they feared scandal, and for this and other reasons they desired to be joined in marriage.   The pope therefore granted another dispensation and declared their offspring legitimate: *Hist. Manuscripts Commission, XII. Report*, App. VIII, 122, 123.   In another case, 1459, the earl of Rothes declares on oath that he had within the last year obtained certain knowledge of the impediment of consanguinity as set forth in his libel, and that formerly, for the space of thirteen years after birth of the last of his living children, he was altogether ignorant of it: *ibid., IV. Report*, 507.

[3] In general see CIGOI, *Unauflösbarkeit*, 149 ff.; PERRONE, *De mat. christ.*, III, 376 ff., 389 ff., 398 ff.; GODOLPHIN, *Repartorium canonicum*, 61, 62, 492-512; ESMEIN, *Le mariage en droit canonique*, II, 295 ff., 308 ff.; SCHULTE, *Lehrbuch*, 359-61; LECKY, *Democracy and Liberty*, II, 193, 196, 197; GLASSON, *Le mariage civil et le divorce*, 216, 217; SCHEURL, *Das gem. deut. Eherecht*, 275, 276, where the canons adopted at the twenty-fourth session are given.

[4] By the bishop of Barcelona, who proposed the word *separatio* for divorce *quoad torum:* ESMEIN, *op. cit.*, II, 309.   On the misleading names for the two kinds

those who should deny the indissolubility of wedlock as a
necessary consequence of its sacramental nature; and a like
curse was fulminated against any who shall dare to say that
the church errs in allowing divorce *quoad torum et cohabitationem*, temporarily or perpetually, for any cause besides
unfaithfulness.[1]   But neither at the council nor since has
there ever been made any essential change in the law relating to the papal power of dispensation.[2]

II.   THE PROTESTANT DOCTRINE OF DIVORCE

a) Opinions of Luther and the continental reformers.—
With the rejection of the sacramental theory of marriage at
the Reformation it was inevitable that more liberal ideas
respecting divorce should arise.   The mother-church was
accused of fostering vice by professing a doctrine too severe;[3]
while at the same time she was bitterly reproached with a
scandalous abuse of her own jurisdiction through which in

of separation see POLLOCK AND MAITLAND, *Hist. of Eng. Law*, II, 392 n. 5.   However,
a "modern distinction of some Catholic writers between *anullatio* and *separatio*
removes all ambiguity."—WOOLSEY, *Divorce*, 124.

[1] "viii.   Si quis dixerit . . . . vel Ecclesiam errare, dum ob alias causas, praeter
adulterium, facit divortium quoad thorum seu cohabitationem, ad tempus vel
perpetuo: anathema sit."—THEINER, *Acta*, II, 313: ESMEIN, *op. cit.*, II, 309 n. 1.

[2] Distinction is made between *dispensatio super matrimonio*, that is, for dissolving an unconsummate marriage; and *dispensatio matrimonialis*, that is, to remove
an impediment which otherwise would invalidate a proposed contract.   In all cases
of dispensation careful judicial inquiry as to the grounds of application is made:
GEARY, *Marriage and Family Relations*, 510–14.   *Cf.* WOOLSEY, *op. cit.*, 122, 123; and
especially the convenient manual of POMPEN, *De dispensationibus*, 122–68.   For a full
discussion of the intricate law and custom as to dispensation see ESMEIN, *op. cit.*,
II, 315–68; FREISEN, *Geschichte des can. Eherechts*, 891–906; SCHEURL, *Das gem. deut.
Eherecht*, 281 ff.   In the oriental church dispensation from the forbidden degrees is
in general not allowed, ZHISHMAN: *Das Eherecht der orient. Kirche*, 709–17.

[3] The writings of Luther, Milton, and other Reformation and Puritan writers
abound in examples of such charges.   "For no cause, honest or necessary," says
MARTIN BUCER, "will they permit a final divorce: in the meanwhile, whoredoms and
adulteries, and worse things than these, not only tolerating in themselves and others,
but cherishing and throwing men headlong into these evils.   For although they also
disjoin married persons from board and bed, that is, from all conjugal society and
communion, and this not only for adultery, but for ill usage, and matrimonial duties
denied; yet they forbid those thus parted to join in wedlock with others: but, as I
said before, any dishonest associating they permit."—"The Judgment of Martin
Bucer," in MILTON'S *Prose Works*, III, 292.

effect the forbidden degrees had become an open door to divorce for the use of the rich and powerful. Accordingly, the leaders of Protestantism took intermediate ground. On the one hand, while Luther and some other reformers sanctioned temporary separations[1] of husband and wife, there was a strong tendency to reject entirely perpetual divorce *a mensa et thoro* as being a "relatively modern invention" unknown to the ancient church; and a condition of life incompatible with the true ideal of wedlock.[2] On the other hand, they generally favored complete divorce *a vinculo*, admitting two or more grounds according as they interpreted strictly or more liberally the scriptural texts. For they still appealed to authority rather than to reason and experience in their attempts to solve a great social problem. They were thus often sorely embarrassed. Their writings, indeed, reveal not a little of the casuistry and self-deception which so often vitiate the reasoning of the canonists and their predecessors.[3]

From the outset the continental reformers took a bold stand;[4] for the Protestant doctrine of divorce, like the Protestant conception of the form and nature of marriage, was shaped mainly by the thought of Martin Luther. Yet revolutionary as were his teachings, he did not go so far in his departure from the orthodox rule as did some of his contemporaries and successors. The analysis of Richter has disclosed two distinct tendencies in the doctrine and practice

[1] GOESCHEN, *Doctrina de mat.*, 60; also MEJER, "Zur Geschichte des ält. prot. Eherechts," in *ZKR.*, XVI, 47; HUBRICH, *Das Recht der Ehescheidung*, 139 ff.

[2] *Cf.* ESMEIN, *Le mariage en droit canonique*, II, 308, 309. Throughout his *Doctrine and Discipline of Divorce*, as elsewhere in his writings, MILTON insists that a real marriage implies a full spiritual as well as conjugal companionship, with which the theory of separation without dissolution is inconsistent; and this is the common Puritan view.

[3] For example, see MILTON's specious argument, following the allegorical method of some of the early theologians, to show the scope of the term "fornication" as used by Jesus and Moses: "Doctrine and Discipline of Divorce," *Prose Works*, III, 251–58, 394–401.

[4] See MILTON's summary of their views: "Tetrachordon," *loc. cit.*, 423–33.

of the Reformation period.[1]   In the sixteenth century the
more rigid or conservative direction is taken by Luther and
the more influential Protestant leaders, among whom are the
theologians Brenz, Bugenhagen, Chemnitz, Calvin, and Beza,
with the jurists Kling, Beust, and Schneidewin.[2]   All are
agreed that absolute divorce should be granted for adultery,
although some of them, like Chemnitz, appear to discriminate against the woman in this regard.[3]   Malicious desertion
is also generally admitted as a second cause for the full dissolution of wedlock, following the same Bible text which gave
rise to the *casus apostoli* of the canonists.[4]   It is characteristic of Luther and the representatives of the more rigid
tendency that, rather than multiply the number of admissible
grounds of divorce, an effort was made by hard logic to
broaden the definition of desertion so as to give to it a wide
range without seeming to transgress the letter of scriptural

[1] RICHTER, *Beiträge zur Gesch. des Ehescheidungsrechts in der evang. Kirche*, 11 ff.,
15 ff., 56 ff. ; *idem, Kirchenrecht*, 1177.

[2] Adultery and desertion are the only grounds of full divorce recognized by
BRENZ, *Wie yn Ehesachen . . . . zu Handeln*, in SARCERIUS, *Vom heil. Ehestande*,
152–57, and *idem, Corpus juris mat.*, 183 ff. ; with which may be compared the passages
from the writings of BRENZ quoted by RICHTER, *Beiträge*, 19–23; BUGENHAGEN, *Vom
Ehebruch und Weglauffen:* in SARCERIUS, *Vom heil. Ehestande*, 138–51; or *Corpus
juris mat.*, 171–84; CHEMNITZ, *Examen conc. trid.*, II, 430; Calvin, in RICHTER, *op. cit.*,
25, 26; BEZA, *Tract. de repud. et divort.* (Geneva, 1569), 228 ff., 275 ff.; KLING, *Tract.
mat. causarum* (Frankfort, 1577), 89 ff.; BEUST, *Tract. de jure connub.; idem, Tract.
de spons. et mat.*, 147 ff.; SCHNEIDEWIN, *Com. in inst.; idem, De nupt., lib. primi com.*
(Jena, 1585), §§ 7 ff.

These and other writers are discussed by RICHTER, *Kirchenrecht*, 1175 ff.; *idem,
Beiträge*, 15 ff.; MEJER, *Zum Kirchenrechte der Reformat.*, 147 ff.; HAUBER, *Ehescheid.
im Reformat.*, II, 209 ff. In general, compare GREVE, *Ehescheidung*, 225 ff.; POPP,
Ehescheidung, 80 ff.; STRIPPELMANN, *Das Ehescheidungsrecht*, 54 ff., 128 ff.; STÖLZEL,
Ehescheidungsrecht, 9 ff.; GLASSON, *Le mar. civ. et le divorce*, 224, 225, 329, 330;
SCHEURL, *Das gem. deut. Eherecht*, 291 ff.; BUCHKA, *Das meckl. Ehescheidungsrecht*,
20 ff.; HUBRICH, *Das Recht der Ehescheidung*, 43 ff.; FRIEDBERG, *Lehrbuch*, 366–78;
idem, "Beiträge," *ZKR.*, VII, 56–127; and SCHULTE, *Lehrbuch*, 414–28.

[3] CHEMNITZ, *Examen conc. trid.* (Frankfort, 1615), II, 430 says : " We have, then,
two cases in Scripture where the bond of matrimony is dissolved — not as by men, but
by God himself. 1. On account of adultery a man lawfully, rightfully, and without
sin, can repudiate his wife." 2. Desertion of the believer by the unbeliever, according to 1 Cor., 7. *Cf.* WOOLSEY, *Divorce*, 131; RICHTER, *Beiträge*, 27, 28. On the
adoption of these two general causes at the Reformation see HUBRICH, *Das Recht der
Ehescheidung*, 44 ff.

[4] 1 Cor. 7:15.

authority.[1]   In this way, for instance, *saevitia*, or cruelty, was included, as was also refusal of conjugal duty, eventually giving rise to the doctrine of "quasi-desertion."   But for this last cause a marriage must not be dissolved except on failure of all prescribed means, however cruel, to induce reconciliation or submission.   For it was a natural result of the carnal theory of wedlock that theological dogma and church ordinance alike in effect permitted a brutal husband, through the aid of fine, exile, or imprisonment, to force an unwilling wife to render him her "conjugal duty."[2]

Only two general causes of full divorce on alleged scriptural authority were thus admitted by Luther and his immediate followers.   Other offenses, except as by logical fiction brought under the definition of desertion or adultery, were merely accepted as grounds of temporary separation

[1] As early as 1520 in his *Von dem bab. Gefängniss der Kirche* (STRAMPFF, 349, 350, 381, 382) LUTHER admits the two grounds of divorce, adultery and desertion; the latter when either spouse abandons the other "über zehen Jahr oder nimmer wiederkommen." Two years later, in his *Vom ehelichen Leben*, he appears to regard refusal of conjugal duty as equivalent to desertion. "We may find an obstinate woman," he says, "who stiffens her neck, and if her husband should fall ten times into unchastity, cares nothing about it. Here it is time for a man to say, 'if you won't, another can be found that will. If the wife will not, let the maid come.' Yet let it be so that the husband give her two or three warnings beforehand, and let the matter come before other people, so that her obstinacy may be known and rebuked before the congregation. If she will not, let her be gone, and procure an Esther for yourself and let Vashti be off, as Ahasuerus did."—As rendered by WOOLSEY, *Divorce*, 130, 131. For the original see STRAMPFF, 350, 351, 394, 395; LUTHER'S *Kleinere Schriften*, II, 26–31; and SARCERIUS, *Vom heil. Ehestande*, 137, 138. *Cf.* RICHTER, *Beiträge*, 16; SCHEURL, *Das gem. deut. Eherecht*, 300 ff. In LUTHER'S *Von Ehesachen* (1530) the refusal of conjugal duty is not mentioned; but it is doubtless included under malicious desertion; and besides in 1531 he commends the book of Brenz in which this position is taken. *Cf.* RICHTER, *op. cit.*, 18, 19; STRAMPFF, 394. In the *Tischreden* flight on account of theft is regarded as desertion: RICHTER, *loc. cit.* On the use made of "definition" by the Protestants see HUBRICH, *Das Recht der Ehescheidung*, 51.

[2] *Quasi malitiosa desertio* comprehends not only refusal of conjugal duty, but also applies to the case of a defendant who abandoned a consort, but who does not necessarily, as in malicious desertion, remain in a place unknown or one beyond the reach of judicial process: STRIPPELMANN, *Ehescheidungsrecht*, 146 ff. *Cf.* DIETRICH, *Evang. Ehescheidungsrecht*, 25 ff.; HUBRICH, *Das Recht der Ehescheidung*, 80, 88 ff. See especially LUTHER, *Vom ehel. Leben:* STRAMPFF, 394, 395, who says the "weltliche Ubirkeit das Weib zwingen oder umbbringen" soll.

from bed and board, subject to reconciliation.[1] On the other hand, the representatives of the more liberal tendency anticipated in many ways modern ideas as to the grounds of absolute dissolution of the marriage bond. Avoiding to some extent the indirect method of attaining practical ends by juggling with definitions, they were inclined to appeal for authority directly to Roman imperial legislation; and so, "since the other direction is connected with the canon law, we have here a phase of the struggle" between that system and the Roman jurisprudence.[2] The first step in the liberal direction is taken by Erasmus, who sustains a rational method of dealing with the divorce problem through appeal to the teachings of the early Fathers, notably those of Origen; and this brought him in contact with the principles of the old Roman law.[3] His influence, as Richter strongly urges, seems to have been felt by Zwingli, who, with his disciple Bullinger, argues that in admitting adultery as a cause of divorce the Scriptures sanction as such all equal or graver offenses.[4] Accordingly, in the Zurich marriage ordinance of 1525, "adultery, malicious desertion, and plotting against the life of a consort are not regarded as

---

[1] Luther does not allow absolute divorce on account of anger or incompatibility, *insidiae*, or attempts upon life, exile, sickness, incurable disease, misfortune to an innocent spouse, or similar grounds: see his *Von Ehesachen*, in STRAMPFF, 398, 399; *Vom ehel. Leben: ibid.*, 400; *Predigt von dem Ehestande* (1525): *ibid.*, 400; and *Auslegung des 17. Cap. 1 Cor.* (1523): *ibid*, 397, 398, where only temporary separation is allowed, unless one of the parties refuses reconciliation and the other "kunnt nicht halten;" but in this case the "separation has the refusal of conjugal duty as a consequence, or it has become malicious desertion": STRAMPFF, 396, 351, 352, 382 ff. *Cf.* BRENZ, *Wie yn Ehesachen . . . . zu Handeln:* in SARCERIUS, *Vom heil. Ehestande*, 155 ff.; DIETRICH, *Evang. Ehescheidungsrecht*, 31 ff.; HAUBER, *Ehescheid. im Reformat.*, II, 242 ff.

[2] RICHTER, *Beiträge*, 14, who points out that, through reaction against the papal system the theologians for the most part were in favor of the Roman law, while the majority of the jurists were opposed to it. The Protestant leaders are thus divided on the question whether the canon law should be accepted as binding: HUBRICH, *Das Recht der Ehescheidung*, 45. On the admission of other grounds of divorce see STRIPPELMANN, *Ehescheidungsrecht*, 151 ff.; SCHULTE, *Lehrbuch*, 416.

[3] ERASMUS, *Annot. in Nov. Test.* (Basel, 1515); quoted by RICHTER, *Beiträge*, 8-10.

[4] RICHTER, *op. cit.*, 6 ff.; BULLINGER, *Der christ. Ehestand* (ed. 1579), 1f. 102.

the only causes, but rather as the standard causes of divorce, and to the judge it is left to decide what others shall be put by their side. And not only this, but cruelty, madness, leprosy, are mentioned as causes which the judge can take into account."[1] Lambert of Avignon is likewise conspicuous for liberal ideas regarding the causes of divorce. Anticipating the principle so often enforced by modern legislation, he holds that when a wife is forced by intolerable suffering to leave the husband who mistreats her and denies her proper support, this should be counted as repudiation by the man, and not as desertion by the woman, who should therefore be allowed to contract another marriage.[2] Similar views are held by Bucer,[3] Melanchthon,[4] and the jurist Monner.[5] All accept the two general causes, and each admits several other grounds.

With no exception in case of divorce, the continental reformers appear to sanction the remarriage of the innocent man or woman without any delay or other condition.[6] The

[1] WOOLSEY, *Divorce*, 132; also THWING, *The Family*, 84. For the ordinance see RICHTER, *op. cit.*, 6, 7. Similar causes are approved by BULLINGER, *Der christ. Ehestand*, 102, appealing to the laws of the "holy Constantine, Theodosius, Valentinian, Anastasius, and Justinian."

[2] LAMBERT OF AVIGNON, *De sacro conjugio* (Strassburg, 1524): cited by RICHTER, *op. cit.*, 31, 32.

[3] See his *De regno Christi* (1557), II, 25 ff.; and the elaborate dissertation entitled *Etlicher gelerten Theologi bedencken von der Ehescheidung:* in SARCERIUS, *Vom heil. Ehestande*, 161 ff.; also *ibid.*, *Corpus juris mat.*, 196 ff., which RICHTER, *op. cit.*, 34 ff., ascribes to Bucer; though MEJER, *Zum Kirchenrecht*, 183, doubts the correctness of this view. On Bucer's doctrines see the discussion of Milton below.

[4] MELANCHTHON, "De conjugio," *Opera Omnia* (Erlangen, 1828), I, pars II, 236 ff.; or in SARCERIUS, *Vom heil. Ehestande*, 159 ff.; or *ibid.*, *Corpus juris mat.*, 190 ff. *Cf.* also RICHTER, *Beiträge*, 32–34; and especially MEJER, *Zum Kirchenrecht*, 179–82, who compares the view of Melanchthon with that of Luther, showing that the former goes back to the Theodosian code.

[5] MONNER, *Tract. de mat. et clandes. conjugiis* (Jena, 1561): *ap.* RICHTER, *Beiträge*, 40, 41. Representatives of the more liberal tendency in the sixteenth century are Chyträus, Hunnius, Wigand, Osiander, and the Danish theologian Hemming: RICHTER, *op. cit.*, 42, 43, 28.

[6] Of course, after regular process was somewhat developed, as will presently be shown, the *toleramus* or permission of the magistrate concluding the decree was requisite to the remarriage even of the innocent person.

earliest church ordinances confer the same privilege;[1] but regarding the question whether an adulterous spouse should be suffered to contract further wedlock the Protestant leaders are not agreed. The majority would have the magistrate deal with the offender according to the harsh principle of the Jewish law. Such is the view of Bugenhagen, who opens his discussion with the curt remark that were the adulterer hanged there would be small need of further parley.[2] Lambert of Avignon insists that the culprit ought to be stoned, warning the sluggish magistrates that they themselves perish even because they do not administer this punishment.[3] Beust, on the contrary, prides himself that in the land of the Saxons there is no flinching in this regard, and so the divorce question in that country is solved. Beza and Brenz are both eager for the death penalty.[4] Melanchthon appears to favor the same treatment, or else exile of the guilty spouse in case the political magistrate is unwilling to proceed with such rigor; for he says the "condemned is as one dead" to his innocent spouse.[5]

[1] The *Renovatio ecc. Nord.* (1525): RICHTER, *Kirchenordnungen*, I, 20, tolerates the second marriage of a person whose spouse has committed adultery. The Prussian *Landesordnung* of the same year expressly sanctions the divorce and remarriage of the injured spouse whose partner has committed the same offense: RICHTER, *op. cit.*, I, 32. In 1531 the church ordinance of Goslar and that of Lübeck, drafted by Bugenhagen, recognize malicious desertion as a second ground for dissolving wedlock: RICHTER, *op. cit.*, I, 156, 148; and a similar provision appears in the Pommer ordinance of 1535, also drafted by Bugenhagen: RICHTER, *op. cit.*, 250. Compare SCHULTE, *Lehrbuch*, 414–28, who gives an account of the provisions of the many ordinances regarding divorce and remarriage.

[2] "Wenn der Ehebruch bey dem halse gestraffet würde, so bedürffte man hie nicht viel fragens": BUGENHAGEN, *Vom Ehebruch und Weglauffen:* in SARCERIUS, *Vom heil. Ehestande*, 138.

[3] RICHTER, *op. cit.*, 31, 45; citing LAMBERT OF AVIGNON, *De sacra conjugio*, who recommends excommunication in case the magistrate does not execute the criminal.

[4] On Beust, Beza, and Brenz see RICHTER, *op. cit.*, 45, 46. Compare BEUST, *Tract. de spons. et mat.*, 140, where he declares that the penalty for adultery is death; and BRENZ, *Wie yn Ehesachen . . . . zu Handeln:* in SARCERIUS, *Vom heil. Ehestande*, 152, where he leaves the offender to the temporal magistrate, urging rigorous punishment; and in cases of negligence advising excommunication by the parish priest.

[5] MELANCHTHON, "De conjugio," *Opera Omnia*, I, pars II, 238: "Respondeo: magistratus politicus adulteria punire debet: ideo persona condemnata, si non punitur durius, pellenda est ex iis locis, ubi vivit persona innocens: cui altera, videlicet condemnata, velut mortua existimanda est; et haec severitas ad politicum magistratum pertinet."

Similar is the position of Luther, who "insists with great energy that death ought to be the penalty for adultery, but since the civil rulers are slack and indulgent in this respect, he would permit the criminal, if he must live, to go away to some remote place and there marry again. So Calvin, in several places, declares that death ought to be inflicted for this crime, as it was by the Mosaic code, but if the law of the territory stop short of this righteous penalty, the smallest evil is to grant liberty of remarriage in such cases."[1]

Thus far we have dealt with doctrine and opinion as disclosed by the legal and theological writings of the century of Luther. The legislation of this period reveals a like difference of view regarding the grounds of divorce and the privilege of remarriage; although the majority of the church ordinances contained in the collection of Richter appear to follow the more rigid direction.[2] Usually the two general causes, adultery and desertion, are allowed; but in a few instances only the first-named ground is admitted.[3] On the other hand, as Goeschen has pointed out,[4] the number of causes is sometimes increased, either by adding new grounds,[5] by appeal to common imperial law,[6] or by leaving the deci-

[1] WOOLSEY, *Divorce*, 138, 139. See Luther, *Vom ehel. Leben:* in STRAMPFF, 363, 364; or in SARCERIUS, *op. cit.*, 137. On Calvin see STRIPPELMANN, *Ehescheidungsrecht*, 69, 70. The same view is expressed by HOOPER, *Early Writings*, 383; and by Bucer: MILTON'S *Prose Works*, III, 299.

[2] RICHTER, *Die evangelischen Kirchenordnungen des sechszehnten Jahrhunderts*. In many Protestant lands these ecclesiastical statutes or provisions, with the sanction of the civil authority, took the place of the old canon law. For a discussion of their contents see especially the monographs of GOESCHEN, *Doctrina de mat.*, 59 ff.; *idem*, in HERZOG'S *Encyclopädie*, III, 702 ff.; DIETRICH, *Evang. Ehescheidungsrecht;* and compare HAUBER, *Ehescheid. im Reformat.*, II, 219 ff.; RICHTER, *Beiträge*, 51 ff.; *idem*, *Kirchenrecht*, 1177, 1178; STRIPPELMANN, *Das Ehescheidungsrecht*, 78 ff.; GREVE, *Ehescheidung*, 298 ff.; THWING, *The Family*, 84, 85; WOOLSEY, *Divorce*, 136-38.

[3] For example, by the *Renovatio ecc. nord.* (1525) : RICHTER, *Kirchenordnungen*, I, 20; the Würtemberg ordinance of 1537: *ibid.*, I, 280; the ordinance of the "Niederländer in London": *ibid.*, II, 115; that of the foreign "Gemeinde zu Frankfurt": *ibid.*, 157.

[4] GOESCHEN, *Doctrina de mat.*, 61, 62, notes.

[5] As by the Prussian ordinance of 1584: RICHTER, *op. cit.*, II, 468.

[6] As by the Brandenburg ordinance of 1540: *ibid.*, I, 330; that of Pfalz-Neuburg: *ibid.*, II, 146, 147.

sion to the judge's discretion.[1] Furthermore, during the seventeenth century, under influence of such writers as Bidembach and Mentzer,[2] divorce legislation follows the conservative lines laid down in the Würtemberg ordinances of 1534 and 1553.[3] The beginning of a new and more liberal treatment of the subject is first seen in the Würtemberg ordinance of 1687, which, besides adultery, desertion, and quasi-desertion, sanctions several other grounds of absolute divorce.[4] This change in the tone of the law-maker is mainly due to the rise of more generous doctrinal views, especially those of Hülsemann, who taught that marriage is dissolved by every offense which, like adultery and desertion, destroys the physical unity of the wedded pair or violates the conjugal troth constituting the safeguard of that unity.[5]

The acceptance of Luther's teaching that marriage is not a sacrament, but a "worldly thing," led at once to the rejection of the jurisdiction of the existing ecclesiastical courts. A dual problem thus arose for solution: Is marriage dissolved *ipso facto* through the commission of the offenses recognized as grounds of divorce; or, if any intervention of public authority is requisite, what is that authority, and what

[1] As by the ordinance of Zurich, 1529: *ibid.*, I, 22; that of Basel, 1529: *ibid.*, 126. *Cf.* GOESCHEN, *Doctrina de mat.*, 63 n. 218, 29 n. 105.

[2] BIDEMBACH, *De causis mat.* (Frankfort, 1608), 81-93; and MENTZER, *De conjugio* (Wittebergae, 1612), 190 ff., allow as causes only adultery and desertion. Other representatives of the conservative tendency in the seventeenth century, as enumerated by RICHTER, *Beiträge*, 58 ff., are the theologians Gerhard, Havemann, Calovius, and Hollaz, and the jurists Cypräus, Carpzov, Nicolai, Brunnemann, and Schilter; while the more liberal direction is taken by the theologians Brochmand, Hülsemann, Calixtus (J. U.), Dannhauer, and Quenstedt, and the jurists Henning Arnisaeus, Forster, Kitzel, Pufendorf, Samuel Stryk, and Bruckner.

[3] For the ordinance of 1553, drafted by Brenz, see RICHTER, *Kirchenordnungen*, II, 130. By this act full divorce is allowed only for adultery and desertion, including refusal of marital duty: and separation *a thoro et mensa* is not permitted even for *saevitia*. *Cf.* RICHTER, *Beiträge*, 57.

[4] See *Des Herzogthums Wirtemberg erneuerte Ehe- und Ehe-Gerichts-Ordnung* (Stuttgart, 1687), 22 ff., 82 ff., 100-111.

[5] HÜLSEMANN, *Extensio breviarii theologici* (3d ed., Leipzig, 1655), 502: cited by HUBRICH, *Das Recht der Ehescheidung*, 54-56, 119 ff.; RICHTER, *Beiträge*, 57, 63; *idem*, *Kirchenrecht*, 1177.

is its exact function? The researches of Stölzel have clearly established that in the beginning the reformers returned to the principle of self-divorce prevailing among the ancient Romans and Hebrews, and accepted by some of the early church councils. According to the modern conception, he declares, a marriage may normally be dissolved during the lifetime of the parties by the sentence of a judge in a legally constituted court after due process of law. Only in exceptional cases is a resort to a political magistrate allowed. The judicial decree is the medium of the dissolution; and it implies, without express permission, the right of each of the divorced persons to remarry, unless the statute has otherwise provided. The divorce law of the Reformation starts from a different, almost an opposite, conception. When an adequate cause exists, a marriage is thereby dissolved in favor of the innocent person without any magisterial authority whatsoever. If in certain cases, in order to establish the existence of the grounds of dissolution, any action is needful, it is regarded as extra-judicial; and when gradually such informal proceedings have grown into an orderly process dealing directly with the question of divorce, this process concludes with a decree; not that the marriage *is* thereby dissolved, but that it *has* already been dissolved in consequence of the grounds now established. Nor did the divorce of itself involve the right of remarriage. That privilege was always in practice, if not in theory, denied to the guilty spouse; and after a regular process arose it was usual, even as late as the eighteenth century, to grant it to the innocent person only by special magisterial permission or "toleramus."[1] From the beginning in some German lands the only purpose of the judicial action was to determine the fact that the marriage was already dissolved in order to justify this license.[2]

[1] STÖLZEL, *Ueber das landesherrl. Ehescheidungsrecht*, 9-19; or the same in *ZKR.*, XVIII, 1-4; DIETRICH, *Evang. Ehescheidungsrecht*, 39.

[2] STÖLZEL, *op. cit.*, 10, 11.

Luther and other Protestant leaders accepted the theory just explained that a marriage is "broken" or dissolved when a proper cause intervenes; and if without exception[1] they insisted that the married persons should not separate themselves, but appeal to public authority, they had in mind, as Luther plainly shows, the establishment of the fact of wedlock already broken in order, where it was desired, to grant the permission of marrying again.[2]

The seeds from which would eventually spring a new public jurisdiction in matrimonial causes were nevertheless in this way planted by Luther. For a time the practice was uncertain and informal. Cases were taken before various officials or bodies, with the prince or sovereign as final authority. The *Pfarrer* or parish priest, who is especially commended by Luther[3] for such business, was often called in; and on hard questions opinions were solicited from jurists and theologians, those of Luther having all the weight of the decisions of a court of last resort. As a result, during this early period jurisdiction came more and more into the hands of the church. Only gradually, following the example of Wittenberg in 1539, were consistorial courts[4] created under

[1] SCHULTE, *Lehrbuch*, 416.

[2] STÖLZEL, *op. cit.*, 11-19, where the proof is given from the writings of Luther and others; and DIETRICH, *Evang. Ehescheidungsrecht*, 37 ff. See STRAMPFF, 363-65, 353, 375.

[3] LUTHER, *Von Ehesachen:* in STRAMPFF, 297, 298, 392, where he names *Pfarrer* and *Oberkeit* as co-ordinate authorities in such causes. On the significance of *Oberkeit* (temporal magistracy) see STÖLZEL, *Entwicklung des gelehrten Richterthums*, I, 207 ff.; and compare *idem*, *Ueber das landesherrl. Ehescheidungsrecht*, 22, 23.

[4] On the rise of the Wittenberg consistory and its influence as a model for others see MEJER, "Anfänge des Witt. Consistoriums," *ZKR.*, XIII, 28-123; and *idem*, "Zur Geschichte des ält. prot. Eherechts," *ibid.*, XVI, 35-106. These two papers, revised and enlarged, with a chapter on the establishment of the consistory at Rostock, may also be found in MEJER'S *Zum Kirchenrechte des Reformationsjahrhunderts*, 3 ff. 146 ff. Compare SCHLEUSNER, "Zu den Anfängen prot. Eherechts," *ZKG.*, VI, 390 ff., 412 ff.; GEFFCKEN, "Zur ält. Geschichte und ehegericht. Praxis des Leipzig. Konst.," *ZKR.*, 3. Folge, IV, 7-67; HINSCHIUS, "Beiträge zur Gesch. des Desertionsprocesses nach evang. Kirchenrechte," *ibid.*, II, 1-38; and DIETRICH, *Evang. Ehescheidungsrecht*, 37-62, who gives a clear account of the development of matrimonial process and jurisdiction.

sanction of the civil power; and these bodies were composed of both lay and ecclesiastical members.[1]

A true idea of the position of German Protestantism regarding the divorce problem cannot be obtained merely from an examination of its doctrines or its legislation. These were supplemented in several ways. Their severity regarding the grounds of separation can only be appreciated at its real value by keeping in mind, as already suggested, that the sword of the judge often cut the marriage tie on account of adultery or other crimes; and that some of the reformers, notably Luther, Brenz, and Melanchthon, were inclined in certain cases to tolerate concubinage or even bigamy, in preference to full divorce.[2] But it is especially noteworthy that the judicial decisions in divorce suits, whether consisting in the opinions of the learned or the decrees of the magistrates or consistories, were in general somewhat more liberal and more practical than either the ordinances or the dogmas of the church.[3]

b) Opinions of the English reformers.—The Fathers of English Protestantism as a body are more conservative than their brethren across the channel.[4] By the chiefs of

---

[1] According to STÖLZEL, *Ueber das landesherrl. Ehescheidungsrecht*, 46 ff., *passim*, after the creation of consistories, as well as before, the head of the state — *Landesherr* — retained a right of dispensation as *summus episcopus;* and in Protestant lands his power to grant divorces in certain cases was not entirely superseded by the imperial law of 1875. These points, especially the last, have given rise to a controversial literature: see MEURER, *Das landesh. Ehescheidungsrecht*, 12 ff., who holds that the authority of the *Landesherr* was superseded by the act of 1875; and compare HUBRICH, *Das Recht der Ehescheidung*, 147 ff.; the works cited by STÖLZEL, *op. cit.*, 54 ff.; by MEURER, *op. cit.*, 8 ff.; and those in this connection described in Bibliographical Note XI.

[2] See the proofs presented by RICHTER, *Beiträge*, 46–50; and chap. ix, p. 390, above.

[3] RICHTER, *op. cit.*, 43 ff., cites several cases as evidence. On the other hand, the Wittenberg decisions analyzed by MEJER, *Zum Kirchenrechte*, 196 ff.; and those published by SCHLEUSNER, "Zu den Anfängen prot. Eherechts," *ZKG.*, XIII, 130 ff., 142 ff., follow mainly the conservative direction. In this connection read the "Antwort auff etliche Fragen und Gegenwurff" in SARCERIUS, *Vom heil. Ehestande*, 204 ff.; or in *idem, Corpus juris mat.*, 248 ff.

[4] *Cf.* LECKY, *Democracy and Liberty*, II, 200; GLASSON, *Le mariage civil et le divorce*, 310, 311; and *idem, Histoire du droit*, V, 89 ff.

the really reforming or Puritan party among them, however, ideas scarcely less bold than those of Luther or Calvin are advanced. The same arguments are used and the same causes of separation are admitted. But these ideas ultimately find no place in the canons of the established church. Under Edward VI. the leaders of the Protestant movement defend their position. "Strongly disapproving the excessive liberty of divorce which the ecclesiastical tribunals had for generations afforded to society, they were not less unanimous in condemning the doctrine of the absolute indissolubility of wedlock. If it was wrong on the one hand to allow husbands and wives the liberty of separating on frivolous pretexts, and to provide the fortress of marriage with numerous gates of egress, whose double locks obeyed the pass-keys of perjury and corruption; it was on the other hand no less hurtful to society and impious to God to constrain a pair of human creatures in the name of religion, to persevere in an association, that could not accomplish the highest purposes of matrimony, and debarred the ill-assorted couple from the serene and wholesome pleasures of Christian life."[1]

The average sentiment of the age is quaintly expressed in Bullinger's *The Christen State of Matrimonye*, translated by Bishop Miles Coverdale in 1541. "That is called iuste diuorce, when as nether partye maye take the tother agene, so it is in the lybertye of the fawtlesse partye to mary another." Such a "divorce is permitted of god for the welth and medicine of man and for amendment in wedlok. And like as all maner of medicynes and specially some as they that go nyest death as to cut of whole membres . . . . are very terrible. So is divorce indede a medicyne, but a perilous and pitefull. . . . . The papistes haue forbydden the innocent and vnguiltye parte to marye after the diuorce

<hr/>

[1] JEAFFRESON, *Brides and Bridals*, II, 316. This summary really gives the gist of MILTON's argument in his "Doctrine and Discipline of Divorce," *Prose Works*, III, 169-273.

made: Which yt was no thinge els but euen violently to cast a snare about poore peoples neckes, and to drawe them vnto vyce and synne. For the diuorced coulde not refrayne, and mary they were not permitted, therfore with violence were they forced into whordome." [1]

The favorite metaphor of the reformers is also employed by Master Henry Smith. In his *Preparation to Marriage*, written in the reign of Elizabeth, divorce is described as the "rod of mariage" and the "medicine of adultery." If duty be done, he says, "then I need not speake of divorcement, which is the rod of mariage and divideth them which were one flesh, as if the bodie and soul were parted asunder. But because all performe not their wedlocke vowes, therefore He which appointed mariage hath appointed divorcement, as it were, taking a privilege from us when we abuse it. As God hath ordained remedies for every disease, so He hath ordained a remedie for the disease of mariage. The disease of marriage is adultery, and the medicine thereof is divorcement." [2]

Nearly all the English reformers of the sixteenth century agree in rejecting separation from bed and board as a "papist" innovation; and they are equally unanimous in allowing the man for unfaithfulness to put away his wife and contract another marriage. [3] Prevailing opinion appears also to have accorded the same privilege to the woman on like provocation; but there were undoubtedly some in the Protestant ranks who were not so liberal in her behalf. In particular this seems to be the correct inference to be drawn from the antagonism and excitement caused by the bold

[1] *The Christen State of Matrimonye*, lvs. lxxvi, lxxvii.

[2] MASTER HENRY SMITH, *Preparation to Marriage:* quoted by JEAFFRESON, *Brides and Bridals*, II, 294, note.

[3] *Cf.*, for example, BECON'S "Catechism," *Works*, II, 647; and his "Prayers," *ibid.*, III, 532; TYNDALE, *Expositions*, 51, 52; Bucer in MILTON'S *Prose Works*, III, 299, 300, who grants this cause to both parties.

position of Hooper,[1] who won a perilous distinction through his sensible demand for even justice to the sexes in this regard.[2] According to the common view, malicious desertion on the part of either spouse is a second scriptural ground for the complete dissolution of wedlock. The singular logic through which the words of Paul are made to sustain this distinctively Protestant doctrine may be illustrated by a typical example. "But to our purpose," exclaims Tyndale, "what if a man run from his wife and leave her desolate? Verily, the rulers ought to make a law, if any do so and come not again by a certain day, as within the space of a year or so, that then he be banished the country; and if he come again, to come on his head, and let the wife be free to marry when she will." But how is this liberty to be reconciled with the words of Paul who allows a brother or sister a divorce when deserted by an unbelieving spouse? Easily; for elsewhere "he saith, 'If there be any man that provideth not for his, and namely for them of his own household, the same denieth the faith, and is worse than an infidel.' And even so is this man much worse to be interpreted for an infidel, that causeless runneth from his wife." [3]

[1] Hooper's teaching caused great excitement: see the letter of JOHN AB ULMIS to BULLINGER, in *Original Letters relating to English Reformation*, 416. Bullinger is said to hold the same views: *ibid.*, 422. At his trial one of the charges against Hooper was that he taught that the bond of wedlock may be dissolved for adultery: HOOPER, *Later Writings*, xxiii.

[2] HOOPER, *Early Writings*, 382-87, declares, on the authority of Mark 10:12, that the woman as well as the man may divorce for adultery. To those who deny this according to the Mosaic law he says: "I grant the same, but I am sure the poor woman was not compelled to live with her adulterous husband; for the law commanded such a villain to be slain, and so put the honest party to liberty; and so should it be now-a-days, and then the question of divorcement would be ended" (383). Again, to those who say if woman had this right "marriage could never be sure nor constant, for women would change still at their pleasure," he replies, "there is given no such liberty to man or woman by the word of God," meaning, doubtless, separation at pleasure, except for cause established in court. In a letter to Henry Bullinger he defends his doctrine of divorce as to the woman: *Original Letters rel. to English Reformation*, 64.

[3] TYNDALE, *Expositions*, 54, 55. A similar illustration of the straits to which the Protestant was brought in his necessity of appealing to authority is afforded by Bucer, in MILTON'S *Prose Works*, III, 309: "Hither may be added, that the Holy

Far more daring than any of the English writers before Milton is Martin Bucer, of Strassburg, whose doctrines of divorce comprised in the book dedicated to Edward VI. are almost as bold as those of Zwingli.   According to this famous theologian, for two years professor at Cambridge, and greatly venerated by his contemporaries, divorce is a divine institution; and it ought to be granted not merely for unfaithfulness and desertion, but for many other reasons as well. It is curious, but thoroughly in keeping with the mental habits of his age, to see how he persuaded himself that the causes of divorce sanctioned by the decrees of the "pious emperors" from Constantine to Justinian are not "contrary to the word of God;" may therefore "be recalled into use by any Christian prince or commonwealth;" and are thus "by divine approbation" valid among Christians at the present hour.[1]   Usually in his treatise he advocates equal liberty of

Spirit grants desertion to be a cause of divorce, in those answers given to the Corinthians. . . . . But some will say, that this is spoken of a misbeliever departing. But I beseech ye, doth not he reject the faith of Christ in his deeds, who rashly breaks the holy covenant of wedlock instituted by God? And besides this, the Holy Spirit does not make the misbelieving of him who departs, but the departing of him who disbelieves, to be the just cause of freedom to the brother or sister. Since therefore it will be agreed among Christians, that they who depart from wedlock without just cause, do not only deny the faith of matrimony, but of Christ also, whatever they profess with their mouths; it is but reason to conclude, that the party deserted is not bound in case of causeless desertion, but that he may lawfully seek another consort, if it be needful to him, toward a pure and blameless conversation." *Cf.* also the argument of MILTON, "The Doctrine and Discipline of Divorce," *Prose Works*, III, 258, 259.

[1] BUCER, in MILTON'S *Prose Works*, III, 302, 303, 292, 293, 306-8. By some of his brethren he was regarded as a fanatic on this subject as the following letter from JOHN BURCHER to HENRY BULLINGER shows: "Strasburgh, June 8, 1550: Bucer is more than licentious on the subject of marriage. I heard him once disputing at table upon this question, when he asserted that a divorce should be allowed for any reason, however trifling; so that he is considered, not without cause, by our bishop of Winchester as the author of the book published in defence of the Landgrave. I am ignorant as to what the hireling Bucer, who fled from this church before the wolf came in sight, is plotting in England."—*Original Letters rel. to the Eng. Ref.*, 655, 656.

"Philip, landgrave of Hesse, in addition to Christina, the daughter of the late duke George, to whom he had been united many years, and by whom he had a large family, married on March 3, 1540, a lady named Margaret de Sala, and this with the consent of the landgravine under her own hand and seal. Previous to this he sought to obtain the sanction of Luther, Melanchthon, and Bucer, whose want of firmness in this painful case has called forth the most violent invectives from Vorillas and Bossuet, bishop of Meaux."—*Ibid.*, 666, note.

divorce for both consorts; but, in contradiction to the spirit
of his own teaching, in one chapter he sets forth a doctrine
which would place the wife absolutely at the mercy of a licentious or despotic lord.   A passage from the prophet
Malachi Bucer renders: "'Take heed to your spirit, and let
none deal injuriously against the wife of his youth.   If he
hate, let him put away, saith the Lord God of Israel.   And
he shall hide thy violence with his garment'—that marries
her divorced by thee."[1]   On this authority he concludes
that "by these testimonies of the divine law . . . . the Lord
did not only permit, but also expressly and earnestly commanded his people, by whom he would that all holiness and
faith of marriage covenant should be observed, that he who
could not induce his mind to love his wife with a true conjugal love, might dismiss her, that she might marry to
another."[2]   Verily this is naïve morality.   Such singular
care for the wife's happiness finds scarcely a parallel, unless
indeed it be in the ethics of John Milton, to which we must
presently recur.

But positive evidence of the views of the Reformation
Fathers has been preserved for the time of Edward VI.
Under Henry VIII. the principles of the canon law touching
divorce remained in full force, except that by restricting the
number of forbidden degrees to those recognized by the
Levitical code, and through the abolition of pre-contracts,
the chances for escaping the ties of marriage by crooked

[1] Mal. 2:15, 16, which in the James version is given: "Therefore take heed to
your spirit, and let none deal treacherously against the wife of his youth. For the
Lord, the God of Israel, saith that he hateth putting away: for one covereth violence with his garment," etc. It may be noted that MILTON, "Doctrine and Discipline of Divorce," *Prose Works*, III, 196, following "Calvin and the best translations,"
renders the passage from Malachi, "he who hates, let him divorce," thus agreeing
essentially with Bucer.

[2] BUCER, in MILTON, *Prose Works*, III, 297. *Cf.* JEAFFRESON, *Brides and Bridals*,
II, 329-32, who believes that these sentiments of Bucer, however shocking to us, were
accepted by the most "virtuous and devout" in the sixteenth and seventeenth centuries.

ways were somewhat lessened.[1] The restoration of pre-contracts[2] under Edward VI., however, caused the reformers to fear lest the old evils growing out of clandestine unions and nullification of false wedlock on the pretext of previous *sponsalia de praesenti* would also be revived; and this quickened their desire for a formal settlement of the law of divorce in harmony with the altered views of the English church. Accordingly, an act of Parliament authorized the appointment of a commission of thirty-two persons to prepare a "complete code of ecclesiastical laws."[3] The commission selected in pursuance of this statute comprised the most learned divines and lawyers of the Protestant party. Their task was well performed; and their report, drafted mainly by Cranmer and translated into Latin by Dr. Haddon and Sir John Cheke, was submitted in 1552 under the title of *Reformatio Legum Ecclesiasticarum*.[4]

This code, though it was never put in force, perhaps in consequence of the king's death, is regarded as a faithful index of Protestant opinion. Before referring to its treat-

---

[1] By 32 H. VIII, c. 38. *Cf.* REEVES, *Hist. of Eng. Law*, IV, 333-36; GLASSON, *Hist. du droit*, V, 89.

On Henry VIII.'s divorce see POCOCK, *Records of the Reformation: The Divorce, 1527-1533*, containing the original documents; BURNET, *Hist. of the Reformation*, I, 26-123; GEARY, *Marriage and Family Relations*, 596-602; THWING, *The Family*, 87; WOOLSEY, *Divorce*, 168, 169; JEAFFRESON, *Brides and Bridals*, I, 114, 124; II, 312 ff., who defends the king on the ground that the pope did not grant him the indulgence which private citizens constantly enjoyed, especially when they were able to pay for it. There is a valuable bibliography of Henry's divorce in HUTH, *Marriage of Near Kin*, 404-11.

[2] By 2 and 3 Ed. VI, c. 23.

[3] By 3 and 4 Ed. VI, c. 11. *Cf.* the account by JEAFFRESON, *op. cit.*, II, 317, 318.

[4] The report was published in 1571 under supervision of Archbishop Parker; and then in an Oxford reprint of 1850: WOOLSEY, *Divorce*, 170, note. I have followed the excellent summary by JEAFFRESON, partly containing the Latin text: *op. cit.*, II, 318-23; and REEVES, *Hist. of Eng. Law*, V, 74-80, gives a good analysis. *Cf.* also HALLAM, *Const. Hist.*, I, 101, 102, note; LINGARD, *Hist. of England*, IV, 284; HAMMICK, *Marriage Law*, 6; GEARY, *Marriage and Family Relations*, 8 n. 6, 578; *Report of the Divorce Commission, Parl. Papers*, 1852-53, 4; *Report of the Ecc. Courts Comm.*, 1883, xxxi-xxxiii, xxxvi; BISHOP, *Marriage, Divorce, and Separation*, I, § 1496; MACQUEEN, *Practical Treatise* (London, 1842), 467; *Law Review* (English), I, 356-58; BURN, *Ecc. Law*, II, 503 ff.; LECKY, *Democracy and Liberty*, II, 175; LUCKOCK, *Hist. of Marriage*, 175, 176; MORGAN, *Marriage, Adultery, and Divorce*, II, 227-29.

ment of the question of divorce, some of its general provisions may be mentioned. These often show the strong common-sense and lofty moral purpose of its framers. The consent of the parent or guardian is made necessary to a valid marriage. Children whose reasonable desires in matrimony are hindered by the caprice or unkindness of those having authority over them are granted the right of appeal to the ecclesiastical magistrate, who may give redress. Aged women are advised to forbear from wedlock with young men. A marriage secured through fear or violence is rendered void. An attempt is also made through severe penalties to check those crimes against women which, as elsewhere shown, were first effectively dealt with during the Puritan Commonwealth.[1] "They ordered that the betrayer of a virgin should be excommunicated until he had married his victim, if it was in his power to wed her; or until he had assigned to her a third of his property, or made some other sufficient arrangement for the support of her offspring," if on account of legal impediment he could not make her his wife.[2]

Hereafter, according to the report, spiritual affinity is not to count as an impediment to matrimony. Separation *a mensa et thoro* is not recognized; but complete divorce *a vinculo matrimonii* is granted "in cases of extreme conjugal faithlessness; in case of conjugal desertion or cruelty; in cases where a husband, not guilty of deserting his wife, had been for several years absent from her," provided there be reason to believe him dead; "and in cases of such violent hatred as rendered it in the highest degree improbable that the husband and wife would survive their animosities and again love one another;"[3] but separation is not permitted

---

[1] See chap. x, sec. i, pp. 421-23 above.

[2] JEAFFRESON, *op. cit.*, II, 322.

[3] "Inter conjuges si capitales intercedant inimicitiae tamque vehementer exarserint, ut alter alterum aut insidiis aut venenis appellat, aut aliqua vel aperta vi, vel occulta peste, vitam velit eripere, quamprimum tam horribile crimen probatum fuerit, rite in juditio divortio volumus hujuscemodi personas distrahi."— *Ref. leg. ecc.*: *ap.* JEAFFRESON, *op. cit.*, II, 320, 321, note.

for frequent, though not incessant or vehement, quarrels.[1] Divorce is denied where both partners are guilty of unfaithfulness; and when one is guilty, only the innocent spouse is permitted to contract another marriage. Self-divorce is forbidden. In all cases it is the province of the ecclesiastical court to determine whether there exists a just cause for separation.[2] Finally, it may be noted that adultery as a crime is severely dealt with, though the commissioners do not go to the length of prescribing capital punishment, as some of the English reformers would have desired. The guilty husband, if a layman, shall "restore to his injured wife whatever possessions she had brought him, and also surrender to her one-half of all his other property. He was, moreover, sentenced to exile or imprisonment for life. Convicted of the same offence, the wife lost her dower and all interest in her husband's property, and was consigned to life-long imprisonment or banishment." For this crime and similar offenses "clerical delinquents" are treated with even greater severity.[3]

The report prepared by the commission never received the sanction of the king; nor does it appear that any authoritative change in the canon law relating to divorce was ever made until the present century. Nevertheless the *Reformatio Legum* "is a work of great authority, showing the recognized opinion and sentiment of the church of England at that time and containing the views of the first reformers."[4] The principle represented by it was carried out in practice, though it may well be doubted whether, as is sometimes urged,[5] the

---

[1] "Parva contentiones, nisi perpetuae sint, divortium non inducunt."—*Ref. leg. ecc.: ap.* JEAFFRESON, *op. cit.,* II, 321.

[2] JEAFFRESON, *op. cit.,* II, 321.

[3] *Ibid.,* 322, 323.   [4] GEARY, *Marriage and Family Relations,* 8 n. 6.

[5] So by Sir John Stoddart in his evidence before the Lords' Select Committee, 1844: "Therefore I apprehend that the *Reformatio legum* having been published as a work of authority, although not of absolute legislative authority, it must have been, and in all probability was, followed: and for that reason *in the Spiritual Courts there were dissolutions of marriage.* Because *I believe that from about the year 1550 to the year 1602 marriage was not held by the Church, and therefore was not held by the Law, to be indissoluble."—Minutes of Evidence,* 27: *Law Review* (Eng.), I, 358, 359.

decrees of the ecclesiastical court ever went so far as expressly
to grant dissolution of wedlock.   According to the ancient
form of judgment, divorce was probably still pronounced
only *a mensa et thoro;* but, whatever the shape of the decrees,
there is strong evidence that from about 1548 to 1602, except
for the short period of Mary's reign, "the community, in
cases of adultery, relied upon them as justifying a second act
of matrimony."[1]   For already in 1548—four years before
Edward's commission had completed its report—the new
doctrine had been in a measure sustained by the well-known
case of Lord Northampton, brother of Queen Catherine Parr.
After obtaining a decision of an ecclesiastical court separating him from his wife, Anne Bourchier, the marquis had
contracted another union with Elizabeth Brooke, daughter of
Lord Cobham.   Subsequently a commission of delegates,
headed by the archbishop of Canterbury, declared the second marriage valid, "because the former contract had been
absolutely destroyed" by Anne Bourchier's infidelity;[2] and
in 1552 this decision was confirmed by an act of Parliament[3]
which declares the marriage valid "by the law of God,—any
decretal, canon ecclesiastical, law, or usage to the contrary
notwithstanding."[4]

[1] *Law Review* (Eng.), I, 359.   *Cf.* JEAFFRESON, *op. cit.*, II, 323.

[2] JEAFFRESON, *op. cit.*, II, 323, 324.   Cranmer examined the Fathers and other
authorities on divorce for adultery; and the material which he thus collected grew
into a large book, which Burnet, who gives a summary, says he has seen: *Hist. of
Reformation*, I, 330 ff.   Burnet's summary is also given by GEARY, *Marriage and
Family Relations*, 577, 578.   *Cf.* MACQUEEN, *Practical Treatise*, 468, 469.

[3] 5 and 6 Ed. VI., c. 4.

[4] MACQUEEN, *op. cit.*, 469.   "This bill is often, but erroneously, referred to as the
earliest example of parliamentary divorce (SHELFORD, 373).   It is not a divorce bill;
neither did it proceed upon the principle of a divorce bill.   Its object was merely to
declare that the adultery of the first wife, followed by the ecclesiastical sentence,
entitled the Marquis to take a second wife.   The principle on which the act passed
assumed the jurisdiction of the Church Court, to dissolve the marriage *proprio
vigore.*   The act did not divorce the parties, but merely declared them to be *already*,
by the ecclesiastical sentence, sufficiently divorced to admit of the Marquis marrying
again."—*Ibid.*, 469 n. e.   On this case see also *Law Review* (Eng.), I, 358, 359; *Report
of the Royal Commission on Divorce, Parl. Papers*, 1853, 57 ff.; GEARY, *op. cit.*, 17;
WOOLSEY, *Divorce*, 169–71; LECKY, *Democracy and Liberty*, II, 174, 175; BURN, *Ecc.
Law*, II, 503a–503b; REEVES, *Hist. of Eng. Law*, V, 80, 81; MORGAN, *Marriage, Adultery, and Divorce*, II, 229 ff.

This is, indeed, convincing evidence of the changed opinion of the English church. Nor can it be questioned that throughout nearly the whole of Elizabeth's reign popular practice was in harmony with the doctrine thus proclaimed.[1] New marriages were freely contracted after obtaining divorce from unfaithful partners.[2] Clear evidence of this fact is afforded by Bunny, himself strongly opposed to the liberal tendency.[3] As a matter of fact, popular custom, sustained by the profound sentiment of the Reformed clergy, was fast ripening into a law as valid as any which a legislature could enact. Such a tendency, however, could not fail to become more and more obnoxious to many of the leaders of the established clergy, as Elizabeth's reign progressed. Archbishop Whitgift defends the ancient divorce jurisdiction of the spiritual courts against Cartwright,[4] and the Puritan party is treated with ever-increasing rigor. Still the reactionary canons passed by the Chamber of Convocation in

[1] According to the *Report of the Commissioners, 1852-3*, 5, divorce was allowed during the period 1550-1602.

[2] See, however, WOOLSEY, *Divorce*, 170, 171, 313, who, insisting that the ancient canon law was unchanged, remarks that "for a number of years, although remarriage after divorce was null and void, so that the issue would not be legitimate, no civil penalties were attached to it, and it was punishable only by ecclesiastical censures." Hence many married "without scruple." *Cf.* CRAIK, *Romance of the Peerage*, I, Appendix, upon whom Woolsey relies; and JEAFFRESON, *Brides and Bridals*, II, 323, 324, who holds that the decision of the delegates in the Northampton case was "good law" until 1602.

[3] BUNNY, *Of Divorce for Adulterie, and Marrying againe: that there is no sufficient Warrant so to do* (Oxford, 1610). This book had been written many years before. The preface is dated Dec. 13, 1595; and in it Bunny refers to the state of public opinion and to events, notably in Yorkshire, of a still earlier time. In "a Sermon," he says: "I breefly noted, that the libertie, that in these our daies many doe take, of divorcing their wiues for adulterie and marying of others, had not such warrant in the worde of God as they thought that it had." Just before delivering this discourse a gentleman who desired to put away his wife for adultery and marry again, "and having already gotten (into a little paper-book of his) the handes of sundrie of the Preachers of those parts," had come to him for similar support. He further notes that "a few yeeres" earlier not less than "fowre several persons" of one of the greatest families in "those parts" had married again after divorce; and in general his "Advertisement to the Reader" leaves the impression that the new doctrine was, on the whole, the prevailing one; although, according to law, "neither those second women were allowed any dowrie, nor their children to be legitimate."

[4] WHITGIFT, "Defence of the Answer," *Works*, III, 267 ff. *Cf.* BULLINGER, *Decades*, IV (V), 511.

1597, doubtless designed to check what was already looked upon as a dangerous abuse, bear witness to its continued existence; if indeed by implication, as is powerfully argued, they do not directly sanction the dissolution of marriage through divorce.[1]

Similar testimony is afforded by the celebrated Foljambe case in 1602, when a court sitting in the Star Chamber incidentally pronounced invalid a marriage which had been contracted after separation from bed and board by decree of an ecclesiastical judge; and this decision follows the advice of a council of the "most sage divines and civilians assembled by Archbishop Whitgift at Lambeth, declaring in harmony with the ancient law that remarriage after judicial separation is null and void." [2]

---

[1] These ordinances are known as the "Ecclesiastical Constitutions" of 1597. Canon 105 urges greater care in matrimonial causes, especially in cases where marriage "is required to be *dissolved* or *annulled*;" and it is strictly charged "that in all proceedings in *divorce* and *nullities of marriage*, good circumspection and advice be used, and that the truth may, as far as possible, be sifted out by depositions of witnesses and other lawful proofs; and that credit be not given to the sole confession of the parties themselves, howsoever taken upon oath either within or without the court." The 107th canon requires a bond to be given in case of "sentences pronounced only for divorce and separation *à thoro et mensâ*," that "the parties so separated shall live chastely, and neither shall they, during each other's life, contract matrimony with other persons." From these canons it has been inferred with some plausibility that both "dissolving divorce" and "nullifying divorce" are contemplated as valid and customary; and that the requiring of a bond implies that the marriage which the bond is intended to prevent would have been valid: see *Law Review* (Eng.), I, 359, 360, and the opinions there cited; also *Plea for an Alteration in the Divorce Laws* (London, 1831), 3 ff.

[2] The Foljambe case has given rise to much controversy. It is commonly regarded as marking the formal abandonment of the more liberal *law* of the Reformation period and a return to canonical principles. This view is mainly traceable to the statements of SALKELD, *Reports of Cases in the King's Bench* (Philadelphia, 1822, from 6th London ed.), III, 137, who commits several errors, and is otherwise misleading. He is followed by JEAFFRESON, *Brides and Bridals*, II, 324; GEARY, *Marriage and Family Relations*, 12; MACQUEEN, *Practical Treatise*, 470, 471; HARRISON, *Probate and Divorce*, 115; and especially BISHOP, *Marriage and Divorce* (5th ed.), I, §§661, 705. On the other hand, WOOLSEY, *Divorce*, 172, note, 310–13, following the researches of CRAIK, *Romance of the Peerage*, I, Appendix, regards the decision as merely confirming existing law. He criticises Bishop for being misled by Salkeld, whereas the facts appear to be more correctly given in NOY'S *Reports*, 100; and particularly in MOORE'S *Cases* (2d ed. folio, London, 1688), 683, which may be translated from the law-French as follows: "Feb. 13, *anno* 44 Eliz. In the Star Chamber it was declared by all the court, that whereas Foljambe was divorced from his first wife

Strictly speaking, it may not be correct to say, as is commonly done by law writers, that the Foljambe case marks a change in the law of divorce by requiring a return to the doctrine of the ancient church; but from it, at any rate, two important inferences may be drawn. On the one hand, it shows that the custom of remarriage after separation *a mensa et thoro* was continued to the very end of Elizabeth's reign. On the other hand, it constitutes a stage in the development of a more conservative policy. As such it may have had something to do with the legislation of about a year later. By royal authority in 1603 the canons of 1597 were re-enacted "word for word," and consequently, as already suggested, they incidentally bear witness to the Reformation theory and practice as to divorce and remarriage, while seeming to admit the possibility of a valid dissolution of wedlock by judicial decree.[1] For the first time in English history a statute of 1604 makes bigamy[2] in the modern sense

for incontinence of the woman [in fact, for his own adultery], and afterwards had married Sarah Poge [Page], daughter of Rye, in his former wife's life-time, this was a void marriage, the divorce being *a mensa et thoro*, and not *a vinculo matrimonii*. And John Whitgift, then Archbishop of Canterbury, said that he had called to himself at Lambeth the most sage divines and civilians, and that they had all agreed therein." It is concluded, therefore, that this decision of the "sage divines and civilians" must have been incidental to a case under trial in the Star Chamber, and that the law was merely declared and not changed. See, however, the sixth edition of BISHOP's work, I, § 1498 n. 3, where the author insists on the essential correctness of his original view. *Cf.* also *Law Review* (Eng.), I, 361, 362; *Report of the Commissioners* (Divorce), 1852-53, 4-6; and MORGAN, *Marriage, Adultery, and Divorce*, II, 233.

[1] *Law Review* (Eng.), I, 362. One of these canons "provided that no persons separated *a toro et mensa* should, during their joint lives, contract matrimony with other persons, and that the parties requiring the sentence of divorce should give sufficient caution and security into the court that they would not transgress this restraint. Another canon required the judge who should grant divorce, without observing these rules, to be suspended for one year by the archbishop or bishop, and declared his sentence utterly void."—WOOLSEY, *Divorce*, 171, 172. *Cf.* LUCKOCK, *Hist. of Marriage*, 177 n. 2; MORGAN, *Marriage, Adultery, and Divorce*, II, 233 ff.

[2] By the act of 1 James I., c. xi, "bigamy" is used in the modern sense. In mediæval law a "bigamist" is one who marries again *after* his first wife's death; the word "polygamist" being employed for the person who takes another woman *before* the death of the first spouse. By 4 Ed. I., 1276 (*Stat. de bigamis, Stat. at Large* [Pickering], I, 116), benefit of clergy is denied him who is a bigamist, *i. e.*, has contracted a second marriage after death of the first wife: JEAFFRESON, *Brides and Bridals*, II, 327. Compare GLASSON, *Hist. du droit*, III, 184, 185.

"As for the crime of polygamy [the modern bigamy], it hath not been made a felony punishable with death; but there are exceptions to the operation of the act which tell strongly in favor of the view that the custom of remarriage after judicial separation had been something more than tolerated. It is expressly provided that the penalty fixed by the act shall not extend to a man or woman who has contracted a new marriage after seven years' desertion; nor to "any person or persons that are or shall be at the time of such marriage divorced by any sentence had or hereafter to be had in the ecclesiastical court."[1] Here it is clear that dissolution of wedlock by

penal by any statute, till the time of James the First. A canon of Pope Gregory the Tenth had taken away all clerical privileges from a bigamist, as the marrying a second wife was considered by the ecclesiastical law, to be proof of a most incontinent disposition; this regulation having been adopted in England, the clergy had a doubt, whether a person, who had been guilty of this offence before the canon law took place, might claim the indulgence of the common law; this statute [4 Ed. I.], therefore, retrospectively declares, he shall not be entitled to such privilege."— Barrington, *Observations upon the Statutes* (4th ed., London, 1775), 106; also Jeaffreson, *op. cit.*, II, 327, note. But it may be noted that by 1 Ed. VI., c. 12, sec. 16: *Stat. at Large* (Pickering), V, 265, 266, benefit of clergy is restored in terms which may leave it in doubt whether bigamy in the modern sense is intended. This privilege is granted to offenders, "although they or any of them have been divers and sundry times married to any single woman or single women, or to any widow or widows, or to two wives or more." On the ancient meaning of "bigamy" see also Glasson, *op. cit.*, III, 184.

[1] 1 James I., c. xi: *Stat. at Large* (Pickering), VII, 88, 89.

However, inferences as to the law in the preceding period must be made with caution. The case of Stephens v. Totty, decided at the Michaelmas term, 44 and 45 Eliz., shows that a husband and a wife divorced *a mensa et thoro* were still married: Croke's *Reports* (Elizabeth), 908. *Cf.* on this act especially Hale, *Hist. of the Pleas of the Crown* (London, 1800), I, 691-93; also Woolsey, *Divorce*, 171; *Law Review* (Eng.), I, 362. Furthermore, Raynolds, a strong advocate of absolute divorce, in his *Defence of the Judgment of the Reformed Churches* (1609), appears to make no claim that his doctrine is sustained either by law or custom. So also in the quaint treatise, *The Lawes Resolutions of Women's Rights* (London, 1632), 64 ff., full divorce is not recognized; although, referring to the fact that legally "no crime dissolueth marriage," the compiler (67) seemingly approves Conrad Lagus who says, "seeing that in Contracts of Wedlock we regard as well what is decent and conuenient, as what is lawfull, I cannot tell why we be not bound in dissoluing of it to follow the like equitie; and for example, if a Wife cannot dwell with her husband without manifest danger of death . . . . why may not she be separated iudicis ordinarij cognitione precedente?"

On the other hand, Spence, *Equitable Jurisprudence*, I, 702, believes that the bond not to marry required by the canons of 1603 was the only hindrance to remarriage after divorce; and from this time onward he thinks it "not unlikely that the court of chancery decreed divorces *a vinculo;* and that the American courts of equity brought this doctrine (or right) with them." This view is rejected by Scribner, *Treatise on the Law of Dower*, II, 545-47, although he agrees as to the effect of the bond.

sentence of nullity is not intended; for this is provided for by another exception in the act itself. It is equally clear that all cases of divorce by judicial decree *are* comprehended, whatever the cause of separation assigned. The law as then interpreted seems to have remained unchallenged until 1637, when in Porter's case the court of King's Bench, without squarely deciding the point, expressed a doubt whether a woman remarrying after divorce for cruelty was exempt from punishment under the proviso of King James's statute; because, "if this should be suffered, many would be divorced upon such pretence, and instantly marry again, whereby many inconveniences would arise. Whereupon she was advised not to insist upon the law, but to procure a pardon to avoid the danger; for it was clearly agreed by all the civilians and others, that the second marriage was unlawful."[1] Nevertheless, the hesitation of the court does not appear to be justified either by the plain words of the act or by the weight of legal authority.[2]

III. LAW AND THEORY DURING THREE CENTURIES

a) The views of Milton.—With the opening of the Stuart era, therefore, a reactionary policy with respect to divorce was established. For two centuries and a half thereafter the principles of the ancient canon law were administered by the English spiritual courts. In fact, it was now more difficult than before the Reformation to escape the marriage

---

[1] Porter's case, Easter term, 12 C. I.: CROKE'S *Reports* (Charles I.), 461-63.

[2] See the strong argument of Holburn and Grimston for the defendant who justly claim that a "divorce *causa saevitiae* is grounded *ex jure naturae*, and is in the same manner and nature as a divorce *causae adulterii:* CROKE'S *Reports* (Charles I.), 463. HALE, *Hist. of Pleas of the Crown*, I, 693, remarks "certainly the divorce intended" by James's act "is not *a vinculo matrimonii*;" and then further observes, in Porter's case "it was doubted, whether a divorce *causâ saevitiae* were such a divorce as was within this exception, because it seemed rather to be a provisional separation for the wife's safety and maintenance, than a divorce; but it was never resolved." *Cf.* also *Co. Lit.*, 235; MARCH, *Reports of New Cases*, 101; COKE, *Institutes*, III, 89; KELYNG, *Report of Divers Cases* (Dublin, 1789), 27; GEARY, *Marriage and Family Relations*, 12.

tie;[1] for the papal dispensation could grant no relief, and in consequence of the decrease in the number of restraints to a valid marriage, the decree of nullity was not so often a convenient subterfuge. Only the rich or noble were able to afford the costly remedy of a special act of Parliament to cure their matrimonial ills. Hence it is not a little surprising that the Puritan Revolution brought with it no change in this regard. One would naturally expect the Independents under Cromwell's leadership, by whom the remarkable civil-marriage law of 1653 was conceived, to relegate the whole matter of divorce and nullity to the temporal courts under proper legal conditions; yet there seems to be no record of such a course.

But if the Puritan statute-book was silent, Puritan thought produced the boldest defense of the liberty of divorce which had yet appeared. If taken in the abstract and applied to both sexes alike, it is perhaps the strongest defense which can be made through an appeal to mere authority. For, in spite of their casuistry, their inconsistencies, and their injustice to woman, the writings of John Milton may be said to have about exhausted the resources of theological argument and the learning of his age on this subject.[2] He goes farther than Zwingli, Bucer, or any other reformer in admitting grounds for the absolute dissolution of marriage. According to Milton, divorce is a "law

[1] JEAFFRESON, *Brides and Bridals*, II, 315, perhaps with too much emphasis, thus describes the effects of 32 H. VIII., c. 38: "It rendered wedlock easier of entrance, but closed all the many gates which had hitherto afforded spouses the means of escape from conjugal wretchedness. . . . . The Elizabethan jest, that compared matrimony to a public rout, was no less applicable to wedlock in Catholic than to marriage in Protestant England; but whereas our ancestors before the Reformation could always get out of the press by a few permissible falsehoods and the payment of money, the marriage law of Protestant times declared that, having once forced their way into the crowd, they should remain in it till death came to their relief."

[2] His four principal works dealing with divorce are the "Doctrine and Discipline of Divorce" (*Prose Works*, III, 169–273); supplemented by "The Judgment of Martin Bucer" (*ibid.*, 274–314); "Tetrachordon" (*ibid.*, 315–433); and the "Colasterion" (*ibid.*, 434–61). See also *Prose Works*, IV, 243–49; I, 259.

of moral equity," a "pure moral economical law . . . . so clear in nature and reason, that it was left to a man's own arbitrement to be determined between God and his own conscience;" and "the restraint whereof, who is not too thick-sighted, may see how hurtful and distractive it is to the house, the church, and the commonwealth."[1] It is lawful to Christians "for many other causes equal to adultery," such as cruelty, idolatry, and "headstrong behaviour" on the part of the woman, as also for desertion.[2] For "what are these two cases [adultery and desertion] to many other, which afflict the state of marriage as bad, and yet find no redress?" Hence he spurns a narrow construction as contrary to reason. "What hath the soul of man deserved, if it be in the way of salvation, that it should be mortgaged thus, and may not redeem itself according to conscience out of the hands of such ignorant and slothful teachers as these, who are neither able nor mindful to give due tendance to that precious cure which they rashly undertake; nor have in them the noble goodness, to consider these distresses and accidents of man's life, but are bent rather to fill their mouths with tithe and oblation?"[3] Nor is this the only time when Milton speaks the language of the modern social reformer, though sometimes his strongest arguments from the standpoint of reason are ill sustained by the authority upon which he relies. From the law of Moses, with which he insists that the law of Jesus must agree, he thus reaches the conclusion that just ground of divorce is "indisposition, unfitness, or contrariety of mind, arising from a cause in nature unchangeable, hindering, and ever likely to hinder the main benefits of conjugal society, which are solace and

---

[1] MILTON, " Doctrine and Discipline of Divorce," *Prose Works*, III, 241, 242.

[2] MILTON, "Colasterion," *Prose Works*, III, 423-33, where the views of many reformers are quoted; and "Doctrine and Discipline of Divorce," *ibid.*, 251-58, where Jesus's words are examined.

[3] MILTON, "Colasterion," *Prose Works*, III, 425.

peace."[1] To this ideal of the true end of wedlock he returns again and again. Rejecting the gross and carnal conception of the Fathers and canonists, their glaring contradiction between marriage as a "defilement" and a sacrament,[2] he urges that matrimony is a society "more than human," centering "in the soul rather than in the body;" a companionship resting upon the "deep and serious verity" of "mutual love," without which wedlock is "nothing but the empty husks of an outside matrimony, as undelightful and unpleasing to God as any other kind of hypocrisy."[3] Hence, where such society does not exist, where mutual affection has given place to deceit, the legal bond of the sham wedlock ought to be dissolved.

Unfortunately, there is another and less pleasing aspect of Milton's teaching. Beyond question saturated as he is in the sentiments of the Hebrew law, Milton has a very low ideal of womanhood. Almost invariably it is the husband's grievances which excite his compassion. Scarcely by implication does he ever admit that the wife may initiate proceedings, private or public, to rid herself of an unwelcome spouse. It is not quite clear whether he would allow her to put away even the unfaithful husband against his will;[4] while repudiation for lack of sympathy, for "loneliness," on account of

[1] MILTON, "Doctrine and Discipline of Divorce," *Prose Works*, III, 185.

[2] The doctrine of indissolubility compels uncongenial minds to "fadge together, and combine as they may to their unspeakable wearisomeness, and despair of all sociable delight in the ordinance which God hath established to that very end. . . . . All which we can refer justly to no other author than the canon law and her adherents, not consulting with charity, the interpreter and guide of our faith, but resting in the mere element of the text; doubtless by the policy of the devil to make that gracious ordinance become unsupportable, that what with men not daring to venture upon wedlock, and what with men wearied out of it, all inordinate licence might abound."—"Doctrine and Discipline of Divorce," *Prose Works*, III, 181.

[3] *Ibid.*, 210, 211, 195. For similar expressions see *ibid.*, 181, 182, 185, 267.

[4] However, chap. xxxiv of BUCER'S work, entitled "That it is lawful for a wife to leave an adulterer, and to marry another husband," Milton disposes of with the remark that "this is generally granted, and therefore excuses me the writing out": "The Judgment of Martin Bucer," *Prose Works*, III, 300. But this must be considered in connection with his positive claim of entire jurisdiction for the man in divorce causes, below referred to. Occasionally he drops a word from which possibly it may be inferred that he believes in a reciprocal right of the sexes; but it is

failure to realize that comfort and full spiritual society upon
which he so fondly dwells, is apparently the sole privilege of
the man.   In his opinion the man is emphatically the head
of the woman, who was created by God expressly "to comfort and refresh him against the evil of solitary life."[1]   No
disciple of Hillel was ever more thoroughly persuaded that
mere dislike is adequate cause for putting away a wife at the
sole command of the husband than was he.   "No libertine, for
the sake of wickedness and gratification of low desire, ever
demanded greater license in marriage than Milton in the
name of religion demanded for Christian men, in order that
they might find meet-helps, and escape the grievances of
uncongenial wedlock," though doubtless his sole aim was the
attainment of domestic purity and happiness.[2]

That this judgment is scarcely too severe is clearly
proved by Milton's theory of proper divorce procedure.[3]
Rejecting all aid of court or magistrate, he goes back to the

amazing how adroitly he avoids a direct statement to that effect. *Cf.*, for example,
"Doctrine and Discipline of Divorce," *Prose Works*, III, 182, where he seems to
approve the liberal laws of the Christian emperors; *ibid.*, 247-49, where he refers to
Beza's view that divorce is for the benefit of the woman; "Tetrachordon," *Prose
Works*, III, 359, 372, where he touches lightly upon the mutual rights of husband and
wife.

[1] MILTON, "Doctrine and Discipline of Divorce," *Prose Works*, III, 181. "And
what his chief end was of creating woman to be joined with man, his own instituting words declare, and are infallible to inform us what is marriage, and what is
no marriage; unless we can think them set there to no purpose: 'It is not good,'
saith he, 'that man should be alone.   I will make him a help meet for him.' "—*Ibid.*,
187. Beza holds, says Milton, that divorce (by the Jewish law) is created "only for
the help of wives." This leads him to exclaim: "Palpably uxorious! Who can be
ignorant, that woman was created for man, and not man for woman, and that a
husband may be injured as insufferably in marriage as a wife! What an injury is it
after wedlock not to be loved! What to be slighted! What to be contended with in
point of house rule who shall be the head; not for any parity of wisdom, for that
were something reasonable, but out of a female pride! 'I suffer not,' saith St.
Paul, 'the woman to usurp authority over the man.' If the apostle could not suffer
it, into what mould is he mortified that can?"—*Ibid.*, 247; *cf.* also *ibid.*, 209.

[2] JEAFFRESON, *Brides and Bridals*, II, 333. He was not solely actuated by irri-
tation against his wife, Mary Powell, whom he had put away; for he retained his
views after taking her back and to his life's end: *ibid.*, II, 333.

[3] For MILTON's theory of divorce procedure, as summarized in the text, see
"Doctrine and Discipline of Divorce," *Prose Works*, III, 263-73. *Cf.* JEAFFRESON,
Brides and Bridals, II, 335-38.

ancient principle of self-divorce.[1] For it was an "act of papal encroachment" to "pluck the power and arbitrement of divorce from the master of the family, into whose hands God and the law of all nations had put it, and Christ so left it, preaching only to the conscience, and not authorizing a judicial court to toss about and divulge the unaccountable and secret reason of disaffection between man and wife, as a thing most improperly answerable to any such kind of trial." For the sake of "revenue and high authority" the "popes of Rome" have "subjected that ancient and naturally domestic prerogative to an external and unbefitting judicature." Differences "in divorce about dowries, jointures, and the like, besides the punishing of adultery," ought indeed to be referred to the magistrate; yet "against the will and consent of both parties, or of the husband alone," the "absolute and final hindering of divorce" cannot rightly "belong to any civil or earthly power." For "ofttimes the causes of seeking divorce reside so deeply in the radical and innocent affections of nature, as is not within the diocese of law to tamper with." Among such "deep and serious regresses of nature" is hate, "of all things the mightiest divider." Moreover, the lord of the family cannot go wrong in acting from such motive; "for although a man may often be unjust in seeking that which he loves, yet he can never be unjust or blamable in retiring from his endless trouble and distaste, whenas his tarrying can redound to no true content on either side."[2] All this despotic power is placed

---

[1] SCHEURL, *Das. gem. deut. Eherecht*, 294 ff., forcibly argues that the conception of divorce through magisterial intervention, as opposed to self-divorce, is a mark of Reformation thought. According to Luther, God speaks through the civil magistrate. Hence in case of divorce from the bond of wedlock by judicial decree it is not "man," but God himself, who parts man and wife. Therefore the command of Jesus is not broken. So here we have another illustration of the casuistry necessitated by the appeal to authority.

[2] Accordingly MILTON justifies Parliament and the clergy in consenting to Henry VIII.'s putting away Anne of Cleves, "whom he could not like after he had been wedded half a year."—"Doctrine and Discipline of Divorce," *Prose Works*, III, 266.

in the husband's hands for the woman's good; for it is "an unseemly affront to the sequestered and veiled modesty of that sex, to have her unpleasingness and other concealments bandied up and down, and aggravated in open court by those hired masters of tongue-fence. . . . . It is true an adulteress cannot be shamed enough by any public proceeding; but the woman whose honour is not appeached is less injured by a silent dimission, being otherwise not illiberally dealt with, than to endure a clamouring debate of utterless things." Whether it would be well to shame the adulterer by publicity we are not informed.   Power would thus be restored to the "master of the family," where it was divinely placed.   For its exercise there is but one condition needful among Christian men.   The repudiation should take place in "the presence of the minister and other grave selected elders."   These are to "admonish" him; and he in turn is to declare solemnly by "the hope he has of happy resurrection, that otherwise than thus he cannot do, and thinks himself and this his case not contained in that prohibition of divorce which Christ pronounced, the matter not being of malice, but nature, and so not capable of reconciling."   He must not be restrained further.   To do so "were to unchristian him, to unman him, to throw the whole mountain of Sinai upon him, with the weight of the whole law to boot, flat against the liberty and essence of the gospel."   The procedure thus provided for by Milton, remarks Jeaffreson, is a "strictly private trial in which the husband discharged the function of prosecutor, furnished the evidence, and played the part of a judge."   But Milton is conscious that the denial of a reciprocal liberty to the wife may require some defense.   This he supplies by a singular piece of logic, which in its effect would sanction and encourage the basest tyranny for even the vilest purposes, though he does not appear to see it.[1]   "The law can only appoint the just

---

[1] *Cf.* JEAFFRESON'S suggestion, *Brides and Bridals*, II, 337.

and equal conditions of divorce," he declares, "and is to
look how it is an injury to the divorced," that is to say, to
the repudiated wife.   But in truth, he hastens to add, "as a
mere separation" it can be no injury to her; "for if she
consent, wherein has the law to right her? or consent not,
then is it either just, and so deserved; or if unjust, such in
all likelihood was the divorcer: and to part from an unjust
man is a happiness and no injury to be lamented.   But
suppose it be an injury, the law is not able to amend it,
unless she think it other than a miserable redress, to return
back from whence she was expelled, or but entreated to be
gone;" or else, if not formally separated, "to live apart still
married without marriage, a married widow."   The circular
argument is thus complete.   "The poet, whose Adam prayed
the Almighty to give him an *equal inferior* for his com-
panion in the happy garden, does not appear to have conceived it possible for a woman in her right mind to wish to
put away her lord and master."[1]

b) *Void and voidable contracts.*—It is a striking illustration of the completeness with which in social questions
the English mind was dominated by theological modes of
thought that no change in the law of divorce was effected
until the present century.   Yet there was crying need of
reform.   The rigid tightening of the bonds of wedlock
seems to have produced its natural fruit.   Immorality grew
apace.[2]   The lot of the married woman became harder even
than before the Reformation.   To the anomalies of the
mediæval system, some of which survived, were added others
not less harmful.   Chief among them were those arising in
the dualism, amounting sometimes to antagonism, subsisting

---

[1] *Ibid.*, 338.   A representative Catholic writer, REV. WILLIAM HUMPHREY, S. J.,
defending the sacramental doctrine of marriage, transposes Milton's phrase, declaring the woman in paradise and "as she is now" to be the "subordinate equal of
man."—*Christian Marriage*, 16.

[2] *Cf.* JEAFFRESON, *op. cit.*, II, 339, 340.

between the civil and the spiritual law. Theoretically, of
course, the temporal judge had no divorce competence at all.
Still where dower or inheritance was involved a policy had
to be defined. "Ultimately the common lawyers came to
the doctrine that while the divorce *a vinculo matrimonii*
did, the divorce *a mensa et toro* did not deprive the widow
of dower, even though she was the guilty person."[1] Such
was the law onward from the days of Edward III.[2] Earlier,
according to Glanville, and apparently also according to
Bracton, the woman "divorced for her misconduct can claim
no dower;"[3] and even at a time when she was not deprived
of dower through the fact of divorce, she might have the
right to claim it taken away as a punishment for her crime,
if she "eloped and abode" with her paramour.[4]

Especially disastrous in its effects was the absurd distinction, maintained after as well as before the Reformation,
between *void* and *voidable* marriages.[5] This had its origin

[1] POLLOCK AND MAITLAND, *Hist. of Eng. Law*, II, 392: *Co. Lit.*, 32a, 33b, 235a.

[2] *Year Book*, 10 Edw. III., fol. 35 (Trin. pl. 24): POLLOCK AND MAITLAND, *op. cit.*, II, 392.

[3] GLANVILLE, *Tractatus*, VI, 17; BRACTON, *De legibus*, fol. 92, 304. BRITTON, II, 264, seems to say, though his statement is somewhat confusing, that in case of divorce *a mensa et thoro* "if verified or not denied, the wife shall not recover any dower." Were not that interpretation of the law in the highest degree improbable, Britton's context might appear to show that such a divorce worked a complete dissolution of marriage. "In the recorded cases it is often difficult to see whether the divorce that is pleaded is a dissolution of marriage; e. g., Note Book, pl. 690. It is believed however that *divortium*, standing by itself, generally points to a divorce [nullification] *a vinculo*, e. g., in Lit. sec. 380."—POLLOCK AND MAITLAND, *op. cit.*, II, 392 n. 5. BISHOP, *Marriage, Divorce, and Separation*, I, §§ 1497, 1498 n. 3, appears to think that the "effect of a divorce for adultery . . . . was to dissolve the marriage" bond, because the guilty woman may "not be heard upon a claim of dower" (BEAMES, *Glanville*, 133). But this view is surely wrong, as the researches of POLLOCK AND MAITLAND have finally established: *op. cit.*, II, 372–95. Their results are thus summarized (373): "If however we can not argue that a woman was not married because she can not claim dower, still less can we argue that a union is a marriage because the issue of it will—or is not a marriage because the issue of it will not—be capable of inheriting English land."

[4] As by the statute of Westminster, II, c. 34, under Ed. I.: POLLOCK AND MAITLAND, *op. cit.*, II, 392, 393.

[5] The term "voidable" as applied to marriage is still used in various senses besides the special meaning referred to in the text. For a full discussion see BISHOP, *Marriage, Divorce, and Separation*, I, chap. xiii, §§ 252–92.

in the canonical doctrine of "putative" wedlock.[1]   A union
unlawful on account of some diriment impediment, such as
affinity or consanguinity, was held not to be *ipso facto* void,
but only voidable, if it had been solemnized with the proper
rites of the church; and the temporal courts assumed the
validity of all such marriages until they were declared null
by an ecclesiastical decree.   The happiness of an innocent
family was thus put in jeopardy.   At any moment a fatal
flaw in the union might be discovered or for money invented,
when *pro salute animarum* a separation of the parties would
be enforced.   In that case the canonists declared that the
issue should not suffer.   If one or both of the parents were
ignorant of the impediment at the time the children were
born, these were held to be legitimate.   This rule was
adopted by the secular courts in determining questions of
inheritance.   "As late as 1337 English lawyers still maintained that the issue of a *de facto* marriage, which was
invalid because of the consanguinity of the parties, were
not bastards if born before divorce.[2]   Later, however, they
developed a different doctrine which was enforced after the
Reformation.   Taking "no heed of good or bad faith," the
temporal law even in Protestant times made the "legitimacy
of the children depend on the fact that their parents while
living were never divorced."[3]   The persons separated for
spurious wedlock were permitted to contract new marriages;
but in that event they were exposed to one of the innumer-
able hardships caused by the fine-spun theories of the canonists.   The "validity of the first marriage was always an

[1] See the excellent discussion of the relation of the spiritual and temporal law
in cases of "putative" wedlock by POLLOCK AND MAITLAND, *op. cit.*, II, 373 ff.

[2] *Ibid.*, 375; *ap. Year Book*, 11-12 Ed. III., xx-xxii; for the early period see
GLANVILLE, *Tractatus*, VI, 17; BRACTON, *De legibus*, fol. 63.   *Cf.* also WOOLSEY,
Divorce 124.

[3] POLLOCK AND MAITLAND, *op. cit.*, II, 375 n. 3.   *Cf.* BLACKSTONE, *Commentaries*, I, 440; *Co. Lit.*, 233, 235; also GLASSON, *Hist. du droit*, IV, 152; BURN, *Ecc.
Law*, II, 501b-501c.

open question, and new evidence might at any time reverse
the decree. In this case the second marriage would be a
nullity and the first would recover its obligatory force, so
that now two separations, it might be, would be demanded
by canonical law."[1] But from the reign of James I.,
through intercession of the temporal courts, the action for
voidance of false wedlock had to be brought during the
joint lives of the consorts.[2] After the death of either
spouse the spiritual judge was prevented from issuing a
decree. For all practical purposes the spurious marriage
then became a valid marriage, and the unlawful issue became
legitimate;[3] though, absurdly enough, the surviving consort
might be punished for the sin of wedding within the forbidden degrees.[4]

Such remained the state of the law until the appearance
of Lord Lyndhurst's act in 1835.[5] This statute declares,
because "it is unreasonable that the state and condition of
the children of marriages between persons within the pro-

---

[1] WOOLSEY, op. cit., 124.

[2] See First Report of Commissioners (affinity), 1847-48, v; also HAMMICK, Marriage Law, 32. Originally the decree might be rendered after the death of one or
both of the persons, without, of course, affecting the status of the children.

[3] See Pride v. The Earls of Bath and Montague (1695): in 1 SALKELD'S Reports,
120, declaring that the reason why the spiritual court cannot give sentence to annul a
marriage after the death of the parties is "because sentence is given only pro salute
animae, and then it is too late." Cf. GEARY, Marriage and Family Relations, 10, 11;
BLACKSTONE, Commentaries, I, 444; JEAFFRESON, Brides and Bridals, II, 262-64.

[4] Harris v. Hicks (1694): in 2 SALKELD'S Reports, 548, where such consort may
be proceeded against for incest. "Our forefathers, with exquisite inconsistency,
were of opinion that the survivor might (for his or her soul's good) be proceeded
against and punished in a spiritual court, for having committed sin in respect of the
marriage which might not be adjudged a sinful nullity."—JEAFFRESON, op. cit., II,
264. Cf. GEARY, op. cit., 10, 11, 32.

[5] 5 and 6 W. IV., c. 54; also in HAMMICK, Marriage Law, 281. Compare
HANSARD'S Parl. Debates, 3d series, XXXVIII, 203-7; XXX, 661, 662. In general, see
GEARY, op. cit., 10, 11, 32; BURN, Ecc. Law, II, 501c-501e; HAMMICK, op. cit., 32, 33,
23; ERNST, Marriage and Divorce, 183, 184; LUCKOCK, Hist. of Marriage, 300-307;
JEAFFRESON, op. cit., II, 264-66; BISHOP, Marriage, Divorce, and Separation, I,
§§ 288, 289, 753; Tracts Issued by the Mar. Law Defence Union, II, 91-104.

The act extends to Ireland. "By the law of Scotland the distinction between
void and voidable marriages was never recognized, all marriages within the prohibited degrees being void ab initio."—HAMMICK, op. cit., 33 n. a.

hibited degrees of affinity should remain unsettled during so
long a period" as the joint lives of the parents, therefore
"all marriages which may hereafter be celebrated between
persons within the prohibited degrees of consanguinity or
affinity" ought to "be *ipso facto* void, and not merely
voidable;" and accordingly it is so enacted. With respect
to existing unions of this kind a distinction is made between
"affinity" and "consanguinity." Marriages within the forbidden degrees of affinity already celebrated may not "hereafter be annulled for that cause by any sentence of the
ecclesiastical court," unless pronounced in a pending suit;
while existing marriages within the prohibited degrees of
consanguinity are not so exempt.[1] Voidable wedlock in the
sense here employed[2] thus disappears from the English law,
except in those minor cases where "canonical" impediments
are still recognized.[3]

Lord Lyndhurst's act was especially designed to put an
end to marriage with a deceased wife's sister.[4] Such unions,
clearly unlawful, appear to have become very common since
the age of the Stuarts.[5] For where no property or other

[1] This liberal exception, mainly in favor of existing unions with a deceased
wife's sister, is of course denounced by writers such as LUCKOCK, *op. cit.*, 305, as a
"mischievous concession and compromise principle."

[2] For the special senses in which the term is used see the discussion of BISHOP,
op. cit., I, §§ 252-92, already cited.

[3] The only surviving canonical impediment for which a marriage may be voidable, but not void, is impotence. The same principle is also applied to marriages
secured by force: GEARY, *op. cit.*, 34, 203 ff., 212; HAMMICK, *Marriage Law*, 48, 49.

[4] Marriage with a deceased wife's sister or a husband's brother is included in the
table of forbidden degrees approved by Archbishop Parker in 1563. It purports to
be based on the Levitical code; and it was accepted as the law of the English
church by the ninety-ninth canon of 1603: HAMMICK, *op. cit.*, 32 ff., 350; *Tracts Issued
by the Mar. Law Defence Union*, I, 51 ff.

[5] JEAFFRESON, *op. cit.*, II, 258-66. These marriages were called "Altona marriages" (from Altona in Denmark, where they were sometimes solemnized), and are
the counterpart of the "Gretna marriages," except that the latter were valid and
the former were not: *ibid.*, II, 259, 260. The case of Brook *v.* Brook (House of
Lords, March, 1861) grew out of a marriage celebrated near Altona, June, 1850:
Tracts Issued by the Mar. Law Defence Union, II, 313 ff.

interests were at stake a man's marriage with his sister-in-law was likely to go unchallenged until the death of husband or wife made it perfectly valid.   Doubtless in such cases, through delay in "collusive suits," greedy relatives may sometimes have been prevented from securing estates which by natural justice, if not by law, belonged to the children or other heirs; for "no fresh proceedings could be initiated so long as any suit of a similar kind was pending."[1] But the avowed purpose of the act is its best justification, if the times were not ripe for a more liberal remedy.   If this class of marriages could not be legalized in harmony with the practice of most other civilized peoples, it was perhaps well in this way to make an attempt to relieve their innocent offspring from the uncertainty which "hung over them sometimes for years like a sword of Damocles."[2]   The attempt, however, did not prove successful.   "In 1847 a Royal Commission was appointed to inquire into the state and operation of the law of marriage as relating to the prohibited degrees of affinity.   In their report the commissioners state that of marriages within the prohibited degrees by far the most frequent class was that of marriage of a widower with a sister of his deceased wife, so that in fact it formed the most important consideration in the whole subject; and that as these so-called marriages will take place, especially among the middle and poorer classes, when a concurrence of circumstances gives rise to mutual attachment, the commissioners were of opinion" that Lord Lyndhurst's act "had failed to attain its object."   They furthermore declare, even at this early date, that such unions are permitted, "by dispensation or otherwise, in nearly all the

---

[1] LUCKOCK, op. cit., 303, 304, who holds that sometimes by such collusion the "ends of justice were defeated, and persons defrauded of their rights."   Cf. the remarks to this effect of Lord Selborne in the House of Lords, 1873, in Tracts Issued by the Mar. Law Defence Union, II, 168.

[2] LUCKOCK, op. cit., 304.

continental states of Europe," as well as in most of the
states of the American Union.[1]

No legislation followed the commissioners' report. Nor,
despite repeated efforts, has the perennial "deceased wife's
sister's bill" ever yet become a law. It is, indeed, curious to
see a noble senate capable of accepting the liberal civil marriage law of 1836 still stubbornly resisting in this particular
the secularizing of marriage which a recent writer observes
"is an evident accompaniment, if it is not a consequence, of
the progress of democracy."[2] There "can be little doubt,"

[1] *First Report of the Commission of 1847–8,* v, vi, xii; HAMMICK, *Marriage Law,*
33 n. *b;* GEARY, *Marriage and Family Relations,* 11, 30 n. 3. See HUTH, *Marriage
of Near Kin,* 129 n. 1.

According to the *Report* (viii), since the Lyndhurst act (1835) there had been
1,364 marriages within the prohibited degrees, of which nine-tenths were with a
deceased wife's sister. Only in 88 cases had the act prevented an intended marriage;
and of these 32 resulted in open cohabitation. Ten of the 88 cases were among the
lower classes. See the epitome of evidence, xvii–xxxix; the minutes of evidence,
1–120; and the interesting letters and papers in the Appendix, 121–65.

[2] LECKY, *Democracy and Liberty,* II, 214. There is already an immense literature
relating to the question of marriage with a deceased wife's sister. The most complete bibliography of the subject is comprised in Mr. HUTH'S "Bibliography of Works
on the Impediments to Marriage" appended to his *Marriage of Near Kin,* 393–449;
also in part previously published by the *Index Society,* IV, 1st App. to 1st Report. In
the *Church Quarterly Review,* XV, 426, may be found a table showing the results of the
various attempts to pass the deceased wife's sister's bill during the period 1842–82.

The absurdities and anomalies of the system are described in his trenchant
manner by LECKY, *op. cit.,* II, 214–23. With his account should be read the able
discussion by HUTH, *op. cit.,* 124–26. The peculiar arguments of the opponents of a
change in the law, mainly resting upon the alleged authority of the Old Testament,
are best seen in the two volumes of *Tracts Issued by the Mar. Law Defence Union*
(London, 1889); while the antidote may be found in T. PAYNTER ALLEN'S *Opinions
of the Hebrew and Greek Professors of the European Universities* (London, 1882), prepared for the Marriage Law Reform Association. The speeches in the two houses of
Parliament in 1849, 1851, 1855, 1873, 1883, 1895, and whenever a bill on the subject has
been under consideration, may of course be found in HANSARD'S *Parliamentary
Debates;* and the *Report of the Royal Commission* of 1848 (London, 1848) is especially
important. A strong partisan in favor of the existing law is LUCKOCK, *Hist. of Marriage,* Part II, 213 ff., particularly 250 ff., 292 ff., 300 ff. For his and similar arguments
from the standpoint of Hebrew law a partial remedy, on the homeopathic plan,
is afforded by the curious essay of REV. GEORGE ZABRISKIE GRAY, *Husband and
Wife* (2d ed., Boston, 1886). Starting with the scriptural premise that man and wife
are "one flesh," not "by his becoming part of her flesh, nor by both forming a new
flesh, but by her entering into his flesh," the author, arguing with an ingenuity which
would have done credit to Peter Lombard in his palmiest days, reaches the trium-
phant conclusion that a widower may properly marry his sister-in-law. In the same
way he shows that by divine intent a woman may not divorce her husband under any
circumstances, for "a member can not put away the head" (90); though she may

adds the same author, "that the opposition to these marriages
rests mainly upon theological grounds."[1]   Yet even on such
grounds it is hard to see why the Protestant theologian or
lawgiver should retain them in the table of degrees of affinity
prohibited by the code of Moses, while other provisions of
that law far more clearly enjoined are rejected or ignored.
"The Jews themselves maintain that this kind of marriage is
not forbidden in the Old Testament, and great numbers of
the most eminent Christian divines concur in their opinion."[2]

"leave" him—secure a separation *a mensa et thoro*—if he is "cruel or unclean"
(100).

On the general controversy see especially *Colloquii über die Frage: Ob Gott ver-
botten oder zugelassen habe dass einer seines verstorbenen Weibes Schwester heyraten
möge* (Oettingen [1681]), 12 ff.; and KETTNER (L.F.E.), *Judicia und Responsa von der
Ehe mit des Weibes Schwester* (Quedlinburg [*ca.* 1710]), 1 ff., neither of which appears
in HUTH's list; also ZEIDLER, *De mat. cum defunctae uxoris sorore*, published with
his *De polygamia* (Helmstadt, 1698); and MICHAELIS *Abhandlung von den Ehegesetzen Mosis* (Göttingen, 1768). Among the vast number of tracts and books on the subject for England a few of the more important are KEBLE, *Against Profane Dealing
with Holy Matrimony* (Oxford, 1849); FOSTER, *Review of the Law* (London, 1847);
PUSEY, *Letter on the proposed Change in the Laws prohib. Mar. between Near Kin*
(Oxford, 1842); *idem, Evidence given before the Commission* (Oxford, 1849); *idem,
God's Prohibition* (Oxford and London, 1860); BINNEY, *The Men of Glasgow and the
Women of Scotland* (London, [1850]); GIBSON, *Mar. Aff. Question* (Edinburgh, 1854);
DUKE, *The Question of Incest* (2d ed., London, 1883). This question, with others, is
also dealt with by FRY, *The Case of Mar. between Near Kindred* (London, 1756, 1773);
ALLEYNE, *The Legal Degrees of Mar.* (London, 1774, 1775); MACRAE, *Script. Law of
Mar.* (2d ed., Edinburgh, 1862); MEYER, *Uxor christiana* (Amsterdam, 1688), 2d
dissertation; and KETTNER (J. J.), *Zwei Abhandlungen* (Leipzig, 1780), 67 ff.   For
discussion of related questions of kinship compare BUTLER, *Marriage of Cousin
Germans* (Oxford, 1619); the same in Latin under the leading title *Suggeneia* in
FLORENS, *De nuptiis consobrinarum* (Frankfort, 1643); DUGARD, *Marriage of Cousin
Germans* (Oxford, 1673); JOHNSTOUN, *Juridical Dissertation* (London, 1734); PATON,
Mar. with a Dec. Brother's Wife (London, 1869), and in general read *Observations on
the Mar. Laws*, 126 ff.; LAWRENCE, in *Revue de droit int.*, II, 65 ff.; JEAFFRESON,
Brides and Bridals, II, 258 ff.; HAMMICK, *Marriage Law*, 23, 30–40; GEARY, *Mar. and
Fam. Rel.*, II, 30–32; WHARTON, *Exposition of the Laws*, 200, note; BISHOP, *Mar., Div.
and Sep.*, I, §§ 736 ff., 747, 750, 752, 753, 875 ff.; *Law Mag.*, XXI, 371–82 (May, 1839); *Quarterly Review*, LXXXV, 156–82 (July, 1849); *Ecc. Review*, new series, II, 735–48.

[1] LECKY, *Democracy and Liberty*, II, 214, who cites "the very candid confession
of the Bishop of Winchester": HANSARD's *Debates*, 3d series, CCLXXX, 1671.

[2] LECKY, *op. cit.*, II, 215, citing T. PAYNTER ALLEN's pamphlet already mentioned.
There is a weak criticism of this work in the *Tracts Issued by the Mar. Law Defence
Union*, I, 177–96.   On its high authority see HUTH, *Mar. of Near Kin*, 129.
    "It is certain that the Old Testament does not directly condemn such marriages,
and it is very doubtful whether it condemns them even by inference.   It is not at all
doubtful that it sanctions, and sometimes eminently blesses, polygamy; that it
strictly enjoins that, in every case of adultery, both parties should be put to death;

The Catholic is far more consistent and liberal in this respect; for he "regards the prohibition as resting, not on direct Divine or natural law, but merely on an ecclesiastical command, and his Church therefore claims and constantly exercises the right of dispensing with it."[1] The arguments on either side of the controversy need not here be summarized. Those in favor of the prohibition rest almost wholly upon authority. Only secondarily is an attempt made to defend it on social, political, or moral grounds. For most people of the civilized world[2] the subject is already "ancient history." Hence the modern student who first takes this controversial literature in hand is amazed to find men of high repute still earnestly speaking the language of the Middle Ages; still juggling with the casuistry and quibbles which satisfied Tancred and his predecessors.[3]

The nature of the problem and the way it is conceived by the English theological mind are thus strongly stated by Lecky in the fine paragraph with which he closes his interesting discussion of these marriages: "It would be difficult to overstate the extravagance of the language which has been sometimes employed in England by their opponents. One gentleman, who had been Lord Chancellor of England, more

that it makes it a capital offence for a man to have intercourse with a woman who, though unmarried, was betrothed to another; that it commands that a man who had defiled an unbetrothed virgin should be compelled to marry her; that it forbids marriage with aliens in religion; that it not only permits, but enjoins a man to marry the widow of his deceased brother if she had no children, or only daughters, which could scarcely be the case if such marriages of affinity were in their own nature incestuous. It is not easy to understand the process of mind which, among all these provisions of the Jewish code, selects a very doubtful inference condemnatory of marriage with the deceased wife's sister as alone binding on the conscience of the Imperial Parliament."—LECKY, *op. cit.*, II, 216, 217.

[1] LECKY, *op. cit.*, II, 215; *cf.* ALLEN, *Opinions*, 36.

[2] Russia appears to be the only important European exception: HUTH, *op. cit.*, 130, 131.

[3] For abundant proofs of what Mr. Lecky would call the "insularity" of the English mind in this regard, see the mass of matter—letters, speeches, and declarations of prelates, noblemen, and private persons—contained in that marvelous monument of mediævalism, the two volumes of *Tracts Issued by the Mar. Law Defence Union.* Mr. Gladstone's speeches are a conspicuous example: *ibid.*, II, 174 ff.

than once declared that if marriage with a deceased wife's sister ever became legal 'the decadence of England was inevitable,' and that, for his part, he would rather see 300,000 Frenchmen landed on the English coasts.[1] Pictures have been drawn of the moral anarchy such marriages must produce, which are read by American, colonial, and continental observers with a bewilderment that is not unmixed with disgust, and are, indeed, a curious illustration of the extreme insularity of the English mind. The truth seems to be that there are cases in which the presence of a young and attractive sister-in-law in a widower's house would, under any system of law, produce scandal. There are others where, in all countries, a sister-in-law's care and presence would seem natural. There are cases where every murmur is silenced by the simple consideration that the two parties are at perfect liberty to marry if they please. Experience—the one sure guide in politics—conclusively shows how quickly the best public opinion of a country accommodates itself to these marriages; how easy, natural, and beneficent they prove; how little disturbance of any kind they introduce into domestic relations. They will long be opposed on the ground of ecclesiastical traditions, and apart from all considerations of consequences, by a section of theologians in England, in America, and in the Colonies. Those who consider them wrong should abstain from contracting them, and a wise legislature will deal gently with the scruples of objecting clergymen, as it has done in the case of the marriage of divorced persons. But the law of the land should rest on other than ecclesiastical grounds, and a prohibition that has

---

[1] HANSARD, 3d series, CCLXXX, 1675. This was Lord Hatherley: see *Tracts Issued by Mar. Law Defence Union*, II, 161, 162, where he repeats the statement. Compare the views of the bishop of Exeter, in the same *Tracts*, I, 19, who predicts an orgy of incest if the law be changed: "At the present, no doubt, there is a strong natural instinct against the marriage of a man with his own mother. It is awful to think of. The marriage of a man with his own blood sister is fearful. But this instinctive protection of our domestic purity, how far does it go if we begin to pare the edges off." The Metropolitan (1880) indulges in like forebodings: *ibid.*, I, 97, 98.

no foundation in nature or in reason is both unjust and oppressive.   It is not for the true interests of morals or of family life that the law should brand as immoral, unions which those who contract them feel and know to be perfectly innocent, and which are fully sanctioned by the general voice of the civilised world, by an overwhelming majority of the English race, by a great and steadily increasing weight of public opinion at home, and by repeated majorities in the House of Commons.   In an age when most wise and patriotic men desire that the influence and character of the Upper House should be upheld and strengthened, few things can be more deplorable than that this House should have suffered itself to be made the representative of a swiftly vanishing superstition, the chief instrument in perpetuating a paltry and an ignoble persecution."[1]

c) *Parliamentary divorce.*—More than twenty years were yet to pass before the appearance of the first English statute providing for divorce through regular civil process. Proximately the act of 1857 owes its origin to the anomaly of parliamentary divorce, whose glaring inconsistency but served to accent the evils fostered by the canons of 1603. In theory marriage continued to be absolutely indissoluble. Only by giving bond not to marry again could a person secure even a judicial separation.   No matter how grave the offense, or how notorious the breach of the nuptial vow, the parties in most legal respects were chained for life.   At most they might be suffered to dwell apart.   Obviously the proper remedy would have been a general law of civil divorce whose benefits should be placed within the easy reach of rich and poor alike.   Instead, a resort was had to special acts of Parliament whose advantages could be enjoyed only by a fortunate class.[2]   The practice originated in

[1] LECKY, *Democracy and Liberty*, II, 221-23.

[2] The only special work on parliamentary divorce is that contained in MAC-QUEEN's *Practical Treatise*, 463-68, comprising a clear historical "Introduction;"

the last years of the seventeenth century, though it may
have been suggested by prior instances of legislative intervention in matrimonial questions.   As early as 1436 a
marriage obtained by force was declared void.[1] More clearly
analogous is the opposite case of Lord Northampton, already
mentioned, whose second marriage after decree of separation
was pronounced valid in 1552.   This, however, is not an
instance of parliamentary divorce.[2] Nor, strictly speaking,
is that of Lord Roos in 1670, which Macqueen regards as
the first "genuine example;" for the bill is entitled merely
"an act for John Manners, called Lord Roos, to marry
again;" and does not as alleged expressly effect a "rescission
of the contract."[3] The earliest clear precedents are the case

the "Action at Law;" the "Petition and Bill;" the "General Preparation of the
Case;" the "Second Reading and Subsequent Proceedings;" and an interesting
"Selection of Leading Cases." See also *Law Review*, I, 362 ff.; LECKY, *Democracy
and Liberty*, II, 200-202; GEARY, *Marriage and Family Relations*, 17, 18; HAMMICK,
Marriage Law, 18; SHELFORD, *Law of Marriage and Divorce*, 373-79; BISHOP,
Marriage, Divorce, and Separation, I, §§ 1422 ff.; WOOLSEY, *Divorce*, 172-74;
JEAFFRESON, *Brides and Bridals*, II, 340-44; LUCKOCK, *Hist. of Marriage*, 178-81;
WHARTON, *Exposition of Laws Relating to Women*, 471-84; GLASSON, *Le marriage
civil et le divorce*, 318, 319; BURN, *Ecc. Law*, II, 503b, 503c; HIRSCHFELD, "The Law
of Divorce in England and in Germany," *Law Quarterly Review*, XIII, 398, 399;
MONTMORENCY, "The Changing Status of a Married Woman," *ibid.*, 191; *Plea for
an Alt. in the Divorce Laws*, 5 ff.; SCRIBNER, *Treatise on the Law of Dower*, II, 542 ff.;
and especially the full account by MORGAN, *Marriage, Adultery, and Divorce*, II,
237-313.

[1] GEARY, *Marriage and Family Relations*, 17: *Rot. Parl.*, 15 H. VI, Nos. 14, 15.

[2] MACQUEEN, *Practical Treatise*, 469. *Cf.* n. 4, p. 80, above.

[3] The act, being private, was never printed in the collections of statutes; but a
writer in the *Law Review*, I, 363 n. 1, publishes it from the "House copy in the
parliament office." *Cf.* MACQUEEN, *op. cit.*, 471-73, 551-61, who discusses the case,
giving Bishop Cozen's argument, but he does not appear to have had a copy of the
statute before him. See EVELYN, *Diary* (London, 1878), II, 49 n. 3, who declares that
the Roos divorce bill was carried under influence of corrupt political motives; and
he is followed by KEBLE, *Sequel to the Argument*, 212 ff.; and MORGAN, *Marriage,
Adultery, and Divorce*, II, 237 ff. For a number of instructive details relating to
this case, extending over the years 1662-70, taken from the manuscripts of the House
of Lords, see *Reports of Hist. MSS. Com.*, VII, 165, 166; VIII, 102a, 117a, App. I, 141a;
XII, App. V, 8; App. VII, 69. The last entry runs: "1669, March 14. News letter.
Lord Roos presses for liberty to marry again, urging precedent of Marquess of
Northampton. All the bishops oppose except the B. of Durham." It is here noted
that the act finally passed April 11, 1670; 22 Car. II., 1, Private Acts. The case gave
rise to *The Case of Divorce and Re-Marriage thereupon* (London, 1673), in which a
"Reverend Prelate of the Church of England" denies, and a "private Gentleman"
maintains, the right of remarriage on scriptural authority.

of the Earl of Macclesfield in 1698 and that of the Duke of
Norfolk, two years later, in each of which the act provides
for a dissolution of marriage.[1]   Ultimately (1798) a standing
order of the House of Lords requires that "all bills of
divorce shall be preceded by a sentence of separation *a
mensa,* issuing out of the ecclesiastical court;"[2] and usually
such bills must be preceded also by the action at law against
the guilty paramour for damage.[3]   Thus a vast power was
placed in the hands of the spiritual courts to hinder an
aggrieved husband or wife from resorting to Parliament for
redress.   This fact is illustrated in the history of the cases
already cited.   Lord Roos had previously secured a decree
of separation, no mention being made of an action for
damage.   In Lord Macclesfield's case the bill for divorce
was sustained neither by a judgment at law nor by an
ecclesiastical sentence.   For "in consequence of the skilful
opposition set up by the countess in the spiritual courts, and
the narrow antiquated maxims which there prevailed, she
contrived to baffle all her husband's efforts to obtain a
sentence of divorce *à mensâ et thoro.*   The circumstances of
the case, however, were so scandalous and flagrant, that it
would have been an outrage upon every principle of justice
to withhold relief."   In like manner for seven years the

[1] On these two cases see MACQUEEN, *op. cit.,* 473, 562–76; and *Law Review,* I, 364.
The proceedings in the Norfolk case are contained in Vol. II, 59–324, appended
to ARCHBISHOP ABBOT'S *The Case of Impotency;* also in HOWELL'S *State Trials,*
XII, 883–948; and in part in the *Reports of Hist. MSS. Com.,* XIV, 17–27, 278, where, in
addition, arguments of the counsel are given.   Sir W. Williams, counsel for the
duchess, calls this case the "first precedent."

[2] MACQUEEN, *op. cit.,* 474, 496; LUCKOCK, *Hist. of Marriage,* 179, note; WHARTON,
Exposition of Laws rel. to Women, 471, 472; MORGAN, *Marriage, Adultery, and Divorce,* II, 244 ff.   The "earliest specimen of a dissolving statute passed by the Legislature, *after* sentence of divorce in the ecclesiastical court" is the "Act to dissolve the
marriage of Ralph Box with Elizabeth Eyre, and to enable him to marry again,"
1701.   This form was followed ever after: *Law Review,* I, 364, 365.

[3] Since about 1800: MACQUEEN, *op. cit.,* 489.   *Cf.* WHARTON, *op. cit.,* 472, 483;
GLASSON, *Le marriage civil et le divorce,* 318.   For examples of these actions for
"criminal conversation" see *Cases of Divorce* (London, 1715), 1 ff. (Feilding), 41 ff.
(Dormer); and *Crim. Con. Actions and Trials,* 10 ff., containing a good historical
introduction.

Duke of Norfolk tried in vain to obtain a decree of separation, although he "recovered damage at law from the adulterer, Sir John Jermayne."[1]   But in no other case save these two has there been a successful resort to Parliament without first obtaining the sentence of an ecclesiastical judge;[2] and the clumsy, almost farcical, nature of the procedure in divorce suits may be more fully appreciated when it is borne in mind that an aggrieved spouse desirous of securing a divorce from a guilty partner through an act of Parliament was compelled, before he could "get through the ecclesiastical courts, to pledge himself not to remarry."[3]

In consequence of the standing order of the House of Lords, Parliament was unable to grant relief, except on the one ground of conjugal infidelity; for the spiritual court declined to issue a decree of separation for malicious desertion, unless in connection with acts of cruelty.[4]   "On a retrospect of one hundred and seventy years, since the establishment of the system of parliamentary divorce *a vinculo*," says Macqueen, writing in 1842, "I find no case in which that remedy has been awarded or sought, without a charge of adultery.   There is no example of a bill of divorce for malicious desertion," although from the Reformation onward this has been a clearly recognized ground for dissolution of wedlock in other Protestant lands.[5]   Furthermore, with respect to the rights of the wife Parliament was more illiberal than the spiritual courts themselves, refusing, even after the ecclesiastical sentence of separation, to free her from a dissolute husband, unless his offense were attended by "aggravating" conduct, such as cruelty.   In no case was the woman granted relief merely for the husband's

---

[1] *Law Review*, I, 364; MACQUEEN, *op. cit.*, 473.   [2] MACQUEEN, *op. cit.*, 550.

[3] *Plea for an Alt. in the Divorce Laws*, 5, referring to the security required by the canons of 1603.

[4] HAGGARD, *Consistory Reports*, 120; MACQUEEN, *op. cit.*, 474.

[5] MACQUEEN, *op. cit.*, 473, 474.

unfaithfulness, however flagrant and shameless his conduct
might be.   Indeed, for the entire period during which the
practice existed, there were but three or four examples of
legislative divorce at the instance of a woman, and in each
case the man's infidelity was attended by other offenses.[1]
In two other cases the bill of the wife was rejected by the
Lords, although the grievous wrong which she had suffered
was established by the clearest proof.[2]   Parliament appears
to have accepted the view of Dr. Johnson that there is a
"boundless" difference between the infidelity of the man
and that of the woman.   In the husband's case, according to
that philosopher, there is no danger of a "confusion of
progeny;" and this, he says, "constitutes the essence of the
crime."[3]   Therefore, "wise married women don't trouble
themselves" about such mere peccadilloes.[4]

The sphere of parliamentary divorce was greatly narrowed
in still other ways.   As a matter of fact, for the century and
a half during which the practice prevailed perhaps not more

[1] The first three cases are those of Mrs. Addison, 1801; Mrs. Turton, 1831; and
Mrs. Battersby, 1840: MACQUEEN, *op. cit.*, 474-80, 594-98, 657, 658; also *Law Review*, I,
371; and LECKY, *Democracy and Liberty*, II, 200, 201. There appears to have been a
fourth case: GEARY, *Marriage and Family Relations*, 18; and in several instances
Parliament interfered by bill to nullify marriage or to grant separation *a mensa:*
MACQUEEN, *op. cit.*, 475, note.

[2] The cases of Tewsh, 1805; and Mrs. Moffat, 1832: MACQUEEN, *op. cit.*, 480, 482,
602-4, 658-60.   These are discussed in *Law Review*, I, 371-74.   Lord Chancellor
Brougham opposed Mrs. Moffat's bill; but later he took the opposite and more
liberal view: BROUGHAM, *Speeches*, III, 446.

[3] "He said, confusion of progeny constitutes the essence of the crime; and
therefore a woman who breaks her marriage vow is much more criminal than a man
who does it.   A man, to be sure, is criminal in the sight of God, but he does not do
his wife any material injury if he does not insult her; if, for instance, he *steals
privately* to her chambermaid.   Sir, a wife ought not greatly to resent this.   I would
not receive home a daughter who had run away from her husband on that account.
A wife should study to retain her husband by more attention to please him."—
BOSWELL, *Life of Johnson*, III, 46 (ed. 1835).   Some recent writers, who ought to
know better, indulge in similar sophistry; *cf.* NISBET, *Marriage and Heredity*, 18 ff.;
AP RICHARD, *Marriage and Divorce*, 25, 34, 35.

[4] BOSWELL, *Life of Johnson*, VII, 288.   For discussion of Dr. Johnson's philosophy
see JEAFFRESON, *Brides and Bridals*, I, 338, 339; II, 278-88; MACQUEEN, *op. cit.*, 482,
483; *Law Review*, I, 369, 370.

than two hundred such separations were granted.[1]   In the first place, the rules of evidence observed in the spiritual courts tended to thwart justice even in cases of the most cruel and scandalous wrongs.   Two witnesses were invariably required; whereas in the lay tribunals one witness is accepted as sufficient when no more can be had.[2]   On such testimony, for instance, damage may be awarded in the suit at law for adultery, when the same evidence is rejected as insufficient in the ecclesiastical action for separation.   Yet it is precisely in cases of adultery that a "*penuria testium* is most likely to occur.   To require two witnesses of facts almost necessarily secret is, in most cases, to ensure a denyal of justice.   Of this constant examples are to be found in the records of the ecclesiastical courts."[3]

Again, the relief granted by Parliament was effectively placed beyond the reach of all save the plutocracy.   The triple cost of the law action, the ecclesiastical decree, and the legislative proceedings was enormous.   How utterly the luxury of divorce was placed beyond the wildest dreams of the poor man clearly appears when one understands that it could

[1] Sixty between 1715 and 1775; 14 between 1775 and 1780; 110 between 1800 and 1852: GEARY, *Marriage and Family Relations*, 18; MORGAN, *Marriage, Adultery, and Divorce*, II, 239, 240; *Report of Commission* (divorce), 1852-53.

[2] "One witness (if credible) is *sufficient* evidence to the jury of any single fact, though undoubtedly the concurrence of two or more corroborates the proof.   Yet our law considers that there are many transactions to which only one person is privy; and therefore does not *always* demand the testimony of two which the civil [and ecclesiastical] law universally requires. '*Unius responsio testis omnino non audiatur.*' To extricate itself out of such absurdity, the modern practice of the civil law courts has plunged itself into another.   For, as they do not allow a less number than two witnesses to be *plena probatio*, they call the testimony of one, though never so clear and positive, *semi-plena probatio* only, on which no sentence can be founded.   To make up, therefore, the necessary complement of witnesses, when they have one only to a single fact, they admit the party himself (plaintiff or defendant) to be examined in his own behalf; and administer to him what is called the *suppletory* oath; and if his evidence happens to be in his own favour, this immediately converts the half proof into a whole one." — BLACKSTONE, *Commentaries*, III, 370.   *Cf.* also BISHOP, *Marriage, Divorce, and Separation*, II, § 456; *Law Review*, I, 378, 379.

[3] *Law Review*, I, 379, 380.   See the illustrative case of Evans *v.* Evans in *Notes of Cases in Ecc. and Mar. Courts*, II (1842-43), 470-76.   *Cf.* BISHOP, *op. cit.*, I, § 1532; BURN, *Ecc. Law*, II, 503e-503g.

be obtained only through the expenditure of a fortune sometimes amounting to thousands of pounds.[1]   The shameful
injustice of the system has never been so vividly brought out
as in the often-quoted words of Justice Maule in a case tried
before him in 1845: "The culprit was a poor man who had
committed bigamy.   The defence was that when the prisoner
married his second wife he had in reality no wife, for his
former wife had first robbed, and then deserted him, and
was now living with another man.   The judge imposed the
lightest penalty in his power, but he prefaced it with some
ironical remarks which made a deep and lasting impression.
Having described the gross provocation under which the
prisoner had acted, he continued: 'But, prisoner, you have
committed a grave offence in taking the law into your own
hands and marrying again.   I will now tell you what you
should have done.   You should have brought an action into
the civil court, and obtained damages, which the other side
would probably have been unable to pay, and you would
have had to pay your own costs—perhaps 100 *l.* or 150 *l.*
You should then have gone to the ecclesiastical court and
obtained a divorce *a mensa et thoro*, and then to the House
of Lords, where having proved that these preliminaries had
been complied with, you would have been enabled to marry
again.   The expenses might amount to 500 *l.* or 600 *l.* or
perhap 1000 *l.*   You say you are a poor man, and you probably do not possess as many pence.   But, prisoner, you must

[1] According to the writer in the *Law Review*, I, 367, two thousand pounds is not
an overcharged estimate. " In some cases even the preliminary proceedings in Doctors' Commons will cost nearly as much.   From the evidence of Mr. Swaby, the Registrar of the Admiralty Court, before the Select Committee, p. 33, it appears that
even in an ordinary litigation, with moderate opposition, and where the witnesses
are at hand, the expense of obtaining a definitive sentence of divorce à *mensâ* may
reasonably amount to 1700 *l.*; and this merely to lay a foundation for the proceedings
before Parliament, and quite independently of the action at law.   It is well known
that Lord Ellenborough's divorce cost 5000 *l.*" — *Ibid.*, 367 n. 6.   At the same time the
cost of a divorce *a vinculo* in Scotland was only 25 *l.*: *ibid.*, 367, 368.   But in the *Evidence before the Select Committee of the House of Lords, 1844,* 39, the expense of getting
a full divorce is then put at about 800 or 900 pounds.

know that in England there is not one law for the rich and another for the poor.'"[1]

d) *The present English law.*—It is, indeed, wonderful that a great nation, priding herself on a love of equity and social liberty, should thus for five generations tolerate an invidious indulgence, rather than frankly and courageously to free herself from the shackles of an ecclesiastical tradition! But even in England, so far as the state is concerned, the dogma that marriage is an indissoluble bond has finally run its course. A partial remedy for the scandals and hardships of the existing system was at last grudgingly provided in the civil divorce law of 1857. By this act,[2] which during a whole session of Parliament was stubbornly resisted, mainly on religious grounds,[3] the entire jurisdiction in matrimonial questions hitherto belonging to the spiritual courts, except "so far as relates to the granting of marriage licences," is transferred to a new civil "Court for Divorce and Matrimonial Causes;" and since 1873 this tribunal has given

---

[1] LECKY, *Democracy and Liberty*, II, 201, 202; also cited by JEAFFRESON, *Brides and Bridals*, II, 342, 343, note. For this case see MORGAN, *Marriage, Adultery, and Divorce*, II, 234–313.

On the law before 1857 see POYNTER, *Doctrine and Practice of Ecc. Courts in Doctors' Commons*, 68 ff. Against the proposed alteration is KEBLE, *Sequel of the Argument against immediately repealing the Laws which treat the Nuptial Bond as indissoluble* (Oxford, 1857), 196–220; while strongly in favor of a reform are the anonymous authors of *Plea for an Alt. in the Divorce Laws* (London, 1831), 1 ff.; and *Observations on the Marriage Laws* (London, 1815); as well as much earlier SALMON, *Crit. Essay Concerning Marriage* (London, 1724), 109 ff.

[2] 20 and 21 Vict., c. 85: *Statutes at Large*, XCVII, 532-46. In general on the present English law of divorce see GLASSON, *Le mariage civil et le divorce*, 317–27; HARRISON, *The Laws of Probate and Divorce*, 115 ff.; GEARY, *Marriage and Family Relations*, 237–430; BROWNING, *Practice and Procedure*, 1 ff.; LECKY, *Democracy and Liberty*, II, 202 ff.; THWING, *The Family*, 194; ERNST, *Marriage and Divorce*, 55 ff.; WOOLSEY, *Divorce*, 174–78; GLASSON, *Hist. du droit*, VI, 177–84; NEUBAUER, "Ehescheidung im Auslande," *ZVR.*, VII, 297–99; MONTMORENCY, "The Changing Status of a Married Woman," *Law Quart. Rev.*, XIII, 189–92; HIRSCHFELD, "The Law of Divorce in England and in Germany," *ibid.*, XIII, 399–405.

[3] HANSARD'S *Parl. Debates*, 3d series, CXLIV-VIII. "The discussions on the subject were curious as showing how powerfully, even to that late period, theological methods of thought and reasoning prevailed in the British Legislature. There were speeches that would seem more in place in a church council than in a lay Parliament."—LECKY, *Democracy and Liberty*, II, 202.

place to the "Probate, Divorce, and Admiralty Division" of the "High Court of Justice."[1] It is "a court for England only," its competence not extending to Ireland, Scotland, or the Channel Isles.[2]

By the law of 1857, supplemented in various ways through subsequent statutes, three forms of separation are recognized. First, on petition of either consort the court is empowered to grant a complete dissolution of wedlock; but in this respect the provisions of the act are conceived in the same narrow spirit that actuated the policy of legislative divorce. The woman is treated with precisely the same injustice. For while the husband may secure an absolute divorce on account of the simple adultery of the wife, the wife is unable to free herself from an unfaithful husband unless his infidelity has been coupled with such cruelty as "would have entitled her to a divorce *a mensa et thoro;*" or "with desertion, without reasonable cause, for two years and upwards;" or with certain other aggravating offenses.[3] Friends and enemies of the bill alike joined in condemning the unequal position in which man and wife were placed. Gladstone, who tenaciously resisted the act on theological grounds, declared: "If there is one broad and palpable principle of Christianity which we ought to regard as precious it is, that it has placed the seal of God Almighty upon the equality of man and woman with respect to everything that relates to these rights."[4] On the other hand, the attorney-

---

[1] 36 and 37 Vict., c. 66, secs. 16, 31.

[2] See GEARY, *Marriage and Family Relations*, 238 ff., for the jurisdiction and procedure of these courts. *Cf.* also HARRISON, *The Laws of Probate and Divorce*, 191 ff.

[3] 20 and 21 Vict., c. 85, sec. 27: *Statutes at Large*, XCVII, 537. But various "absolute" or "discretionary" bars may be pleaded against a decree. On these see GEARY, *op. cit.*, 267-304; HARRISON, *op. cit.*, 130 ff.; WOOLSEY, *Divorce*, 175.

[4] HANSARD, *Parl. Debates*, 3d series, CXLII, 394 ff. See the suggestive paper of HIRSCHFELD, "The Law of Divorce in England and in Germany," *Law Quart. Review*, XIII, 400-403, giving illustrative passages from the debates relating to the unfair treatment of the wife.

general, who introduced the measure, found it necessary to apologize for this defect. "If this bill," he says, "were thrown aside and the whole law of marriage and divorce made the subject of inquiry, I should be the last man to limit the field of discussion or to refuse to consider a state of law which inflicts injustice upon the women most wrongfully and without cause, and which may be considered opprobrious and wicked;" moreover, he continues, the "present bill need not be the end-all of legislation upon the subject."[1]

In judicial practice, however, the terms "cruelty" and "desertion" have acquired a rather broad meaning.[2] In particular through the doctrine of "constructive" and "moral" cruelty there is a "strong tendency to equalize the positions of the two" sexes.[3] Nevertheless, the woman is still in a relatively unfavorable position; and the sphere of divorce *a vinculo* is exceedingly narrow. There are doubtless many other causes besides infidelity for which the welfare of society and the happiness of individuals require that marriage may be dissolved. "It is a scandal to English legislation," ob-

[1] HANSARD, *op. cit.*, 3d series, CXLVII, 1545.

[2] Thus adultery, if long persisted in, ripens into "desertion." For a detailed discussion of "cruelty" and "desertion" according to definition and judicial precedent, and particularly on "constructive" and "moral" cruelty, see GEARY, *op. cit.*, 323 ff., 330 ff. *Cf.* BISHOP, *Marriage, Divorce, and Separation*, I, §§ 1524 ff., especially 1532; HARRISON, *op. cit.*, 138 ff.

[3] "From the meaning of pain inflicted on the body it [cruelty] has in recent years attained the extended meaning that includes pain inflicted on the mind. Coldness and neglect may now almost of themselves constitute such cruelty as, coupled with misconduct, will give the right of divorce. The time may very reasonably be looked forward to when almost every act of misconduct will in itself be considered to convey such mental agony to the innocent party as to constitute the cruelty requisite under the Act of 1857. The difference already is very marked when we compare the 'cruelty' of today with the thrashing by the husband that constituted cruelty thirty years ago. Probably in those days the doctrine of a husband's right to administer physical correction to his wife was not entirely discredited. Today it is possible for a woman, with celerity and at little cost, to separate herself from her husband if she be able to prove that he is either a brute or a monster. Forty years ago the vast majority of women were indissolubly tied to their husbands though the whole world knew them to be both brutes and monsters. It is a great change in a short period."— MONTMORENCY, "The Changing Status of a Married Woman," *Law Quart. Review.* XIII, 191, 192.

serves Lecky, that divorce "should not be granted when one of the partners has been condemned for some grave criminal offence involving a long period of imprisonment or penal servitude, or for wilful and prolonged desertion, or for cruelty, however atrocious, if it is not coupled with adultery. In all continental legislations which admit divorce a catalogue of grave causes is admitted which justify it."[1]

While depriving the ancient spiritual tribunals of the monopoly of matrimonial jurisdiction which they had so long possessed, Parliament made a proper concession to the scruples of the regular clergy. By the act a divorced person, whether guilty or innocent, is permitted to marry again if he likes; but a clergyman of the "United Church of England and Ireland" is not compelled to solemnize the marriage. Should he refuse, however, he cannot legally prevent a brother-minister of the establishment from using his church or chapel for the celebration; and this last provision has in our own day become a standing grievance on the part of those who denounce such a celebration as a "defilement" of the sanctuary.[2]

[1] LECKY, op. cit., II, 202, 203.

[2] Read, for instance, the complaint of Right Rev. G. F. Browne, bishop of Stepney, in his Marriage of Divorced Persons in Church: Two Sermons Preached in St. Paul's Cathedral on Feb. 16 and 23, 1896. The author seems to pine for the good old days before the act of 1857 when "things were different;" when, thanks to the singular merits of the old system, the "difficulty and cost of a special Act" of Parliament made separations a vinculo very few; when that evil statute had not yet caused a "horrible familiarity with the idea of divorce" (42). Compare LUCKOCK, Hist. of Marriage, 197-209, who likewise laments the desecration of the church through the celebration of the marriage of divorced persons; while he also condemns the alleged "connivance on the part of the Church of England" in the violation of the doctrine of indissolubility through the "issue of licences to divorced persons to remarry from Diocesan Registrars, ostensibly with the sanction of our own Bishops." He gives extracts from the Report of the lower house of the York Convocation (1894), which denounces the two practices mentioned, as also the "admission of persons who have entered into such unions to Holy Communion." Technically such a license is a "dispensation" which the bishop may refuse. It is often refused, as in the "Instructions issued to Surrogates in the Diocese of Lichfield": HAMMICK's Marriage Law, 362, and n. a. On these questions see GEARY, Marriage and Family Relations, 577-93, giving extracts from the proceedings of the Lambeth Conference, (1888), and the Convocation of Canterbury at various times, as also from the opinions of individual bishops and ministers.

The act of 1857 directs that, before granting a decree, the court shall "satisfy itself, so far as it reasonably can, not only as to the facts alleged," but also whether there has been any collusion between the petitioner and either of the respondents, or whether there is any bar or counter-charge against the petitioner.[1]   But no special procedure was created for making the inquiry suggested, "nor could a stranger without any legal private interest intervene."[2]   The necessary machinery for that purpose was provided by the Matrimonial Causes Act[3] of 1860, which rests upon the theory "that the public is interested in seeing that no marriage is dissolved except on certain grounds."[4]   Two distinct stages in the proceedings for a dissolution of wedlock are prescribed. If a sentence of divorce be rendered, it must always in the first instance be a decree *nisi*.   Only after an interval of six months, unless a shorter time be set by the court, can such a decree be made *absolute*.   In the meantime, the queen's proctor, or any member of the public, whether interested in the suit or not, may "intervene" to show collusion or the suppression of material facts;[5] and in case of such interven-

[1] 20 and 21 Vict., c. 82, secs. 29–31: *Statutes al Large*, XCVII, 538.

[2] So decided in Y. *v.* Y. (1860): 1 Swabey and Tristram, *Reports*, 598–600; Geary, *op. cit.*, 249, 261.

[3] 23 and 24 Vict., c. 144.   For the discussion of the bill see Hansard, *Parl. Debates*, 3d series, CLX, 1628–31, 1734–42.   *Cf.* also Glasson, *Le mariage civil et le divorce*, 322 ff.; Geary, *op. cit.*, 261 n. 6; Harrison, *The Laws of Probate and Divorce*, 141 ff.

[4] Lord Hannen, in the celebrated case of Crawford *v.* Crawford (1886), 11 P. D., 150–58, where the queen's proctor is allowed to intervene to prove a previous decision unjust.   See also Geary, *op. cit.*, 257 n. 2, 262, where this case is summarized.

[5] 23 and 24 Vict., c. 144, sec. 7.   The "intervener cannot be the respondent, or any one actually instigated by him or her, or his or her nominee; but the mere fact that the intervener may be (as he usually is) the friend or relative of the respondent is no objection."— Geary, *op. cit.*, 263, 264:   Howarth *v.* Howarth (1884), 9 P. D., 218–31; Forster *v.* Forster (1863), 3 Swabey and Tristram, *Reports*, 158–60. The queen's proctor may intervene as one of the public.   Only the petitioner can apply to have a decree *nisi* made absolute, but in long default of such application the respondent may ask to have the petition dismissed.   Decrees *nisi* "only apply to petitions for dissolution of marriage and not to judicial separations, restitution of conjugal rights, or jactitation;" but by 36 Vict., c. 31, they do apply to nullity suits: Geary, *op. cit.*, 249, 250 nn. 355, 356.

tion the court shall deal with the cause "by making the decree absolute, or by reversing the decree *nisi*," or by conducting further examination, as "justice may require."

Secondly, the present English law allows a decree for "judicial separation" with the "same force and the same consequences" as the former sentence of divorce *a mensa et thoro*, which is abolished by the act of 1857.[1] To such a decree either the husband or the wife is entitled on the ground of adultery, cruelty, or two years' desertion;[2] provided no legal bar to the petition such as condonation, cruelty, or a separation deed, be established. At the prayer of the petitioner, or when the evidence is insufficient to warrant a decree of complete divorce, a judicial separation may be granted in a suit brought for dissolution of marriage.[3] After such separation the wife is considered as a *feme sole* with respect to property, contracts, wrongs, suing and being sued; and her husband is not liable for her engagements.[4] In place of the old action at law for "criminal conversation" a prayer for damage against the wife's paramour may be joined with the petition for judicial separation or for dissolution of wedlock; or the aggrieved husband may make separate application for indemnity.[5] Adultery thus becomes a mere "private injury" and not a crime. The damage recovered may be "applied by the court for the benefit of the children of the marriage or for the maintenance of the wife."

---

[1] 20 and 21 Vict., c. 85, secs. 7, 16, 23, 25, 26: *Statutes at Large*, XCVII, 533, 534, 536, 537. On the law for judicial separation see GEARY, *op. cit.*, 352-59; HARRISON, *The Laws of Probate and Divorce*, 148-53; WOOLSEY, *Divorce*, 175.

[2] By the Matrimonial Causes Act of 1884, 47 and 48 Vict., c. 68, sec. 5, failure to respond to a decree for restitution of conjugal rights, even for a less time than two years, is made equivalent to desertion.

[3] GEARY, *op. cit.*, 353, 354.

[4] Except when alimony has been decreed and is in arrear the husband is liable for necessaries furnished his wife: 20 and 21 Vict., c. 85, secs. 25, 26: *Statutes, at Large*, XCVII, 537. *Cf.* HARRISON, *op. cit.*, 152, 153; GEARY, *op. cit.*, 424.

[5] 20 and 21 Vict., c. 85, sec. 33: *Statutes at Large*, XCVII, 539. *Cf.* Mason *v.* Mason (1883), 8 P. D., 21-23, C. A.; also WOOLSEY, *Divorce*, 177; GEARY, *op. cit.*, 354, 255-61; HARRISON, *op. cit.*, 182, 183.

When the wife is the guilty person and is entitled to property in possession or in reversion, the court, at its discretion, may settle "such property, or any part of it, on the innocent party, or on the children of the marriage."[1] The rules, principles, and procedure observed in the old ecclesiastical courts are to be followed by the civil judge in a suit for judicial separation except as otherwise provided by statute.[2]

In the third place, by the existing law provision is made for what is commonly called "magisterial separation." The "separation order," presently to be considered, is one of several remedial devices introduced by various statutes in the injured wife's behalf. Thus the act of 1857 enables a woman deserted by her husband to apply to a local court of summary jurisdiction, or, if she prefer, to the high divorce court of the kingdom, for an order to protect her subsequently acquired earnings or property from being seized by him or any of his creditors.[3] By this "protection order" the wife is to be in the same position as to property and contracts, suing and being sued, as if she had obtained a decree of judicial separation.[4] In all respects she is treated as a *feme sole*. For a number of years after it was first introduced the protection order was a means of real redress; for then, according to the principles of the barbarous laws of the Middle Ages which still survived, a married woman without settlements had practically no property rights at all during her husband's lifetime. Her landed property at marriage passed into his control; her chattels and personal

---

[1] WOOLSEY, *Divorce*, 177; 20 and 21 Vict., c. 85, secs. 33, 45: *Statutes at Large*, XCVII, 539, 541.

[2] 20 and 21 Vict., c. 85, sec. 22: *Statutes at Large*, XCVII, 536; *cf.* also HARRISON, *op. cit.*, 117.

[3] Application may be made to a police or petty sessional court and to the Court for Divorce and Matrimonial Causes or its successor, the Probate and Divorce Division. *Cf.* 20 and 21 Vict., c. 85, sec. 21: *Statutes at Large*, XCVII, 535, 536; also GEARY, *op. cit.*, 360 ff., 425 ff.; HARRISON, *op. cit.*, 176, 177; GLASSON, *Le mariage civil et le divorce*, 323: ERNST, *Marriage and Divorce*, 53.

[4] 20 and 21 Vict., c. 85, sec. 21: *Statutes at Large*, XCVII, 536.

effects of every description became absolutely his; and she
had no legal power to dispose even of the wages of her own
toil.[1] The protection order merely gave the wife her own,
preventing the man who had basely abandoned her without
making any provision for her support from appropriating the
wages or the property which she might thereafter gain.
More than this it did not do. "So to a poor wife a protection order was but little, if any, advantage, and now seems
absolutely useless. For it did not relieve her from cohabitation, it did not compel the husband to pay her any alimony,
and it did not permit her to pledge his credit for necessaries."[2]
Since the Married Women's Property Acts, therefore, notably those of 1870 and 1882, by which many of the worst
evils of the old system have been remedied,[3] the protection
order has been of little avail. Accordingly, a new measure
of relief was adopted. The act of 1886,[4] in case of desertion,
provides that any two justices in petty sessions or any
stipendiary magistrate may make a "maintenance order"
when they "are satisfied that the husband, being able wholly
or in part to maintain his wife and family has wilfully refused
and neglected to do so." The maintenance order requires
the husband to "pay to the wife such weekly sum, not
exceeding two pounds, as the justices or magistrate may consider to be in accordance with his means and with any means
the wife may have for her support and the support of her
family;" and the payment of the sum so ordered may be

----

[1] For a good summary of the old law as to property rights of married women
see GLASSON, *Hist. du droit*, II, 284; IV, 157-59; V, 103 ff.; VI, 162; GEARY, *op. cit.*,
184 ff.; and especially SWINDEREN, " Ueber das Güterrecht der Ehefrau in England,"
ZVR., V, 275 ff.

[2] GEARY, *op. cit.*, 363, 364.

[3] On these and other statutes giving the married woman control of her property
see SWINDEREN, *op. cit.*, 278 ff.; GLASSON, *op. cit.*, VI, 193 ff.; and MONTMORENCY'S
valuable article, " The Changing Status of a Married Woman," *Law Quart. Review*,
XIII, 192 ff.

[4] 49 and 50 Vict., c. 52. On the " maintenance order " see GEARY, *op. cit.*, 363,
368-70; HARRISON, *op. cit.*, 178, 179.

enforced by distress or by imprisonment if necessary.[1] Unlike
the protection order, the order for maintenance is not expressly
declared to be equivalent to a judicial separation; so it is
inferred that a husband may "at any moment terminate the
desertion," and require to be taken back by the wife who
will "be in default" for refusal.[2]

By the protection and maintenance orders a deserted wife
is secured in the enjoyment of her own property or is given
a just share in her delinquent partner's goods. In the
meantime, a statute of 1878 attempts to shield her from
a husband's brutality through the so-called "separation
order."[3] The court is authorized in case of "aggravated
assault," if "satisfied that the future safety of the wife is in
peril," to order that she shall no longer be bound to live
with her husband; that he shall render to her such weekly
alimony[4] as may seem just; and to place the children in her
custody.[5] This order for "magisterial separation," as it is
called, has the "effect in all respects of a decree of judicial
separation on the ground of cruelty." Like the protection,
and probably also the maintenance, order, it does not pre-
clude the wife's right, when she sees fit, to apply for a
judicial separation or even for a dissolution of marriage.[6]

[1] It is to be enforced as under an order of affiliation; but that is by distress, or,
in default of distress, by imprisonment: GEARY, op. cit., 366, 369, 415.

[2] Ibid., 370.

[3] 41 Vict., c. 19. On the separation order see GEARY, op. cit., 364 ff., 424, 425;
HARRISON, op. cit., 177, 178.

[4] The weekly amount and the manner of enforcing payment are expressed in
exactly the same terms as later adopted in the act of 1886 for the maintenance order.

[5] This order, like that for maintenance, may be discharged or varied on proof of
the wife's adultery; and the weekly sum may be varied in amount with an alteration
in the amount of the wife's or husband's means: GEARY, op. cit., 366, 367, 369, 370.

[6] "If the husband goes out of the jurisdiction and leaves no tangible goods that
are physically seizable, the wife is without remedy, however large be the husband's
property in stocks and shares, etc., or by way of interest under a settlement." She
may then apply for a judicial separation or a dissolution of marriage, when "she
will obtain alimony in the usual way; and this will be indeed her only effectual
course if; the husband absconds."—GEARY, op. cit., 367. Compare Gillet v. Gillet
(1889), 14 P. D., 158.

PART III

MATRIMONIAL INSTITUTIONS IN THE UNITED STATES

CHAPTER XII

OBLIGATORY CIVIL MARRIAGE IN THE NEW ENGLAND COLONIES

[BIBLIOGRAPHICAL NOTE XII.—For this chapter a large quantity of files and records of Massachusetts colonial and provincial courts has been examined. In the office of the Clerk of Courts for Middlesex county (Cambridge) have been used the *Records of the County Court for Middlesex,* 1649-86, 4 vols., MSS. folio, Vol. II missing; supplemented by the *Files of the County Court for Middlesex,* 1655-99; and followed by the *Records of the Court of General Sessions of the Peace for Middlesex,* 1692-1822, 9 vols., MSS. folio, the ninth volume containing also *Records of the Court of Pleas and General Sessions of the Peace,* October 1686, to March, 1688. In the office of the Clerk of the Supreme Judicial Court for the County of Suffolk (Boston) have likewise been examined the *Records of the Court of General Sessions of the Peace,* 1702-32, 4 vols., MSS. folio, with a fifth volume of fragments, 1738-80; the *Minute Books of the Court of General Sessions of the Peace,* January 3, 1743, to August 3, 1773, 5 vols., MSS. folio; the *Records of the Superior Court of Judicature, Court of Assize* and *General Goal Delivery in the Province of Massachusetts Bay,* 1692-1780, 33 vols., MSS. folio, Vol. II containing also the records of certain courts during the Andros period, 1686-87; and the *Early Court Files of Suffolk,* 1629-1800 — being papers of colonial and provincial courts held in Suffolk county, of the Superior Court of Judicature held in the several counties, and of the Supreme Judicial Court prior to last century, with miscellaneous papers, the whole collection comprising several hundred volumes, of which only those for the period 1629-1730 have been covered by this investigation. Careful examination has also been made of the MSS. folio volume of *Records of the County Court of Suffolk,* October 1671, to April, 1680, in the possession of the Boston Athenæum.

Very important are the published *Colonial Records of Plymouth* (Boston, 1855-61); *Massachusetts Bay* (Boston, 1853-54); *New Haven* (Hartford, 1857-58); *Connecticut* (Hartford, 1850-87); *Rhode Island* (Providence, 1856 ff.); and the *Provincial, Town, and State Papers of New Hampshire* (Concord, 1867-83).

The necessary complement of the records is of course found in the various compilations of statutes. For Massachusetts it has seemed best to cite by preference Whitmore's fine facsimile edition of the

Colonial Laws (Vol. I, 1660–72, Boston, 1887; Vol. II, 1672–86, Boston, 1889), which should be used in connection with his *Bibliographical Sketch of the Laws of the Massachusetts Colony*, 1630–86 (Boston, 1890); and Ames and Goodell's *Acts and Resolves* (5 vols., Boston, 1869–86), which with the three supplementary volumes (Boston, 1892–96), cover the period of the provincial charter and carry us beyond the Revolution. The following original digests have also been employed: *The Book of the General Lawes and Libertyes of the Massachusetts Colony* (Boston, 1660); *The General Laws and Liberties* (Boston, 1672) — these two earliest codes being those reprinted by Whitmore; *Acts and Laws*, 1692–1714 (Boston, 1714); *Acts and Laws*, 1692–1765 (Boston, 1769); *Acts and Laws* (Boston, 1759); and the collection entitled *Charters and General Laws of the Colony and Province of Massachusetts Bay* (Boston, 1814). The first digests of New Haven and Connecticut plantations are comprised in Trumbull's *True Blue Laws* (Hartford, 1876). There is also a reprint of the *Code of 1650, to which is added extracts from Laws and Judicial Proceedings of New Haven Colony commonly called Blue Laws* (Hartford, 1822); and a facsimile reprint of *The Book of the General Laws of 1673* (Hartford, 1865). For the eighteenth century we have the *Acts and Laws of his Majesties Colony of Connecticut in New England* (New London, 1715); *Acts and Laws of his Majesties English Colony of Connecticut* (New London, 1750); *Acts and Laws* (New Haven, 1769); and the *Acts and Laws* (New London, 1784). For New Hampshire, the "Province Laws" published in Vol. VIII of the *New Hampshire Historical Society Collections;* the *Acts and Laws passed by the General Court or Assembly*, 1696–1725 (Boston, 1726); the *Acts and Laws* (Portsmouth, 1761); and the *Acts and Laws*, 1696–1771 (Portsmouth, 1771), have been cited. To follow the tangled thread of Rhode Island legislation on any subject is a perplexing task; but the development of the written marriage law may be traced with tolerable clearness in the published digests. See Staples's *Proceedings of the First General Assembly . . . . and the Code adopted by that Assembly in 1647* (Providence, 1847); Rider's facsimile reprint of the code of 1705, entitled *Laws and Acts of his Majesties Colony of Rhode Island, 1636–1705* (Providence, 1896); his facsimile reprint of the code of 1719, entitled *The Charter and the Laws of his Majesties Colony of Rhode-Island in America* (Providence, 1895); also the original *Acts and Laws* (Newport, 1730); with Rider's facsimile reprint, entitled *Supplementary Pages to the Digest of 1730* (Providence, [1898]); the original folio editions of the *Acts and Laws* dated respectively 1745, 1752, 1767 (Newport); and Gregory's facsimile reprint of the compilation of 1772, entitled *Acts and Laws . . . . passed since the Revision in June 1767* (Providence, 1893). The Plymouth codes are printed in Vol. XI of the *Colonial Records* of that colony; and they are given in convenient form in Brigham's *Compact, with the Charter and Laws of New Plymouth* (Boston, 1836).

Original material has also been gleaned from the *Collections* (Boston, 1806–97) and the *Proceedings* of the Massachusetts Historical Society (Boston, 1879 ff.); Bradford's *History of Plymouth Plantation* (Boston, 1856); Winthrop's *History of New England*, 1630–49 (Boston, 1853); Hutchinson's *History of Massachusetts*, 1628–1774 (Vol. I, Salem, 1795; Vol. II, Boston, 1795; Vol. III, London, 1828); Cotton Mather's *Magnalia Christi Americana* (Hartford, 1820); Increase Mather's *Answer of Several Ministers* (Boston, 1695), on marriage with wife's sister; *The Andros Tracts* (Boston, 1868–74); Young's *Chronicles of the Pilgrims*, 1602–25 (2d ed., Boston, 1844); *Historical Collections of the Essex Institute* (Salem, 1896); Lechford's *Note-Book, 1638–71* (Cambridge, 1885), *idem, Plain Dealing* (Boston, 1867); reprinted also in 3 *Mass. Hist. Soc. Collections*, III; Dunton's *Life and Errors* (Westminster, 1818); his *Letters from New-England* (Prince Society, Boston, 1867); the "Town Records of Boston," 1634–1777; and the "Town Records of Dorchester," both in the *Reports of the Boston Record Commission;* "Town Records of Salem," 1634–59, in Vol. IX of *Hist. Coll. Essex Inst.;* especially Sewall's "Diary," in 5 *Mass. Hist. Coll.*, V, VI, VII (Boston, 1878–80); and his "Letter-Book," in 6 *Mass. Hist. Coll.*, I, II (Boston, 1886), both of which afford a wealth of illustration for almost every phase of wedding and other social customs.

Among recent writings relating to the general subject most important are Shirley, "Early Jurisprudence of New Hampshire," in *Proceedings of the New Hamp. Hist. Society*, 1876–84 (Concord, 1885); Earle, *Customs and Fashions in Old New England* (New York, 1894); Weeden, *Economic and Social History of New England*, 1620–1789 (Boston, 1891); Goodwin, *Pilgrim Republic* (Boston, 1888); Howe, *Puritan Republic* (Indianapolis, 1899); Arnold, *History of Rhode Island* (New York, 1874); Friedberg, *Eheschliessung* (Leipzig, 1865); Cook, "Marriage Celebration in the Colonies," in *Atlantic Monthly*, LXI (Boston, 1888); Bishop, *Marriage, Divorce, and Separation* (Chicago, 1891); Lodge, *Short History of the English Colonies* (New York, 1882); Trumbull, *History of Connecticut* (New Haven, 1818); Hollister, *History of Connecticut* (Hartford, 1857); Atwater, *History of the Colony of New Haven* (New Haven, 1881); Freeman, *History of Cape Cod* (Boston, 1869); Bailey, *Historical Sketches of Andover* (Boston, 1880); Bliss, *Side Glimpses from the Colonial Meeting-House* (Boston, 1896); *idem, Colonial Times on Buzzard's Bay* (Boston, 1888); Brooks, *The Olden Time Series: The Days of the Spinning-Wheel in New England* (Boston, 1886); articles by Scudder, Whitmore, Edes, McKenzie, Morse, and Goddard, in *Memorial History of Boston* (Boston, 1882–83); and Newhall, *Ye Great and General Court* (Lynn, 1897).

Illustrative material has likewise been gathered from a large number of writers, among whom are Palfrey, *History of New England* (Boston, 1888–90); Carlier, *Le mariage aux États-Unis* (Paris, 1860); Oliver, *Puritan Commonwealth* (Boston, 1856); Doyle, *English Colonies* (New York, 1882–87); Ellis, *Puritan Age* (Boston, 1888); Dexter, *Congregationalism* (New York, 1880); Bacon, *Genesis of the New England Churches* (New York, 1874); Belknap, *History of New Hampshire* (Dover, 1812); Green, *Short History of Rhode Island* (Providence, 1877); Sanford, *History of Connecticut* (Hartford, 1888); Hawthorne, *Grandfather's Chair* (Boston, 1893); Campbell, *The Puritan in Holland, England, and America* (New York, 1892); Hildreth, *History of the United States* (New York, 1882); Snow, *History of Boston* (Boston, 1824); Shurtleff, *Topographical and Historical Description of Boston* (Boston, 1872); Gilman, *The Story of Boston* (New York, 1889); Drake (S. G.), *History and Antiquities of Boston* (Boston, 1854); Drake (S. A.), *Old Landmarks of Boston* (Boston, 1889); Drake (S. A.), *The Making of New England* (New York, 1887); Prime, *Along New England Roads* (New York, 1892); Read, in the *Collections of the Old Colony Historical Society*, No. 2 (Taunton, 1880); and Brigham, in *Proceedings of the Mass. Hist. Society*, IV.

Among the works drawn upon in the treatment of special topics are Stiles's *Bundling* (Albany, 1871); supplemented by his *History of Windsor* (New York, 1859); and the very suggestive paper of Charles Francis Adams, *Some Phases of Sexual Morality and Church Discipline in Colonial New England*, reprinted from the *Mass. Hist. Soc. Proceedings*, June, 1891 (Cambridge, 1891); while there is an interesting passage relating to the same custom in Burnaby's *Travels through the Middle Settlements in North America*, 1759–60 (London, 1798); as also a characteristic reference in Irving's *Knickerbocker History of New York* (Philadelphia, 1871). For the first time the history of the stigma of the "scarlet letter" has been treated from the sources in Davis's careful monograph, *The Law of Adultery and Ignominious Punishments* (Worcester, 1895). In connection with the influence of the Levitical law on the New England conception of marriage and the family, Amram's *The Jewish Law of Divorce* (Philadelphia, 1896), and Mielziner's *The Jewish Law of Marriage and Divorce* (Cincinnati, 1884) are important. Of most service for the legal character of New England slave marriages are Moore's *Notes on the History of Slavery in Massachusetts* (New York, 1866); his "Slave Marriages in Massachusetts," in the *Historical Magazine*, XV (1869), containing a significant ritual used by Rev. Samuel Phillips, minister at Andover, 1710–71; and Steiner's "History of Slavery in Connecticut," in *Johns Hopkins University Studies*, XI (Baltimore, 1893). The originality of the system of civil registration created by the New England settlers is appreciated by Kuczynski, "The Registration Laws in the Colonies of Massachusetts Bay and New Plymouth," in *Publications of the Am. Statistical Ass.*, VII, 65–73 (Boston, 1901). See also Bibliographical Note XV.]

I. THE MAGISTRATE SUPERSEDES THE PRIEST AT THE NUPTIALS

THE continuity of English law and custom in the New England colonies is not more striking than the innovation. First of all it would indeed be strange if the planting of new states in the wilderness should not have afforded to thoughtful men a rare opportunity for freeing themselves from the trammels of antiquated methods and traditions which the "inertia of vested interests" might yet for ages sustain in the native land. In some instances the influences of a new and primitive environment might cause an unconscious return to the practices of earlier days. Religious and ecclesiastical ideas must necessarily play the leading part. In fact, the zeal with which the Pioneers of Plymouth and Massachusetts Bay proscribed the ceremonies and usages of the Roman and Anglican churches has had much to do with the character of civil institutions in the United States. On the part even of the Puritan there was thus sometimes a strong reaction in favor of the temporal power in matters hitherto regarded as exclusively pertaining to the spiritual jurisdiction. The sway of the so-called theocracy in Massachusetts and New Haven tended, sometimes inadvertently, to foster the growth of the American idea of complete separation of church and state. Thereby the forces of local self-government were quickened. Thus for a time the town-meeting and the congregation were practically one and the same; but authority was exercised in the name of the lay township and not in that of the ecclesiastical parish. So also the probate of wills, the administration of estates, the exercise of chancery jurisdiction,[1] and the

---

[1] In Massachusetts the county courts had an equity jurisdiction; *Mass. Col. Rec.*, V, 477, 478; *Acts and Resolves*, I, 75, 356; WASHBURN, *Judicial Hist. of Mass.*, 34, 166, 167; HOWARD, *Local Const. Hist.*, I, 330, 331. See the able article by WOODRUFF, "Chancery in Massachusetts," *Law Quarterly Review* (London, 1889), V, 370–86.

supervision of primary and secondary education[1] were taken out of the hands of the church and vested mainly in the local community. The process of secularization in legal functions proceeded with rapid strides.

In no respect was the change more remarkable than in the administration of matrimonial law and in the conception of the marriage contract. Here, as in so many other instances, our ancestors anticipated the thought and the legislation of the mother-country by more than two hundred years.[2] It will be remembered that in the beginning of the seventeenth century—and ever since the thirteenth—English marriage law was in an anomalous and most chaotic state. The Reformation in England had brought no real change in the canonical conception of the form of wedlock, though its sacramental nature was denied. On the one hand was the church at the demand of the state trying to enforce ecclesiastical rites and to secure publicity by requirement of banns, parental consent, and registration; on the other was the "irregular" or common-law marriage, entered into without any of these safeguards, by mere private agreement; and the validity of the latter was not squarely impeached by the church, though the disregard of the priestly office was punished by spiritual censure. All this is changed in the colonies. In place of

---

[1] An important epoch in the history of social progress is reached when our New England ancestors recognized the support of popular education as a proper function of local government. The event is all the more remarkable because it led the development of thought in the mother-country by more than two centuries and a half. However, the primary motive of the Massachusetts act of 1647 for the establishment of elementary and grammar schools was to provide religious knowledge. "It being one cheife p'iect of yᵗ ould deluder, Satan, to keepe men from the knowledge of yᵉ Scriptures, as in formʳ times by keeping yᵐ in an unknowne tongue, so in these lattʳ times by p'swading from yᵉ use of tongues, yᵗ so at least yᵉ true sence & meaning of yᵉ originall might be clouded by false glosses of saint seeming deceivers, yᵗ learning may not be buried in yᵉ grave of oʳ fathʳˢ in yᵉ church & comͫonwealth," etc.— *Mass. Col. Rec.*, II, 203. *Cf.* also HOWARD, *Local Const. Hist.*, I, 66–70; and *idem*, "The State University in America," *Atlantic Monthly*, LXVII (1891), 332 ff.

[2] Many of the enactments of the colonies are described by Lord Campbell as "anticipating and going beyond most of the salutary amendments which have been adopted in the reigns of William IV. and Victoria."— GOODWIN, *Pilgrim Republic*, 251.

confusion and complexity is found simplicity.   In New England particularly civil rites, civil registration, and uniform theory of marriage tend at once to prevent the manifold evils growing out of a lax or uncertain law.   The conception of wedlock which existed there from the beginning was identical with that which later found expression in the writings of Milton and the legislation of Cromwell.   Marriage was declared to be, not a sacrament, but a civil contract in which the intervention of a priest was unnecessary and out of place.

Governor Winthrop, in commenting upon "a great marriage to be solemnized at Boston," in 1647, expresses the sentiment prevailing during the first three-quarters of a century after the settlement.   The bridegroom was "of Hingham, Mr. Hubbard's[1] church," and the latter "was procured to preach and came to Boston to that end.   But the magistrates, hearing of it, sent to him to forbear.   The reasons were, 1. for that his spirit had been discovered to be averse to our ecclesiastical and civil government, and he was a bold man, and would speak his mind.   2. we were not willing to bring in the English custom of ministers performing the solemnity of marriage, which sermons at such times might induce, but if any ministers were present and would bestow a word of exhortation, etc., it was permitted."[2]   The last remark reminds us of the benediction of the early Christian priest, who, like the Puritan, discriminated between the religious act and the marriage.   Sermons, however, were originally proscribed at the nuptials, though they were permitted at the betrothal.[3]

The early colonial laws, generally, required that all marriages should be celebrated before a justice of the peace

---

[1] Peter "Hobart": GOODWIN, *Pilgrim Republic*, 596; DEXTER, *Congregationalism*, 458 n. 166; YOUNG, *Chronicles of the Pilgrims*, 402 n. 2.

[2] WINTHROP, *History of New England* (ed. SAVAGE, 1853), II, 382 (313).

[3] See especially DEXTER, *Congregationalism*, 458, who has pointed out the error of Mr. Savage (WINTHROP, *Hist. of New England*, II, 382 n. 2) in confusing the nuptials with the "contraction."

or other magistrate, sometimes under penalty of nullity for
those solemnized in any other way.[1] Where no statutory
provision to the contrary existed the common-law marriage
by private consent was valid.[2] The question now arises as
to the causes which determined the establishment of civil
marriage in the New England colonies. Was it set up in
imitation of the practice in Holland? Did it come as a
natural result of the general tendency of Protestant, and
especially of Puritan, thought? Or was it perhaps the
product of both influences combined? Already in the
middle of the eighteenth century colonial historians were at
a loss to account for it. Thus Governor Hutchinson makes
a difficulty of understanding why the lay celebration was
introduced. "Their laws concerning marriage and divorce,"
he says, "are somewhat singular. I suppose there had been
no instance of a marriage, lawfully celebrated, by a layman
in England, when they left it. I believe there was no
instance of marriage by a clergyman after they arrived,
during their charter; but it was always done by a magistrate, or by persons specially appointed for that purpose.
. . . . It is difficult to assign a reason for so sudden a
change, especially as there was no established form of the
marriage covenant."[3]

On the other hand, Governor Bradford believed that the
civil celebration was introduced by the Pilgrims directly

[1] The fact that ministers as such were not allowed to celebrate in New England
until near the end of the seventeenth century is, of course, well known to students.
Very many, however, who now insist on the religious ceremony are ignorant of the
fact; and it is not a little surprising to find so reputable a writer as AUGUSTE
CARLIER, speaking of the "émigrants dans la Nouvelle Angleterre," declaring that
marriage "se formait sous les yeux et avec l'approbation du chef de famille; il était
consacré par le pasteur; d'après les prescriptions impératives de la loi, mais surtout
pour obéir à la conscience d'un devoir religieux."—Le mariage aux États-Unis, 8, 9.

[2] BISHOP, Marriage, Divorce, and Sep., I, 176, 178; FRIEDBERG, Eheschliessung,
471, 472.

[3] HUTCHINSON, Hist. of Mass., I, 392. Compare COOK, "Mar. Celebration in the
Colonies," Atlantic Monthly, LXI, 351, who, following Hutchinson, thinks that the
colonists instituted "a form of marriage celebration unique in modern times."

from Holland. The first marriage in Plymouth Plantation
—that of Edward Winslow and Susannah White'—occurred
on May 12 (22), 1621. This, he declares "according to y^e
laudable custome of ye Low-Cuntries, in which they had
lived, was thought most requisite to be performed by the
magistrate, as being a civill thing, upon which many questions
aboute inheritances doo depende, with other things most proper
to their cognizans, and most consonante to ye scriptures,
Ruth 4, and no wher found in ye gospell to be layed on y^e
ministers as a part of their office. 'This decree or law about
marriage was published by ye State of ye Low-Cuntries
An^o: 1590. That those of any religion, after lawfull and
open publication, coming before ye magistrats in ye Town or
Stat-house, were to be orderly (by them) married one to
another.' Petits Hist. fol: 1029. And this practiss hath
continued amongst, not only them, but hath been followed
by all ye famous churches of Christ in these parts to this
time,—An^o: 1646."[2]

The testimony of Bradford must, indeed, command our
earnest attention, though in the matter of dates he is apparently misled by his authority. For, as already seen,[3] two of
the Netherland provinces had established civil marriage as
early as 1580; while it was not extended to them all until
seventy-six years later. Nor is the mere fact that, seemingly
without discussion, civil marriage was adopted by Massachusetts and her daughter-colonies, as well as by Plymouth,
necessarily a fatal objection to this theory of origin, though
it has a bearing upon the question which must be carefully

---

[1] On this marriage see also GOODWIN, *Pilgrim Republic*, 181; SHIRLEY, "Early
Jurisprudence of New Hampshire," *Procds. New Hamp. Hist. Soc.* (1876-84), 309;
BACON, *Genesis of the New England Churches*, 339-41; YOUNG, *Chronicles of the
Pilgrims*, 201.

[2] BRADFORD, *Hist. of Plymouth*, 101. The work mentioned by Bradford, accord-
ing to Mr. Deane, "is probably *La grande Chronique ancienne et moderne de
Holland, Zélande, Westfrise, Utrecht*, &c., by Jean-François le Petit, 1601, and 1611."
—BRADFORD, *op. cit.*, 101, note by the editor.

[3] See chap. x, sec. i.

considered. For the New England Pilgrim and Puritan alike were simply doing what their brethren did a few years after when they found their opportunity in the days of the Commonwealth. If America owes the institution of civil marriage to Holland, it is so not merely because of the residence of the Scrooby congregation at Leyden, but because of the profound influence which Dutch Puritanism exerted upon the Puritanism of England for a hundred years after the Spanish and Tudor persecutions began. It can scarcely be doubted that in various ways Dutch ideas made themselves felt in the remarkable legislative and constitutional experimentation of Cromwell's reign.[1] Moreover, the argument is strengthened by the fact that the Fathers of the English Reformation, unlike Luther and his followers, do not seem to have raised a single voice in favor of the lay ceremony.

Nevertheless, though Dutch custom undoubtedly furnished a direct precedent which should not be ignored, it seems highly probable that without the influence of Holland the early establishment of civil marriage in New England was inevitable. It was required by the spirit of Protestantism. Under favorable conditions, which New England did and old England did not afford, it was sure to arise as a consequence of rejecting the sacramental theory of wedlock.[2] There is another factor of the problem which must be reckoned with. The New England Puritans were steeped to the marrow in Hebraism; and, as we shall presently see,

---

[1] The evidence for the influence of Holland upon English and American institutions is presented in CAMPBELL, *The Puritan in Holland, England, and America* (New York, 1892), an able and timely work, calling attention to many facts strangely neglected by previous writers, but too sweeping in its general conclusion that American law and institutions, in their essential characteristics, are not Anglo-Saxon, but Dutch. For the interrelations of the Puritans in England and Holland see especially *op. cit.*, I, 485 ff.; II, 44 ff.

[2] At a very early day the English Separatists are found advocating civil marriage: see BACON, *Genesis of the New England Churches*, 107, who states Greenwood's view (1587).

the growth of a sentiment in favor of lay marriage was fostered by the example of the Jewish law.[1] It is vain to apologize for them on the ground that under the influence of the Mosaic code they really regarded the officiating magistrate as the "minister of God." In his "judicial" capacity the magistrate may, indeed, have been looked upon as a divine agent.[2] That is the well-known casuistry by which Luther and the early Protestants persuaded themselves that absolute divorce through the temporal court is not forbidden by the scriptural precepts.[3] But it is a grave error to suppose that the seventeenth-century Puritan had this in mind when he rejected the priestly ceremony. Doubtless he did not forget that marriage from its social and ethical sides is something higher than a *mere* civil contract. Yet for more than half a century after the settlement so intent was he in emphasizing its secular character that in the statutes the words "holy" or "sacred" as applied to it very seldom, if ever, appear. "Honorable" or some similar epithet is the strongest term usually employed. Even the publication of banns, as will hereafter be seen, was at first ordinarily required to be made, not on the sabbath, but at public "lecture" or on training day.[4]

The difference between the colonists and their Anglican adversaries in this regard is brought out in an interesting way through the experience of Edward Winslow, whose second marriage has just been mentioned. In 1634 he was sent on public business to England, where, partly in the interest of Merry-Mount Morton, Mason, and Sir Ferdinando

---

[1] See sec. iv, below.   [2] ELLIS, *Puritan Age*, 185.   [3] See chap. xi, sec. ii.

[4] But publication of banns on the sabbath was not ordinarily *prohibited*, the laws being usually silent as to that, while naming other days. Probably in some towns from the beginning sabbath publication may have been customary, as it was, apparently, at Andover: BAILEY, *Hist. Sketches of Andover*, 75. *Cf.* BACON, *Genesis of the New England Churches*, 339-41, who also seems to misapprehend the attitude of the Separatist and Puritan in his anxiety to show that early New England marriages were not "godless."

Gorges, he was accused by Archbishop Laud—whose scheme for setting up a governor-general and a bishop in the colonies seemed likely to be frustrated by Winslow's petition relative to the encroachments of the French and Dutch—of "teaching in yᵉ church publickly," and of performing the marriage ceremony. The latter offense he had committed in his capacity as magistrate. In reply to the charge he excused himself on the ground that the colonists were "necessitated so to doe, having for a long time togeather at first no minister; besids, it was no new-thing, for he had been so maried him selfe in Holland, by yᵉ magistrats in their statthouse."[1] But "with more courage and candor than caution, he proceeded to defend the practice on its merits, declaring that he knew no scriptural ground for confining this office to the clergy; while from the relations which marriage often had to property and to business obligations, there seemed good reason for making it a civil contract, as in Holland."[2] As a consequence Winslow was imprisoned in the Fleet for seventeen weeks.[3]

It appears certain, then, that in the two older colonies the lay ceremony was invariably required from the beginning.[4] But in neither case does there seem to have been any direct legislation on the subject for many years. Indeed, were there no prudential reason,[5] a positive legal sanction may well have been deemed superfluous while public opinion was so sensitive and so united. The first extant order of the general court of Plymouth requiring celebration before

---

1 BRADFORD, *Hist. of Plymouth Plantation*, 327–30.

2 GOODWIN, *Pilgrim Republic*, 386.

3 *Cf.* PALFREY, *Hist. of New England*, I, 543.

4 WEEDEN, *Ecc. and Soc. Hist. of New England*, I, 217 ff., has some interesting gleanings on the civil contract.

5 " To make a law that marriage should not be solemnized by ministers is repugnant to the laws of England; but to bring it a custom by practice for the magistrate to perform it is by no law made repugnant."—WINTHROP, *Hist. of New England*, II, 313, 314 (382). *Cf.* COOK, in *Atlantic Monthly*, LXI, 351.

a civil officer was passed, it is said,[1] in 1671. But in this jurisdiction, as in Massachusetts, the assistants or "magistrates" had always exercised this function; and it had long been the custom for the general court to appoint commissioners in the particular towns to join persons in marriage.[2] The earliest statute of Massachusetts relating to the celebration is the act of 1646, providing "that no person whatsoever in this Jurisdiction, shall joyne any persons together in Marriage, but the Magistrate, or such other as the General Court, or Court of Assistants shal Authorize in such place, where no Magistrate is neer."[3] In practice the last provision of this act was carried out in various ways. Thus, for example, any citizen might be appointed for a particular town during the pleasure of the court.[4] Or, in absence of the regular officer, a commission might be issued

---

[1] By BRIGHAM, *Mass. Hist. Soc. Proceedings*, IV, 283, 284. In general on civil marriage in New England see LECHFORD, *Plain Dealing* (Boston, 1867), 86, 87, or in 3 *Mass. Hist. Coll.*, III, 94; DUNTON, *Life and Errors* (1686), in 2 *Mass. Hist. Coll.*, II; *Mem. Hist. of Boston*, I, 196; READ, in *Coll. of Old Col. Hist. Soc.*, No. 2, 9; FRIEDBERG, *Eheschliessung*, 470-78; DRAKE, *Making of New England*, 98; OLIVER, *Puritan Commonwealth*, 415; HILDRETH, *Hist. of U. S.*, I, 192; WEEDEN, *Ecc. and Soc. Hist. of New England*, I, 217 ff., and Index; COOK, "Marriage Celebration in the Colonies," in *Atlantic Monthly*, LXI, 350 ff.; and especially the excellent chapter in EARLE's *Customs and Fashions of Old New England*, 36-81.

SEWALL's *Diary*, in 5 *Mass. Hist. Coll.*, V, VI, VII; and his *Letter Books*, in 6 *Mass. Hist. Coll.*, I, II, are a mine of information on social usages connected with dowers, courting, and wedlock. For very interesting records of marriages celebrated by magistrates at Salem in the seventeenth century see *Hist. Coll. Essex. Inst.*, I, II.

[2] *Plym. Col. Rec.*, II, 155; IV, 10, 22, 43, 65, 73, 74, 108, 186; VI, 217, etc. *Cf.* 3 *Mass. Hist. Coll.*, II, 270. In one instance we find the court abrogating a commission: FREEMAN, *Hist. of Cape Cod*, I, 208.

[3] WHITMORE, *Colonial Laws of Mass.* (1660-72), 172; *ibid.* (1672-86), 102. *Cf. Mass. Hist. Soc. Procds.*, IV, 283, 284. Compare NEWHALL, *Ye Great and General Court*, 367.

[4] So, in 1646, the court "granted comission to Mr Edwd Rawson to see people ioyne in marriage in Newberry," during pleasure, Watertown receiving a similar commission: *Mass. Col. Rec.*, II, 166. In 1651, on petition, Captain William Gerrish was similarly appointed for Newbery: *ibid.*, III, 256; IV, Part I, 65; *cf. ibid.*, IV, Part II, 63; V, 483. Such commissoners were usually so appointed at the request of the inhabitants. See two further examples for 1654, *ibid.*, III, 345, 346. On May 29, 1663, we find a "humble request by two men to *General Court* that Lieu. Goodinnough be authorized to marry their son and daughter. Granted with addition that Goodinnough be authorised to marry all who apply to him in that town [Sudbury?] and who have been properly published."— *MSS. Early Court Files of Suffolk*, No. 519.

to perform the ceremony in specified cases; as when Henry
Chickering was given authority to marry "two or three
couples, legally published at Dedham."[1] In one instance
we find a curious optional commission in which are inserted
the names of three persons, either one of whom is empowered
to join "M[r.] John Apleton and M[rs.] Priscilla Glover" in
marriage.[2] But, as a rule, one or more of the three commissioners, chosen for the ending of small causes in towns
where no assistant resided, was authorized by the county
court to perform this duty.[3]

The law and custom of the other New England colonies
were essentially the same as those already discussed. Everywhere marriage was regarded as a civil contract and the
celebration was performed by a civil magistrate. In New
Hampshire members of the council could act.[4] In Rhode
Island, besides the magistrate, "none but Quakers[5] and

---

[1] *Mass. Col. Rec.*, IV, Part I, 407. In October, 1647, Captain Wm. Hathorne was
commissioned to marry Thomas Jeggles and Abigail Sharpe, in the absence of "y[e]
major Gennerall."— *Mass. Col. Rec.*, III, 115. The *MSS. Early Court Files of Suffolk*,
No. 221, under date of Nov. 13, 1655, contains the following: "Order by the deputies in
General Court for appointing Captain Hathorne to join together in marriage at
Salem such as desire it, there not being in or near there any Magistrate. The Magis-
trates judge meet that the Deputies of Salem be authorized to join in marriage.
The Deputies judge meet to leave the choice to the town of Salem."

[2] *Mass. Col. Rec.*, IV, Part I, 74; *cf. ibid.*, 407; and SHIRLEY, "Early Jurisprudence of New Hamp.," in *Procds. of New Hamp. Hist. Soc.* (1876-84), 308.

[3] At a "County Court at Charlestown," June 25, 1658, "Mr. Richard Russell at
the request of the freemen of Charlestown is empowered to solemnize marriages and
to take oaths in civil cases."— *MSS. Records of the County Court of Middlesex*, I,
133. See also *Mass. Col. Rec.*, IV, Part I, 255 (1656), 322 (1658). The "associates,"
who sat with the "magistrates" to compose the county court, were often commanded
to join persons in marriage: *ibid.*, V, 139, 145, 101.

[4] See the Cutt Code in *Provincial Papers*, I, 396, 397; also *New Hamp. Hist. Soc.
Coll.*, VIII, 23, 117, 118; *cf.* SHIRLEY, "Early Jurisprudence of New Hamp.," *Procds.
New Hamp. Hist. Soc.* (1876-84), 307 ff.

[5] "A good story is told of Wm. Wanton—governor of Rhode Island, 1732-3—in
Deane's Scituate. Before his removal from that place to Newport, prior to 1700, he
had married Ruth Bryant, daughter of a Congregational deacon. Wanton's family
were Quakers. Religious objections were made to the match on both sides. He
said, ' Friend Ruth, let us break from this unreasonable bondage—*I* will give up *my*
religion, and *thou* shalt *thine*, and we will go over to the Church of England, *and go
to the devil together*.' They fulfilled this resolution so far, says our author, as to go to
the Church of England, and marrying and adhering to the Church of England during
life."— ARNOLD, *Hist. of Rhode Island*, II, 113, note.

clergymen of the Church of England could perform the ceremony," and these were given such authority by special grant of the king.[1] The law of New Haven, 1648, is peculiar in requiring not only that the marriage be performed before a magistrate or someone expressly allowed by the general court; but when the persons to be united are "able to go forth," that it be solemnized in some public place,[2] under penalty of five pounds for "every such miscarriage."[3] In Connecticut, likewise, compulsory civil marriage was adopted.[4]

During the "usurpation" period, beginning in 1686, the laws requiring civil marriage were set aside. Joseph Dudley, who entered upon his duties as president of New England in May of that year, published "an order of council, authorizing and empowering ministers and justices of the peace, the order says, 'to consummate marriages,' after three several times publication or licence from the president or deputy."[5]

[1] GREEN, *Short Hist. of Rhode Island*, 152, 153; ARNOLD, *Hist. of Rhode Island*, II, 113. By the code of 1647 marriages were to be celebrated ("confirmed") before the "head officer of the towne": STAPLES, *Proceedings of the First Gen. Assembly, 1647* (Providence, 1847), 47, 48; *R. I. Col. Rec.*, I, 187. On the head officer see HOWARD, *Local Const. Hist.*, I, 88, 89. According to the law of 1663 the intentions are to be published, and " afterwards before one of the Gener[ll] officers shall they be married ": in RIDER'S reprint of the *Laws and Acts* (1705), 12. But in RIDER'S reprint of *The Charter and the Laws* (1719), 12, it is declared lawful for " any Assistant, Justice of the Peace, or Warden " to perform the ceremony. The act cited is one of a group dated 1662; and it appears to be a modification of the law just cited from the collection of 1705. The act of 1701 reserves the right of Quakers and members of the Church of England to be married according to their own usage: RIDER, *Charter and Laws* (1719), 48; also in *Acts and Laws* (Newport, 1730), 44, 46.

[2] "This requirement was sufficiently answered when spectators were present; and usually marriages were solemnized at the home of the bride."— ATWATER, *Hist. of the Colony of New Haven*, 363.

[3] *New Haven Col. Rec.*, II, 599, 600.

[4] The civil-marriage form is recognized by the code of 1650: see TRUMBULL, *Blue Laws*, 167; COOK, in *Atlantic Monthly*, LXI, 351; SANFORD, *Hist. of Conn.*, 125; and HOLLISTER, *Hist. of Conn.*, I, 438. By the code of 1673 no person is to solemnize marriages "but the Magistrates, or such other as the General Court shall Authorize in such places where no Magistrate is near ": see the reprint of *The Book of the General Laws of 1673* (Hartford, 1865), 46.

[5] HUTCHINSON, *Hist. of Mass.*, I, 392, note; *cf.* SNOW, *Hist. of Boston*, 172, 173, 192; DRAKE, *Hist. of Boston*, 472, 473; SHIRLEY, "Early Jurisprudence of New Hamp.," *Procds. New Hamp. Hist. Soc.* (1876–84), 308; WHITMORE, in *Mem. Hist. Bost.*, II, 1, 2.

With this compromise Governor Andros was not satisfied; and it was his intention to allow marriages to be performed only by the Episcopal clergy. To do this at once, however, was impracticable. "Magistrates," says Hutchinson, "still continued to give people in matrimony. Other provision could not immediately be made." For at the time there was but one Episcopal clergyman in the country; and "Sir Edmund considered the Congregational ministers as mere laymen. Randolph wrote to the bishop of London, 'I press for able and sober ministers, and we will contribute largely to their maintenance; but one thing will mainly help, when no marriages shall hereafter be allowed lawful but such as are made by the ministers of the church of England."[1] Another restraint upon marriage was accounted a still more serious hardship. "None were allowed to marry except they entered into bonds with sureties to the governor, to be forfeited in case there should afterwards appear to have been any lawful impediment."[2]

---

[1] HUTCHINSON, *Hist. of Mass.*, I, 318; *cf.* ARNOLD, *Hist. of Rhode Island*, I, 498, 499; GREEN, *Short Hist. of Rhode Island*, 103. TRUMBULL, *Hist. of Conn.*, I, 372, followed by HOLLISTER, *Hist. of Conn.*, I, 317, makes the following extraordinary statement: "Magistrates only were allowed to join people in the bands of wedlock. The governor (Andros) not only deprived the clergy of the perquisite from marriages, but soon superseded the laws for their support."

[2] HUTCHINSON, *Hist. of Mass.*, I, 318. At least twenty-two of these bonds are extant. One, dated Jan. 11, 1686-87, given "unto Edward Randolph, Esq., Secretary of his Majesty's Territory and Dominion," may be found among the "Usurpation Papers" in 3 *Mass. Hist. Coll.*, VII, 170; and also in *New Hamp. Provincial Papers*, II, 18. The other twenty-one are in the *Early Court Files of Suffolk*, Nos. .29996-30016. Following is a copy of the first:

"Know all men by these presents that Wee John Harris of the Isle of Shoales ffisherman and Jabesh Negus of Boston Carpenter are houlden and firmely bound vnto his Excellency Sr Edmund Andros Knt Capt Gñall and Governour in Cheife vnder his most Sacred Maty James the Second King of England ec in and over the Territory & Dominion of New England ∽ In two Hundred pounds Currant money of New England aforesaid to be paid to his said Excellency Sr Edmund Andros his Executors Adminrs or Assignes To which payment well and truly to be made Wee bind ourfelves and each of vs and each of our heires Executors and Administrators Joyntly and feurally in the whole and for the whole firmely by these presents Dated the 24th day of June Anno Dni 1587 Annoq R R Jacobii Secdi nunc Anglice ec Tertio.

"The Condicon of this Obligãcon is fuch That if hereafter there fhall not appeare any Lawfull Lett or Impediment by reason of any precontract Consanguinity Affinity or any other Lawfull meanes whatsoeur But that the above said John Harris

This requirement in many cases amounted to a practical prohibition.[1]

The "first marriage at Boston with prayer-book and ring" occurred on May 18/28, 1686, just four days after Dudley received his commission as president of New England.[2] But there is evidence that zealous opposition to the religious ceremony existed up to the very beginning of this period. Thus, according to Savage, "Lawrence Vanderbosk, a Huguenot clergyman, undertook to solemnize marriages in Boston in 1685."   But he was brought before a tribunal for this enormity and promised "to do no more such things," yet in September, says Judge Sewall, "he joined together Giles Sylvester and Hannah, widow of Benjamin Gillam.   The reverend offender went to New York the same week."[3]

and Mary Sparks of Ipswich Spinster may Lawfully folemnize Marriage togeather; And in the fame afterwards Lawfully remaine and Continue Like man and wife ⁓ according to the Lawes in that behalfe made and provided That then this Obligaĉon to be void or else to Remaine in full force & virtue.

"Signed Sealed and Deliured   [Signed] John Harris | Seal |

"In the presence of vs.   ["   ] Jabesh Negues | Seal |

[Signed] " Jn Bonamy
["   ] Wm Marshall "

The earliest bond is dated June 24, 1687 (1587 in the MS.), and the latest Oct. 24, 1688. They are alike in all essential respects, differing very slightly from the above sample either in form or wording. They are all for £200; and all are executed in Boston, as shown by the names of the witnesses, although only six are "dated in Boston." Seventeen of them were witnessed by John Bonamy, and thirteen by Pe[ter] Heyman. These seemingly were men who made a business of witnessing in Boston; and all the other witnesses appear in connection with them. The bridegroom is always a bondsman. In one case, that of the fifteenth bond, dated March 5, 1687/8, the other signer is a woman, but not the bride. The other bondsman is never of the same name as the bride to be. The places of residence are Salem, Boston, Piscataqua, Nevis, and Plymouth; the counties of Bristol, Suffolk, and Plymouth; while in one case the man is from "Rhode Island."

1 TRUMBULL, Hist. of Conn., I, 372; HOLLISTER, Hist. of Conn., I, 317.

2 GOODWIN, Pilgrim Republic, 596; DRAKE, Hist. of Boston, 472; DOYLE, Eng. Colonies, III, 232.

3 Note by WHITMORE, Andros Tracts, II, 37. " 'Tis confessed," says Increase Mather referring to this incident, "that once or twice a Debauched Priest has appeared amongst them; particularly one Vardenbosch, who, besides the good work of Baptizing a noted whore or two of his acquaintance, made private Marriages without any previous publication of Banes (which is a nusance & Bane to all humane society); and yet so tender was the government as only to give them some Orall

Gradually, however, the stern Puritanism of the colonists became softened; the prejudice against ecclesiastical rites rapidly subsided; marriages were solemnized even by the Congregational clergy;[1] and soon after the struggle for the charters, laws were enacted allowing the ministers of all denominations to perform the ceremony. Yet, in Rhode Island, it was not until 1733 that the "settled and ordained ministers and elders of every society and denomination of Christians" were permitted to join persons in marriage, the legal fee therefor being fixed at three shillings.[2]   By an act of October, 1694, the same privilege was conferred upon the "ordayned ministers of the severall plantations" of Connecticut—in order, says the general court, to satisfy "such as are conscienciously desirous to be" so joined.[3]   For Massachusetts a similar statute was passed in 1692, authorizing all "settled ministers" to solemnize marriages, but only in their "respective towns;" while, on the other hand, the authority of the justice of the peace extended throughout the county.[4]   The careful limitation of the respective dis-

---

Rebukes, upon which the guilty Knaves have run away."—MATHER, "A Vindication of New England," *Andros Tracts*, II, 36, 37. For the passage in SEWALL's *Diary* referred to, see 5 *Mass. Hist. Coll.*, V, 98. There is a discussion of the first clerical marriage in New England, with reference to Vanderbosk, in *Historical Magazine and Notes and Queries*, VIII, 279, 348.

1 During the Andros period Rev. Charles Morton—who was installed as pastor of the church in Charlestown, Nov. 5, 1686—began to solemnize marriages. He was probably the first Congregational minister in New England who did so. See EDES, *Mem. Hist. of Boston*, II, 315.

2 *Rhode Island Col. Rec.*, IV, 490; RIDER, *Supp. Pages to the Digest of 1730*, 258, 259; *Acts and Laws* (1745), 176. *Cf.* ARNOLD, *Hist. of R. I.*, II, 113; GREEN, *Short Hist. of R. I.*, 152, 153.

3 *Conn. Col. Rec.*, 136. As the law stood in 1769, marriages might be solemnized by magistrates and justices, each within his own county, and by any ordained minister within his town or society during his continuance in the work of the ministry: *Acts and Laws* (New Haven, 1769), 144.

4 *Acts and Resolves*, I, 61. On this act JUDGE SEWALL makes the following characteristic entry in his *Diary*: "Nov. 4, 1692. Law passes for Justices and Ministers Marrying persons. By order of the Committee, I had drawn up a Bill for Justices and such others as the Assembly should appoint to marry: but came new-drawn and thus alter'd from the Deputies. It seems they count the respect of it too much to be left any longer with the Magistrate. And salaries are not spoken of; as if one sort of men might live on the Aer. They are treated like a kind of useless, worthless folk."—5 *Mass. Hist. Coll.*, V, 368. The marriage fee was fixed by this act at three shillings.

tricts of the minister and magistrate was doubtless intended to act as a check upon clandestine unions, as by the more stringent act of 1695.   By this statute none may join any persons in marriage who are not inhabitants or residents of the county or town; nor without a proper certificate of due publication and parental consent from the clerks of the towns where the parties respectively dwell.   For celebrating a marriage contrary to the act the minister or justice suffers a penalty of fifty pounds and is forever disabled to join persons in marriage, with the added liability of prosecution from the parent or guardian.[1]   By several subsequent acts the powers of the clergy are still further enlarged.   Thus in 1763 they are empowered to solemnize marriages in "parishes" and "districts" composed of "parts of towns" in "as ample a manner" as in the several towns where they dwell.[2] In 1773 they are allowed to perform the ceremony, not merely within their official districts, but for any whose "ministerial taxes" they are entitled to receive; or if for any cause a parish is without a minister, or if the incumbent himself desires to get married, then the next minister of the same denomination in the town may lawfully act.[3]

So it appears that the proclamation of President Dudley in 1686 marks an epoch of some importance in institutional history.   For by it the principle of American law, generally recognized at present by the statutes of the various states, and imitated by English legislation, was first recognized. Almost everywhere in this country the lay and the religious celebrations are equally valid; and it is not without interest to note that long before the Revolution the priest had once

---

[1] *Charters and General Laws* (Boston, 1814), 285; *Acts and Resolves*, I, 209, 210. In Nov., 1704, James Gardner, "preacher of the Gospel" at Dartmouth, that town being destitute of an "ordained minister," was allowed to solemnize marriages: *ibid.*, VIII (Appendix, Vol. III), 92.

[2] *Acts and Resolves*, IV, 622; *Charters and Laws*, 655. *Cf.* the earlier act of 1716-17: *Acts and Resolves*, II, 60.

[3] *Acts and Resolves*, V, 231; *Charters and Laws*, 679.

more practically superseded the magistrate at the nuptials.[1] It was already regarded as good social "form" to have the nuptials solemnized by religious rites.

No prescribed marriage ritual existed. The intention of the persons entering into the covenant might be expressed in any fitting words.[2] In the early period weddings were usually celebrated quietly in the home of the bride. But it must not be understood that all festivity was for long rigorously proscribed. Soon feasting was added to prayer and the singing of psalms.[3] A sumptuary law of 1637, forbidding the sale of buns and cakes in the markets, victualling houses, and elsewhere, carefully makes an exception of "such cakes as shalbee made for any buriall, or marriage, or such like speciall occation."[4] The ancient practice of our teutonic ancestors of "bedding" the newly married pair was maintained in some quarters. Judge Sewall had that experience when he took his second wife.[5] "In Marblehead bridesmaids and groomsmen put the wedded couple to bed;" and we are told that "along the New Hampshire and upper Massachusetts coast, the groom was led to the bridal chamber clad in a brocaded night-gown. This may have occasionally taken place among the gentry," comments Mrs. Earle, "but I fancy brocaded night-gowns were not common wear among New England country folk."[6] Another "survival" was the sham "bride-stealing" which was long kept

[1] In Hutchinson's time marriages were usually performed by the clergy. "Although," he says, "the law admits of its being done by a justice of the peace, yet not one in many hundred is performed by them;" and he adds in a note: "Perhaps, in a few years, the people of England will be equally well satisfied with the provision made by the late marriage act, and no body will be at the pains of a journey to Scotland to avoid conformity to it."—HUTCHINSON, *Hist. of Mass.*, I, 392, 393.

[2] See GILMAN, *The Story of Boston*, 177, 178, for an account of the marriage ceremony in the time of the Mathers.

[3] LODGE, *Short History*, 462.

[4] *Mass. Col. Rec.*, I. 214; *cf.* ATWATER, *Hist. of the Col. of New Haven*, 363; BAILEY, *Hist. Sketches of Andover*, 74, 75; WEEDEN, *Ecc. and Soc. Hist. of N. E.*, I, 113.

[5] SEWALL, *Diary*, in 5 *Mass. Hist. Coll.*, VII, 233.

[6] EARLE, *Customs and Fashions*, 73, 74.

up in the Connecticut valley. "The last bride stolen in Hadley was Mrs. Job Marsh, in the year 1783;" and to this day "in certain localities in Rhode Island, the young men of the neighborhood invade the bridal chamber and pull the bride downstairs, and even out-of-doors, thus forcing the husband to follow to her rescue. If the room or house-door be locked against this invasion, the rough visitors break the lock."[1] Furthermore, numerous instances of "smock marriages" in New England are recorded. Here the English superstition elsewhere mentioned[2] took the special form that "if the bride were married 'in her shift on the king's highway,' a creditor could follow her person no farther in pursuit of his debt."[3]

In the eighteenth century weddings were accompanied by much revelry and extravagance. Gloves, rings, and scarves, as at funerals, were given away in such profusion as to call for legislation to check the abuse.[4] Unstinted feasting and drinking were the order of the day. "Sack-posset" appears to have been the favorite wedding beverage.[5] "All

[1] EARLE, *Customs and Fashions*, 77. "A poem, by Mrs. Emma Willard, entitled 'Bride-Stealing, a Tale of New England's Middle Ages,' is preserved in Everest's *Poets of Connecticut*. It gives a poetical account of one among many instances of 'stealing the bride' that occurred in the early days of the colony."— HOLLISTER, *Hist. of Conn.*, I, 438, note. See also STILES, *Windsor*, 475; WEEDEN, *Ecc. and Soc. Hist. of N. E.*, I, 295; and HUNTINGTON, *Celebration of the 200th Anniversary of Hadley* (Northampton, 1859), 43.

[2] See above, chap. x, sec. ii, p. 441, note 3.

[3] EARLE, *Customs and Fashions*, 77–79, where several instances are discussed. See also PRIME, *Along New England Roads;* WEEDEN, *Ecc. and Soc. Hist. of N. E.*, II, 538.

[4] NOURSE, *Hist. of the Town of Harvard, Mass., 1732–1893* (Harvard, 1894), 498, gives details as to marriage fees received and entered in his record by the local clergyman. At first John Seccomb usually had 5 shillings; later, about 1750, his fee became "one pound old tenor;" still later generally "a dollar," or "half a dollar," and once a "pistareen." From 1760 Rev. Joseph Wheely usually records "2£ 5s." During the Revolution the ordinary charge was six shillings legal money.

[5] Sack-posset was compounded of milk, spirits, and other ingredients; and it was eaten with a spoon: SEWALL'S *Diary*, in 5 *Mass. Hist. Coll.*, VI, 403, note. On the wonderful mixed drinks of the New England Puritans see MRS. EARLE's delightful chapter on "Old Colonial Drinks and Drinkers," *Customs and Fashions*, 163–83; and also BLISS, *Side Glimpses from the Colonial Meeting-House*, 12–28.

the friends were entertained at the bride's home with a collation or supper, and afterward a dance; while in the country they were the most important social events. The banns were proclaimed in church, and all the neighbors were invited from the pulpit to attend the ceremony. On the day of the wedding muskets were fired, a procession was formed, and marched to the bride's house, where the marriage took place; and then came a dinner, a dance, and great merrymaking. Usually these wedding feasts lasted through the day and evening, but they were sometimes kept up for two or three days. On one occasion at New London there was a great wedding dance on the day after the marriage, when ninety-two ladies and gentlemen assembled and proceeded to dance ninety-two jigs, fifty-two contra-dances, forty-five minuets, and seventeen hornpipes. This was probably an extreme case; but all over New England weddings were great occasions, and were celebrated with much pomp and rejoicing." [1]

Of the New England marriage celebration at the beginning of the eighteenth century we have some vivid, though imperfect, sketches from the inimitable pen of Judge Sewall. Next to funerals, weddings seem to have been his chief recreation. The brief and naïve entries in his *Diary* reveal to us the mingled praying, psalm-singing, and posset which enlivened those festive occasions. Thus on October 22, 1713, he writes: "I go to Salem . . . . See Mr. Noyes marry Mr. Aaron Porter and Mrs. Susan Sewall, at my Brother's. Was a pretty deal of Company present . . . . Mr. Noyes made a Speech, said Love was the Sugar to sweeten every condition in the married Relation. Pray'd once. Did all very well.

---

[1] LODGE, *Short History*, 462, 463; *cf.* SANFORD, *Hist. of Conn.*, 125. BAILEY, *Hist. Sketches of Andover*, 74–78, gives interesting details as to weddings and marriage settlements; and BROOKS, *Olden Time Series: Days of the Spinning-Wheel*, 32, 33, reprints specimens of marriage notices taken from newspapers of the eighteenth century. On these festivities, advertisements, and settlements see also EARLE, *Customs and Fashions*, 60–77.

After the Sack-Posset, etc., Sung the 45th Psalm from the 8th verse to the end, five staves. I set it to Windsor Tune. I had a very good Turkey-Leather Psalm-Book which I look'd in while Mr. Noyes Read: and then I gave it to the Bridegroom saying, 'I give you this Psalm-Book in order to your perpetuating this song: and I would have you pray that it may be an Introduction to our Singing with the Choir above.' "[1]

Again in 1720 we find him solemnizing the marriage of his daughter, Mrs. Judith Sewall, with Mr. William Cooper. "I said to Mr. Simeon Stoddard and his wife, Sir, Madam, The Great Honor you have conferr'd on the Bridegroom and the Bride, by being present at this Solemnity does very conveniently supercede any further enquiry after your Consent. And the part I am desired to take in this Wedding, renders the way of my giving my Consent very Compendious: There's no maner of room left for that previous Question, Who giveth this Woman to be married to this Man? Dear child, you give me your Hand for one moment, and the Bridegroom forever. Spouse, You Accept and receive this Woman now given you, etc. Mr. Sewall pray'd before the Wedding, and Mr. Coleman after. Sung the 115. Psalm from the 9. verse to the end, in the New Hall, St. David's which I set. Then we had our Cake and Sack-posset."[2]

II. BANNS, CONSENT, AND REGISTRATION

It is a fact of great historical interest that in the New England colonies the administration of matrimonial law was relegated to the sphere of local self-government. The requirement of previous publication, parental consent, and registration was everywhere carried into effect by the officers of the town as a part of their regular functions; and by-laws for their guidance were enacted in town-meeting.

[1] SEWALL'S *Diary*, in 5 *Mass. Hist. Coll.*, VI, 403.   [2] *Ibid.*, VII, 253.

The first extant statute for the regulation of marriage is contained in the revision of the Plymouth laws made in 1636, and repeated under a slightly altered form in the revision of 1658. It is a model of brevity and precision; and it marks an epoch in the history of English jurisprudence, attempting, as it does in few words, a remedy for many of the evils which continued for two centuries to vex the mother-country. No one "under the covert of parents" is allowed to marry without their approbation. But in case such approval "cannot be had then it shall be with the consent of the Goveř or some assistant to whom the persons are knowne whose care it shall be to see the marriage be fitt before it be allowed by him." After the consent of parent or magistrate has thus been obtained, the marriage is to be published in "meeting" three several times before it is solemnized. Or, if there is no meeting, then fifteen days' notice by posting in the usual public place shall be sufficient; provided the "writing be vnder some magistrats hand or by his order."[1]

The Old Colony, likewise, made careful provision for registration. By an act of 1646 it is declared the duty of the town clerk to keep a register of the "day and yeare of the marriage, birth, and buriall of euery man, woman, and child" within his township. He is to have "thripence apece for each particular person soe registered." The persons marrying are themselves required, within one month, to report their marriage to him under penalty of three shillings for neglect— one-half to the Colony and the other half to the register "upon his complaint." The clerk must also submit annually to the general court at its March meeting a written report of all registrations made by him during the year. By this act, moreover, the publication of banns was devolved upon him.[2]

[1] *Plym. Col. Rec.*, XI, 13, 190; *cf.* PALFREY, *Hist. of New England*, II, 20; and BRIGHAM, *Plym. Col. Laws*, 44, 272.

[2] *Plym. Col. Rec.*, XI, 189, 190; *cf. ibid.*, 52, 53. Records of births, deaths, and marriages are printed *ibid.*, VIII. The record of marriages was sometimes included in the proceedings of the general court: *ibid.*, I.

The laws of the other colonies differed only in details from those of Plymouth. In Massachusetts the first order of the general court on the subject was passed in 1639. The intention is to be thrice published, not at divine service on the sabbath, it may be noted, but in town-meeting or at "publike lecture" in "both the townes where the parties, or either of them, do ordinarily reside." If no public lecture is held in the town, then fourteen days' notice may be given in writing on "some poast standing in publike viewe" and used solely for this purpose.[1] The "poast" is to be provided by the town under penalty of ten shillings for default.[2] Later it became customary for the town clerk or his deputy to publish the banns on Sunday, "after the blessing to the evening exercise was pronounced;" and so in 1696–97 we find the town-meeting of Charlestown ordering that "publishments should be made 'on Lecture days or any other public times, and not restrained to Sabbath Days only.'"[3] Sometimes on petition the legislature granted to individuals special permission to marry.[4] Originally the registration of births, deaths, and marriages devolved upon the town clerk; but it seems to have been neglected by him. For in 1642

[1] In the edition of the laws, 1660, notice is to be placed "upon some post of their Meeting-house door": WHITMORE, Col. Laws of Mass. (1660–72), 51, 52: cf. ibid. (1672–86), 101.

[2] Mass. Col. Rec., I, 275; WHITMORE, Col. Laws of Mass. (1660–72), 51, 52; ibid. (1672–86), 101.

The meeting-house on Sunday or lecture-day was a general clearing-house for news and gossip; and not the least inviting topics were supplied by the marriage notices. "There they read, as from an old newspaper, of an intention of marriage between persons known to everybody; and although the town clerk had stood up in the congregation and screamed it at the top of his voice, it was an endless subject of comment, especially if the woman had as publicly renounced the intention — as women sometimes did."— BLISS, Colonial Times on Buzzard's Bay, 77, 78.

[3] EDES, in Mem. Hist. Bost., II, 315, and n. 2.

[4] For instance, on May 22, 1651, such a petition from Mary Longe was allowed, provided "she be published according to law": Mass. Col. Rec., III, 232. Sept. 7, 1643, "Jacob Sheath & Margaret Webbe are permitted to joyne in marriage, though but twice published": ibid., II, 46. May 30, 1644, "without further publishment," Robert Parke "hath libertye to proceed in marriage with Alice Tompson": ibid., III, 3.

the general court laid this duty upon the clerk of the writs
in each town, under penalty for default, requiring him to
make annual return of all names registered to the recorder
of the county court.[1] A similar report to the same officer is
to be submitted each year by all magistrates or persons
appointed to solemnize marriages; and the "new married
man" shall likewise, within one month, bring in to the clerk
of the writs a certificate of his marriage.[2] Under the
Province laws the duties of recorder were again performed
by the clerk of the township; and under severe penalty
persons might not be joined in marriage without presenting
a proper certificate of publication and satisfactory evidence
of parental consent.[3]

Previous to 1692, of course, the legal history of New
Hampshire is in the main identical with that of Massachusetts.[4] But in the pioneer stage the township was sufficient
unto itself. "Dover and Portsmouth, for nearly twenty
years, had no central authority.[5] They had no ministry in

[1] *Mass. Col. Rec.*, II, 15; IV, Part I, 290; *cf. ibid.*, I, 275, 276; and WHITMORE, *Col.
Laws of Mass.* (1660–72), 188; *ibid.* (1672–86), 130. But town clerks continued to act:
Salem Town Rec., 148. The office of "Clark of the writts" seems to have been created
in 1641, primarily to issue summons and attachments: *Mass. Col. Rec.*, I, 344, 345. See
also "Province Laws of New Hampshire," in *Coll. of New Hamp. Hist. Soc.*, VIII,
31. Originally clerks of the writs were appointed by the general court; but later it
was ordered that they should be licensed by the shire court or court of assistants.
Those presented for license were first nominated in town-meeting: *Mass. Col. Rec.*,
II, 188; *Dorchester Town Rec.*, 116; *Salem Town Rec.*, 148, 195; *Boston Town Rec.*
(1660–1701), 100, 103, 130, 197. *Cf.* HOWARD, *Local Const. Hist.*, I, 90, 91, 331.

[2] WHITMORE, *Col. Laws of Mass.* (1660–72), 188; *ibid.* (1672–86), 130; *Mass. Col.
Rec.*, II, 59.

[3] See the acts of 1692 and 1696: *Acts and Resolves*, I, 61, 209, 210. By the former
statute ministers and justices are required to make a quarterly report of marriages
solemnized by them to the clerk of the sessions of the peace. The act of 1716, referred to in SEWALL's *Diary*, provides that the town clerk shall send in to the same
officer an annual transcript of marriages recorded by him. "The volume of such
returns for Suffolk County has very recently (written 1882) been transferred to the
custody of the city registrar of Boston."—SEWALL's *Diary*, in 5 *Mass. Hist. Coll.*,
VII, 112, and the note by the editors.

[4] Intentions of marriage were to be published three times, or else on fourteen
days' written notice: "General Lawes and Liberties of New Hamp.," *Coll. New Hamp.
Hist. Soc.*, VIII, 23. See also the Cutt Code, *Provincial Papers*, I, 396, 397.

[5] DOYLE, *English Colonies*, II, 201 ff.; LODGE, *Short Hist.*, 397 ff.; HILDRETH,
Hist. of U. S., I, 200; BANCROFT, *Hist. of U. S.*, I, 217, 218, 262.

any form, nor any magistrates, except such as might be created by any mining hamlet in an unorganized territory, or afterward as the result of forming themselves into societies. This, however, did not prevent people either from marrying or dying. The result was that marriage in New Hampshire has borne from the outset not only the character of a civil contract, but the impress of our township system."[1] After the establishment of the royal province the contract might be solemnized by "virtue either of publishment, or of a licence from the Governor. The granting of these licences was accounted a part of the royal prerogative;"[2] and it was complained of as leading to abuse.[3]

The statutes of Connecticut contain a curious provision, which will receive further notice hereafter. Distinction is made between the "contract" and the "covenant." Eight days' public notice of the proposed engagement must be given; and after the contract the betrothed pair must "forbeare" for a second period of eight days before joining in the covenant.[4] By the code of 1673 persons are not to be joined in wedlock "before the intention . . . . hath been sufficiently published at some publick Lecture or Town meeting in the Towns where the parties or either of them do ordinarily reside, or be set up in Writing . . . . upon some post of their Meeting House Door in publick view, there to stand so as it may be read eight days before such marriage."[5]

[1] SHIRLEY, "Early Jurisprudence of New Hampshire," *Procds. New Hamp. Hist. Soc.* (1876–84), 309.

[2] BELKNAP, *Hist. of New Hampshire*, III, 211.

[3] *Provincial Papers*, IV, 832 (1737).

[4] *Conn. Col. Rec.*, I, 47, 48 (1640), 540; TRUMBULL, *True Blue Laws*, 106. Compare *The Code of 1650* (Hartford, 1836), 67, 68.

[5] *The Book of General Laws of 1673* (Hartford, 1865), 46. The *Acts and Laws* (New London, 1715), 75, require three publications or eight days' posting; while by the *Acts and Laws* (New Haven, 1769), 144–47, intentions are to be announced only eight days before the celebration " in some public Meeting or Congregation on the Lord's Day, or on some public Fast, Thanksgiving, or Lecture Day, in the Town, Parish, or Society where the Parties or either of them do ordinarily reside," or else posted eight days, as before.

In general, the marriage laws of both Connecticut[1] and New Haven[2] on the topic considered are plainly modeled upon those of Massachusetts, and so need not here receive further analysis.

Some interesting details may be gleaned from the matrimonial legislation of Rhode Island. The code of 1647 requires the publication of banns at two town-meetings, confirmation before the head officer, and registration in the town clerk's book; otherwise the marriage is void. It is further enacted that the "man that goes contrarie to this present Ordinance . . . . shall forfeit five pounds to the parents of the Maid, and be bound to his good behaviour; and all the accessories shall forfeit five pounds a man, halfe . . . . to the grieved parents and the other halfe to the Town."[3] Thus was established at an early day, says Arnold, a system of registration "such as recent legislation has attempted to revive."[4] In 1656 it was permitted either to publish marriages at town-meeting, or "on a traininge day at yᵉ head of yᵉ Companie,"[5] or by a "Writinge under yᵉ Magistrates hands fixed upon some noted place in yᵉ Towne."[6] If "the

[1] For the law of registration see *Conn. Col. Rec.*, I, 48, 105, 106, 551; Trumbull, *op. cit.*, 123.

[2] *New Haven Col. Rec.*, II, 599, 600, 607; Trumbull, *op. cit.*, 241, 242, 255; Atwater, *Hist. of New Haven Colony*, 363.

[3] *R. I. Col. Rec.*, I, 187; Staples, *First Proceedings*, 47, 48.

[4] Arnold, *Hist. of Rhode Island*, I, 208.

[5] Publication on training day seems to have been customary elsewhere in New England, doubtless that day being one of the " public times " referred to in the Massachusetts laws.

[6] This practice may be illustrated by the following anecdote concerning the marriage of Ruth Wilkinson and William Hopkins at Providence, related by Mr. C. C. Beaman in *Hist. Coll. Essex Inst.*, II, 116: " The lovers could not muster courage enough to speak to the ' awful Justice,' for Mr. Wilkinson (Ruth's father) held that office so dignified in former days. In the house or office it was the custom to post up ' Intentions of Marriage.' The timid lovers, who had often looked with an envious or emulous eye upon such important steps preliminary to a ' consumation devoutly to be wished,' wrote a notice of their ' intentions,' and placing it unobserved upon the table of the ' Justice,' watched to see how it would be regarded. 'Squire Wilkinson, as they saw by a peep through the door, took up the paper, read it, and deliberately posted it up in the proper location. There were some blushes on the cheeks of Ruth that day, probably, but the desired approbation thus ingeniously obtained soon led on to marriage."

banns were forbidden, the case was to be heard by two
magistrates; should they allow it, the parties might marry;
but if not, the general Court of trials were to decide."[1]   A
later version of the law of 1647, of uncertain date, is somewhat more detailed.   The "man y^t hath A respect to a maid
& doth desi[re] to Obtaine her in Marriage . . . . shall
first acquaint her Parents thereof & upon their consenting
thereto he shall have Baines of matrimony set up in a Publick Place in ye Town or be Published two sever^{ll} times
In A Public Assembly In the Town & then remaine from
After ye first Publication Tenn Days."   Afterward, "before
one of the Gener^{ll} officers" the celebration may take place
according to "ye usuwal Custome of this place & then a Certificate Shall be given by ye Officer y^t Ioynes them togeather
in Marriage to ye party So married who shall Carry it to the
Clarke of ye Town where ye Marriage was Solemnized &
have it Placed upon Record."   For violation of the act the
same penalties are imposed on the principals and accessories
as in 1647; and the children "y^t any shall have wthout this
due & orderly Course of Law . . . . shall be looked at not
to be Legitimate."[2]   It appears that the execution of the
laws was sadly neglected, and so by an act of 1698 all marriages thus far solemnized, but not duly registered, are declared valid.   Persons married in future are ordered within
ten days to make return to the town clerk; while the latter
is required to submit annually to the head officer of the town
or to the chief justice of the peace a report of all births,
marriages, and deaths by him recorded.[3]   Three years later
a more stringent statute appears.   Persons from another
colony or township must present to the officer performing the
ceremony a magistrate's certificate of proper publication and

[1] ARNOLD, *Hist. of R. I.*, I, 260; *R. I. Col. Rec.*, I, 330.

[2] RIDER'S *Laws and Acts* (1705), 12.

[3] *R. I. Col. Rec.*, III, 362; also in RIDER'S *Laws and Acts* (1705), 44.

qualification.[1] "Fine and suspension from office were the penalties for any violation of this act by a magistrate, and fine, imprisonment, or whipping, is the punishments for the principals who disregard it."[2] After various changes[3] the law of the provincial era reached its full development in the code of 1767. A dual system of banns and lay publication is provided. If application be made to a "settled and ordained" minister of any denomination, he shall "openly and by public speaking" proclaim the banns on three several Sundays, holidays, or days of public worship "in the Meeting in the Town, where the Parties respectively belong." If lay publication be preferred, the assistant, warden, or justice, under his hand and seal, is required to post a notice in some public place in each of the towns where the parties dwell fifteen days before the wedding.[4] A method of "under-writing" in case of objection is prescribed. With leave of any assistant, justice, or warden, the person opposing the marriage is to make the objection "in writing under his or her Hand, therein assigning the Impediment, and affix the same under the Publication;" but in case of oral banns the written objection, in the presence of two witnesses, is to be delivered to the minister or elder who proclaimed the banns. The person forbidding the marriage must enter into recognizance with two good sureties to appear at the next court of general

---

[1] *R. I. Col. Rec.*, III, 436; *cf. ibid.*, IV, 395, 396; RIDER, *op. cit.*, 50.

[2] ARNOLD, *Hist. of R. I.*, II, 3; *R. I. Col. Rec.*, III, 436, 437. By this act fourteen days' notice is required of those living in the jurisdiction.

[3] Compare RIDER'S *Charter and Laws* (1719), 12, 13, 47, 48; *Acts and Laws* (1745), 30, 31, 176, 177 (1733), 100 (registration act of 1727); and RIDER'S *Supp. Pages to the Digest of 1730*, 258, 259 (act of 1733).

[4] The prescribed notice is in the following form:
"Know all Men by these Presents, that A. B. of —— and C. D. of —— have declared unto me their Intention of Marriage: I do therefore hereby make public the said Intention. If any Person knows any just Cause or Impediment why these Two Persons shall not be joined together in Marriage, they may declare the same as the Law directs. Given under my Hand and Seal at —— this —— Day of —— *Anno Domini*——."—*Acts and Laws* (Newport 1767,), 172, 173.

sessions of the peace and there "make good and prove" his allegations, or, in default, pay to the persons to be wedded "all such Damages as they shall sustain by Means of staying their Marriage." A certificate of publication must be produced; two credible witnesses to the ceremony are required; the person conducting the celebration must give a certificate[1] thereof to the newly wedded pair; and he is entitled to a fee of three shillings. Only fines are imposed for violation of the act by the solemnizer or by the parties. Neither by this law nor apparently by any statute subsequent to the act of 1663 is a contract declared void for non-observance of legal forms.[2]

In conclusion it may be noted that generally throughout New England neglect of the prescribed forms did not invalidate marriage, though the offender against the law might be punished.[3] It is historically probable, where words of nullity were not contained in the statute, that the irregular contract by simple present agreement, without intervention of a minister or magistrate, was valid. But this is a disputed point which will hereafter be considered in connection with the history of common-law marriage in the United States.[4]

---

[1] The marriage certificate is in the following form:

"I Hereby certify, That A. B. of —— Son of —— and C. D. of —— Daughter of —— were lawfully joined together in Marriage on the —— Day of —— Anno Domini —— by me the Subscriber."

[2] *Acts and Laws* (Newport, 1767), 172-75.

[3] See the case of Usher *v.* Troop (Throop), 1724-29, in *MSS. Records of the Superior Court of Judicature* (Mass.), 1725-30, folio 236. In 1724 John Usher, of Bristol, a minister of the Church of England, convicted in the inferior court of common pleas of marrying a couple without certificate of the town clerk, was fined 50 pounds and "forever thereafter disabled to Joyn Persons in Marriage." On appeal it was found: "If the Constitutions and Canons Ecclesiastical of the Church of England are sufficient to support the Appellant here, in Joyning Persons together in Marriage without such certificate . . . . Then the Jury say the Applt is not Guilty; otherwise they say he is Guilty." The appeal was finally dismissed (1729) on default of the "appellee."

[4] See chap. xviii, i.

III.   COURTSHIP, PROPOSALS, AND GOVERNMENT OF SINGLE
PERSONS

It may be an exaggeration to say that the Mosaic code
was the *corpus juris* of the Puritan.[1]   But it is certain that
the early private law of New England was profoundly
influenced by it.   The family in many respects took on
a patriarchal character.   The sway of the house-father,
though in the main just, became in theory despotic.   Even
the conception of marriage as a civil contract gained support from the Jewish law.[2]   Our ancestors loved to cite the
book of Ruth and other scriptural texts in its favor; and
their view of the proper relations of husband and wife, those
of parent and child, or those of man and woman before
marriage, was derived directly from the biblical ordinances.[3]

Thus "old bachelors," though rare in early New England, were looked upon with disfavor.   They were regarded
almost as "suspected criminals."[4]   Connecticut "in 1636
would not allow any young unmarried man to keep house."[5]
A special order of the town of Windsor was necessary, in

[1] " Il y avait même un tel mélange de la religion à toutes les circonstances de la
vie civile, que la législation, en certaines matières, en référait à la Bible qui était,
pour ainsi dire, le *corpus juris* des émigrants dans la Nouvelle-Angleterre.   La
famille, où ils avaient puisé le sentiment religieux, était forte parce qu'elle était
unie; et le père, qui ressemblait en quelque sorte au patriarche d'autrefois, avait une
autorité incontestée qu'on aimait, car elle était composée de bienveillance et de
justice."—CARLIER, *Le mariage aux États-Unis*, 7, 8.

[2] " Between these two extreme views—that of marriage as merely a civil contract and marriage as a sacrament—stands that of the Jewish law.   The act of concluding marriage is there certainly also considered as a contract, which requires the
consent of both parties and the performance of certain formalities, similar to other
contracts, and which, under certain circumstances, can be dissolved.   But, inasmuch
as marriage concerns a relation which is based on morality and implies the most
sacred duties, it is more than a mere civil contract."— MIELZINER, *The Jewish Law
of Marriage and Divorce*, 25, 26.   But "the presence of a rabbi or minister is, according to the Talmudic Law, not required at the betrothal or the nuptials.   The prescribed benedictions were pronounced either by the bridegroom or by any of the
friends present.   Such was also the Jewish custom during the Middle Ages."—*Ibid.*,
84.   *Cf.* AMRAM, *The Jewish Law of Divorce*, 39.

[3] See SHIRLEY'S comments on the Cutt Code, "Early Jurisprudence of New
Hampshire," *Procds. New Hamp. Hist. Soc.* (1876–84), 273 ff.

[4] EARLE, *Customs and Fashions*, 36.

[5] WEEDEN, *Ecc. and Soc. Hist. of N. E.*, I, 230; *Conn. Col. Rec.*, I, 8.

1682, to permit "Isaac Sheldon and Samuel Rockwell to keep house together, 'so they carry themselves soberly and do not entertain idle persons to the evil expense of time by day or night.'"[1] Hartford taxed "lone-men" twenty shillings a week "for the selfish luxury of solitary living."[2] Even in the eighteenth century a general statute of Connecticut, under the same penalty of twenty shillings a week, forbade any "house-keeper" or "master of a family," without "allowance of the selectmen," to give "entertainment or habitation" to a single person; and "such Bourders, Sojourners, and Young persons" are required to "attend to the Worship of God" in the families where they live and "to be subject to the domestick Government of the same," or else forfeit five shillings for every breach of the law.[3] In Rhode Island in one instance "single persons of three months' residence paid five shillings, while the 'rate of faculties and personal abilities' was left at the discretion of the assessors."[4] According to a New Haven law, in order to "suppress inconvenience" and disorders inconsistent with the "mind of God in the fifth commandment," single persons, not in service or dwelling with their relatives, are forbidden to diet or lodge alone; but they are required to live in "licensed" families; and the "governors" of such families are ordered to "observe the course, carriage, and behaviour, of every such single person, whether he or she walk diligently in a constant lawful imployment, attending both family duties and the publick worship of God, and keeping good order day and night or otherwise."[5]

Similar measures were adopted by the other colonies. The law of Plymouth provides that "wheras great Incon-

---

[1] WEEDEN, *loc. cit.*; STILES, *Windsor*, 54.   [2] EARLE, *Customs and Fashions*, 37.
[3] *Acts and Laws* (1715), 60; see also *Conn. Col. Rec.*, I, 538; TRUMBULL, *Blue Laws*, 104.
[4] In 1682: WEEDEN, *op. cit.*, I, 272; MUNRO, *Bristol, R. I.*, 115.
[5] *New Haven Col. Rec.*, II, 608; TRUMBULL, *op. cit.*, 258.

venience hath arisen by single persons in this Collonie being
for themselues and not betakeing themselues to live in well
Gou^rned famillies. It is enacted by the Court that henceforth noe single person be suffered to liue by himselfe or in
any family but such as the Celectmen of the Towne shall
approue of; and if any person or persons shall refuse or
neglect to attend such order as shalbe giuen them by the
Celectmen; that such person or persons shalbe sumoned to
the Court to be proceeded with as the matter shall require."[1]
"Whereas," runs a statute of Massachusetts, "there is a
loose and sinful custom of going or riding from town to
town, ... oftimes men and women together, upon pretence of going to lectures, but it appears . . . . merely to
drink and revel in ordinaries and taverns, which is in itself
scandalous, and it is to be feared a notable means to debauch
our youth and hazard the chastity of those that are drawn
fourth thereunto: for prevention whereof," it is ordered
"that all single persons who merely for their pleasure take
such journeys . . . . shall be reputed and accounted riotous
and unsober persons, and of ill behavior . . . . and shall be
committed to prison for ten days, or pay a fine of forty shillings for each offence," unless they can "give bonds and sufficient sureties for good behavior in twenty pounds."[2] Earlier
it was decreed that the "Select men of every Town, in the
several precincts, and quarters where they dwel, shal have a
vigilant eye over their brethren and neighbours, to see,
first that none of them shall suffer so much barbarism in any
of their families, as not to endeavour to teach, by themselves
or others, their children & apprentices, so much learning, as
may enable them perfectly to read the english tongue &
knowledg of the Capital laws." Once a week children and
apprentices are to be catechised "in the grounds and prin-

[1] *Plym. Col. Rec.*, XI, 223.
[2] WHITMORE, *Colonial Laws of Mass.* (1672-86), 236, 237.

ciples of Religion," or at least taught "some short orthodox catachism without book;" and they are to be bred and brought up "in some honest Lawfull calling . . . . profitable for themselves and the Common-wealth," if their parents or masters "will not, or cannot train them up in learning to fitt them for higher imployments." If parents and masters neglect their duty, "whereby children & servants become rude, stubborn & unruly, the sayd Select men with the help of two Magistrates or the next County Court for that Shire, shall take such children or apprentices from them," and until they come of age place them with persons who will more strictly look after their government as the law directs.[1] It was further enacted that every town shall order and dispose to service or otherwise all "single persons and inmates" within its borders, anyone feeling aggrieved thereby "to have Liberty to appeale to the next County Court."[2]

These laws were not wholly a dead letter, as shown by the judicial records. Thus on April 2, 1672, "Thomas Henshaw and Thomas Hall, singlemen, being convicted of living from under family government . . . . , are ordered forthwith to submit themselves" to such government "and to appear at the next court and bring with them certificate thereof."[3] Nevertheless complaint is made that the town officers are negligent. In 1668 the legislature directs the clerk of each shire court to send "to the Constables of the Towns" within the shire an order which they are "enjoyned faithfully to execute." In the preamble it is recited that the neglect of the laws, "as by sad experience from Court to Court abundantly appears, doth occasion much sin and prophaness to increase among us, to the dishonour of God, and the ensnaring of many Children and Servants, by the dissolute lives and practices of such as do live from under Family

---

[1] *Ibid.* (1660–72), 136.   [2] *Ibid.*, 196; *ibid.* (1672–86), 148; *Mass. Col. Rec.*, I, 186.
[3] *MSS. Records of the County Court for Middlesex*, III, 21.

Government, and is a great discouragement to those Family
Governours, who conscientiously endeavour to bring up their
Youth in all Christian nurture, as the Laws of God and this
Common wealth doth require: These are therefore . . . . to
require you to acquaint the Select men of your Town, that
the Court doth expect and will require, that the said Laws
be accordingly attended . . . . : and you are also required
to take a list of the names of those young persons . . . . who
do live from under Family Government, *viz.*, do not serve
their Parents or Masters, as Children, Apprentices, hired
Servants, or Journey men ought to do, and usually did in
our Native Country, being subject to their commands and
discipline." [1]

The manuscript files of Middlesex show that lists[2] of
delinquent single persons were taken by the constables as
required; and that some of them were summoned to appear
before the court. Following is the "answer" of Robert
Williams, whose name is in the list given in the margin:

"I do desire to liue under family gouernment and haue
so desired euer sinc my time was out with my master that I
liued with and all the time sinc commited myself into mens
housis of good report as neer as I could and do desir to walk
inofenciue to all men and furder I do hop that the men
which I do work with will say as I do if the honered court
will desir it indeed I am not a saruant yet do submit myself
to family ordor I [will] do as a saruant what els the honered

---

[1] WHITMORE, *op. cit.* (1660–72), 260; also *ibid.* (1672–86), 149. There is a copy of
one of the orders sent to the constables, differing slightly in capitalization and
punctuation from the above, in the *MSS. Files of the County Court for Middlesex*,
Dec., 1668.

[2] Here is the list from Marlboro:

"Samuell Goodenow, from under family Gouernment, Liuing upon his oune
ground.

"Isaius Tailer and Will Tayler, Renters . . . .

"John Howard . . . . out of his time . . . . and Entending as fast as he can to
settell himselfe: so to liue under family gouernment.

"Rober Williams . . . ."— *MSS. Files of the County Court for Middlesex*, Dec.
1668.

court would haue me do mor I hope I shall be willing to obay the finil power."[1]

In a society where marriages were formed very early, girls often wedding at sixteen or less, and where widows were wooed almost at the bier of the dear departed,[2] it is perhaps not surprising if "old maids" were ridiculed and sometimes despised. A woman became an "antient maid" at twenty-five.[3] In an often quoted passage of his *Life and Errors*, John Dunton thus praises a woman who remained single, not from "necessity," but from "choice," and who knew that time is a "dressing-room for Eternity, and therefore reserves most of her hours for better uses than those of the Comb, the Toilet, and the Glass":

"It is true an *old* (or super-annuated) maid in Boston is thought such a curse as nothing can exceed it (and look'd

---

[1] The selectmen of "Billerica" thus "strove to free themselves of all blame": "To the Honᵈ Court . . . .

"Whereas Aaron Jaquese, a single prson liuing in our towne, who hath for sometime liued from vnder family gouernment contrary to Court Order, being sum̄uned by yᵉ Constable to appear before this Honored Court: These are to enforme . . . . that . . . . Aaron Jaquese hath bin much complained of by seuerall of our inhabitants, for negligence in his calling, hauing obserued him much giuen to idleness; also shifting from house to house, & vnfaithfull to his Couenants & promises with such prsons, with whom he has engaged service, vpon which Complaints the selectmen haue endeauered acording to law, to place him foorth in service, but cañot effect it. Our Humble request to this Hon'd Court is, that they would please to despose of . . . . Aaron to service, or otherwise to order something concering the same as may be effectuall to render him to a more regular Course of life, as yᵉ wisdome of this Court shall judg best. So shall we pray &c.
Your humble seruants."
The *MSS. Files of the County Court for Middlesex*, April, 1669, also contain a certificate of the selectmen of Charlestown to the effect that John Swain had given satisfaction for orderly behavior.

[2] Thus Judge Sewall went home with Widow Denison from her husband's funeral and "prayed God to keep house" with her: *Diary*, in 5 *Mass. Hist. Coll.*, VII, 179 (March 26, 1718). *Cf.* also EARLE, *Customs and Fashions*, 45, 46.

"The colonists married early and they married often. Widowers and widows hastened to join their fortunes and sorrows. The father and mother of Governor Winslow had been widow and widower seven and twelve weeks respectively, when they joined their families and themselves in mutual benefit, if not in mutual love. At a later day the impatient governor of New Hampshire married a lady but ten days widowed."—EARLE, *op. cit.*, 36. On early marriages see WEEDEN, *Ecc. and Soc. Hist. of N. E.*, II, 541, 739.

[3] EARLE, *op. cit.*, 38.

upon as a *dismal spectacle*); yet she, by her good-nature, gravity, and strict virtue, convinces all (so much as the fleering Beaus) that it is not her necessity, but her choice, that keeps her a Virgin. She is now about thirty years (the age which they call a *Thornback*), yet she never disguises herself, and talks as little as she thinks of Love. She never reads any Plays or Romances, goes to no Balls, or Dancing-match, as they do who go (to such Fairs) in order to meet with Chapmen. Her looks, her speech, her whole behaviour, are so very chaste, that but once (at Governor's Island, where we went to be merry at roasting a hog) going to kiss her, I thought she would have blushed to death."[1]

But bachelors and "thornbacks" were not the only people who caused the lawmaker anxiety. He kept a sharp eye on married persons living away from their mates. An act of the Massachusetts general court, in 1647, after reciting that diverse married persons are living in the jurisdiction, whose wives or husbands are in England or elsewhere, and who are guilty of making love to women, of attempting marriage or even attaining it, or are under "suspition of uncleannes" —the vice which seems to have sorely vexed the good people of those days—and all of whom are a great dishonor to God and a reproof to religion, commonwealth, and church— orders that every such person shall be incontinently sent back "by ye first oportunity of shiping," unless present on transient business or to "make way" for the family to come over.[2] Such complaints were by no means groundless and the courts were often called upon to execute the law. Under the circumstances bigamy was easily committed, though not

[1] DUNTON's *Life and Errors* (Westminster, 1818), I, 102, referring to Boston in 1686. In DUNTON's *Letters from New-England* (ed. by WHITMORE for the Prince Society, Boston, 1867), 99, where this passage appears in a modified form, the age of a "thornback" is reduced to twenty-six years. The paragraph is also quoted by WEEDEN, *op. cit.*, I, 299, 300; and EARLE, *op. cit.*, 38, 39.

[2] *Mass. Col. Rec.*, II, 211, 212; WHITMORE, *Col. Laws of Mass.* (1660-72), 172; *ibid.* (1672-86), 216.

always permanently concealed. On December 3, 1639, the pretended marriage of James Luxford was declared void; "all that hee hath" was given to his victim; and he himself was fined, set in the stocks, and ordered "sent away to England by the first opportunity."[1] In 1644 the "marriage of John Richardson to Elizabeth Frier was annulled upon proof that he had a former wife living in England."[2] Henry Jackson—whose case seems to justify the act of 1647—was presented in 1672–73 "for lying, in saying he was single and attempting marriage with several," though since confessing that he has a wife beyond the sea; "for living from under family government; and for carrying a fire brand at night near a hay stack;" on all of which counts, we are prepared to hear, he got twenty stripes, had to pay costs, and was ordered away to "England by the next ship."[3]

More numerous are the cases of "living apart." For example in 1637 the general court decreed that Isaac Davies should be sent home to his wife in England.[4] Three years later "Willi Wake" in like manner was advised to seek his consort.[5] Edward Iron in 1651 "upon promise to take some effectual course to send for his wife now in England" was "granted liberty to abide in the country until the next return of ships." Should his attempt fail, then he was "ordered to depart out of this jurisdiction by the next opportunity."[6] For similar absence from his spouse James Underwood in 1654 was fined at Salem.[7] In 1663 for the same offense Christopher Blake was presented by the grand jury of Suffolk, although in his petition he avers that for

---

[1] *Mass. Col. Rec.*, I, 283.

[2] *Ibid.*, II, 86. [3] *MSS. Records of the County Court of Suffolk*, 113.

[4] *Mass. Col. Rec.*, I, 198. [5] *Ibid.*, 311.

[6] *MSS. Records of the County Court of Middlesex*, I, 18. Apparently Edward's attempts were a failure; for on Oct. 4, 1653, he was "granted liberty to use what more effectual means he may or can to send for his wife from England": *ibid.*, I, 32.

[7] *Mass. Col. Rec.*, III, 349, 350. But on petition, in order to present further testimony, the general court granted a respite.

three years he had "been desirous of getting his wife across but she refused to come;" and that he had never "presented himself as a single man, but always openly manifested the true state of his condition." Accordingly the general court ordered the prosecution "stayed for a year."[1] In 1671 Paul Hall, presented in the same county, "appeared and declared he was informed his wife was dead." The court, being skeptical, commanded him to "repair to the last place of her abode or bring in a certificate of her death."[2] Delinquent wives were looked after with equal vigilance. In 1668 the constable of Boston is ordered to summon "before the county court two women and one man for living apart from their spouses contrary to law."[3] A presentment of Sarah Pickering failed in 1674 because she produced evidence that her husband had renounced her.[4] Even when both partners were in the jurisdiction the law was not less harshly administered. On June 17, 1672, for "disorderly living apart," Michael Smith and wife, "inhabitants of Charlestoun" were "admonished and ordered to pay costs."[5] The case of "Abr. Hagborne" in 1663 is more remarkable. Although he had come to the colony twenty-two years before; had lived contentedly with his wife for fourteen or fifteen years until she "did depart" for England; had sent for her to return home and provided for her transportation, "whereby the innocence of Living Apart is on your peticoners part;" and "had no idea the law against living apart would apply to the known settled inhabitants, brethren and free-men whose wives unnaturally desert them;" yet the county court "was pleased to require him to depart the Countrie &

---

[1] MSS. Early Court Files of Suffolk County, No. 531. This case is also partially reported in Mass. Col. Rec., IV, Part II, 84; and quoted in SHIRLEY, "Early Jurisprudence of New Hampshire," Procds. New. Hamp. Hist. Soc. (1876-84), 310.

[2] MSS. Records of the County Court of Suffolk, 9.

[3] MSS. Early Court Files of Suffolk, No. 867.

[4] MSS. Records of the County Court of Suffolk, 279.

[5] MSS. Records of the County Court of Middlesex, III, 63.

to repayre vnto his wife." So he "humbly petitions" the general court that he may not be compelled to return to England and that he may "not be put vpon [religious] temptacoñs or aboue his strength or any kind of iniunc̃con [injunction] of going to Serue other Gods;" but may be "allowed to continue his Abode here . . . . vnder the Shadow of that happie Gouernment in Com̃onwealth and Churches . . . . those few days of his pilgrimage that remayne." A gracious answer, it is perhaps needless to add, was the meet reward of so just and so skilful a prayer.[1]

In like spirit single women and wives in the absence of their husbands were forbidden to "lodge any inmate or sojourner," except with the approval of the selectmen or other magistrates.[2] Of course, these were pioneer days. The peace of the settlements was probably disturbed by loose and riotous adventurers, outcasts from the society of the Old World. Doubtless these measures, aside from religious motives, were in some degree useful police ordinances; as were also those prohibiting the husband from beating his wife, and the wife from striking her spouse.[3]

[1] *MSS. Early Court Files of Suffolk*, No. 527. For similar legislation see *New Haven Col. Rec.*, II, 600; TRUMBULL, *Blue Laws*, 243.

[2] *Mass. Col. Rec.*, V, 4; SHIRLEY, *Early Jurisprudence of New Hamp.*, 310, 311. The harboring of "strangers"—and "stranger" might be a father, daughter, or son from a neighboring town—gave the good people of the colonies a great deal of trouble. See the illustrations in WEEDEN, *Ecc. and Soc. Hist. of N. E.*, I, 272; and HOWARD, *Local Const. Hist.*, I, 87, 88, where the town records are cited.

[3] WHITMORE, *Col. Laws of Mass.* (1660-72), 51, 171; *ibid.* (1672-86), 101. *Cf. Mass. Col. Rec.*, III, 212 (1650). In 1638 John Emerson, of Scituate, was tried before the general court for abusing his wife: *ibid.*, I, 232; the same year for beating his wife, Henry Seawall was sent for examination before the court at Ipswich: *ibid.*, 233; and in 1663 Ensigne John Williams, of Barnstable, was fined by the Plymouth court for slandering his wife: GOODWIN, *Pilgrim Republic*, 596.

It would seem that the husband, too, really needed some legal protection. The early court records disclose the sad fact that husband-beating was painfully frequent in colonial times. Thus in Plymouth jurisdiction Joan, the wife of Obadiah Miller of Taunton, was presented "for beating and reviling her husband, and egging her children to healp her, bidding them knock him in the head, and wishing his victials might c̃oake him."—*Plym. Col. Rec.*, III, 75.

The bad practice was not unknown among the "good wives" of Salem. For example, in 1637, at the fifth quarter court, it was decreed: "Whereas Dorothy the

But the colonists went farther and prescribed the death penalty for disobedience to parents, following the precepts of the Mosaic law.[1] Furthermore, they attempted to regulate courtship by statute, in a way which, however wholesome, would scarcely be relished by the young men and maidens of our generation.   Thus the general court of Plymouth prohibits "any motion of marriage to any man's daughter or mayde servant" without having "first obtayned leaue" of the parents or master under penalty of fine and corporal punishment in the discretion of the bench.   But appeal is allowed to the magistrate, when the master "through any sinister end or couetous desire," witholds his consent.[2]   The courts were not wholly without business growing out of this legislation, as appears from illustrations collected by Mr. Goodwin. "In 1652 Jonathan Coventry was indicted for 'making a motion of marriage' to Katherine Bradbury, servant to Mr. Bourne, of Marshfield, without the latter's consent.[3] Coventry left the Colony before arrest. . . . . In 1648 Thomas Dunham was ordered to abstain from visiting or sending to Martha Knott, of Sandwich, from October 4 till the first Tuesday of December, that the Court may bet-

wyfe of John Talbie hath not only broak that peace & loue, wch ought to haue beene both betwixt them, but also hath violentlie broke the king's peace, by frequent Laying hands vpon hir husband to the danger of his Life, & Condemned Authority, not comīng before them vpon command, It is therefore ordered that for hir misdemeaner passed & for prvention of future evills that are feared wilbe comītted by hir if shee be Lefte att hir Libertie.   That she shall be bound & chained to some post where shee shall be restrained of hir libertye to goe abroad or comminge to hir husband till shee manefest some change of hir course. . . . . Only it is pmitted that shee shall come to the place of gods worshipp, to enjoy his ordenances."   Later "Dorothy" was punished again for a similar offense: *Hist. Coll. Essex Inst.*, VII, 129, 187.   *Cf.* HOWARD, *Local Const. Hist.*, I, 326, 327.   For further illustrations see WEEDEN, *Ecc. and Soc. Hist. of N. E.*, I, 294.

[1] WHITMORE, *Col. Laws of Mass.* (1660-72), 129; *New Haven Col. Rec.*, II, 578, and TRUMBULL, *Blue Laws*, 201; *Conn. Col. Rec.*, I, 515, and TRUMBULL, *op. cit.*, 69; *New Hamp. Hist. Coll.*, VIII, 12; SHIRLEY, *Early Jurisprudence of N. H.*, 311; *Andros Tracts*, III, 13.   *Cf.* a similar law for early New York: *Duke of Yorke's Laws*, 15.

[2] *Plym. Col. Rec.*, XI, 29, 108, 190, 191.

[3] For the case see *ibid.*, III, 5: "Wee psent Jonathan Couentry . . . . for makeing mocion of marriage vnto Katheren Bradberey, servant vnto Mr Burne, of the same town, without her master's consent, contrary to Court orders."

ter learn of his pretended contract, unless the Governor, on
the clearing of things, give him leave.   A romantic case was
that of Governor Thomas Prence against Arthur Howland,
Jr., nephew of the Pilgrim.[1]   The tolerant course of the
elder Arthur Howland toward the Quakers had earned
Prence's hearty ill-will; and when, in 1660, he found that
Arthur, Jr., had wooed his daughter Elizabeth, he had the
swain before the General Court, where he was fined £5 for
making love without her father's permission.   The couple
remained constant, for in 1667 the irate Governor once more
brought up young Arthur, who was again fined £5 because
he had 'disorderly and unrighteously endeavored to obtain
the affections of Mistress Elizabeth Prence,' and was put
under bond of £50 to 'refrain and desist.'   But Prence, like
Canute, was unable to control the forces of Nature.   This
action was in July; but before the next spring the imperious
Governor seemed to have been forced to capitulate, for
Arthur and Elizabeth were united."[2]   On the other hand,
the right of a lover to appeal to the magistrate, in case his
"motion" were hindered through "sinister end or couetous
desire," was occasionally of practical value.   In 1646, for
instance, Richard Taylor complained to the general court
of Plymouth that he was prevented from marrying Ruth
Wheildon by her father Gabriel; but when before the court
Gabriel yielded and promised no longer to oppose the marriage.[3]   The records show that parents might be held accountable for "miscarriages" resulting from unreasonable opposition.[4]

[1] See *ibid.*, IV (1666/7), 140, 158, 159.

[2] GOODWIN, *Pilgrim Republic*, 598; *cf.* PALFREY, *Hist. of New England*, II, 21.

[3] GOODWIN, *op. cit.*, 597.

[4] Dec. 16, 1679.   At a court held at Charlestown, George Parminter and his wife
convicted of fornication before marriage, court respited their sentence till next
court, and ordered that their parents be summoned then to appear to give answer
why they denied them the consummation of their marriage for so many months after
they were in order thereto: *MSS. Records of the County Court of Middlesex*, III, 316.

To the close of the colonial era a law of Connecticut provided that "if any Man shall directly or indirectly endeavour to draw away the affections of any Maid . . . . , on pretence of Marriage, before he hath obtained Liberty and Allowance" from her parent, governor, or guardian, should there be any, "he shall forfeit the sum of *Five Pounds* to the Party grieved; double that amount for the second offence; and for a third transgression suffer imprisonment, besides paying the costs of prosecution."[1]

An elaborate statute of New Haven, for the regulation of proposals, provides "that whosoever within this jurisdiction shall attempt, or endeavor to inveagle, or draw the affections of any maide, or maide-servant, whether daughter, kinswoman, or in other relation, for himself, or for any other person, without the consent of father, master, governor, or such other, who hath the present interest, or charge, or (in absence of such) of the nearest magistrate, whether it be by speech, writing, message, company-keeping, unnecessary familiarity, disorderly night meetings, sinful dalliance, gifts, or any other way, directly or indirectly, every such person (besides all damages which the parent, governor, or person intrusted or interested, may sustain by such unlawful proceedings) shall pay to the plantation forty shillings for the first offence; and for the second offence towards the same party four pounds; and for the third offence he shal be further fined, imprisoned, or corporally punished, as the plantation court, or court of magistrates considering all circumstances, shal determine."[2]

The foregoing act was probably suggested by the Massachusetts law of 1647, which is likewise here presented. It

---

[1] *Acts and Laws of Conn.* (New Haven, 1769), 144. Substantially the same provision appears in the *Code of 1643*: TRUMBULL, *Blue Laws*, 106, 107; *Conn. Col. Rec.*, I, 92; in *The Book of General Laws, 1673* (Hartford, 1865), 46; and in *Acts and Laws* (New London, 1715), 75.

[2] *New Haven Col. Rec.*, II, 600; TRUMBULL, *op. cit.*, 242. *Cf.* ATWATER, *Hist. of Col. of New Haven*, 362.

is declared that, "whereas God hath committed the care and power into the hands of parents for the disposing their Children in Marriage, so that it is against rule, to seek to draw away the affections of young maidens under pretence of purpose of marriage, before their parents have given way and allowance in that respect; and whereas it is common practise in divers places for young men irregularly and disorderly to watch all advantages for their evil purposes, to insinuate into the affections of young Maidens by coming to them in places and seasons unknown to their parents for such ends, whereby much evil hath grown amongst us, to the dishonour of God and damage of parties; for prevention whereof for time to come. It is further Ordered, that whatsoever person from henceforth shall endeavour, directly or indirectly, to draw away the affection of any mayd in this jurisdiction, under pretence of marriage, before he hath obtained liberty and allowance from her parents or Governors or in absence of such of the nearest magistrate, he shall forfeit for the first offence five pounds, for the second towards the partie ten pounds, and be bound to forbeare any further attempt and proceedings in that unlawful designe, without or against the allowance aforesayd. And for the third offence upon information or complaint by such parents or Governors to any Magistrate, giving bond to prosecute the party, he shall be committed in prison, and upon hearing and conviction by the next court, shal be adjudged to continue in prison, untill the Court of Assistants shall see cause to release him."[1]

The courts were not without employment under this statute. In 1658 Paul Wilson appeared before the county court of Middlesex, sitting in Charlestown, "to answer the complaint of Deacon Upham for violent soliciting his

[1] WHITMORE, *Col. Laws of Mass.* (1660-72), 172; *ibid.* (1672-86), 101; *Mass. Col. Rec.*, II, 207. *Cf.* FRIEDBERG, *Eheschliessung*, 477, note; NEWHALL, *Ye Great and General Court*, 349-65, giving interesting examples.

daughter against his will." Whereupon the tribunal "admonished Wilson of his evil behavior towards the said Upham and his daughter Priscilla, and ordered him to give bond of ten pounds for his regular behavior towards the said parties." Accordingly the culprit gave bond "yt he will no more frequent the company of Priscilla Upham, nor by no means whether direct or indirect, make any more addresses vnto her without her fathers leave first orderly had & obteined."[1] For a similar offense, in 1672, the county court of Suffolk fined Benjamin Scott five pounds.[2] Two years later, before the same tribunal, Thomas Irons was presented "for procuring Richard Barnum to publish a marriage" between himself and Mary Arnold without her father's leave;[3] while the next February, as we learn from the record, John Lorin stood "convict on his own confession of making love to Mary Willis without her parents consent and after being forwarned by them, £5."[4]

Although parents might be prosecuted for "unreasonably denying any child timely or convenient marriage,"[5] it is evident that lovers had to be very circumspect in old colonial days. In a community where power to dispose of a son or daughter in wedlock was believed to be the gift of heaven,

---

[1] *MSS. Records of the County Court for Middlesex*, I, 131.

In 1662 Marmaduke Johnson, who by his own confession had a wife in England, was convicted of trying to steal the affections of the daughter of Samuel Green without his knowledge and consent; and he was ordered to join his spouse by the first oportunity: *ibid.*, I, 206. The next year Johnson was "fined £20 unless he give security" so to depart, in the meantime being "committed until the order is performed": *ibid.*, 249. It may be further noted that on April 7, 1674, a Marmaduke Johnson is spoken of as "late constable of Cambridge": *ibid.*, III, 87.

[2] *MSS. Records of the County Court of Suffolk*, 106.

[3] Irons was fined 20 shillings, and Barnum half that sum: *MSS. Records of the County Court of Suffolk* (July 28, 1674), 255, 256. On the same day "Edward Peggy being bound over for using indirect means 'by powders or other wayes unlawfull to Engage the affections or desires of women kinde to him' and for begetting a bastard child "—in particular for illegally "drawing away the affections of two girls "—was assessed 10 pounds and put under bonds for good behavior: *ibid.*, 261.

[4] *Ibid.* (Feb. 4, 1674–75), 301. The records of the court of assistants in *Mass. Col. Rec.* (Sept. 1, 1640), I, 299, 300, contain a similar case.

[5] Law of 1641: WHITMORE, *Col. Laws of Mass.* (1660–72), 137.

it is not strange that "allowance" was sometimes hard to gain.   Praising the chaste reserve of the gentle "old maid" of Boston whom he had learned to admire, John Dunton thus expresses the dominant view: "I am sure this is most agreeable to the *Virgin modesty*, which should make Marriage an act" rather of "obedience" than "choice."   "And they that think their Friends too *slowpaced* in the matter give certain proof that lust is the sole motive."[1]   Nor was the average New England house-father at all likely to allow sentiment to get the better of prudence in seeking a match for his child.   He was more apt to be governed by a spirit of cold calculation which never for an instant lost sight of the "main chance."   Judge Sewall, for example, can hardly be called "slowpaced" in providing his daughters with wooers. He superintends the whole "business" of love-making with never-flagging zeal.   Poor, timid daughter Betty is fairly worried into matrimony, perhaps as the only sure way of escaping her father's nagging.   What a procession of "captains" and "persons of worth" he parades before the reluctant girl before he succeeds in gaining his will!   The first who "wished to speak with her" is Captain Tuthill, who appears as a suitor when she is but seventeen years of age.   After the judge had made careful and satisfactory inquiry as to the captain's estate—which he finds valued at £600 or £700— and the young man "in good Business, and like to be in better;"[2] and after having his daughter read to him about the courtship of Adam and Eve "as a soothing and alluring preparation for the thought of matrimony,"[3] the lover is invited to call.   Of this visit and its surprising result Sewall thus writes in his *Diary:* "At night Capt. Tuthill comes to speak with Betty, who hid her self all alone in the coach

---

[1] DUNTON, *Life and Errors*, I, 103; *idem*, *Letters from New England*, 101, 102.

[2] SEWALL's *Diary*, in 5 *Mass. Hist. Coll.*, V, 490.

[3] EARLE, *Customs and Fashions*, 57.

for several hours till he was gon, so that we sought at several houses, till at last came in of her self, and look'd very wild."[1] A number of others in rapid succession have little better luck with the coy maiden. The next fall, however, on returning from a journey to Rhode Island, the judge finds his "family in health, only disturb'd at Betty's denying Mr. Hirst." A month later he sadly records that he supposes even this suitor has "taken his final leave."[2] Nevertheless two days after, on October 26, 1699, he addresses Betty at "Brantry," where she had gone on a visit, the following characteristic letter:

"Mr Hirst waits upon you once more to see if you can bid him welcome. It ought to be seriously considered, that your drawing back from him after all that has passed between you, will be to your Prejudice; and will tend to discourage persons of worth from making their Court to you. And you had need well to consider whether you are able to bear his final Leaving of you, howsoever it may seem grate-full to you at present. When persons come toward us, we are apt to look upon their Undesirable Circumstances mostly; and therefore to shun them. But when persons retire from us for good and all, we are in danger of looking only on that which is desirable in them to our wofull Disquiet. Whereas 'tis the property of a good Balance to turn where the most weight is, though there be some also in the other Scale. I do not see but that the Match is well liked by judicious persons, and such as are your Cordial Friends, and mine also.

"Yet notwithstanding, if you find in yourself an imovable, incurable Aversion from him, and canot love, and honour, and obey him, I shall say no more, nor give you any further trouble in this matter. It had better be off than on. So praying God to pardon us, and pity our Undeserving, and to direct and strengthen and settle you in making a right Judg-

---

[1] SEWALL'S *Diary*, in 5 *Mass. Hist. Coll.*, V, 491.   [2] *Ibid.*, 503.

ment, and giving a right Answer, I take leave, who am, dear child, your loving father. Your mother remembers to you."[1]

Either this letter had the desired influence or Betty was unable to endure the "wofull disquiet" of a "final leaving;" for a year later it stands written that "Mr. Grove Hirst and Elizabeth Sewall are married by Mr. Cotton Mather."[2]

IV. PRE-CONTRACTS, BUNDLING, AND SEXUAL IMMORALITY

The colonists were extremely anxious to restrain vice by legislation. The whole field of private morals was brought under the purview of the magistrate. Unchastity and sexual crimes, especially, they were determined to prevent at all hazards; and, in consequence, the early colonial and court records are far from pleasant reading. Conjugal infidelity is especially abhorred by the lawmaker. Originally, in all the New England colonies save Rhode Island and Plymouth, death was the penalty prescribed for adultery with a "married or espoused wife." In the New World the Puritan thus actually realized what Luther, Hooper, and other Reformation Fathers ardently desired as an ideal fulfilment of the Mosaic code.[3] The capital law of Massachusetts, at any rate, was not a dead letter, as is clearly shown by the records of the early period. The only attempt to put in force the original act of 1631 was, indeed, a failure. It appears that in 1637 two men and one woman were con-

---

[1] SEWALL'S *Letter-Book*, in 6 *Mass. Hist Coll.*, I, 213.

[2] SEWALL'S *Diary*, in 5 *Mass. Hist. Coll.*, VI, 24. In like spirit the judge manages the marriage of his daughter Mary with Sam Gerrish: SEWALL'S *Letter-Book*, in 6 *Mass. Hist. Coll.*, I, 379; *Diary*, in 5 *Mass. Hist. Coll.*, V, xxxviii; VI, 250, 251, 263. On these and other illustrations of New England courtship see EARLE, *Customs and Fashions*, 56 ff.

[3] *Mass. Col. Rec.*, I, 92 (1631) ; WHITMORE, *Col. Laws of Mass.* (1660-72), 55 (" Body of Liberties," 1641), 128; *ibid.* (1672-86), 15; *New Haven Col. Rec.*, II, 577; TRUMBULL, *Blue Laws*, 200; *Conn. Col. Rec.*, I, 77; TRUMBULL, *op. cit.*, 60; *New Hamp. Prov. Papers*, I, 385 (Cutt Code). Beginning with the " Body of Liberties," 1641, the capital law of Massachusetts cites Lev. 20:19;18:20; Deut. 22:23, 24; and the laws of the other colonies are supported by the same or like passages of the Jewish Code.

victed; but on the ground that the statute had been "made by the court of assistants by allowance of the general court," and for fear lest it had not been "sufficiently published," the extreme penalty was not administered. Instead the culprits were whipped and then banished on pain of death should they return.[1] The act of 1631 was, however, at once confirmed,[2] and it remained in force until superseded by the "Body of Liberties," whose provision on this point was not abrogated during the period of the colonial charter. Under the law as thus constituted two persons were condemned and executed in 1644.[3] Further, in his *Magnalia* Cotton Mather mentions the execution of an adulterer from Weymouth.[4] These are the only cases of capital punishment for this offense yet discovered; but a number of persons narrowly escaped it, where the evidence seems sufficient to warrant the death penalty. Apparently the courts shrank from pronouncing sentence according to the full rigor of the law,[5]

[1] The "elders" being appealed to promptly decided that the three persons then lying in prison should be put to death, "if the law had been sufficiently published." But for the reasons named in the text the general court thought it was "safest that these persons should be whipped and banished": WINTHROP, *Hist. of New England*, I, 309; *Mass. Col. Rec.*, I, 198, 202, 203, 225. Compare the excellent monograph of DAVIS, *The Law of Adultery and Ignominious Punishments*, 6–11, who gives the details regarding this case and the law of 1631; and calls attention to the English act of 1650, which classes incest and adultery among felonies, citing thereon PIKE, *Hist. of Crime in England*, II, 182; and BLACKSTONE, *Commentaries*, IV, 64.

[2] March, 1637–38. "The law against adultery made by the Particular Court in October, 1631, is confirmed, that whosoever lieth with another man's wife, both shall be punished by death; and this is to be promulgated."—*Mass. Col. Rec.*, I, 225. This law was confirmed in 1640, the act of 1631 being then formally repealed: *ibid.*, I, 301.

[3] In 1643–44, at a quarter court held in Boston, "James Brittanie being found guilty of adultery with Mary Latham, he was condemned to death. Mary Latham being found guilty of adultery with James Brittanie, she was condemned to death." —*Record of the Court of Assistants of Mass. Bay Colony*, 1641–44 (from the Barlow MS.) in WHITMORE'S *Bibliographical Sketch of the Laws of Mass.*, xlii. According to WINTHROP, *Hist. of New England*, II, 157–59, these persons were executed.

[4] DAVIS, *The Law of Adultery*, 15, 16.

[5] Thus on Sept. 7, 1641, for adulterous practices a man was "censured to bee sent to the gallos wth a roape about his neck, & to sit upon the lather an houre, the roapes end throwen over the gallos, so to returne to prison."—*Mass. Col. Rec.*, I, 335; *cf.* DAVIS, *op. cit.*, 15. In 1645 Henry Dawson came near suffering the extreme penalty: WINTHROP, *op. cit.*, II, 305. Three years later the "Corte acquit Elisa: Pennion of the capitall offence charged upon her by 2 sev'rall inditements for adultery," but

satisfying themselves with lesser punishments, such as imprisonment, banishment,[1] or whipping.

In Plymouth the death penalty for adultery seems never to have been established.[2] Instead, the "scarlet letter," a punishment even more terrible to bear, was there adopted as a permanent badge earlier than in any other colony; while in England it appears never to have been so employed for any crime.[3] So far as known, the oldest typical case of bearing such a "stigma" continuously for adultery occurred

sentence her to be "whiped" in Boston and again "at Linn w^{thin} one month" (1648): *Mass. Col. Rec.*, II, 243. Still more striking are the cases of Elizabeth Hudson and Bethia Bulloine (Bullen), "married women and sisters," carried from the county court at Boston before the assistants in 1667. On a special verdict by the jury the latter tribunal sentenced each "to be by the Marshall Generall . . . . on ye next lecture day presently after the lecture carried to the Gallowes & there by ye Executioner set on the ladder & with a Roape about her neck to stand on the Gallowes an half houre & then brought . . . . to the market place & be seriously whipt wth tenn stripes or pay the Sume of tenn pounds," standing committed till the sentence be performed": *MSS. Early Court Files of Suffolk* (Sept. 11, 1667), No. 821. Whether this sentence was for adultery as charged or for "lascivious carriage" we are not informed. In NOBLE'S *Records of the Court of Assistants*, I, 56, 57, 70, 71, 73, 74, 114, 115, 240, 252, are ten cases of punishment by rope and gallows and whipping instead of death, the jury plainly avoiding the penalty for adultery under the law.

[1] Under date of Sept. 2, 1674, the Suffolk Files contain a petition from a husband praying that his wife—for adultery banished to Rhode Island the preceding year—might "be allowed to return in peace." His petition was denied, although he avers that through his wife's absence "his life is most uncomfortabell," having "no Relation at all that liveth with him and it being low with him and not abell to . . . . pay Rent in seuerall places & not willing to Remaine away from the things of god . . . . to goe to liue in a place and with such as he never delighted in."—*MSS. Early Court Files of Suffolk*, No. 1325.

[2] But the law is not entirely clear: see *Plym. Col. Rec.*, XI, 12; and the comments of DAVIS, *The Law of Adultery*, 16.

[3] See the facts collected by DAVIS, *op. cit.*, 16-32. For Massachusetts, between 1633 and 1681, are a number of sentences to wear a badge for offenses other than adultery, such as drunkenness, theft, wanton behavior, incontinence, or the disturbing of public worship. In most instances the mark is to be worn temporarily; but in three cases it is a continuous punishment. Thus on March 4, 1633–34, for drunkenness, Robert Coles is "sentenced to be disfranchised, and to wear about his neck, and to hang about his outer garment a D made of red cloth set upon white, to continue for a year and not to leave it off at any time when he should come among company."—DAVIS, *op. cit.*, 18; *Mass. Col. Rec.*, I, 112. This appears to be the earliest reference to a *red* badge placed upon the outer garments. See also the case cited by Davis from JOSSELYN'S *Account of Two Voyages to New England* (VEAZIE'S reprint, Boston, 1865), 178, 179, occurring either in Massachusetts or Plymouth prior to 1671; the similar case of sentence to wear a "Roman B cut out ridd cloth," for unclean and lascivious behavior and blasphemous words: in *Plym. Col. Rec.*, III, 111, 112 (March 5, 1656–57); and one in *Mass. Col. Rec.* (Sept. 3, 1639), 269.

in 1639. In that year a woman was sentenced to be "whipt at a cart tayle" through the streets, and to "weare a badge vpon her left sleeue during her aboad" within the government. If found at any time abroad without the badge, she was to be "burned in the face wth a hott iron."[1] Two years later a man and a woman for the same offense were severely whipped "at the publik post" and condemned while in the colony to wear the letters *AD* "vpon the outeside of their vppermost garment, in the most emenent place thereof."[2] So the custom was already developed in judicial practice when the oldest statute providing for the "scarlet letter" appeared in 1658. It was then enacted "that whosoeuer shall comitt Adultery shalbee seuerly punished by whiping two seuerall times; viz: once whiles the Court is in being att which they are convicted of the fact and 2^{cond} time as the Court shall order; and likewise to weare two Capital letters ziz; AD cut out in cloth and sewed on theire vpermost Garments on theire arme or backe; and if at any time they shalbee taken without the said letters whiles they are in the Gou^{r}ment soe worn to bee forth with taken and publickly whipt."[3]

The Plymouth statute was copied into the Cutt Code for New Hampshire in 1679–80.[4] By the act of 1701, taken from the Massachusetts law of 1694, the initial letter is still prescribed;[5] and down to its repeal in 1792 the law was frequently enforced by the courts.[6]

It is an evidence of the more humane tendency of Rhode Island legislation that neither death nor the scarlet badge seems ever to have been prescribed for adultery, although

[1] *Plym. Col. Rec.*, I, 132.   [2] *Ibid.*, II, 28 (1641).   [3] *Ibid.*, XI, 95, 172.
[4] *New Hamp. Prov. Papers*, I, 384–86.

[5] By the marriage act of 13 W. III., 1701: *New Hamp. Prov. Papers*, III, 224. This act is retained in *Acts and Laws of New Hamp.* (Portsmouth, 1761), 53, 54; and *ibid.* (Portsmouth, 1771), 10, 11.

[6] There is a discussion of several cases in SHIRLEY, "Early Jurisprudence of New Hamp.," *Procds. New Hamp. Hist. Soc.* (1876–84), 279 ff.

the offense was otherwise harshly punished.   The culprit is to be "publickly set on the Gallows in the Day Time, with a Rope about his or her Neck, for the Space of One Hour; and on his or her Return from the Gallows to the Gaol, shall be publickly whipped on his or her naked Back, not exceeding Thirty Stripes; and shall stand committed to the Gaol of the County wherein convicted, until he or she shall pay all Costs of Prosecution."[1]

In Connecticut a brand appears to have superseded the death penalty at least by 1673, as shown in the code of that year.   The provision of this code is retained almost exactly in the compilation of 1769, requiring "that whosoever shall commit adultery with a Married Woman or one Betrothed to another Man, both of them shall be severely Punished, by Whipping on the naked Body, and Stigmatized or Burnt on the Forehead with the Letter *A*, on a hot Iron: And each of them shall wear a Halter about their Necks, on the outside of their Garments, during their Abode in this Colony, so as it may be Visible: And as often as either of them shall be found without their Halters, worn as aforesaid, they shall, upon Information, and Proof of the same, made before an Assistant or Justice of the Peace, ... be Whipt, not exceeding Twenty Stripes."[2]

As a detail of interest it may be observed that nowhere save in Connecticut is the continuous wearing of a halter provided for by statute; although for offenses other than adultery several decisions show that during the seventeenth century this punishment was employed in the Bay Colony.[3]

[1] Act of 1749: in *Acts and Laws of R. I.* (Newport, 1767), 6; also *ibid.* (Newport, 1752), 67, 68.   By the earlier statute as given in *Acts and Laws* (1745), 118, the punishment is thirty-nine stripes or a fine not exceeding 10 pounds.

[2] *Acts and Laws of Conn.* (New Haven, 1769), 7; *The Book of Gen. Laws, 1673* (Hartford, 1865), 2, 3; nearly the same in *Acts and Laws* (New London, 1715), 4, and *ibid.* (New London, 1750), 7.

[3] In 1654, for rape, a man, besides being whipped in Boston and again in Watertown, is sentenced during the court's pleasure to wear a rope around his neck, the end of it "hanging downe two feete long."   If found at any time without the rope

Furthermore, in Connecticut, as will hereafter appear, the law of incest differs from that of adultery in not requiring a rope to be so worn.

The statute of Massachusetts prescribing the death penalty for adultery did not survive the fall of the charter. So in 1794 the scarlet letter was substituted.[1] The act published on June 20 of that year, and remaining in force until after the close of the provincial era, varies in several important details, though not essentially, from the laws of Plymouth and Connecticut already presented. The offenders "shall be set upon the gallows by the space of an hour, with a rope about their neck, and the other end cast over the gallows; and in the way from thence to the common goal shall be severely whip'd, not exceeding forty stripes each." Also the offenders "shall forever wear a capital A, of two inches long and proportionate bigness, cut out in cloth of a contrary color to their cloaths, and sewed upon their upper garments, on the outside of the arm, or on their back, in open view." If "found without their letters so worn, during their abode in this province, they shall, by warrant from a justice of peace, be forthwith apprehended and ordered to be publicly whip'd,

"aboue forty rodd from his house," he is to be whipped: *Mass. Col. Rec.*, IV, Part I, 212. There is a similar case in 1642: DAVIS, *The Law of Adultery*, 30. That such sentences were executed is shown in a realistic way by a petition of 1670 preserved in the Suffolk Files. William Stacey, suffering for some offense not mentioned, prays "that the rope which he is forced to wear around his neck may be taken off. In answer the Secretary is required to send a copy of the Court's sentence to the Constable of Charlestoun that he may see that the sentence requiring the rope to be worn outside the clothes is carried out."—*MSS. Early Court Files of Suffolk*, No. 988. On May 6, 1646, "Elizabeth Fairefeild" petitioned the court of assistants that her husband might be discharged "from yᵗ pte of yᵉ censure inflicted on him for his notorious evills, of wearing yᵉ rope about his necke." He was, however, compelled to wear the rope six years more; for it was not until 1652 that his faithful wife's prayer was granted: *Mass. Col. Rec.*, III, 67, 161, 273.

[1] Already in 1673, for having an illegitimate child and imposing it on her husband, a woman had been sentenced by the court, "if found in this Colony two months after this date that shee stands in the markett place on a stoole for one hower wᵗʰ a paper on hir breast wᵗʰ yᵉ Inscription THVS I STAND FOR MY ADVLTEROVS AND WHORISH CARRIAGE and that on a lecture day next after the lecture and then be seuerely whipt wᵗʰ thirty stripes."—NOBLE'S *Records of the Court of Assistants*, I, 10.

not exceeding fifteen stripes, and so from time to time, *toties quoties*."[1]

Apparently writers have thus far failed to discover positive evidence that the provision of this act regarding the capital letter was ever carried out. A search in the manuscript records of the superior court of judicature, however, has disclosed several interesting cases. The earliest sentence occurred in March, 1707, when Mathew Fuller and Hannah Parker were indicted before a superior court at Plymouth. In the exact terms of the statute Hannah was sentenced to be set on the gallows, receive thirty stripes upon her naked back, and forever after to wear the capital *A*. But, singularly enough, her paramour was acquitted, no reason being assigned therefor either in the court record or in the files.[2] Again in 1721 Jemima Colefix, for sinning with a free negro and bearing a mulatto child, received a similar sentence; and in this case also the accused man was acquitted of being the putative father as had been charged.[3] The next case is dated February 9, 1730–31; and it shows that men as well as women had to endure this penalty. Before a court held in Boston "the jurors present John Warren, miller, and Rachel Gould for adultery," both being married persons. Although they pleaded not guilty, they were each set on the gallows, given thirty-nine stripes, and condemned to wear the capital

---

[1] *Acts and Resolves*, I, 171. This provision seems to have been retained until it was omitted in the act of Feb. 17, 1785: *The Perpet. Laws of the Com. of Mass.* (Boston, 1789), 203, 204.

[2] *MSS. Records of the Superior Court of Judicature*, III (1700–14), fol. 206. This decree may not actually have been carried out. The record concludes, "she being big with child the sentence was suspended for the present."

[3] *Ibid.* (May 2, 1721), IV, foll. 355, 356. According to the *MSS. Early Court Files of Suffolk*, No. 15,180, the order of execution to the sheriff says she was convicted on her own confession and accused the negro Humphers of being the father. The woman was apparently an experienced sinner. Fifteen years earlier "Jemima Colefix . . . . being presented . . . . for whoredom with a Negro, appeared and owned the same but that it was before marriage with her present Husband." Severely whipped twenty stripes, costs, and stands committed: *MSS. Records of the Court of General Sessions of Suffolk* (Jan. 27, 1706), I, 144.

letter.[1] Twenty years later, on September 26, 1752, "Daniel Bayley, cooper, and Mary Rainer" received the same punishment, except that they each suffered forty stripes, the full number allowed by the statute.[2] Finally after the lapse of thirty years more, just as the War of Independence was drawing to a close, we learn from the records that, following the usual stripes and exposure on the scaffold, Jerusha Doolittle was condemned to wear the fatal *A* as a badge of shame "forever."[3]

This closes the list of cases found in which the stigma is referred to. On the other hand, there are a number of sentences for adultery, or for what would ordinarily be so regarded, where this penalty is not imposed. These are the cases of semi-adulterous conduct, nominally provided for by the act of 1694, in which there is either no charge or not sufficient evidence of absolute transgression.[4] Usually one

[1] *MSS. Records of the Superior Court of Judicature* (1730-33), fol. 49.

[2] *Ibid.* (1752-53), fol. 190. The *MSS. Early Court Files of Suffolk*, No. .29,729, show that on this conviction without further proof "George Rainer [Raynord]," Mary's husband, got a complete divorce. The statutory limit of forty stripes was originally fixed according to the "law of God": WINTHROP, *Hist. of N. E.*, II, (ed. 1825-26), 250.

[3] *MSS. Records of the Supreme Judicial Court* (1781-82), leaf 41. Besides the cases of conviction discussed in the text, there are in the records a number of instances of acquittal for the same offense. In the *MSS. Early Court Files of Suffolk* (May 28-30, 1700), No. 4715, is an interesting example of extradition for adultery; and the survival of the ancient "chattel" interest of the husband in the wife is revealed by three damage suits for trespass on account of alleged assault upon, and in one for detaining, the wife: *MSS. Records of the Superior Court of Judicature* (1763-64), fol. 70; *ibid.* (1767-68), fol. 163; *ibid.* (1775-78), fol. 144; *ibid.* (1739-40), fol. 286. A similar case of "drawing away the affections" of a daughter may be found in *MSS. Early Court Files of Suffolk* (1671-72), No. 1100.

[4] These convictions are usually not for "adultery," but for being in bed together, according to a clause of the act of 1694 providing that when a man is found in bed with another person's wife each offender shall receive not more than thirty stripes, unless one was surprised and not consenting. For examples, some of them acquittals and some convictions, see *MSS. Records of the Superior Court of Judicature*, I (Oct. 30, 1694), fol. 129; *ibid.*, III (May 7, 1700), foll. 10, 11; *ibid.*, 1736-38 (Aug. 8, 1738), fol. 209; *ibid.*, 1757-59 (Aug. 1, 1758), 391; *ibid.*, 1757-59 (Feb. 21, 1759), 554; *ibid.*, 1760-62 (Sept. 16, 1760), foll. 122, 123; *ibid.*, 1763-64 (Jan. 25, 1763), fol. 11; *ibid.*, 1763-64 (April 26, 1763), fol. 44; *ibid.*, 1767-68 (April 12, 1765), fol. 164; *MSS. Records of Gen. Sessions of Suffolk* (April 2, 1717), II, 151.

For the earlier period the Athenæum copy of the *MSS. Records of the County Court of Suffolk*, 34 (March 17, 1671-72), 113 (Jan. 28, 1672-73), 585 (May 5, 1679), 633 (Jan. 27, 1679-80), contains four analogous cases; and there is one in *MSS. Records of the County Court of Middlesex* (April 1, 1684), IV, 97.

and sometimes both of the culprits are married. Fines, stripes, and occasionally banishment are the penalties imposed. As in the early period, there is manifestly a hesitation to urge conviction for "adultery" so as to involve the extreme penalty of the scarlet letter. The courts thus seem to favor a strict construction of the statute, giving the accused the benefit of the more lenient interpretation. In several cases the jury declines to convict for the offense charged where the evidence would clearly seem enough to sustain a verdict.[1]

Throughout New England, Rhode Island alone excepted, persons guilty of incest—that is to say, of uniting within the degrees of consanguinity or affinity legally forbidden— were stigmatized with an initial letter precisely as in the case of adultery. An act of Massachusetts in 1692, "for the punishing of capital offenders," makes this offense a felony punishable with death.[2] Because some of the "articles" dealing with capital crimes, among which is incest, "were conceived in very uncertain and doubtful terms," and because in such cases the penalty of death was not "conformable to ye Laws of England," the act was disallowed by the privy council in August, 1695.[3] However, in June of the same year a new act for the prevention of incestuous

---

[1] Thus at a superior court held at Falmouth for Cumberland and Lincoln counties, June 28, 1763, the "jurors present John Lawrence, husbandman, and Mary Lawton, *both married*, for adulterously dwelling together for five years, frequently lodging together in the same bed knowing each other to be married, being found adulterously in bed together and not surprised but consenting, and having carnal knowledge together. John was arraigned, pleaded not guilty, and the jury returned a verdict of guilty except to the charge of having committed adultery. 30 stripes and recognition in £100 to keep the peace." [Mary not tried.]—*MSS. Records of the Superior Court of Judicature* (1763-64), fol. 90. So also before a superior court held at Worcester, April 20, 1773, Joshua Phillips, laborer, presented by the jury for "committing *adultery*" with Mary, wife of Edward Rice, was acquitted. Then the jurors present them both "for being found at divers times in bed together. . . . . They pleaded not guilty. Convicted. Joshua fined £20 and costs. Mary 20 stripes and costs."—*Ibid.* (1773-74), foll. 36, 38.

[2] *Acts and Resolves*, I, 56 (Oct. 29).

[3] See the "Letter from the Privy Council," *Acts and Resolves*, I, 56, note; and compare DAVIS, *The Law of Adultery*, 12, 13.

marriages had been adopted by the general court; and this remained in force during the provincial era. By it the forbidden degrees are enumerated in harmony with the English ecclesiastical law. For violation of its provision exactly the same penalty in the same words is imposed as by the statute of 1694 for the punishment of adultery, except that in place of *A* a capital *I* is to be continuously worn.[1] This act of 1695 was adopted by New Hampshire in 1714,[2] and by Connecticut in 1702, the provision regarding the initial letter reappearing in the statute books of the latter commonwealth until 1821.[3]

In Massachusetts the legal stigma for incest was often imposed by judicial sentence. As already noticed by Davis, such a sentence in 1743 was executed upon Andrew Fleming, of Groton, who had first been set on the gallows for an hour and whipped forty stripes.[4] Hitherto no other examples of wearing the capital *I* seem to have been discovered. But a careful search in the manuscript records of the superior court for the period ending in 1780 has brought to light five additional cases. The first of these occurred in 1729 and the last in 1759. In every instance the culprit is punished with rope and gallows, stripes, and the scarlet letter.[5]

---

[1] *Acts and Resolves*, I, 208–10.

[2] By 13 Anne: in *Acts and Laws* (Portsmouth, 1761), 55, 56; and *ibid.* (Portsmouth, 1771), 42, 43,

[3] Revision of 1702, 73; *Acts and Laws* (New London, 1715), 74–76; *ibid.* (New London, 1750), 145; *ibid.* (New Haven, 1769), 145; *ibid.* (New London, 1784), 136.

[4] This case is in *MSS. Records of the Superior Court of Judicature* (1740–42), fol. 264. From the Suffolk Files (360–66, 557) DAVIS, *The Law of Adultery*, 13, 14, quotes the warrant of the sheriff for the execution; and also a notice of the case from the *Boston Weekly News-Letter* of Thursday, Feb. 10, 1743, stating that the daughter Elizabeth, with whom the crime was committed, had absconded.

[5] The five cases are as follows: (1) Salem, Oct. 28, 1729: Peter Harding, tailor, for having carnal knowledge with his daughter; gallows an hour, thirty-nine stripes, and capital *I*; *MSS. Records of the Superior Court of Judicature* (1725–30), fol. 274. (2) Worcester, Sept. 19, 1752: Jonathan Fairbanks, husbandman, and Sarah Armstrong, his wife's daughter; Jonathan sentenced as above, except twenty stripes: *ibid.* (1752–53), fol. 181. (3) Springfield, Sept. 24, 1754: Joseph Severance and Eunice Classon, his wife's sister; Joseph sentenced as above, except thirty stripes. (4) Eunice, *particeps criminis* in the preceding case, receives the same sentence, except twenty stripes: *ibid.* (1755–56), fol. 341. (5) Cambridge, Aug. 7, 1759: Judah Clark and Huldah Dudley, his wife's daughter; Huldah sentenced as above, except thirty stripes: *ibid.* (1757–59), 655.

The New England Puritans were, of course, very serious in their efforts to check sexual immorality. Their laws are characteristic of the age. As yet small progress had been made in enlightened theories of crime and its punishment. Besides they were steeped to the core in Hebraism. More or less as a religious duty they accepted and re-enacted the harsh precepts of the primitive Jewish code. It is not a little curious, however, to see them preserving an ancient English usage, almost extinct in the mother-country—in some instances regulating it by statute—which "thwarted their endeavors for complete propriety."[1] This was the custom of pre-contract, contraction, or betrothal, which everywhere in New England was celebrated with due solemnity. Such was the case in Massachusetts.[2] By the Connecticut statute, as already noted, the "contract" was carefully distinguished from the "covenant;" and because many persons entangle themselves by rash and inconsiderate promises for their future joining in marriage, the act of 1640 requires eight days' public notice of the betrothal, after which a second period of eight days must elapse before the covenant is sealed.[3] The pre-contract was in use also in New Hampshire[4] and Plymouth. In the latter jurisdiction the "couple—having the consent of the parents or guardians, in the case of minors—made before two witnesses a solemn promise of marriage in due time, the ceremony having the formality of the magisterial weddings then in vogue."[5]

[1] GOODWIN, *Pilgrim Republic*, 599, 600.

[2] COTTON MATHER, in his life of Danforth, says: "After his Contraction, according to the old usage of New England, unto the virtuous daughter of Mr. Wilson (whereat Mr. Cotton preached the sermon), he was married unto that gentle-woman, in the year 1651."—MATHER, *Magnalia*, IV, c. 3, §6, Vol. II, 50. *Cf.* DEXTER, *Congregationalism*, 458 n. 166, who cites also a statement in MATHER's *Ratio*, 112; likewise WINTHROP, *Hist. of New England*, II, 382 n. 2, whose mistake has already been mentioned. Compare EARLE, *Customs and Fashions*, 68 ff., who gives the "texts" of some of the betrothal sermons.

[3] *Conn. Col. Rec.*, I, 47, 48.

[4] SHIRLEY, "Early Jurisprudence of New Hamp.," *Procds. New Hamp. Hist. Soc.* (1876–84), 308.

[5] GOODWIN, *Pilgrim Republic*, 600; *cf. Plym. Col. Rec.*, XI, 172.

Undoubtedly pre-contract was derived from the English "espousals," which, it has already appeared, were a direct survival of the *beweddung* of the Anglo-Saxon laws. But in New England the betrothal gained a peculiar legal significance. "The betrothed woman was put, both by law and social custom, one step above the woman who was not betrothed, and one step below the woman who was married. This was so both as respects the civil and the criminal law."[1] In Massachusetts, Connecticut, and New Haven the "espoused wife" like the married wife is to suffer death for adultery;[2] while for fornication, on the other hand, the single woman and her partner in guilt are much less severely punished. The betrothed woman "was sentenced to wear the brand of the 'scarlet letter,' precisely as if she were married."[3]

Thus in New England the betrothal regained a sanction similar to that which it possessed according to primitive Germanic custom. It was, in fact, a kind of marriage. The espoused couple were separated from the world and placed in a relation whose sacredness might not be violated as respects others without the most serious consequences. On the other hand, it was entirely in harmony with this theory that when they "were guilty of incontinence with each other after pre-contract before marriage, their punishment was in general one half, or less than one half, what it would have been had there been no betrothment."[4] By the statute of Plymouth, for example, the

---

[1] Shirley, *loc. cit.*, 308.

[2] Whitmore, *Col. Laws of Mass.* (1660-72), 55, 128; *Conn. Col. Rec.*, I, 77; *New Haven Col. Rec.*, II, 577; Trumbull, *Blue Laws*, 60, 200.

[3] Shirley, *loc. cit.*, 308. This is true of Connecticut for the entire provincial period: *Acts and Laws* (New Haven, 1769), 7, but apparently not of Massachusetts under the second charter. In New Hampshire under the Canfield Code, 1682, the betrothed woman is still treated as married, but whipping is dispensed with: *New Hamp. Prov. Papers*, I, 444, 445. But by the act of 1701 she is punished for fornication as a single woman: *ibid.*, III, 224.

[4] Shirley, *loc. cit.*, 308.

penalty in such cases was fifty shillings for each person and imprisonment for a period not exceeding three days, or if the guilty persons "will not or cannot" pay the fine, they are to suffer "corporal punishment by whipping" instead; while for transgression before contract the fine was twice as much.[1] This was, in effect, to place a premium[2] upon wrong-doing committed between the espousals and the nuptials. Naturally the immorality of such offenses seemed thus to be lessened; and, as will presently appear, a vast amount of sexual license was the natural result.

The evil consequences of this anomalous state of the law were rendered all the more serious through the custom of "bundling" which obtained a wide prevalence in New England as it did also in New York and the other middle colonies. According to Stiles, who has produced the only general history of the subject, bundling "was practiced in two forms; first, between *strangers*, as a simple domestic makeshift arrangement, often arising from the necessities of a new country, and by no means peculiar to America; and, secondly between *lovers*, who shared the same couch, with the mutual understanding that innocent endearments should not be exceeded."[3] It is the second form with which we are

[1] The whole of this curious law may prove instructive. It is enacted "That any person or persons that shall Comit Carnall Copulation before or without lawfull contract shalbee punished by whiping or els pay ten pounds fine apeece and bee Imprisoned during the pleasure of the Court soe it bee not aboue three daies but if they bee or wilbee married [*i. e.*, a "delayed" marriage voluntarily solemnized or else marriage prescribed as a penalty] the one to the other; then but ten pounds both and Imprisoned as aforsaid; and by a lawfull Contract the Court vnderstands the mutuall consent of parents or guardians if there bee any to bee had; and a sollemne promise of marriage in due time to each other before two competent witnesses [this being the regulation of pre-contract already mentioned in the text]; and if any person or persons shall Comitt carnall Coppulation after contract and before Marriage they shall pay each fifty shillings and bee both Imprisoned," etc.— *Plym. Col. Rec.*, XI, 172, 95, 46. Originally the punishment for fornication was left in the discretion of the magistrates: *ibid.*, 12.

[2] *Cf.* SHIRLEY, *loc. cit.*, 308, 309.

[3] STILES, *Bundling in its Origin, Progress, and Decline* (Albany, 1871), 13, 14. GROSE, *Dictionary of the Vulgar Tongue*, thus explains the practice: "A man and a woman lying on the same bed with their clothes on; an expedient practiced in

here most concerned; and in its origin this likewise appears to have been "a custom of convenience." It was long regarded as a gross or licentious practice peculiar to New England. Thus Irving taunts the people of Connecticut with having tried to deprave the manners of the "Dutch lasses of the Nederlandts" through the introduction of that "horrible" usage.[1] But the Dutch maidens needed no lessons from their Yankee sisters in this regard; for in their "queesting" they had brought with them a form of bundling from Holland.[2] Indeed, it is not at all improbable that in this case Pilgrim and Puritan alike may have been strongly influenced by Dutch precedent, as they certainly were in more important institutions. Such an inference seems all the more justifiable, for as yet no trace of bundling has been reported "in any localities of England itself, the mother country;"[3]

America on a scarcity of beds, when, on such occasions, husbands and parents frequently permitted travelers to *bundle* with their wives and daughters." This applies, of course, only to the first named and less interesting form of the custom. In almost the same words as those used by Stiles, Masson, *Journeys in Belochistan, Afghanistan*, etc., III, 287, describes the bundling of lovers among the Afghans: see Adams, *Some Phases of Sexual Immorality*, 31, note. In general on this custom consult Earle, *Customs and Fashions*, 62-64; Weeden, *Ecc. and Soc. Hist. of N. E.*, II, 739, 864.

[1] Irving, *Knickerbocker's Hist. of New York* (Philadelphia, 1871), Book III, chaps. vii, viii, 217-28; *cf.* Stiles, *Bundling*, 45 ff.; Adams, *Some Phases of Sexual Immorality*, 31.

[2] *Queesting* (a seeking, similar to English "quest") seems to have existed until last century on the islands of Vlie, Wieringen, and perhaps elsewhere in Holland. "At night the lover has access to his mistress after she is in bed; and, upon an application to be admitted upon the bed, which is of course granted, he raises the quilt, or rug, and in this state *queests*, or enjoys a harmless chit-chat with her, and then retires. This custom meets with perfect sanction of the most circumspect parents, and the freedom is seldom abused. The author traces its origin to the parsimony of the people, whose economy considers fire and candles as superfluous luxuries in the long winter evenings."—Stiles, *op. cit.*, 35, 36, citing Carr, *The Stranger in Ireland* (1807).

[3] Adams, *Some Phases of Sexual Immorality*, 33. Mr. Adams, however, while pointing out the "singular and to me unaccountable, fact" that traces of bundling, found so widely in the New England colonies, have not yet been discovered in England, thinks that it "could hardly have found its way as a custom" from Holland or the other countries named; and he mentions, by way of supporting his conclusion, its great prevalence in Cape Cod where, according to Palfrey, until about 1825, "there was a purer strain of English blood to be found . . . . than could be found in any county of England." But wherever the Dutch settled the custom of bundling was tenacious, lasting in Pennsylvania at least until 1845: Earle, *Customs and Fashions*, 63: and in New York at least until 1804: Stiles, *op. cit.*, 111.

though in Ireland, Scotland, and Wales evidences of its recent existence are not wanting,[1] and the custom seems clearly to be deeply planted in the ancient usage of the German race.[2]

In New England, however, it was by no means confined to Connecticut.[3] It prevailed in the sister-provinces, and especially in both western[4] and eastern Massachusetts, down to the revolutionary period and perhaps for a good many years to come. Burnaby,[5] writing of his visit to that colony in 1759–60, gives a lively account of the custom, under the name of "tarrying," significantly observing that it takes place between the permission to pay court and the banns. In his view, bundling is on the whole an innocent practice, seldom being attended by evil consequences. On the other hand, that veracious historian, Rev. Samuel Peters, reproves Burnaby for presenting the custom in "an unfavorable light, and as prevailing among the *lower class* of people;" whereas, according to Peters, it exists among "all classes, to

[1] STILES, *op. cit.*, 14–35, who cites various authorities for Wales, especially PRATT, *Gleaning through Wales, Holland, and Westphalia* (3d ed., London, 1797), I, 105–7; and BINGLEY, *North Wales* (London, 1804), II, 282. *Cf.* also ADAMS, *op. cit.*, 32; and BRAND, *Popular Antiquities*, II, 98.

[2] Bundling probably has its origin in the "proof-nights" which formerly were widely prevalent among the Teutonic peoples of Europe: see FISCHER, *Ueber die Probenächte*, 12 ff., 24 ff., 32–36.

[3] STILES, *Windsor*, 495; WEEDEN, *Ecc. and Soc. Hist. of N. E.*, II, 739.

[4] JUDD, *Hadley*, 247.

[5] "When a man is enamoured of a young woman and wishes to marry her, he proposes the affair to her parents. . . . . If they have no objection, they allow him to tarry with her one night, in order to make his court to her. At their usual time the old couple retire to bed, leaving the young ones to settle matters as they can; who, after having sate up as long as they think proper, get into bed together also, but without putting off their undergarments, in order to prevent scandal. If the parties agree, it is all very well; the banns are published, and they are married without delay. If not, they part, and possibly never see each other again; unless, which is an accident that seldom happens, the forsaken fair one prove pregnant, and then the man is obliged to marry her, under pain of excommunication."— *Travels in North America*, 110, 111. Elsewhere he says that, while at first the practice may "appear to be the effects of grossness of character, it will, upon deeper research, be found to proceed from simplicity and innocence."—*Ibid.*, 144. *Cf.* ADAMS, *op. cit.*, 31, note; and LODGE, *Short History*, 438. The word "tarrying" is not always equivalent to "bundling," having a more general meaning. Nor was tarrying or bundling always restricted to one night; see STILES, *Bundling*, 70, 71.

the great honor of the country, its religion and ladies."[1]
Again in 1777 Lieutenant Anbury, "a British officer, who
served in America during the Revolutionary War, and whose
letters preserve many sprightly and interesting pictures of
the manners and customs of that period,"[2] chats racily of
an invitation to bundle which he received at Williams-
town, Mass.—a courtesy brought about through the scarcity
of beds for the entertainment of strangers.[3]   Charles
Francis Adams finds positive proof of the existence of the
custom "within a ten-mile radius of Boston" at least until
1781;[4] and he also quotes a reference to it from a letter of
Abigail Adams written three years later.[5] Nor apparently
was bundling entirely abandoned in eastern Massachusetts
until nearly fifty years thereafter, Cape Cod having the
"dubious honor" of holding out against the "advance of
civilization" in this regard until 1827.[6] The next year, in

[1] See STILES, op. cit., 51-60, for a long extract from the lively account of Peters,
who says that in Connecticut bundling is "as old as the first settlement in 1634;"
and that "about the year 1756 Boston, Salem, Newport, and New York, resolving to
be more polite than their ancestors, forbade their daughters *bundling* on the bed
with any young men whatever, and introduced a sofa to render courtship more
palatable and Turkish;" but with more "natural consequences than all the *bundling*
among the boors with their *rurales pedantes* through every village in New England
besides." Of course, all this must be swallowed with a very large "grain of salt."

[2] STILES, op. cit., 66.

[3] ANBURY, *Travels through the Interior Parts of America; in a Series of Letters*
(new ed., London, 1781), II, 37-40: cited by STILES, op. cit., 66 ff. In a subsequent
letter Anbury plagiarizes the passage from Burnaby which we have quoted in a
preceding note.

[4] According to WORTHINGTON's *History of Dedham* (1827), 109—"a town only ten
miles from Boston—I find that the Rev. Mr. Haven, the pastor of the church there,
alarmed at the number of cases of unlawful cohabitation, preached at least as late
as 1781 'a long and memorable discourse,' in which, with a courage deserving of
unstinted praise, he dealt with 'the growing sin' publicly from his pulpit, attribut-
ing 'the frequent recurrence of the fault to the custom then prevalent of females
admitting young men to their beds who sought their company with intentions of
marriage.'"—ADAMS, op. cit., 35. STILES, op. cit., 75-77, note, gives a long extract
from Worthington, who represents Haven's sermon as having had a powerful influence in setting aside the custom of bundling. But already before this Jonathan
Edwards had raised his voice against it.

[5] ADAMS, op. cit., 35; citing MRS. JOHN ADAMS's *Letters* (1848), 161.

[6] STILES, op. cit., 110, note, where personal testimony is adduced.

Franklin county, Me., a letter to the Portland *Yankee* reveals the custom existing in full vigor.[1]

According to the judgment of Stiles, bundling "came nearest to being a universal custom from 1750 to 1780." Contrary to the popular view,[2] it appears to have been confined to the more humble and less cultivated classes; "to those whose limited means compelled them to economize strictly in their expenditure of firewood and candlelight."[3] No evidence has yet been produced showing that it made its appearance in the main centers of New England civilization.

Though bundling could arise only in a comparatively rude state of society, it seems in itself to have been neither very vicious nor very immoral. Yet manifestly it was easily capable of abuse. Under dangerous conditions it might readily degenerate into coarseness and vice. Such conditions were not wanting throughout the colonial era. The general tone of sexual morality was not high. The laws and usages already presented, which in effect invited transgression on the part of engaged lovers, afforded a constant temptation.[4] Bundling thus has its chief moral significance as an adjunct

[1] See the Appendix to STILES, *op. cit.*, 113-25, where an article from the *Yankee*, of Aug. 13, 1828, containing the letter mentioned, is quoted. A search in the manuscript court records reveals not a single clear case of bundling. On Jan. 30, 1709-10, Jane Lee, widow, was presented and acquitted in Charlestown for conduct resembling bundling: *MSS. Records of the Court of Gen. Sessions of Suffolk*, I, 202. There is a more probable example in the *MSS. Records of the Court of General Sessions of Middlesex* (Dec. 15, 1702), I, 137.

[2] Thus SHIRLEY, "Early Jurisprudence of New Hamp.," *Procds. New Hamp. Hist. Soc.* (1876-84), 308, declares that "the practice prevailed very largely in New England, among the rich and the poor, the educated and the uneducated, the cultivated and the uncultivated."

[3] STILES, *op. cit.*, 65, 106. ADAMS, *op. cit.*, 31, 32, 36, reaches the same conclusion. "It was," he says, "a practice growing out of the social and industrial conditions of a primitive people, of simple, coarse manners and small means," and probably did not exist in Boston, Salem, or Plymouth.

[4] So also in Holland, it is interesting to note, bundling appears in connection with the practice of public betrothals as the cause of ante-nuptial transgressions. See Townshend's speech on the Hardwicke act in COBBETT-HANSARD, *Parliamentary Debates*, XV, 56-59.

of pre-contract which must be held responsible for a very large share of the sexual misconduct revealed in the judicial records.   Before the general court of Plymouth the cases of "uncleanness" after contract and before marriage are very numerous.   According to Goodwin, they averaged one a year; and this appears to be a conservative estimate.   By actual count the records of that colony, for the twenty-eight years between 1633 and 1661, show at least twenty-four sentences for ante-nuptial offenses, chiefly after betrothal; while during the seventeen years following 1661 there are not less than forty-one such judgments.   Members of some of the most illustrious families of New England were guilty of indiscretions in this regard.[1]   In several of the early cases the husband was publicly whipped in view of the wife, who sat near in the stocks.[2]

The manuscript records of two counties of Massachusetts for a portion of the seventeenth century appear to demonstrate that such "miscarriages" before complete wedlock were not less frequent in the Bay Colony.[3]   A thorough

[1] "There was Peregrine White, the first-born child of the Colony and stepson of Governor Winslow; Thomas Cushman, Jr., son of the elder; James Cudworth, Jr., son of the future general and deputy-governor, and Jonathan, his brother; Samuel Arnold, Jr., son of the Marshfield pastor; Isaac Robinson, Jr., grandson of the great Leyden pastor; Thomas Delano; Nathaniel Church; and other scions of leading families."— GOODWIN, *Pilgrim Republic*, 600, who, thinks it a mistake to suppose that generation " below the present in general purity of life;" since the pre-contract was " a sort of semi-marriage " and " such cases were ferretted out and recorded " with "impartial diligence."

[2] GOODWIN, *op. cit.*, 600; *cf. New Hamp. Prov. Papers*, I, 386, 445.   FREEMAN, *Hist. of Cape Cod*, I, 167, 168, gives the following forms of sentence : "A. F. for having a child born six weeks before the ordinary time of women after marriage, fined for uncleanness, and whipt, and his wife set in the stocks." "C. E., for abusing himself with his wife before marriage, sentenced to be whipt publicly at the post, she to stand by whilst the execution is performed.   Done, and he fined five pounds for the trouble."

[3] In addition the records of the court of assistants for the early period contain six cases, in each instance the husband alone being punished; two cases in 1635, one in 1637, one in 1639, two in 1640: *Mass. Col. Rec.*, I, 163, 193, 269, 296, 297; and three cases where both husband and wife were fined, condemned to stand in the market place, or to confess on Lecture Day: *Rec. of the Court of Assistants, 1641—1643/44*, in WHITMORE, *Bib. Sketch*, xxxi, xxxiii, xxxvii.

analysis of the records of the county court of Suffolk, covering the ten years 1671–80, brings to light twenty of these cases, while during the same period there are forty-three instances of transgression by "single women."[1] Now, it is important to remember that the statutes of Massachusetts, unlike those of Plymouth, do not discriminate between the offenses of single persons and those committed with each other by espoused lovers.[2] The question therefore arises as to whether the *custom* of pre-contract—for pre-contract was not established by *law* in that province—can be held in any way accountable for these facts. A comparison of the penalties imposed in the two classes of cases, as exhibited in Tables I and II, shows that an affirmative answer must be given. The sins of betrothed persons are in general punished with far less rigor than those of single men and women. Thus twenty-one out of forty-three single women, and eight out of thirteen single men, are sentenced to stripes alone, nineteen of them receiving each from fifteen to forty lashes;

[1] These are in the Athenæum copy of the *MSS. Records of the County Court of Suffolk, 1671-80.* There is also a unique example in the *MSS. Early Court Files of Suffolk* (1675), No. 1412. This is a case of appeal to the assistants from the county court at Salisbury, where John Garland and wife had been fined £5 for having a child eleven weeks too early. On his appeal John says, significantly: " I and She had parents Concent to marry and Legally published & Stayed after publication a Considerable time, that had any Such Act been comĩted by us we could haue preuented it by marrying sooner ; " and he further alleges that it was an untimely birth caused by the wife's fall. In reply, the attorney for the county of Norfolk said Garland had pretended to quote "Aristottle" to prove a child might come in the seventh month, but that if the court "please to Cast an eye vpon John garland . . . . they will judg Him to be no deepe man in phylosophie." Whereupon the worthy barrister, rejecting pagan learning, imparted the following bit of strictly orthodox biology: "It was well knowne to the Honored Court at Salisbury that the usuall time of woman was a set time As in genesis the 18 and the 10 compared with 2 of kings the 4th & the 16 verse, the Honored Court likewise knew that that time wast aboue seauen month as is the first of luke the 36 vers compared with the 39 & 40 and 56 & 57 verse of that chapter." The "jury" reversed the decision of the lower court.

[2] "If any man commit fornication with a single woman, they shall be punished, either by enjoining marriage, or fine, or corporal punishment, or all or any of these," as the court may determine: WHITMORE, *Col. Laws of Mass.* (1660-72), 153. Later disfranchisement, in the case of a freeman, was added: *ibid.*, 231. See also WHITMORE, *op. cit.* (1672-86), 54, 208 ; *Conn. Col. Rec.*, I, 527 ; *New Haven Col. Rec.*, II, 590 ; *Plym. Col. Rec.*, XI, 12, 46, 95, 172.

TABLE I

Cases of Fornication before Marriage in the County Court of
Suffolk County, Mass., 1671-80

1. Fine only - - - - - -	3 married couples	
£5 (both) - - - - - - 1	"	"
£3 " - - - - - - 1	"	"
40s. " - - - - - - 1	"	"
2. Fine and confession before the congrega-		
tion or stripes - - - - - 2	"	"
3. Fine or stripes - - - - - 15	"	"
a) Fine—		
£5 (both) - - - - - - 3	"	"
£4 " - - - - - - 3	"	"
£3 " - - - - - - 1	"	"
50s. " - - - - - - 1	"	"
40s. " - - - - - - 7	"	"
b) Stripes—		
20 - - - - - - -	2 husbands	0 wives
15 - - - - - - - 12	"	2 "
10 - - - - - - - 1	"	13 "

TABLE II

Cases of Fornication by Single Persons in the County Court of
Suffolk County, Mass., 1671-80

The most noticeable feature of these cases is the tendency on the part of single
men to confess the crime and accept punishment, besides becoming bound as putative fathers. All the convictions for fornication are by confession or pleading guilty.

1. Single women convicted	43	30 - - - -	2
a) Fine or stripes -	22	20 - - - -	11
£15 or 20 stripes -	1	15 - - - -	4
£5 or { 20 " -	1	10 - - - -	2
{ 15 " - -	4	2. Single men, confession -	13
£3 or { 20 " -	1	a) Fine or stripes -	5
{ 15 " - -	3	£5 or 20 stripes - -	4
50s.or { 15 " -	3	40s. or 15 stripes -	1
{ 10 " - -	2	b) Stripes alone - -	8
40s.or { 15 " -	2	30 - - - -	3
{ 10 " - -	4	20 - - - -	5
b) Stripes alone -	21	c) Putative fathers -	17
40 (20 each in two places)	2		

while in no case is a single man or woman merely fined. On the other hand, out of twenty married couples punished for ante-nuptial misconduct, fifteen are given the choice of fines or stripes, three are merely fined; and in no instance is whipping alone the penalty decreed. Furthermore, the fines are on the average smaller in these cases than in others, although as regards both fines and stripes the sentences are sadly lacking in uniformity. The conclusion seems irresistible that, in harmony with popular sentiment, the courts, exercising the discretion granted by the statute, were inclined to deal more leniently with the faults of the betrothed than with those of less favored bachelors and spinsters.

Similar evidence is afforded by the incomplete records of the county court of Middlesex for the period 1629–86, supplemented by the Files. These contain in all thirty cases of transgression before marriage, eight of which fall within the ten years covered by the Suffolk records already considered. Most of the severe sentences (Table III) occur in this period and the six years immediately following, although the heaviest fine, twenty pounds for the couple, is imposed in 1663.[1] Seemingly, from the few cases known, single persons were treated more harshly than those who were betrothed.[2]

[1] June 16, 1663. At a county court at Charlestown, "Daniel Weld and Bertha his wife convicted of fornication before marriage, appeared and made humble acknowledgment of their sin craving the favor of the court. Admonished seriously to consider their great sin and fined £10 apiece. Execution respited during the pleasure of the court."— MSS. Records of the County Court of Middlesex, I, 243. On the same day before the same court John Roy and wife were convicted of the same offense, and "pleaded that it was committed a fortnight after their solemn contract in marriage and being hindered of marriage were overcome by the temptation." They had to pay only 40s.: ibid., 241.

[2] In these volumes there are five cases of fornication by single persons. In the first, April 4, 1654, the two culprits got each twelve stripes; in another, April 1, 1684, a married man and a girl were parties, the man being sentenced to pay £20 or receive thirty stripes, the woman, £5; and in one instance, October 2, 1677, the woman was "whipt fifteen stripes." More cruel was the fate of Sarah Pore. On July 7, 1785, for refusing to name the father of her two children, she was condemned "to be whipt severely twenty stripes and to lie in the house of correction for twelve months, there to be kept at hard labor and to be whipt once a month until she confess." Of course, on August 14, she named the man. For these cases see MSS. Records of the County Court of Middlesex, I, 39; III, 107, 194; IV, 97, 171, 173.

On presentment by the grand jury[1] or voluntarily confessions were made by wives and husbands before the court; and these documents contain evidence of the close relation

TABLE III

CASES OF FORNICATION BEFORE MARRIAGE IN THE COUNTY COURT OF
MIDDLESEX COUNTY, MASS., 1649–86 [EXCEPT 1663–71]

During the same period these records contain five cases of fornication by single persons.

1. Fine only   -   -   -   -   -   -   15 married couples
     £20 (together)   -   -   -   -   -   1   "   "
     £5   "   -   -   -   -   -   3   "   "
     £4   "   -   -   -   -   -   6   "   "
     £3   "   -   -   -   -   -   2   "   "
     40s.   "   -   -   -   -   -   3   "   "
2. Fine or stripes
     a) Fine   -   -   -   -   -   -   10   "   "
       £10 (together)   -   -   -   -   -   5   "   "
       £6   "   -   -   -   -   1   "   "
       £4   "   -   -   -   -   3   "   "
       £3   "   -   -   -   -   1   "   "
       50s. (wife)   -   -   -   -   -   1
     b) Stripes   -   -   -   -   -   10   "
       20   -   -   -   6 husbands   0 wives
       15   -   -   -   -   1   "   0   "
       10   -   -   -   -   3   "   10   "
3. Stripes only
     15   -   -   -   -   1   " (the wife 50s. or whipped)
4. Confessions and petitions -   -   -   -   3 married couples
5. Convicted and respited -   -   -   -   1   "   "

existing between the colonial church and state. On October 31, 1671, for instance, Christopher Wheaton and Martha his wife were sentenced in Boston to make an acknowledgment "in publique at Hull to yᵉ Satisfaction of yᵉ Congregation, & pay twenty Shillings fine," on pain of being whipped

[1] See the long petition and confession of Samuel and Elizabeth Manning, who had been presented by the grand jury of Middlesex. It is expressed in perfervid pious phrase, much like the "church confession" presently referred to: *MSS. Files of the County Court of Middlesex*, June, 1664.

ten stripes each by the constable.[1] An elaborate "church confession," found among the Middlesex Files, would seem to prove that in another case the decree of the court was obeyed; and that the written acknowledgment made before the congregation was returned to the court for record.[2]

The files and records of the same two counties, supplemented by the record of the superior court, may next be examined for the period of the second charter. The impression made by their contents is decidedly disagreeable and depressing. The coarser and more heinous sexual crimes are growing more frequent, although due allowance must be made for the increase of population. Indeed, the bulk of the records of the general sessions appears to be concerned with sexual immorality of almost every kind.[3] Inquiry is, however, here restricted to the two classes of cases thus far considered. For convenience the material is treated chronologically in two divisions. The first division covers the

---

[1] *MSS. Records of the County Court of Suffolk*, 22. There was another sentence of this kind at the same session of this court.

[2] See the acknowledgment of Samuel Wright and Lydea his wife beginning: "for as much as wee are heere called to confese our sine before God and his people wee doe therefore heere accnowlidg that wee haue sined in that wee haue brokne the seuenth comandmente in neglecting our deuty therein required and comitinge the sine forbiddene: to the dishonour of God and Scandalizinge of the gospel;" and so on in scriptural phrase to the extent, in the author's copy, of a large typewritten page: *MSS. Files of the County Court of Middlesex*, Oct., 1664.

[3] There are (1) many cases of bastardy, the woman being usually fined or whipped and the man in most cases sentenced merely to contribute to the child's support; for a few examples see *MSS. Records of the Court of Gen. Sessions of Suffolk*, I, 112 (1705), 190, 192 (1709); II, 234 (1719); III, 154, 308 (1724); IV, 331 (1731): *MSS. Records of the Court of Gen. Sessions of Middlesex*, II, 197, 203, 204 (1729–30); (2) killing of bastard, at least ten convictions between 1692 and 1725, in nine of which the woman was sentenced to death; and not less than a dozen presentations and one capital sentence after 1725: see examples in *MSS. Records of the Superior Court of Judicature*, II (1686–1700), 49, 50; III (1700–1714), fol. 270; *ibid.* (1725–29), fol. 111; *ibid.* (1772), fol. 98; *ibid.* (1757–59), 295; (3) miscegenative fornication, a number of cases, the white woman almost always receiving twenty stripes: examples in *MSS. Records of the Court of Gen. Sessions of Suffolk*, I, 144 (1706), 206 (1710); II, 43, 45 (1713); (4) rape, at least two cases: *MSS. Records of Superior Court of Judicature* (1739–40), fol. 225; *ibid.* (1767–68), fol. 261; (5) prostitution of wife, one case: *MSS. Minute Books of the Court of Gen. Sessions of Suffolk*, III, Dec. 3, 1756. The darker crimes were, however, not unknown to the period of the first charter. Between 1674 and 1681 in Massachusetts four persons were sentenced to death for rape: NOBLE, *Records of the Court of Assistants*, I, 21, 50, 74, 199.

period ending in 1725; and the second the years 1726–80. Within the former period (Table IV) the records of the general sessions of Suffolk for the years 1702–25, inclusive,

TABLE IV

SUMMARY OF FORNICATION CASES BEFORE THE GENERAL SESSIONS OF SUFFOLK COUNTY, 1702–25, AND THE GENERAL SESSIONS OF MIDDLESEX COUNTY, 1692–1725

Between 1702 and 1725 the following cases brought conviction before the general sessions for Suffolk county:

Cases of fornication where the woman alone was sentenced -	104
Cases of conception before marriage with fine, and in a few cases fine or whipping for husband, or both husband and wife - - - - - - - - -	48
Cases of woman fined or whipped, and putative (or acknowledged) father sentenced to maintenance of child - -	44

Between 1692 and 1725 there were the following convictions before the general sessions for Middlesex county (each case stands for both man and woman if both were tried):

Cases of fornication - - - - - - - -	135
Cases of fornication and conception before marriage - -	155

yield forty-eight cases of conviction of married couples for pre-nuptial misconduct, as compared with 148 cases of single women sentenced for the same offenses.[1] The corresponding

---

[1] Here are two typical cases:

Aug. 27, 1711: "Joseph Holbrook and Mary Cooke . . . . being presented . . . . for fornication, He appeared and owned the same; and that he is since Married to her. Ordered That [he] . . . . shall pay a Fine of Three pounds in behalf of himself and his 2d Wife & Costs . . . . standing Comitted."— *MSS. Records of the Court of Gen. Sessions of Suffolk*, I, 234.

April 4, 1721: "Mary Shaw the Wife of Benjamin Shaw . . . . being presented for having a child in September last, about five Months after Marriage, appeared and owned the same. Ordered That [she] . . . . pay a fine of Forty Shillings . . . . Costs . . . . standing committed."—*Ibid.*, III, 83.

A sentence that includes the alternative of whipping is rare; for an example (July, 1702) see *ibid.*, I, 4. The proceedings in the case of Benjamin and Hopestill Allen, March 5, 1696–7—Nov. 23, 1698, are especially instructive. They were presented by the grand jury of Bristol for having a child within six months after publishment. Hopestill was fined 50 shillings, or to be whipped ten stripes. On appeal to the superior court the legality of the marriage was called in question. The privilege of appeal was granted by special act of the legislature: with the *MSS. Early Court Files of Suffolk*, No. 3728, compare the *MSS. Records of the Superior Court of Judicature*, II, 198; and the petition and act regarding appeal in *MSS. Mass. Archives*, XL, 476, 478, 483.

records of the general sessions of Middlesex for the years 1692–1725 contain the extraordinary number of 155 cases of the first class, as compared with 135 of the second. In a great many instances the husband or both husband and wife appear "freely and voluntarily" and confess their guilt.

TABLE V

FORNICATION CASES BEFORE THE GENERAL SESSIONS OF MIDDLESEX COUNTY, MASS., FOR EACH QUINQUENNIUM, 1726–80[1]

	QUINQUENNIUM											TOTAL
	26–30	31–35	36–40	41–45	46–50	51–55	56–60	61–65	66–70	71–75	76–80	
Single women......................												523
Appeared and confessed............	..	13	2	4	12	4	10	6	5	13	21	...
Confessed on recognizance.........	2	3	12	3	9	7	9	6	4	2	2	...
Pleaded guilty..	9	2	3	12	10	4	11	11	13	5	2	...
Pleaded guilty and named man.....	1	3	1	4	5	6	21	18	16	7	3	...
Conf. on recogniz'nce and named man	10	4	6	4	3	6	16	11	15	9	1	...
Appeared, confessed, and named man	4	15	5	1	5	4	3	9	15	16	45	...
Married couples												160
Appeared and confessed............	37	65	16	3	1	..	1	..	..	..	..	...
Pleaded guilty	15	9	8	1	1	..	..	..				...
Pleaded not guilty, but convicted ..	2	...	1	..								...
Wives[2]												31
Appeared and confessed............	2	1	3	..	1	..	..	..	1	..	..	...
Pleaded guilty	3	...	...	..	1	2	6	7	4	..	..	...
Total...........................	85	115	57	32	48	33	77	68	73	52	74	714

This is especially true during the decade following 1715, there being five such confessions at one sitting of the court, four of them on one page of the record.

The results for the later period (Table V) are still more striking. Before the Middlesex court alone, during the fifty-five years commencing in 1726, were 523 cases of single

[1] In addition to the 714 cases comprised in the table, during the same period 73 single men, perhaps all involved in those cases, were before the court as follows: putative fathers, 54; settled out of court, 9; appeared and gave bond to save the town, 8; fornication, pleading guilty, 2. Of these one (1750) was fined £5; and one (1732) was given the choice of 10 shillings or ten stripes.

[2] Fornication before marriage (presumably with husband).

women and 191 cases of married couples; but 189 of these couples were tried during the twenty-five years ending in 1750—there being but two isolated cases of confession after that date—and 181 within the first fifteen years. On the

TABLE VI

PENALTIES IMPOSED IN CASES COMPRISED IN TABLE V[1]

Fine	Single Women	Married Couples	Wives	Fine	Single Women	Married Couples	Wives
£12½....	..	1	..	20s.......	43	3	..
£9.......	1	..	..	15s.......	20	..	..
£6.......	1	2	..	10s.......	96	2	2
£5.......	18	37	..	5s.......	169	..	16
£4.......	48	61	3	4s.......	11	..	..
£3.......	6	..	..	3s.......	13	..	2
50s.......	10	..	1	2s.......	7	..	..
40s.......	24	2	4	1s.......	10	..	1
30s.......	9	..	3	Total ..	494	109	32
25s.......	8	1	..				

other hand, 337 single women were convicted during the twenty-five and 257 during the same fifteen years. Again, 118 out of the 181 married couples tried between 1726 and 1740 appeared and, presumably, freely confessed their faults. The leading years in this regard are 1730 with twelve, 1732 with twenty-nine, and 1734 with sixteen confessions. The leading quinquennium is the second (1731–35) with sixty-six confessions as compared with thirty-nine in the first

[1] In general the later the date of the case, the smaller the fine. With few exceptions fines of 25 shillings or less are after 1745; and most of those for 5 shillings or under are many years later. The "married couples" and the "wives" are only fined. Eight "single women" have the alternative of fine or stripes as follows: One (1734), £5 or 5 stripes; two (1755, 1770), £3 or 10 stripes; two (1746, 1756), 50 shillings or 10 stripes, the first being an "old offender;" one (1751), an "old offender," 40 shillings or 10 stripes; one (1758), 10 shillings or 10 stripes; one (1761), 5 shillings or 10 stripes. One woman (1747), whose child is a mulatto bastard, is given 20 stripes and sold into "service." In two similar cases (1759, 1772) 10 and 20 stripes respectively are deemed sufficient; while in another instance (1761) an "old offender" is sentenced to 20 lashes. In the later years, it will be noted, stripes decrease in money value. On the other hand, with the progress in humanism, they are probably lighter and therefore worth less.

(1726–30) and nineteen in the third (1736–40). To offset these figures we find thirteen presumably voluntary confessions by single women in the second quinquennium, none in the first, and two in the third. These facts seem to point directly to the action of special causes in producing this kind of immorality, or, at any rate, its confession. Whether this action was local for Middlesex cannot positively be determined from these documents alone; although, as will soon appear, other evidence shows that this cannot be assumed. After 1725 the records for Suffolk are incomplete; but it is surprising that during the seven years (September, 1725, to October, 1732) covered by Table VII there were in that county only seven convictions of married couples, not one of whom freely confessed, as compared with forty-eight cases of single women, including one confession.

There can be little doubt that in the eighteenth century, just as in the age preceding, the general cause of this antenuptial immorality — and probably also of some part of the similar misconduct of single persons whose engagements were not followed by wedlock — was the custom of solemn pre-contract which still survived. During the second quarter of the eighteenth century the penalties were relatively severe, though not so rigorous as during the period of the first charter; but the facts exhibited in Table VI show that the courts still treated pre-nuptial offenders more mercifully than those who were not married.

To determine the special cause of the sudden rise in the number of confessions during the same period is a more difficult matter. It is not improbable that a suggestion of Charles Francis Adams, regarding another aspect of the problem, may give us a clue to its right solution. Already the practice of church confession of these offenses, in obedience to judicial decree, has been noticed ; and independently of the courts, as a religious expiation, such acknowledgments

were required by the authority of particular churches.   In
the eighteenth century, if not earlier, under the "seven
months rule," the culpable parents were forced to humble

TABLE VII

FORNICATION CASES BEFORE THE GENERAL SESSIONS OF SUFFOLK COUNTY,
MASS., SEPTEMBER, 1725, TO OCTOBER, 1732[1]

	YEAR								TOTAL
	1725	1726	1727	1728	1729	1730	1731	1732	
Single women :									
Confessed............................			1						1
£3 or 10 stripes.....................			1						..
Pleaded guilty									8
£4 or 10 stripes				2					..
£3 or 10 stripes				2		1			..
£2 or 10 stripes				1		1		1	..
Pleaded not guilty, but convicted									3
£5 or 10 stripes						1			..
10 stripes....				1		1			..
Pleaded guilty and named man									35
£5 or 10 stripes		1							..
£4 or 10 stripes	2	2	1		2				..
£3 or 10 stripes	1	2	2	5	3	4	3	1	..
£2 or 10 stripes				1	1		1	3	..
Came in freely and accused a man									1
£2 or 10 stripes							1		..
Married couples :									
Fornication before marriage, man alone accus'd	..	..	..						2
20s. or 10 stripes						1	1		..
Fornication before mar'ge, woman alone accus'd	..	..							5
40s. or 10 stripes		1			1	1			..
20s. or 10 stripes	1	1							..
Total............................	4	7	8	8	7	10	6	5	55

themselves before the whole congregation or else expose their
innocent child to the danger of eternal perdition.[2]   Yet, in

[1] During the period are also fifteen cases of putative fathers. Voluntary accusa-
tions of putative fathers were looked on with suspicion. In the fragments of later
records of Suffolk it is not uncommon for the court to refuse to put the woman on
her oath in such cases.

[2] By this rule children born in less than seven months after marriage were
refused baptism, that is, were put in peril of eternal damnation, unless the parents
made public confession of their fault before the whole congregation: ADAMS, *Some
Phases of Sexual Immorality*, 20 ff.

In like spirit other offenses were subjected to church discipline.   For minor spite of the fact that the clergy had thus devised a punishment more terrible to bear than the fines or stripes imposed by the criminal law, during the very period under consideration the church records show a great increase in the number of confessions. Adams suggests that an explanation may be found in the religious excitement which generally prevailed during the second quarter of the eighteenth century, the period which includes the "Great Awakening" under Whitefield in 1740, the Northampton revival of 1735, "engineered and presided over by Jonathan Edwards," and earlier "harvests" of the same character.[1] At Braintree, for example, there was a vast increase in the number of church confessions during the pastorate of John Hancock, 1726–43. It was "everywhere noticed that the women, and especially the young women, were peculiarly susceptible to attacks of the spiritual epidemic. Jonathan Edwards for instance mentions, in the case of Northampton, how the

shortcomings, such as cheating, the culprit, after examination, was required to give "christian satisfaction" by public confession of penitence. If he refused, he was "suspended" from the communion. For adultery the penalty was "excommunication" on refusal to confess: and this punishment in Puritan New England meant as complete a social ostracism as it did in old England during the Middle Ages. Sometimes the most shameful wrongs resulted from these church trials; and this is well illustrated by the case of Abigail Muxon who, in 1783, on the unsworn testimony of two gossips, was condemned for alleged misconduct, thirty years after she was "suspended" on the same charge. She positively declared the evidence of the witnesses false. She was then an old woman; but "there was no friend or attorney to represent her before the self-righteous tribunal; and without cross-examining the unsworn witnesses, the church voted (men only were allowed to vote) that she is guilty of the charge." For weeks she refused to "confess," although she was "admonished" by the parson and "labored" with by the brethren. At last before a tribunal of six ministers "her excommunication was pronounced by Parson Everitt, who in his condemnation describes her 'as being visibly a hardened and impenitent sinner out of the visible Kingdom of Christ, one who ought to be viewed and treated by all good people as a heathen and publican in imminent danger of eternal perdition'": For a full discussion of this case see the fascinating book of BLISS, *Colonial Times on Buzzard's Bay*, 99–101, 111–14.

[1] ADAMS, *op. cit.*, 26 ff. The following scarce works are in the Harvard library: JONATHAN EDWARDS, *Thoughts concerning the Present Revival of Religion in New England* (London, 1745); CHAUNCEY, *A Letter from a Gentleman to Mr. George Wishart . . . . concerning the State of Religion in New England* (Edinburgh, 1742), criticising Tennant and Whitefield; *The State of Religion in New England* (Glasgow, 1742); and especially the *Letter from New England* (1742), 4, describing the symptoms of "conversion."

young men of that place had become 'addicted to night-walking and frequenting the taverns, and leud practices,' and how they would 'get together in conventions of both sexes for mirth and jollity, which they called frolicks ; and they would spend the greater part of the night in them ;' and among the first indications of the approach of the epidemic noticed by him was the case of a young woman who had been one of the greatest 'company keepers' in the whole town, who became 'serious, giving evidence of a heart truly broken and sanctified.'   This same state of affairs doubtless then prevailed in Braintree, and indeed throughout New England.   The whole community was in a sensitive condition morally and physically." [1]   The morbid quickening of the conscience would thus naturally result in a greater number of confessions rather than in an increase of sexual license ; and this same cause seems adequate to explain the extraordinary number of confessions which we have found in the contemporary court records. [2]   Besides, after the sin had been disclosed before the congregation, an acknowledgment in court would almost necessarily follow.   It would be very strange, however, if there were not a considerable increase in immorality.   The practice of bundling, as

[1] ADAMS, op. cit., 28.

[2] The church confessions of married couples and single persons continued long after confession ceased to be made in court.   In Groton the "seven months rule" was put in force in 1765 and not abrogated until 1803.   Under its operation "the records of the Groton church show that out of two hundred persons owning the baptismal covenant in that church during the fourteen years between 1761 and 1775 no less than sixty-six confessed to fornication before marriage.   The entries recording these cases are very singular.   At first the full name of the person, or persons in the case of husband and wife, is written, followed by the words 'confessed and restored' in full.   Somewhat later, about the year 1763, the record becomes regularly 'Confessed Fornication' which two years later is reduced to 'Con. For.;' which is subsequently still further abbreviated into merely 'C. F.'   During the three years 1789, 1790, and 1791 sixteen couples were admitted to full communion ; and of these nine had the letters 'C. F.' inscribed after their names in the church records."   The practice existed at Dedham, Roxbury, and probably throughout Massachusetts: ADAMS, op. cit., 20–23, citing BUTLER, History of Groton, 174, 178, 181 ; WORTHINGTON, History of Dedham, 108, 109 ; and Report of Boston Record Commission, vi, 93, passim.

Adams believes,[1] may have afforded ready opportunity. Any violent or protracted disturbance of the mental or nervous equilibrium, often tending to produce sexual excesses, would be sure to find "vent" in so dangerous a custom, especially when sanctioned by the recognized doctrine of betrothal.

Finally it is not without interest to note that the higher legal significance of the "contraction," as compared with that of the English *sponsalia*, is due mainly to the influence of the Jewish law. The code of Moses mentions no fixed ceremonies for concluding marriage.[2] But precisely the same relation as by the Puritans is fixed between marriage and betrothal. For criminal assault upon the betrothed "damsel that is a virgin" and for adultery the death penalty is prescribed.[3] Later, however, the rabbinical law establishes "certain legal formalities for the act of concluding marriage. The act consisted of two distinct parts, intervened by the lapse of a certain time, the betrothment and the nuptials."[4] To constitute a legal betrothment the mere consent of the parties did not suffice. The performance of a solemn act was required. This consisted in the man's giving to his chosen bride in the presence of two witnesses either a written instrument, *sh'tar*, or a piece of money, *kaseph*, and saying: "Be thou consecrated (wedded) to me."[5] The contract thus made is not a "mere promise

---

[1] Adams, *op. cit.*, 31 ff., 34. Judd, *History of Hadley* (Northampton, 1863), 247, note, mentions Jonathan Edwards's sermon against bundling.

[2] Mielziner, *The Jewish Law of Marriage and Divorce*, 75.

[3] Deut. 20:7; 22:22-29.   [4] Mielziner, *op. cit.*, 75.

[5] *Ibid.*, 78. "As the formality of contracting marriage by money had in the Rabbinical Law merely a symbolical character, a coin of the least value (the *peruta*, the smallest used in Palestine), and even any other object representing such a value, could be used."— *Ibid.*, 79. The practice may have been derived from the Roman *coemptio*. "The rabbinical formality differs, however, from the Roman in this, that the act is done by the man only; *he* gives the money or its value, and *he* speaks the formula, while her consent is expressed by her silent acceptance of both. This passivity on her side is in consequence of the Talmudic principle based on the expression used in the Mosaic law: 'If A Man Taketh A Wife;' he takes and she *is* taken; he is the active and she the passive party."— *Talm. Kiddushin*, 2b and 3b: Mielziner, *op. cit.*, 78 n. 2. During the Middle Ages it became customary to use a plain ring instead of the piece of money: *ibid.*, 79, 80.

to marry," with civil consequences for non-fulfilment. "It is the very initiation of marriage. The betrothed parties are in some respects regarded as married, though not yet entitled to the marital rights nor bound to fulfil any of the mutual duties of conjugal life. . . . . The betrothment could be dissolved only through death or a formal bill of divorce." [1]

Among the Jews it was quite customary for the betrothal to be preceded by an "engagement," but it was not legally required.[2] The Puritan went farther in this regard, regulating proposal and courtship, as well as the pre-contract and nuptials, by statute.

V.   BREACH OF PROMISE AND MARRIAGE PORTIONS

The New England contraction or public betrothal, when its social and legal consequences are considered, is thus seen to be an institution of far more historical interest than the scanty attention it has hitherto received would lead one to infer. This is all the more apparent when the accompanying practice of legal courtship is kept in view. Never, perhaps, in any modern society has parental control been so pronounced. But if consent were once given and sealed by a contract in due form, it could not be lightly withdrawn. The early records abound in notices of suits for breach of promise. The colonists were a litigious people; and members even of some of the best families do not hesitate to drag their matrimonial difficulties into court. Sometimes a jilted lover sues his fickle sweetheart; or a forlorn maiden seeks satisfaction from her betrothed spouse. Thus the Massachusetts court "orders that Joyce Bradwicke shall giue unto Alex: Becke the some of xx^s, for promiseing him marriage wthout her ffrends consent, & nowe refuseing to

---

[1] Mielziner, *The Jewish Law of Marriage and Divorce*, 76.

[2] *Ibid.*, 77. "Since the third century it was regarded as improper to effect a betrothment without a previous engagement."—*Ibid.*, 77.

pforme the same."[1] Likewise in the Plymouth jurisdiction we find John Sutton complaining "against Mary Russell, in an action of the case, to the damage of two hundred pounds, for engageing herselfe to another by promise of marriage, whenas shee had engaged herselfe by promise of marriage vnto the said John before. The jury find for the plaintiffe fifteen pounds damage, and the cost of the suite which came to 1[lb] 10[s] 6[d]."[2] But this did not entirely end the matter. In 1662–63 the case was taken up for review, Mary having in the meantime become the wife of John Jacob. After a careful rehearing, the court reaches the curious decision that Mary's "actinges haue bine such . . . . as may not reflect vpon her disparagement, wee apprehending that what wrong hath bine vnto John Sutton heerin hath bine rather occationed by her father than by . . . . herselfe, shee haueing heard such thinges concerning the said Sutton as might justly discurrage her, although the truth of these reports wee see not cause to determine." Whereupon, oddly enough, it is decreed "that the abouesaid John Sutton doe pay vnto John Jacob . . . . the sume of fifty shillings."[3]

Sometimes a parent joins with his aggrieved child in seeking reparation; as when "Richard Siluester, in the behalfe of his daughter, and Dinah Siluester in the behalfe of herselfe" recover twenty pounds and costs from John Palmer, "for acteing fraudulently against the said Dinah, in not pforming his engagement to her in point of marriage."[4]

The proceedings of the Massachusetts courts contain the record of many similar suits under a variety of conditions. Some are ordinary cases of breach of promise.[5] In 1735 a woman was awarded two hundred pounds and costs at the

---

[1] *Mass. Col. Rec.*, I, 104. [2] *Plym. Col. Rec.*, VII, 101.
[3] *Ibid.*, 109. [4] *Ibid.*, 101.

[5] For examples see *MSS. Records of the County Court of Middlesex* (Apr. 2, 1661), I, 185; *MSS. Early Court Files of Suffolk* (1663), No. 573; *MSS. Records of the Superior Court of Judicature* (1725–29), fol. 333; *ibid.* (1725–30), fol. 338; *ibid.* (1730–33), fol. 196.

expense of her betrothed who after jilting her had married another, although he had first beguiled her into deeding him a piece of land "worth £100."[1]   Hopestill Aldrich in 1764 was not so successful.   The higher court on appeal declined to give her damage, because after beginning her action against the faithless Darius Daniels she had married David Bowin, "who is still living and is her lawful husband."[2]   A number of cases afford further evidence of the danger lurking in the New England doctrine of espousals, the indemnity sought being intended in part to punish personal wrongs committed under cover of pre-contract.[3]

Puritan lovers did not always hesitate to prosecute their parents for refusing marriage when permission had once been given.   Such was the fate of Hope Allen, who admitted before the Massachusetts court that "he did give his consent y^t ye said Mr. Deacon should haue his daughter;" and accordingly for breaking his word he was censured, and had to pay a fine of ten pounds for his "irregular procedure."[4] The action might take a still more interesting form, including both the recreant parents and the promised consort in the same complaint.   In this way Richard Sutton alleges "against Moses Symonds and Sarah, his wife, and Elizabeth theire daughter, that shee, the said Elizabeth, hath made a promise of marriage vnto him, and is hindered by the parents . . . . from proceeding with her therin."   The court after due consideration decides that Moses ought to pay the said Richard "the sume of three pounds, for satisfaction for his

[1] *Ibid.* (1735-36), fol. 243.

[2] Case of Daniels *v.* Bowin *et ux.*: *ibid.* (1764-65), fol. 4.

[3] Thus in 1686 John Row was sentenced for "committing folly with Martha Beale, then servant to his father, & publishing himself in marriage to her and now denying to accomplish the marriage." — *MSS. Records of the County Court of Middlesex*, IV, 218.   For other cases of this kind see *MSS. Records of the Superior Court of Judicature* (1730-31), fol. 1; *ibid.* (1745-46), fol. 253; *MSS. Early Court Files of Suffolk* (Nov. 19, 1663), No. 600.

[4] *Mass. Col. Rec.*, IV, Part II, 458.

time and charges spent about the pmises;" but not without kindly releasing the couple from their engagement,
"vnless on second considerations they shall see cause to renew theire former couenants."[1]

These illustrations would seem to show that the blighted
hopes and disappointed affections of New England lovers
were not judicially reckoned at an extortionate figure. But
those were the days of "small change" in all domestic affairs. As a matter of fact, the colonists were a close-fisted,
bargaining race;[2] and in no respect perhaps were they more
prudent than in their matrimonial transactions. Sometimes
very careful contracts were executed in court regarding the
property rights of the future husband and wife.[3] Often before betrothal and almost invariably before wedlock an exact
arrangement was made between the parents touching the
marriage portion on either side. The "higgling of dowries,"
suggests Weeden, was one of the most "singular practices"
of New England life.[4] Even paupers were provided a marriage portion at the county's charge.[5] No shrewder hand at

[1] *Plym. Col. Rec.*, V, 116.

[2] For many proofs of the niggardly economy and exceeding "nearness" of the
old New Englander see BLISS, *Colonial Times on Buzzard's Bay;* WEEDEN, *Ecc. and
Soc. Hist. of N. E.;* and especially the *Diary* and *Letter-Book* of SAMUEL SEWALL.

[3] An example is afforded by the *Plym. Col. Rec.*, IV, 163, where a stipulation is
entered into between a widow and a widower about to marry. By this agreement the
children are to remain "att the free and proper and onely dispose of theire owne
naturall parents, as they shall see good to dispose of them." The wife is to retain
"all her house and land goods & cattles, that shee is now possessed of, ... to dispose of them att her owne free will." If the husband die first, she is to have "one
third pte . . . . of his estate that hee dieth possessed of . . . . during her life;"
while in case of her death, the husband's property is to go to his heirs, "excepting
her wearing apparrell and her bed and bedding . . . . which shee shall and may
giue att her death to whom she pleaseth." For another such marriage agreement
see *MSS. Early Court Files of Suffolk* (1671), No. 1063. In the *MSS. Records of the
Superior Court of Common Pleas for Middlesex* (1707), I, 103, is a suit to recover a gift
made to a fiancée as legacy.

[4] WEEDEN, *Ecc. and Soc. Hist. of N. E.*, I, 413; *cf. ibid.*, I, 420, II, 541 ff.; also
EARLE, *Customs and Fashions*, 62 ff., 43 ff.

[5] Thus in 1638 "Mary Joanes was consented to be taken care of by the countrey,
and at the countreyes charge."—*Mass. Col. Rec.*, I, 230. Four years later "It was
ordered the Treasurer should give Mary Joanes five pounds against her Marriage."—
Ibid., II, 20.

a bargain existed than Judge Sewall, whose *Diary* and *Letter-Book* are crowded with illustrations of this and other matrimonial customs. In 1712 we find him planning a match between his daughter Mary and young Samuel Gerrish. So he dines with the father and "discourses" with him "about my Daughter Mary's Portion. I stood for making £550 doe: because now twas in six parts, the Land was not worth so much. He urg'd for £600. at last would split the £50. Finally Feb. 20. I agreed to charge the House Rent and Difference of Money, and make it up to £600."[1]

The worthy magistrate was not less thrifty in managing his own courtships, never for a moment allowing mere sentiment to get the better of prudence. From the outset he was lucky; for in 1676, according to tradition, he received as a dowry with his first wife, Hannah Hull, her weight in pine-tree shillings, which her father, the mint-master, measured out to him against her body in his own scales. In reality, his wife brought him much more than this fabled treasure; for six years after the wedding he came into the enjoyment of the mint-master's large estate, thus laying the foundation of his own fortune and official career.[2] Hannah lived with him more than forty years, bearing him seven sons and seven daughters. On her death the judge writes to a friend: "Wife expired on Satterday Oct. 19th, a little before Sun-Sett; and I lost my most constant lover, my most laborious Nurse; which produc'd a Flood of Tears in our Bed Chamber."[3]

[1] SEWALL, *Diary*, in 5 *Mass. Hist. Coll.*, VI, 336. In like spirit the judge "dickers" with Joseph Dudley, whose daughter had been sought in marriage for Samuel Sewall, Jr.: *idem, Letter-Book*, in 6 *Mass. Hist. Coll.*, I, 279-81; *Diary*, in 5 *Mass. Hist. Coll.*, VI, 80.

[2] "Her father died in six years, leaving his fortune, which was large for that time, to his daughter and his widow. It was practically one estate for the mother lived in the most affectionate intimacy in Judge Sewall's family."—WEEDEN, *Ecc. and Soc. Hist. of N. E.*, I, 420; *cf.* HAWTHORNE, *Grandfather's Chair* (Boston, 1893), chap. vi, 459-64.

[3] SEWALL's *Letter-Book*, in 6 *Mass. Hist. Coll.*, II, 83, 84 (letter of Jan. 25, 1718, referring to his wife's death in 1717) ; *cf.* the *Diary*, in 5 *Mass. Hist. Coll.*, VII, 143, 144.

Soon, however, he was able to stem the torrent of his grief, for on the sixth day of the next February he enters in his diary: "Wandering in my mind whether to lead a Single or a Married Life."[1] Indeed, several weeks before this, when his wife was hardly two months dead, his mind and feet had begun to wander in the direction of Madam Winthrop,[2] upon whom, in his usual kindly way, he had bestowed certain tokens of his regard.[3] But for the present the charms of Widow Winthrop had to yield to those of Widow Dennison, whose goodly estate he had come to admire through having drawn her husband's will.[4] Attending her home from the funeral of her late consort, he "prayed God to keep house with her."[5] This was in March. Presently he opens serious negotiations. He makes her numerous presents, among which are "A pound of Reasons and Proportionable Almonds;" a "Psalm-Book neatly bound in England with Turkey-Leather;" the "last two News Letters;" "Dr. Mathers Sermons very well bound," and "told her in it we were invited to a wedding;" a "pair of Shoe-buckles, cost 5s 3d;" and "Two cases with a Knife and a fork in each; one Turtle shell tackling: the other long with Ivory handles Squar'd, cost 4s 6d."[6] In November, after much visiting and chaffering, he came to the point. "I told her 'twas time now to finish our Business: Ask'd her what I should allow her; she not speaking; I told her I was willing to give Two [Hundred] and Fifty pounds per añum, during her life, if it should please God to take me out of this world before her. She answer'd she had better keep as she was, than give a Certainty for an uncertainty; she should pay dear for dwelling at Boston. I desired her

[1] SEWALL'S Diary, in 5 Mass. Hist. Coll., VII, 165.   [2] Ibid., 151, 163, 164.

[3] Feb. 3, 1718, he writes: "I sent Madam Winthrop, Smoking Flax Inflamed, the Jewish Children of Berlin, and my small vial of Tears."—Diary, in 5 Mass. Hist. Coll., VII, 164. On March 14 he sends her a copy of the Berlin Jewish Converts, ibid., VII, 177.

[4] Ibid., 177 (March 19, 1718), 180.

[5] Ibid., 178, 179 (March 26, 1718).   [6] Ibid., 182, 187, 188, 189, 190, 199.

to make proposals, but she made none. I had Thoughts of Publishment next Thorsday, the 6ᵗʰ. But I now seem far from it. May God, who has the pity of a Father, Direct and help me."[1]

This is by no means the end. The courtship drags along, and they continue to "higgle like hucksters and pedlers."[2] "She said she thought twas Hard to part with *All*, and have nothing to bestow on her Kindred. I said, I did not intend anything of the Movables, I intended all the personal Estate to be to her. She said I seem'd to be in hurry on Satterday . . . . which was the reason she gave me no proposals. Whereas I had ask'd her long before to give me proposals in Writing; and she upbraided me, That I who had never written her a Letter, should ask her to write." So the thrifty judge, although his "bowels" did "yern toward Mrs. Dennison," must even decide that God "in his Providence" directed him to "desist."[3] Later the widow grew more kind. On the following Lord's day she came to see him in the evening, walking all the way from Roxbury. She "ask'd pardon if she had affronted me;" and plainly let it be seen that she was not averse to the match, if only she were not called upon to "put all out of her Hand and power" and could "reserve something to bestow" on her deceased husband's friends "that might want." But, says Samuel, "I could not observe that she made me any offer of any part all this while." So "she went away in the bitter Cold, no Moon being up, to my great pain. I saluted her at parting."[4]

Then the judge turned to Widow Tilly, whom he married on the next Thanksgiving day (October 29, 1719), though she pleaded her "Unworthiness of such a thing with much

---

[1] *Ibid.*, 202 (Nov. 1, 1718).

[2] WEEDEN, *Ecc. and Soc. Hist. of N. E.*, II, 542.

[3] SEWALL, *loc. cit.*, 205 (Nov. 28, 1718).   [4] *Ibid.*, 206, 207 (Nov. 30, 1718).

Respect."[1] But the union was short-lived; for in May of
the next year "a very Extraordinary, awful Dispensation"
came to the Judge. "About midnight," he writes, "my dear
wife expired to our great astonishment, especially mine."[2]

Already by the following December he wants God to "yet
again provide such a good Wife for me, that I may be able
to say I have obtained Favour of the LORD."[3] For in the
meantime his mind has been "wandering" again toward
Catherine Winthrop. But the gentle widow is now very coy
and close at a bargain. After many visits and some interesting love passages,[4] the judge writes, she "was Courteous
to me; but took occasion to speak pretty earnestly about my
keeping a Coach: I said 'twould cost £100. per añum: she
said twould cost but £40."[5] Clearly the issue was getting
too sharply joined; and it is not wholly surprising that the
lady was a trifle cool at her suitor's next visit.[6] Later he
asked her "when our proceedings should be made publick:
She said they were like to be no more publick than they were
already. Offer'd me no Wine that I remember." She did
not offer to help him on with his coat, nor at his request
would she send her servant Juno to light him home.[7] It is
to be feared that Catherine had not forgiven her suitor for
leaving her for Widow Dennison, and was now getting
"even." But the judge stood manfully to his arms. At the
next meeting "I told her . . . . I was come to enquire
whether she could find in her heart to leave that House and

---

[1] *Ibid.*, 225, 232, 233.   [2] *Ibid.*, 255 (May 26, 1720).

[3] Letter of Dec. 13, 1720, to Alexander Dummer, in SEWALL'S *Letter-Book*, in 6
Mass. Hist. Coll., II, 122, 123.

[4] "Asked her to Acquit me of Rudeness if I drew off her Glove. Enquiring the
reason, I told her twas great odds between handling a dead Goat and a living Lady.
Got it off. . . . . Told her the reason why I came every other night was lest I should
drink too deep draughts of Pleasure. She had talked of Canary, her Kisses were to
me better than the best Canary."—SEWALL'S *Diary, loc. cit.*, 267.

[5] *Ibid.*, 269.   [6] *Ibid.*, 270.

[7] "I pray'd her that Juno might light me home, she open'd the shutter, and said
twas pretty light abroad; Juno was weary and gon to bed."—*Ibid.*, 271.

Neighborhood, and go and dwell with me at the South-end;
I think she said softly, Not yet. I told her it did not ly in
my Lands to keep a coach. . . . . Told her I had an Antipa-
thy against those who would pretend to give themselves;
but nothing of their Estate. I would [give] a proportion of
my Estate with my self. And I supos'd she would do so."[1]
It goes without saying that when Sewall made his next call
the lady was "not at home." After one or two more futile
efforts[2] at coming to terms the grapes began to sour. The
aged wooer somewhat spitefully closes this unlucky chapter
of his courtships with the ungallant remark that "I did not
bid her draw off her Glove as sometimes I had done. Her
dress was not so clean as sometimes it had been. Jehovah
jireh."[3] Thus Eros regained his sight.

Several other attempts prove not more successful in providing the venerable widower with a suitable place to rest
his "weary Head in Modesty."[4] But at last, humbly confessing himself, "aged, and feeble, and exhausted," he offers
himself as a husband to Mrs. Mary Gibbs, of Newton, who
is all too yielding in her reply.[5] For with this gentle dame
the astute wooer, erstwhile so meek, at once proceeds to drive
the sharpest bargain in the long history of his courtships.
As she had no property to leave him by will, he insists upon
the following harsh conditions: "I Rode to Newtown in the
Coach, and visited Mrs. Gibbs. Spake of the proposals I
had intimated per Mr. H. Gibbs; for her Sons to be bound
to save me harmless as to her Administration; and to pay
me £100. provided their Mother died before me: I to pay
her £50. per añum during her Life, if I left her a Widow.
She said 'twas hard, she knew not how to have her children
bound to pay that Sum; she might dye in a little time. Mr.

---

[1] SEWALL, *loc. cit.*, 272.   [2] *Ibid.*, 273, 274.   [3] *Ibid.*, 275.
[4] EARLE, *Customs and Fashions of Old New England.*
[5] SEWALL's *Diary, loc. cit.*, 299 (Jan. 12, 1722), 300.

Cotton, whom she call'd spake to the same purpose, spake of a Joynture. I said I was peremptory as to the indemnifying Bond; Offer'd to take up with that alone, and allow her forty pounds per aฬum."[1]

These terms, "hard" as they were and again insisted upon with most unromantic bluntness,[2] were at length accepted by the amiable Mary; who, surviving her kindly though grasping spouse, was no doubt by his side, according to his wish, to "carry it tenderly"[3] with him when he passed to his last reckoning.

VI. SELF-GIFTA, CLANDESTINE CONTRACTS, AND FORBIDDEN DEGREES

The Separatist and the Puritan, regarding marriage as "purely a civil contractual relation," logically conceded that "the parties may marry themselves as they may make other contracts." But, "like all other civil institutions, this may be regulated by municipal law. It should therefore be sanctioned by the civil authority;" and for that reason persons may be fined for marrying without observing the forms prescribed by the statutes.[4] Nevertheless such legal

---

[1] *Ibid.*, 300, 301.

[2] "Madam, These are kindly to salute you, and to say, that the Omission of Answering one or two of my Letters, and of coming to Town, makes it needful to enquire, what the plain meaning of your letter of Jany. 30th may be. 'I do chuse to comply with your last proposal, of Releasing my children, and Accepting of the sum you proposed.' The last Proposal was, For your children, or some in their behalf, to give Bond, to indemnify me from all debts contracted by you before the Marriage; and from all matters respecting the Administration. This I told you, I peremptorially insist on. I was to secure you Forty pounds per aฬum during the term of your natural Life, in case of your Survival. This proposal must be taken entirely, every part of it together, and if the words '*Releasing my Children*' intend a Releasing them from this Bond, my last Proposal is not accepted by you."—*Ibid.*, 303 (Feb. 10, 1722).

[3] The judge was almost tempted to bargain with his intended spouse for affectionate treatment. Speaking with "Mr. Dan Oliver," Feb. 2, 1722, he says: "Told, I hoped she was nat so Attached to her children, but that she would carry it Tenderly to me; or else there would soon be an end of an Old Man. I said, I suฬosed they would clothe her, Answered, no question; And would be Tender of me."—*Ibid.*, 302. On Sewall's courtships and New England wedding customs see HOWE, *The Puritan Republic*, chap. v, 111 ff.

[4] SHIRLEY, "Early Jurisprudence of New Hamp.," *Procds. New Hamp. Hist. Soc.* (1876-84), 307.

restraint, however wholesome and reasonable, seems to have been resented by the more radical as an interference with individual liberty; though doubtless the disregard of the marriage laws was in part due to the rudeness of an early society.

Instances of self-betrothal and self-*gifta* seem to have been frequent in all the New England colonies. Thus, in 1678, Edward Wanton was fined £10 by the general court of Plymouth for "marrying himself," and Thomas Boarman paid £5 for the same offense. In 1684 William Gifford was fined fifty shillings for contracting a "disorderly marriage."[1] More interesting is the case of Edward Perry, on Cape Cod, who appears to have been guilty of self-marriage in 1654. For this he was fined £5; and Thomas Tupper, of Sandwich, for neglecting to perform the ceremony, "was 'disallowed' by the court from solemnizing marriages in future."[2] Then "magistrate Prence, when passing by on his return from court to Eastham, was to marry him rightly. Perry refused to be re-married, and was fined £5 more, with the discouraging notice that his fine would be repeated every three months till he complied."[3]

Marriages by the primitive form of "hand-fasting" were not unknown in Massachusetts. An intelligent French refugee, who visited Boston two years after the revocation of the Edict of Nantes, writes that "there are those who practice no Formality of Marriage except joining Hands, and so live in Common."[4] But the most celebrated instance of self-*gifta* is the case of Governor Richard Bellingham, who in 1641 entered into a private marriage with Penelope Pelham, herself "about forming a contract with another."[5] "Two errors more," says Winthrop, "he committed upon it.

[1] For these cases see GOODWIN, *Pilgrim Republic*, 599.

[2] FREEMAN, *Hist. of Cape Cod*, I, 208.   [3] GOODWIN, *loc. cit.*

[4] SHURTLEFF, *Top. and Hist. Description of Boston*, 51.   [5] GOODWIN, *loc. cit.*

1. That he would not have his contract published where he dwelt, contrary to an order of court. 2. He married himself contrary to the constant practice of the country."[1] The governor was therefore indicted for his offense by the grand jury; but "he declined to leave his place on the bench" over which he presided, "in order to take a position in the dock, and thus 'escaped both trial and punishment.'"[2] The secretary "postponed the case amidst excitement, and it was not again called up."[3]

In spite of the constantly increasing severity of the penalties, clandestine marriages gave the lawmaker much trouble.[4] This is plainly revealed by the laws, already cited, relating to banns, consent, registration, and celebration,[5] especially by those of Rhode Island. The act of 1647 provides "that no contract or agreement between a Man and a Woman to owne each other as Man and Wife, shall be owned from henceforth threwout the Whole Colonie as a lawfull marriage, nor their Children or Issue so coming together to be legitimate or lawfullie begotten," but such as conform to the statute.[6] The clause relating to the issue of irregular

---

[1] WINTHROP, *Hist. of New England*, II, 51, 52. One might cheerfully forgive Governor Winthrop, had his sense of historical propriety suffered him to go farther into the details of the marriage customs. He apologizes parenthetically: "I would not mention such ordinary matters in our history, but by occasion of some remarkable accidents."

[2] MORSE, in *Mem. Hist. Bost.*, IV, 572. The *MSS. Records of the County Court of Middlesex* (Apr. 1, 1656), I, 80, contain the following case: "Mr. Joseph Hills being presented by the grand jury for marrying of himself contrary to the law of the Colony (page 38 of the old book); freely acknowledged his offence and his misunderstanding the grounds whereon he went, which he now confessed to be unwarrantable. Admonished by the court."

[3] GOODWIN, *loc. cit.* See further on Bellingham's marriage HILDRETH, *Hist. of U. S.*, I, 279; *Mem. Hist. Bost.*, I, 575.

[4] Complaints of clandestine marriages may be found in the New Hampshire records: see *Provincial Papers*, IV, 832; *New Hamp. Hist. Coll.*, VIII, 117, 118. There is an unsettled case of alleged clandestine marriage in the *MSS. Early Court Files of Suffolk* (March, 1699–1700), Nos. 4590, 4663.

[5] See *Conn. Col. Rec.*, I, 47, 48, 540; *New Haven Col. Rec.*, II, 599; and the Massachusetts laws relating to the districts of ministers and justices, mentioned above.

[6] *R. I. Col. Rec.*, I, 187; and STAPLES, *Proceedings of the First Assembly*, 47, 48.

marriages is noteworthy; for it is contrary to the usual tenor of the colonial laws, which—anticipating the policy of William III.—usually imposed severe penalties upon the offenders without affecting the legitimacy of the children. But even so stringent a remedy did not suffice. A new law in 1665 enforces that of 1647, adding the penalty prescribed for "fornication" for non-observance; but making the important exception in favor of existing irregular marriages "that any persons now living within the confines expressed in our late charter, ... that are reputed to live together as man and wife by the common observation or account of there neighbours before this act was passed, shall not come vnder any of the censures, fines, or penaltyes in any of the fore premised acts or orders, or in this present [order] concearning marriages," though "there may have been some neglect of the due observation of the rules and directions to that end therein contained."[1] It appears that "some persons" had "taken advantage of the law" to render the children of unregistered marriages illegitimate. An explanatory statute was therefore enacted in 1698 declaring such marriages lawful;[2] and in the subsequent legislation of this colony the lawmaker was content to punish the parties to irregular marriages without affecting the status of the offspring.[3]

The clergy of New England, and especially those of Massachusetts, were much agitated over the question of the degrees of relationship which should be prohibited in wedlock. Marriage of first cousins, by affinity as well as by blood, and with a deceased wife's sister was strongly opposed. That of cousins german had been legalized by a statute of Henry VIII. in 1540;[4] and the earliest fruit of this act was the

---

[1] *R. I. Col. Rec.*, II, 104.

[2] *Ibid.*, III, 361, 362; also in RIDER's reprint of the *Laws and Acts* (1705), 44.

[3] See the act of 1701: *R. I. Col. Rec.*, III, 435, 436. Compare RIDER's *Laws and Acts* (1705), 50; and his reprint of *Charter and Laws* (1719), 12, 13.

[4] By 32 H. VIII., cap. 38: *Statutes at Large* (London, 1763), II, 298; SEWALL's *Letter-Book*, in 6 *Mass. Hist. Coll.*, I, 351-53, 369, 370.

marriage of that monarch with Catherine Howard, first cousin of Ann Boleyn, his former wife.[1] Within less than two years thereafter Catherine lost her head; and Sewall, who like the Mathers regarded such marriages as incestuous, draws a grim moral from her fate.[2] Indeed, the Puritans, were in sore straits, fearing lest the "English Nation," while rejecting the excessive strictness of the Roman church in this regard, had gone "beyond the golden mean towards the other Extream."[3] In their anxiety to obey the Mosaic law they even exceeded its requirements.[4] Already in 1679 the general court, in reply to interrogation, had decided that marriage with a deceased wife's sister was unlawful,[5] thus taking the position which has been stubbornly maintained ever since by the English House of Lords.   Interest in the matter seems, however, to have culminated in 1695. In that year a meeting of the ministers of Boston, Charlestown, and Dorchester, with Increase Mather at their head, came to the same conclusion as the general court in 1679.[6] This led directly to the passage of the celebrated law against incestuous marriages of the following June,[7] by which the general

---

1 "The greatest good the Land got by this Match, was a general leave to marry Cousin Germans, formerly prohibited by the *Crown*, and hereafter permitted by the *Com̄on Law*. A door of lawfull liberty, left open by God in Scripture; shut by the Pope for his privat profit; opend again by the King, first, for his own admittance . . . and then for the service of such Subjects as would follow him." — FULLER, *English Worthies* (London, 1840), II, 352; SEWALL's *Letter-Book*, in 6 *Mass. Hist. Coll.*, I, 369. Compare his letter of Feb., 1603/4, in *op. cit.*, 290–93.

2 "They that will, from this Example, be fond of Marrying Cousin-Germans, Let 'em!" — *Ibid.*, II, 19.

3 *Ibid.*; *cf. ibid.*, I, 290–93, where Sewall opposes the marriage of his cousin John Sewall with the *widow* of the latter's cousin german; also *ibid.*, I, 17; and his *Diary*, in 5 *Mass. Hist. Coll.*, V, 96, 424, for further illustrations.

4 The Mosaic code does not clearly prohibit marriage with a *deceased* wife's sister: Lev., chaps. 18, 20; Deut., chaps. 23, 27. *Cf.* MIELZINER, *Jewish Law of Marriage and Divorce*, 31–40; and chap. xi, sec. ii, *b.*

5 WHITMORE, *Col. Laws of Mass.* (1672-86), 102; *Mass. Col. Rec.*, IV, Part II, 454.

6 They published the decision in a printed tract of eight pages: *The Answer of Several Ministers to that Case of Conscience whether it is Lawful for a man to Marry his Wife's own sister:* GODDARD, in *Mem. Hist. Bost.*, II, 415 n. 2.

7 "Friday, June 14. The Bill against Incest was passed with the Deputies, four and twenty Nos, and seven and twenty Yeas, The Ministers gave in their Arguments yesterday in Writing; else it had hardly gon, because several have married their

court, though not taking "in hand to determine what is the whole breadth of the divine commandment," proceeded, among other prohibitions, to forbid marriage with a wife's sister or niece.[1] For violation of the law, we have already seen, the culprit was condemned, as in the case of adultery, to wear the "scarlet letter."   This act[2] remained nominally in force until after the Revolution; but the statute of 1785 in which these prohibitions do not appear was adopted seemingly without discussion.[3]

The colonial laws on this subject were not allowed to slumber.   From the records of the Connecticut court of assistants, for instance, it appears that in May, 1694, Nathaniel Finch is complained of "for that he hath unlawfully married to Elizabeth Hemmeway," sister "of the said Finch his first wife."   The pleas of Finch's attorney are "esteemed to be insufficient, and also of an offensive nature."   Accordingly, having considered all the facts of the case, the "rules of God's word, the judgment of most able Divines, and the Laws of this colony," the court finds the "said marriage to be incestuous and unlawful," and therefore declares it "to be wholly null and void;" further relegating the case to the county court to be held at New Haven the next June, "to lay such punishment on the said Finch for his said offence as the nature thereof doth require."[4]

---

wives sisters, and the Deputies thought it hard to part them. 'Twas concluded on the other hand, that not to part them, were to make the Law abortive, by begetting in people a conceipt that such Marriages were not against the Law of God."—SEWALL, *Diary*, in 5 *Mass. Hist. Coll.*, V, 407; *cf.* MCKENZIE, in *Mem. Hist. Bost.*, II, 197.

1 But, on the other hand, marriage with a husband's brother or nephew is not expressly prohibited; *cf.* 5 *Mass. Hist. Coll.*, V, 407, note.

2 *Acts and Resolves*, I, 209; also *Charters and General Laws of Mass.*, 283. GODDARD, *Mem. Hist. Bost.*, II, 415 n. 2, is plainly in error when he says that this act "suggested the leading incident of HAWTHORNE's *Scarlet Letter*."   It probably originated in the similar law, already mentioned, for the punishment of adultery which is expressed in nearly the same words: see *Acts and Resolves*, I, 171.

3 5 *Mass. Hist. Coll.*, V, 407 n. 1.

4 *Historical Magazine and Notes and Queries*, II, 301.

While the Massachusetts act of 1695 does not expressly prohibit a woman from wedding her husband's brother, a passage in Sewall's *Diary* shows that such unions were already treated as unlawful. On December 25, 1691, he writes, the "marriage of Hana Owen with her Husband's brother, is declar'd null by the court of Assistants. She commanded not to entertain him; enjoin'd to make a confession at Braintrey before the Congregation on Lecture Day, or Sabbath, pay fees of court and prison," and "to be dismissed." [1]

VII. SLAVE MARRIAGES

Finally in this connection a word regarding the treatment of slave marriages in New England may not be wholly out of place. With respect to the morality of slavery and the slave trade as viewed by the Puritan the record is perfectly clear. He was no better and no worse than his contemporaries. In his eyes the commerce in human chattels, whether red, black, or white,[2] was as legitimate a business as the handling of West India molasses; though like the Spaniard he may sometimes have excused or extolled it as affording a field for missionary work. "The seventeenth century," observes Weeden, "organized the new western countries, and created an immense opportunity for labor. The eighteenth coolly and deliberately set Europe at the task of depopulating whole districts of Africa, and of transporting the captives, by a necessarily brutal, vicious, and horrible traffic, to the new civilizations of America. . . . . New England entered upon this long path of twisted

[1] SEWALL'S *Diary*, in 5 *Mass. Hist. Coll.*, V, 354. For the case see NOBLE's *Recs. of the Court of Assistants*, I, 361. Samuel Newton, of Marlborough, married his uncle's widow and had two children by her. This marriage was judged void "by the word of God, as also by the law of England ": *ibid.*, 342. *Cf.* COWLEY, *Our Divorce Courts*, 30, 31.

[2] On white slaves in New England, and elsewhere in America, see the valuable article of BUTLER, "British Convicts Shipped to American Colonies," *American Historical Review*, II, 12–33.

social development—the wanton destruction of barbaric
life in the hope of new civilized life, this perversion of the
force of the individual barbarian into an opportunity for
social mischief—with no more and no less consciousness
than prevailed elsewhere at that time. The Winthrops
and other Puritan colonists asked and received Indian
captives for slaves as freely as any partisan went for loot
or plunder." [1]

With respect to matrimonial rights nothing can be more
misleading than the self-gratulations of writers who have
treated colonial history from what Charles Francis Adams
has aptly called the "filio-pietistic" point of view. [2] Thus
in his early edition Bancroft, referring to the alleged miti-
gating character of Massachusetts legislation, securing to
the slave such protection "as the Hebrew scriptures seemed
to enjoin," declares that "this brought about a total modification of the character of negro slavery by giving to the
slave the rights of marriage and the family." [3] Palfrey goes
even farther in his zeal, solemnly assuring us that "from the
reverence entertained by the Fathers of New England for
the nuptial tie, it is safe to infer that slave husbands and
wives were never parted." [4] In like spirit statesmen, jurists,
and historians have reiterated the assertion that slavery was
not hereditary in Massachusetts. "In all her annals," says
Charles Sumner, "no person was ever born a slave" on her
soil; and if, in fact, "the issue of slaves was sometimes held
in bondage, it was never by sanction of any statute or law of
Colony or Commonwealth." [5] Similar statements are made

[1] WEEDEN, *Ecc. and Soc. Hist. of New England*, II, 449, 450. *Cf.* his entire discussion of the "African Slave Trade" in New England, *ibid.*, 449-72; and BANCROFT,
Hist. of U. S. (New York, 1888), II, 268-80.

[2] See his admirable *Massachusetts: Its History and Historians* (Boston, 1893).

[3] Compare MOORE's article "Slave Marriages in Mass.," in DAWSON's *Hist. Mag.*,
2d series, V (Feb., 1869), 135, to which I am much indebted.

[4] PALFREY, *Hist. of New England*, II, 30, note; *cf.* MOORE, *loc. cit.*, 135-37.

[5] SUMNER, in his speech in the Senate, June 28, 1854: *Works*, III, 384.

by Hurd, Washburn, and Belknap.[1] Justice Gray declares
that "previously to the adoption of the State Constitution
in 1780 negro slavery existed to some extent, and negroes
held as slaves might be sold, but all children of slaves were
by law free."[2] The unsupported dictum of Palfrey is
equally confident. "In fact," he says, "no person was ever
born in legal slavery in Massachusetts."[3]

Since the appearance of Moore's able monograph it is
perhaps needless to explain that the facts are against these
comfortable theories. Slavery was authorized by statute in
Massachusetts under sanction of the Mosaic law; and so the
children of slave mothers were also slaves.[4] The evils of the

---

[1] According to HURD, *Law of Freedom and Bondage*, I, 225, " the involuntary
servitude of Indians and negroes in the several colonies originated under a law not
promulgated by legislation, and rested upon the prevalent views of universal jurisprudence, or of the *law of nations*, supported by the express or implied authority of
the home Government." Compare WASHBURN, "The Extinction of Slavery in Mass.,"
4 *Mass. Hist. Coll.* (1857), IV, 333–46; the same in *Procds. Mass. Hist. Soc.* (1855–58),
188 ff.; and BELKNAP'S answer to TUCKER'S *Queries* (1795), in 1 *Mass. Hist. Coll.*, IV,
191–211, which on the points under consideration is very superficial and misleading.

[2] See Justice Gray's note to the case of Oliver *v.* Sale: *Quincy's Reports*, 29. The
authorities there cited are misleading and do not establish the assertions quoted.
The well-known apology for Massachusetts slavery by NATHAN DANE in his *Abridgment*, II, 413, 426, 427, is equally unsupported by the facts. The same view as that of
Gray is taken by Chief Justice Dana in Littleton *v.* Tuttle (1796): 4 *Mass. Reports*, 128,
note; by Chief Justice Shaw in Commonwealth *v.* Aves: 18 *Pickering's Reports*, 208,
209; and it is repeated in *Cushing's Reports*, 410. On the other hand, in Winchendon
v. Hatfield: 4 *Mass. Reports* (1806), 123, Chief Justice Parsons correctly says "slavery
was introduced " in Massachusetts "soon after its first settlement, and was tolerated until the ratification of the present constitution " in 1780. "The issue of the
female slave, according to the maxim of the civil law, was the property of her master." The same opinion is held in Perkins, Town Treasurer of Topsfield *v.* Emerson
(1799): DANE'S *Abridgment*, II, 412; and by Chief Justice Parker in Andover *v.* Canton
(1816): 13 *Mass. Reports*, 551, 552. In 1865 the errors of Gray, Dane, Webster, and
others were fully exposed by MOORE, *Notes on the History of Slavery in Mass.*, 10 ff.,
22 ff., 94 ff., 98 ff.; yet it is curious to see BISHOP, *Marriage, Divorce, and Separation*
(Chicago, 1891), I, 179 n.1, 282, still accepting Gray's dictum as authority.

[3] PALFREY, *Hist. of New England*, II, 30, note.

[4] Compare sec. 91 of the " Body of Liberties," upon which the apologists have
mainly rested their case, with the later version of the provision: WHITMORE, *Col.
Laws of Mass.* (1660–72), 53, 125; *ibid.* (1672–86), 10; and read MOORE'S convincing
argument as to the significance of the altered wording: *Notes on the Hist. of Slavery
in Mass.*, 10–18. For Connecticut see FOWLER, " The Historical Status of the Negro,"
in DAWSON'S *Hist. Mag.*, 3d series, III, 12–18, 81–85, 148–53, 260–66; STEINER, "Hist. of
Slavery in Conn.," *J. H. U. S.*, XI, 371–452; and HURD, *Law of Freedom and Bondage*,
I, 267 ff.

institution may, indeed, have been somewhat mitigated by
the simple industrial conditions which then prevailed. The
climate and soil were ill suited to slave labor. Occasionally
there may have been a mind far enough ahead of the age to
perceive dimly the social danger lurking in the system.
Almost the only clear voice raised against it is that of
Samuel Sewall,[1] whose practice nevertheless was not always
consistent with his doctrine.[2] Mixture of race was not
favored. But not until 1705 was intermarriage between a
white person and a negro or mulatto forbidden by statute.[3]
Through Sewall's influence the prohibition was not then
extended to Indians;[4] and he succeeded in having a clause
retained in the act enjoining that "no master shall unreasonably deny marriage to his negro with one of the same
nation."[5] A passage in his diary shows that the laws relat-

[1] In 1700 Sewall, then a judge of the superior court, wrote an anti-slavery tract
entitled *The Selling of Joseph.* It is reprinted in the *Procds. Mass. Hist. Soc.*
(1863–64), 161–65; with the *Diary* in 5 *Mass. Hist. Coll.*, VI, 16–20, note; and in MOORE,
Notes on Hist. of Slavery in Mass., 83–87. The next year JOHN SAFFIN, a judge of the
same court, replied to Sewall in *A Brief and Candid Answer* (Boston, 1701); reprinted by MOORE, *op. cit.*, 251–56. Compare SEWALL's letter *To the Revd. & aged
Mr. John Higginson* (Apr. 13, 1706), and his extract from the *Athenian Oracle*, II,
460–63, both reprinted by MOORE, *op. cit.*, 89–94. Sewall favored a law requiring
"that all importers of Negroes shall pay 40 shillings per head to discourage the
bringing of them." *Cf.* BLISS, *Side Glimpses from the Col. Meeting-House*, 21;
WEEDEN, *Ecc. and Soc. Hist.*, II, 450.

[2] According to Bliss, "as time passed on and the slave trade flourished,"
Sewall "must have dismissed his anti-slavery opinions;" for the following adver-
tisement appears in the Boston *News-Letter* of June 23, 1726: "To be sold by Mr.
Samuel Sewall at his House in the Common, Boston, several likely young Negro
Men & Boys Just Arrived."—*Side Glimpses from the Col. Meeting-House*, 21.

[3] "An Act for the better preventing of a spurious and mixt issue" (Dec. 5, 1705):
Acts and Resolves, I, 578, 579; *Charters and Gen. Laws*, Appendix, 748: "Be it enacted
. . . . that none of her majesty's English or Scottish Subjects, nor of any other
Christian nation within this province, shall contract matrimony with any Negro or
Molatto: nor shall any . . . . presume to join any such in Marriage, on pain of for-
feiting . . . . *fifty pounds.*"

[4] By the act of 1786 intermarriage of whites with Indians, negroes, and mulattoes is forbidden.

[5] Of the bill for the act of 1705 SEWALL writes: "Deputies send in a Bill against
fornication or Marriage of White men with Negros or Indians; with extraordinary
penalties. . . . . If it be pass'd, I fear twill be an Opression provoking to God, and
that which will promote Murders and other Abominations. I have got the Indians
out of the Bill, and some mitigation for them [the Negroes] left in it, and the clause
about their Masters not denying their Marriage." *Diary:* in 5 *Mass. Hist. Coll.*,
VI, 143.

ing to banns, as also, it is safe to infer, those regarding celebration and registration, were applied in the case of such unions; while at the same time we are given a pleasing picture of the humane treatment which slaves sometimes received from their masters. On September 26, 1700, he records that "Mr. John Wait and Eunice his Wife, and Mrs. Debora Thair come to Speak to me about the Marriage of Sebastian, Negro Servt of said Wait, with Jane, Negro Servt of said Thair. Mr. Wait desired they might be published in order to Marriage. Mrs. Thair insisted that Sebastian might have one day in six allow'd him for the support of Jane, his intended wife and her children, if it should please God to give her any. Mr. Wait now wholly declin'd that, but freely offer'd to allow Bastian Five pounds, in Money p̄ añum towards the Sup̄ort of his children p̄ said Jane (besides Sabastians cloathing and Diet). I persuaded Jane and Mrs. Thair to agree to it, and so it was concluded; and Mrs. Thair gave up the Note of Publication to Mr. Wait for him to carry it to Wm Griggs, the Town Clerk, and to Williams in order to have them published according to law."[1]

Examples of such kindly usage were doubtless not uncommon among New England slave-owners, just as they were often found at all times in the South. But it is vain to apologize for a system, wicked and corrupting in itself, on the ground of individual benevolence or of laws which inconsistently in certain particulars seem to recognize the spiritual and social equality of human chattels. In a com-

[1] *Ibid.*, 22. The *MSS. Records of the General Sessions of Suffolk* (Jan. 30, 1709–10) contain the following evidence: "Upon reading the Petition of Jack Negroman Servant . . . . relating to his . . . . being Married to Esther a Negro Woman Servant [to another master] . . . . Ordered that [he] . . . . be not denyed marriage provided he attend the Directions of the law for the Regulation of Marriages." Compare "Flora's case" (1758) in *MSS. Records of the Superior Court of Judicature* (1757–59), 295, where the court held that the child of a female slave "never married according to any of the Forms prescribed by the Laws of this Land," by a person supposed also to be a slave, was not a bastard. From this decision it is argued that in Massachusetts all actual marriages were deemed good without any formal solemnization or the presence of priest or magistrate. *Cf.* BISHOP, *Mar., Div., and Sep.*, I, 179.

munity where a black man or woman for sexual misconduct with a member of the favored race was condemned by statute to be sold into another province;[1] where Indian prisoners were divided among the captors, and sold as legitimate spoil;[2] where African fathers and mothers, bought on their native soil for watered rum with short measure, were shipped across the ocean in stifling death-traps,[3] to be "knocked down" from the auction block to the highest bidder,[4] it seems rather more than absurd to assume that under the benign influence of Puritan religion and morality slave wives and husbands were never parted through the lust or greed of their owners. Nor in general was the alleged hope of converting the "benighted heathen to enjoy the blessings of a Gospel dispensation" more than a soothing balm to quiet the incipient throes of a rudimentary conscience in this regard.[5] Nay, in New England as elsewhere, the Christianizing of the blacks was sometimes actually discouraged, lest it should put in jeopardy the white man's property in them. During the seventeenth and eighteenth centuries a typical "case of conscience" arose. Would not the baptism of a slave in effect be a dangerous admission of his spiritual equality with the master? "Could

---

[1] By the act of 1705 already cited: *Acts and Resolves*, I, 578.

[2] So in the Pequot War: 4 *Mass. Hist. Coll.*, III, 360; in King Philip's War; and by the *Articles of Confederation* (1643), in *Plymouth Col. Rec.*, IX, 4. Compare MOORE, *Notes on Hist. of Slavery in Mass.*, 1–10, 30–40.

[3] For an interesting discussion of this point see BLISS'S chapter on "Rum and Slavery," *Side-Glimpses from the Col. Meeting-House*, 12 ff.; and WEEDEN, *Ecc. and Soc. Hist.*, II, 449–72. Such men as Peter Faneuil and Thomas Amory, of Boston, were "deep" in the rum and slavery business: BLISS, *op. cit.*, 15.

[4] For examples of advertisements of slave auctions in New England see BLISS, *op. cit.*, 15–19.

[5] "A deacon of the church at Newport esteemed the slave trade with its rum accessories as home missionary work. It is said that on the first Sunday after the arrival of his slaves he was accustomed to offer thanks ' that an overruling Providence had been pleased to bring to this land of freedom another cargo of benighted heathen to enjoy the blessings of a Gospel dispensation.'" — BLISS, *op. cit.*, 22. In general on the slave trade as missionary work see FROUDE, *History of England*, VIII, 439.

an intelligent being, who, through the Mediator, had participated in the spirit of God, and by his own inward experience had become conscious of a Supreme Being, and of relations between that Being and humanity be rightfully held in bondage? From New England to Carolina, the 'notion' prevailed that 'being baptized is inconsistent with the state of slavery;' and this early apprehension proved an obstacle to the 'conversion of these poor people.' The sentiment was so deep and so general that South Carolina in 1712, Maryland in 1715, Virginia repeatedly from 1667 to 1748, set forth by special enactments that baptism did not confer freedom." [1]

Naturally the Puritan was deeply exercised by the same scruples. He sorely dreaded lest through extending the means of grace to his serf Christ should inadvertently be put "in bondage." But he solved the problem in the same way as his southern brother—at the expense of the bondman. In Massachusetts as in Rhode Island slavery was consecrated "without regard to the religion of the slave." [2] Accordingly in 1696 "the ministers of Boston" submitted to the general court "That yᵉ wel-knowne Discouragemᵗ upon yᵉ endeavours of masters to Christianize their slaves, may be removed by a Law which may take away all pretext to Release from just servitude, by receiving of Baptisme." But to the credit of the court, we are told, "this proposal was not noticed." [3] Over forty years later a different result was reached by the clergy of Connecticut. At a meeting of the General Association for that colony in 1738, "It was

[1] BANCROFT, *Hist. of U. S.* (New York, 1888), II, 275, 276. On this subject see BRUCE, *Economic Hist. of Virginia*, II, 94-98; the discussion by FISKE, *Old Virginia and Her Neighbors*, I, 16; II, 192-94; and GOODWIN, *The Colonial Cavalier*, 178, who says: "Baptism was permitted to the slave, but with the distinct understanding that it was to make no difference in the condition of bondage of these brothers in Christ." The Virginia law of 1667 will be found in HENING, *Statutes*, II, 260.

[2] It was consecrated "sans égard à la religion de l'esclave": CARLIER, *Histoire du peuple américain*, I, 364; *cf.* also HILDRETH, *Hist. of U. S.*, I, 372.

[3] BLISS, *op cit.*, 92.

inquired — whether the infant slaves of Christian masters may be baptized in the right of their masters — they solemnly promising to train them in the nurture and admonition of the Lord: and whether it is the *duty* of such masters to offer such children and thus religiously to promise. Both questions were affirmatively answered."[1] Thus the negro of Connecticut was admitted to the covenant of grace without jeopardizing his owner's chattel interest in his body.

The attitude of Massachusetts slave-owners on this problem is revealed in Sewall's "question" from the *Athenian Oracle*: "What then should hinder but these be *Baptized?* If only the Covetousness of their Masters, who for fear of losing their Bodies, will venture their Souls ; which of the two are we to esteem the greater *Heathens?* Now that this is notorious Matter of Fact, that they are so far from persuading those poor Creatures to Come to *Baptism*, that they discourage them from it, and rather hinder them as much as possible, though many of the wretches, as we have been informed, earnestly desire it ; this we believe, none that are concern'd in the Plantations, if they are ingenuous, will deny, but own they don't at all care to have them Baptized. Talk to a *Planter* of the *Soul* of a *Negro*, and he'll be apt to tell ye (or at least his *Actions* speak it loudly) that the Body of one of them may be worth twenty Pounds ; but the Souls of an hundred of them would not yield him one Farthing ; and therefore he's not at all solicitous about them, though the true Reason is indeed, because of that Custom of giving them their Freedom, after turning Christians." Whether this custom be "reasonable" the writer doubts ; for neither the "Father of the *Faithful*" nor St. Paul commands masters to liberate their slaves and

[1] Taken from MOORE, *Notes on Hist. of Slavery in Mass.*, 92, note, who cites *Records as Reported by Rev. C. Chapin, D.D., Quoted in Jones's Religious Instruction of the Negroes*, 34. *Cf.* STEINER, "Hist. of Slavery in Conn.," *J. H. U. S.*, XI, 386.

Christianity does not "alter any *Civil Right*." In the "mean time, if there be such a Law or Custom for their *Freedom*, to encourage 'em to Christianity, be it reasonable or otherwise, this is certain, that none can excuse those who for that Reason should in any way hinder or discourage 'em from being Christians; some of whose excuses are almost too shameful to repeat, since they seem to reflect on the Christian Religion, as if that made Men more untractable and ungovernable, than when bred in Ignorance and Heathenism." [1]

Much of the same casuistry is manifested in dealing with the question of slave marriages. A bondman might be made amenable to the law of banns and celebration; but his continued enjoyment of marital rights and family life was absolutely precarious. As Moore suggests, the proviso of the act of 1705 forbidding the "unreasonable denial of marriage to negroes is very interesting. Legislation against the arbitrary exercise and abuse of authority proves its existence and the previous practice." [2] Besides, the adoption of that law was prompted perhaps as much by self-interest as by regard for morality. It was in effect a prudent police ordinance. Masters were liable for the legal fines imposed on their slaves for sexual offenses. It might be cheaper and less troublesome to allow orderly wedlock. "Moreover it is too well known," writes Sewall, "what Temptations Masters are under, to connive at the Fornication of their Slaves; lest they should be obliged to find them Wives, or pay their Fines. It seems to be practically pleaded that they might be Lawless; 'tis thought much of, that the Law should have satisfaction for their Thefts, and other Immoralities; by which means, *Holiness to the Lord* is more rarely engraven upon this sort of servitude. It is likewise

---

[1] *Athenian Oracle*, II, 460-63 : in MOORE, *Notes on Hist. of Slavery in Mass.*, 93, 94.

[2] MOORE, *op. cit.*, 55.

most lamentable to think, how in taking Negroes out of *Africa*, and selling of them here, That which God has joined together, men do boldly rend asunder ; Men from their Country, Husbands from their Wives, Parents from their Children.   How horrible is the Uncleanness, Mortality, if not Murder, that the ships are guilty of that bring great Crouds of these miserable Men and Women.   Methinks when we are bemoaning the barbarous Usage of our Friends and Kinsfolk in *Africa* : it might not be unreasonable to enquire whether we are not culpable in forcing the *Africans* to become Slaves amongst ourselves."[1]

For another reason families were in constant danger of being separated.   The breeding of slaves was not generally regarded as convenient or profitable in New England. According to Belknap, "negro children were considered an incumbrance in a family ; and when weaned, were given away like puppies," and they were "publickly advertised in the news-papers" to be so disposed of.[2]

That there was something grotesque in using the solemn ritual of the church in the marriage of slaves was faintly realized.   In 1748 Rev. Noah Hobart "challenged the want of flexibility in the forms of the Liturgy of the Church of England, as tending 'to introduce irreligion and profaneness'— especially in the use of the office of Matrimony for marriages contracted between slaves."   The use of the phrase "with all my worldly goods I thee endow, in the name of the Father, and of the Son, and of the Holy Ghost" he regarded as particularly sacrilegious, although the prayers employed by the Congregational minister at slave weddings were equally profane.[3]

---

[1] SEWALL, *The Selling of Joseph:* in 5 *Mass. Hist. Coll.*, VI, 17, 18.

[2] BELKNAP's answer to TUCKER's *Queries:* in 1 *Mass. Hist. Coll.*, IV, 200 ; *cf.* MOORE, *Notes on Hist. of Slavery in Mass.*, 57.

[3] MOORE, *Slave Marriages in Mass.*: DAWSON's *Hist. Mag.*, 2d series, V, 136, reprinting HOBART's *Serious Address to the Episcopal Separation in New England*

In at least one instance a sufficiently flexible special ritual was composed which very frankly discloses the idea of its author, and probably also that of a majority of his brethren, as to the real character of a slave marriage. According to Moore, it was discovered at Northampton, N. H., in 1868, by Mr. J. Wingate Thornton; and it was prepared and used by Rev. Samuel Phillips, of Andover, Mass., whose ministry there, beginning in 1710 and ending with his death in 1771, was a prolonged and eminently distinguished service of more than half of the eighteenth century." This "Form of a Negro-Marriage" is a decidedly safe and practical service from the master's point of view. The minister says:

"You S: do now in the Presence of God, and these Witnesses, Take R: to be your *Wife;* Promising that so far as shall be consistent with ye Relation wch you now sustain, as a Servant, you will Perform ye Part of an *Husband* towards her; And in particular, you Promise, that you will *Love* her: And that, as you shall have ye Opport^{ty} & Ability, you will take a proper *Care* of her in Sickness and Health, in Prosperity & Adversity: And that you will be True & *Faithfull* to her, and will Cleave to her *only, so long* as God, in his Provd^{ce}, shall continue your and her abode in Such Place (or Places) as that you can conveniently come together." Similar words are repeated to the woman ; and when each in turn has sealed this unique troth-plight, the minister continues: "I then agreeable to your Request, and wth ye Consent of your Masters & Mistresses, do Declare, that you have Licence given you to be conversant and familiar together, as *Husband and Wife,* so long as God shall continue your Places of abode as aforesaid ; and so

(1748), 77, 78; and quoting in reply DR. JOHN BEACH's *Calm and Dispassionate Vindication*, 39, who in logic characteristic of the age argues in " substance that as a Slave was capable of being made free, and so of having property in a large estate, there was no profaneness " in the use of the phrase mentioned.

long as you shall behave your-selves as it becometh Servants
to doe :   For you must, both of you, bear in mind, that you
Remain Still as really and truly as ever, your Master's
Property, and therefore it will be justly expected, both by
God and Man, that you behave and conduct your-selves, as
Obedient and faithfull Servants towards your respective
Masters & Mistresses for the Time being."[1]

Through this ingenious device, it is clear, the permanence
of the slave's nuptial bond, with all his connubial and
family rights, was made absolutely dependent upon his
owner's will.

[1] "And finally," continues the minister, " I exhort & charge you to beware lest
you give place to the Devil, so as to take Occasion from the Licence now given you,
to be lifted up with *Pride*, and thereby fall under the Displeasure, not of Man only,
but of God also; for, it is written, that God resisteth the Proud, but he giveth Grace to
the humble.

" I shall now conclude w[th] *Prayer* for you, that you may become good Christians,
and that you may be enabled to conduct as such; and in partic[r], that you may have
Grace to behave suitably towards each Other, as also dutifully towards your Masters
& Mistresses, not wth Eye-Service, as Men-pleasers, but as y[e] serv[ts] of Chr[t], doing
y[e] will of God from y[e] heart."   Published by MOORE, *Slave Marriages in Mass.:* in
DAWSON'S *Hist. Mag.*, 2d series, V, 137.

CHAPTER XIII

ECCLESIASTICAL RITES AND THE RISE OF CIVIL MARRIAGE IN THE SOUTHERN COLONIES

[BIBLIOGRAPHICAL NOTE XIII.—For Virginia the chief materials have been drawn from Hening's *Statutes at Large* (Richmond, 1809–23), and the laws comprised in *Acts of the Assembly* (fol., Williamsburg, 1769). The third volume of O'Callaghan, *Documents Rel. to the Col. History of New York*, has an interesting memorial of the bishop of London written in 1677; and there are some references to marriage in Strachey, *For the Colony in Virginea Britannea: Lawes Diuine, Morall, and Martiall*, being "Dale's Code" (London, 1612): in Force, *Tracts*, III; Spotswood, *Letters*, constituting Vols. I and II, new series, of the *Collections of the Va. Hist. Soc.* (Richmond, 1882–85); Beverley, *History of Virginia* (reprint, Richmond, 1855); and the acts of the assembly of 1619 contained in the *Colonial Records of Virginia* (Richmond, 1874). Cooke, *Virginia* (Boston, 1884), gives a curious proclamation of Governor Wyatt for the regulation of courtship. In Vol. IV of the *Va. Magazine of Hist. and Biog.* (Richmond, July, 1896) there is a unique "Marriage Agreement" which throws some light on the economic affairs of the provincial household; and further illustrations of domestic and social customs may be found in Goodwin, *The Colonial Cavalier* (Boston, 1895); and Fiske, *Old Virginia and Her Neighbors* (Boston, 1898).

The principal sources for Maryland are Browne, *Archives of Maryland* (Baltimore, 1883–91); Bacon, *Laws of Maryland* (fol., Annapolis, 1765); and, to supplement these, the *Laws of Maryland made since 1763* (fol., Annapolis, 1777); or the same (fol., Annapolis, 1787). Streeter, "Papers Rel. to the Early Hist. of Maryland," in *Md. Hist. Soc. Publications* (Baltimore, 1876), publishes a record of the first wedding in the colony, with the marriage license bond. The matrimonial doctrines of the Labadists are discussed by James, "The Labadist Colony in Maryland," in *J. H. U. S.*, XVII (Baltimore, 1899); and the character of the episcopal clergy is described by Browne, *Maryland* (Boston, 1884), and by Lodge, *Short History* (New York, 1882).

On this subject, as on most topics for the period, the extremely valuable *Colonial Records of North Carolina* (Raleigh, 1886–90) are a mine of information; and they are enriched by Colonel Saunders's "Prefatory Notes." The first matrimonial statute, passed by the assembly of Albemarle in 1669, is also contained in Chalmers, *Political Annals:*

in Carroll, *Hist. Coll. of South Carolina* (New York, 1836); and in Hawks, *History of North Carolina* (Fayetteville, 1857–58), likewise of service on other points.   The various statutes of the eighteenth century may be consulted in Iredell-Martin's *Public Acts of the Gen. Assembly* (Newbern, 1804); in Swan's *Revisal* (ed. 1752); or Davis's *Revisal* (ed. 1773).   Similar collections of laws for South Carolina are Cooper and McCord's *Statutes at Large* (Columbia, 1837–41), and Brevard's *Alphabetical Digest* (Charleston, 1814)—both of which contain useful editorial notes.   Constitutional provisions are, of course, found in Poore, *Charters* (Washington, 1877).   The works of Friedberg and the *Atlantic* article of Cook, elsewhere mentioned, are still of service; and Weeks in his valuable monograph, "Church and State in North Carolina," in *J. H. U. S.*, XI (Baltimore, 1893), has traced from the sources the struggle of the Presbyterian with the Episcopalian government party for the privilege of using their own rites in the celebration of marriage.]

I.   THE RELIGIOUS CEREMONY AND LAY ADMINISTRATION IN
VIRGINIA

THROUGHOUT the colonial period in Virginia the religious marriage ceremony, according to the rites of the Church of England, was prescribed by law.   Indeed, it was not until 1794 that the lay celebration before a magistrate was permitted, and then only in certain exceptional cases.   But in two important particulars, even in the earliest statutes, there is a remarkable advance upon the custom of the mother-country.   In the first place, it is noteworthy that the administration of matrimonial law is gradually intrusted to the county officers and the local courts.   Here, as in New England, there is a quickening of the forces of local self-government; and the lay tribunals gained important functions which in England belonged to the ecclesiastical courts.   Again, the legislation of 1631–32 embodies the essential principles of the Hardwicke act of 1753.   The institution of marriage begins to be protected and defined by careful statutory provisions and is no longer left to the perils of uncertain custom.   Banns or license, parental consent, certificate, and registration are all soon introduced.   Marriage becomes in effect a civil contract long before it is squarely acknowledged to be such by the law.

The brief act of 7 Charles I., 1632, provides that "no mynister shall celebrate matrimony betweene any persons without a facultie or lycense graunted by the Governor, except the baynes of matrimony have beene first published three severall Sundays or holydays in the time of devyne service in the parish churches where the sayd persons dwell, accordinge to the booke of common prayer." The minister is forbidden to "ioyne any persons soe licensed in marriage at any unreasonable tymes, but only betweene the howers of eight and twelve in the forenoone." If the marriage is after publication of banns without license, and the persons are under twenty-one years of age, the consent of parents is required before legal celebration.[1] It was also enacted that all marriages should be solemnized in church "except in case of necessity."[2]

The act of 1632 determined the broad outline of the marriage law of Virginia until after the Revolution. But two or three important modifications were made by subsequent legislation. Thus, an act of the Commonwealth period, 1657–58, enforces the provision that "ministers only shall celebrate marriages;" and significantly adds that they shall not do so without license or publication of banns "as formerly," under a penalty of "tenne thousand pounds of tobacco to ease the leavye of that county." No license is to be granted "without certificate vnder the hands of the parents, masters, or guardians of the parties to be married."[3] Again, the first act of the Restoration, 1661–62, requires license or "thrice publication according to the prescription

[1] HENING, *Statutes*, I, 156, 157. See also the act of 8 Chas. I., expressed in about the same terms, *ibid.*, 181.

[2] *Ibid.*, 158, 183.

[3] *Ibid.*, 433. By the act of 1646 the penalty for celebration without license or banns was 1,000 pounds of tobacco: *ibid.*, 332.

of the rubric in the common prayer booke, which injoynes that if the persons to be marryed dwell in severall parishes the banes must be asked in both parishes, and that the curate of one parish shall not solemnize the matrimony untill he have a certificate from the curate of the other parish, that the banes have been there thrice published, and noe objection made" to the union. For violation of the law by the minister the penalty of 1657–58 is retained. But this statute goes farther and declares that "any pretended marriage *hereafter* made by any other then a minister" shall be "reputed null, and the children borne out of such marriage of the parents" shall be "esteemed illegitimate and the parents suffer such punishment as by the laws prohibiting fornication ought to be inflicted."[1] This act of the Restoration, like that of the Duke of York, 1665, was probably invalid as transcending the requirements of the English common law.[2] In part it may have been intended to punish violation of the marriage law by dissenters, and its severity must have been keenly felt. At any rate, it was repealed in 1696 and replaced by an "act for the prevention of clandestine marriages." The preamble recites that "many great and grievous mischeifes have arisen and dayly doe arise by clandestine and secret marriages to the utter ruin of many heirs and heiresses," and that "the laws now in force . . . . do inflict too small a punishment for so heinous and great an offence." The minister guilty of violating the provision for banns or license, which is re-enacted, is to suffer imprisonment "for one whole year without bayle or mainprize and shall forfeitt and pay the sume of five hundred pounds currant money, one moyety thereof to our sovereign lord the king, ... and the other moyety to him or them that shall

---

[1] *Ibid.*, II, 49–51. By the law of 1788 the issue of even "incestuous" marriages are made legitimate: *ibid.*, XII, 689.

[2] See chap. xiv, i, *b*), below.

sue or informe for the same." No licenses are to be granted without a certificate from the clerk of the county court; and the certificate may not be issued by the clerk without the consent of the parent or guardian given in person or by writing attested by two witnesses, under penalty of a year's imprisonment and the payment of a fine of five hundred pounds current money. The clause of the preceding act making the issue of irregular marriages illegitimate is not repeated in this act or subsequently — an admission, seemingly, that the provision was originally null and void. But a female between the ages of twelve and sixteen contracting such a marriage forfeits during coverture her inheritance to the next of kin. After the death of her husband the inheritance reverts to her or those who should have claimed "in case this act had never been made."[1] This clause was retained in subsequent legislation.[2] By the act of 1705 still more careful provision is made for license and certificate; and if any minister, contrary to the spirit of the law, shall "go out of this her majesty's colony and dominion" and there join in matrimony "persons belonging to this country," without license or publication, he is to suffer the same penalty as if the offense had been done in the province.[3]

No relaxation in the illiberal rule requiring solemnization by a clergyman of the establishment was made until after the Revolution. First in 1780 the court of each county was authorized to license not more than four ministers of any religious society to solemnize marriages. In 1784 ministers of all denominations, except itinerants, were put on the same level in this regard. Already the preceding year laymen "in the western waters" had grudgingly been empowered to act, provided they make use of the ritual of the English

[1] HENING, *Statutes*, III, 149-51.
[2] See the act of 1705, *ibid.*, 443, 444; and that of 1748, *ibid.*, VI, 83.
[3] *Ibid.*, III, 441, 442.

church; but it was not until 1830 that it became possible, when the court saw fit, to appoint laymen for this purpose in all counties of the commonwealth; and this policy has survived to the present hour.[1]

But if the Anglican clergy during the entire colonial period were given a monopoly of matrimonial business, it by no means follows that the dissenters, whose numbers were constantly gaining, ever tamely submitted. On the contrary, they often took the law into their own hands and had their marriages celebrated before their own ministers, or resorted to the local magistrates. This fact is made clear by the act of 1780 and subsequent statutes, by which marriages irregularly contracted are declared valid. Indeed, as early as 1677 we have evidence that dissenters refused to observe an unjust and probably invalid law. A memorial of the bishop of London in that year laments that in Virginia there is a great "defect in the execution of those two wholesome laws . . . . of the Assembly, the one prohibiting all marriages to be solemnized without a lawful minister imposing the punishment due for fornication on the parties & making their children illegitimate & so not capable of inheriting, the other prohibiting any persone the ministeriall Function without proveing himself to have first received Orders from some Bishop in England."[2]

As already stated, the matrimonial laws of Virginia were from an early day locally administered, and mainly by the civil magistrate. The minister of every parish was required to keep a "booke wherein shall be written the day and yeare of every christeninge, wedding, and buriall;"[3] and annually on the first day of June it was the duty of the church wardens and ministers to make a return to the quarter court of all

---

[1] See chap. xvi, where this legislation is treated in detail.

[2] O'CALLAGHAN, *Doc. Rel. to Col. Hist. of N. Y.*, III, 253.

[3] HENING, *Statutes*, I, 158, 182, 183 (1632).

marriages solemnized during the year.[1]   By the act of 1642
the report is to be made to the "commander of every
monethly court;"[2] and in 1661–62 the duty of registration
is laid upon the reader equally with the minister.[3]   At
length, in 1780, the officiating minister is required to transmit a certificate of every marriage solemnized by him to the
clerk of the county court for record.[4]   It was the minister's
duty to publish the banns thrice, as required by law.   But
in consequence of the scarcity of clergymen of the established
church, in some places it became practically impossible to
comply with the statutes.   So, in 1705, the clerk or reader
in any parish having no minister was empowered to publish
banns and, "if no objection be made," to grant a certificate
thereof to the officiating minister.[5]

In Virginia, as we have seen, the governor's license
instead of banns takes the place of the license of the English
bishop.   Licenses are not to be issued "without certificate
under the hands of the parents, masters or guardians."[6]   On
account of the rapid growth of population, in which was an
ever-increasing proportion of dissenters, and on account of
the scarcity of ministers of the established church, the
demand for licenses became so great that, in 1661, the
clerks of the county courts were empowered to issue them.
"Whereas," runs the statute, "many times lycences are
granted and the persons are marryed out of the parishes,
which lycences have been usually granted by the governor,
whose knowledge of persons cannot possibly extend over the
whole country," therefore persons desiring to be married by
license are required to give bond to the clerk that there is no
lawful impediment.   The clerk is then to write the license

[1] *Ibid.*, 155.

[2] *Ibid.*, 242.   *Cf.* the act of the Commonwealth, 1657–58, *ibid.*, 433.

[3] *Ibid.*, II, 54.   [4] *Ibid.*, X, 362.

[5] *Ibid.*, III, 442.   *Cf.* the act of 1748: *ibid.*, VI, 82.

[6] Act of 1657–58: *ibid.*, I, 433.

and certify to the first justice in the commission for the county, or else to the person appointed for this business by the governor, who shall sign it.[1] Later the personal or written consent of the parent or guardian is required before the clerk may issue certificate.[2] But by the act of 1705 a bond is required in all cases, and parental consent only in the case of minors. The license is then issued by the clerk for the signature of the magistrate or the governor's deputy.[3]

The granting of licenses was an important source of income for the governor, he receiving two hundred pounds of tobacco or twenty shillings for each license issued. Such, for example, was the law in the days of Beverley.[4] These fees were collected by the sheriff and turned over to the governor or secretary of the colony.[5] At the beginning of the Revolution, in order to provide for the expense of the militia, a tax of forty shillings was laid by the assembly upon each marriage license;[6] and in the next year the law granting license fees to the governor was repealed.[7] The legal fee allowed the minister was twenty shillings or two hundred pounds of tobacco for each marriage when celebrated by license, and five shillings or fifty pounds of tobacco when celebrated by banns.[8] In 1792, however, the uniform fee for a marriage was fixed at one dollar.[9]

Marriages within the "levitical degrees prohibited by the laws of England" were forbidden;[10] and curious and strin-

---

[1] HENING, op. cit., II, 54, 55; cf. 28 (1660–61). Only the clerk of the county in which the woman, her parents, or guardians dwell may act: ibid., 281.

[2] Ibid., III, 150 (1696).   [3] Ibid., 442, 443.

[4] BEVERLEY, Hist. of Va., 211, 212; also 1 Mass. Hist. Coll., V, 136; and HENING, op. cit., III, 445; VI, 84, 85; II, 55.

[5] Ibid., II, 28.

[6] Ibid., IX, 66 (1775). The tax was raised to ten pounds in 1780: ibid., X, 245.

[7] Ibid., 225.

[8] SPOTSWOOD, Letters, I, 128 n. 90; BEVERLEY, Hist of Va., 211; HENING, op. cit., III, 45; VI, 84, 85, etc. Earlier the marriage fee was 2 shillings: ibid., I, 160, 184.

[9] Acts of the Gen. Assembly, 203.

[10] HENING, op. cit., IV, 245 (1730). Marriage with a deceased wife's sister is forbidden: ibid., XII, 689 (1788).

gent regulations concerning the secret marriage of indented servants were made. Thus in 1642–43, since "many great abuses & much detriment hath been found to arise both against the law of God and likewise to the service of manye masters of families in the collony" by secret marriage of servants, it is provided that a man servant contracting a secret marriage with a maid servant shall serve an additional year after the completion of the term of indenture; while a maid servant so offending is to double the time of her service. A freeman for secretly marrying an indented maid servant must double the value of her service and pay a fine of five hundred pounds of tobacco to the parish where the offense is committed.[1] The unjust discrimination against female servants was done away with in 1657–58.[2] A still more rigorous law was passed in 1661–62. The minister is prohibited under a penalty of ten thousand pounds of tobacco from either publishing the banns or celebrating the contract of marriage without a certificate of consent from the masters of both the persons, who are each to suffer the penalty of a year's extra service, as before; while the freeman clandestinely marrying a servant is to pay to the master fifteen hundred pounds of tobacco or a year's service.[3] But in 1748 for the offending parties the year's extra service is commuted at "five pounds current money."[4] It may be noted that in this Virginia legislation there is no provision like that of Plymouth for compelling the consent of stubborn masters.

The matrimonial history of Virginia begins with the nuptials of Ann Burras and John Laydon, celebrated in

---

[1] *Ibid.*, I, 252, 253.

[2] *Ibid.*, 438. By this act either the man or the woman suffers a penalty of one year's extra service.

[3] *Ibid.*, II, 114. The penalty for a freeman was made 1,000 pounds of tobacco in 1705: *ibid.*, III, 444.

[4] *Ibid.*, VI, 83, 84.

1608.[1]   A few years later, in Dale's code, appear the first marital regulations, though to what extent they were ever carried out must remain uncertain.   Every minister is required to "keepe a faithful and true Record, or Church Booke, of all Christnings, Marriages, and deaths of such our people, as shall happen within their Fort, or Fortresse, Townes or Towne at any time, vpon the burthen of a neglectfull conscience, and vpon paine of losing their Entertainment."[2]

The statutes of the Dominion are silent as to the celebration of pre-contract or espousals; and the penalties prescribed for adultery and fornication are in marked contrast with those of early New England.   Persons were presented for these offenses by the church wardens at the annual visitations;[3] and the culprits were punished by fines or whipping.[4]   Nor do the laws concern themselves with the regulation of courtship and "sinful dalliance" in New England style; although a proclamation of Governor Wyatt

[1] On this marriage see WINSOR, *Nar. and Crit. Hist.*, III, 132; HOLMES, *Annals*, I, 162; CAMPBELL, *Hist. of Va.*, 65.

[2] WILLIAM STRACHEY, *For the Colony in Virginea Britannea, Lawes Diuine, Morall, and Martiall*, 11: in FORCE, *Tracts*, III.

[3] HENING, *op. cit.*, I, 240, 310, etc. The following curious judgment was rendered by the governor and council sitting as a court in 1627 : "Upon the presentment of the church-wardens of Stanley Hundred for suspicion of incontinency betweene Henry Kinge and the wife of John Jackson, they lyinge together in her husband's absence ; it is thought fitt that the sayd Kinge shall remove his habitation from her, and not to use or frequent her company until her husband's return."—*Ibid.*, 145, note. This may be compared with the following record of the same court in 1631 : "Because Edw. Grymes lay with Alice West he gives security not to marry any woman till further order from the Governor and Council."—*Ibid.*, 551.

[4] *Ibid.*, 433 ; III, 74, 139, 361 ; *Acts of the Gen. Assembly*, 287. The first representative assembly, which met at Jamestown in the summer of 1619, enacted, "Against excesse in apparell that every man be cessed in the church for all publique contributions, if he be unmarried according to his owne apparell, if he be married according to his owne and his wives, or either of their apparell."—*Col. Rec. of Va.* (ed. BANCROFT), 20. The same assembly provided that "All Ministers in the Colony shall once a year, namely in the moneth of Marche, bring to the Secretary of Estate a true account of all Christnings, burials and marriages, upon paine, if they faill, to be censured for their negligence by the Governor and Counsell of Estate; likewise where there be no ministers, that the comanders of the place doe supply the same duty."—*Ibid.*, 26.

shows that his excellency was willing to supply the law's defect in this regard. He announces that "every minister should give notice in his church that what man *or woman* soever should use any word or speech tending to a contract of marriage to two several persons at one time," such "as might entangle or *breed scruples* in *their consciences*, should for such their offense, either undergo *corporal correction*, or be punished by fine or otherwise, according to *the quality of the person so offending*."[1]

Very little material has been collected regarding wedding customs in Virginia.[2] But this sketch may be concluded by reference to a curious "marriage agreement" which took place in Eastville, Northampton county, in 1714, and which throws light on domestic economy in the Old Dominion. Mr. John Custis and Frances, his wife, having fallen out, are inspired with hope and faith that they may renew "perfect love and friendship" by bond and covenant. First, therefore, it is duly stipulated that "the sd Frances shall return to the sd John all the money, Plate and other things what soever that she hath from him or removed out of the house upon oath and be obliged never to take away by herself or any other, anything of value from him again or run him in debt without his consent, nor sell, give away or dispose of anything of value out of the family without his consent, upon the condition that the plate and damaske linen" shall not be given away or otherwise disposed of by the said John during her life, but be delivered to his children "by the said Frances immediately after her decease." Next it is agreed that "Frances shall henceforth for bear to call him ye sd John any vile names or give him any ill language, Neither shall he give her any," but they are "to live lov-

---

[1] Quoted by COOKE, *Virginia*, 149 ; also FISKE, *Old Virginia and Her Neighbors*, I, 246, 247.

[2] See, however, GOODWIN, *The Colonial Cavalier*, 45 ff. ; and on social customs in general FISKE, *op. cit.*, II, 174, 269.

ingly together and to behave themselves to each other as a
good husband & good wife ought to doe.   And that she shall
not intermeddle with his affairs but that all business belonging to the husband's management shall be solely transacted
by him, neither shall he intermeddle in her domestique
affairs but that all business properly belonging to the management of the wife shall be solely transacted by her."
Again, after settling his debts, John gives bond in the sum
of one thousand pounds that he will keep "true and perfect
accounts of all the profitts and disbursements of his whole
Estate," present and future, in Virginia or the rest of the
world, and that he will "produce the same accounts yearly
if it be required upon oath.   And that after all debts hereafter necessarily accrueing ; for buying cloaths, tools and all
the necessary [things] for the servants and the plantations,
paying leavys and Quitt-rents & making necessary repairs of
his whole estate and alsoe all other necessary charges acrew-
ing for the use & benefitt of the estate which is to descend to
the child of ye said Frances are deducted and paid he shall
freely & without grudging allow one full moity . . . . of
his whole estate" to her annually, "for clothing herself and
the children with a reasonable proportion thereof and the
remainder to be all laid out in the education of the children
& for furnishing . . . . all things . . . . necessary for
house keeping (that are to be brought from England) and
Phisick," so long as she remains peacefully with him ; and
that he shall allow for her maintenance and that of the family "one bushell of wheat for every week and a sufficient
quantity of Indian Corn and as much flessh of all kinds as
the stocks of Cattle, Sheep and hoggs" will stand, with
"sufficient quantity of Cyder and Brandy if so much be made
on the plantation."   But if Frances exceed her allowance,
then it is to cease, and the "bond to be voyd."   Out of her
allowance Frances is to have "free liberty to keep a white

servant if she shall think fitt;" also the usual colored servants, among whom are mentioned "Jenny," "Queen," and "Billy boy," who are to "tend the garden, goe of errands or with the coach, catch horses, and doe all other necessary works" both in and about the house. Moreover, with impulsive generosity, "ye sd John" binds himself, not only to allow Frances "fifteen pounds of wool and fifteen pounds of fine dresst flax or fifteen pounds of wool in lieu thereof every year to spin for any use in the family she shall think fit;" but even to suffer her "to give away twenty yards of Virginia cloth every Year to charitable uses *if soe much remain after the servants are clothed.*" Finally, pending the marketing of the tobacco crop in England, which will take twelve months, Frances is graciously endowed by John with fifty pounds in money for support of herself and the family, if there should happen to be so much left when all the debts are paid.[1]

II. OPTIONAL CIVIL MARRIAGE AND THE RISE OF OBLIGATORY RELIGIOUS CELEBRATION IN MARYLAND

The earliest extant record of a marriage in Maryland, we are told, is that of William Edwin and Mary Whitehead, dated March 26, 1638. They were married by license, with security to the Lord Proprietor for the payment of "one thousand weight of merchantable tobacco, to be paid upon demand, in case the said William Edwin hath precontracted himself to any other woman than Mary Whitehead (spinster)," or in case there is any other lawful impediment to the marriage.[2] According to Bozman, many similar marriage-license bonds have been preserved.[3] The requirement of a

---

[1] For this document see *The Virginia Mag. of Hist. and Biog.*, IV (July, 1896), 64-66.

[2] STREETER, *Papers Rel. to the Early History of Md.*, 278, 279. This license may be compared with the bonds required by Governor Andros in New England or by the New York governors: see chaps. xii and xiv.

[3] In the "book in the land office, entitled, *Liber* No. 1": BOZMAN, *Hist. of Maryland*, II, 604, who gives the following example: "November 2d, 1638. This day came

"caution," in such cases, is enforced in the act of the assembly passed in 1640.[1]   No marriage may be solemnized without banns "three days before published in some Chappell or other place of the County where publique instnts are used to be notified, or else afore oath mad & caution entered in the County Court that neither partie is apprentice or ward or precontracted or within the forbidden degrees of consanguinity or under goverm[t] of parents or tutors and certificate of such oath & caution taken from the Judge or Register of the Court."[2]

By the act of 1658, passed during the Fendall government, the civil ceremony is made legal. Persons desiring to be married have liberty to apply either to a magistrate or to a minister; but in all cases, under severe penalty, a certificate of the publication of banns at the county court, or in some church, chapel, or meeting, is required.[3] Banns or a

William Lewis, planter, and made oath, that he is not precontracted to any other woman than Ursula Gifford, and that there is no impediment of consanguinity, affinity, or any other lawful impediment to his knowledge, why he should not be married to the said Ursula Gifford; and further he acknowledgeth himself to owe unto the lord proprietor 1000 lb. tobacco in case there be any precontract or other lawful impediment whatsoever as aforesaid, either on the part of the said William Lewis or the said Ursula Gifford."

[1] Among the thirty-six bills of the assembly of February, 1639/40, which according to Bozman were engrossed for a third reading, but not finally enacted into laws, was one giving the so-called "county court" jurisdiction in "all causes matrimonial, for as much as concerns the trial of covenants and contracts, and the punishment of faults committed against the same; and all offences of incest; attempting of another's chastity; defamation; temerarious administration; detention of legacies; clandestine marriage without banns thrice published or bond entered in the court."—BOZMAN, *op. cit.*, II, 106, 128, 129. Since at this time there was but one organized county, St. Mary's, and this "county court" is made a tribunal of appeal in all civil common-law cases, the body is really the supreme provincial court, and it is given about the same jurisdiction thereafter exercised by the latter.

[2] *Archives of Md.: Proceedings and Acts of the General Assembly*, 1637-64, 97.

[3] *Ibid.*, 374. The fine for each of the parties violating the statute is 1,000 pounds of tobacco; for the magistrate or minister, 5,000 pounds, one half to the Lord Proprietor, the other half to the informer. In 1650 it is provided that adultery shall receive punishment as the court may see fit, but "not extending to life or member": *ibid.*, 286. The penalty is the same in 1654: *ibid.*, 344. In the last-named year "the names of all that shall be borne, married or buried . . . , shall be Exhibited to the Clarke of Every Court who shall Iust Register thereof who shall be allowed five pounds of Tobacco as a ffee due to him for every such Regist[r] made and kept."—*Ibid.*, 345.

license from the governor or lieutenant-general is prescribed by the act of 1662; and, as before, the ceremony may be performed by either a minister or a magistrate, but in presence of two witnesses. Otherwise the marriage is void.[1] Thus far no form of words at the nuptials had been prescribed. Therefore in 1666, by a statute which was to remain in force three years, a modification of the English ritual was adopted.[2]

The general provisions of the law of 1662 are repeated in the act of 1676, except that the intention to allow complete liberty with respect to the form of celebration is more accented. Instead of a "minister or magistrate," as in the former act, any "priest, minister, pastor, or magistrate" may now conduct the celebration; and, as before, a marriage not so solemnized is declared null and void; though it is highly probable that such a requirement was invalid as being inconsistent with the English common law.[3]

Up to this point, under the Catholic proprietors of the palatinate, absolute toleration had prevailed. Optional civil or ecclesiastical rites were sanctioned. But now arose a struggle for supremacy between the toleration party composed of Catholics and Quakers, who began to take strong root in the province, and a bigoted Protestant faction. "As happened twenty years before, a minority in the colony, in sympathy with the dominant party in England, wished to control in matters of religion, and, backed by the home government, renew a policy of intolerance in their own interests. Now, of course, this minority was composed of Protestants of the Established Church, instead of Puritans,

---

[1] *Ibid.*, 442, 443. This act is approved in 1664: *ibid.*, 537.

[2] "The man taking the woman by the R^t hand shall say I A B doe take thee C D to my wedded wife To have and to hould from this day forward for better for worse for Rich or for Poore in sickness & in health till death us do part and thereto I plight thee my troth which being finished lett her hand goe." Similar words are to be used by the woman: *ibid.*, 1664–76, 148.

[3] *Ibid.*, 1666–76, 522, 523

as in the days of the Commonwealth."[1] The Episcopal
minority triumphed with the establishment of the royal
government in 1692, the Church of England was set up, and
Catholics and dissenters were taxed for its support. A reactionary policy was begun with respect to the marriage celebration, and we have in this instance the only clear example
of such retrogression that can be found in American history.[2]
Only in Maryland was civil marriage entirely abrogated after
it was once introduced.[3]

The change did not take place all at once. A beginning
was made by the law of 1692 which in part deprived members of the established church of the privilege of the civil
celebration, but as yet did not interfere with the liberty of
others. As under the preceding acts, either a minister or
a magistrate may perform the ceremony; but now it is provided that he "shall joyn them in manner and forme as is
sett down & expressed in the Liturgy of the Church of England wch being finished the Minister, Pastor, or Magistrate
shall say I being hereunto by Law Authorized do pronounce
you lawfull man and wife."[4]

A more rigorous statute, affecting members of the establishment, appears in 1702. To "prevent all illegal and
unlawful Marriages, not allowable by the Church of Eng-

---

[1] LODGE, *Short History*, 105. Elsewhere this writer says the Episcopal church in
Maryland was as " contemptible an ecclesiastical organization as history can show."
" It is not easy to conceive the utter degradation of the mass of the Maryland clergy.
Secure in their houses and glebes, with a tax settled by law, and collected by the
sheriffs for their benefit, they set decency and public opinion at defiance. They
hunted, raced horses, drank, gambled, and were the parasites and boon companions
of the wealthy planters. A common jest was the question:

    ' Who is a monster of the first renown?
    ' A lettered sot, a drunkard in a gown.'

" They extorted marriage fees from the poor by breaking off in the middle of the
service, and refusing to continue until they were paid."—*Ibid.*, 123, 120–24; *cf.*
BROWNE, *Maryland*, 184 ff.

[2] See, however, the case of North Carolina below, where the original toleration
of the early years was later somewhat curtailed; and that of West Virginia.

[3] Compare COOK, " Mar. Cel. in the Colonies," *Atlantic*, LXI, 356, 357.

[4] *Archives of Md.: Procds. and Acts of the Gen. Assem.*, 1684–92, 450, 451.

land," it is enacted that "no Minister, Priest or Magistrate shall presume to join together in Marriage, any persons whatsoever, contrary to the Table of Marriages, by this Act appointed to be set up in every Parish-Church within this Province," under penalty of five thousand pounds of tobacco for violation, and with a like punishment for each of the parties to such a marriage.   To "prevent any Lay-Persons" from acting "where any Minister or Priest can be had, and to ascertain what shall be paid for Marriages," it is provided that "in every Parish where any Minister or Incumbent shall reside and have charge of souls therein, no Justice or Magistrate, being a Lay-Man, shall join any Persons in Marriage, under penalty of Five Thousand Pounds of Tobacco . . . . to our Sovereign Lord the King." The marriage fee is fixed at five shillings sterling, provided the persons to be married come to the parish church or chapel at time of divine service.[1]

In 1717 was passed a more elaborate act, which remained in force throughout the colonial period, but which did not extend to "persons of different persuasions from the Church of England," who are still to enjoy their own "manner of proceedings" unaltered.   "Persons who desire Marriage" are to "apply themselves to a Minister . . . . and shall cause due Publication to be made, according to the Rubrick of the Church of England, of their Intent to marry, at some Church or Chapel of Ease belonging to the Parish" wherein the woman resides.   In "case there be no Minister, Curate or Reader in such Parish, an Advertisement or public Notification . . . . shall be set up at the Court-house Door of the County, where such Marriage shall be intended, there to remain for the Space of Three Weeks at the least." The clerk of the county court is required to make a certificate of publication, on presenting which any "qualified" minister

[1] BACON, *Laws of Maryland*, 1702, chap. i, §§ iv, v.

is empowered to solemnize the marriage "according to the Liturgy of the Church of England." For proceeding without certificate of publication or the governor's license, the minister and each of the parties shall severally forfeit five thousand pounds of tobacco, as under the act of 1702; and for evasion of the law by getting married in any place outside the province, except where the woman is a resident, the man is to suffer the same penalty.[1] But it is important to note that neither the act of 1702 nor that of 1717 invalidates an irregular or clandestine marriage.

Another statute of 1717 prescribes severe penalties for miscegenation. Any free negro or mulatto intermarrying with a white person shall become a slave for life, unless the free mulatto in question be "born of a white woman," when he is merely condemned to service for seven years. On the other hand, servitude for this same period is the punishment prescribed in case a white man or woman intermarry with a negro or mulatto.[2] Two years before a law provides that for joining any negro whatsoever or a mulatto slave to any white person the minister, pastor, or magistrate shall forfeit five thousand pounds of tobacco, one half to the use of free schools, and the other half to the informer.[3]

It is significant that throughout the whole colonial period all persons in Maryland, except members of the establishment, should have had unrestricted liberty to contract civil marriage, only to have that liberty taken away after the Revolution began. By the reactionary law of 1777, "the rites of marriage between any white persons, subjects or inhabitants of this State, shall not be celebrated by any person within this State, unless by ministers of the Church of England, ministers dissenting from that Church, or Romish

---

[1] BACON, *op. cit.*, 1717, chap. xv, §§ i–v. The fee for marriage after license is "10 shillings and no more;" after publication of banns it is 100 pounds of tobacco or 6 shillings and 8 pence current money.

[2] *Ibid.*, chap. xiii, § v.　　　　[3] *Ibid.*, 1715, chap. xliv, § xxv.

priests, appointed or ordained according to the rites . . . . of
their respective churches, or in such manner as hath been
heretofore used and practiced in this State by the society
of people called Quakers."[1] This monument of religious
conservatism has survived to our own time.

No attempt is here made to describe wedding customs in
the colonial era;[2] but the *Archives of Maryland* contain a
unique document, entitled "Articles of Courtship," which
may serve as companion-piece and counterpart to the "Marriage Agreement" with which the domestic economy of Virginia, half a century later, has already been illustrated. In
this instance Robert Harwood essays by formal indenture to
compound a lawsuit and at the same time reclaim the reluctant affections of Elizabeth Gary, despite the fact that
ungallantly he had sought to requite her fickleness through
"slanders and unhandsome attempts."   From the "Articles
of agreement . . . . made the 24th of September 1657
between Peter Sharpe of Putuxent County in the Province
of Maryland Chirurgeon of the one pte, and Robert Harwood of the Same County planter of the other parte," it
appears that "there hath been a Suit Commenced by the
Said Peter Sharpe before the Governour and Councell . . . .
a gainst the abovenamed Robert Harwood on the behalf of
Elizabeth Gary Daughter of Iudith now the wife of the Said
Peter Sharpe, for reparation for Slanders, and undhandsome
attempts charged to be acted and reported by the Said
Robert Harwood to the great Detriment of the Said Elizabeth, and of the Said Peter Sharpe his wife and family;"

[1] KILTY, *Laws*, 1777, chap. 12, sec. 5; also *Laws of Md.*, 1763-87 (Annapolis, 1787),
chap. xii, sec. v; *cf.* COOK, " Mar. Cel. in the Colonies," *Atlantic*, LXI, 357.

[2] The Quakers were strong in Maryland and practiced the same rites as their
brothers elsewhere. The Labadists, who had a colony in the province, thoroughly
disliked the Friends, though in some respects the doctrines of the two bodies were
strikingly alike. The Labadists were even more narrow than the Pennsylvania
Friends regarding intermarriage with gentiles. A convert was expected to leave his
unregenerate spouse behind when he joined the society; see JAMES, " The Labadist
Colony in Maryland," *J. H. U. S.*, XVII, 12 ff., 17 ff.

and, on the other side, that Robert, "for his own Vindication, doth much insist upon a former promise of Marriage Grounded upon a Mutuall declared affection" between him and Elizabeth, "obtained after a long familiaritie and Sollicitation;" with which engagement the said Peter and Judith his wife "are much dissatisfied," but which they are nevertheless willing to see followed by wedlock, if Elizabeth really have the proper "affection and resolution of marriage to and with the Said Robert."

Therefore it is duly stipulated that the insistent suitor shall have a fair chance to ensnare the coy damsel on neutral ground. "Imprimis the said Peter Sharpe doth for himself and his heirs . . . . agree that the Said Elizabeth Gary shall within fifteen dayes . . . . be conveyed to the house of m^r Thomas Davis at the Cliftes and there she is to remaine for the Space of six weekes," the said Robert "during all the Said Time" being given "full free and perfect Liberty (bringing one or more of the Neighbours with him) to have all freedom of discourse" with her, and "to use all faire and Lawfull Endeavours" to win her consent to marry him. That Robert's "nerve" and zeal were confidently relied upon is revealed by the proviso that "one or more of the Neighbours" are "alwayes to be present" with the lovers at the above specified courting, the "Said Robt Harwood paying for the Said Elizabeth Gary her Entertainment during her Stay at the Said Davis his house."

Next it is covenanted by Peter, "if it should by Gods permission, So happen" that Elizabeth shall "within the Said prefixed time give her consent," that he will not directly or indirectly, "neither by himself nor by any other person or persons," try to hinder the marriage, which "shall be permitted to take effect without obstruction." On his part Robert doth agree that, if in the time set he fail to gain Elizabeth's consent to "intermarry with him," he "will from thence forth totally and absolutely discharge the Said Elizabeth" from all former promises; and will "never after by himself, or any other person or persons, either by words Letters or any other way directly or indirectly Endeavour to gain" her affections, "or to procure any familiaritie of discourse with her or willingly to Come into her Company." But if "Robert and Elizabeth shall entermarry," the docile bridegroom "shall first enter into Good Caution and Securitie not to upbraid or deride or any other way Exercise, or use any bitherness" toward the bride, "for or in relation to any former passages between them;" and in case of "breach of this his Engagement he shall from thenceforth be absolutely disabled and made uncapable of Entermedling with or disposing of any part of the Estate now belonging to the Said Elizabeth, or any part of the produce thereof."

Finally it is stipulated that "in the Cause forme^{r}ly depending and now to be withdrawen" Robert is to "beare his own Charge," as well as those "on th^e plaintiffes behalf," if the marriage take place, otherwise Peter is to pay his own costs. Thereupon the instrument is "signed, sealed and delivered in the presence of Thomas Turner Clerk," under date of September 26, 1657.[1]

III. THE STRUGGLE FOR CIVIL MARRIAGE AND FREE RELIGIOUS CELEBRATION IN NORTH CAROLINA

From the outset the colony of North Carolina had a population of diverse nationalities and various religious creeds. The "Fundamental Constitutions" of 1669, granted by the Earl of Clarendon and his colleagues, provided, hesitatingly, for the establishment of the English church;[2] but it was not until after the beginning of the eighteenth century that an

---

[1] *Archives of Md.: Judicial and Testamentary Business of the Provincial Court*, 1649/50-57, 531-33.

[2] "Fundamental Constitutions," c. 96: POORE, *Charters*, II, 1406. The charter of 1663 allows the proprietors to use their discretion in dispensing from the liturgy and ceremonies of the English church: *ibid.*, 1389. The supplementary charter of 1665

attempt was made to enforce the Episcopal system by statute.
In the meantime, the regular clergy were few, and dissenters
came in large numbers; for lest "Jews, heathens, and other
dissenters from the purity of the Christian religion may be
scared and kept at a distance," the Constitutions had inconsistently guaranteed a qualified religious freedom.[1]   Among
the sects represented were Protestants from Germany, Hu-
guenots from France, and Independents from New England.
Later the Quakers and Presbyterians became relatively
strong; and they stoutly resented the bigoted tyranny of
the Episcopal minority, which was sustained by the government by whom the matrimonial legislation was shaped.   The
intolerance was the harder to bear because of the low character of the English clergy, some of whom in vice and
dissipation being worthy rivals of the brawling and cock-
fighting parsons of Maryland and Virginia.   To this class
belonged Rev. Daniel Brett, the first Episcopal clergyman
who came to the colony; and Rev. John Boyd, notorious for
open drunkenness.[2]

During nearly half a century following the charter[3] there
was in practice full toleration as to the form of the marriage

declares that no one shall be "in any way molested, punished, disquieted or called
in question, for any differences in opinion, or practice in matter of religious concernments, who do not actually disturb the civil peace." All are to enjoy "judgment
and conscience in matter of religion."—*Ibid.*, 1397.

[1] After thus expressing the motive for toleration, the Constitutions curiously
provide that any seven or more persons agreeing in any religion may form themselves into a "church or profession;" and no person over seventeen years of age
"shall have any benefit or protection of the law, or be capable of any place of profit
or honor, who is not a member" of such a church or profession, "having his name
recorded in some one, and but one religious record at once."—*Ibid.*, 1407.

[2] *N. C. Col. Records*, IV, 264; HAWKS, *Hist. of N. C.*, II, 341. For Virginia see
LODGE, *Short History*, 60 ff.   *Cf.* HOWARD, *Local Const. History*, I, 133, 134.

[3] Paragraphs 45 and 84 of the Fundamental Constitutions (1669) provide for
matrimonial jurisdiction and for registration. Paragraph 87 declares that "no
marriage shall be lawful, whatever contract and ceremony they have used, till both
parties mutually own it before the register of the place where they were married,
and he register it, with the names of the father and mother of each party."—POORE,
Charters, II, 1402, 1406. Compare HEWITT, *An Hist. Account of the Rise and Progress
of South Carolina and Georgia* (London, 1779), 321–47.

celebration. The very first statute of the "Assembly of Albemarle," the first legislative body after the "Fundamental Constitutions" went into effect, provides in characteristic American style for the solemnization of marriage. "Forasmuch," runs this act, "as there may be divers people that are minded to be joyned together in the holy state of Wedlock and for that there is noe minister as yet in this County by whom the said Partyes may be joyned in Wedlock according to the rites and customs of our native Country the Kingdome of England;" therefore, that "none may be hindred from this soe necessary a worke for the preservation of Mankind and settlement of this County it is enacted And be it enacted by the Pallatine and Lords Proprietors of Carolina by and with the advice and consent of the Present Grand Assembly . . . . that any two persons to be joyned together in the holy state of matrimony takeing three or fower of their Neighbors along with them and repairing to the Governor or any one of the Councell before him declaring that they doe joyne together in the holy state of Wedlock And doe accept one the other for man and wife; and the said Governor or Councellor before whom such act is performed giveing certificate thereof and the said certificate being registered in the Secretary's Office or by the Register of the Precinct or in such other Office as shall hereafter for that use be provided. It shall be deemed a Lawfull Marriage and Partyes violating this Marriage shall be punishable as if they had binn marryed by a minister according to the rites and customs of England."[1]

This timely act was ratified by the Proprietors, January 20, 1669/70; and there can be no doubt of its validity. It is a straightforward and sensible measure, such as the pioneer, forced to resort to self-help, has so often shown

---

[1] *N. C. Col. Rec.*, I, 184; also in HAWKS, *Hist. of N. C.*, II, 152, 153; and CARROLL, *Hist. Coll. of S. C.*, II.

himself capable of throughout the history of the Anglo-Saxon race. Its clear expression, good English, and respectable spelling speak well for the training and intelligence of the first settlers of Carolina; although the act has been sneered at and ridiculed by some people who ought to know better.[1]

From the beginning the Quakers seem to have been allowed to solemnize marriage in their own way; and this they contrived to do even after the English forms were prescribed by statute. According to Hawks, the "Friends were entitled, by express grant from the proprietors, thus to adhere to their peculiar usage; for they had declared to them as an inducement to emigrate, 'there is full and free liberty of conscience granted to all, so that no man is to be molested or called in question for matters of religious concern; but every one to be obedient to the civil government, worshipping God after his own way.'"[2] The records of the monthly meeting in North Carolina reveal the Friends using the same simple rites as elsewhere in the colonies. The betrothed man and woman proclaimed their own banns, "passing the meeting" twice as in Pennsylvania. Thus at a monthly meeting of Friends "in Pasquotank yᵉ 11ᵗʰ of yᵉ first month 1707/8," held "as their manner is, to Inspect into yᵉ affairs of yᵉ

---

[1] Thus DOYLE, *Eng. Colonies*, I, 453, says the acts of the assembly of 1669/70, of which the marriage act is one, tended to make North Carolina "an Alsatia for ready and profligate adventurers." So also GEORGE CHALMERS, *Political Annals of the United Provinces:* in CARROLL, *Hist. Coll. of S. C.*, II, 291, concludes, "From this remarkable law we may judge of their state of religion and morals." On the other hand, HAWKS, *Hist. of N. C.*, II, 152, 153, says of this statute: "It has given rise to some abortive efforts at wit, which, if genuine, would, we think, be sadly misplaced; and has, besides, sorely troubled the over-sensitive and camel-swallowers who thank God they are 'not as other men are;'" justly adding: "It is difficult to conjecture any other course, which under the circumstances, they could reasonably have adopted. The very fact that any plan was devised to afford a legal and decent mode of entering into the marriage contract, certainly implies that the moral sense of the community revolted at general concubinage." *Cf.* also WEEKS, *Church and State in N. C.:* in *J. H. U. S.*, XI, 244.

[2] HAWKS, *op. cit.*, II, 154. These are nearly the words of the charter of 1665: POORE, *op. cit.*, II, 1397. *Cf.* also WEEKS, *op. cit.*, 244, 245.

Church," Zachariah Nixon and Elizabeth Symons appear the "second time & declare their Intentions of taking Each Other in Marriage and being approved by the said meeting are left to their liberty to take each other."[1]

It appears, then, that civil marriage, side by side with religious marriage according to the rites of each denomination, was lawful until 1715. By the so-called "Vestries Act" of that year, for the establishment of the Church of England in the province, magistrates are authorized to join people in wedlock only in "such parishes where no minister shall be resident." If any layman, except in such parishes, presume to act, he shall be fined five pounds, one-half to the parish for the use of the poor, and one-half to the resident minister or incumbent. After license or banns no marriage may be lawfully celebrated by minister, priest, or magistrate contrary to the table of marriages, which the church wardens and vestry are to have set up in every church or chapel.[2] But there is no invalidating clause for neglect. Already in 1704 some provision had been made by statute for registration.[3] Now it is enacted that the "inhabitants and freemen of each precinct" by majority vote are to elect three freeholders, from whom the governor or commmander in chief is to choose one as register of deeds; and until there be a clerk of the parish church, such register is to record betrothals and marriages. Every "master or mistress of a family who shall neglect to register the birth or death of any person born or dying within his or her house or plantation; and every married man who shall neglect to remit to the said register

---

[1] "Records of the Friends Monthly Meeting in Pasquotank Precinct": in *N. C. Col. Rec.*, I, 688. There is a similar entry in 1711: *ibid.*, 813. Two years earlier we find a "precinct" court — about the only part of the machinery of the "Fundamental Constitutions" which was ever made use of (HOWARD, *Local Const. Hist.*, I, 129)— sentencing for adultery: "Ordered that Ellinor Mearle be punished by receiving Ten Stripes on her Back well laid & pay cost also Exō."—Records of Perquiman's Precinct Court, in *N. C. Col. Rec.*, I, 626 (1705).

[2] *N. C. Col. Rec.*, II, 212, 213.   [3] *Ibid.*, 877, 878.

a certificate of his marriage and cause the same to be registered, for longer than one month," must pay a fine of one
shilling a month for the period of delay, provided the whole
penalty do not exceed twenty shillings.[1]

The act of 1715 fixes the minister's marriage fee at five
shillings; and to retain a monopoly of this perquisite at all
hazards was the unswerving purpose of the Episcopal clergy
throughout the colonial period. The governors, too, found
the stipend for issuing marriage licenses a lucrative source
of revenue. In 1730 the royal instructions to Governor
Burrington declare, "to the end Ecclesiastical Jurisdiction
of the Bishop of London may take place in that our Province
so far as may be We do think fit that you give all countenance
& encouragement to the exercise of the same excepting only
the collating the Benefices Granting licenses for Marriages
and probate of Wills which we have reserved to you our
Governor and to the Commander in chief of our said
Province for the time being as far as by law we may."[2] The
license fee was fixed at ten shillings.[3]

A new law was passed in 1741, which, though it does not
expressly forbid dissenting ministers from performing the
marriage ceremony, at any rate, as Weeks insists, makes
"dissent burdensome and humiliating," puts a "premium on
conformity," and constitutes "religious persecution."[4] "To
prevent clandestine marriages" it is enacted "that every
Clergyman of the Church of England, or for want of such,
any lawful magistrate, within this Government" may join
persons in the "holy state of matrimony." By implication
this provision widens the area within which a magistrate is
empowered to act, for by the law of 1715 a layman may not

[1] IREDELL-MARTIN, *Public Acts of the Assembly* (Newbern, 1804), I, 18, 19.

[2] *N. C. Col. Rec.*, III, 110, 111.

[3] *Ibid.*, 160. According to COOK, "Colonel Byrd, writing about 1728, says that
in North Carolina, 'for want of men in holy orders, justices of the peace and members of the council were empowered to celebrate marriage.'"—*Op. cit.*, 355, 356.

[4] WEEKS, *Church and State*, 244, 245.

perform the ceremony in any parish where a "minister or priest" resides, thus probably including dissenters, who in the present case do not count. The next clause gives still further chances for lay celebration; for, while a justice of the peace may not join in marriage "any persons whatsoever in any parish where a minister shall reside and have a cure," still by implication he may do so in any parish in the colony by obtaining permission from the minister, and, of course, in all cases turning over to said minister the legally prescribed fee.[1]   Another provision of this statute may perhaps justify the inference that dissenting ministers are not absolutely excluded.   To prevent "that abominable mixture and spurious issue" which would follow, it is enacted, "That if any white man or woman, being free, shall intermarry with an indian, negro, mustee, or mulatto man or woman, or any person of mixt blood, to the third generation, bond or free, he shall, by judgment of the county court, forfeit and pay the sum of fifty pounds, proclamation money, to the use of the parish;" and any persons, including dissenting ministers, are forbidden to solemnize such marriages, under the same penalty.[2]   The marriage of servants indented or by custom is also dealt with.   It is provided "That if any minister or reader shall willingly publish, or cause or suffer to be published, the banns of matrimony between any servants, or between a free person and a servant; or if any minister or justice of the peace shall willingly celebrate the rites of matrimony between any such, without a certificate from the master or mistress of such servant, that it is done by their consent; he shall forfeit and pay five pounds, proclamation money, to the use of the master or owner."   Every

---

[1] The justice shall not act in any parish where a minister resides and has cure, "without permission first had and obtained from such Minister under penalty of five pounds proclamation money, to the use of the minister."—IREDELL-MARTIN, *Public Acts.* I, 45; for the fee see *ibid.*, 46.

[2] *Ibid.*, 46; SWAN's *Revisal* (ed. 1752), 127-30; *cf.* WEEKS, *op. cit.*, 244, 245.

servant so married without consent shall serve the master or mistress "one whole year, after the time of service by indenture or custom is expired." [1]

Regarding the scope and intent of the law of 1741, Weeks remarks that "in this, as in the former cases, the Assembly did not undertake to give" the right of celebrating marriages to the established clergy, "but simply recognized it as resting on prescription. But they might have granted this right to Dissenters as they proposed doing in the act of 1770. The Quakers seem to have been allowed to marry after their own fashion from the first," and why not grant the same privilege "to Presbyterians and Baptists"? Instead of taking such a just and tolerant course, "their preachers were debarred from performing the ceremony even among their own flocks. They were thus put to grave inconvenience, and the law of 1766 recites that the Presbyterians refused to consider themselves as bound by its provisions." Surely there was good reason to take this position, considering the previous law and custom of the colony. The Episcopalian government party seems to have been conscious of this fact, as appears from the discussion of the clergy bill of 1762. "The governor and council," continues Weeks, "tried to force on the lower house a clause by which it was enacted that 'no Dissenting minister of any denomination whatever shall presume on any pretence to Marry any person, under the penalty of forfeiting £50.' The law does not seem to have been successful, but it is a clear statement of the tendency of the act of 1741, and shows the position of a certain element in the province." [2]

The assembly rested from further matrimonial legislation until the passage of the act of 1766, already mentioned,

---

[1] IREDELL-MARTIN, *op. cit.*, I, 45.

[2] WEEKS, *op. cit.*, 245; *cf. N. C. Col. Rec.*, VI, 881, 952, 954.

which gave some relief to the Presbyterians, but not to any other dissenting body. Aside from the greed for the marriage fees, the principal motive leading to its passage was not justice, as will presently appear, but a desire to reward and strengthen the sympathy of the Presbyterians for the government in its struggle with the Regulators. The preamble of the act recites that because "the presbyterian, or dissenting clergy, conceiving themselves not included in the restrictions mentioned" in the act of 1741, have "joined many persons together in holy matrimony, without either licence or publication; whereby the payment of the just and legal fees to the governor on such occasions, has been eluded, and the validity of marriages may be endangered:" therefore all such marriages now celebrated or to be celebrated before the first day of January next are declared valid. Henceforth no minister of the Church of England or justice of the peace may celebrate marriage without a certificate of three times publication of banns, or a license from the governor or the commander in chief, "who is authorized hereby to grant the same, on certificate of the county court" of the person's "having taken and filed . . . . the usual bond," under the "penalty of fifty pounds, proclamation money; with condition that there is no lawful cause to obstruct the marriage for which such license is given." Presbyterian missionaries or itinerants in the western parishes, as well as all other dissenters in the province, are in effect excluded by the provision that after January 1 any Presbyterian minister regularly called to any congregation in this province may celebrate matrimony "in their usual and accustomed manner." But in all cases a license from the governor is requisite; and the marriage fee, it is carefully added, is always reserved to the clergyman of the Church of England having cure of any parish, no matter whether a dissenting minister or a justice performs the ceremony. Furthermore, a marriage celebrated without a license is declared "illegal and void."[1]

Governor Tryon, who approved the act of 1766, was not overfond of the Presbyterians as such, and all other "sectaries" he looked upon "as enemies to society and a scandal to common sense."[2] The next year, writing to the Earl of Shelburne, he says the law of 1766 "has more objects in view than appears on the sight of it." The Marriage Act of "1741 to which it has relation entitles every Justice of the Peace to marry by licence. In abuse of this privilege many Justices performed the marriage ceremony without licence . . . . and took the fee allowed to the Governor, most generally dividing the spoil between the Justice and the Clerk of the county who gave the bond and certificate. Another tendency of this Act was to prevent the frequent abuses of rascally fellows who travelled thro' the province under the title of ministers of the Presbyterian and other sectaries and who being beggars in conscience as well as in circumstances sought all opportunities to perform that sacred office to the great prejudice of the country. It is also to be observed most of the justices in the back or western settlements are Presbyterians, who by the Act of 1741 had the power to marry by licence: Therefore upon the whole I do not conceive the allowing the Presbyterian ministers the privilege to marry in their usual and accustomed manner can be of any real prejudice to the established Church especially as the marriage fee is reserved to the ministers of the parish; and the licence to be granted under the hand and

---

[1] IREDELL-MARTIN, *op. cit.*, I, 157, 158; DAVIS, *Revisal* (ed. 1773), 350.
"It was proposed to limit this law to three years, which was not done. It provided for no Dissenters *except* Presbyterians. But it seems that the original intention was to cover the case of all Dissenters. The second section probably read 'dissenting *or of the dissenting Presbyterian clergy*.' The clause in italics was stricken out and the phrase ' dissenting or Presbyterian clergy ' took its place, thus excluding all Dissenters except Presbyterians."— WEEKS, *op. cit.*, 245 n. 2; *cf. N. C. Col. Rec.*, VII, 411, 329, 331.

[2] SAUNDERS, " Prefatory Notes," *N. C. Col. Rec.*, VIII, xlv.

seal of the Governor, this last provision prevents the former abuses in the application of the fee collected.   The Act also provides a summary and effectual method for the Governor to oblige the county court clerks to account for the fees due to him: a recovery tho' an equitable one, was never yet secured but in temporary laws."[1]

The Presbyterians were by no means satisfied with the reward their loyalty had received.   Especially did the "rascally" missionaries of the western frontiers feel themselves abused.   Petitions protesting in strong terms against the act were presented by the clergy.   Those of Mecklenburg, for instance, regard themselves as "highly injured and aggrieved" by the statute, "the preamble whereof scandalizes the Presbyterian clergy."[2]   The petitioners of Tryon county say they are "much aggrieved," the law depriving them of a privilege "which a million of our fellow-professors in America now enjoy . . . . neither was it ever taken from Dissenters in America until it was taken from us by this act."[3]   The "manly protest from the inhabitants of Orange and Rowan claims that the right of 'dissenting ministers' to perform the marriage ceremony after their own fashion was a 'priviledge they were debarred of in no other part of his majesty's Dominions; and as we humbly conceive, a priviledge they stand entitled to, by the Act of Toleration, and in fine, a priviledge granted even to the very Catholics in Ireland and the Protestants in France.'"[4]

The vigorous resistance aroused by the unjust law of

[1] " Letter from Governor Tryon to Earl of Shelburne, Brunswick, 31st January 1767," *N. C. Col. Rec.*, VII, 432, 433. On this act see also SAUNDERS, "Prefatory Notes," *ibid.*, VIII, xlv.

[2] See the petition for repeal *ibid.*, X, 1015; *cf.* WEEKS, *op. cit.*, 246, 247, who has collected these passages.

[3] *N. C. Col. Rec.*, VIII, 80b. There was also a petition from the people of Anson: *ibid.*, 78.

[4] *Ibid.*, 82; WEEKS, *op. cit.*, 246, 247. This petition was presented to Tryon by " Herman Husband the leader of the Regulators ": WEEKS, *op. cit.*, 247, 248, referring to SWAIN, " War of Regulation," *N. C. University Mag.*, IX (1859-60), 339.

1766, and the continued services rendered by the Presbyterian pastors to the governor in his struggle with the Regulators had the desired result. In December, 1770, a legislative committee brought in a report recommending a new law. "Upon perusing the several Acts of Assembly concerning the solemnization of the rites[1] of matrimony and considering the great number of Presbyterian Inhabitants settled in the western Frontier Counties in this Province and the difficulties and expenses they must necessarily be under," the committee "Can't but think that the restraints and penalties in the Said Acts are in some measure hard and oppressive and that they have a just and reasonable claim to the attention of the Legislative body for granting to them a religious toleration in that particular, and that it is well becoming the Catholic and liberal principles of the Members of the House Representatives of this Colony, to appoint a Committee to prepare and bring in a Bill for impowering all regular Presbyterian Ministers in this Province to Solemnize the rites of Marriage, according to the Westminster confession of Faith, by publication in their religious Assemblies, where the parties are best known, and by License, without any Tax or Fees to the Clergy of the Establishment."[2] Such a bill was accordingly brought in and passed with the governor's approval, "but with a clause suspending its operation until the pleasure of the King should be known."[3]

No relief was offered by this act to the other dissenters; and the report of Governor Tryon shows that he felt himself under special obligations to the Presbyterians. According to Saunders, he said that the act was an "indul-

---

[1] It is "rights" in the text, but this appears to be a "slip," for lower down the proper spelling is used.

[2] *N. C. Col. Rec.*, VIII, 322 (Dec. 17, 1770).

[3] SAUNDERS, "Prefatory Notes," *N. C. Col. Rec.*, VIII, xlv; also *ibid.*, VIII, 297, 300; IX, 7.

gence" to which they were well "entitled because of the attachment they had shown to the Government;" and it appears, aside from the "merits of the case," that something was due from Tryon to the Presbyterians "for the support their pastors gave him in 1768." Certainly "the letters in which all the Presbyterian pastors in the Province united to praise Tryon and denounce the Regulators were as strong in language as they were opportune in point of time. Indeed, old Parson Micklejohn of the Established Church was not more pronounced in enforcing the duty of obedience to 'the powers that be' as being of divine origin than the Presbytarian pastors were. The Governor in his report put him" and these ministers "on the same footing in this regard."[1]

The act had passed the house and received the governor's signature; but the battle was not yet won. It is perhaps not surprising that the ear of George III., in the days immediately following the Stamp Act, should have inclined more to the desires[2] of the loyalist clergy of the English church than to the complaints of "sectaries" in a rebellious province. Accordingly, the marriage act was disallowed by his Majesty; and the law of 1766 remained in force until 1778, two years after the constitution of 1776 had brought the establishment to an end.[3]

---

[1] Saunders, op. cit., xlv.

[2] " It is interesting to note with what satanic disregard of the rights of man the leaders in the Establishment can write. Says Reed [minister in Craven County]: 'The bill was pushed by the dissenting interest, and [because of] the dangerous situation of the province from such formidable number of malcontents [Regulators], the governor acted with the greatest prudence in passing the bill with a suspending clause. . . . . Should this act receive the royal assent it would be a fatal stroke to the Church of England, but as the insurrection is entirely quelled,┃I flatter myself with hopes that the act will meet with a repulse.' "—Weeks, op. cit., 247; N. C. Col. Rec., IX, 6. Later the Board of Trade wrote that the law was in effect a "bounty to the tolerated religion at the expense of the established," and petitioned for its disallowance: N. C. Col. Rec., IX, 7, 245, 251, 284, 366.

[3] Saunders, op. cit., xlv, errs in saying that the law of 1766 was repealed soon after its passage.

IV. EPISCOPAL RITES BY LAW AND FREE CIVIL OR RELI-
GIOUS CELEBRATION BY CUSTOM IN SOUTH CAROLINA AND
GEORGIA

The history of marriage in South Carolina runs much the
same course as in the northern province; except that we
hear of no struggle by the privileged establishment to enforce
the statutes eventually enacted in its behalf. For a time,
under the same charters, the two colonies were ruled in the
same way by the proprietors; and in South Carolina for
over three decades there was apparently full toleration with
respect to matrimonial rites. That such was the case near
the close of the seventeenth century may be inferred from
the registration act of 1696. It is required that "every
man which hereafter shall be married according to the
rubrick of the Church of England, or by any other contract
or ceremony," shall record his marriage in the register's
office within thirty days after celebration, or else forfeit
"one royall" for neglect. But at the time of registration
he must produce "a certificate from under the hand of the
parson, minister, magistrate, or otherwise," attested by "six
persons at least met and congregated at such religious meate-
ing" where the ceremony took place. For neglecting to file
the certificate the register forfeits his office.[1]

The Church of England was established by law in 1704.
In the act for that purpose it is declared that "no justice
or magistrate, being a layman, shall presume to join any
persons in marriage, under penalty of one hundred pounds
currant money of this province." Vestries are to provide a
fit person as register of births, christenings, marriages, and
burials, except those of "negroes, Mullatoes, and Indian
slaves;" and a fine is prescribed for wedding contrary to the
table of forbidden degrees.[2] All these provisions are re-

---

[1] COOPER, *Statutes at Large*, II, 120, 121 (act of March 1695/6).

[2] *Ibid.*, 242, 243; also in *N. C. Col. Rec.*, II, 867-82.

peated in the new act of 1706 for the "establishment of
religious worship" in the province.[1] Six years thereafter
the full text of the law of Henry VIII., "for marriages to
stand notwithstanding Pre-Contracts" is adopted; and it
appears again and again in the statute book until recent
days.[2]

No further important change was made in the law before
the Revolution.   The act of 1706, giving a monopoly of the
business of solemnizing matrimony to the established clergy,
remained nominally in force.   A fine could be levied for
neglect of its provisions.   But in the "Up" or "Back"
country it was quietly disregarded ; and, apparently without
a contest, custom sanctioned the optional civil ceremony or
optional ecclesiastical rites according to the usage of each
denomination.   "In the early stages of our juridical and civil
history," says Brevard, "the laws of the province on this
subject were in conformity to the English; but as the population . . . . encreased by emigrants from all countries, and
of different religious denominations, this adherence to Episcopal regulations and forms was gradually relaxed, and at
length generally disregarded."   The church act of 1706, he
adds, must have gone into "effectual and general operation."
But, except partially, "it seems never to have extended
farther than about sixty miles from Charleston."[3]

What has just been said regarding South Carolina applies
equally to Georgia, whose territory had belonged to South
Carolina since the original grant of 1663.   But the charter
issued to James Oglethorpe and his associates in 1732

[1] Cooper, *op. cit.*, II, 289-91 ; also in Brevard, *Alphabetical Digest of Laws of
S. C.*, 41-44. In both these acts elaborate provision is made for registration.

[2] Cooper, *op. cit.*, II, 475, 476, where 32 H. VIII., c. 38, is put in force; and it is
retained in *Revised Statutes* (Columbia, 1873), 481. In 1712, likewise, a part of the
statute 1 Jac. I., c. 11, regarding bigamy was adopted: Cooper, II, 508.

[3] Editorial note in Brevard, *Alphabetical Digest of Laws of S. C.*, II, 41, 42,
notes.

expressly abrogates the laws of the parent colony,[1] and gives the power to enact new laws to the corporation of associates as trustees for the colony.   The Episcopal system was introduced, but it was not rigidly enforced.   The charter to Oglethorpe "guaranteed liberty of conscience to all except papists,[2] and the spirit exhibited in ecclesiastical legislation was one of toleration.   Hence a considerable Puritan element was drawn to the Colony."[3]   The preamble of the act of 1785 shows that it had been the custom for justices, ministers, and "preachers of the gospel" to solemnize marriage. Such marriages are made valid and the practice legalized for the future.[4]

It appears, then, that throughout the southern colonies matrimonial legislation was tending in the same direction. Everywhere, except in Maryland, the optional civil ceremony was legally or practically recognized, though under various restrictions.   Marriage was already a civil contract of mutual partnership; and, notwithstanding an occasional invalidating clause for neglect of the prescribed forms, the common-law marriage by mutual consent was probably valid, though, so far as it appears, the records of the provincial courts are almost entirely silent on that question.[5]   In short, in its

---

[1] With an exception relating to military power: POORE, *Charters*, I, 373, 374. Georgia was made a royal province in 1751; but the policy of toleration was maintained: HOLMES, *Annals*, II, 45; STORY, *Commentaries*, I, 102. In early days the province suffered the usual evils from scarcity of women: *Coll. Georgia Hist. Soc.*, II, 105; III, 32, 144.

[2] POORE, *Charters*, I, 375.

[3] COOK, "Mar. Cel. in Col.," *Atlantic*, LXI, 356.

[4] *Digest of the Laws of Georgia* (Philadelphia, 1801), 314.

[5] Even in Virginia civil marriages were frequent before the Revolution, though liable to penalty. For Maryland the view of the text as to the common-law contract was sustained in the case of Cheseldine v. Brewer, 1 Har. and McH., 152 (1739). This decision was, however, overruled in Denison v. Denison (1871), 35 *Md.*, 361, 379, in which Justice Alvey says: "We think we are safe in saying that there has never been a time in the history of the state, whether before its independence of Great Britain or since, when some ceremony or celebration was not deemed necessary to a valid marriage. In the early days of the province, it was not absolutely necessary that a minister of religion should officiate,— a judge or magistrate could perform

principal elements, throughout the South matrimonial law had reached or was strongly tending toward the existing American type.

the ceremony — but still, in all cases, some formal celebration was required." Of course, the opinion of a judge long after the colonial era, not professing to be based on evidence, can have little weight in settling the present historical problem. Though the laws of the Maryland assembly, like those of Connecticut and Rhode Island (STORY, *Commentaries*, I, §171), were not required to be submitted to the king for approval, it cannot be assumed that such laws could deprive a person of any liberty secured by the common law, but they might bestow greater privileges. *Cf.* BISHOP, *Mar., Div., and Sep.*, I, §416.

A statute of North Carolina, in 1715, declared that the common law should be in force in that province (IREDELL, *Laws*, 1715, 18, 19; STORY, *op. cit.*, I, §142). Yet in this century it has been held that the common law of the state recognizes no marriage not according to the statutes; as to which statement, "the court observed in a subsequent case, 'we express no opinion.' But such, all agree, is not the common law of England."—BISHOP, *op. cit.*, I, §412; citing State *v.* Samuel, 2 Dev. and Bat., 177; and State *v.* Ta-cha-na-tah, 64 *N. C.*, 614.

Several decisions of the courts of Tennessee have regard to the colonial laws of North Carolina, the parent commonwealth, and on the whole sustain the view that informal marriages were good despite the statutes. In the case of Bashaw *v.* the State, 1829 (1 Yerger, 177-97), which gives a history of North Carolina matrimonial legislation for the period 1715-1829, it was held that the celebration must be according to the statutes which had superseded the common law. The same view is taken two years later in Grisham *v.* the State (2 Yerger, 589, 592). But in Andrews *v.* Page, 1868 (3 Heiskell, *Tenn. Reports*, 653, 667), the opposite position is taken, the court holding rightly that the acts of 1741 and 1778 do not expressly prohibit the common-law marriage.

The common-law principle of marriage by mutual consent prevailed in South Carolina (compare 10 McCord, *Statutes*, 357, ed. note; and the case Vaigneur *v.* Kirk, 2 *S. C. Equity Reports*, 640-46, with H. W. Desaussure's note, 646). Referring to the law of South Carolina, generally, BREVARD, *Alphabetical Digest*, II, 41, note, says: "How far the informality of a marriage may afford ground for questioning its validity, on a trial for polygamy, may perhaps admit of some doubt." Historically, however, the doubt is exceedingly small that such an informal contract would be valid.

It is doubtful whether there were any courts in the southern colonies vested with full matrimonial jurisdiction: see BISHOP, *op. cit.*, I, §§115-49.

CHAPTER XIV

OPTIONAL CIVIL OR ECCLESIASTICAL MARRIAGE IN THE MIDDLE COLONIES

[BIBLIOGRAPHICAL NOTE XIV.—The *New York Colonial MSS.*, of more service for the history of divorce, afford several important documents available for the present chapter. The use of these papers is facilitated by O'Callaghan's *Calendar of Historical Manuscripts* (Albany, 1866). Among the treasures also preserved in the State Library at Albany may be found the MS. copy of the *Dongan Laws*, including the marriage act of 1684 concerning which there has been much discussion; and some forty volumes of *MSS. Marriage License Bonds*, of interest to the genealogist and historian. The use of these is made easier by the published *Names of Persons for Whom Marriage Licenses Were Issued by the Secretary of the Province of New York, Previous to 1784* (Albany, 1860), to which O'Callaghan has given an *Introduction*.

The most important source for the province is the *Documents Relating to the Colonial History of New York* (Albany, 1856-83), edited by O'Callaghan and Fernow. Original material may also be found in the *Records of New Amsterdam* (New York, 1897); Munsell's *Annals of Albany* (Albany, 1850-59); the same compiler's *Collections on the History of Albany* (Albany, 1865-71); and Valentine's *Manual of the Corporation of the City of New York* (New York, 1843 ff.). For the Dutch period we have O'Callaghan's *Laws and Ordinances* (Albany, 1868); for the proprietary government, "The Duke of Yorke's Book of Laws," in Linn's *Charter and Laws* (Harrisburg, 1879); earlier in Vol. I of the *Collections of the New York Historical Society for the Year 1809* (New York, 1811); and recently in Vol. I of the *Colonial Laws of New York* (Albany, 1894), while the last-named collection covers the period of the royal province, and is enriched by Cumming's *Historical Note* and his comments on the various statutes and papers. The celebrated "Lauderdale Peerage Case," so important for understanding the marriage law of New York for the period between 1691 and 1772, may be found in the English *Law Reports*, X (London, 1885); and also abridged in Cook, *Reports of Cases Decided by the English Courts*, XXXVII (Albany, 1887). In connection with this case several members of the American bar submitted written opinions, and three of those published are in the New York State Library: see Fowler, *Letter and Opinion* (New York, May 11, 1885); Seward, *Answers to the*

Interrogations of Brodie and Sons (New York, June, 1885); and Webster, *Opinion on the Law of Marriage in the Colony of New York* (New York, May 26, 1885). But far more conclusive than the views of the witnesses and expert advisers called at the trial is the remarkable paper of Rev. John Rodgers, found in the cabinet of President Stiles by the historian Holmes, entitled "A brief view of the state of religious liberty in New York 1773," in 2 *Mass. Hist. Coll.*, I (Boston, 1838).

For the history of bundling, besides the mention in Valentine's *Manual*, should be consulted the case of Seger *v.* Slingerland in Caine's *Reports*, II (New York and Albany, 1860), where the custom was judicially considered; also Lamb, *History of the City of New York* (New York and Chicago, 1877); and especially Stiles, *Bundling* (Albany, 1871). Stiles, *History of the City of Brooklyn* (Brooklyn, 1867–70), gives an account of the restrictions put on the remarriage of widows in the old Dutch wills; and there are some notices of marriage law and customs in Grant, *Memoirs of an American Lady* (New York, 1809); Weise, *History of the City of Albany* (Albany, 1884); Watson, *Annals and Occurrences of New York City and State* (Philadelphia, 1846); Vanderbilt, *Social History of Flatbush* (New York, 1882; new ed., 1899); Ostrander, *History of the City of Brooklyn and King's County* (Brooklyn, 1894); Gerard, *The Old Stadt Huys of New Amsterdam* (New York, 1875); Hazard, *Annals of Pennsylvania* (Philadelphia, 1850); and especially Earle's *Colonial Days in Old New York* (New York, 1896). In 1786 a brief account of wedding customs in New York state was given by Hannah Thompson, "Letters," in *Pa. Mag. of Hist. and Biog.*, XIV (Philadelphia, 1890); and in 1748 the governor's lucrative monopoly of marriage-license fees is described by the Swedish botanist Kalm, *Travels in North America* (Warrington, 1770): see Hart, *Source-Book of American History* (New York, 1899), extract 50. Cook, "The Marriage Celebration in the Colonies," *Atlantic*, LXI (Boston, 1888), discusses the subject for the middle provinces; and for the historical background Brodhead, *History of the State of New York* (New York, 1853–71); O'Callaghan, *History of New Netherland* (2d ed., New York, 1855); Friedberg, *Eheschliessung* (Leipzig, 1865); and his *Geschichte der Civilehe* (Hamburg, 1877), have been of most service.

For New Jersey, Leaming and Spicer, *Grants, Concessions, and Original Constitutions* (2d ed., Philadelphia, 1881), is of first-rate importance. This collection is supplemented by the documents in *New Jersey Archives* (Newark, 1880–86); and Smith, *History of the Colony of Nova-Caesaria or New Jersey* (Burlington, 1765; reprint, 1877); while the law of 1719 may be found in *Acts of the General Assembly* (Woodbridge, 1752); or in Allinson, *Acts of the General Assembly, 1702–1776* (Burlington, 1776).

The early legislation of Pennsylvania is contained in Linn's convenient *Charter to William Penn, and Laws of the Province of Pa., 1682–1700* (Harrisburg, 1879), which is supplemented by Nead's valuable *Historical Notes.* Some illustrations of judicial and administrative proceedings have been gleaned from the *Colonial Records of Pa.* (Harrisburg, 1838–53); and the marriage laws enacted from 1700 onward are cited in Carey and Bioren, *Laws* (Philadelphia, 1803); the *Laws of the Commonwealth of Pa.,* 1700–1810 (Philadelphia, 1810); and Pepper and Lewis, *Digest* (Philadelphia, 1896). For the doctrines of the Friends one must go to the founder. William Penn's *Select Works* (1 vol. fol., London, 1771; 5 vols., 8vo, London, 1782) are a mine of information on every phase of Quaker teaching; and the same is true of William Sewel's *History of the Rise, Increase, and Progress of the Christian People called Quakers* (original Dutch ed., Amsterdam, 1717; first English ed., London, 1722), a work whose scrupulous accuracy has never been impeached. On the other hand, for the false charges brought against the Friends by their orthodox antagonists one should read Thomas Underhill, *Hell broke loose: or an History of the Quakers Both Old and New* (London, 1660), who has raked together scandals of every description; Nathaniel Smith, *The Quaker's Spiritual Court* (London, 1668); and Gerard Croese, *Historia quakeriana* (Amsterdam, 1695; English ed., London, 1696), the book whose errors called forth Sewel's *History.* More recently Quaker rites and wedding customs have been described by Watson, *Annals of Philadelphia* (last ed., Philadelphia, 1881); Hallowell, *Quaker Invasion of Mass.* (Boston, 1883); Applegarth, "Quakers in Pennsylvania," *J. H. U. S.*, X (Baltimore, 1892); and in a lively sketch, drawn mainly from records of the Monthly Meeting, by Earle, "Among Friends," in *New England Magazine*, XIX (Boston, 1898). There is a typical Quaker marriage certificate of 1692 in Vol. XIII of the *Pa. Mag. of Hist. and Biog.* (Philadelphia, 1889). A brief summary of the matrimonial laws of the colony may be found in Gordon, *History of Pennsylvania* (Philadelphia, 1829).]

I.   NEW YORK

THE history of matrimonial institutions in the middle colonies is on the whole less attractive than in New England. At any rate, it is less interesting in the sense of being less eventful. The original materials from which to construct it are less abundant. There is nothing equal to the *Diary* of the inimitable Sewall from which it may be filled out and embellished. It is not quickened by the struggle to maintain or to introduce diverse forms of celebration resting upon opposing theories as to the nature of the nuptial contract. There is little answering to the Puritan thoroughness in regulating the conduct of domestic life, even among the Quakers.   Hence the legislative and judicial records are relatively meager.   In New York, notably, between 1684 and the Revolution the law-book is a complete blank.   On the other hand, in Pennsylvania, after the establishment of the proprietary government, the predominance of Quaker sentiment enables the original usages and the early statutes regarding wedlock to run their even course for generations without essential change.   Still the study of marriage in the middle section of the English colonies is not devoid of social interest.   There, on account of mixed population and diverse religious sects, toleration in the main prevailed.   The quaint records of the Dutch and the homely ceremonial of the Friends may even prove entertaining, while in this field, as in every other, the thought and experience of New York and Pennsylvania have done much to form and fix the types of law and administration now prevailing in the United States.

a) *Law and custom in New Netherland.*—Long before the first plantations were established on the Hudson, as already seen, optional civil marriage had been sanctioned in several of the Dutch states, and as early as 1656 it was extended to the United Netherlands.   In Holland independents of both old and New England found encouragement and also a model in the effort to realize similar ideas born of their common Protestantism.

It is therefore strange at first glance that a thorough-going civil-marriage law should not have been introduced in New Netherland from the beginning.   The laws of the mother-country, even after 1656, varied considerably in details among the different provinces.   In their content they

generally rested on the basis of the later Roman statutes.[1]
From the desire to check the evils of clandestine contracts,
in many instances rigorous measures had been adopted.
Usually parental consent, often publication of banns, was
made essential to a valid marriage.[2] The laws of Guelderland were especially severe;[3] and these according to Fernow, "naturally prevailed" in New Netherland; for a
"majority of the early settlers" came from that province.
"In Guelderland," he declares, "a marriage was void, if the
express consent of the father, or if dead of the mother had
not been obtained for the marriage of a son. With regard
to daughters the law was still more rigorous; even a marriage,
entered into by a girl with parental consent, did not eman-
cipate her from parental authority, if she was still under
age at her husband's death: she had to place herself again
under the guardianship of her father or mother. Neither
were parents obliged to give before a Court of Justice any
reasons in case they refused consent. This law had its
foundation in the Codex Justinianus."[4]

In all respects except the celebration optional civil or
ecclesiastical marriage was sanctioned in New Netherland.
It is doubtless safe to assume that during the early years of
the Dutch colony banns and parental consent, probably
according to the law of Guelderland, were required; but
legally, so far as the evidence at hand shows, the covenant
had to be solemnized by a minister with religious rites.
The first legislation by the local authorities appears to have
been enacted only ten years before the first establishment of
English rule. The occasion was the violation of the "custom

---

[1] O'CALLAGHAN, *Introduction to Names of Persons for Whom Marriage Licenses Were Issued*, p. iii.

[2] FRIEDBERG, *Eheschliessung*, 478 ff., 485 ff., gives the details, citing the Dutch authorities.

[3] Compare the summaries of FRIEDBERG, *op. cit.*, 487, 488, 491.

[4] FERNOW, *Doc. Rel. to Col. Hist. of N. Y.*, XIV, 243, note.

of our Fatherland" in the publication of banns by the magistrates of Gravesend, as appears from the following letter addressed to them by Peter Stuyvesant:[1]

"Worthy and dear friends.

"I received in due time your letter of the 13th inst. sent to me by the Fiscal, which has been communicated to the High Council. We have been very much astonished that you arrogate to yourself the publication of marriage-proclamations within your village without our or the Council's knowledge, in cases where both parties live beyond the jurisdiction of your village. As to the allegation made by you, that the person is a freeman of your village, he is the same in the City of *Amsterdam* and here in this City and for this reason must the marriage-proclamation be reported and published here as well as there according to the customs of our Fatherland. We do not deny, that matrimony is ruled by divine and by human laws, but they who enter upon this state must do it according to these divine and human laws, with the consent or knowledge of their parents, tutors or guardians and then notify thereof the Commissary, appointed by higher authority, at the place where they reside or where they have previously been living during the last year. Your final request, that we should send you a copy of the order and power of attorney, which his [evidently Johannis van Beeck's] father has given us concerning this son, is not complied with, as we do not think ourselves bound to do it, considering yours being a subordinate jurisdiction and subject to us; besides the father would be displeased and it would be unreasonable in us, to communicate to others, what an honest and prominent man has written to us in a detailed letter.

"Thus much in answer to your open letter. This further serves as cover of the enclosed order and resolution made

[1] *Ibid.* The letter is dated Jan. 20, 1654.

by us and the Council, which you must promptly obey, not because we wish to prevent the marriage, but that according to divine and human laws and ordinances they may be put in practice, proclaimed and affixed, at the proper place and without infraction of anybody's rights.

"Relying thereupon we commend you with cordial greetings to God's protection and remain

Your well-affected friend and Governor

P. Stuyvesant."

The ordinance mentioned in the letter bears date of January 19, 1654/5, and runs as follows:

Since the magistrates at Gravesend "have presumed and undertaken publickly to post notices of marriage" of persons "domiciled in and about this city of *New Amsterdam*," far beyond their proper district; therefore the "Director General and Council order and notify the aforesaid Magistrates of Gravesend and all others within this Province, to annul such posting of intentions of Marriage, and on sight hereof to withdraw the same, and in all cases to proceed with and confirm no such Marriage, either privately or publickly, before and until such persons, according to *Netherland* style, have entered and received their bans and proclamations of marriage where they are dwelling and have resided the last years."[1]

This important measure was supplemented by another four years later. The preamble recites that it had become common for betrothed persons to put off marrying for a long time after the proclamation of their banns, "which is directly in contravention of, and contrary to the excellent order and customs of our Fatherland." Therefore it is ordered that thenceforward all persons must be married within one month

---

[1] O'CALLAGHAN, *Laws and Ordinances*, 152, 153. For this ordinance see also *New York Colonial MSS.*, XII, 40; and compare *ibid.*, IV, 456; V, 197; VIII, 647. Consult WEBSTER, *Opinion on the Law of Marriage prevailing in the Colony of N. Y.*, 1772, 19, 20 (Lauderdale Peerage Case), who discusses these ordinances.

after publication, unless they can give a good excuse.[1] Light
is thrown on the real motive for the adoption of this act by
its provision that no man and woman are henceforth to live
together until lawfully married. It seems to have been the
custom, in too many instances, for betrothed couples whose
banns had been asked the first time to begin living together
as if already man and wife. They looked upon themselves
as at least half married; and we are thus confronted by a
state of affairs strikingly similar to that which we have
found existing in New England in consequence of the laws
governing pre-contract. Doubtless couples through indifference, the refusal to fulfil the contract on the part of an
unscrupulous lover, or for other reasons, were now and then
led to protract the irregular marital relation beyond the
completion of the term prescribed for the publication of
banns. Moreover, as in New England, the custom of queesting or bundling imported from the old home may have
proved a snare for the unwary feet of the young men and
maidens of New Netherland. Indeed, the practice of bundling has been assigned by New York writers as the proximate
cause of the singular provision referred to. "It was one of
the ordinances of the time," says Valentine, "that upon an
agreement of marriage, the bans should be published from
the pulpit three times, before the marriage could be solemnized. Impatient of the delay, however, the youthful couple
were often inclined to be satisfied with their moral obligations towards each other, and to waive the immediate fulfill-
ment of the legal ceremony; in the meantime . . . . the
indulgence of cohabitation, then called 'bundling,' was
practiced. It was for a long time winked at by the community, but its violence against the tenets of propriety was
obvious, and at the time [1656] before spoken of, in which

[1] Brodhead, *Hist. of the State of N. Y.*, I, 639. For the text of the ordinance of
Jan. 15, 1658, see *N. Y. Col. MSS.*, XVI, 40, 129; also O'Callaghan, *op. cit.*, 328, 329;
and *Law Reports*, X (1885), 729 (Lauderdale Peerage Case).

the city authorities resolved to set themselves to the reformation of abuses, this custom came under their prohibatory
decrees." There were "those who still maintained its
advantageous results, even though the contract of marriage
were subsequently violated. The latter instances, it was
contended, were comparatively few, and were set off by the
increase of population which came" through this means.
Yet the reformers "triumphed, and in 1658 it was ordered,
that henceforth the mere publication of bans should not
justify cohabitation."[1] The custom of bundling was, however, too tenacious to be stopped by a decree of the legislator.
For more than a century in New York it continued to
flourish, and sometimes to bear evil fruit, as is clearly
revealed in the case of Seger *v.* Slingerland, which was
decided in 1804.[2] Another action shows that forty years
later the practice existed in the neighboring state of Pennsylvania. In this instance the plaintiff admits that "the
custom in courtship which he has denominated bundling"
prevails "very generally" in the part of the country where
the interested persons reside; and in this suit, as in the New
York case, the defendant won on appeal because of the
connivance of the parents in the misconduct of their
daughter.[3]

According to the old Dutch law, enforced in New Netherland, all persons desiring to form a valid union were required
to appear before the minister or the court, as they saw fit, in

---

[1] VALENTINE, *Manual of the Corporation*, 1858, 497, 498; *cf.* also LAMB, *History of
the City of N. Y.*, I, 183.

[2] CAINE, *Reports*, II, 219, 220. This was a case on appeal by the original defendant who had been sued for damage for debauching the plaintiff's daughter. The
defendant won on the ground of connivance of the parents of the girl. "We lay out
of view," says the court, "the custom which it is agreed prevails in that part of the
country for young people, who are courting, to sleep together." "Nor is it an excuse
for the parent to say that promises of marriage had been exchanged." *Cf.* also
STILES, *Origin and Hist. of Bundling*, 44 ff., 109-11.

[3] Case of Hollis *v.* Wells (1845), 3 *Pa. Law Journal* (Philadelphia, 1872), 29-33.
Under head of "A Custom Must be Moral," these two cases are discussed in LAWSON
(J. D.), *The Law of Usages and Customs* (St. Louis, 1881), 58-60.

the place where they had "their fixed domicil for the last year and day, and to apply there, for three Sundays or market days, when publication of the banns was to be made in the church or the court-house, or other place where the court of justice was held; and every one who had any impediment to propose, was obliged to state the same in the mean time, on pain of being otherwise deprived of that right."[1]

The following document of 1655, contained in Fernow's collection relating to the plantations on the Delaware when under the Dutch jurisdiction, may serve to illustrate the prescribed formality in applying for publication of banns:

"Appears Toms Broen, as father and guardian of his daughter, Jannetje Tomas and consents to the marriage between her and Willem Mauritz here present and requests that their legal bans might be published; the names being, of the bridegroom Willem Mauritz, bachelor, from Walle Schier, about 33 years old, of the bride Jannetje Tomas, spinster, born in New-Netherland, about 16 years old. Witness Stuyte Andries."[2]

From the same collection, two years later, we learn that "Laurens Pieters bachelor from Lier and Catlyne Jans of Gottenburch in Sweden were confirmed in marriage after proclamation of banns on the previous Sundays."[3]

The civil courts in New Netherland possessed full jurisdiction in all suits or matrimonial causes, including cases of separation and divorce.[4] For an understanding of the relation of the lower and higher courts, the procedure in

[1] O'Callaghan, *Names of Persons for Whom Marriage Licenses Were Issued*, p. iii.

[2] Addressed to the vice-director and his council: Fernow, *Doc. Rel. to Col. Hist. of N. Y.*, XII, 137 (Dec. 29, 1655). For a similar application see *ibid.*, XII, 153, 154. For further record of entry of banns before the "mayor of New York" (1670-71) see *Records of New Amsterdam*, VI, 262, 334.

[3] Dec. 24, 1657: Fernow, *loc. cit.*, 156.

[4] For a discussion of the divorce jurisdiction of the Dutch courts see chap. xv, below.

such cases, and the details of the law, the often-mentioned
case of Johannis van Beeck and Maria Verleth is instructive.
The facts in this case appear to have been the proximate
cause of the ordinance of 1654/5 and the letter of Stuyvesant
already submitted.   It is all the more interesting because it
involves the double question of irregular banns and unlawful celebration, as shown by the final decree.   On January
26, 1654, takes place the first step in the proceedings.   Cornelis van Tienhoven, the schout, lodges formal complaint
before the burgomasters and schepens of New Amsterdam
against the court of Gravesend for illegally "granting and
confirming the Banns of Matrimony betwixt Johan van
Beeck and Maria Verleth, who both have their domicil in
and about this city of New Amsterdam;" suggesting that
such conduct tends to the infringement of the good policy
of the fatherland, as also the privileges and jurisdiction of
the city, and to prepare a way for sons and daughters to go
secretly and get married.   In reply, says the record, the
"Burgomasters, and Schepens . . . . do hereby refer the
foregoing complaint and proposition made by Cornelis van
Tienhoven, in quality as Schout, to their High Mightinesses
the Director-General and Councillors of New Fetherland."[1]
But this did not end the matter.[2]   On February 10, pending
the decision of the higher court, van Beeck petitioned the
burgomasters and schepens "that his bans with Maria Var-

[1] Valentine, *Manual of the Corporation*, 1845-46, 368; *Records of New Amster-dam*, I, 155.

[2] While these proceedings were in progress, another appeal, growing out of the case, came from the schout, burgomasters, and schepens, in the city hall, special session of Feb. 8, 1656. Case of " Maria Verleth, pltf. v. Joost van Beeck, deft." The defendant maintains, as the marriage between Johannis van Beeck and Maria Ver-leth is not yet declared legal, that certain "letters are not her's, until the marriage be legalized." But should the marriage be declared lawful by the court, supreme council, and consistory, he consents that she shall have them. He only wants his right. The court lets Maria have the letters provisionally, because it has never been informed that the marriage has been declared illegal, and it has already announced that it must respect the proclamation of the church and the "marriage tie of said Young people."—*Records of New Amsterdam*, II, 36.

leth may be entered and be properly proclaimed here" in New Amsterdam. Whereupon the court "engage to do same because it is usual and custom of Fathld to have publcts where domicil is and married where he pleases."[1] After a little delay, the court keeps its promise. On February 19 the burgomasters and schepens solemnly examined the petition, noting (1) who instituted marriage and the apostles' teaching; (2) the proper ages and the attained ages of both parties; (3) consent of parents on the girl's side; (4) distance between this and fatherland; (5) that "matters by long delay might come to be disclosed . . . . which would bring disgrace on both families;" therefore that "proper ecclesiastical proclamations . . . . ought to be made at the earliest opportunity and followed afterwards by their marriage."[2] This resolution seems a trifle indiscreet, in view of the fact that the original case had been referred to their High Mightinesses. It is therefore not strange that a communication signed by Stuyvesant himself should express surprise that van Beeck should have affixed by a poster "that his marriage, contracted not only without his father's knowledge, but contrary to his express prohibition to marry abroad has been declared lawful and proper by Resolution of the Burgomasters and Schepens . . . .; of which Resolution the Director General and Council are ignorant;" at the same time requesting an "authentic copy" of the resolution, with "written reasons" for failing to submit the same for approbation of the higher court.[3] This was on March 2, 1654. Apparently, after republication of the banns, van Beeck had had the marriage ceremony performed outside of the Dutch jurisdiction, probably because of the doubtful

---

[1] *Ibid.*, I, 159, 160.

[2] *Ibid.*, 164, 165. Earlier on the same day, the record says, van Beeck prays "that disposal be made of petition and remonstrance;" but no action was taken because the bench was not complete: *ibid.*, 163, 164.

[3] *Records of New Amsterdam*, I, 173, 174.

legality of the course taken by the officials of New Amsterdam. The records are silent as to the further proceedings in the case, except as they may be inferred from the following decree of the higher court, rendered not earlier, apparently, than 1656, which leaves us in doubt as to how the original complaint against the magistrates of Gravesend was disposed of:

"Whereas, the Director-General and Council of *New Netherland* have heard the charge of the Fiscal against *Johannis van Beecq*, a free merchant and inhabitant of this City of *New Amsterdam*, defendant, who has been duly summoned by the Court Messenger *Elslandt* in the name of the Fiscal on three Court days and who has had himself married by an unauthorized countryman, named *Goodman Crab*, living at *Greenwich*, against the laudable laws and customs of the *United Netherlands* and, as the Fiscal further states and proves in his charge, contrary to the advice and command of his lawful guardian,[1] the Honble Director-General, also without previously publishing the bans and who has so far failed to make his appearance,

"And whereas the Fiscal demands by his motion, exhibited on the 1st of September, 1654, that the said *van Beecq* be condemned in contumacy,

"Therefore, after proper invocation of the Lord, the Director-General and Council of *New Netherland*, in the name and behalf of their Noble High: Might: the Lords-States-General of the *United Netherlands* and of the Noble Lords-Directors of the Privileged West India Company administering justice at the requisition of the Fiscal, declare, that the Fiscal's charges are true and founded in law and therefore the marriage of *Johannis van Beecq* and *Maria Verleth*, solemnized at *Greenwich* and confirmed by an unauthorized person contrary to the laudable laws and customs

---

[1] See the reference to power of attorney in Stuyvesant's letter, p. 269, above.

of *Netherland* and without previous publication of the bans, is hereby declared . . . . unlawful and the said *Jan van Beecq* and *Maria Verleth* are commanded to live separate under penalty of being punished according to law for living in concubinage."[1]

From the evidence already presented it is perhaps not rash to infer that marriage by mere private consent, in words of the present tense, was not valid in New Netherland. Publication of banns and celebration before an authorized person were essential. The principle, therefore, of the English common-law marriage did not obtain. It had been superseded by statute. These records afford other evidence to sustain this conclusion. Thus in February, 1662, William Beeckman, of "Fort Altena on the South-River," writes to Stuyvesant and the council, complaining that one Laers, a Finnish priest, who was granted a divorce from his wife two months before, has "married himself again last Sunday" — an act "which in my opinion (under currection) he has no right to do. I expect your Honors' orders, how to conduct myself in regard to it."[2] As a result the marriage was declared to be "null, void, illegal;" seemingly on the ground that self-marriage was not tolerated by the usages of the Reformed church. Clearly in the opinion of the court the performance of the ceremony by a person legally competent was necessary to a valid contract. It is possible, however, that the decree was unjust because of unfair representation of the facts by Beeckman, who is accused of being a tyrant. In a letter to Stuyvesant, remonstrating against his treatment, Laers says: "I cannot discover anything illegal in it [his conduct]. I acted just in the same manner as I had done before in respect to others; exactly as others do who are not prosecuted for it, and I can conscientiously

---

[1] FERNOW, *Doc. Rel. to Col. Hist. of N. Y.*, XIV, 291.

[2] *Ibid.*, XII, 359, 360. The case is also discussed by GERARD, *The Old Stadt Huys of New Amsterdam*, 390, 391.

assure you that it was done without any evil intentions.
Had I known that my marrying myself in this manner should
have been so unfavorably interpreted, I should have submitted to the usage of the Reformed Church.   But I did
not know it.   Wherefore I pray once more the honorable
general that he will vouchsafe me his aid." [1]

Another case, or rather pair of cases, occurring during
the restoration of Dutch rule in 1674, seems conclusive as
to the severity of the law.   On the fifth of February of that
year, as the fiscal alleges, Jacob Fabricius, a Lutheran
preacher, had "contrary to the laws of this government
married Ralph Doxy and Mary van Harris . . . . without
having any lawful authority thereto and without publication
of bans."   For this offense it is suggested in the complaint
that the culprit be severely whipped and "forever banished
this government *cum expensis*."   After hearing the fiscal's
charge, the confession of Fabricius, and a "report" of the
latter's previous bad behavior, the court decides not to
"proceed against him in the most rigorous manner, considering his age and late position, but they condemn him
and declare him incapable to perform the functions of a
minister and what is connected with them within this
province for the time of one year.   After this time has
elapsed Deft. shall be held to ask for a special 'consent'
before he shall be re-admitted to the performance of the said
functions." [2]

---

[1] GERARD, *op. cit.*, 391, who says Laers was not legally bound to conform to the
usage of the Reformed church. See also the documents in this case in O'CAL-
LAGHAN, *op. cit.*, XII, 358, 359, 363, 366, 367.

[2] FERNOW, *op. cit.*, XII, 512: case of the Fiscal *v.* Jacob Fabricius, March 1, 1674,
before Governor-General Colve and the council. A version of the case is also given
by O'CALLAGHAN, *op. cit.*, II, 693, who translates " license " where Fernow uses
" consent " in the last sentence.

It is greatly to be feared that Brother Fabricius was a rather uncomfortable
inhabitant; for at the same session of the court the fiscal charges that he did " beat
and use force and violence against Marretie Jurians, in her own house," for which it
is thought he ought to be " condemned in a fine of five Beavers with costs." The
defendant admits the charge; " but says that the above named Marretie Jurians did

The case against Ralph Doxy is complicated by additional charges. The fiscal makes no direct reference to the unauthorized celebration or to the failure to publish the banns, though from the judgment of the court we perceive that these offenses were considered; but accuses him of entering "in an unlawful manner, into the married state with Mary van Harris, making use for that purpose, of a forged certificate," further alleging that he "hath still a wife alive who resides in New England;" for which delinquencies he ought to be severely whipped and "banished the country forever, with costs." In his reply, Doxy "denies ever having been married to a woman before," but confesses "his guilt as regards the forged certificate," saying "that through love for Mary Harris he had allowed it to be executed by a certain Englishman, now gone to the Barbadoes, and therefore prays forgiveness." The court declared the marriage unlawful on the two counts for which Fabricius was suspended; but "finding the charge against him of having a second (*sic*) wife in New England unfounded, he is therefore permitted to confirm himself in wedlock with the abovenamed Mary, according to the laws of the government." For the forged certificate "he is pardoned for this time on his promise of improvement, and request for forgiveness."[1]

With the exception of the restriction put upon bundling, if that were indeed the purpose of the act of 1658, the Dutch

provoke him with harsh language." Their honors, however, deemed it just to assess him "two Beavers with costs": O'CALLAGHAN, *loc. cit.*, 693. Later Fabricius was accused of riotous conduct at Newcastle on June 4, 1674, but he denied the charge and offered to bring witnesses: FERNOW, *op. cit.*, XII, 521. Possibly religious bickerings had something to do with his troubles. At any rate on June 1, 1675, the Lutherans on the Delaware petitioned that he be confirmed as pastor: *ibid.*, 529. On April 18, following his suspension for marrying Doxy, he had the hardihood to ask that the sentence be mitigated, so that "he might be at least allowed to baptize, if he may not preach and act as minister;" but the court declined his request: *ibid.*, 512.

[1] O'CALLAGHAN, *op. cit.*, II, 691, 692. On these two cases see FOWLER, *Letter and Opinion*, 60 ff. (Lauderdale Peerage Case).

law-makers do not seem to have busied themselves with the regulation of courtship. Sexual transgressions were severely dealt with, although not with the same rigor as in New England or even in early Virginia. Neither the death penalty nor the scarlet letter appears. Fornicators, if single, were required to contract marriage or pay a heavy fine.[1] Adulterers fared worse. Some illustrations from the judicial records in such cases have been gleaned by Cowley from the *Colonial Manuscripts*. Among these are the sentence to whipping and banishment of Ytie [Yutie] Jansen, "for living in adultery with Jan Parcel, and also the sentence of Laurens Duyts, who, for selling his wife, Yutie Jansen, and forcing her to live in adultery with another man, and for living also himself in adultery, was 'to have a rope tied around his neck, and to be severely flogged; to have his right ear cut off, and to be banished for fifty years.' John Parcel, for living in adultery with this Yutie Jansen, whom he had thus bought from her own husband, was 'to be placed at the whipping-post, with two rods in his arm,' to be banished twenty years and pay a fine of a hundred guilders [forty dollars], with costs. The fourth party, Geesje Jansen, for living in adultery with Laurens Duyts, was 'to be conducted to the whipping-post, and fastened thereto, the upper part of her body being stripped naked, and two rods placed in her hand; to be afterwards conducted, in that wise, outside the city gates, and banished the province for the term of thirty years, with costs.' Moreover, Iva Dircksen, for adultery, was 'to be conducted to the place where justice is administered, and there to witness the punishments inflicted this day, and then to be banished for the term of fifty years.'"[2]

---

[1] O'CALLAGHAN, *Laws and Ordinances*, 495.

[2] COWLEY, *Our Divorce Courts*, 33, 34; citing *New York Colonial MSS.*, *1630–1664:* Dutch: Part I, Vol. VIII, 1049, 1051, 1653, 1055, 1057.

Breach of promise suits are not infrequent. Sometimes it is the faithless swain who is prosecuted for his broken troth; as in 1669, when Elizabeth Stedwill called Jan Hendrix van Gunst to account;[1] or when Maria Besems seeks pecuniary satisfaction for the like offense of Boudewyn van Nieuwland.[2] Sometimes it is the maid who asserts the woman's privilege, if not her legal right, to change her mind; as in the case of Pieter Koch *v.* Annetie Cornelissen van Vorst, which took place in New Amsterdam, 1653–54, and may serve as an example. On February 24 the defendant's stepfather delivers her "papers" to the burgomasters and schepens, who order that each party shall have a copy of the other's papers, and that the defendant shall appear in person. Then the case drags along for nearly a year, over no less than eight sessions of the court, before the pleadings and other preliminaries are finished. At last, on February 19, 1654, the papers are sent by the lower court to the director-general and council for advice. Apparently in consequence of this advice the documents are then submitted to a special committee of three men, who hand in their report on the 18th of the following May. Upon this report the decision of the burgomasters and schepens was based, though they resolved to keep the judgment in "abeyance" until "requested" by the parties to the suit. From the records it appears that there was an oral promise of marriage; that the plaintiff had given presents to his betrothed; and that she, because of his "misbehaviour," was not disposed to keep her engagement. The court, however, decided that a promise once given should remain in force. Neither person without the consent of the other and the approbation of the court should marry. The defendant was allowed to keep her

[1] *Records of New Amsterdam*, VI, 203.

[2] Gerard, *The Old Stadt Huys*, 27. *Cf. ibid.*, 26, 27, where cases of breach of promise are mentioned in 1642, 1644, 1653, and 1656.

presents until marriage or until, with the knowledge of the magistracy, the betrothed should set each other free. Costs were to be borne equally by the parties.[1]

It is not surprising that among a people so thrifty and sensible as the pioneers of New Netherland the remarriage of a widow or a widower should be accompanied, or anticipated, by prudential measures, designed to protect the interests of the children of the first union. For this reason the wills and marriage contracts, specimens of which have been preserved, are of peculiar interest. According to Stiles, a well-known investigator of deeds and wills in Williamsburgh[2] makes the remark "that the old Dutch wills seem not to trust the widow in a second marriage. The restraints placed upon remarriages, by wills, were generally in favor of the children of the first marriage; and the widows thus restricted generally signed consents to accept the bequests in lieu of dower, for the good reason that propriety did not allow them to refuse so soon after the death of their first husband, and because the devises and bequests in lieu of dower vested an estate for life, or three thirds of the estate subject to a contingency in their own control, instead of one third absolutely. The will of Cornelius van Catts of Bushwick, dated in 1726, and expressed in a sort of half Dutch dialect, devises to his wife Annetjie, his whole estate . . . .

---

[1] *Records of New Amsterdam*, I, 54; see *ibid.*, 167, 199, 200. It may perhaps be inferred that the couple concluded to release each other; for only seven years after the trial (May 24, 1661) "Annetje Dircks, widow of Pieter Koch," is mentioned; *ibid.*, III, 310; and similar phrase is twice repeated: *ibid.*, 403; IV, 34.

There are other cases. "In 1654 Greetje Waemans produced a marriage ring and two letters, promissory of marriage, and requested that on that evidence Daniel de Silla be 'condemned to legally marry her.' He vainly pleaded his unfortunate habit of some days drinking too much, and that on those days he did much which he regretted; among other things his bacchanalian love-making of Greetje. François Soleil, the New Amsterdam gunsmith, another recreant lover, swore he would rather go away and live with the Indians (a terrible threat) than marry the fair Rose whom he had left to droop neglected — and unmarried."—EARLE, *Colonial Days in Old New York*, 51; and for mention of other cases, in connection with Dutch wedding gifts, see *ibid.*, 52, 53.

[2] J. M. STEARNS.

while she remains his widow—both real and personal. 'But if she happen to marry, then I geff her nothing of my estate, neither real nor personal. I geff to my well-beloved son, Cornelius, the best horse that I have, or else £7, 10s., for his good as my eldest son. And then my two children, Cornelius Catts and David Catts, all heef [half] of my whole effects, land and movables, that is to say, Cornelius Catts heef of all, and David Catts heef of all. But my wife can be master of all for bringing up to good learning my two children. . . . . But if she comes to marry again, then her husband can take her away from the farm, and all will be left for the children, Cornelius Catts and David Catts, heef and heef.'"[1]

It was not, however, the first husband alone who took such precautions. After betrothal careful marriage contracts were often drawn up when either a widow or a widower was about to re-enter wedded life. The following is a sample of these stipulations, dated July 27, 1656:

"Appears Geertruyt Jacops, widow of the late Mr. Roeloff de Haes, now betrothed to Jacob Crabbe and declares her intention of proving and assigning their father's inheritance to the children, left by him, Mr. de Haes, and

---

[1] Stiles, *History of Brooklyn*, I, 233, 234.

The author adds: "So also in the will of John Burrows, of Newton, July 7, 1678, he devises to his son John his then dwelling-house, farm, orchard, out-houses, and lands, etc. 'But not to dispossess my beloved wife during the time of her widowhood. But if she marry, then her husband must provide for her as I have done.' So also the will of Thomas Skillman, of Newton, in 1739."—*Ibid.*, 233, 234.

"Often joint-wills were made by husband and wife, each with equal rights, if survivor. This was peculiarly a Dutch fashion. In Fordham, in 1670 and 1673, Claude de Maistre and his wife Hester du Bois, Pierre Cresson and his wife Rachel Cloos, Gabriel Carboosie and Brieta Walferts, all made joint-wills. The last-named husband in his half of the will enjoined loss of property if Brieta married again. Perhaps he thought there had been enough marrying and giving in marriage already in that family, for Brieta had had three husbands,—a Dane, a Frieslander, and a German,—and his first wife had had four, and he—well, several I guess; and there were a number of children; and you couldn't expect any poor Dutchman to find it easy to make a will in all that confusion. In Albany may be found several joint-wills, among them two dated 1663 and 1676; others in the Schuyler family."—Earle, *Colonial Days in Old New York*, 54, 55.

born in wedlock by her, Geertruyt Jacops, to wit Johannes
de Haes, old about 10 years, Marrietje de Haes, old about
9 years, and Annitje, old about three years, and assigns
herewith to each of the aforesaid children the sum of 6
carolus guilders, declaring at the same time upon her conscience, in place of an oath that she, affiant, hereby satisfies
the aforesaid children out of their father's inheritance and
this declaration is made in presence and with the consent of
her affianced husband Jacobus Crabbe, and she Geertruyt
Jacops, has nominated, constituted, and appointed . . . .
as guardians of the aforesaid children the Worthy Oloff
Stevensen and Hendrick Kip, both burghers and inhabitants
of the Manhattans."[1]

b) *Law and custom under the Duke of York.*—In 1664
New Netherland passed into the hands of the Duke of York,
whose patent from Charles II. directed him to establish
authority "not contrary to but as neare as conveniently may

[1] Before the vice-director on the Delaware: FERNOW, *Doc. Rel. to Col. Hist. of
N. Y.*, XII, 149, 150.

Here is a somewhat more elaborate contract in which one party is a widower:

"In the name of the Lord Amen, be it known by the contents of this present
instrument, that in the year sixteen hundred and sixty-three the eighteenth day of
May, appeared before me, Johannes La Montagne in the service of, etc., Meyndert
Frederickse [Smith], widower of the late Cataryna Burger, who declares in the
presence of the aforesaid witnesses, that for God's honor he has contracted a future
marriage with Pietertien Teunise, spinster (jonge dochter), and before the consummation of the same, he, the subscriber, assents to the following conditions, firstly,
that the aforesaid betrothed persons, for the maintenance of said marriage, will
collect and bring together, all such existing estates and effects of whatever nature;
in whatever place, and with whatever persons, the same may be lying or deposited,
nothing excepted, which each now has and posesses, to be by them possesed in
common, according to the law of our Fatherland, except that out of the bridegroom's
estate, to-wit, from the estate left by Caterina Burger deceased, be reserved the sum
of eight hundred guilders payable in beavers, for the children left by her; to wit
Frederick Meyndersen aged six years, and Burgert Meyndersen aged three years,
being their maternal (matrimonial) inheritance; moreover said married persons
shall be holden to bring up said children in the fear of the Lord, to teach them to
read and write in the schools, to maintain them in food and clothing till their
majority or married state, without diminishing their maternal estate, which the
subscriber promises without craft or guile, and for the same binding his person and
estate, real and personal, present and future, nothing excepted, subject to all laws
and judges." In the presence of the children's guardians and the "orphan master."
—MUNSELL'S *Collections on the Hist. of Albany*, IV, 321. For similar contracts see
ibid., 311 (Sept. 23, 1662), 345.

bee agreeable to, the Lawes Statutes and Government of this our Realme of England."[1] After studying the New England laws, especially those of Connecticut and Massachusetts, Colonel Richard Nicholls, the duke's deputy governor, promulgated a code which was in force on Long Island, or Yorkshire, from March 1, 1665.[2] On August 6, 1674, Governor Andros ordered the duke's laws to be enforced throughout "New York" except "such as shall have apparent inconveniences in them,"[3] and in 1676 they were established in the Delaware region, "except the constables' courts, county rates, and some other things peculiar to Long Island."[4] It follows that for a short time after the conquest, in the province and on the Delaware, the Dutch laws were still observed; and, of course, the old usages and customs long survived.

By the duke's code optional civil marriage was established in New York. "Whereas," declares the preamble, "by the Law of England no Marriage is Lawfully Consummated without a Minister whose office it is to join the parties in Matrimony after the Banes thrice published in the Church or a Lycence first had and obtained from some person thereunto Authorized, All which formality cannot be duly practiced in these parts. Yet to the end that a decent rule therein may be preserved It is Ordained that from henceforth the names and surnames of each Party who sue for

[1] See the charter in *New York Colonial Laws*, I, 1-5; and compare Cook, "The Mar. Cel. in the Colonies," *Atlantic*, LXI, 360 ff.

[2] Brodhead, *Hist. of N. Y.*, II, 18, 63, 66, 67; *Colonial Laws of N. Y.*, I, xii, 100, 101. The code of the Duke of York has been thrice published: in *Collections of N. Y. Hist. Soc.*, I, 305-97, for the year 1809 (New York, 1811); in the recent *Colonial Laws of New York* (Albany, 1894), I, 6-100, where a critical note on the original copies may be found; and as the *Duke of Yorke's Book of Laws*, a part of Linn's *Charter and Laws of Pennsylvania* (Harrisburg, 1879), the edition here cited by preference.

[3] O'Callaghan, *Doc. Rel. to Col. Hist. of N. Y.*, III, 226, 227; *N. Y. Col. Laws*, I, xii, xiv, 107 (Andros's order). *Cf.* Dongan's report in O'Callaghan, *op. cit.*, III, 390 (1686); also see Hildreth, *Hist. of U. S.*, II, 44 ff., 76 ff.; Lodge, *Short Hist.*, 297-99; Brodhead, *Hist. of N. Y.*, II, 273; Howard, *Local Const. Hist.*, I, 105, notes.

[4] Hazard, *Annals of Pa.*, 427; *N. Y. Col. Laws*, I, xii.

Marriage shall be Publiquely read in their Parish Church or place of usuall Meeting, where they both then Inhabit, three severall Lords days successively." An optional procedure by license or by ecclesiastical banns was thus introduced; but in one respect the liberality of the Dutch law was not imitated. Unqualified permission to publish intentions of marriage by civil notice, instead of banns in church, was not granted. Yet, in effect, such discretion is often allowed; for "where no Church or Meeting place shall happen to bee," fourteen days written notice on "three doors of each parish" where the parties respectively dwell, namely on the doors of the constable, and two of the overseers, is declared sufficient.

Optional religious or civil celebration is established. After proper notice, as already described, the ceremony may be performed by "any minister" or "any justice of the peace," but on one important condition: the parties are required to "purge themselves by oath before the minister or justice that they are not under the bonds of matrimony to any other person living;" and in case of obtaining a "double marriage" by perjury, we catch a glimpse of the influence of New England thoroughness on Colonel Nicholls, in the barbarous provision that the persons "offending shall bee boared through the tongue with a read hot Iron and moreover proceeded against as in Case of Adultery." But the party "approved innocent" and "ignorant of the other's wicked fraud" may recover damages against the "nocent," and is permitted to contract a new marriage as if nothing had happened.[1] For the marriage of any "Daughter, Maid, or Servant" the "known consent" of the parent, master, or dame is required; and for celebration without such consent,

[1] *Duke of Yorke's Book of Laws:* in *Charter and Laws,* 19, 36; *Col. Laws of N. Y.,* I, 45, 46. In at least one case this provision was carried out: on Oct. 5, 1672, Dan Sutton, for perjury and bigamy was sentenced to have his tongue bored through with a red-hot iron: *Law Reports,* X, 733 (Lauderdale Peerage Case); for the text of the duke's marriage law of 1664/65 see *ibid.,* X, 730, 731.

or without preceding banns or other legal notice, or the governor's license in place of notice, the minister or justice is to "forfeit twenty pounds and be put out of his office."[1]

The declaration of the preamble that "by the Law of England no Marriage is Lawfully Consummated without a Minister" may prove misleading, unless the vital distinction between "legality" and "validity," already emphasized, be kept in mind. In 1665 a marriage in England without a minister was valid, but it was not lawful and might be punished. In the present instance, however, all doubt as to the meaning of the law is set at rest by the further provision that "if any man shall hereafter presume to Marry contrary to these Lawes prescribed the Person offending shall be proceeded against as for Adultery or fornication, ... the Children so begotten shall be Reputed Bastards, And the Parents suffer such paines and penalties by fines or Punishment as they have deserved."[2] Since this provision is clearly contrary to the existing law of England, it would seem to be invalid as transcending the legislative power granted to the duke by the royal charter; and even the king could not have changed the law of England.

Later in 1665 provision is made relative to the legal age for matrimony. All persons are to be "accompted of fitt age to Marry, when the Man shall attaine to the age of twenty one, and the Women of Eighteene years."[3] In the next year the not very lucid interpretation is vouchsafed that this law is to be understood "of such persons onely as are under guardianshipp, and itt is not in any wayes to take of the naturall bounds of Duty and obligation which Children owe to their parents."[4] If this declaration has any sense, it may perhaps mean that, without consent, only orphans under guardianship, and not those whose parents

---

[1] *Duke of Yorke's Book of Laws*, 37.
[2] *Ibid.*   [3] *Ibid.*, 65.   [4] *Ibid.*, 70.

are living, have full authority to marry at the ages mentioned.

A system of registration is likewise provided for. The names and surnames of all the inhabitants of every parish in the government are to be registered; and "to prevent future inconveniences which may arise about the age of Orphants, The Certaine Marriage of Men and Women or the decease of persons imported into this Country whereof no positive Certificate can be granted, as to the age of one, Marriage of another or the Death of another, The Minister or Town Clark of every parrish shall well and truly and plainly" record all births, marriages, and deaths happening within his district "in a Book to be provided by the Church-wardener for that purpose." If a master of a family or anyone concerned fail, within one month, to report the birth, marriage, or death of a person related to him, he shall pay a fine of five shillings.[1]

Another provision reveals the tender solicitude of the English common law for the wife in a way which a century later would have warmed the heart of Sir William Blackstone himself. "No man shall harbour, conceal or detain Contrary to the concent of the Husband any Married woman, upon penalty of five Shillings for every hour" that she "remains under his Roof." Still there really might be occasions when even a "married woman" could reasonably claim some share of public protection. For has not the "common law" itself, in certain emergencies, placed her on a level with the bondwoman? Therefore it is provided "always that any woman flying from the barbarous Cruelty of Her Husband to the House of the Constable or one of the Overseers of the same Parish; may be protected by them in the manner as is Directed for Servants in such Cases, and not otherwise."[2]

---

[1] *Duke of Yorke's Book of Laws*, 13, 14; *Col. Laws of N. Y.*, I, 19.

[2] *Duke of Yorke's Book of Laws*, 36; *Col. Laws of N. Y.*, I, 46.

Again on producing a "sufficient" certificate "from any forraigne parts" under the "hand and seal of some creditable person and known magistrate," that either spouse is dead, the other is free to marry again. The same liberty is accorded the survivor when either party has been absent for five full years without knowledge on a journey by sea or land usually made in "a year or less or in a few days." But in that case a veritable trap is laid for the feet of Enoch Arden, in a provision, imitated from the laws of New England, the stupidity of which is only less surprising than the fact that in substance it has survived in statutes of far more recent times. It is "provided always that if either the man or the woman shall at any time after the Expiration of five years Returne and bring full Testimony that hee or shee have divers wayes endeavoured by writings or Messages to make known to his wife, or her Husband, that Shee or hee were then living, or that they were by Imprisonment or Bond Slavery with the Turks or other Heathen, Lawfully hendred from giving such information;" then such person may "Challenge his or her premarriage, and obtain an order for their Cohabiting as formerly." But "if neither shall sue for such an order," they "may by mutuall agreement Enter a Release to each other in the office of Records, and both remain free from their former obligations."[1]

One or two incidents gleaned from the records for the period of the duke's laws may serve to illustrate the difficulties of matrimonial administration on the Delaware. Thus in 1678, in a case similar to that of Laers above cited, the minister, reader, and churchwardens present to the local court at Newcastle Walter Wharton, justice of the peace, for marrying himself or being married "contrary to the Knowne Lawes of England & alsoe contrary to the Lawes

[1] *Ibid.*, 46, 47; *Duke of Yorke's Book of Laws*, 36, 37. "The father onely of the Children as are begotten in Lawfull Marriage," continues the statute, "is to provide for such Children as shall be adjudged in the Court of Assizes only."

and customes of this place and Province;" as likewise for granting certain lands without proper authority. The said "Mr. Wharton not appearing in three following Court dayes, and to the end the Reproach may bee taken away from the River and that Such notorious breatches of yᵉ Lawes and disorders may for the future not passe unpunished, especially in pʳsons of Lesser qualitys whoe if this [conduct] of Mʳ Whartons [whoe" being "in Commission" and bearing "the office of a Justice of yᵉ peace ougt to give good examples to others] had not been Reguarded, migt att all tymes" hold it for a "bad president": the court do therefore submit the "pʳmisses to the Judgemᵗ of his Honoʳ the Governoʳ for to Inflict such punishment" as he "shall thinke fitt & expedient." We are only informed in the record that the accused is "to bee out of the Commission of Justices & left to the Law."[1] One regrets that we are not told whether the "law" treated his marriage as void.

The Delaware papers, for the next year, contain also a long letter to Governor Andros from Luke Watson, of "Whoorekill"—whose spelling is, if possible, more ingenious than usual even for that fertile region—complaining of the many shortcomings of Captain John Avery, magistrate and president of the court. It seems that the captain was fond of having his own way; sometimes, when his colleagues on the bench presumed to give a contrary "judgment," going out of the court "in a greate Rage and feury, ... Cursing and swaring," and even suggesting that they were "ffooles, Knaues, and Rouges." He is accused, moreover, of taking upon himself "to grant a Licence to Marry Daniel Browne to Sussan Garland, widdow, without any publiqueation, which Marrige was effected, notwithstanding it is Generally knowne or at Least the said Daniel confesses that

[1] Fernow, *Doc. Rel. to Col. Hist. N. Y.*, XII, 596; mentioned also by Hazard, *Annals of Pa.*, 451, 454, 455. On the same day the local court fined him ten pounds and costs for neglecting his judicial duties: Fernow, *loc. cit.*, 596, 597.

he knows no other but that he haue a wife living in England." This was not the captain's worst indiscretion in the discharge of his official matrimonial duties. We learn that in taking "vpon himselfe to Marry the widdow Clament to one Bryant Rowles, without publiquecation notwithstanding she was out aske at Least a Month to another man, namly Edward Cocke," he prepared a sad tragedy in real life. For when the "said Cocke" heard that the widow had jilted him he said "it would be his death." So he "went home, fell sick, and in forty eight hours after dyed," declaring in his last breath "that her marrying was the cause of his dyeing."[1]

At this time Governor Andros, replying to the inquiries of the Lords of Trade, reports that because of the "scarcity of Ministers & [the] Law admitting marriages by Justices no acc^t cann be giuen of the number marryed." He adds that "ministers haue been so scarce" and "Religions" so many that he can give no statement of the number of births or christenings.[2] In 1695 Mr. Miller, an English clergyman, "complains that many marriages are by a justice of the peace."[3]

The duke's code makes no provision for the celebration of marriage except before a minister or a justice of the peace. The Quakers of Long Island, who earlier had suffered severely from the intolerance of the Dutch,[4] continued never-

---

[1] *Ibid.*, 624, 625.

[2] O'CALLAGHAN, *Doc. Rel. to Col. Hist. of N. Y.*, III, 261 (1678); VALENTINE, *Manual of the Corporation*, 1851, 453. The year before the bishop of London complains that the Virginia marriage laws are not enforced: O'CALLAGHAN, *op. cit.*, III, 253 (July 17, 1677).

[3] EARLE, *Col. Days in Old New York*, 60.

[4] See O'CALLAGHAN, *Hist. of New Netherland*, II, 345-55, 450-57. Under the lead of the clerical bigots, Drisius and Megapolensis, the Reformed church in New Netherland banished Lutherans and tormented the Quakers. A number of Friends, expelled from Massachusetts, arrived in New Amsterdam in 1657, and were at once persecuted with fiendish cruelty. Nevertheless, the Quakers grew apace in numbers, settling by preference in Jamaica and Flushing on Long Island. Among them was John Bowne, a recent convert and signer of the petition quoted in the text. In 1662

theless to practice their own simple but solemn rites.   For so doing they were harshly dealt with by the courts, as appears in a petition to Governor Andros and his council from two of their number in 1680,[1] praying for the "Remission of a Fine imposed for Contravention of the Marriage Laws." The paper is in the form of an "address from Henry Willis and John Bowne, Concerning the proceedings of a Court of Sessions against vs, who said they fined us 10 lbs a peece for suffering our daughters to marrie contrary to their law, which proceeding we are satisfied is without precedent and we can count it noe lesse but a mistake or hasty oversight and though we have endeaverd for its removall yet Execution is eished forth and Jos. Lee vndershiref hath seazed Hen: Willis barne of corn and since taken from Jo. Bowne 5 good milch cowes and drove them away by night and kept them pownded from food" more than a night and a day, so that the neighbors were "generally troubled at it." Then the petitioners proceed to reason with the enemy, using the soft word which turneth away wrath.   "Now in simplisity, we doe seriously entreat all that may be conserned herein seriously to consider it and in the cooleness of your spirits without anger or hard thoughts truly to waye it in the balance of Equity where the witness of God may arise in every Contience to testifie, whether If such things should goe on . . . . it would not be to the rewenating of families and to the kindling of Gods anger against a place or people which we truly desire may be prevented, by takeing away yᵉ ocation." So they make their appeal to the "cheife," know-

---

he was fined for allowing his house to be used as a Quaker conventicle; and in the next year he was banished to Holland.   This resulted in calling down upon the head of Stuyvesant a severe and just rebuke from the directors.   See also BRODHEAD, *Hist. of N. Y.*, I, 636, 705; O'CALLAGHAN, *op. cit.*, 338-42, 428; EARLE, *op. cit.*, 260; and WALLER, *Hist. of Flushing*, 37-47, 77, note.   It is a pity that a writer of such merit as Mr. Waller should have reiterated (46, 47) the baseless and long since exposed slanders against the Quakers in New England.

[1] FERNOW, *op. cit.*, XIV, 752, 753; also in *New York Colonial MSS.*, XXIX, 202.

ing that a magistrate's "authority is to preserve mens persons
and Estates, but yᵉ prerogative of the contience that belongs
to God and we dare not but yeald obedience thereunto;" for
"we do not act—as sometimes resented (*sic*)—in stobourness
obstainancy or contempt of authority but in simplisity."[1]

From this evidence it would seem that the magistrates of
Long Island were not less thrifty in their zeal than were
their brethren in Massachusetts from whose pious robbery
and legal cruelty the Wardwells suffered.[2] It is noticeable,
too, that only fines are spoken of.   Nothing is said of invalidating marriages celebrated in the Quaker fashion.   From
this the suggestion already made gains support that the nullifying clause in the duke's code was illegal; and we may,
perhaps, also infer that it was not attempted to be carried
out in practice by the courts.   Certain it is that in 1661,
only four years before the adoption of the duke's laws, a
marriage celebrated in England according to Quaker rites
was held legal in a trial which took place at the Nottingham
assizes.[3]   The marriage law of 1665, at least so far as it was

---

[1] The petition concludes with the following exhortation: "and we earnestly
desire yᵉ Lord may perswade your hearts, vnto whome we are now concerned, that
yᵉ may remoue yᵉ cause of this our address and open that eye in you that can see vs
as we are, who can pray for those thats in authority that vnder them we may live a
peaceable holy and Godlike life

Yᵉ 4ᵗʰ day of yᵉ 7ᵗʰ mo: 1680

" Henry Willis
John Bowne."

[2] HALLOWELL, *Quaker Invasion of Massachusetts*, 99–104.

[3] *New York Colonial MSS.*, XXIX, 203 (New York State Library). Regarding
this decision, which settled the character of marriage law in England, SEWEL, *History . . . . of the Quakers*, 292, has a striking passage: "It happened about this
Time in England, that some covetous Persons, to engross Inheritances to themselves,
would call the Marriages of those called Quakers in question. And it was in this
Year that such a Cause was tried at the Assizes at Nottingham; a certain Man
dying, and leaving his Wife with Child, and an Estate in Copyhold Lands: When the
Woman was delivered, one that was near of kin to her deceased Husband, endeavoured to prove the Child illegitimate: And the Plaintiff's Council willing to blacken
the Quakers, so called, asserted the Child to be illegitimate, because the Marriage
of its Parents was not according to Law; and said bluntly, and very indecently, That
the Quakers went together like brute Beasts. After the Council on both sides had
pleaded, the Judge, whose name was Archer, opened the Case to the Jury, and told
them That there was a Marriage in Paradise, when Adam took Eve and Eve took

valid, remained in force until the passage of the so-called
"Dongan" act of 1684.[1]   This statute[2] was one of the thirty-
one acts receiving the governor's signature and passed at the
second session of the first representative assembly of New
York, elected in 1683 under the reluctant and grudging
sanction of the Duke of York.[3]   By it no striking change
is made in the broad outline of matrimonial administration;
but in the details several important alterations appear.   The
provision regarding optional civil or ecclesiastical banns is
identical with that of the earlier law, except that posting on
the constable's door in each parish, instead of on "three
doors," is deemed sufficient.   License "under the hand and
seale of the governour" in place of banns is still allowed.
As before, any minister or justice within the province is
authorized to perform the ceremony; but now the persons
are required to "bring a Certificate from under the ministers hand that published them or under the Constable hand
on whose doores their names were affixed which Certificate
shall be sent to the office of the Register of the County and

Adam; and that it was the Consent of the Parties that made a Marriage. And
as for the Quakers (said he) he did not know their Opinion; but he did not believe
they went together as brute Beasts, ... but as Christians; and therefore he did
believe the Marriage was lawful, and the Child lawful Heir. And the better to satisfy the jury, he related to them this Case: A Man that was weak of Body, and kept
his Bed, had a Desire in that Condition to Marry, and did declare before Witnesses
that he did take such a Woman to be his Wife; and the Woman declared, that she
took that Man to be her Husband. This Marriage was afterwards called in question: But all the Bishops did at that time conclude it to be a lawfull Marriage." The
jury found for the child.

[1] In 1674 the duke's laws were ordered put in execution "except those requiring
amendment or alteration ": *Colonial Laws of N. Y.*, I, xiv, 107. On Nov. 9, 1674, Governor Andros issued a proclamation to that effect: *ibid.*, xiv, 107, 108.

[2] "The original of this act is not in the office of the Secretary of State. This
copy was made from the manuscript compilation of the 'Dongan laws' formerly in
the office of the Secretary of State, but now in the New York State Library. The
date of its passage, as October 23, 1684, is given by E. B. O'Callaghan, in *Hist. Int.
to Journals of the Legislative Council of N. Y.*, p. 12."—CUMMING'S note to the act,
Col. Laws of N. Y., I, 150.

[3] See his two letters to Andros (1675 and 1676 respectively) in *Col. Laws of N. Y.*,
I, xiv, xv; and also the instruction to Dongan, 1682, allowing a general assembly
to be summoned: *ibid.*, xv, 108-10. The duke's letters are also in O'CALLAGHAN, *Doc.
Rel. to Col. Hist. of N. Y.*, III, 230, 235.

there Entred on Record together with a Certificate of their Marriage with the day and date thereof from the party by whom they were marryed there to remaine in perpetuam rei memoriam;" and it is provided, further, that the persons purge themselves by oath, if required, that they are not already under bonds of matrimony. But in this connection, instead of the clause as to boring through the tongue with a red-hot iron, it is declared that "if it shall afterwards happen to be proved that either . . . . of the said partyes" has thus contracted a bigamous marriage through false swearing, he "shall suffer as in Cases of perjury and further be proceeded against as in Cases of polygamy."[1] The act is liberal in another respect. At last the Quakers are granted relief in a provision which in substance finds many repetitions in American legislation during the two centuries to come. Nothing, we are told, is "intended to prejudice the Custome and manner of marriage amongst the Quakers, but their manner and forme" shall be judged lawful; provided they allow "none to marry that are restrained by the Law of God contained in the five bookes of Moses; and that they permitt none to be marryed within their Congregation or meeting of any other persuasion then themselves," except after banns or license and record made according to law.

There is in this act one essential variation from that of 1665, which it is of the highest importance to note, and which has been entirely overlooked by writers[2] who have discussed the character of the marriage law of New York after 1684. The invalidating clause, unless by implication, in case of neglect of the required forms and procedure, does not appear. It is merely declared that if "any man Shall p'sume

---

[1] *Col. Laws of N. Y.*, I, 150, 151. This seems to be a decided mitigation of the original penalty: see "An act to prevent wilfull Perjury," passed by the Assembly Nov. 1, 1683: *ibid.*, 129-31.

[2] By COOK, for instance, who says the Dongan act was " substantially a re-enactment of the Duke's Laws of 1664, and seems not to have been repealed prior to the Revolution."—" Marriage Celebration in the Colonies," *Atlantic*, LXI, 360.

to marry contrary to the Law prescribed the person offending shall be proceeded against as for fornication;" and the minister or justice performing the ceremony shall forfeit twenty pounds and be suspended from his benefice or office.[1] The penalty for fornication according to the duke's law, which seems to have been still in force, was "enjoyning Marriage, fine, or Corporal punishment" at the "discretion of the Court."[2]   Thus by any fair interpretation of a penal statute, after 1684, an irregular marriage *per verba de praesenti* was illegal though valid in New York, just as it was in the mother-country.

c) *Law and custom in the Royal Province.*—The Dongan act of 1684, continuing as it does the general provisions of the duke's law, and indeed differing but little—except perhaps in the matter of lay celebration—from the earlier usage of the Dutch, is in harmony with the administrative practice which prevailed in New York until the Revolution; though, as will presently appear, there is good reason to believe that it was repealed in 1691.   The provision regarding certificate and registration corresponds with the custom, though the local officers were negligent and the records are far from complete.[3]   Perhaps, as a rule, marriage was preceded by banns or civil notice; but license must have been popular, especially among the well-to-do, and a lucrative source of income to the governors, as the forty manuscript volumes of marriage-license bonds, preserved among the treasures of the State Library at Albany, amply bear witness.[4]

[1] *Col. Laws of N. Y.*, I, 151.

[2] *Ibid.*, 35. The view presented in the text as to the penal clause in the act of 1684 is sustained by the opinion of Lord Watson in the Lauderdale Peerage Case: COOK, *Reports of Cases Decided by the Eng. Courts*, XXXVII, 357, 358.

[3] For example, a marriage record was continuously kept at Trinity Church, New York, only for the years 1746-64. In general, the records were imperfect at a much later period: see MYRON A. MONSON, in *Hist. Genealog. Register*, XLI, 93.

[4] These MSS. are a rich mine for the genealogist. For this purpose they are made easily accessible through the *Names of Persons for Whom Marriage Licenses Were Issued*, printed by order of Gideon J. Tucker, secretary of state, Albany, 1860. On the period covered by the New York licenses see HOFFMAN, *Chancery Practice*, 15; and *Law Reports*, X, 728 f.

An instructive piece of evidence as to the importance of the license fee is given by Professor Peter Kalm, the Swedish botanist and traveler, writing in 1748. He mentions the small salary allowed the royal governor by the assembly, the whole of which is sometimes lost through "dissension with the inhabitants;" and he declares that but for three "stated profits" the governor "would be obliged either to resign his office, or to be content with an income too small for his dignity; or else to conform himself in everything" to their inclinations. These extraordinary sources of income are the fees for passports, permission to keep public houses, and marriage licenses. "Few people," he says, "who intend to be married, unless they be very poor, will have their banns published from the pulpit; but instead of this they get licenses from the governor, which impower any minister to marry them. Now for such a license the governor receives about half a guinea, and this collected throughout the whole province, amounts to a considerable sum."[1]

In fact, just as in England in our own day,[2] it was "deemed most plebeian, almost vulgar, to be married by publication of the banns for three Sundays in church, or posting them according to the law, as was the universal and fashionable custom in New England." This notice from a New York newspaper, dated December 13, 1765, will show how widespread had been the aversion to the publication of banns:

"We are credibly informed that there was married last Sunday evening, by the Rev. Mr. Auchmuty, a very respectable couple that had published three different times in Trinity church. A laudable example and worthy to be followed. If this decent and for many reasons proper method of publication was once generally to take place, we should have no

---

[1] KALM, *Travels in North America* (translated by JOHN REINHOLD FORSTER, Warrington, 1770), I, 259–62; see also the extract in HART, *Source-Book of American History*, 128–30; and for the dates *ibid.*, 100.

[2] See chap x, sec. iii, above.

more clandestine marriages; and save the expense of licenses, no inconsiderable sum these hard and depressing times."

For another reason the times became more "hard and depressing" and banns more economical, perhaps more patriotic, as Mrs. Earle further shows by an extract from Holt's *New York Gazette and Post-boy* for December 6, 1765:

"As no Licenses for Marriage could be obtained since the first of November for Want of Stamped Paper, we can assure the Publick several Genteel Couple were publish'd in the different Churches of this City last Week; and we hear that the young Ladies of this Place are determined to Join Hands with none but such as will to the utmost endeavour to abolish the Custom of marrying with License which Amounts to many Hundred per annum which might be saved."[1]

The character of the governor's license may be seen in the following sample, issued in 1732:

"By his excellency William Cosby, Esq., Captain general and governor in chief of the provinces of New York, New Jersey, and territories thereon depending, in America, vice-admiral of the same, and colonel in his majesty's army, &c.

"To any Protestant Minister:

"Whereas there is a mutual purpose of marriage between Jacob Glenn of the City of Albany, merchant, of the one party, and Elizabeth Cuyler of the same city, spinster, of the other party, for which they have desired my license, and have given bond upon conditions, that neither of them have any lawful let or impediment of pre-contract, affinity, or consanguinity to hinder their being joined in the holy bands of matrimony; these are therefore to authorize and empower you to join the said Jacob Glenn and Elizabeth Cuyler in the holy bands of matrimony and them to pronounce man and wife."[2]

A goodly store of folklore relating to wedding customs

[1] EARLE, *Col. Days in Old New York*, 58, 59.
[2] MUNSELL'S *Annals of Albany*, II, 182.

among the Dutch and English of New York has been gathered by Vanderbilt, Earle, and other writers. There was no lack of feasting and pastime. As in the fatherland, maypoles were set up before the door in honor of newly wedded pairs. The fashion of "coming out bride," "that is the public appearance of bride and groom, and sometimes of entire bridal party in wedding array, at Church the Sunday after the marriage," was observed with due pomp and splendor. Collections for the parish poor or to build a church were received from the guests on the bridal day; and bumpers of "sack-posset" seem to have been as keenly relished by the worthy burghers of New York as by good old Samuel Sewall and his Massachusetts brethren.[1] At wedding time there was "open house" and plenty of feasting; but the festivity does not appear to have reached the excess practiced by the Pennsylvania Friends.[2] Hannah Thompson, wife of the secretary of Congress, while residing in New York in 1786, wrote to John Miflin, of Philadelphia, that the "Gentleman's Parents keep open house just in the same manner as the Brides Parents. The Gentlemen go from the Bridegrooms house to drink Punch with and to give joy to his Father. The Brides Visitors go In the same manner from the Brides to his Mothers to pay their Compliments to her. There is so much driving about at these times that in our narrow streets there is some danger. The Wedding-House resembles a bee-hive. Company perpetually flying in and out."[3]

---

[1] For these customs and others see EARLE, *op. cit.*, 60 ff.; and compare VANDERBILT, *Social Customs of Flatbush*, 149 ff.; WATSON, *Annals and Occurrences of New York City and State*, 211-17 (written in 1828 regarding customs twelve years before the Revolution); OSTRANDER, *History of the City of Brooklyn and King's County*, I, 79-83; *New York Hist. Coll.*, Fund Series, 1880, XIII, 355, where Rev. John Sharpe tells us that negroes are married merely by mutual consent without blessing of the church; and *ibid.*, Second Series, II, 347-49, where courtship among the New York Indians is described.

[2] See sec. ii, *b*) below.

[3] HANNAH THOMPSON, *Letters:* in *Pa. Mag. of Hist. and Biol.*, XIV, 35.

But in the main domestic life was peaceful and prosaic. Family woes were seldom dragged into court. The "capital laws" contained in the duke's code do, indeed, show their New England origin by prescribing death as the penalty alike for denying God or the king's titles, or wantonly smiting a parent; but these were practically a "dead letter."[1] Mrs. Grant bears witness to the happiness and tranquillity of marital life in Albany. "Inconstancy or even indifference among married couples was unheard of, even where there happened to be considerable disparity in point of intellect. The extreme affection they bore their mutual offspring was a bond that forever endeared them to each other. Marriage in this colony was always early, very often happy, and very seldom indeed interested. When a man had no son, there was nothing to be expected with a daughter but a well brought-up female slave, and the furniture of the best bed-chamber. At the death of her father she obtained another division of his effects, such as he thought she needed or deserved, for there was no rule in these cases."[2]

So much for custom and the actual legal practice. We may now turn to the controversy as to whether subsequently to 1691 there was any valid statutory regulation of marriage in New York until after the close of the provincial period. The uncertainty arose in consequence of the following resolution of the assembly, April 24, 1691: "Upon an information . . . . That the several Laws made formerly by the General Assembly, and his late Royal Highness, James Duke of York;" and also "the several Ordinances or reputed Laws made by the preceding Governors and Councils, for the Rule of their Majesties Subjects within this Province, are reported amongst the people, to be still in force;" it is resolved, *nemine contradicente*, that the first-named laws of

---

[1] *Duke of Yorke's Book of Laws*, 14, 15; *cf.* WEISE, *Hist. of Albany*, 195, 196.

[2] GRANT, *Memoirs of an American Lady*, 48; quoted also by EARLE, *op. cit.*, 55, 56.

the assembly, "not being observed, and not ratified and approved by His Royal Highness, nor the late King, are null, void, and of none effect;" as also are the "several Ordinances made by the Governors and councils, being contrary to the constitution of England, and the practice of the government of their Majesties other plantations in America."[1]

The terms of the resolution are very clear; but unfortunately, so far as has yet been discovered, no record exists of its having been placed before the governor and council for approval. Nor does the validity of this resolution or that of the act of 1684 ever appear to have been tested in the provincial courts. Singularly enough, this dual question was not judicially considered until the "Lauderdale Peerage Case," in 1885, which grew out of a marriage solemnized one hundred and thirteen years before—on the very eve of the Revolution. The record of the trial and judgment in this case is really equivalent to a treatise by learned jurists on the matrimonial law of New York, from the Dutch Ordinance of 1654 to the adoption of the constitution of 1777. Moreover, distinguished American lawyers were called as expert witnesses or to submit written opinions.[2] From the record in the case[3] it appears that on July 11, 1772, two days before his death, Colonel Richard Maitland

[1] See CUMMING'S "Historical Note," *Col. Laws of N. Y.*, I, xix. CUMMING cites the note of ROBERT LUDLOW FOWLER to *Fac Simile of the Laws and Acts of the General Assembly . . . . as printed and sold by William Bradford, 1694,* 78 ff.

[2] American witnesses for the claimant were E. J. Phelps, the United States minister, S. P. Nash, and C. Cary, of the American bar. Those for the counter-claimant were R. L. Fowler, of the American bar, and G. F. Edmunds, chairman of the Committee on Judiciary of the United States Senate: *Law Reports*, X, 728 n. 1. See also WEBSTER, *Opinion on the Law of Marriage in the Col. of N. Y.* (New York, May 26, 1885); SEWARD, *Answer to Interrogations of Brodie and Sons* (New York, June, 1885); and FOWLER, *Letter and Opinion* (New York, May 11, 1885). Copies of these three opinions are in the State Library, Albany. Written opinions were also submitted by James C. Carter and William Evarts, of New York.

[3] In *Law Reports*, X (1885), 692-762; and in COOK, *Reports of Cases Decided by Eng. Courts*, XXXVII, 341-69. The case was referred by the House of Lords to the Lords' "Committee for Privileges" for hearing.

and Mary McAdams were married in New York city by
Rev. John Ogilvie, an ordained clergyman of the Church of
England, and then assistant minister of Trinity Church.
The main question at issue, and the only one with which we
are here concerned, was the requisites for a valid marriage
in the province of New York in that year. As recited in
the syllabus, there were produced, *inter alia*, in support of
the marriage from the custody of the family a certificate in
legal form; an affidavit, signed by the mayor of New York,
to the effect that the officiating minister had made oath of
the truth of the statements in the certificate; a will of date
anterior to the marriage, by which Colonel Maitland left all
his property to his wife and the children then born; copies
of letters showing that one of the executors wrote to his co-
executors in England, a brother of the bridegroom, stating
that he was a witness to the ceremony of marriage; that the
woman signed herself in the man's surname; that the
children were recognized and taken care of by members of
the man's family; and also war office records showing that
the woman received a pension as Maitland's widow.[1] But
evidence was not forthcoming of previous license or publication of banns. Did the neglect of license or banns invalidate
the marriage? It was contended by the witnesses and
advisers of the counter-claimant that the statute of 1665 and
that of 1684 rendered license or banns indispensable, and
that such continued to be the law of New York down to the
marriage in 1772.[2]

Thus in his written opinion Mr. Sidney Webster, in
answer to the question "whether the law of marriage in New
York, in 1772, was contained in Dongan's law of 1684, supplemented, where defective, by the older laws of the Duke
of York and of the Dutch?" says that he thinks the "fundamental law" of the colony of New York when the case arose,

---

[1] *Law Reports*, X, 693.   [2] *Ibid.*, 794.

was made up of so much of the Dutch law as was unrepealed
and remained in force; so much of the English common law
as had been established after the conquest in 1664; so much
of the English parliamentary statutes[1] as had been enacted
and specially made applicable; and the colonial statutes
legally enacted and sanctioned by the crown. "I have not
seen nor heard," he continues, "of a denial that the . . . .
law of 1684 was a valid enactment" at the date of its passage.
"In so far as it covered matters and also punishments
embraced in any previous statute, or ruled by the common
law, and was inconsistent therewith, it repealed or abrogated
both by implication." Any contract of marriage made in
"palpable violation" of the requirements of either of these
laws, while in force, would be void; and "if it could be found
that the marriage law of 1684 was repealed prior to 1828,
then, in the absence of any positive law to the contrary," the
duke's law "would by implication be revived."[2] So he concludes that in 1772, for a valid contract, there must be
previous banns or license, as well as solemnization by a
clergyman or magistrate.[3] With this conclusion the opinion

[1] This opinion is not convincing; for the common law had not been "established," in the sense of enacted or declared; nor were there any British statutes
which bore upon the marriage celebration in New York.

[2] By the law of 1828 it was declared that a marriage, "so far as validity is concerned," is a civil contract "to which the consent of parties capable in law of contracting, shall be essential."—*Revised Statutes*, 1827-28, II, 138.

[3] WEBSTER, *Opinion*, 2 ff., 55, 59, 70. He cites Fenton v. Reed (4 JOHNSON, *Reports*,
51), in favor of validity of consensual or common-law marriage; and Milford v. Worcester (7 *Mass. Rep.*, 48), on the opposite side. In substantial agreement with Webster are the opinion of SEWARD, *Answer*, 1-53; and that of FOWLER, *Letter and
Opinion*, 60, 61, *passim*, who to prove the validity of the duke's law cites the cases
of Fabricius and Ralph Doxy, above discussed.

The counter-claimant also produced the case of Dan Sutton, sentenced for
bigamy and bored through the tongue with a red-hot iron in 1672—a case plainly
irrelevant, so far as the question of marriage contract is concerned; and likewise
the case of Mary Jones, 1680, for having a bastard child, "she pretending to be married before delivered; but without either license or publication. She was fined £5
or to receive twenty stripes on the back"—a sentence which perhaps tells on the
claimant's side, for it punishes an illegal act, but says nothing of nullifying the
marriage; or, if the marriage may be regarded as invalidated by implication, the
sentence is illegal as contrary to English law. For these citations see *Law Reports*,
X, 733.

of Mr. Evarts coincides. "The statute of the Assembly in
1684," he says, "unquestionably was in force in 1772. The
essentials of a valid marriage according to the law of New
York in 1772, were that the ceremony should be performed
by a minister or a justice of the peace, and that such marriage could be lawfully performed only after the publication
of the banns prescribed by the act of . . . . 1684, or in
default of such publication . . . . , by a license from the
governor."[1]

For the claimant also a mass of evidence was presented.
Important decisions were cited;[2] and it was pointed out that
in the acts of the legislature published after 1684 neither
the statute of that year nor the duke's law appears; "nor in
fact" were "any of the laws prior to 1691" printed in subsequent collections.[3]   Sir. F. Herschell, counsel, urged that
"unless it is expressly provided that the failure to comply"
with the requirement of the statutes in question "shall
render a marriage null and void, the courts will not so con-
strue;" and he holds that the resolution of the assembly,
1691, was valid; for "everybody" acted as if the laws repealed
by it were not in force.[4]   In short, "the substantial effect of
the evidence of those called for the claimant," as summarized
in the report of the case, was "that the law prevailing in
New York with regard to the requisites for a marriage in the
year 1772 was the common law of England as interpreted by
the American courts, i. e., that there should be a contract of

---

[1] Evarts's opinion cited by COOK, "Mar. Cel. in the Colonies"—*Atlantic*,
LXI, 361.

[2] The American witnesses for the claimant cited Jackson v. Gilchrist (15 JOHN-
SON, *Rep.*, 89) ; Constantine v. Windle (6 HILL, *Rep.*, 176) ; Humbert v. Trinity
Church (24 WENDELL, *Rep.*, 625): HOFFMAN, *Chancery Practice* (2d ed., New York,
1843) ; *Revised Statutes of N. Y.* (ed. 1830), 729; and Fenton v. Reed (4 JOHNSON, *Rep.*,
52), the leading case for "common-law" marriage.

[3] *Law Reports*, X, 728. The act of 1684 is preserved in MS. in the New York State
Library ; and this I have examined through the courtesy of Mr. Griswold.

[4] *Law Reports*, X, 734. Herschell cites King v. The Inhab. of Birmingham (8 B.
& C., 29) ; and Dr. Lushington in Caterall v. Sweetman (1 ROBERTSON, *Ecc. Reports*,
321).

marriage per verba de presenti; and that the 35th article of the constitution of the state of New York, adopted in 1777, ... shewed that the common law of England, as then understood, governed this subject."[1]

Such was the unanimous decision of the committee of Lords constituting the court, whose members submitted their opinions separately. The Earl of Selborne doubted whether the acts of 1665 and 1684 were in force in 1772 and significantly suggests that, if they were in force, failure of banns and license would not invalidate a marriage. He further argues strongly that in the present instance there is no absolute proof that banns or license was lacking; for the church records are often imperfect. In any event, therefore, the rule *omnia praesumunter rita acta* ought to govern the case; for one cannot conceive of any circumstance more properly requiring its application.[2] In harmony with this view was the able opinion of Lord Blackburn, which in effect maintained the validity of the common law in New York subsequent to 1684. The original English settlers, he argues, "carried with them all the immunities and privileges and laws of England. . . . . That being so, from the time when the colony of New York was first settled it had primâ facie the marriage law of England such as it was in the latter part of the seventeenth century;" and in England at that time a marriage "solemnized according to the form of the Church of England, and by a clergyman of the Church of England . . . . was valid to constitute matrimony: although if it was a clandestine or irregular marriage without banns or a license,

---

[1] *Law Reports*, X, 728. The reference to the thirty-fifth article of the constitution of 1777 adds little weight to the argument. Except as concerns any established denomination of Christians or the sovereignty of the crown, that article provides that "such parts of the common law of England, and of the statute law of England and Great Britain, and of the acts of the legislature of the colony of New York," as together did form the law of that colony on April 19, 1775, should be the law of the state: POORE, *Charters*, II, 1337, 1338.

[2] *Law Reports*, X, 742.

the clergyman who performed it might be liable to censure"
and punishment. In addition his lordship significantly
raises a doubt as to whether the Duke of York had power to
introduce a new law of marriage essentially different from
that of England as regards the absolute requirement of
license or banns.[1]

Accordingly, the other judges agreeing, the laws of 1665
and 1684 were set aside as not in force; and the claim of
Major Frederick Henry Maitland, descendant of Colonel
Richard Maitland, to the earldom of Lauderdale was sustained.[2]

There can be little doubt that this was a righteous judgment, in harmony with the entire history of the English
decisions down to the case of the Queen v. Millis, whose
character has already been considered.[3] Furthermore, its
justice is rendered almost certain by a witness, not called in
the trial, but whose evidence given in 1773, the very next
year after the marriage in question, is assuredly worthy of
more attention than any produced by the American experts
in 1885. This testimony is given by Rev. John Rodgers,
in a paper read before the "Reverend General Convention
of the Delegates from the Associated Churches of Connecticut, and the Synod of New York and Philadelphia," met at
Stamford, September, 1, 1773; the manuscript being found
in the cabinet of President Stiles by the historian, Abiel
Holmes:

[1] *Law Reports*, X, 744-49.

[2] *Ibid.*, 762. Of course, the question as to whether the presence of a clergyman
at the ceremony was essential to a valid marriage was not raised; and if it had been
raised in 1885, the court might possibly have decided that it was requisite, in harmony with the judgment in the Queen v. Millis. History must, however, decide the
other way. But compare the conclusion of COOK, "Mar. Cel. in the Col.," *Atlantic*,
LXI, 361, who infers from this decision that "this 'common-law marriage,' falsely
so-called — the 'free marriage' of the later Roman law, of the canon law, and of the
Scotch law,—did not exist in New York (or, indeed, in any of the other colonies)
prior to the Revolution."

[3] See Vol. I, 316-20, above.

"There has no law been made in this province relating to marriages, nor do any of the English statutes concerning them extend to it. They stand therefore on the common law of the land; and as words de presenti constitute a marriage by that law, the courts of judicature, on any contest, must leave the question *married or not* to the jury of the county upon the proofs that are offered, as they do with respect to any other enquiry relating to matter of fact. This is attended with some inconvenience; but the politicians contend that they would be greater, if the legislature should interpose by a law to prevent clandestine marriages; and it is much to be doubted, whether the several branches would be brought to any unanimity on the subject, were it attempted. The rites of marriage were at first celebrated by the justices of the peace, as well as the clergy, either upon the governor's licence, or the publication of bans thrice in some place of worship. This was the case till the year 1748, before which time the licences ran, *to all Protestant ministers;* but upon application of the Episcopal clergy who meant to monopolize this business, they are since directed *to all Protestant ministers of the Gospel,* and from the time of this alteration the justices do not intermeddle, except in such counties where clergymen are scarce. But marriages are celebrated by clergymen of all denominations without distinction, and yet for any law to the contrary, a marriage with or without licence or publication, and with or without the aid of a clergyman or magistrate, will be valid in law. A contract in words de presenti, proved by witnesses and subsequent cohabitation as man and wife, constitutes a marriage of legal validity, as already suggested."[1]

After this it seems only necessary to add that if it should appear strange that the legal practice in the administration

---

[1] RODGERS, *A Brief View of the State of Religious Liberty in the Colony of New York:* in 2 *Mass. Hist. Coll.*, I, 152. On the authorship, see *ibid.*, II, 270.

of matrimonial law, during the provincial period, harmonizes
in the main with that prescribed by the laws of 1665 and
and 1684, it is sufficient to say that this is so by force of
custom; while, so far as license is concerned, that was maintained by virtue of the power granted to the royal governors
in their instructions.[1]

II.   NEW JERSEY, PENNSYLVANIA, AND DELAWARE

a) *Law and custom in New Jersey.*—The population of
New Jersey was far more homogeneously English than was
that of New York and Pennsylvania.   It was composed of
members of various religious sects.   Some Quakers settled
in East New Jersey and more in West New Jersey, but they
were never numerically strong.   The vast majority of the
people were Scotch Presbyterians and New England Con-
gregationalists; so that family law shows decided traces of
Puritan influence.[2]   Circumstances, however, favored toleration in this regard; and hence only in details were the New
Jersey matrimonial law and custom different from those
which existed in New York.

The legal history of the province begins in the year of
the English conquest of New Netherland.   In 1664 a very
liberal plan of government, called the "Concessions and
Agreement," was established by the proprietors, Lord
Berkeley and Sir George Carteret.   All "faithful subjects
of the king" are admitted to "plant and become freemen"
of the said province of New Jersey.   No one is to be

---

[1] In their instructions the governors are directed to issue marriage licenses, and
usually to hang up the "table of marriages" according to the English canons:
O'CALLAGHAN, *Doc. Rel. to Col. Hist., N. Y.*, III, 372 (instructions to Dongan, May
29, 1686), 688 (to Sloughter, Jan. 31, 1689), 821 (to Fletcher, March 7, 1691/92); *ibid.*,
IV, 288 (to Bellomont, Aug. 31, 1697), 558 (Bellomont's instructions to Lieutenant-
Governor Nanfan), 766 (a letter of Bellomont to secretary of Board of Trade, telling
of the trick by which Rev. Symon Smith got a license for Baldridge, the pirate,
Oct. 19, 1700); *ibid.*, V, 135 (instructions to Hunter); *ibid.*, VII, 830 (Governor Moore
to Lords of Trade, mentioning his power to license, June 12, 1766).

[2] Compare COOK, "Mar. Cel. in the Colonies," *Atlantic*, LXI, 358, 359.

"molested, punished, disquieted or called in question, for any difference in opinion or practice in matters of religious concernments," provided he do not disturb the "civil peace."[1]

Under this instrument in 1668 the first matrimonial legislation appears. "For the preventing of unlawful marriages, it is ordered . . . . that no person or persons, son, daughter, maid, or servant, shall be married without the consent" of parents, masters, or overseers, "and three times published . . . . at some public meeting or kirk, where the party or parties have their most usual abode;" or their "purpose" be set up in writing "on some publick house where they live," there to "abide" for the space of fourteen days before the celebration, which, "if possible" is to be performed in a public place. "None but some approved minister or justice of the peace within this Province, or some chief officer, where such are not, shall be allowed to marry or admit of any to join in marriage, in their presence;" under the penalty of twenty pounds[2] and removal from office for neglect. But in place of banns or civil notice, the governor may grant his license to "any that are at their own disposing," if they "clear themselves by oath or certificate;" or to any others "under tuition," provided the parents, masters, or overseers are present to give their consent, or such consent be "attested by some public officer" before the license is issued.[3]

This act, which, it may be noted, does not contain a clause expressly invalidating a marriage for non-observance of its provisions, seems to have remained in force for fifteen years. But in 1682 "that part of the province called East

[1] For the Concessions see SMITH, *Hist. of the Col. of Nova-Caesaria, or New Jersey*, 512 ff.

[2] Later reduced to ten pounds: *Acts of the Assembly*, 1693, 332.

[3] LEAMING AND SPICER, *Grants, Concessions, and Original Constitutions*, 81, 82 ("Laws in Cartaret's Time").

New Jersey came by purchase into the possession of William Penn and other Quakers," who formed an association called the Twenty-four Proprietors.   By these a body of rules known as the "Fundamental Constitutions" was established, containing a provision for the celebration of marriage, after the Quaker fashion, very similar to the law for Pennsylvania made in England the same year by Penn and his associates.[1] All marriages "not forbidden in the law of God shall be esteemed lawful where the Parents or Guardians being first acquainted, the Marriage is publickly intimated in such Places and Manner as is agreeable to Mens different Perswasions in Religion, being afterwards still solemnized before creditable Witnesses, by taking one another as Husband and Wife, and a certificate of the whole, under the Parties and Witnesses Hands, being brought to the proper Register for that End, under a Penalty if neglected."[2]   In March of the same year a statute was passed differing in several respects from the preceding.   Parents or guardians are to be consulted and give their consent.   "Intentions" are to be published for "at least three weeks" before solemnization, which "shall be performed by and before some justice of the peace or other magistrate," unless he "refuse to be present;" the certificate shall be entered "in the register of the town and county" where the marriage takes place; and a record of publication is likewise to be kept by the clerk of the "assembly" or public place where it occurs.[3]

---

[1] *Cf.* COOK, *loc. cit.*, 359; and LINN, *Charter and Laws*, 101.

[2] "Fundamental Constitutions," sec. xx: in *New Jersey Archives*, I, 408; and LEAMING AND SPICER, *Grants*, etc., 164.

[3] A "Bill for the General Laws of the Province of East New Jersey," March, 1682/83: LEAMING AND SPICER, *op. cit.*, 236.   By this act marriage within the degrees there named is declared void: *ibid.*, 243.

The "Fundamental Constitutions" had provided that there should be a "register in each county for births, marriages, burials, and servants, where their names, times, wages, and days of payment" should be recorded: LEAMING AND SPICER, *op. cit.*, 163; and already in 1675, under the first proprietors, the "clerk of each town within this Province," in a book provided by the town, is to record "all births, marriages, and deaths" in his district: *ibid.*, 100.

Cook thinks this statute may "have been a compromise between the Quaker and the Puritan practice, that left out the very feature in each which was most desirable. For the parties were to take each other as husband and wife, but not 'before creditable witnesses;' while, on the other hand," by the terms of the law, if the "justice or magistrate refused to be present, it would appear that the parties could marry themselves."[1] But *that* they could undoubtedly do under the former law, since there is no nullifying clause, and the only penalty mentioned is clearly for failure to file the certificate.

Already in 1676[2] West New Jersey was also acquired by Quaker proprietors; and in May, 1682, by an act of the general assembly, "for the preventing of clandestine and unlawful marriages," a system much like that of the eastern province was established. Justices within their jurisdictions are authorized to solemnize, when the persons have caused their intentions to be previously published for fourteen days in "some public place appointed for that purpose," and the "parents or trustees" show "no lawful reason against it." For celebrating without such consent, if it "may be reasonably obtained," the magistrate is to be fined at the discretion of the general assembly. Provision is likewise made for registration.[3]

It will be observed that in all these measures for the two provinces of New Jersey civil marriage is recognized. It is optional under the act of 1668; but under the Quaker régime, of course, solemnization by a minister is not mentioned.

For about twenty years after the legislation just presented the proprietary rule was maintained in the two prov-

---

[1] COOK, *loc. cit.*, 359.

[2] See the "concessions" to West New Jersey: in SMITH, *Hist. of N. J.*, 521 ff.

[3] LEAMING AND SPICER, *op. cit.*, 446, 447.

inces.   During the latter part of the period there was more
or less friction and dissatisfaction.   The jurisdictions, though
not the property rights, were turned over to Governor-
General Andros in 1688.   Four years later all the interests
of the proprietors were absolutely surrendered to the crown.
The united colony was then joined with New York under
the same governor, but with a council and assembly of its
own; and this arrangement was continued until 1738, when
New Jersey became an independent royal province.[1]

After the union with New York, with characteristic
intolerance, the Church of England was established; "but
as the Episcopalians were a small minority of the population, and had but little zeal, the Establishment remained
barely more than nominal."[2]   To the "end the ecclesiastical
jurisdiction of the said Lord Bishop of London, may take
place in our said province, so far as conveniently may be"—
run the instructions to Governor Cornbury in 1702—"we
do think fit that you give all countenance and encouragement to the exercise of the same, excepting only the collating to benefices, granting licences for marriages, and probate
of wills, which we have reserved to you."   The table of
marriage according to the English canons is to be "hung
up in every orthodox church, and duly observed."   For its
"strict observance" the governor is to try to get a law
passed by the assembly, if none already exists.[3]

The attempt to force the rites of the English church and
the jurisdiction of the bishop of London on the people of
New Jersey proved a failure.   So, March 27, 1719, a new
act appears, which shows that serious abuses, notably in the
issue of licenses, must have existed during the orthodox rule.

[1] For the instrument of surrender see SMITH, *Hist. of New Jersey*, 211-19.   There
was a petition to separate from New York as early as 1728: *ibid.*, 421 ff.   *Cf.* also
COOK, *loc. cit.*, 359; THWAITES, *Colonies*, 211, 213, 214.

[2] COOK, *loc. cit.*

[3] Instructions to Lord Cornbury, 1702: in LEAMING AND SPICER, *op. cit.*, 639; also
in SMITH, *op. cit.*, 253.

"Whereas of late Years," says the preamble, "several Young
Persons have been, by the Wicked Practices of evil disposed
Persons, and their Confederates, inticed, inveigled and
deluded, led away and clandestinely so Married," to the
"great Grief of their Parents and Relatives," it is therefore
enacted that, under forfeit of five hundred pounds, no license
shall be granted to a person under twenty-one years of age
without consent of the parent or guardian, "signified by a
certificate in writing" under his hand; which certificate
must be filed in the office of the secretary of the province.
The person presenting the certificate of parental consent,
before issue of license, must "take an Oath upon the Four
Holy Evangelists, of Almighty God, or if really of Tender
Conscience, shall make a Solemn Affirmation and Declaration," that it is genuine; and besides, as in New York, he is
required to execute a bond to the governor, with two
sufficient sureties, in the penal sum of five hundred pounds.[1]
In case of celebration by banns instead of license the procedure is the same.   The certificate of consent must be presented by the persons to the clerk of the peace or to the
county clerk; they must take the oath on the evangelists,
and execute a bond of the same tenor as that already
described.   Thereupon the clerk, within fourteen days,
"shall affix a Writing in a fair legible Hand, in the *English*
Tongue, at three the most publick Places in said County,
setting forth the Persons names, Places of Abode, and
Intentions of Marriage."   All religious societies may celebrate according to their own rites; and by implication ministers of the gospel, justices of the peace, and "others" may
perform the ceremony.[2]

---

[1] 5 Geo. I., in *Acts of the General Assembly* (Woodbridge, 1752), 79 ff.   The form
of bond is given p. 81.   This statute is also in ALLINSON'S *Acts of the Gen. Assem.*,
1702–76 (Burlington, 1776), 53–57.

[2] Under penalty of £200, ministers, justices, or others are forbidden to join
persons in marriage without banns or proper license: *Acts of the Gen. Assem.* (1752),
79, 80, 82, 84.

At this point legislation rested.   No further change was made in the matrimonial law of New Jersey until long after the Revolution.[1]   However, in 1765 a vain attempt was made by the Episcopal clergy, though a small minority in the province, to monopolize the income derived from the celebration of marriages on the governor's license, showing that they were not less greedy nor selfish than were their brethren of New York seventeen years before.   In a letter to the Lords of Trade the "Bishop of London at the request of the clergy of . . . . New Jersey begs leave to represent, ... that by an old Law the Licences for Marriages are directed to any Protestant Minister or Justice of the Peace, which however necessary at the first Establishment of the Colony to facilitate Marriages, when there were few Ministers in the Country, seems at present not only prejudicial to the clergy, who are depriv'd of a considerable part of their Income, but gives occasion to many Inconveniences and abuses."   It appears, as the letter further shows, that in 1760 the clergy petitioned Governor Boone to "alter the Direction of the Licences."   The petition was declined on the ground that authority to make the change belonged to the Lords of Trade on application of the bishop of London. The request being now made to the bishop, the latter hopes that the lords "will take the matter into Consideration, and if they see no particular Objections will give their Instructions to the Governor of that Province, that for the future Marriage Licences may be directed only to a Protestant Minister of the Gospel."   The Bishop's communication was forwarded by the Lords of Trade to Governor Franklin of New Jersey, with a sensible letter in which certain pertinent questions are so forcibly raised as seemingly to bring the correspondence to a speedy end.   Their lordships see no

[1] Until the act of March 4, 1795, by which the act of 1719 was repealed: *Laws of the State* (Newark, 1800), 160.

objection to what the bishop proposes, "if there is no Law in force by which the Civil Magistrate is authorized to perform the Marriage Rites, or if long usage and custom has not established such a practice." But they add, "as it does not appear to Us from any Information we can collect here, how the case stands in respect to this matter, we desire you will by the first opportunity acquaint Us, whether the civil Magistrates in New Jersey do or do not perform those Ceremonies; and if they do; whether it is by virtue of any declared Law or by usage only; and if the latter, whether such practice may in your opinion be altered in the manner proposed by the Bishop of London without Inconvenience or Complaint."[1]

It is evident what a truthful answer from the governor must have been; but we hear no more of the matter.

b) Law and custom in Pennsylvania and Delaware.—It was one of the many false charges originally brought against the Quakers by their orthodox adversaries that they did not celebrate marriage in an orderly and decent way. They were even accused of repudiating the marital relation and of indulging on principle in licentious conduct.[2] There is no ground whatever for such slanders, unless the rejection of the ring, with the peculiar observances of the English church, and the insistence that marriage, as a divine ordinance, is a

---

[1] *New Jersey Archives*, First Series, IX, 504, 520, 521.

[2] See, for example, the curious pamphlet of THOMAS UNDERHILL, *Hell broke loose: Or An History of the Quakers Both Old and New. Setting forth many of their Opinions and Practices. Published to Antidote Christians against Formality in Religion and Apostasie* (London, 1660), 16, 37, where, contradictorily, they are accused of believing, "that we sould endeavor to be perfect; and therefore to forbear *all carnall acts* of *Generation*, as being of *Sin* and of the *Devil;* and therefore *Husband* and *Wife* should *part asunder*, or *abstain;*" and that "marriage was made by Man;" while one of them is charged with defending a woman who went naked and confessing " *That of late he went to bed with a woman, who was not his wife, and that he did it without sin.*"

Read also *The Quakers Spiritual Court Proclaimed* (London, 1668), 5, 6, by "Nathaniel Smith Student in Physick, who was himself a Quaker, and conversant among them for the space of about XIV years": "Not long before this, they spoke against Marriage, and said, That it was for Lust; and that men ought to live soverly,

matter between man and his own conscience, in which the priest shall have nothing to do, may be counted a justification. The Quakers always held the institutions of marriage and the family in great esteem. From the beginning they have exacted due publicity in the celebration which was attended by a modest, though devout and severe, ceremonial. So important, indeed, was the nuptial contract in their eyes, as will presently appear, that the Pennsylvania Friends were too much inclined to extravagant display in the wedding festivities. One may well marvel what was Masson's notion of a religious rite when he wrote that the Quakers "had no religious ceremony in sanction of marriage."[1] "Professor Masson, as his context proves, had ample opportunity to avoid this blunder, and it can only be accounted for on the theory that his mind is prejudiced by the still popular notion that the presence and offices of an ordained minister are necessary to make a marriage ceremony religious and to secure the Divine sanction of the nuptial rites. The Quakers thought otherwise. They repudiated the claims of the clergy, and believed that God alone can join men and women in the solemn covenant."[2]

From their founders we may learn their doctrine of matrimony. "We marry none," says George Fox, "but are witnesses of it; marriage being God's joining not man's."[3] In harmony with this is Penn's declaration that the Quakers

For all Lust came of the Devil: and so they spoke against Marriage in general; but this continued not above three or four Years, at which time they began to Marry in Prison: and there was the first Marriage that I ever knew of. After this, that their Ministers did marry in Prisons, then the Common sort would marry in the Meeting: And it was after this Manner; Those two that were resolved to go together, (and many times there was not one that did know it besides themselves,) the Man and the Woman would stand up in the midst of them, or in some convenient place; the Man declaring after this manner, *I take this Woman to Wife:* and after, departed and went together as Man and Wife."

[1] MASSON, *Life and Times of Milton*, V, 25; *cf.* HALLOWELL, *Quaker Invasion of Mass.*, 23.

[2] HALLOWELL, *op. cit.*, 23, 24.

[3] APPLEGARTH, "Quakers in Pennsylvania," *J. H. U. S.*, X, 402.

believe marriage to be "an ordinance of God, and that God only can rightly join men and women" in wedlock.[1] Elsewhere he declares that ceremonies the Friends "have refused not out of humor, but conscience reasonably grounded; inasmuch as no Scripture-example tells us, that the priest had any other part, of old time, than that of a witness among the rest, before whom the Jews used to take one another; and therefore this people look upon it as an imposition, to advance the power and the profits of the clergy; and for the use of the ring, it is enough to say, that it was an heathenish and vain custom, and never practiced among the people of God, *Jews* or *primitive Christians.*"[2] Again, he claims that wedlock is a union which should only grow out of mutual inclination. "Never marry but for love," is his advice, "but see that thou lovest what is lovely."[3] Similar evidence is given by Sewel, the Quaker historian. "In their Method of Marriage," he says, "they also depart from the common Way: For in the Old Testament they find not that the Joyning of a Couple in Marriage ever was the Office of a Priest, nor in the Gospel any Preacher among Christians appointed thereto. Therefore it is their Custom, that when any intend to enter into Marriage, they first having the Consent of Parents or Guardians, acquaint the respective Mens and Womens Meetings of their Intention, and after due Enquiry, all Things appearing clear, they in Publick Meeting solemnly take each other in Marriage, with a Promise of Love and Fidelity, and not to leave one another before Death separates them. Of this a Certificate is drawn, mentioning the Names and Distinctions of the Persons thus joyned, which being first signed by themselves, those then that are present sign as witnesses."[4]

[1] Penn, *Rise and Progress* (Manchester, 1834), 25, 27; *cf.* Applegarth, *op. cit.*, 402.
[2] Penn, *Select Works*, V, 225: cited by Applegarth, *op. cit.*, 401, 402.
[3] Penn, *op. cit.*, V, 129: quoted by Applegarth, *op. cit.*, 401.
[4] Sewel, *History* (London, 1722), 691.

Commenting on this passage, Hallowell says: "This custom is still in force, and with some unimportant verbal amendments, the phraseology of early Friends is still preserved. After an appropriate silence, the groom and bride rise, and taking each other by the hand, each in turn repeats, 'In the presence of the Lord and this assembly, I take thee to be my wife (or husband), promising, with Divine assistance to be unto thee a loving and faithful husband (or wife) until death shall separate us.' For religious solemnity and tender, touching simplicity, the Quaker marriage ceremony has always challenged comparison, and if anyone desires to *feel* and realize the presence of God in a public or private gathering, let him attend a Quaker wedding."[1]

These principles are revealed in the early legislation for Pennsylvania; for, while believing it an ordinance of God, the Friends held that the regulation and protection of marriage belong to the civil authority. In the "Laws agreed upon in England" May 5, 1682, it is provided "that all marriages (not forbidden by the law of God, as to nearness of blood and affinity . . . .) shall be encouraged; but the parents or guardians shall be first consulted, and the marriage shall be published before it be solemnized, and it shall be solemnized by taking one another as husband and wife, before credible witnesses, and a certificate of the whole, under the hands of parents and witnesses, shall be brought to the proper register of that county, and shall be registered in his office."[2]

This is a clear statement of the desires of the proprietor and his associates. Accordingly in a law enacted by the assembly in December, 1683, there is a provision regarding

---

[1] HALLOWELL, *op. cit.*, 24, 25.

[2] "Laws Agreed upon in England": in LINN, *Charter and Laws*, 101. *Cf.* NEAD'S *Historical Notes: ibid.*, 472. This law also provides for a "register of births, marriages, burials, wills, and letters of administration, distinct from the other registry." —*Ibid.*, 101.

marriage only differing in details from the declaration made beyond the sea. The purpose of the act, as expressed in the preamble, is "to prevent Clandestine, Loose, and unseemly proceedings" in the province and its "territories." As before, marriage is to be encouraged; parental consent is required; the parties must clear themselves "from all other engagements assured by a Certificate from some Credible persons where they have lived;" affix their "intentions of Marriage on the Court, or Meeting-house Door of the County where they Dwell, one Month before the solemnization thereof;" the marriage shall be celebrated "by taking one another as husband and wife, before Sufficient Witnesses;" and a "certificate of the whole under the hands of parties and witnesses (at least twelve,) shall be brought to the Register of the County" where the marriage takes place and be with him filed for record. For neglect of the requirements of law the parties are to be fined ten pounds, and the "person so joining others in Marriage" twice that amount.[1] The "Great Law" of 1682, punishes adultery severely, sanctions divorce for that offense,[2] and contains the declaration, unique since old English days, that "no person, be it either widower or widow, shall contract marriage, much less marry, under one year after the decease of his wife or her husband."[3]

This provision of 1682 is declared fundamental, and by it in fact the main principles of the marriage law of Pennsylvania were defined. Still one or two important changes were subsequently made. Thus, in 1684, the certificate of their "clearness of all engagements" is to be produced to the "religious society" to which the persons "relate;" or to

---

[1] Linn, *Charter and Laws*, 151. See the same provision as to penalty (1684), *ibid.*, 171, and (1693), 229.

[2] *Ibid.*, 109; *cf.* 194.

[3] This is chap. 35 of the Great Law as given by Hazard, *Annals of Pa.*, 626, 627; but it was not engrossed and does not appear in Linn's edition, which follows Patrick Robinson's copy: Nead, *Historical Notes:* in Linn, *op. cit.*, 481 n. 3.

a justice of the peace of the county where they live.[1]   From this requirement it may doubtless be inferred that either civil celebration before a magistrate or religious celebration according to the rites of any denomination was contemplated.   Such is expressly declared to be the case by the act of 1693, which runs in nearly the same words as the preceding, except that now, after mentioning the twelve witnesses, it is provided that at least one justice of the peace of the county must be present at the solemnization; and provided also that "this Law shall not extend to any who shall marry or be marryed by any person authorized by the Church of England, so as they observe the methods of publication, Licensing & Solemnization" required by English law, "nor to any persons that marry in their own Society in the absence of a Justice of the peace."[2]   With the exception of a provision in 1730, forbidding the justice in case of minors to subscribe as witness without a certificate of parental consent,[3] the law of 1693, re-enacted in 1700 and again in 1701,[4] still governs the nuptial celebration in Pennsylvania;[5] and previous to 1788 the marriage law of Delaware was practically the same.[6]

It remains to give a few illustrations of administrative practice and social custom.   So far as it appears, the courts and magistrates were not given much employment in domes-

---

[1] LINN, op. cit., 171.   [2] Ibid., 229.

[3] Cf. COOK, op. cit., 358.   This act of Feb. 14, 1729/30, is contained in Laws of the Comm. of Pa., 1700–1810, I, 180, 181.

[4] BIOREN, Laws, I, 7, 34; LINN, op. cit., 229, note; also Laws of the Comm. of Pa., 1700–1810, I, 21–23.

[5] PEPPER AND LEWIS, Digest (1896), II, 2878 ff.

[6] See the act of 1700 in FRANKLIN AND HALL'S Laws of the Government of New Castle, Kent, and Sussex, upon Delaware (Philadelphia, 1752).   It is especially provided that if any servant marry without the consent of his or her master, he or she shall, for such offense, serve for one year after the time of his or her servitude by indenture has expired; and if any free person marry a servant without consent of the master, he or she shall pay to the master, if the servant is a man, 12 pounds, and if a woman, 6 pounds, or one whole year's service; and the servant so marrying shall serve an additional year.   Adultery is punished with a fine of 50 pounds or 21 lashes "well laid on."   The penalty for fornication is 3 pounds or 21 lashes: ibid., 74.

tic controversies.   But the provincial council seems to have exercised jurisdiction in divorce and matrimonial causes. For example, in 1685 we learn that "information being given to this board of yᵉ unlawfull Marriage of Rᵈ Noble, of yᵉ County of New Castle, Ordered that yᵉ Justices of that County have notice given by yᵉ Secrt^{rs}, to Inspect the same and give report thereof to this board."[1]   Again, in 1703 Andrew Bankson, one of the justices of Philadelphia county, on complaint of the president, got himself into trouble "for irregularly marrying a couple lately according to law, but against yᵉ Prohibitions of yᵉ Parents."   When called to account before the council, the justice declared that he was "wholly ignorant of its being illegal, & was heartily sorry for what was done, promising that wether he should continue in Commission, or otherwise, this should be such a caution to him as to prevent him of committing the like for yᵉ future, & being severely checked was dismissed."[2]

Celebration on the president's license in place of civil notice similar to the plan existing in the royal provinces was introduced as early as 1684 and the practice was continued to the Revolution;[3] although marriages thus solemnized were looked at askance by the Quakers as hardly orthodox,[4] and there are the usual complaints of extortion.[5]   The

---

[1] Col. Records of Pa., I, 144.

[2] Col. Records of Pa. (Jan. 1703/4), II, 114, 115; also quoted by APPLEGARTH, Quakers in Pa., 413, note.

[3] Pa. Col. Rec., I, 121.   "The Board then took into their Consideration the alterations proper to be made in the forms of Marriage Lycences."—Ibid., V, 69 (1747). Again, "Order'd, That the President sign all Marriage Lycences."—Ibid., V, 71 (1747).

[4] See the passage from WATSON, Annals of Phil., III, 434, below cited.

[5] On Sept. 29, 1755, in an address to the governor, the assembly declares that "they [the assembly] are not, however, chargeable with exacting Money from the people which by law they had no right to exact, as we apprehend the Governor does in the Fees for Marriage Licenses, by which many thousand Pounds have been drawn from the Inhabitants of this Province.   If this be not dispensing with Law 'tis making Law, and we presume the Governor alone has no more right to do the one than the Assembly alone the other."—Pa. Col. Rec., VI, 633, 634.   Cf. ibid., II, 455; IV, 175; and Pa. Archives (1728), I, 235, 236, where the bishop of London says that "some occasional perquisites that the Clergy us'd to enjoy, are now cut off" in the matter of licenses.

marriage certificate was itself an elaborate document of historical interest, not only because of the full statement therein
of all the previous stages in the transaction, but because in
simple phrase we catch many a glimpse of Quaker sentiment
and teaching in regard to the nuptial covenant.   Sometimes
even at the marriage of persons of humble station, this instrument was signed by many persons; as in the case of John
Roades and Hannah Willcox, in 1692, whose wedding certificate bears the names of fifty witnesses.[1]

In the first half of the eighteenth century the Pennsylvania Friends, like the New England Puritans, were much
worried over the question of forbidden degrees.   They were
sorely disturbed concerning marriage "between first cousins,
or one person marrying two sisters, or a man marrying his
wife's first cousin, or justices of the peace undertaking to
marry people by virtue of licenses obtained to that end, or

[1] "Whereas John Roades of the County of Philadelphia and Hannah Willcox
daughter of Sarah Willcox of Schoolkil in the County aforesaid having declared
theire Intentione of Takeing Each Other as Husband and Wife before several Men
and Womens Meetings of the People called Quakers whose Proceedings Therein
after deliberate Consideration Thereof and Consent of parties and Relations concerned being approved by the said Meeting.

"AND alsoe the said John Roades and Sarah Willcox having Published theire
said Intentions in Writing according to the Lawes of thiss province Whereby the
said Law is fulfilled. . . . ;

"Now these are to CERTIFIE all Persons whome it may concern that
for the full Determination of their Intentions this tenth day of the Ninth
Month in the Yeare One Thousand Six Hundred and Ninety and two, they the
said John Roades and Hannah Willcox in an Assembly of the aforesaid people Mett
together for that end and purpose at the Dwelling House of Sarah Willcox aforesaid,
according to the Example of the primitive Christians Recorded in the Scriptures of
Truth did take each Other as Husband and Wife in Manner following (viz) he the
said John Roades takeing the said Hannah Willcox by the Hand said friends in the
feare of the Lord and Before you his people I take this my friend Hannah Willcox
to be my wife promising as the Lord shall Inable mee to be unto her a faithfull and
Loving Husband till Death shall part us. . . . . And the said Hannah Willcox in like
Manner takeing the said John Roades by the Hand said friends I Likewise do in the
fear of the Lord and in the presence of You his people take John Roades to be my
Husband promising to be unto him a faithfull and Loving Wife till Death separate
us. . . . . AND the said John Roades and Hannah Willcox as a farther Confirmation
thereof did then and there to these presents Set theire Hand. AND wee whose Names
are hereunto Subscribed are Witnesses of the Same the Day and Yeare abovesaid."—
In the Pa. Mag. of Hist. and Biog., XIII (1889), 112.

The custom of many witnesses signing the certificate survived to recent times:
WATSON, Annals of Phil., III, 434.

marriages by members of the sect with others not of that persuasion, in young couples 'keeping company' without the consent of their parents. In 1725 and 1731, Chester and Burlington Monthly Meetings sought the advice of Yearly Meeting upon these subjects," and decisions were subsequently rendered in the negative on every point.[1]

A register of marriages was kept through a custodian appointed by the monthly meeting. From the records of the Philadelphia society, which have been preserved "for the first thirty-two years of the city," it appears that the first marriage solemnized was that of Thomas Smith and Priscilla Allen in 1682; and they, says Watson, "had before passed one Meeting in the Isle of Wight."[2] The monthly meeting was a mighty power, and it kept a sharp eye on all the social goings and comings of its members.[3] In fact, the constant surveillance of the meeting over the daily life of the individual reminds one of the way in which domestic conduct and private business were dealt with by provincial law and town ordinances in the New England colonies.[4] Courtship, espousal, and marriage were looked after much in the same spirit. The Quaker maid was lucky if she might receive her lover on the "stoop" in presence of father and mother.[5] The Friends were not content with the publicity given by posting the intention of marriage as prescribed by

---

[1] WATSON, *op. cit.*, III, 434.   [2] *Ibid.*, I, 503; III, 434.

[3] The meeting sometimes took part in the civil administration. Thus committees were frequently appointed by the Philadelphia meeting to lay out roads; *ibid.*, I, 305.

[4] *Cf.* HOWARD, *Local Const. Hist.*, I, 53 ff.

[5] EARLE, "Among Friends," *New Eng. Mag.*, Sept., 1898, 20. "Courtship and marriage were closely hedged around. Friends were enjoined against proposing marriage without the consent of the meeting, against marrying any but a Friend, against 'keeping unreasonable company' with any woman not a Friend; against going to weddings of any who marry out of meeting; against being 'married by a priest.' They were enjoined also 'to be clear of one before being concerned with another,' in an engagement of marriage. Widows and widowers were reminded not to marry again too swiftly; 'not to let their minds out soon to another husband or wife ;' and kinship was to be carefully regarded in thinking of wedding."—*Ibid.*, 19, 20; *cf.* WATSON, *Annals of Phil.*, III, 434.

the law.   In addition, it was the duty of the betrothed couple
to ask their own banns, or to "pass the meeting," as it was
called in solemn phrase.   "In the intense silence of the
Quaker assembly the man arose from his seat on his side of
the meeting and said formally: 'I intend to take Dorcas
Macy to be my wife if the Lord permit.'   Dorcas then arose
on the woman's side of the aisle or partition and said in
turn: 'I intend to take Jonathan Coffin to be my husband if
the Lord permit.'[1]   A committee of 'weighty men and
women' was then appointed to learn 'the conversation and
clearness of the parties'—that is to learn specially whether
either were entangled in any other matrimonial engagement.
If the report of these inspectors proved favorable, the 'continuance of the intention of marriage' was permitted, they
were 'liberated to proceed according to the devout order of
truth,' and the engaged pair were said to have 'passed meeting.'   But sometimes the committee of inspectors discovered
obstacles, or 'disorderly walking,' or a previous flirtation.
There still was redress; the offender had to make a self-
condemnation and apology for his offense, in meeting, the
next First day, in some such words as these: 'Friends, I am
very sorry for my transgression, and desire mercy from God
and forgiveness of all the people of God whom I have
offended.'   The marriage was usually then permitted.   If a
sober young Friend sought a wife in another town, his home
meeting sent him off fortified with a certificate enumerating
his virtues.   One such ran partly thus:

'He is of sober and orderly behaviour; a frequenter of our
Meetings and in good Eunity with us; is clear of all Women
hereaway on account of Marriage so far as we can find; soe

---

[1] It seems to have been customary, at least in some meetings, to file the notice
in writing for permanent record. The form was as follows:
"We the subscribers, A.B.. son of C., and D. B.; and F. G., daughter of H.,
and I. G., purpose taking each other in marriage, which we hereby offer for the
approbation of Friends."—APPLEGARTH, "Quakers in Pennsylvania," *J. H. U. S.*,
X, 402.

we recommend him to your further Care in accomplishing their Intending Marriage.'"[1]

Faithful Friends were enjoined by the meeting not to marry out of the society; and so the worldly lover was sometimes forced to turn Quaker or "lose his bride." On the other hand, says Earle, if a Friend took a wife "out of meeting, he might by profoundly humbling himself, and acknowledging his error, still be retained in the society, though for a time not in good report. No Quaker groom could express contrition for an offense in 'marrying out of meeting,' nor indeed submit patiently to discipline for it without unmanly disloyalty to his confiding consort. . . . . One reads thus:

"'To the Monthly Meeting of friends now in meeting at So. Kingston. I through Inattention to the Lights of Christ have Married a wife out of the good order of Friends, neither was she a member of their Society. Therefore now being Sincible that their Rules and orders therein is Consistant with truth, and Seeing the Error of My Doings, am sorry for my Transgression therein, and Desire friends to pass by my offense, and still Continue their Care for me, desiring I may be preserved to walk according to good order for time to come.'"[2]

As already suggested, the Pennsylvania Friends indulged in much good cheer and sometimes in lavish display at the wedding time. A description given us by the annalist Watson may serve for the purpose of comparison between their nuptial festivals and those practiced by their New England contemporaries. "The wedding entertainments of olden times, he says, "were very expensive and harassing to the wedded. The house of the parent would be filled with company to dine; the same company would stay to tea and to supper. For two days punch was dealt out in profusion.

---

[1] EARLE, "Among Friends," *New Eng. Mag.*, Sept., 1898, 20.   [2] *Ibid.*, 21.

The gentlemen saw the groom on the first floor, and then ascended to the second floor, where they saw the bride." Every man present, even though hundreds were invited, was privileged to kiss the bride and to repeat the process each day while the feast lasted. These were the same persons who had signed the marriage certificate in the meeting. Sometimes the "married pair for two weeks saw large tea parties at their home, having in attendance every night the groomsman and bridesmaids." All this was not enough. "When these . . . . entertainments were made, it was expected also that punch, cakes, and meats should be sent out very generally in the neighborhood even to those who were not visiters in the family."[1] In some towns another writer tells us, "the custom was after a wedding to set a table in front of the house and feast all passers-by. In the country Quaker brides had an 'infare' or wedding treat, often so liberal as to be a serious drag on the family that provided it." Moreover, it should be noted that the great wedding festival had been preceded by a similar feast or "treat" at the first "passing of the meeting," when the banns were published.[2]

Such excesses seem inconsistent with traditional Quaker sobriety. One is astonished that they could have been tolerated so long. But at length it was decided that "passing" in one meeting should suffice.[3] To lessen the expenses the Philadelphia society in 1716 "advised no extraordinary provision for weddings, and the avoidance 'as much as may be of inviting those not under our discipline.'"[4]

---

[1] WATSON, *Annals of Phil.*, I, 178, 503.

[2] EARLE, *loc. cit.*, 21. "In Philadelphia not only did the friends of the bride and groom come and eat and drink and all kiss the bride, but every evening for a week the entire bridal party received friends, and again the bride ran a gauntlet of kisses. When Mrs. Robert Erwin received her wedding visitors, four hundred gentlemen came in two days, ate the wedding cake, drank the wedding punch and, doubtless, all kissed her."—*Ibid.*, 21.

[3] WATSON, *op. cit.*, I, 504.   [4] EARLE, *loc. cit.*

So the old frivolities "were relegated to the limbo of exploded vanities, and matrimonial alliances were attended with no other ceremony than that of the parties taking each other by the hand in public meeting and avowing their willingness to enter the connubial state."   The certificate was then entered in the record book of the meeting and the celebration was complete.[1]

[1] APPLEGARTH, "Quakers in Pa.," *J. H. U. S.*, X, 402, 403, who gives a discussion of Quaker weddings, following WATSON. GORDON, *Hist. of Pa.*, 70, 557, has a brief, concise account of the marriage law of the province.

CHAPTER XV

DIVORCE IN THE AMERICAN COLONIES

[BIBLIOGRAPHICAL NOTE XV.—The most valuable original material for the history of divorce in Massachusetts during the period of the first charter is afforded by the decisions of the court of assistants in the exercise of its primary jurisdiction. These may be found in Vol. I of the *Colonial Records*, to September 7, 1641; the Barlow *MS. Records of the Court of Assistants*, October 28, 1641, to March 5, 1643/44; published by Whitmore in *Bibliographical Sketch of the Laws of the Mass. Colony* (Boston, 1890); and, after an interval for which the record is missing, in Noble's *Records of the Court of Assistants*, March 3, 1673, to March 23, 1691/92 (Boston, 1901). A number of cases have been found in the *MSS. Early Court Files of Suffolk*, supplemented by the *MSS. Records of the County Court of Suffolk*, and the *MSS. Records of the County Court of Middlesex*. The *Massachusetts Colonial Records* are, of course, very important. There is an instructive passage in the first volume of Hutchinson's *History of Mass.* (Salem, 1795); and much aid has been given by Whitmore in the work already cited; Newhall, *Ye Great and General Court* (Lynn, 1897); Goodwin, *Pilgrim Republic* (Boston, 1888); and Cowley, *Our Divorce Courts* (Lowell, 1880). The last-named work in part had already appeared in the *Albany Law Journal*, XX (Albany, 1879). It may be read in connection with the same writer's *Famous Divorces of All Ages* (Lowell, 1878); and his *Browne's Divorce and its Consequences* (Lowell, 1877). For the period of the second charter the divorce record is missing until 1739. Between that date and 1760 the *Suffolk Files* already mentioned yield eleven cases. From 1760 to 1786 there is a continuous and apparently complete record in a MS. "Divorce" book in the office of the clerk of the supreme judicial court for Suffolk county.

An interesting petition may be found in the eighth volume of the *Collections of the New Hampshire Historical Society;* and in general for all the New England colonies the records and the various collections of laws mentioned in Bibliographical Note XII have been used. Durfee, *Gleanings from the Judicial History of Rhode Island* (Providence, 1883), and Arnold, *History of the State of Rhode Island* (New York, 1874), are also helpful. Trumbull, *Appeal to the Public* (New Haven, 1788), gives some statistics in connection with the alleged laxity of Connecticut divorce laws; but historically his statements are misleading and very inaccurate.

In the southern colonies the English divorce laws were in abeyance, except in case of separate alimony. The meager materials existing for a "negative" sketch are therefore derived almost wholly from the judicial decisions. Among these—cited more fully in the footnotes—the most instructive are: for Virginia, Fulcher *v.* Fulcher, in 1 Palmer's *Calendar of Va. State Papers* (Richmond, 1875), 29; Purcell *v.* Purcell, 4 Hening and Munford's *Reports* (Richmond, 1854), 506; and Almond *v.* Almond, 4 Randolph's *Reports*, 662, or 15 *American Decisions*, 781. For Maryland, Galwith *v.* Galwith, 4 Harris and McHenry's *Md. Reports* (Annapolis, 1818), 477; Farnshill *v.* Murray, 1 Bland's *Reports*, 479, or 18 *American Decisions*, 344; Helms *v.* Franciscus, 2 Bland's *Reports*, 544, or 20 *American Decisions*, 402; Wallingsford *v.* Wallingsford, 6 Harris and Johnson's *Reports*, 485; Macnamara's case, Scott's case, Govane's case, all in 2 Bland's *Reports*, 566, 568, 570; Crane *v.* Meginnis, 1 Gill and Johnson's *Ch. Reports*, 468, or 19 *American Decisions*, 237; Wright *v.* Wright's Lessee, 2 *Md. Reports*, 429, or 56 *American Decisions*, 723; and Jamison *v.* Jamison, 4 *Md. Ch. Reports*, 289, 295. For Georgia see Finch *v.* Finch, 14 *Georgia Reports*, 362; and especially Head *v.* Head, 2 Kelly's *Reports*, 191.

The *New York Colonial MSS.* preserved in the State Library at Albany have yielded several documents of importance for the chapter. Cadwallader Colden, the last governor of the province, has an instructive passage in his *Letters on Smith's History of New York: Collections New York Historical Society*, Fund Series, I, 1868, showing that in the early period divorces were granted by the royal governors. Various cases and illustrations have been gleaned from Gerard, *The Old Stadt Huys;* Valentine, *Manual of the Corporation; Records of New Amsterdam;* Munsell, *Annals of Albany; Duke of Yorke's Book of Laws; New Jersey Archives;* O'Callaghan, *Ordinances;* and especially O'Callaghan and Fernow, *Documents*—all of which have been described in Bibliographical Note XIV. A number of extracts from old records have been borrowed from Alice Morse Earle's excellent book *Colonial Days in Old New York* (New York, 1896); and among the decisions cited, Chancellor Kent's opinion in Williamson *v.* Williamson, Johnson's *Chancery Reports*, 488, 491; and that of Chancellor Walworth in Wood *v.* Wood, 2 Paige's *Chancery Reports*, 108, 111, bearing on the validity of the common law in the province, are of special interest.

The materials for Pennsylvania are furnished by Linn, *Charter and Laws;* the *Colonial Records of Pennsylvania;* Bioren, *Laws* (Philadelphia, 1803); and Gordon, *History of Pennsylvania* (Philadelphia, 1829). Lastly, for the entire group of colonies, Kent, *Commentaries* (Boston, 1884); Story, *Commentaries* (Boston, 1891); and particularly Bishop, *Marriage, Divorce, and Separation* (Chicago, 1891), have been of service.]

I.   IN NEW ENGLAND

UNDER normal conditions civil divorce is the counterpart of civil marriage.   Naturally, in the New England colonies the same influences which determined the rise of civil marriage secured also the adoption of a liberal policy respecting divorce.   In each case there was a reaction against the forms and abuses of the ancient canonical and ecclesiastical systems; while at the same time the innovations were in a measure sustained by appeal to the Levitical code.   Everywhere as a result the ideas of the Reformation Fathers—the general trend of Protestantism—found effective expression in statute and judicial decree.   For in most respects throughout New England the broad modern doctrines of the *Reformatio Legum* of Edward VI.'s commission, though scarcely even now completely victorious in the mother-land, were from the outset put in practice by both Puritan and Separatist.   The American legal conception of divorce as pertaining, not to the criminal, but exclusively to the civil jurisdiction, had its birth in the seventeenth century.[1]   In all the New England colonies the canonical decree of separation from bed and board was practically, though not entirely, abandoned.   On the other hand, a dissolution of the bond of matrimony was freely granted for various causes, such as desertion, cruelty, or breach of the marriage vow; and usually, though not always, the husband and wife were dealt with as equals before the law.   These general principles will be illustrated, somewhat in detail, by reference to the history of the particular provinces.

a) Massachusetts.—For the Bay Colony we have a concise summary from the pen of Governor Hutchinson, who presided in the divorce court for many years.   "In matters of divorce," he says, "they left the rules of the canon law

---

[1] On the "divorce suit as civil or criminal" see, however, BISHOP, *Marriage, Divorce, and Separation*, II, secs. 483-88, pp. 218-20; also KENT, *Commentaries*, 100.

out of the question; with respect to some of them, prudently enough. I never heard of a separation, under the first charter, *a mensa et thoro*. Where it is practised, the innocent party often suffers more than the guilty. In general what would have been cause for such a separation in the spiritual courts, was sufficient, with them, for a divorce *a vinculo*. Female adultery was never doubted to have been sufficient cause; but male adultery, after some debate and consultation with the elders, was judged not sufficient. Desertion a year or two, when there was evidence of a determined design not to return, was always good cause; so was cruel usage of the husband. Consanguinity they settled in the same degrees as it is settled in England and in the levitical laws." [1]

By the code of 1660 the court of assistants, sitting twice a year, is given authority to hear and determine "all causes of divorce." [2] This is the only extant law on the subject for the period of the first charter. It is, however, almost certain that the assistants in the "quarter courts," or other tribunals, possessed such jurisdiction from the beginning. It is probably intended to be covered by the authority conferred on the quarter courts in 1639; [3] and the evidence of the Halsall case shows that as early as 1656 "the power of divorce doth properly belong" to the court of assistants. From the same case it has been inferred that the code of 1649 may have contained a like provision. [4]

---

[1] HUTCHINSON, *Hist. of Mass.*, I, 393.

[2] WHITMORE, *Col. Laws of Mass.* (1660–72), 36; (1672–86), 143.

[3] It is ordered "that such of the magistrates as shall reside in or near Boston, or any 5, 4, or 3 of them, the Governor or Deputy to be one, shall have power to assemble together upon the last fifth day of the eighth, eleventh, second, and fifth month, every year, and then and there to hear and determine all civil causes whereof the debt or trespass and damages shall not exceed £20, and all criminal causes *not* extending to life, or member, or banishment, according to the course of the Courts of Assistants, and to summon juries out of the neighboring towns."—*Mass. Col. Rec.*, I, 276. In 1648 the number of such courts was reduced to two: *ibid.*, II, 286; III, 175.

[4] In the petition for divorce in the Halsall case the counsel for the plaintiff says: "But considering the power of divorce doth properly belong to the Honored

Neither the right of appeal nor the causes or kinds of divorce are defined by the statutes. Information regarding these important points must be sought in the cases themselves. As a result of the failure of positive legislation, there is a lack of precision and harmony in the judicial practice of the entire colonial and provincial eras. For the period 1639–92, as shown in Table I, forty actions for divorce or annulment of marriage have been discovered. Thirty-one of these are mentioned by Newhall, Whitmore, Goodwin, and Cowley, not less than eighteen being found by the latter in the assistants' records for the years 1673–92, since edited by Mr. Noble.[1] The remaining nine cases are here added from further search in the court records and the Suffolk Files. The records of the court of assistants from 1644 to 1673 are missing; else doubtless the list might be considerably enlarged.

The first case thus far brought to light is that of James Luxford, elsewhere considered. On December 3, 1639, his bigamous marriage was declared void by the "Court of Assistants or Quarter Court;" and very righteously "all that he hath" as a kind of alimony was given to the woman last married and to her children.[2] A similar instance of having two wives was dealt with in November, 1644.[3]

Court of assistants as is expressed in an order of the general Court (May 16, 1656) & a president ther is for it (namly Mr. freeman sometimes of Watertowne) & the law admitts it (page 17)."—MSS. *Early Court Files of Suffolk*, No. 257. From the last phrase (in which he reads "submitts" for "admitts") WHITMORE thinks it "a reasonable surmise that this clause stood in the code of 1649, under the title Courts": *Bibliog. Sketch*, 101, note. The general court, referring to the same case, declares that it "doth properly belong" to the court of assistants: *Mass. Col. Rec.*, IV, i, 272. COWLEY, *Our Divorce Courts*, 10, mentions the error of PALFREY, *Hist. of U. S.*, II, 17, who says the superior "courts had jurisdiction in cases of divorce."

[1] COWLEY, *Our Divorce Courts*, 28–31; WHITMORE, *Biog. Sketch*, 99–101, note; NEWHALL, *Ye Great and General Court*, 380–84; GOODWIN, *Pilgrim Republic*, 596.

[2] *Mass. Col. Rec.*, I, 283. For this case and that of Frier v. Richardson see above, chap. xii, p. 159.

[3] Elizabeth Frier v. John Richardson: *Records of Court of Assistants*, 1641–1643/44 (Barlow MS.): published in WHITMORE, *Bibliog. Sketch*, xlii; also in *Mass. Col. Rec.*, II, 86.

TABLE I

CASES OF DIVORCE AND ANNULMENT OF MARRIAGE IN MASSACHUSETTS, 1639-92

No.	Where Found[1]	Date	Case	Cause	Court	Decree
1	C. R., I, 283	Dec. 3, 1639	Second wife v. Jas. Luxford	Another wife	Assistants	Marriage void
2	W., 42	Mar. 5, 1643/4	Anne v. Dennis Clarke	Desertion, adultery	Assistants	Mar. dissolved
3	W., 42; C. R., II, 86	Nov. 13, 1644	Eliz. Frier v. J. Richardson	Another wife	Assistants	Marriage void
4	C. R., IV, i, 32	Oct. 16, 1650	Wm. v. Eleanor Palmer	remarriage	General court	Mar. dissolved
5	C. R., III, 277, IV, i, 89	May 26, 27, 1652	Dorothy v. Wm. Pester	Deser., remarriage	General court	Leave to marry
6	C. R., III, 350, IV, i, 190	May 14, 1654	Dorcas v. Jno. Hall	Long absence	General court	Mar. dissolved
7	Suff. Files, 257	Before 1656	Sam. and Apphia Freeman	Desertion, adultery?	Assistants	Mar. dissolved
8	IV, i, 272, 380, 401; C. R.,	1655-59	Joan v. Geo. Halsall	Adultery	Assists. to general ct.	Mar. dissolved; reversed on ap.
9	C. R., I, 85, IV, i, 259, 269	June 9, 1656	Petition of Wm. Clements	None given	Co. ct. on ref. of g. ct.	Denied
10	C. R., IV, i, 282	Oct. 14, 1656	Petition of Mary Batchiler	Deser., remarriage	Co. ct. on ref. of g. ct.	None appears
11	C. R., IV, ii, 8	May 22, 1661	Rachel v. Jos. Langton	None given	General court	Mar. dissolved
12	C. R., IV, ii, 91	Oct. 21, 1663	Mary v. E. White	"Deficiency"	General court	Denied
13	Suff. Files, 651	Sept. 9, 1664	Petition of Sarah Helwis	Adult., cruelty of h.;	Assistants	Mar. dissolved
14	Suff. Files, 913	Jan. 28, 1668/9	Christ. and Eliz. Lawson	bad cond. of wife	Assists. from co. ct.	None appears
15	Plym. Rec., v. 33	Aug. 3, 1670	James v. Eliz. Skiffe	Desertion, adultery	General court	Mar. dissolved
16	C. R., IV, ii, 465	Oct., 1670	Eliz. v. Henry Stevens	Desertion, adultery?	General court	Mar. dissolved
17	Suff. Files, 1148; N., 32	Oct., 1672	Kath. v. Ed. Nailer	Adultery, cruelty	Assistants	Mar. dissolved
18	Suff. Files, 1360; N., 30	Mch. 4, 1674/5	Mary v. Wm. Sanders	Deser., remarriage	Assistants	Mar. dissolved
19	Suff. Files, 1644; N., 91	1673-77	Hugh and Mary Drury	Disease and imp. of h.	Assistants	Sep. b. b.?
20	Rec. Suff. co. ct., 506	Before 1678	Philip and Mary Wharton	See text	See text	Mar. dissolved
21	Suff. Files, 1741; C. R., V, 205; N., 127.	Sept. 9, 1678	Hugh v. Dorcas March	Another husband	Assists.; app. to g. ct.	Denied on app.
22	C. R., V, 188	May 9, 1678	Mary v. Henry Maddox	Long absence	General court	Leave to marry
23	N., 127	1678	Hope v. Sam. Ambrose	Desertion, adultery, failure to provide	Assistants	Mar. dissolved
24	N., 138	1678	Rebeckah v. Rich. Cooly	None given	Assistants	Mar. dissolved
25	Suff. Files, 1807; C. R., V, 248, 249	Oct. 15, 1679	Mary v. Aug. Lyndon	None given	General court	Mar. dissolved
26	N., 144	1679	Mary v. Job Bishop	Deser., remarriage	Assistants	Mar. dissolved
27	N., 147	1679	Mary v. Jos. White		Assistants	
28	N., 168	1680	Sus. v. Ed. Goodwin	Deser., fail. to prov.	Assistants	Mar. dissolved
29	N., 197	1681	Sam. v. Mary Holton	Adultery, desertion	Assistants	Mar. dissolved
30	N., 200	1681	Dorcas v. Christ. Smith	Deser., fail. to prov.	Assistants	Mar. dissolved
31	N., 208	1681	Rachel v. Lawrence Clenton		Assistants	Mar. dissolved
32	N., 227	1682	Petition of Ann Perry	Bigamy	Assistants	Mar. dissolved
33	N., 229	1683	Eliz. v. Robt. Street		Assistants	Denied
34	N., 240	1683	Sarah v. Nich. Maning	Incest, desertion	Assistants	Mar. dissolved
35	N., 256, 258	1684	Sarah v. Thos. Cooper		Assistants	Mar. dissolved
36	Suff. Files, 2347	Sept. 17, 1685	Petition of Thos. Winsor	Adultery	Assistants	Mar. dissolved
37	N., 323	1690	Phillip v. Hannah Goss	Deser., remarriage	Assistants	Mar. dissolved
38	N., 242	1690-91	Mary v. Sam. Stebbins	Adultery (bro's wife)	Assistants	Mar. dissolved
39	N., 361	1691	Hannah and Josiah Owen	Affinity (bro's wife)	Assistants	Marriage void
40	N., 342	1690	Sam. and Reb. Newton	Affinity (uncle's wid.)	Assistants	Marriage void

[1] N. = NOBLE's Records of the Court of Assistants, I; W. = Record of the Court of Assistants, in WHITMORE's Bibliog. Sketch.

Earlier in the same year "Anne Clarke" was released from her husband Dennis for desertion, "refusing to accompany with hir," and for living in adultery with another woman.[1] The case of Joan and George Halsall, 1655–59, is especially enlightening regarding the early law and procedure in divorce suits. Joan's original petition was presented to the general court, by which, as already noted, the matter was referred to the assistants for "final determination." In a later petition to the last-named tribunal the injured wife complains not only of her husband's "frequent abusing himself with Hester Lug," but "also of his wicked, constant & unsufferable expense" in "mulled sack and otherwise" with another woman of equally bad reputation, humbly asking that she "may be dismissed from her intolerable burden—an uncleane yoake-fellow."[2] The decree of the court is missing, but elsewhere we learn that her prayer was granted.[3] The fact is noteworthy; for seemingly this marriage was dissolved solely for the man's adultery.[4] If so, down to 1776, as will later appear, it is the only known clear exception to the rule mentioned by Governor Hutchinson. The case was, however, not yet ended. Halsall appealed to the general court; and so, on November 12, 1659, after the decree of the assistants had been in force for three years, it was declared void and George was allowed to "have and enjoy the said Joan Halsall, his wife, again."[5]

Jurisdiction on appeal thus belonged to the general court. This is further shown by the peculir case of Hugh

---

[1] *Records of Court of Assistants*, 1641–43 (Barlow MS.): published in WHITMORE, *op. cit.*, xlii.

[2] The two petitions are in the *MSS. Early Court Files of Suffolk*, No. 257; and the reference of the general court in *Mass. Col. Rec.*, IV, i, 272.

[3] *Mass. Col. Rec.*, IV, i, 401.

[4] Of course, the alleged "wicked expense" may possibly have been admitted as a second ground.

[5] *Mass. Col. Rec.*, IV, i, 401. The reason for Halsall's petition is not stated. Was it, perhaps, that "male adultery" was not a sufficient ground of divorce?

and Dorcas March. In 1678, for "ye peace & satisfaction" of his conscience, Hugh asked the court of assistants to decide whether he might legally retain Dorcas as his wife, alleging that her former husband was living and hinting that a divorce from him had never been secured. With much parade of law and logic, in a long and vague petition, probably drafted by his attorney, he betrays far more anxiety to get rid of his spouse than to quiet the throes of an outraged conscience. The secret of this is clearly disclosed by Dorcas in the counter-petition, written by her own hand, and proving her to be a better lawyer than her husband's counsel. It seems she had been "for some yeares ye wife of Benoni Blackleach," with whom she had formerly lived in Connecticut. About nine years before the present action Blackleach "was taken in a crime worthy of death by ye Law," but he escaped from his captors. Six months thereafter he sent her a letter saying he dared not call her his wife, and subscribing himself her "friend not husband." Later, not knowing for six years whether he was living or dead, Dorcas came to her friends in Massachusetts, bringing with her, on the advice of "ye honored Gouernor Winthrop," the "testimonys" sworn against her guilty consort. These, together with a petition for the determination of her status, she laid before "ye honord Court in Boston," Governor Winthrop being present when the case was "agitated." This tribunal adjudged her a "free woman," as "some of ye honored Magistrates did tell" her.[1] Presently she was solicited in marriage by March, he giving her an "Ingagement vnder his hand of one hundred pounds of ye best of his estate," promising "y^t he would remove his children from him y^t they might not make any disturbance between" them. Then they were "published," joined in wedlock

---

[1] The petition and decree here mentioned are not in the *Suffolk Files*. Perhaps further search in the *Mass. Archives* would bring them to light.

"by yᵉ honord Deputy Governor," and thereafter "Lived comfortably." Next we reach the heart of the business. Hugh's children "liveing in yᵉ familie" did "shamefully slight" her, purloining from her box the said "writing" of a hundred pounds; and their father disowned her as his wife. This conduct, she suggests, is due to a desire to "please his children" rather than to the scruples of a tender conscience. The magistrates were not moved by her plea. According to the record, "It was put . . . . whither Hugh March & said Dorcas might still lawfully live as man & wife;" and "the Court Resolved it in the Negative."[1] With this decree Hugh was not content. So on October 2, 1678, he prays the general court "to put a full Determination to the case." After a fortnight that body responded by over-ruling the lower court's decision, and declaring that the "sajd March ought to take the sajd Dorcas & reteyne hir as a wife, and to obserue & fullfill the marriage covenant according to his Engagement."[2]

In 1668 a petition to the county court of Suffolk for a "bill of divorce" was referred to the assistants, because it "was not proper to the cognizance" of the former body.[3] On the other hand, in the exercise of its superior authority a case might be sent to the lower court with power to render a final decree. Thus in May, 1656, was so referred "unto County Court of Charlestown" the petition of William Clements of Watertown, "craving a divorce from his wife who for several years hath refused marriage fellowship with him."[4] The lower court proved conservative. Not only was

---

[1] *MSS. Early Court Files of Suffolk*, No. 1741 (Sept. 9).

[2] *Mass. Col. Rec.*, V, 205.

[3] Case of Christopher and Elizabeth Lawson: *MSS. Early Court Files of Suffolk*, No. 913. Though the decree in this case has not been discovered, it is certain that it came before the assistants; for the papers in the proceedings are marked "*vera copia* E[dward] R[awson] S[ec.]". In the Nailer case, mentioned below, there was similar reference from the county court to the court of assistants.

[4] *Mass. Col. Rec.*, IV, i, 259, 269; *cf.* WHITMORE, *Col. Laws of Mass.* (1660-72), 100, note.

a divorce denied, but the couple were commanded to "own each other according to their marriage covenant," on pain of being "severely punished" for refusal.[1]

The general court was at once the legislature and the supreme judicial tribunal of the colony. In relegating the trial of divorce suits to the court of assistants it by no means surrendered its right to exercise the primary jurisdiction. A number of cases make it almost certain that it entertained and decided such cases in the first instance. William Palmer was so divorced in 1650.[2] Two years later Dorothy Pester, having waited "wth patience tenn yeeres for the retourne of her husband" William, prays "that she might not still be held in such bondage." Whereupon the court mercifully granted her "libertje to marry when God by his providence shall afoord her an Oppertunitje."[3] In the same way in 1654 Dorcas Hall was released on account of the desertion and other misconduct of her spouse.[4] "Rachel Langton, or Verney," was set "free from her late husband, Joseph," in 1661, no cause being assigned.[5] In 1663 the petition of Margaret Bennet in behalf of her daughter Mary White was denied.[6] A decree was granted in a peculiar form in 1670. In answer to the petition of Elizabeth Stevens, whose husband had deserted her and been guilty of "familiarity" with another woman, the "Court judgeth it meete to declare, that the petitioners marrying again another man shall not be indangered thereby as a transgression of our lawes."[7] The petition of Mary Maddox in 1678 alleges that her husband Henry had been absent unheard of for "a thirteen yeares." She was

---

[1] *MSS. Rec. of the County Court of Middlesex*, I, 85. In the same year the case of "Mary Batchiler" was referred for settlement to the county court of York: *Mass. Col. Rec.*, IV, i, 282.

[2] *Ibid.*, 32.   [3] *Ibid.*, 89; III, 277.

[4] *Ibid.*, III, 350; IV, i, 190.   [5] *Ibid.*, IV, ii, 8.

[6] Mary complained of her husband's "deficjency": *ibid.*, IV, ii, 91.

[7] *Ibid.*, IV, ii, 465.

accordingly freed from the conjugal bond and put "at liberty to dispose of herself as she shall see meete."[1] Very generous alimony is sometimes allowed the injured woman. On October 15, 1679, because Augustine Lyndon "hath in so many Particulars Broken Covenant," his wife Mary is granted a full divorce, besides being awarded two-thirds of her husband's lands and the "small matter that now Remaineth in Deacon Allen's hands" for the use of herself and children, "till the County Court shall take further Order." The next day, on a second petition, additional property is decreed to the "late wife of Augustine Lyndon now Mary Sanderson," showing apparently that she was permitted to resume her maiden name.[2] The eight[3] divorces just enumerated are all granted by the general court on petitions precisely similar to those regarding other matters dealt with by that body in the first instance. To all intents and purposes they are "legislative" divorces; as much so, in fact, as are those so often sanctioned by the state legislatures during the present century.

The remaining cases mentioned in the table are for the most part very simple and require but little comment here. Two are only known from incidental notice in other records.[4]

---

[1] *Ibid.*, V. 188.

[2] *MSS. Early Court Files of Suffolk*, No. 1807. This document begins: "At a Generall Court." The case is also in *Mass. Col. Rec.*, V, 248, 249.

[3] The divorce of James Skiffe was also granted "Att a Generall Court held vpon the Vineyard": *Plym. Col. Rec.*, V, 33. See subsection *b*) below.

[4] These are the cases of Samuel Freeman (before 1656) and Philip Wharton (before 1678). The first is mentioned in the Halsall case. *Cf.* WHITMORE, *Col. Laws of Mass.* (1660-72), 100, note, who says: "Samuel Freeman had a wife Apphia, and it has been thought that his widow married Gov. Thomas Prence of Plymouth. It has now been suggested that she was divorced, and married a second time while Freeman stayed in England, but this surmise needs examination." The second case is inferred from the following: "At a Circuit Court at Boston, Apr. 30, 1678, Philip Wharton and Mary Gridley, formerly his wife, bound over to answer for disorderly and offensive cohabiting together, having sued out a divorce. They owned they lived together. Bonds for good behavior until next court, especially to refrain from each other's company."—*MSS. Records of the County Court of Suffolk*, 506. Evidently it was common to resume the maiden name: *cf.* the Nailer and Lyndon cases.

Four are contained in the *Suffolk Files*.[1] In one of these the divorced husband, who had broken the marriage vow and been guilty of "Inhuman Carriage & Satanic Cruelty" toward his wife and children, was banished ten miles from Boston; and later, when he was permitted to visit that town on business, he was required to give bond "to be on good behavior towards his late wife."[2] It is significant that during the seventeenth century not a single clear case of divorce from bed and board has been discovered in any of the Massachusetts records.[3]

During the period of the second charter divorce controversies and all matrimonial questions are to be "heard and determined by the governour and council,"[4] whose decrees may be executed by arresting and committing the "body" of the person disregarding them.[5] By a law of 1641 it had already been provided that the divorced wife, if the innocent party, should retain her right of dower in one-third of the husband's real property for life.[6] A later act makes provision for alimony. The "superior court of judicature" is empowered in case of divorce or nullity to assign the woman "such reasonable part of the estate of her late husband as in

---

[1] Cases of Sarah Helwis, Sept. 9, 1664; Katherine Nailer, 1672; Mary Sanders, March 4, 1674/5; and Thomas Winsor, Sept. 17, 1685: all in *MSS. Early Court Files of Suffolk*, Nos. 651, 1148, 1360, 2347. The Sanders case is also in NOBLE'S *Records of the Court of Assistants;* COWLEY, *Our Divorce Courts*, 28.

[2] The Nailer case. Two years later (March 11, 1674/5) we learn that "Edward Naylor being Complayned on for Intruding into his late wiues Katherin Nannys Company The Court on hearing what was lajd to the sajd Naylors charge doe Judge & declare his bond to be forfeited."—NOBLE'S *Records of Court of Assistants*, I, 32.

[3] It is just possible that in the case of Mary Drury, Oct. 10, 1677, the decree is intended as a separation from bed and board. It is voted "whether the Court [probably the assistants] would declare it a nullity, past in the negative. Whether they would be compelled to Cohabit past in ye Negative."—*MSS. Early Court Files of Suffolk*, No. 1644. Four years earlier (*ca.* March 5, 1673) the following record appears: "In the case of Hugh Drury & Mary His Wife The Court after due hearing of the case & euidences therein produced Doe declare that they Doe enjoine them both to liue together according to the ordinance of God as man and wife."—NOBLE'S *Rec. of Court of Assistants*, I, 91.

[4] Nov. 3, 1692: *Acts and Resolves*, I, 61.   [5] Jan. 13, 1755: *ibid.*, III, 782.

[6] In WHITMORE, *Col. Laws of Mass.* (1672-85), 42, the date is given as 1641; but *ibid.* (1660-72), 146, it is 1647.

their discretion the circumstances of the estate may admit, not exceeding one-third part thereof."[1]   As in the earlier period, the causes and kinds of divorce are not determined by legislation; but an act of 1695 declares that the penalty for "polygamy"—at this time death—shall not apply to those who marry when the husband or wife has been absent wilfully or unheard of "by the space of seven years together."[2] Three years later the term of absence is shortened, the law taking the form it sometimes has in the other colonies.   It is provided that "if any married person, man or woman, has lately or shall hereafter go to sea in a ship or other vessel bound from one port to another where the passage is usually made in three months' time, and such ship or other vessel has not been or shall not be heard of within the space of three full years . . . . , or shall only be heard of under such circumstances as may rather confirm the opinion, commonly received, of the whole company's being utterly lost, in every such case the matter being laid before the governour and council, ... the man or woman whose relation is in this manner parted from him or her may be esteemed single and unmarried; and upon such declaration thereof, and license obtained from that board, may lawfully marry again."[3]

After 1692 the legislature does not seem to have interfered in divorce suits either on appeal or in the first instance. In a few cases the county court of general sessions of the peace is found granting separate maintenance.   Thus in 1710/11, on petition of Elizabeth Goddard, two men are appointed to examine certain accounts of her husband John, and to "take into their hands for the use of the Petitioner what shall appear to be due to him."[4]   In 1725 Dorothy, "the wife of John Jackson of Boston Starchmaker," asks for separate maintenance, alleging that her husband had utterly

---

[1] June 19, 1696: *Acts and Resolves*, I, 209; *cf. Acts and Laws, 1692–1765*, 60.

[2] June 6, 1694: *Acts and Resolves*, I, 171, 172.   [3] Dec. 2, 1698: *ibid.*, 353, 354.

[4] Jan. 29, 1710/11: *MSS. Records of the Court of Gen. Sessions of Suffolk*, I, 225.

refused to provide for her support, and that she "would run the hazzard of her life in case she should attempt to Enter into his house." The court orders Jackson to take his wife home, support her according to his ability, "and keep his Majesty's Peace." On refusal, he is required to enter into recognizance in the sum of fifty pounds to make Dorothy a weekly allowance of eight shillings.[1]

TABLE II

DIVORCE CASES BEFORE THE GOVERNOR AND COUNCIL OF MASSACHUSETTS, 1739-60
(Found in *MSS. Files of Suffolk County*, Vol. DCCXCIII)

No.	No. of File	Date	Case	Cause	Decree	Hus. Occupation	Years Mar.
1	.29726	27-12-38	Gill *v.* Mary Belchar	Coer. to mar.		Yeoman	
2	.29727	24- 6-40	Jesse *v.* Grace Turner	Incapacity	M. void	Farmer	5
3	.29728	27- 4-44	Eliz. *v.* Jos. Bredeen	Incapacity		Carp't'r	11
4	.29729	5-12-52	G. *v.* M. Rainer [Raymond]	Adultery	M. diss.	Husb'n	
5	.29730	13- 6-51	Eliz. *v.* Ezekiel Eldridge	Bigamy	M. void		1
6	.29730	26-12-52	Susanna *v.* Ezek. Eldridge	Deser., remar.	M. diss.		8
7	.29731	20- 2-53	Ben. *v.* Jemima Green	Adult., bast.	M. diss.		
8	.29732	9- 4-54	Petition of Hannah Wood	5 yrs. absence	Lv.tom.	Mariner	
9	.29733*a*	1-11-54	Mary *v.* Wm. Clapham	Adult., bast.	Sep.b.b.	Gent.	
10	.29733*b*	-12-54	Mary *v.* Geo. Arthur	Cr'l.. was. est.	Sep.b.b.	Gent.	13
11	.29734	- -57	Dan *v.* May McCarthy	Adultery		Mariner	

The history of divorce legislation is a complete blank for nearly half a century under the provincial charter. Between 1692 and 1739 the record of the governor and council in such suits is entirely missing. For the next twenty-one years, 1739-60, eleven cases have been gathered from the court files (Table II); while during the following twenty-six years, 1760-86, a continuous and apparently complete record, showing ninety-six cases, is contained in a manuscript volume preserved in the office of the clerk of the supreme judicial court for Suffolk county (Table III).

[1] Apr. 26, 1725: *ibid.*, III, 330. For a similar case, see *ibid.*, 311.

In the *MSS. Records of Superior Court of Judicature*, 1725-30, fol. 284, may be found the following entry: At a court held for Barnstable and Duke's Cos., Apr. 21, 1730, "Hannah Marshall, wife of the Rev. Josiah Marshall, complained that she has lived with him for a considerable time past in daily fear of her life, threats of being brained, etc. Josiah appeared and made answer. Hannah admitted to her oath . . . . Court directed and advised her to keep at her father's house until further order from the Court or from the General Sessions. Josiah to find surety for his good behavior." This is the only case in these records between 1725 and 1780.

TABLE III

DIVORCE CASES BEFORE THE GOVERNOR AND COUNCIL, OR THE COUNCIL, OF MASSACHUSETTS, 1760-86

(From MS. Book of "Divorces" in Office of Clerk of Supreme Judicial Court, Suffolk County)

No.	Page	Date of Decree	Case	Cause		Decree	Husband's Occupation	Years Married
				Charge*	Specifications			
1	1	22- 4-60	Wm. v. Eleanor Arbuthnot		Adultery, elopement	Mar. dissolved	Soldier [officer]	3
2	2	9- 6-60	Henrietta v. Hugh Cane		Bigamy, desertion, cruelty	Deferred		¾
3	4	10- 6-60	Jane v. Joshua Eustis		Adultery, desertion	Mar. dissolved		
4	5	5- 6-60	Petition of Eunice Coffin		Five years' absence	Leave to marry	Mariner	
5	6	8-10-60	Mary v. Rich. Hunt		Cruelty	Accommodated	Truckman	12
5a	7	14- 2-61	Mary v. Rich. Hunt		Cruelty, failure to provide	Separate b. b.†		
6	11	11- 3-61	Stephen v. Tabitha Lufkin		Adultery, wasting estate	Mar. dissolved†	Mariner	6
7	15	21- 4-62	Petition of Ruth Woodberry		Four years' absence	Leave to marry	Mariner	
8	16	29- 7-62	Wm. v. Hannah Davidson		Bigamy	Marriage void	Gardener	4
9	18	14- 2-63	Ed. v. Rebecca Holman		Adultery	Mar. dissolved†	Husbandman	8
10	21	13- 7-63	James v. Mary Torrey		Adultery, elopement	Mar. dissolved†		8
11	24	15- 2-64	Eliz. v. Mark Keith		Cruelty, refuses bed	Separate b. b.		2
12	27	7-11-64	Elias v. Bethia Parmenter		Adultery, bastard	Mar. dissolved†	Soldier [captive]	9
13	29	20- 4-65	Ben. v. Lydia Ingersoll		Adultery	Mar. dissolved†	Mariner	
14	32	20- 6-65	Margaret v. Fred Knodle		Cruelty	Dismissed	Yeoman	8
15	33	14- 8-65	Rachel v. John Wormley		Bigamy	Marriage void†		14
16	35	24- 9-66	Russell v. Mary Knight		Adultery	Mar. dissolved	Cooper	17
17	37	6- 5-67	Thos. v. Abigail Hammet		Adultery	Mar. dissolved	Yeoman	13
18	40	16-12-67	Mary v. Jno. Fairservice		Cruelty, adult., att. to poison	Separate b. b.	Trader	
19	44	5- 2-68	Ann v. Cornelius Vansise		Desertion, failure to provide	Separate b. b.		
20	45	15- 6-68	Jas. v. Mary Dougherty		Adultery	Mar. dissolved†	Trader	11
21	48	14- 9-68	Lucy v. Scipio Purnan		Cruel., sells wife, fail. to prov.	Separate b. b.	Truckman	7
22	51	17- 4-70	Jno. v. Anna Bragg	Adultery	Adultery	Mar. dissolved†	Cordwainer	17
23	54	16- 7-70	Wm. v. Susanna Chambers		Adultery	Mar. dissolved†	Mariner	15
24	57	18-10-70	Sam. v. Sarah Lefebure		Bigamy	Marriage void†	Mariner	1
25	59	9- 5-71	Mary v. Henry Bates		Bigamy, desertion	Marriage void†	Mariner[?]	6
26	62	19- 9-71	Mehetable v. Josh. Nicholson		Bigamy	Marriage void†	Ropemaker	2
27	64	23-10-71	Jno. v. Jane Crosley		Adultery, drunkenness	Mar. dissolved†	Husbandman	6
28	66	28-10-71	Cadwell v. Charlotte Ford		Desertion, sequest. fruits of wife's estate	Mar. dissolved†	Physician	3
29	68	17-10-71	Abagail v. Jos. Bradstreet		Adul., threats to life and pr'ty	Separate, b. b.		1½
30	70	10-12-72	Jas. v. Hannah Richardson		Adultery, elopement, bastard	Mar. dissolved	Esquire	20
31	73	3- 2-73	Jos. v. Eunice Price		Adultery, elopement, bastard	Mar. dissolved†	Yeoman	7

TABLE III—*Continued*

No.	Page	Date of Decree	Case	Charge	Cause (Specifications)	Decree	Husband's Occupation	Years Married
32	75	4–3–73	Sarah v. Enoch Kingsley		Desertion, remarriage	Mar. dissolved†	Merchant	13
33	78	2–3–73	Sarah v. Wm. Gould		Cruelty, adult., ven. disease	Mar. dissolved	Turner	13
34	80	4–11–73	Martha v. Adam Air		Adult., fail. to prov.	Mar. dissolved†	Tailor	4
35	83	15–6–74	Martha v. Wm. Jones		Desertion, remarriage	Mar. dissolved	Gentleman	12
36	85	6–7–74	Abigail v. John Pell		Adult., ven, dis., fail. to prov.	Mar. dissolved†		10
37	87	21–11–76	Asaph v. Naomi Leonard	Adultery	Adult., ven, elopement	Mar. dissolved†		28
38	90	7–12–76	J. C. v. Mary Lewis	Adultery	Adultery	Mar. dissolved†	Printer	7
39	92	27–5–77	Isaiah v. Mary Thomas	Adultery	Adultery	Mar. dissolved†		7
40	96	5–9–77	Rosanna v. Wm. Scott	Adultery	Adultery	Mar. dissolved†		11
41	101	30–1–78	Joshua v. Sarah Jay	Adultery	Adultery	Mar. dissolved†	Innholder	19
42	104	14–7–78	Wm. v. Sarah Sturgis	Adultery	Adultery	Mar. dissolved†	Mariner	2
43	107	15–10–78	Jas. v. Hannah Thompson	Adultery	Adultery, squandered estate	Mar. dissolved†	Mariner	3
44	110	25–2–79	Eliz. v. Samuel Bemis	Adultery	Adult., cruelty, fail. to prov.	Mar. dissolved†	Yeoman	9
45	113	30–12–79	Ed. v. Isabella Dawes	Adultery	Adultery, elopement	Mar. dissolved†	Peruke maker	9
46	117	28–2–80	Rose v. Timothy Corles	Adultery	Adultery, failure to provide	Mar. dissolved†	Yeoman	28
47	120	20–2–80	Deborah v. Ashael Owen	Adultery	Ad., des., remar., fail. to prov.	Mar. dissolved†		10
48	122	19–9–80	Chloe v. Luke Welch	Adultery	Adult., deser., fail. to prov.	Mar. dissolved†	Laborer [soldier]†	10
49	126	21–9–80	Alice v. Wm. Gray	Adultery	Adultery, failure to provide	Mar. dissolved†		
50	144	21–9–80	Sarah v. Valentine Wheeler	Adultery	Adultery, desertion	Mar. dissolved†		34
51	131	6–10–80	Mary v. Jno. Marshall	Adultery	Adultery, desertion	Mar. dissolved†		26
52	134	22–12–80	Rebecca v. Jacob Dunnell	Adultery	Adultery, desertion, bastard	Mar. dissolved†	Mariner	7
53	137	24–1–81	Geo. v. Phebe Shearman	Incapacity	Incapacity	Mar. dissolved†		
54	140	25–1–81	Eliz. v. Samuel Bemis	Adultery	Cruelty, ven. disease, adult.	Separate b. b.		1½
55	145	26–5–81	Mary v. Geo. Lobb	Cruelty	Cruelty, failure to provide	Mar. dissolved	Husbandman	2
56	149	29–9–81	Amzi v. Jerusha Doolittle	Adultery	Adultery, elopement	Mar. dissolved	Mariner	
57	150	29–2–81	Belah v. Amos Marsh	Adultery	Adultery, desertion	Mar. dissolved	Husbandman	
58	153	29–11–81	Abigail v. Jno. Daniels	Adultery	Cruelty, adult., wasted estate	Mar. dissolved†		31
59	156	3–5–82	J. P. v. Eliz. Barrere	Adultery	Has bastard	Mar. dissolved		11
60	158	3–5–82	David v. Mary Hoit	Adultery	Adult., bastard, elopement	Mar. dissolved†		14
61	161	5–6–82	Rhoda v. Ben. Pidgin	Adultery	Deser., remar., fail. to prov.	Mar. dissolved†		4
62	163	23–12–82	Eliz. v. Thomas Finnecy	Adult., cruelty	Adultery, cruelty	Mar. dissolved†		3
63	165	25–2–83	Ebenezer v. Anna Tarbox	Adultery	Has bastard	Mar. dissolved	Mariner	12
64	166	15–4–83	Squire v. Dorcas Baker	Adultery	Has bastard	Mar. dissolved†	Sailor [captive]	22
65	168	14–5–83	Ann v. David Gardner	Cruelty	Cruelty, failure to provide	Separate b. b.	Soldier	5
66	170	4–6–83	Mary v. Stephen Holman	Adultery	Adultery, disease, desertion, failure to provide	Mar. dissolved		

TABLE III—*Continued*

No.	Page	Date of Decree	Case	Charges	Specifications	Decree	Husband's Occupation	Years Married
67	172	11- 6-83	Z. W. v. Juda Thayer	Adultery	Desertion, bastard	Mar. dissolved†	Yeoman	11
68	173	18- 6-83	Thos. v. Rosanna Crippen	Adultery	Adultery, elopement	Mar. dissolved		
69	175	18- 6-83	Alice v. Lemuel Hill	Adultery	Adultery, deser., remarriage	Mar. dissolved		6
70	176	19- 6-83	Mime v. T. J. Carnes	Adult., cruelty	Cruelty, bastard	Mar. dissolved		
71	178	3- 7-83	David v. Mary Harwood	Adultery	Adultery, elopement	Mar. dissolved	Husbandman	25
72	179	3- 7-83	Sarah v. Stephen Temple	Adultery	Adultery, esp. with daughter	Mar. dissolved†		15
73	181	17-10-83	Sam. v. Margaret Crafts	Adultery	Adultery, elopement, bastard	Mar. dissolved†	Laborer	5
74	184	17-10-83	Puella v. Sam Kelly	Adultery	Adultery, another wife	Mar. dissolved†		6
75	186	27-10-83	Albert v. Ann Fitch	Adultery	Adultery, elopement	Mar. dissolved†	Mariner	7
76	188	29- 1-84	Phin. v. Sybil Chamberlain	Adultery	Adultery	Mar. dissolved		21
77	189	16- 2-84	Sarah v Abel Sawyer	Adultery	Adultery, venereal disease	Mar. dissolved		14
78	191	16- 2-84	Jeremiah v. Mary Higerty	Adultery	Bastard children	Mar. dissolved†	Mariner	18
79	192	26- 2-84	Andrew v. Eliz. Gage	Adultery	Adultery, cruelty	Mar. dissolved	Mariner	5
80	194	4- 3-84	Mary v. Wm. Pedley	Adultery	Coresp. in 73, desertion	Mar. dissolved†	Mariner	24
81	196	16- 3-84	Hannah v. David Dudley	Adult., cruelty	Turned wife out; took another woman	Mar. dissolved†	Husbandman	11
82	198	16- 3-84	Hannah v. Nehemiah Adams	Adultery	Adultery	Mar. dissolved†		
83	199	18- 3-84	Sarah v. Francis Rust	Adult., cruelty	Adultery, cruelty	Denied	Trader	5
83a	204	11- 6-84	Sarah v. Francis Rust	Cruelty	Cruelty	Separate b. b.		
84	201	10- 5-84	Helena v. Jas. Bayard	Cruelty	Cruelty	Separate b. b.	Mariner	27
85	202	4- 6-84	Sibbla v. G. W. Babcock	Another wife	Another wife	Mar. dissolved†	Mariner	4
86	205	6- 7-84	Mary v. Thos. Smith	Adultery	Adult., deser., fail. to prov.	Mar. dissolved†	Husbandman	12
87	206	18-10-84	Sarah v. Wm. Vernon	Adult., cruelty	Adult., cruelty, fail. to prov.	Denied	Merchant	6
87a	214	21- 7-85	Sarah v. Wm. Vernon	Adultery	Adultery with negress	Mar. dissolved		
87b	222	1- 1-85	Sarah v. Wm. Vernon		Suit for alimony	Denied		
88	208	27-10-84	Appey v. Jno. Pumpelly	Adultery	Deser., remar., fail. to prov.	Mar. dissolved†	Cordwainer	24
89	209	16- 2-85	Patience v Wm. Cornell	Adultery	Adultery, turned wife out	Mar. dissolved†		21
90	211	3- 3-85	Sarah v. Jno. Backus	Adultery	Adult., deser., fail. to prov.	Mar. dissolved†		6
91	212	3- 3-85	Jacob v. Hannah Millard	Adultery	Adultery, elopement	Mar. dissolved†	Yeoman	17
92	216	26-10-85	Hannah v. Moses Elwell	Adultery	Adultery, desertion	Mar. dissolved†	Yeoman	12
93	218	23-11-85	Domin. v. Martha Record	Adultery	Adultery, elopement	Mar. dissolved†		17
94	220	24-11-85	Jno. v. Hannah Wales	Adultery	Adultery, intoxication	Mar. dissolved†		4
95	224	8- 2-86	Anna v. Ebenezer Pelton	Adultery	Bas., remar., des., fail. to pro.	Mar. dissolved†		5
96	226	8- 2-86	Rebec v. Ebenezer Simpson	Adult., cruelty	Adult., cruelty, fail. to prov.	Mar. dissolved†	Blacksmith	20

* Beginning with No. 37, 1776, the record in each suit consists of (1) the charge; (2) the specifications; and (3) the decree. The cause or causes assigned in the charge are usually identical with those named in the decree; but the specifications often contain more points than does the charge. Before 1776 the record has two parts, there being but one instance (No. 22, 1770) of a charge before that date.

† Defendant contumacious: does not appear to defend, though repeatedly summoned.

A glance at the tables exhibiting the more important details connected with these actions discloses several important facts. For the period covered by Table III the average yearly number of cases is less than four, although the number rapidly increases after 1780. It is significant that in twenty-three out of seventy-six instances, for both tables, when the occupation is known, the husband is entered as a "mariner." The wife is plaintiff in sixty-one out of one hundred and seven petitions; and in fifty-three of the ninety-six cases listed in Table III the defendant, though summoned, fails to appear at the trial. The courts, as in the early period, still hesitate to grant the wife a divorce when the husband's adultery is the sole ground assigned. Before 1776 there is not a single clear instance[1] of such a divorce, although after that date marriages are freely dissolved for this cause. Another important innovation is of somewhat earlier date. Twelve out of the one hundred and seven cases entered in the two tables—about one in nine—are separations from bed and board, the two earliest occurring in 1754. In five of these the petitioner asks for either partial or absolute divorce, as the court may determine. Thus in 1767 Mary Fairservice, whose husband was guilty of adultery and cruelty with attempt to poison, "humbly prays . . . . that the Bonds of Marriage . . . . may be dissolved, or otherwise if . . . . this cannot by Law be done, that she may be divorced from Bed and Board." According to the record the husband appears to have been overanxious for a complete release; so the court granted only partial divorce and gave the wife alimony, although she had not asked for it in her petition. On the other hand, in each of the other four cases a full dissolution of the marriage bond was decreed.[2]

[1] However, in Nos. 34 (1773) and 36 (1774), Table III, adultery of the husband is the only reason for the divorce mentioned in the decree, but other grounds are specified in the petition. Perhaps these may be regarded as the earliest cases of divorce for " male adultery " during the eighteenth century.

[2] See Table III, Nos. 18, 32, 33, 36, 58.

Separation from bed and board was prayed for and granted in one instance which reveals the fact that cruelty, however aggravated, was not regarded as sufficient ground for a full divorce. This is the case of Lucy and Scipio Purnan, free negroes, decided in 1768. Although Scipio was in "good business" and lived "in good fashion," as we are told in the petition, he turned his wife out of doors and refused to provide for her support. Furthermore, in 1765, he "sold her to one William Alford who with the help of another man seized bound and gagged her at midnight and carried her off to Province of New York and there sold her 'being a black woman.'" After again being sold "she ran away back to Boston." Nevertheless Lucy sued for a mere separation with alimony and the custody of her child. The court granted her prayer, except that the child is not mentioned in the decree.[1] The conservatism of the court regarding this cause is further disclosed by the case of Sarah Rust in 1784. In her petition she asks for a dissolution of wedlock on the double ground of adultery and extreme cruelty. For lack of evidence as to the first-named offense sufficient to warrant either full or partial divorce, her prayer was denied, nothing being said in the decree concerning the charge of cruelty. Sarah then brought suit for cruelty alone, alleging that on the fifth of June, "as she was going into the yard of a dwelling house where a pitying friend has given her license to take shelter," Francis "waylaid & with a club beat & mangled her in a most atrocious and cruel manner," attempting to take her life. Accordingly the court allowed her a separation from bed and board.[2] An

---

[1] Table III, No. 21. This is the only case where custody of a child is asked for. In all other cases where children are mentioned they are already in the hands of the plaintiff; and in no instance are children referred to in the decree. Separation from bed and board is usually granted for cruelty (see Table III, Nos. 5a, 24, 18, 55, 65, 83a, 84); but a full divorce is never granted for this cause alone.

[2] Table III, Nos. 83, 83a. With this case may be compared that of Sarah v. William Vernon (Nos. 87, 87a, 87b). On October 16, 1784, the wife asked for such

earlier case constitutes a notable exception to the policy of the court touching another ground of action. In 1771 Abigail Bradstreet got a partial divorce from her husband Joseph, who had abandoned her because he had "married a woman with less money than he might have expected." This case is unique; for in no other instance is separation granted where desertion alone without adultery or cruelty is charged.[1]

A few other cases illustrating general facts or principles may be mentioned. In only one instance is the common-law action against the adulterer referred to.[2] Suits for divorce or nullity on the ground of bigamous marriages are of frequent occurrence.[3] On October 15, 1751, Ezekiel Eldridge, indicted for feloniously taking two wives, pleaded guilty and "pray'd the Court that he might be allow'd the Benefit of the Clergy which was Granted him." He was "thereupon burnt in the hand in the face of the Court" and allowed to "go without day Paying Costs." Thereafter one of his victims secured a divorce and his marriage with the other was declared null and void.[4] In six cases the decree is preceded by previous written or oral agreement by the parties.[5]

relief as the "laws of the land" provide, charging her husband with adultery and cruelty. The court found the evidence insufficient for either kind of divorce; but on July 21, 1785, the marriage was dissolved on the ground of adultery alone. Singularly enough, her petition for alimony six days later was denied.

[1] Table III, No. 29. *Cf.* Nos. 32 and 50, where marriage is dissolved for desertion accompanied by adultery (or remarriage).

[2] On April 22, 1760, for this offense "William Arbuthnot, Esq.," secured a divorce from his wife. In his petition he explains "that the reason of his application to this Court, before . . . . Eleanor hath been legally convicted of adultery by the course of Common Law, is, because the said Eleanor before she could be prosecuted absconded . . . . and still continues out of the jurisdiction of the Common Law Courts of this Province": see Table III, No. 1. In Nos. 17, 20, 41, 56, and 57 the decree is based in part on proceedings in other courts; while in Nos. 78 and 80 such proceedings are pleaded.

[3] See Table III, Nos. 2, 8, 15, 24, 25, 26, 74, 85.

[4] *MSS. Early Court Files of Suffolk*, DCCXCIII, No. .29730: see Table II, Nos. 5 and 6.

[5] In Table III, Nos. 11 and 19, after previous written agreement, separation from bed and board with alimony is allowed. The same is true of No. 65, except that the wife retained her right of dower. Nos. 55, 56, and 57 are cases of verbal agreement; but this does not constitute the sole reason for the decree.

The petition in cases of long absence under the act of 1698 is illustrated by the case of Eunice Coffin, in 1760, whose husband had been absent on a whaling voyage for five years without word. "The Petitioner hath the highest reason to imagine that the sloop . . . . was lost at Sea, for . . . . a few day[s] after they sailed there was the most terrible Storm that had been known since Nantucket hath been settled." So the court adjudged Eunice single and granted her "license" to marry again.[1] Finally it may be noted that in one instance a negro slave was granted a divorce by the governor and council in the regular way.[2]

b) New Hampshire, Plymouth, and New Haven.—The Massachusetts act of 1698 regarding desertion or long absence in precisely the same terms is embodied in the laws of New Hampshire,[3] whose policy respecting divorce seems to have been identical with that of the Bay Province. The causes of divorce, except desertion, are not defined by law. As early as 1681, after the establishment of the independent government, the president and council appear to have possessed jurisdiction in such controversies. In that year a quaint petition is presented by Sarah Pearce, "not knowing where to find redress under Heaven but from your honorable council of this province," praying to be "disobliged" from her union with Hubbartus Mattoon with whom for "sundry years past she was married;" because, owing to more than seven years' wilful desertion, aggravated by unfaithfulness, she has been sadly disappointed in her hope of "a comfortable living with him;" and since, unless she mistake, by the "unerring rule of God and the laws of our nation," either or

---

[1] Table III, No. 4; *cf.* Table III, No. 7, and Table II, No. 8.

[2] In 1745 a slave was allowed a divorce for his wife's adultery with a white man: see Gray's note to Oliver *v.* Sale in QUINCY, *Reports*, 29; and BISHOP, *Mar., Div., and Sep.*, I, 282.

[3] *Acts and Laws of* . . . . *New Hamp.*, 1696-1726 (Boston, 1726), 10; *ibid.* (Portsmouth, 1761), 54; *ibid.* (Portsmouth, 1771), 11.

both of the causes assigned should free her from the nuptial bond.   At the same time she humbly requests their honors in their justice to weigh "his strange embracement" of her estate while she lived with him; and his "solemn threatenings" since desertion to destroy her "by poison, or knocking of the head" if she come near him.   Whether the court granted the petition does not appear.[1]

For the other New England colonies a point of special interest is the existence of legislative divorce.   The popular assemblies, bearing the name of "general courts," are seen freely passing decrees of divorce, and this function is usually exercised concurrently with the law tribunals or by way of supplementing their jurisdiction.[2]   From the record of proceedings in such cases many an interesting glimpse is obtained of the social life of the times.   Thus the general court of Plymouth grants dissolution of wedlock for desertion and adultery; but the conservatism of public sentiment in this regard is shown by the fact that for the seventy-two years during which that colony existed as a separate jurisdiction only six instances of divorce have been discovered.   The first case occurred in 1661, when Elizabeth Burge on the scriptural ground was released from her husband Thomas, who for his misconduct was sentenced to be severely whipped at Plymouth and again at Sandwich.   The court took care that Elizabeth's temporal interests should be protected.   Not only did she receive one-third of her late husband's

[1] The petition is in the " Province Records and Court Papers ": *Coll. New Hamp. Hist. Soc.*, VIII, 68.

[2] Woolsey, *Divorce*, 196, says, " At first, divorces were mainly, if not quite exclusively, granted by an act of a colonial legislature, in accordance, perhaps, with the practice then, and until recently, existing in England, for the House of Peers to take cases of dissolution of marriage into their own hands."   This statement is of course too broad; but Cowley is decidedly in error when he declares that the "remark of President Woolsey requires modification with respect to Rhode Island, and still more with respect to Connecticut.   Neither Massachusetts nor New York nor any other Colony or State knew anything of legislative divorce until a much later day." — *Our Divorce Courts*, 22.

"estate, viz., lands, goods, and chattles, as her proper right
forever;" but with his consent she got also "an old cotton
bed and bolster, a pillow, a sheet, and two blankets . . . .
with some other smale thinges . . . . to the value of forty
shillings."[1] The experience of William Tubbs, of Scituate,
is unique. His wife Marcye was notoriously unfaithful to
her nuptial vow and eventually eloped with another man.
So he sought a divorce; and accordingly in 1664, "after the
patriarchal style," as Goodwin observes, William Paybody of
Duxbury gave him a "writing of divorcement," with Lieutenant Nash and John Sprague as witnesses. This document the general court treated as a nullity, fining Paybody
five pounds and each of the witnesses three pounds for their
resort to self-help. But four years later that court came to
his relief in the regular way. In July, 1668, after serving
due notice on the libellee through letters addressed to the
government of "Road Iland"—where "Goodwife Tubbs"
had fled with her paramour—he was pronounced "legally
cleare from his couenant of marriage formerly made with
Marcye, his late wife," with the privilege of marrying again,
"if hee see fit soe to doe;" while she is solemnly declared
to have cut herself off from the "pson" and "estate of the
said William."[2] For similar cause and on the same conditions John Williams was released from his wife Sarah in
1674.[3] The next year "Edward Jenkins, of Taunton, petitioned that his daughter Mary be divorced from Marmaduke
Atkinson, who had been out of the Colony and made no provision for her during seven years or more. The decision was
a singular one; namely that while the court sees no cause to

---

[1] So stated by GOODWIN, *Pilgrim Republic*, 596, 597, who gives a list of the cases,
to which, after independent examination of the *Plymouth Records*, I am unable to
add any new examples.

[2] *Ply. Col. Rec.*, IV, 66 (1664), 187, 192 (1668), 42, 46, 47 (earlier notices). *Cf.* GOOD-
WIN, *op. cit.*, 596.

[3] *Ply. Col. Rec.*, V, 127.

grant a divorce 'yett they doe apprehend her to be noe longer bound, but doe leave her to her libertie to marry if she please.'"[1] This was probably the court's homely way of saying that, the common-law term of seven years' absence without word having expired, it regarded the marriage as *ipso facto* dissolved without judicial process, though a formal decree was the more prudent course in case a second marriage were contemplated.[2] In the Plymouth records, as often elsewhere, the term "divorce," following common-law usage, is employed for a sentence of nullity in case of a void or voidable marriage. Thus in 1680 Nicholas Wade, of Scituate, and his daughter, Elizabeth Stevens, present a petition "wherein they complaine of a great and sore crosse," her husband being a man of "debauged life, expressed by his plurallitie of wifes." Elizabeth was therefore "dismissed" from her conjugal bond; while the "debauged" Stevens for his "abominable wickedness" was "centansed to be seueerly whipt att the post."[3] The last case is that of John Glover of Barnstable whose marriage with Mary his wife was dissolved in 1686 on account of her unfaithfulness.[4] It is significant that four of the six petitions just enumerated are brought against the wife on the scriptural ground and none against the husband for the same cause. From this fact it may perhaps be inferred that in Plymouth Plantation, as at that time in Massachusetts, male adultery was not recognized as a legal ground of divorce.[5]

---

[1] GOODWIN, *op. cit.*, 597. The case is in *Ply. Col. Rec.*, V, 159.

[2] On the Connecticut law as to seven years' absence, SWIFT, *Digest of the Laws of the State of Conn.*, I, 21, says: "By common law, that period of absence unheard of, is presumptive evidence of the death of the person; yet in such cases it would be proper that there should be a divorce before a marriage is had, for if the party should return, the first marriage would undoubtedly be valid, though by the [Connecticut] statute a prosecution for the crime of bigamy could not be sustained."

[3] *Ply. Col. Rec.*, VI, 44, 45.   [4] *Ibid.*, 190.

[5] There are two other references to divorce matters in the *Records*. In 1670, on his wife's confession of legal cause, Samuel Hallowey petitioned for a divorce; but the court, "being not very clear," postponed the case three months to see if the wife

Similar illustrations of the life and thought of the times are afforded by the records of New Haven colony. In that "biblical commonwealth" it is, of course, not surprising that the influence of Judaism should be strongly felt. By the "capital laws" adultery is punished with death; so, before 1648, it is ordered that if "any marryed person proved an Adulterer, or an Adulteresse, shall by flight, or otherwise, so withdraw or keep out of the Jurisdiction, that the course of Justice (according to the mind and Law of God here established) cannot proceed to due execution, upon the complaint, proof, and prosecution, made by the party concerned, and interessed, a separation or Divorce, shall by sentence of the Court of Magistrates be granted," and the innocent party "have liberty to marry again." For physical incompetency marriage may be "declared void and a nullity;" and here we get a glimpse of the carnal motives for wedlock handed down from the Mosaic code and tenaciously surviving in all modern systems of law. Avoidance of marital "duty" is the real ground of action. Therefore should the man deceive the wife as to the fact, then such "satisfaction shall be made to the injured woman, out of the estate of the offender, and such fine paid to the Jurisdiction, as the Court of Magistrates shall judge meet."[1] In like spirit an unusually stringent rule as to desertion is laid down. If either party shall wilfully abandon the other, "peremptorily refusing all Matrimoniall society, and shall obstinately persist therein, after due means have been used to convince and reclaim, the husband or wife so deserted, may justly seek and expect relief,

would persist in her confession or the parties become reconciled. In June the case was referred to two men for examination; but it is not again mentioned: *ibid.*, V, 32, 41, 42. *Cf.* GOODWIN, *op. cit.*, 597. Again, curiously enough, we find here the certified copy of a decree of divorce granted in the Massachusetts jurisdiction to James Skiffe, "late inhabitant of Sandwich, but now att the Viniyard," by a "Generall Court" held on that island. Skiffe's wife had run away to Roanoke with another man: *Ply. Col. Rec.*, V, 33.

[1] This, of course, is practically equivalent to "fraudulent contract" as usually permitted in the modern statutes.

according to 1 Cor. 7: 15."[1] Here no definite term of wilful desertion is fixed. But in 1663 divorce with remarriage is permitted in case of seven years' absence, when the deserted consort has "noe certaine intelligence" of the other's being alive or purposing to return.[2] Whether this comprehends the case of wilful desertion we are not told.

c) *Connecticut.*—The laws of Connecticut relating to divorce gained a surprisingly early maturity. Perhaps in none of the other colonies was so liberal, and on the whole so wisely conservative, a policy adopted. That plantation almost deserves the patriotic eulogy bestowed upon it by Swift, who declares in 1795 that the "institution of a court for the decision of such controversies, and the limitation of their power to such cases as the public good requires to be remedied, gives the practice adopted by" the Connecticut "laws, a decided preference to the practice of all other nations, and renders our mode of granting divorces, as favourable as the other modes have been unfavourable, to the virtue and happiness of mankind."[3] Certainly in the middle of the seventeenth century no state, with the possible exception of Holland, possessed a system so modern in its character. Separation from bed and board was rejected. Only in one instance, it is said, and that by the assembly, was such a decree ever granted.[4] Reasonable and fairly liberal causes of divorce *a vinculo* were clearly specified; husband and wife were treated with even justice; and, although legislative divorce, always liable to abuse, was permitted, the greater

---

[1] For the foregoing orders see *New Haven's Settling in New England. And some Lawes for Government published for the Use of that Colony* (London, 1656): in *New Haven Col. Rec.*, II, 586. They are also embodied in the code of 1655: TRUMBULL, *Blue Laws*, 241, 242. Their date is not given, but it is probably previous to 1648 or 1649: *New Haven Col. Rec.*, II, preface, iv; TRUMBULL, *op. cit.*, 40.

[2] *New Haven Col. Rec.*, II, 479, citing also "1 Cor., 7: 15," as in the order before cited.

[3] SWIFT, *System of the Laws of the State of Conn.* (Windham, 1795), I, 192; *cf. idem, Digest* (New Haven, 1823), I, 24, 25.

[4] SWIFT, *System of the Laws*, I, 193.

part of litigation seems always to have been intrusted to the regular courts. In short, Connecticut, in all the more essential respects, anticipated the present policy of civilized nations by nearly two hundred years.

By the act of 1667 the court of assistants is empowered to grant bills of divorce from the bond of matrimony to either party, with the privilege of remarriage, for adultery, fraudulent contract, three years' wilful desertion with total neglect of duty, or for seven years' "providential" absence unheard of.[1] This law was re-enacted in 1677;[2] and the four causes, with scarcely the change of a word in the terms of the statute, appear in the revision of 1715,[3] and again and again in the succeeding compilations until 1843, when two new grounds—"habitual intemperance" and "intolerable cruelty"—were added.[4] The real scope of this singularly liberal provision for divorce thus early adopted cannot, however, be fully appreciated unless two important facts be kept in mind. First, in judicial practice adultery acquired a very broad meaning. Not only did it cover the misconduct of the husband as well as that of the wife, but the statute was interpreted to allow the latter a divorce for the "criminal connection" of the man with any single women.[5] Secondly,

[1] See *Public Statute Laws of the State of Conn.* (Hartford, 1808), I, 236, editorial note 1; also SWIFT, *Digest*, I, 24, 25.

[2] *Conn. Col. Rec.* (Oct. 18, 1677), II, 328: "It is ordered, by this court that noe bill of divorce shall be granted to any man or woman lawfully married but in case of adultery, fradulent contract, or willful desertion for three years with totall neglect of duty, or seven years' providentiall absence being not heard of after due enquiry made and certifyed, such party shall be counted as legally dead to the other party; in all which cases a bill of divorce may be granted by the Court of Assistants to the aggrieved party who may then lawfully marry or be marryed to any other."

[3] *Acts and Laws* (New London, 1715), 28; *ibid.* (New London, 1750), 43; *ibid.* (New Haven, 1769), 43. Almost the only change during the period mentioned in the text is the substitution of "superior court" for "court of assistants." *Cf. Pub. Stat. Laws* (1808), 236 n. 1. As in Massachusetts, the divorced wife is to have a part of the husband's estate, not exceeding one-third thereof: *Acts and Laws* (1769), 146.

[4] Act of June 6, 1843: *Public Acts* (1843), 20; *Revision of the Stat. of the State of Conn.* (Hartford, 1849), 274.

[5] SWIFT, *Digest*, I, 21.

"fraudulent contract" was construed "according to its plain and natural import, that is a contract obtained by fraud," and not in the very restricted and conventional sense which the courts, perhaps misled by a remark of Blackstone, have in later years sometimes adopted.[1]

Long before the act of 1667, and for one hundred and eighty-three years thereafter, the legislative assembly of Connecticut, side by side with the court of assistants or its successors, reserved to itself the right of granting bills of divorce. This power seems in the main to have been exercised with caution, though there are not lacking signs that it was sometimes abused. The general policy, according to Swift, was only to grant relief in this way in "cases of intolerable cruelty, and inveterate hatred, and such gross misbehaviour and wickedness as defeat the design of marriage, and presumptive proof of a criminal connection . . . . , where the positive proof required by law cannot be had."[2] Yet this wise rule, if legislative divorce is to be allowed at all, does not in all cases seem to have been rigidly followed. The first instance of action by the general court in such questions found in the records occurs in 1655. "Considering the sad complaint of Goody Beckwith of Fairfield, in reference to her husband," and weighing the evidence presented "of ye manner" of his "departure and discontinuance," the assembly declares that if the "said Goody Beckwith, wife

---

[1] This is the view of Swift, *Digest*, I, 21, 22, referring to Blackstone, *Commentaries*, III, 94. Thus a decision of the Connecticut superior court of errors seems to limit "fraud" as a cause of divorce to "corporal imbecility": 1 Day, *Reports*, 111. But in 1848, at the August term of the superior court for Litchfield county, "it was held . . . . upon a consultation with judges of the Supreme Court, that where a woman at the time of her marriage was pregnant with a bastard child, and fraudulently concealed the fact from her husband, this was a sufficient cause for a divorce." —Dutton and Cowdrey's *Revision of Swift's Digest* (New Haven, 1851), I, 22; citing 9 *Conn. Rep.*, 321; and for New York, where a similar practice prevailed, 4 Johnson, *Chancery Rep.*, 343. In the earlier period doubtless a still broader meaning was given to the term "fradulent contract": see the examples for illustration in Swift, *Digest*, I, 22.

[2] Swift, *System of the Laws*, I, 193.

of Thomas, shall uppon her oath testifie to the Magistrates that are shortly to keepe Courte at Strattford, that her husband's departure was as others have testified it to bee; and yᵗ shee hath not heard from him nor of him any wayes since hee deserted her, the said Magistrates may give her a bill of Divorce."[1]   This is, of course, an example of granting the court jurisdiction in a particular case where perhaps the evidence was otherwise insufficient to warrant a decree.   Two years later the general court frees Robert Wade of Seabrook from his "Couenant of marriage" with Joane his "late wife," because of the evidence presented to them of her "unworthy, sinfull, yea, unnaturall cariage" in staying in England and "disowning fellowship" with him for "neare fifteene yeares."[2] Again in 1660, taking time by the forelock in the behalf of Sarah North, the same body orders that if she "hear not of her husband by that yᵉ seauenth year be expired, (he haueing bene absent six already) . . . . then, she shalbe free from her coniugal bonds."[3]   So also two years later, "vpon good consideration and solid reasons"—of what nature the record saith not—Bridget Baxter is likewise released; and because the estate which her late husband left with her "is sold to pay debts, all excepting a bed and her wearing aparell," the creditors of "yᵉ said estate" are prohibited from "seizing extending or any way troubleing yᵉ remainder, vntil yᵉ Court see cause to yᵉ contrary."[4]   In 1670 Hanna Huitt "is at liberty to marry if shee see cause," for the absence of Thomas during "eight years and better."[5]

The case of Elizabeth Rogers is of special interest; for it is much to be feared that the worthy deputies and magistrates regarded "free thinking" as a sufficient cause for dissolution of wedlock.   In 1675 she laid her petition before

---

[1] *Conn. Col. Rec.*, I, 275 (May 17, 1655).   [2] *Ibid.*, 301 (Aug. 12, 1657).

[3] *Ibid.*, 362 (Mch. 14, 1660).   [4] *Ibid.*, 379 (May 15, 1662).

[5] *Ibid.*, II, 129 (May 12, 1670).

the court of assistants, which found "some difficulties as to a present issue finally." Yet the case being one which called "for compassion to the woman under so great distress and hazard," it was referred for settlement to the general court, Mrs. Rogers having liberty meanwhile to dwell with her father.[1] Accordingly, at its next session the assembly, accepting the "allegations and proofes presented to clear the righteousness of her desires," released Elizabeth from her "conjugall bond."[2] A year later provision is made for alimony with custody of the children; and now at last the reason for Goodwife Rogers's "great distress and hazard," thus far carefully omitted from the record, is clearly divulged. "Her husband," runs the order, "being so hettridox in his opinion and practice," and having even "in open Court declared that he did vtterly renounce all the vissible worship of New England, and professedly declare against the Christian Sabboth as a mere invention," the court grants the mother and her father, Mathew Griswold, the care and custody of the children "to be brought up and nurtured by them (in the admonition and fear of the Lord)," also ordering John Rogers to pay "towards the mayntenance of his children, the sume of twenty pownds" in four equal annual instalments. In case "he fayle of payment, the reversion of the land by sayd John Rogers made ouer to Elizabeth his late wife, at Mamacock" is to be held as security.[3]

Another case, that of Richard Edwards, deserves notice, for as late as 1690 it affords us an example of the reference of public questions to the elders. In October of that year Edwards presented a petition for divorce from his wife Elizabeth. The general court "declare they doe not find reason

---

[1] *Ibid.*, 292, note.   [2] *Ibid.*, 292 (Oct. 21, 1676).

[3] *Ibid.*, 293 (Oct. 18, 1677). For two cases of divorce, each for six years' desertion, see *ibid.*, 293 (Oct. 12, 1676), 322 (Oct. 11, 1677); one for five years' desertion, *ibid.*, 327 (Oct. 18, 1677); and another for three years' "wilful" desertion, *ibid.*, III, 23 (1678).

to grant" it.[1]   But Richard is bound to have "releife therein
if the law of God or man will affoarde it him."   So he comes
before the court again "desireing that a councill of able
diuines upon his charge might be called to consider his case
and giue their resolves upon the same to the court."   The
latter, though not "fully sattisfyed to alter their apprehen-
sions from what they were formerly, yet considering the
deplorable state of the petitioner, and the many intolerable
temptations he lyes open too, are willing to doe what they
can for his releife, and to recomend it to the Gen[ll] Court
October next to consider the case, and doe desire that the
Reuerend Mr. Hooker" and five other ministers give their
attendance upon the court "to hear the case and grant what
light they can come at" to guide the issue.[2]   No definite
ground for the petition, it will be observed, is assigned; but
one may safely hazard a guess that "hettridox" opinions
were again involved.   At any rate, Richard's plan was successful.   The next October he was released "from his conjugall tye," the court first "haueing considered the case with
seriousnesse and taken the best advice they could com at by
the word of God and learned and worthy diuines."[3]

As time went on, the cases of legislative divorce became
few and far between.   The courts were felt to be the proper
place for such business.[4]   In 1753 Mary Larkum was freed

---

[1] *Conn. Col. Rec.*, IV, 37 (Oct. 9, 1690).

[2] *Ibid.*, 52, 53 (May, 1691).   [3] *Ibid.*, 59 (Oct. 8, 1691).

[4] In a pamphlet entitled *Appeal to the Public* (New Haven, 1788), full of errors,
TRUMBULL attacks the divorce laws of his state.   According to him (48), there
is no example of divorce in New York from the settlement to 1787; and with equal
inaccuracy he declares (46) that "in the Massachusetts and Connecticut codes
printed at Cambridge 1672, there is no law respecting divorce.   The law of Connecticut relating to it was made five years after, Oct. 11, 1677."   For Connecticut he makes
the further extraordinary statement (46) that "more than forty years from the settlement" elapsed "before any such law was in existence.   No divorce was given by
virtue of the law, till the year 1692.   After this divorces were, for many years, spar-
ingly given.   But as they became customary, as there were no punishments for
delinquents, and as the shame decreased with the growth of the practice, they have,
within this few years, had a rapid increase.   In less than a century [1692-1788], four
hundred and thirty-nine (439) pair . . . . have been separated by divorce.   This

from her husband Job on account of his "barbarous and inhuman carriage toward her."[1] In 1761 the assembly set aside a divorce granted two years before by the superior court for alleged wilful desertion;[2] and at rare intervals that body was appealed to during the next seventy-five years.[3] There was a sudden increase of business in 1837.[4] From that date until 1850 the annual crop of legislative divorces is surprisingly large.[5] Sometimes the "resolve" granting the petition is curt and informal; while often it is entirely silent as to the exact cause of complaint.[6] It would seem that the practice of intrusting proper judicial business to popular political bodies was yielding the usual evil fruit; for at last, in 1849, a statute provides that the "Superior

whole number, forty-eight couple excepted, have been divorced in the short term of fifty-two years. Between twenty and thirty pair . . . . are now annually" thus separated "in the Superior Court, besides those put asunder by the General Assembly. About twenty times as many are now divorced annually, as were in almost sixty years after the first settlement of the State; and about half as many as were divorced through the whole first century. Seventeen pair have been divorced last circuit." It is to be hoped that the statistics are more trustworthy than the history.

[1] *Conn. Col. Rec.*, X, 168 (May, 1753).   [2] *Ibid.*, XI, 544, 545 (May, 1761).

[3] Thus a divorce was granted in 1774: *ibid.*, XIV, 223, 387, 388; and two instances occurred in May, 1821: Swift, *Digest*, I, 23.

[4] An act of 1837 refers incidentally to divorces which have been or shall be "granted, either by the general assembly or by the superior court, on the application of a married woman."—*Pub. Stat. Laws* (1837), 33; also in *Pub. Stat. Laws* (general revision, 1838), 187. Query: Did this act invite and authorize appeal to the assembly in such matters?

[5] For the annual lists of divorces granted by the assembly see *Resolves and Private Acts of the State of Conn.* (1837), 3 ff.; *ibid.* (1838), 13–16; *ibid.* (1839), 28–42; *ibid.* (1840), 9–14; *ibid.* (1841), 23–28; *ibid.* (1842), 4–16; *ibid.* (1843), 10–20; *ibid.* (1844), 8; *ibid.* (1845), 15, 16; *ibid.* (1846), 15–19; *ibid.* (1847), 31–34; *ibid.* (1848), 61–69; *ibid.* (1849), 46–56. The last of these divorces is that of Candace Williams, of New Haven, from F. Walter Williams, May, 1850: *ibid.* (1850), 21.

[6] Here is a typical case, though often the resolve is much briefer:

"Upon the petition of Polly M. Mead of Danbury, Fairfield County, and State of Connecticut, praying a bill of divorce from her husband, Martin Mead of said Danbury, which petition was duly served and returned:

"*Resolved by the Assembly*, that the said Polly M. Mead be, and she is hereby divorced from the said Martin Mead, and is and forever hereafter shall be absolved from all obligations to the said Martin Mead by virtue of the said marriage contract, and is hereby declared to all intents and purposes, sole, single and unmarried.

"Resolved that the said Polly . . . . have the sole charge, care and custody of her only child, and that the said Martin . . . . shall have no power or authority over him, in any way or manner whatsoever."—*Resolves and Private Acts* (1837), 3.

Court shall have sole and exclusive jurisdiction of all petitions for divorce."[1]

d) *Rhode Island.*—It is, however, in the judicial history of Rhode Island that legislative divorce has left its deepest mark and had its worst consequences. In the American colonies and states this practice has perhaps never caused the same hardships or flagrant injustice as it did in England previous to the act of 1857. Ordinarily, as in that country, relief has not in effect and of necessity, owing to the cost of the proceedings, been entirely denied to anyone because he was poor. On the other hand, popular political assemblies, such as American state legislatures, are on other grounds ill fitted for judicial functions. Their ignorance or carelessness may produce results bad for society. For they possess nothing like the legal knowledge and experience of the House of Lords, in which petitions for divorce were first considered. Before the legislative trial, as in England, the facts have not already been fairly well ascertained in the law and spiritual actions; and if the same harsh discrimination between rich and poor does not appear, there is at least equal opportunity for jobbery and favoritism. It is well that the custom practically has long ceased to exist in the United States.

The legislation of Rhode Island begins with a conservative measure in 1650. It is "ordered, that no bill of divorce shall stand legall . . . . butt that which is sued for, by the partie grieved" and not "for any other case but that of Adulterie." This cause may be proved by the injured person, "eyther by the man against the woman, or by the woman against the man, before the Generall Assemblie" which by the act is given exclusive jurisdiction in such questions. After separation "each partie shall be as free from " the other as "before they came together."[2] But in 1655 a change

[1] Act of June 19, 1849: *Pub. Acts of the State of Conn.* (Hartford, 1849), 17.
[2] *Rhode Island Col. Rec.*, I, 231 (Oct. 26, 1650); *cf.* Arnold, *Hist. of R. I.*, I, 322.

is made in jurisdiction, as also by implication, in the legal grounds of divorce. First we have a striking example of the tendency of Rhode Island to vest important functions in the officers of the local community. "It is ordered, that in case of adulterie, a generall or towne magistrate may grant a bill of divorce against yᵉ partie offendinge uppon yᵉ demand of yᵉ partie offended." Furthermore, other grounds of complaint are contemplated, though they are not clearly expressed; for it is declared that "in all other cases of separation or divorce between man and wife, all persons shall addresse themselves for release to yᵉ Generall Court of Commissioners"—the name which the assembly bore during the parliamentary charter. Here we have the usual reservation of special cases to the legislature, among which, it seems clear, separation from bed and board is had in view.[1]

In the early days the assembly did not lack business. At the June session, 1655, John and Elizabeth Coggeshall, who had separated "by mutuall and voluntarie consent," were each allowed on separate petition to contract further marriage.[2] Two other cases occurred the same year;[3] and later examples have been collected. In 1665 the assembly "granted a divorce for the adultery of the wife on her own confession, and at the same time sentenced her to pay a fine and be whipped."[4] At this time is also recorded the pathetic story of Horod Long. In her petition addressed to the royal com-

[1] *R. I. Col. Rec.*, I, 312 (1655). "And if any persons in this Colonie," continues the order, "shall part themselves and marrie again without yᵉ authoritie of yᵉ Court of Commissioners, or be convicted of carnal copulation with any other [bigamy], they shall be punished as in case of adulterie."—*Ibid.*, 312.

[2] *Ibid.*, 319.

[3] Peter Talman got a divorce on his wife's confession of adultery: ARNOLD, *Hist. of R. I.*, I, 320; and it "was ordered that Thomas Genings shall goe and demand his wife to live with him, but in case she refuse, he shall make his addresses to the General Court of Commissioners."—*R. I. Col. Rec.*, I, 312. Ann Talman, the divorced wife of Peter, referred to, was later more than once whipped for her misconduct: *ibid.*, II, 187, 188.

[4] DURFEE, *Gleanings from the Judicial Hist. of R. I.*, 35.

missioners,[1] then in the colony, she says: "I was upon the death of my father sent to London by my mother in much sorrow and griefe of spiritt, and then taken by one John Hickes vnknown to any of my friends, and by the said Hickes privately married in the vnder Church of Paules, called Saint Faith's Church, and in a little while after, to my great griefe, brought to New England, when I was betweene thirteene and fourteene years of age." After living two years and a half at Weymouth the pair came to Rhode Island in 1640. "Not long after," Horod continues, "there happened a difference betweene the said John Hickes and myselfe, soe that the authority that then was vnder grace, saw cause to part vs, and ordered I should have the estate sent me by my mother." Evidently she was allowed to resume her maiden name. Here we catch a glimpse of the earliest known divorce in Rhode Island. After the separation Hickes fled to the Dutch,[2] taking with him, in defiance of the court's order, most of the wife's property. Thus she was "put to great hardshipe and straight;" for she was friendless and "not brought up to labour." To gain a maintenance, therefore, without any formal celebration or other proceedings, she allowed herself to be "drawne by George Gardener," and lived with him as his wife, being so reputed by the neighbors, for near twenty years, bearing him "many children." Clearly, as further shown by the testimony, we have here a case of "common-law" marriage. Yet during this time Horod alleges she had "much oppression of spiritt" regarding her questionable condition; but Gardener, who had enjoyed the remnant of her estate and all her labor, refused either to allow her a separate support or to cease to trouble her. So in her distress of mind she appealed to the com-

---

[1] Carr, Cartwright, and Maverick.

[2] Is this the same "John Hicks" who in New Netherland obtained a divorce in 1655? See sec. iii, below.

missioners for relief, asking separate maintenance for her-self and child, and that "hee may bee restrained from ever meddling with" her. The commissioners referred the matter to the governor, requesting him to "doe justice to the poore petitioner;" and the governor placed it in the hands of the assembly. That body was without compassion; for the woman had "impudently" discovered "her owne nakedness." She and her partner were treated as ordinary offenders, being each fined twenty pounds, and warned henceforth not "to lead soe scandalous a life, lest they feel the extreamest penalty that either is or shall be provided in such cases."[1]

To this same eventful year, 1667, belongs the only case of partial divorce yet discovered. Richard and Mary Pray joined in a petition asking a complete dissolution of their nuptial bond. The assembly denied their prayer, but allowed them to live apart without the right of remarriage.[2] On the powers of the general court at this time Arnold makes the following comment: "Not only were divorces granted and a separate maintenance awarded to the wife, but the whole property of the husband was attached and held by the Assembly, until the provisions of the decree had been satisfied. In the case of John Porter . . . . they went even further, and annulled all transfers of property . . . . made by him since the separation from his wife, which had not already been recorded. Upon his settling a satisfactory estate upon his wife these disabilities were removed."[3]

[1] *R. I. Col. Rec.*, II, 99 ff. At the same time, with astonishing inconsistency, it was enacted that similar offenders shall be amenable to the laws punishing fornication, which are made more stringent; but all present reputed marriages are declared valid and the children legitimate (104, 105). By this rule Horod and George should either have been regularly divorced or ordered to cohabit as husband and wife. In any event their punishment was unjust.

[2] *Ibid.*, 188, 189. In the same year Robert Colwell got a divorce from his wife Mary: *ibid.*, 204.

[3] Arnold, *Hist. of R. I.*, I, 320. This case came before the assembly in 1665: *R. I. Col. Rec.*, II, 119-21; *cf.* Durfee, *Gleanings from the Judicial Hist. of R. I.*, 35.

After the establishment of the royal charter the ordinary jurisdiction in divorce matters was vested in the court of trials, composed of the governor and assistants who formed a part of the assembly; but the latter body continued to act when it saw fit. But "it would seem," says Arnold, "that the separate powers of the magistrates were not distinctly defined or well understood, for a censure was passed upon John Green, Assistant of Warwick, for having granted, by his own authority, a bill of divorce. This proceeding was sharply reproved by the Assembly, as being a usurpation of judicial power in superseding the action of the Court of Trials. The town of Warwick declared the divorce to be legal, and protested against this censure upon their leader."[1] In this case it may perhaps be right to infer that a reminiscence existed of the order of 1655, already cited, vesting jurisdiction in the principal cases of divorce in a single "town" or "general" magistrate, the latter term applying to an "assistant" under the royal charter. The assembly in 1676 released John Belou "from all matrimonial engagements" to his wife Hannah.[2] An entry in the records of Muddy River, Mass., for July 30 of the same year, informs us that John "Lewis came from Road Island where his wife gave him a paper of dismission from her in Novr. last & libertie to marrie another woman & he is now engaged to yᵉ widow Williams to marry her, by theire own confessions."[3]

In 1683 we have an interesting example of the summary punishment of a divorced man by the legislature, doubtless for the misconduct which led to the decree. "The power of the Assembly to expel its members was rarely exercised,

---

[1] Arnold, *Hist. of R. I.*, I, 365 (Nov., 1672). This bill was granted to Richard and Mary Pray, whom the assembly had permitted to live apart in 1667: *R. I. Col. Rec.*, II, 479.

[2] *Ibid.* (1664–77), 543.

[3] The entry is marked "returned to county court": *Early Records of Muddy River*, 69.

but at the adjourned session, a deputy from Warwick, against whom complaints were brought and a divorce granted on petition of his wife," at this time, "was deemed unfit to hold his seat, and was therefore expelled."[1] Two years thereafter a law was passed making "five years neglect or absence of either party" a ground for divorce;[2] but the period was extended to seven years in 1749.[3]

According to Judge Durfee, after power to grant divorces came to the superior court in 1747[4] the jurisdiction of the assembly "languished;" but "it continued, nevertheless, to be invoked in exceptional cases,[5] which either were not provided for by the statute or were too flimsey or too whimsical for judicial treatment. There is an uncanny tradition, still vaguely surviving, that in such cases grave legislators were sometimes plied in the lobby with solicitations and arguments too peculiar for public discussion. After the constitution the more usual course for the assembly was, not to hear the petition, but to authorize the supreme court to hear it by special act, if without such act the court was incompetent. Divorces, however, were granted as late as 1850. In January, 1851, the assembly had several petitions pending before it and transferred them, together with all documents and depositions in support of them, to the supreme court, 'where,' the resolution of transfer tartly

[1] ARNOLD, *op. cit.*, I, 470 (June, 1683). [2] *Ibid.*, 483 (1685).

[3] See *Acts and Laws* (Newport, 1767), 74, containing the changes made in 1749 and 1754. The superior court is authorized in its discretion to grant alimony from the husband's estate.

[4] In that year the court of trials, composed of the governor and assistants or councillors, which with no essential change in composition and functions had existed from about 1644, was superseded by a regular law tribunal, the superior court of judicature: ARNOLD, *op. cit.*, II, 157. But already in 1729 a "Superior Court," composed of at least five members of the upper branch of the legislature, and apparently lower than the court of trials, was established: *ibid.*, 90. In general on the various stages in the history of the court of trials, see *ibid.*, I, 210 (1647), 302 (1663-64), 460 (1680); II, 16 (1704).

[5] In Oct., 1749, a divorce was granted by the assembly; and this is the first Arnold had noticed, probably meaning in that period: *op. cit.*, II, 175.

remarks, 'the said petitions should have been filed,' and at
the same time authorized and required the court to try
them.'"[1]

II. ENGLISH DIVORCE LAWS IN ABEYANCE IN THE
SOUTHERN COLONIES

It is an established principle of jurisprudence that colonists settling in an uninhabited land take with them all the
laws of the mother-country which are suited to their new
circumstances.[2] This doctrine is sustained by the decisions
of the courts.[3] It follows, according to the views strongly
supported by Bishop, "that all such laws of England, relating to marriage and divorce, by whatsoever names there
known, are, as they existed at the respective times of the
settlements here, common law in our several states."[4] The
law of divorce which the American colonists brought with
them in the seventeenth century allowed a separation from
bed and board by decree of an ecclesiastical court, and for
two causes only, adultery and cruelty. Absolute divorce
was not recognized. But while the colonists carried with
them the English law, they did not bring likewise the English courts. Therefore it "results that these laws can practically be administered with us only as far and as fast as
tribunals are established on which, directly or by implication,

---

[1] DURFEE, *Gleanings from the Judicial Hist. of R. I.*, 35, 36. See *Laws of R. I.*
(1851), 796, where petitions for divorce on account of wilful desertion are transferred
by the assembly to the supreme court; and similar reference, *ibid.* (1846), 57, 85.

[2] BISHOP, *Mar., Div., and Sep.*, I, § 116. "If an uninhabited country is discovered
and planted by British subjects, the English laws are said to be in force there, for
the law is the birthright of every subject."—STORY, *Commentaries*, I, §§ 147 ff. *Cf.*
KENT, *Commentaries*, I, 343, 473; and BLACKSTONE, *Commentaries*, I, 107, who regards
the colonies as a conquered country.

[3] BISHOP, *First Book*, §§ 51-59; *idem, Mar., Div., and Sep.*, I, § 117.

[4] The expression "all laws" is used advisedly. Though "in some of the American cases the term 'common law' is used, the broad meaning of the term, not its
narrow and technical one, is intended."—BISHOP, *Mar., Div., and Sep.*, I, § 119; citing
C. *v.* Knowlton, 2 *Mass. Rep.*, 530, 534: Sackett *v.* Sackett, 8 PICKERING, *Reports*, 309,
316. *Cf.* JEFFERSON, *Works*, VI, 65; VIII, 374, 379; IX, 282.

is conferred the jurisdiction." The laws slumber, so to speak, until quickened through the creation of courts by the legislature. "Between the arrival in a colony of the law from the mother-country, and the organization of courts for its enforcement, some space of time must intervene. And during such space the law must be practically in abeyance, or inoperative." Should a "tribunal be created with jurisdiction extending to a part only of the law, such part will become operative, but the rest will remain inert as before."[1] Besides, for our present purpose it is highly important to note that the English courts "have specifically held, that the matrimonial law of the ecclesiastical tribunals is a branch of the law which colonists take with them."[2]

Since, therefore, the church courts were never established in any of our American provinces, it follows by the foregoing rule that there was no tribunal competent to decree a divorce or separation in such of them as had not assigned the jurisdiction in question to some other body. This was the case throughout the southern colonies. Their statute books are entirely silent on the subject of divorce jurisdiction. Judicial separations from bed and board did not exist; nor prior to the Revolution has there been discovered a single case of absolute divorce by legislative act—a practice so common in New England during the same period—although Parliament had set the example before the close of the seventeenth century. On the other hand, separations by mutual consent, or on account of bad conduct, or parol[3] separations in some form, did occur, as they always do occur in any society; and it is from the meager records of judicial actions regarding

---

[1] BISHOP, *op. cit.*, I, §§ 115–37, where the authorities for each step in the argument are cited.

[2] *Ibid.*, §§ 119, 109. See Latour *v.* Teesdale, 8 TAUNT., *Eng. Com. Pleas Rep.*, 830; Rex *v.* Brampton, 10 EAST, *King's Bench Rep.*, 282; Caterall *v* Caterall, 1 ROB., *Ec.*, 580, 581; and Lauderdale Peerage Case, 10 *Law Reports*, 744, 745.

[3] On "parol separation" see BISHOP, *Mar., Div., and Sep.*, I, §§ 1203–52.

separate maintenance in such cases that one learns something concerning the state of southern law and custom before the Revolution.

In Virginia we find the county court, which had gained a share of the equity jurisdiction,[1] hearing and granting petitions for separate alimony. Thus in 1691 the prayer "of Ruth Fulcher for separate maintenance against her husband, John Fulcher," was referred by the governor and council, constituting the "general court,"[2] to the justices of a county court, "who, after hearing the testimony, decided in favour of the plaintiff."[3]

Now, by the English law alimony could not be granted in an independent action, but only as incident to a divorce by decree of the ecclesiastical court. Moreover, in Virginia no colonial statute had ever conferred this portion of the ecclesiastical jurisdiction upon the local courts or upon any other tribunal. How, then, consistently with the principles just stated, could a petition for separate maintenance be entertained by the county magistrates as falling within their equity jurisdiction? From two decisions in the early part of the present century the dual innovation is represented as the result of justifiable self-help under the stress of circumstances; while, in the absence of a statute authorizing it, the assumption of the power of the ecclesiastical court by the equity tribunal is looked upon as a natural and logical course. In the first of these cases, arising in 1810, the superior court of chancery affirms its own jurisdiction in suits for alimony. The chancellor, after conceding that the authorities are in doubt and divided, holds "that in every well-regulated government there must somewhere exist a power of affording a remedy where the law affords none;

[1] HENING, *Stat.*, I, 303; V, 491.

[2] This court was so called since 1662: HENING, *Stat.*, II, 58; *cf.* HOWARD, *Local Const. Hist.*, I, 390 ff.

[3] June 16, 1691: PALMER, *Calendar of Va. State Papers*, I, 29.

and this peculiarly belongs to a court of equity; and as husband and wife are considered as one person in law, it is evident that in this case the law can afford no remedy; which is universally admitted to be a sufficient ground to give this court jurisdiction, and therefore it must entertain the bill."[1]

Thirteen years later this "reasoning of the chancellor on the point of jurisdiction" is pronounced "sound," in a suit for separate maintenance which was carried from the chancery court of Fredericksburg to the Virginia court of appeals. In his opinion Judge Carr says: "I find no case with us, in which the subject has been before this court. Having no Ecclesiastical Tribunal, the powers of that court seem to have been considered as vesting originally in the old General Court. From thence, some of them have been distributed to other courts, as they were branched out. . . . . I know of no law which has given to any court the trial of matrimonial causes, except so far as relates to incestuous marriages, as to which a power is given to the Court of Chancery to annul them." Judge Tucker, he continues, in his edition of Blackstone,[2] "says with respect to suits for alimony after a divorce *a mensa et thoro*, as there is no court in Virginia which possesses jurisdiction in such cases, there can be no room for suits of this nature; unless, perhaps, the High Court of Chancery should sustain them as incidental to its equitable jurisdiction." "I believe," adds Judge Carr, "that in practice the County Courts, sitting as courts of equity, have assumed the power of giving separate maintenance in cases of separation; but by what rule they have been regulated, I know not."[3]

---

[1] Case of Purcell *v.* Purcell (1810), 4 HEN. AND MUNF., *Reports*, 506-19. " It is not commonly thus assumed that a court of equity will take jurisdiction of a subject simply because the common law tribunals do not."— BISHOP, *Mar., Div., and Sep.*, I, §1398, note 5; STORY, *Equity Jurisprudence*, §62.

[2] TUCKER, *Blackstone's Commentaries* (1803), III, 94.

[3] Case of Almond *v.* Almond (1823), 4 RAND., *Rep.*, 662-68; also in 15 *Am. Decisions*, 781.

But the colonial and state courts of equity, in "exercising the authority, not of granting divorces, but alimony, where the latter was the only relief prayed," seem to have acted contrary to the more approved legal rule; and Bishop suggests that their course may have been influenced by a misunderstanding of the policy of the commonwealth. In the time of Cromwell "the ecclesiastical courts were abolished; thereupon the equity judges were expressly authorized, it appears by a clause in their commissions,[1] to decide causes of alimony, and after the Restoration their decrees were by statute confirmed. Misapprehensions of this matter have sometimes led to the inference that the equity courts took cognizance of the question simply as of their own appropriate jurisdiction, because of the extinguishment of ecclesiastical tribunals, or as succeeding to them. But this obviously was not so; since, had the jurisdiction been theirs, they would have exercised it as well when there were ecclesiastical courts as when there were none, for the latter never claimed it, their alimony being only an incident in the divorce suit; and since any jurisdiction which they might assume as successors of the defunct ecclesiastical courts could have been only to decide causes of divorce, with their incidental alimony, not to grant an alimony before unknown." The granting of separate alimony without a divorce is now common in the states;[2] and, from whatever source the courts have derived their power, it is entirely justifiable as satisfying a social need. In the absence of statutory sanction justice may demand that some existing body shall promptly grant relief; though it is doubtless true that the authority to do so cannot be *logically* assumed

---

[1] BISHOP, *op. cit.*, I, §§ 1394, 1395; following FONBLANQUE, *Equity*, 97, note. In Helms *v.* Franciscus, 12 BLAND, 544 ff., it is taken for granted that the equity judges of the commonwealth *assumed* the jurisdiction in question as naturally coming to them; nothing is said of a statute conferring it.

[2] The subject is worked out in detail by BISHOP, *op. cit.*, I, §§ 1383–1421.

as the legitimate inheritance of equity tribunals from the ecclesiastical courts.

The colonial law of Maryland on the subject does not differ essentially from that of Virginia, although there are some divergences of interest. Judicial divorces were not granted. A number of early cases show that the high court of chancery took cognizance of suits for separate alimony as naturally belonging to its jurisdiction in the absence of ecclesiastical courts. Of these perhaps the most important for the facts presented, though the precise ground of the judgment is not clearly expressed, is the action of Galwith v. Galwith which in 1689 came before the provincial court on appeal from the court of Calvert county. The record of the lower tribunal states that at the June term, 1685, "the appellee, being the wife of the appellant," presented a petition "setting forth, that within a few years certain false, evil, and scandalous reports were raised and spread abroad against her by some malicious persons," causing "great dissention and difference between her husband and herself, insomuch that he refused to entertain her in his house, or allow her a competent maintenance elsewhere, by which she was reduced to great poverty and want." Whereupon, in June, 1684, she "applied to the county court for relief and redress therein, at which time the court hearing and considering the premises, granted an order that her husband should allow . . . . her 2000 wt. of tobacco for her maintenance the year next ensuing." Now the "year was completed and ended, and her said husband not being reconciled nor willing" to take back either herself or the child, "which she hitherto had maintained," she "would in a short time be brought to extreme poverty and necessity without further assistance from the court." Therefore she prayed that the court would give order that her husband might "take her home to dwell with him, which she was desirous to do, or else that he might be enjoined to allow her a competent maintenance for herself and child." Accordingly the "said John Galwith" was commanded to "take home his said wife Jane Galwith, to dwell with him as man and wife ought to do; otherwise to allow . . . . her 3000 wt. of tobacco a year, commencing from that day."

John then appealed to the higher tribunal, assigning for errors: (1) that the county court passed judgment against him upon reading the petition without calling him to answer, "so that he is condemned unheard contrary to the law, and against the statute of *Magna Charta;*" (2) that the county court had "no jurisdiction of the matter in difference . . . . , being touching Alimony, which is not recoverable there but in chancery, or the court of the ordinary;" (3) that the county court cannot take "cognizance of matters relating to causes of separation and divorce between man and wife, but such matters are only triable and examinable in the court of the ordinary."[1] The judgment was reversed, but on what particular ground we are not told; so that from the apparent inconsistency of the last two specifications, one might be in doubt, were the fact not well established, whether the high court of chancery had jurisdiction; for surely alimony is strictly a matter "relating to causes of separation and divorce," cognizance of which is said in the report to belong in effect to the bishop of London as ordinary. One point, however, seems clear: the county court had no power in such causes; and that is what one would infer according to the doctrine of the Virginia judges before quoted; for, unlike the county courts of Virginia, those of Maryland had no equity jurisdiction.[2]

[1] Case of Galwith *v.* Galwith, 4 HARRIS AND MCHENRY, *Reports*, 477, 478.

[2] The act of 1639, engrossed but not finally approved, gave the so-called " county court" power in certain matrimonial causes belonging properly to ecclesiastical courts: but this tribunal was really the predecessor of the provincial court: BOZMAN, *Hist. of Md.*, 106, 128, 129, 131, 604.

Some other decisions of a later date throw light on the colonial practice. In Macnamara's case, involving alimony, decided before the Revolution, "the defendant claimed an appeal to the Arches Court in England. His right thereto seems to have been acknowledged, it does not appear on what principle."[1] Again, in 1828, it was declared in Farnshill v. Murray that "there never having been an ecclesiastical court, and no power to grant a divorce by annulling for any cause, a contract of marriage which was originally valid ever having been conferred upon any of the courts of justice, it follows that a divorce can only be granted by an act of the general assembly;" but in the provincial era alimony was customarily granted by the court of chancery.[2] Similar evidence two years later is afforded by the opinion in Helms v. Franciscus, where the parties had a written agreement to live apart. In the absence of the ecclesiastical court it is affirmed, "the high court of chancery always had, even under the provincial government, entire jurisdiction of such claims for alimony, or for separate maintenance out of the husband's estate founded on his misconduct," but chancery may not meddle with causes of marriage and divorce. Moreover, it is laid down, apparently as the rule in the colonial as well as in the modern period, that separate maintenance may be assigned by the equity court only on the two grounds of misconduct admitted in the ecclesiastical tribunals as proper reasons for a divorce *a mensa et thoro*.[3] It may also be noted that the jurisdiction in suits for alimony, assumed prior to the Revolution by the courts of equity, was later confirmed by statute. In 1777 it was enacted that the

---

[1] Macnamara's case, 2 BLAND, 566, note: BISHOP, *op. cit.*, I, § 1396 n. 3.

[2] Case of Farnshill v. Murray, 1 BLAND, 479 ff.; 18 *Am. Decisions*, 344–50. *Cf.* the case of Utterton v. Tewsh, FERGUSON'S *Reports of Consist. Court of Sc.* (1811), 23.

[3] That is, for cruelty and adultery: case of Helms v. Franciscus (1830), 2 BLAND, 544 ff.; 20 *Am. Decisions*, 402 ff. *Cf.* the case of Wallingsford v. Wallingsford, 6 HAR. AND J., 485.

"chancellor shall and may hear and determine all causes for alimony, in as full and ample a manner as such causes could be heard and determined by the laws of England in the ecclesiastical courts there."[1]   Commenting on this act Bishop remarks that "as the ecclesiastical courts in England had no power over alimony except in connection with divorce, it would not have been an extravagant interpretation to derive from this statute authority to decree both divorce and alimony, to the extent exercised in those courts.   But it was held, instead, that the wife could have under it the sort of alimony we are considering, for any cause authorizing in England a divorce from bed and board, and even sometimes for other causes;[2] yet not the divorce."[3]

It is just possible, finally, that absolute divorces were granted in Maryland by the colonial assembly—a common practice after the Revolution.   "In this state," it was held in 1829, "the act of divorcing man and wife has been performed by the legislature, for the want, perhaps, of ecclesiastical authority to effect it, or borrowing, perchance, the power from the parliament of Great Britain. . . . . However this may be, divorces in this state, from the earliest times have emanated from the general assembly, and can now be viewed in no other light than as regular exertions of legislative power."   But no evidence is forthcoming for the "earliest times."[4]

---

[1] By the same act it is provided that "the general court may inquire into, hear and determine, either on indictment or petition of either of the parties, the validity of any marriage, and may declare any marriage, contrary to the table in this act [table of forbidden degrees] or any second marriage, the first subsisting, null and void," with appeal to the "court of appeals."—*Laws of Md.* (Annapolis, 1799), I, Feb., 1777, c. xii, par. xiv, xv.

[2] Jamison *v.* Jamison, 4 *Md. Ch.*, 289, 295.   This case is thus more liberal than Helms *v.* Franciscus just cited.

[3] BISHOP, *op. cit.*, I, § 1396.   *Cf.* Hewitt *v.* Hewitt, 1 BLAND, 101: Crane *v.* Meginnis, 1 GILL AND J., 463, or 19 *Am. Decisions*, 237; Wright *v.* Wright's Lessee, 2 *Md.*, 429, or 56 *Am. Decisions*, 723.

[4] Case of Crane *v.* Meginnis, 1 GILL AND J., 468; 19 *Am. Decisions*, 237-42.   *Cf.* also Wright *v.* Wright's Lessee, 2 *Md.*, 429, or 56 *Am. Decisions*, 723-33.

The law and custom prevailing in the Carolinas are in harmony with those of Virginia and Maryland, and need not here be considered. The same is probably true of Georgia, as appears from the case of Head *v.* Head, which will receive some notice in another connection.[1] From the opinion in this suit we infer that in the colonial period the English common law, including the law administered by the ecclesiastical courts, governed the subject of divorce. By an act of February 25, 1784, the common law and such statutes as were in force "in the Province of Georgia in 1776, so far as they were not contrary to the constitution, laws, and form of government of the state," were adopted. Accordingly, up to 1784 an absolute divorce could not be given, and the only causes recognized for a partial divorce were those of the common law. But even such limited divorces were not granted; for there had been no legislation on the subject, and therefore no courts existed in the colony competent to act. Through exercise of its sovereign power the legislature might, indeed, have granted divorces, partial or complete, after the British model; and according to the opinion in this case the legislature had exercised this function for some time prior to 1798, when the constitution transferred the primary jurisdiction in all cases from the legislative body to the courts. "We have searched in vain," says Justice Nisbet, "for any legislation upon the law of divorce before 1798. If the legislature had passed laws declaring what would be good cause for divorce at any time anterior to 1798, without controversy those laws would have repealed the common law, and the *legal principles* mentioned in the constitution would have been referable to them. But there were no such laws passed. It is true that, before 1798, the legislature . . . . did grant divorces upon special application. . . . . These acts do not even exhibit the grounds upon which they were

[1] See chap. xvii, sec. ii.

passed." Thus far the judge, apparently, is speaking of the period between the Revolution and the constitution of 1798. We are not told by him whether any legislative divorces were granted in the colonial era, though that is highly improbable. At any rate, it is nearly certain that the common law was not repealed by any provincial statute. For "no such laws have come down to us. If there were any . . . . they are too deeply buried beneath the deposits of time for our power of revelation;" though, probably, a "diligent search in the colonial records preserved in England, but not accessible to this court, might convict us of error."[1]

III. ARBITRATION AND DIVORCE IN THE MIDDLE COLONIES

Touching the question of divorce the Middle Colonies held a place much closer to the extreme conservatism of the South than to the broad liberalism of New England. In New Netherland, indeed, it was natural that the Reformation doctrines on this subject should prevail. The civil courts exercised every kind of matrimonial jurisdiction. Already we have seen them trying cases of breach of promise and annulling marriages for the lack of legal forms.[2] So also they possessed full power to dissolve the nuptial bond.

As early as 1655 John Hicks obtained a divorce on account of his wife's adultery, with leave to remarry. Two years later John George Baldingh was granted a similar decree on the same ground. Anneke Adriaens was released from her husband for bigamy in 1664.[3] In 1674, the year of interregnum, Governor Colve, with the fiscal and council, heard the petition of Catrina Lane for "letters of divorce"

---

[1] Case of Head v. Head (1847), 2 KELLY, *Georgia Reports*, 191-211. *Cf.* on the same point, Finch v. Finch, 14 *Ga.*, 362: and Brown v. Westbrook, 27 *Ga.*, 102, which varies from the two other decisions.

[2] See chap. xiv, above.

[3] These three cases are in the *New York Colonial MSS.*, 1630-1664: Dutch: Part First, VI, 49; VIII, 415, 417, 419; X, 291, 293. They were first brought to light by COWLEY, *Our Divorce Courts*, 32, 33.

from her husband Daniel, who, being accused of committing a heinous crime, had broken jail and absconded. After due consideration, the court ordered that a "divorce and separation" should be granted if the husband do not within six months appear and "purge" himself of the charge.[1] The allowance of this delay before a decree of divorce shall take effect, in case of absence of the defendant, appears to be the rule; for in the same year the prayer of Abigail Messenger, deserted wife of Richard Darlin, for divorce with the privilege of remarriage, is for "cogent reasons, provisionally postponed . . . . six months, during which time the supplicant's husband is commanded to purge himself from this accusation," or in default the supplicant shall be permitted to urge her suit.[2] Thirteen years earlier Laers, the Finnish priest who later got himself into trouble by performing his own wedding ceremony, is said, in a "meeting," to have secured a divorce from his wife on account of her elopement with Jacob Jongh.[3]

In 1659 we find what appears to be a cause of separation from bed and board with assignment of alimony. Since "Nicolaas Velthuyzen cannot resolve to live any more in love with his wife," therefore it is decreed "that he shall provisionally supply her with one fat hog, two skepels of maize, according to his own offer for her support, and further disposition shall be made for the maintenance of her and her children."[4] To this same year, also, belongs a case

[1] This was a case of alleged incest: O'CALLAGHAN, *Doc. Rel. to Col. Hist., N. Y.*, II, 704.

[2] Case of desertion and adultery: *N. Y. Col. MSS.* (translation from the Dutch), XXIII, 248; also, with slightly different translation, in O'CALLAGHAN, *op. cit.*, II, 730.

[3] Case of elopement with adultery, Dec. 15, 1661: GERARD, *The Old Stadt Huys*, 386, 387; also in O'CALLAGHAN, *op. cit.*, XII, 359, where we read: "This fine priest demanded with great circumstantiality in the above-mentioned meeting a decree of divorce on account of his wife's flight and received the same, subject to your Honors' approval, on the 15th of December" (letter from Beeckman to Stuyvesant and others, dated at Altona, South River, Feb. 1, 1662).

[4] *Records of New Amsterdam*, III, 73.

which seems to be the complement of the English action for jactitation. The plaintiff brings suit because the defendant has privately accused him of having another wife; where-upon the court orders the accuser to prove his charge.[1] There is also mention of a separation by mutual agreement made originally before the local commissaries at Albany. A record of the higher court at New York in 1670 recites: "Whereas strife and difference hath arisen betweene Albert Andriesen and Gertruyde Vosburgh his wife with yᵉ which yᵉ commissaryes at Albany being acquainted" and, finding their "Inclinations averse from living together as man and wife ought to doe they did by consent make an Agreement of their Seperation as likewise how their estates are to be divided betweene them." Therefore the court doth "Ratifye and Confirme what hath beene Already ordered as to that perticular by yᵉ which each partye is to res[t] satisfyed without giving any further trouble upon this occasion."[2]

"Tender parents," writes Mrs. Earle, "could not unduly shelter a daughter who had left her husband's bed and board. He could promptly apply to the court for an order for her return to him, and an injunction to her parents against harboring her. It has been plain to see in all such cases which I have chanced upon in colonial records that the Court had a strong leaning towards the husband's side of the case."[3] This fact appears in a case coming before the local authorities of New Amsterdam in 1665, which, moreover, affords an illustration of the sensible Dutch custom of arbi-tration in such domestic differences. A trouble having arisen between Arent Jureaensen Lantsman and his spouse Beletje, the burgomasters and schepens refer the matter for adjustment "to reverend Dome. Johannes Megapolenses and

[1] *Ibid.*, 70. *Cf. ibid.*, 370 (1661), for mention of a case of seduction.

[2] At "ffort James in New Yorke the 24th day of October 1670."—MUNSELL, *Annals of Albany*, IV, 20.

[3] EARLE, *Colonial Days in Old New York*, 48.

Dome. Samuel Driesius." If the arbitrators fail to settle the difficulty by next court day, warning is given that "proceedings may be expected according to the Style and custom of law, as an example to other evil housekeepers." Later Lantsman avers that his wife's parents will not listen to the arbitrators; and so he prays that the court may order his wife to return to him. Thereupon Beletje appears and says she will not return because her husband has often broken his promises to amend. So the court takes a hand on the husband's behalf, forbidding the wife's father, Lodowyck Pas, to keep her above fourteen days, during which time the consorts must be reconciled or else apply to the court again. At the same time Lantsman is duly warned that if further complaint of bad behavior be made, he shall be handed over to the "Honorable Governor General to be punished by his Honor in such manner whether by separation from bed and board imprisonment or otherwise as by his Honor shall then be deemed proper as an example to other householders." But the wife's parent seems to have disregarded the mandate. For, later, sworn jurymen decide that "Beletje Lodowyck" must return to her husband, and that her father shall no longer harbor her without the husband's consent; and this verdict is approved by the court.[1] "A curious feature of this marriage quarrel," adds Mrs. Earle, "is the fact that this Lantsman, who was so determined to retain his wife, had been more than recreant about

[1] For this case (July 11, 1665) see VALENTINE, *Manual of the Corporation* (1852), 486, 487, 489, 494.

Some further details are given in the *Records of New Amsterdam*, V, 262–65: "Lodowyck Pas, his wife and daughter (the wife of Arent Jurriaansen Lantsman), entering the aforesaid Lantsman's wife's request to be divorced from her husband, as she cannot keep house with him. Decreed to postpone the matter until the next court day when the said Lantsman is to be heard and the aforesaid Lodowyck Pas was allowed to retain his daughter with him during that time" (262). Then Beletje produces a remonstrance against being obliged to go to her husband (263). Lantsman next appears, and is ordered to produce his witnesses by next court day (264, 265). No further mention of the matter appears in these documents. Whether the proceedings just indicated were preliminary or after failure of arbitration is, of course, not clear; but the former seems more probable.

marrying her. The banns had been published, the wedding-day set, but Bridegroom Lantsman did not appear. Upon being hunted up and reprimanded, his only proffered excuse was the very simple one that his clothes were not ready."[1]

A few other cases of separation, occasionally with arbitration, have been gleaned, some of them occurring long after the English rule began. For example, William Hallet petitions "that his wife may be obliged to live with him agreeably to the decision of referees, or in the case of her refusal to comply, that he be granted a divorce."[2] Whether his prayer was allowed we are not told. In 1697 Daniel Vanolinda prayed "that his wife be 'ordyred to go and live with him where he thinks convenient.' The wife's father was promptly notified by the Albany magistrates that he was 'discharged to shelter her in his house or elsewhere, upon Penalty as he will answer at his Perill;' and she returned to her husband."[3] The same writer from whom the record of this case is borrowed says "Nicasius de Sille, magistrate of New Utrecht and poet of New Netherland, separated his life from that of his wife because—so he said—she spent too much money," and also because "she was too fond of schnapps,—which her respected later life did not confirm."[4] Likewise "when Anniatje Fabritius requested an order of court for her husband to vacate her house with a view of final separation from him, it was decided by the arbitrators that no legal steps should be taken, but that 'the parties comport themselves as they ought, in order that they win back each others affections, leaving each other in meanwhile unmolested'—which was very sensible advice. Another married pair having 'met with great discouragement' (which is certainly a most polite expression to employ on such a

---

[1] Earle, *op. cit.*, 49.

[2] *New York Col. MSS.*, XXIII: *Calendar of Hist. Man.* (1664–1776), 26; *cf. ibid.*, XXIII, 269, 390; XXV, 84, 85.

[3] Earle, *op. cit.*, 48, 49.   [4] *Ibid.*, 50.

subject), agreed each to go his and her way, after an exact
halving of all their possessions."[1]   But the most remarkable
case of reconciliation through help of the court is that of
Anneke Schaets, daughter of Domine Schaets, first minister at Fort Orange.   It seems, according to Mrs. Earle,
that her conduct had in some way scandalized her father's
congregation, so that she "refrained from contaminating
attendance at communion;" whereupon the dominie, out of
resentment, quarreled with the brethren and persisted in
"ripping up new differences and offences."   At last, after
being removed from his clerical office for disobeying a judicial summons, matters were adjusted.   Anneke "was ordered
off to New York to her husband, 'with a letter of recommendation; and as she was so headstrong, and would not
depart without the Sheriff's and Constable's interference, her
disobedience was annexed to the letter.'"   The record of
the court made in July, 1681, runs as follows: "Tho: Da-
vidtse promisses to conduct himself well and honorably
towards his wife Anneke Schaets, to Love and never neglect her, but faithfully and properly to maintain and support
her with her children according to his means, hereby making
null and void all questions that have occurred and transpired
between them, but are entirely reconciled: and for the better
assurance of his real Intention and good Resolution to observe the same, he requests that two good men be named to
oversee his conduct at New York towards his said wife, being
entirely disposed and inclined to live honorably and well
with her as a Christian man ought, subjecting himself willingly to the rule and censure of the said men.   On the other
hand his wife Anneke Schaets, promises also to conduct herself quietly and well and to accompany him to New York
with her children and property, not to leave him any more,
but to serve and help him and with him to share the sweets

[1] *Ibid.*

and the sours as becomes a Christian spouse: Requesting all
differences which had ever existed between them both may
be hereby quashed and brougt no more to light or cast up,
as she on her side is heartily disposed to.   Their Worships
of the Court Recommend parties on both Sides to observe
strictly their Reconciliation now made."[1]

If one may judge from the scattered fragments of court
records thus preserved, the little settlements in New Netherland and early New York were afflicted by their fair share of
domestic ills.   In the main, however, family life was placid
and prosaic.   Few cases of absolute divorce, or even of permanent separation, occurred; and this is probably due, at
least in part, to the system of friendly arbitration and to the
kindly paternalism of the Dutch magistrates.

After the conquest, according to the weight of legal authority,[2] the people of New York province acquired the rights
and privileges of the English common law.   The ecclesiastical courts were "regular tribunals of England, and the law
administered in them" a part of the general law of the land.[3]
But so far as divorce is concerned, in New York, as in the
southern colonies, this law was practically in abeyance
throughout the entire provincial era.   The code of the duke
of York, it is true, does contain a provision on this subject.
It is there declared that "In Cases of Adultery all proceedings shall bee accordinge to the Lawes of England which is
by Divorce (if sùrd) Corporall punishment or fine and Imprisonment."[4]   In substance, therefore, separation from bed
and board, not complete divorce, is thus sanctioned for the

---

[1] Quoted from EARLE, op. cit., 46, 47.

[2] See Chancellor Kent, in Williamson v. Williamson, 1 JOHNSON, Chancery Rep.,
488, 491, 492; and Chancellor Walworth's decisions in Wood v. Wood, 2 PAIGE, Chancery Rep., 108, 111; North v. North, 1 BARBOUR, Chancery Rep., 241, 245: 43 Am. Decisions, 778; and Burr v. Burr, 10 PAIGE, Chancery Rep., 20, 35.   Cf. BISHOP, Mar.,
Div., and Sep., I, §§ 132, 133, notes; and STORY, Commentaries, I, 80, 81.

[3] BISHOP, op. cit., I, § 109.

[4] Duke of Yorke's Book of Laws: in LINN, Charter and Laws, 63.

scriptural ground. But this provision in its practical result does no more than say that the English law regarding judicial separation *a mensa et thoro* shall be recognized in the colony, and such would have been the case without it. From the beginning it must have been a "dead letter;" for no tribunal was clothed by statute with adequate jurisdiction to enforce it. Possibly for a time the old Dutch law and customs were in practice accepted as partially binding. We have just seen evidence of the survival of arbitration in cases of separation, and of marital reconciliations managed and recorded by the courts. But, unless granted on this authority in the brief period of transition, judicial divorce *a vinculo* ceased in New York with the English conquest. According to Chancellor Kent, who may not be quite accurate, "during the period of our colonial government, for more than one hundred years preceding the Revolution, no divorce took place in the colony of New York; and for many years after New York became an independent state, there was not any lawful mode of dissolving a marriage in the lifetime of the parties, but by a special act of the legislature."[1]

Subsequent to the meeting of the first assembly of the province in 1683 the writer has found no evidence of a legislative divorce, though there is preserved a copy of what appears to be a circular letter from King George III. in 1773, commanding the provincial governors "not upon any pretence whatsoever" to give their assent to any bill "that may have been or shall hereafter be passed by the Council and Assembly of the Province under your government for the naturalization of Aliens, nor for the divorce of persons joined together in Holy marriage nor for establishing a Title" to lands originally acquired by aliens before naturalization.[2]

[1] KENT, *Commentaries*, II, 97, 98.

[2] Letter of Nov. 24, 1773: O'CALLAGHAN, *Doc. Rel. to Col. Hist., N. Y.*, VIII, 402; also in *New Jersey Archives*, X, 411, 412.

But if the legislature declined to interfere, during the early period the executive stepped into the breach. Cadwallader Colden, who died in 1776, tells us that "the Governors of New York took on them the power of granting divorces which has been in disuse at least ever since the revolution neither is there any court in this province that can give this remedy tho' in the neighboring Colonies a divorce is more easily obtained than perhaps in any other Christian Country;" and he significantly raises the "Query whether this may not be for the advantage of a new country which wants people. It is certain that the natural increase of People in New England has been very great perhaps more than in any other of the English Colonies."[1]

Colden's declaration that divorces, even by authority of the governor, were not granted after the revolution of 1689 harmonizes with the statement of Chancellor Kent. A petition for such executive relief is preserved among the New York Colonial Manuscripts. In this case Richard Wood, who avers that he has lived in Westchester "about fifteen years," during all which time he "hath endeauoured to demeane himselfe as a true and loyall subject and serviceable in his generation," prays for separation from his wife Mary on account of "her most abominable words and actions" purposely designed to "breed difference" between them. The petition is addressed to Governor General Andros; but no record of his excellency's action in the premises is forthcoming.[2] The granting of divorces by

---

[1] COLDEN, *Letters on Smith's History of New York:* in *Coll. N. Y. Hist. Soc.*, Fund Series, I, 1868, 187.

[2] *New York Col. MSS.*, XXV, 84. Here is the document in full, though some phrases are hard to decipher:

"To the Right Honrble Maij Edmond Andross, Gouevnr Genll of all his Highnes Territories in America:

"The Humble Petiton of Richard Wood:

"Humbly: Sheweth:

"That whereas your Honours Petitioner haueing liue under his Highness Jurisdiction in Westchester about fifteen years, during wch time your petitioner hath

executive authority is unprecedented; and it is just possible that the governors immediately after the English occupation believed their action in such cases in a way sustained by the duke's law; though this hypothesis is scarcely probable.

For the other middle colonies the story is soon told. New Jersey is in the same position as New York under English rule. The statute book is silent on the subject of divorce. If divorces were permitted at all, it must have been by legislative authority; unless, indeed, in the early period, as in the sister-province, the governors assumed the power to act.

The Great Law of 1682 for Pennsylvania authorizes divorce on the scriptural ground. The punishment for adultery prescribed by this statute may be compared with the penalties mentioned in the early New England and New York codes. One convicted of that crime " shall for the first offence be publicly whipt and suffer one whole year's imprisonment in the house of correction, at hard labor, to the behoof of the publick, and longer if the Magistrate see meet. And both he and the woman shall be liable to a Bill of Divorcement, if required by the grieved husband or wife, within the said term of one whole year after Conviction." For a second offense the penalty is "imprisonment in man-

endeauoured to demeane himselfe as a true and Loyall subject and serviceable in his generation, to the best of his power, but through the unchastity and disloyalty of ye petitioners wife by name Mary Wood, sustained great detriment and endured a very troublesome and vexatious liueing to the Dishonour of God, and repugnant to the holy bond of wedlock, she haueing as much as in her lay endeauoured the totall ruine and destruction of your petitioner, by her most abominable words and actions, haueing openly confessed she hath defiled her marriage bedd, and that purposely to breed difference between your petitioner and her selfe, notwithstanding ye petitioner endeauoured to reclaime her, by all means lawfull, who yet continued the same and rather worse, and now purposely absented her selfe by reason she knows her selfe guilty and to prevent that shame and punishment due to her base and wicked actions. . . . .

"Yr Petitioner humbly beggs your Honrs would bee pleased to take your petitioners sad case into consideration, and if it shall seem good in your Honrs sight a sepa_ration may be made, otherwise noe [illegible] can be expected but a sad euent of such deplorable doings.

"and ye Petitioner shall for
"Euer Pray as in Duty bound."

ner aforesaid, During Life." If the husband or wife sins with a person who is unmarried, then for the first offense either shall suffer half a year's imprisonment; and for a second transgression, imprisonment for life.[1] Nearly the same penalties are imposed for incest[2] and for bigamy.[3] It will be noticed that the Great Law, which was re-enacted in later statutes, deals with divorce much in the same spirit as does the duke of York's code. In each case divorce is allowed for the one scriptural cause; but whereas the New York statute plainly intends the separation to be merely from bed and board, "according to the law of England," on the other hand, by its peculiar terms, the Pennsylvania act seems to authorize "bills" for complete dissolution of wedlock. However that may be, in this case, as in the other, the law has no practical significance; for, with one exception below named, the jurisdiction of the English spiritual courts was not devolved upon any of the provincial tribunals. Accordingly, the historian Gordon, in his summary of the laws of the colony, is able to say that these "made no general provision for the dissolution of marriage; and

---

[1] LINN, *Charter and Laws*, 109, 110. This provision was abrogated by William and Mary, 1693, but re-enacted the same year: *ibid.*, 110, note, 194 (the re-enacted law).

By the Dutch code fornicators, if single, are to marry or pay a heavy fine; O'CALLAGHAN, *Ordinances*, 495. Under the duke of York the penalty is marriage, fine, or corporal punishment, in the discretion of the court: *Duke of Yorke's Book of Laws:* in LINN, *Charter and Laws*, 27. The New Jersey laws of "Carteret's time" (*ca.* 1675) contain the same provisions: LEAMING AND SPICER, *Grants*, 107; and the Pennsylvania statutes authorize the county court to impose "all or anie" of these three penalties: LINN, *op. cit.*, 145, 210; BIOREN, *Laws*, I, 2, c. 3.

[2] For incest the guilty person "shall forfeit one-half of his estate, and both suffer imprisonment a whole year, in the house of Correction, at hard labour, and for the second offence, imprisonment in manner aforesaid during life."—LINN, *op. cit.*, 110; abrogated and re-enacted in 1693: *ibid.*, 194; and a similar law was passed in 1700: BIOREN, *Laws*, I, 2, 6.

[3] For bigamy, according to the Great Law, whosoever shall be "Convicted of having two wives or two husbands, att one and the same time shall be imprisoned all their Lifetime in the House of Correction, at hard labour, to the behoof of the former wife and children, or the former husband and children." When one of the persons is single and the other married, the penalty is the same: LINN, *op. cit.*, 110, 111; abrogated and re-enacted in 1693: *ibid.*, 194; and again in substance re-enacted in 1700: BIOREN, *Laws*, I, 2, 6.

divorce from bed and board was allowed in case of bigamy only, on request of the first wife or husband, made in one year after conviction."[1]

Absolute divorces were, however, granted by legislative authority. Of these an example occurs in 1769, when there was laid before the council a "Bill sent up by the Assembly for the Governors concurrence, entitled 'An Act to Dissolve the Marriage of Curtis Grubb, of the County of Lancaster, Iron Master, with Ann, his wife, late Ann Few,'" and to enable them to contract further matrimony. After amendment this bill was approved, and Curtis was allowed to "take to Wife any other woman during the Natural Life of the said Anne, in the same manner as he might or could do if she, the said Anne was actually Dead."[2] In the same way, on March 21, 1772, the "marriage of George Kehmle of the City of Philadelphia, Barber, with Elizabeth, his wife," was dissolved; but on April 27, 1773, the decree was declared void by the king in "an Instrument of Writing under the Privy Seal;" and on the 11th of next October the royal veto was published by a proclamation of the governor, Jonn Penn.[3] There is also extant an example of annulment of wedlock by the legislative body. On March 20, 1772, a bill to declare void the "pretended marriage of Rebecca Vanakin with a Certain John Martin" was presented to the governor; but after six months' deliberation, on September 19, it was returned to the assembly with his excellency's veto.[4] There is no evidence to show, however, that divorces either partial or absolute were at all common in the Quaker province.

---

[1] GORDON, *Hist. of Pa.*, 557. But GORDON (*op. cit.*, 70) is in error when he states that by the Great Law divorce was sanctioned after a " second " offense; and regarding this law some other mistakes occur.

[2] *Pa. Col. Rec.*, IX, 564, 566, 567, 568, 580.   [3] *Ibid.*, X, 26, 42, 104, 105.

[4] *Ibid.*, 40, 53, 54, 55, 104, 105.

CHAPTER XVI

A CENTURY AND A QUARTER OF MARRIAGE LEGISLATION IN THE UNITED STATES, 1776–1903

[BIBLIOGRAPHICAL NOTE XVI.—For this chapter all the statutes relating to marriage enacted in fifty-two states and territories since the Revolution have been examined and compared, Hawaii not being included. The session laws and various compilations of statutes consulted are described in the Bibliographical Index, V, and need not here be named in detail.

Hitherto a history of matrimonial legislation in the United States has not appeared; but summaries of the laws of the various states have been made for particular periods. Of these the most important is the accurate digest for 1887–88—the time of compilation—contained in Wright's *Report on Marriage and Divorce* (Washington, 1889; reprinted without change, 1897). There is also a summary in Stimson, *American Statute Law* (Boston, 1886), I, 664 ff.; and for the sake of completeness may also be mentioned Vanness, *A Digest of the Laws of New York and New England, on Marriage, Dower, Divorce, etc.* (Hartford, 1877); Noble, *A Compendium and Comparative View of the Thirty-Eight State Laws of Marriage and Divorce* (New York, 1882); with the discussion of Cook, "Reform in the Celebration of Marriage," in *Atlantic Monthly*, LXI (Boston, 1888); Convers, *Marriage and Divorce in the United States* (Philadelphia, 1889); Snyder, *The Geography of Marriage or the Legal Perplexities of Wedlock in the United States* (New York, 1889); Ernst, *The Law of Married Women in Massachusetts* (2d ed., Boston, 1897); and Whitney, *Marriage and Divorce* (Philadelphia, New York, Boston, and Chicago, 1894). Consult the parliamentary return of *Marriage Law and Divorce Law* in foreign countries and the colonies (London, 1894); and see also Bibliographical Note XVIII.]

I. THE NEW ENGLAND STATES

THE foundation of the marriage law of the United States was laid long before the War of Independence. Some features have since been pruned away, and others have been changed or added; but the existing forms of celebration, the modes of registration, and the leading principles of matrimonial jurisprudence had already been developed. The century has produced a great mass of legislation; but so far as it is new it is concerned largely with administrative details, often of very great importance as determining the effective character of the law.

a) *The solemnization.*—In New England before the end of the colonial period the religious ceremony had long since been made optional with the lay celebration before a magistrate, which was the only form allowed in the beginning. This system is continued after the Revolution. As elsewhere in the country, the minister and the justice of the peace now share the business between them. The earlier statutes are generally more strict than the later regarding the place of residence and the territorial jurisdiction of the persons authorized to celebrate matrimony. For example, by the Massachusetts act of 1786 any justice of the peace may solemnize lawful wedlock within his own county; while a minister of the gospel, if "stated and ordained," may act only in the "town, district, parish, or plantation where he resides," provided one of the persons lives there too. If a place be destitute of a minister of any denomination, then a neighboring clergyman of the same society may serve; but only in the town or district where the bride or bridegroom dwells.[1] In 1821 such ordained and stated minister, although living outside of the district over which he is settled, may conduct the ceremony at his own place of residence or at that of either of the persons, provided one or both of them is a member of his congregation. If there be no such minister in the place, then the couple desiring to be married may go to any other clergyman in the commonwealth, who in such case is authorized to act.[2] All previous laws on the subject are repealed in 1834, when a new statute empowers the min-

---

[1] *Laws of the Com. of Mass., 1780–1816*, I, 321.

[2] Act of Feb. 12, 1821: *Laws of the Com. of Mass.* (1821), 507. This somewhat extends the provisions of the act of Feb. 20, 1818: *ibid.* (1818), 550.

ister or justice, each in his own place of residence or in that of either of the persons, to perform the ceremony, if at least one of them lives in his official district.[1]   The present law is still broader in its terms.   A marriage may now be solemnized in any place within the commonwealth by Jewish rabbis duly accredited; Friends according to their rites; any minister of the gospel, ordained according to the usage of his denomination, who resides in the commonwealth and continues to perform the functions of his office; or, until a few years ago, by any justice of the peace.[2]   By the act of May 23, 1899, an important change is made.   Henceforth no justice of the peace may solemnize a marriage unless he also holds the office of city or town clerk, city registrar, clerk of a court, or that of assistant in either case; or "unless he shall have been specially designated by the governor."   The latter may at his discretion name justices of the peace "who may solemnize marriages in the city or town in which they severally reside."   Each place is to have at least one such designated magistrate; but otherwise the number is not to exceed one for every five thousand of its inhabitants.   No justice may act without a certificate of designation, which the governor is authorized to revoke whenever he thinks fit; and every year in January the secretary of the commonwealth is required to send to the respective clerks or registrars a list of the justices to which authority is thus granted.[3] However, by the Massachusetts law is prescribed the wise, though unique, condition that the ceremony may be conducted only by a person who is able to read and write the English tongue.[4]

[1] Act of April 1, 1834: *Laws of the Com. of Mass.* (1834), 252-57.

[2] *Pub. Stat.* (1882), 811. The law has remained substantially the same since 1835: see *Rev. Stat.* (1836), 477; *Supp. to Gen. Stat., 1860-1872,* I, 540.

[3] *Acts and Resolves of Mass.* (1899), 379.

[4] Act of April 22, 1896: *Acts and Resolves,* 257. This statute further declares that "no rabbi of the Israelitish faith shall solemnize marriage until he has filed with the clerk or registrar of the town or city where he resides a certificate of the estab-

The course of legislation in the other states has been much the same as in Massachusetts previous to 1899. In all of them throughout the century, except in Rhode Island, justices of the peace in their respective counties have had authority to solemnize marriages. In that commonwealth any justice of the supreme court may now act,[1] as earlier could the assistants, justices of the peace, and justices of the courts of common pleas.[2] For over fifty years the judges of the county and higher courts in Connecticut have had the same power;[3] and so during the assumption period had the councilors, judges, and even the governor and deputy governor, in Vermont.[4] But in that state, after the admission to the Union, the justice of the peace has always been the only lay officer empowered to conduct the ceremony.

The law governing the ecclesiastical celebration has been a matter of slower growth and of much experimentation. That of Massachusetts has already been described. The New Hampshire statute of 1791 provides that marriage may be celebrated by any "ordained minister" in the county where he is settled or has his permanent residence.[5] For many years thereafter no change was made in that requirement.[6] But in 1833 every resident "ordained minister," if in "regular standing" with his denomination, is authorized to act throughout the state, after causing the "credentials of his ordination to be recorded in the office of the clerk of

lishment of the synagogue of which he is rabbi, and of the date of his appointment thereto, and of the term of his engagement."—*Ibid.*, 257. *Cf. Rev. Laws* (1902), II, 1349-50, with somewhat different wording.

[1] Also the wardens of the town of New Shoreham: *Pub. Statutes* (1882), 416; *Gen. Laws* (1896), 621. The justice has power in any town of the state.

[2] *Pub. Laws of R. I.* (1798), 481-83; *ibid.* (1844), 267. By this date the justice of the peace had ceased to act.

[3] *Revised Stat.* (1849), 273; *Stat. of the State of Conn.* (1854), 374, 375; *Gen. Stat.* (1875), 186; *ibid.* (1887), 609; *ibid.* (1902), 1086.

[4] *Slade, State Papers*, 292, 484. *Cf. Laws of the State of Vermont* (1798), 330.

[5] Act of Feb. 15, 1791: *Laws of the State of N. H.* (1797), 295, 296.

[6] *Cf. Const. and Laws* (1805), 296; *Laws of the State* (1815), 350, 351; *ibid.* (1830) 172-74.

common pleas, in the county where he shall solemnize any marriage."[1] The present law is the same in substance, except that the filing of credentials is not mentioned. A nonresident minister, similarly qualified, may now officiate anywhere in the state, on receiving a commission from the governor acting on the advice of the council; and within his own parish, when having a pastoral charge wholly or partly within the state.[2] Authority in the state to join persons in wedlock is granted to "settled" or "ordained" ministers or elders of the leading churches by the Rhode Island laws of 1798;[3] to the ministers or elders of any religious denomination who may be "domiciled" in the state, by the revision of 1844;[4] and by the present law the same elder or minister may obtain a license to join persons in marriage, when he shall have registered his residence, the name of the parish with which he was last "associated, if any, and the name of the religious denomination to which he belongs, in the office of the town clerk of the town in which he resides . . . . in a book to be provided for that purpose," and "shall have subscribed his name thereto."[5]

By the first laws of Maine like authority, in the counties where they dwell, is conferred upon ordained ministers, who shall be duly appointed and licensed during pleasure by the governor with the advice and consent of the council; provided either of the persons resides in the same county.[6] In 1828 this restriction is removed; and the ministers of any denomination of Christians may be so commissioned for counties other than those in which they dwell.[7] The law has since taken a different form. Power is now granted,

---

[1] Laws of N. H. (1833), 88.

[2] Gen. Laws (1878), 428; Pub. Stat. (1891), 494; ibid. (1900), 589.

[3] Pub. Laws (1798), 481–83; same provision, ibid. (1822), 371.

[4] Ibid. (1844), 267.   [5] Gen. Laws (1896), 621.   Cf. Pub. Stat. (1882), 416.

[6] Laws of the State of Maine (1821), I, 341.

[7] Public Acts (1828), 1157, 1158; Laws of the State of Maine (1831), III, 238–40.

during the pleasure of the executive, to every ordained minister of the gospel and to every person licensed to preach by an association of ministers, religious seminary, or ecclesiastical body, who shall be duly appointed and commissioned for that purpose by the governor.[1] Moreover, in this state women, otherwise eligible under the constitution, may in the same way be commissioned to celebrate matrimony.[2] In Vermont during the assumption period similar authority was granted to "settled" ministers in their respective towns while they continue in the ministry.[3] The district of the "ordained" minister was extended to the county in 1797.[4] Three years later, because "irregular itinerant preachers, under pretence of being ordained ministers of the gospel," in remote parts of the county, practiced impositions, and marriages solemnized by them were wholly illegal, it was again restricted to the town;[5] but the act making this change was itself repealed in 1802.[6] By a statute of 1806 a minister is required to file credentials of his ordination with the clerk of the town where he shall solemnize any marriage.[7] But a more liberal provision appears in the revision of 1839, any resident minister of the gospel being then authorized to celebrate wedlock throughout the state.[8] By the law as it now stands the same power is conferred upon a clergyman, ordained according to the usage of his denomination, who resides in the state, or else "labors statedly therein as a minister or missionary."[9]

Ordained ministers of the "several plantations" of Connecticut, as already seen, in 1694 were first allowed to share

---

[1] *Revised Statutes of Maine* (1884), 516, 517. This provision has long existed: see *Acts and Resolves* (1876), chap. 110, sec. 2, pp. 78, 79; *Revised Stat.* (1871), 485; *ibid.* (1857), 391. *Cf.* WRIGHT, *Report*, 53.

[2] *Acts and Resolves* (1875), chap. 56, p. 44; *Revised Stat.* (1884), 517. *Cf.* 62 *Maine Reports*, 596.

[3] SLADE, *State Papers*, 292, 484. [4] *Laws of the State of Vt.* (1798), 330.

[5] Act of Nov. 7, 1800: *Laws of the State of Vt.* (1808), I, 268.

[6] *Ibid.*, 269. [7] *Ibid.*, 272, 273.

[8] *Revised Stat. of 1839* (1840), 319. [9] *Vermont Stat.* (1894), 500.

with the justices of the peace the function of joining persons
in marriage. Their power was restricted to their respective
towns in 1702. It was extended to the county in 1783;[1] and
the clergyman is to have authority "while he continues
settled in the work of the ministry." In 1820 the word
"settled" was dropped. In the revision of 1821 marriages
celebrated according to the rites of any religious denomination were declared valid.[2] Authority to solemnize was
granted in 1847 to any clergyman regularly licensed according to the forms and usages of the denomination to which
he belongs, and having charge of a society for one year or
more.[3] Finally, since 1855, the same power has been conferred upon all ordained or licensed clergymen of Connecticut or any other state while engaged in the work of the
ministry.[4]

The law of Connecticut still retains the broad provision
that marriages celebrated according to the rites of any religious society within the state are valid.[5] This, of course,
includes the Quakers, who in each of the other New England
states are expressly permitted to follow their own usages in
this regard, as also are the Jews in Rhode Island.[6] No form
of ceremony is anywhere prescribed; nor, except in Rhode
Island, are any witnesses required by the statute.[7] In New
Hampshire persons living together and acknowledging each
other as husband and wife, and generally reputed to be such
for the period of three years or until the death of one of

---

[1] *Acts and Laws* (1784), 130.

[2] *Pub. Stat. Laws* (1821), 316; the same provision, *ibid.* (1835), 370.

[3] *Pub. Acts* (1847), 39.

[4] *Gen. Stat.* (1866), 301, note, giving a summary of changes in the law since 1640. *Cf. Gen. Stat.* (1874), 186; *ibid.* (1887), 609; *ibid.* (1902), 1086. See 1 ROOT, 381; 4 *Conn. Reports*, 134, 209.

[5] *Gen. Stat.* (1887), 609.

[6] *Pub. Stat. of Mass.* (1882), 811; *Pub. Stat. of N. H.* (1891), 494; *Gen. Stat. of N. H.* (1867), 331; *Gen. Laws of R. I.* (1896), 622; *Vermont Stat.* (1894), 500; *Revised Stat. of Maine* (1884), 516.

[7] Two witnesses, besides the person solemnizing the marriage, must attend: *Gen. Laws of R. I.* (1896), 624; *Acts and Resolves* (1899), 50, 51.

them, shall thereafter be deemed to have been legally married.[1] Various penalties are prescribed in the different states for unauthorized celebration;[2] but in Maine, Massachusetts, New Hampshire, Vermont, and Rhode Island it is expressly provided that when a marriage has been solemnized by a person professing to be legally authorized, although not so authorized, its validity shall be unaffected by such lack of authority, if it is valid in other respects, and entered into by the parties or one of them in the belief that they were lawfully wedded.[3] It is also enacted in Massachusetts, Maine, New Hampshire, and Rhode Island that the validity of a marriage shall not be affected by any omission or informality in entering the intention to marry.[4]

b) Forbidden degrees: void and voidable marriages.— In none of these states is any definition of marriage laid down in the statutes; but in effect matrimony is treated as a relation partaking of the nature of both status and contract.[5] The age of valid consent to marriage—not to be confused with the so-called "age of consent" under the criminal laws enacted to protect a child from legally agreeing to its own ruin[6]—is prescribed only in New Hampshire, where it is

---

[1] *Pub. Stat.* (1900), 590; *Gen. Stat.* (1867), 332.

[2] In Massachusetts the penalty is a fine not exceeding $500, or imprisonment in jail or in the house of correction for a term not exceeding one year, or both: Act of April 22, 1896: *Acts and Resolves* (1896), 257; in Maine it is $1,000, or not less than five years' imprisonment: *Rev. Stat.* (1884), 517; in New Hampshire it is not exceeding $300, one-half to the complainant: *Pub. Stat.* (1891), 494; *Gen. Laws* (1878), 429; in Vermont, not less than six months' imprisonment or a fine of from $100 to $300; in Connecticut, not to exceed $500, or six months' imprisonment: *Gen. Stat.* (1887), 348; in Rhode Island the fine is $500: *Gen. Laws* (1896), 625.

[3] *Pub. Stat. of Mass.* (1882), 811; *Revised Stat. of Maine* (1884), 517; *Pub. Stat. of N. H.* (1891), 494; *Vermont Stat.* (1894), 502; *Gen. Laws of R. I.* (1896), 625.

[4] *Pub. Stat. of Mass.* (1882), 811; *Rev. Laws of Mass.* (1902), II, 1351; *Rev. Stat. of Maine* (1884), 517; *Pub. Stat. of N. H.* (1891), 494; *Gen. Laws of R. I.* (1896), 625.

[5] For a digest or tabulation of the statutes of all the states and territories relating to definition, age of consent to marriage, age below which parental consent is required, prohibited degrees, void, voidable, and forbidden marriages, as the law stood in 1887, see Wright, *Report*, 28–45.

[6] See chap. xviii, sec. i, *b*), for some account of the laws governing the "age of consent."

fourteen for males and thirteen for females.[1] Elsewhere in
New England the common-law rule of fourteen for boys and
twelve for girls probably obtains.   On the other hand, in all
these states, except New Hampshire, the age below which
parental consent is necessary for a legal contract is named in
the statute.   For males it is everywhere set at twenty-one
years.   For females it is eighteen years in Maine, Massachusetts, and Vermont; and twenty-one years in Connecticut
and Rhode Island.   But in Maine and Massachusetts consent is required only when the minor has a parent or guardian living in the commonwealth.   The Rhode Island law
expressly provides that a license may be issued to a person
of over eighteen years when such person has no parent or
guardian residing in the state;[2] and the same is true in Connecticut of a female under age when a selectman of the
town where she has last resided six months gives his consent.[3] Massachusetts has taken wise precaution regarding
the marriage of minors below a certain age.   By an act of
1894 no town or city clerk is permitted to receive a notice
of the intention of marriage of any male under eighteen or
any female under sixteen years of age, unless the "judge of
probate in each county after due hearing" shall "make an
order allowing the marriage under the age specified;" but
such order may be issued only when the minor resides in the
county where the judge holds court, or when the father,
mother, or guardian gives consent.[4] A law of March 28,
1899, amending the above act, allows the probate judge to

[1] Pub. Stat. of N. H. (1900), 588.

[2] Written consent is requisite in Connecticut, Maine, Rhode Island, and Vermont; but it may be either written or verbal in Massachusetts; and in all cases the
consent is preliminary to issuance of license: Pub. Stat. of Mass. (1882), 810; Rev.
Stat. of Maine (1884), 516; Vermont Stat. (1894), 501; Gen. Stat. of Conn. (1887), 608, 609;
ibid. (1902), 1085; Gen. Laws of R. I. (1896), 623; and Acts and Resolves (1899), 49.

[3] Pub. Acts of Conn. (1895), 474.

[4] Act of May 18, 1894: Acts and Resolves (1894), 453, 454. See also the provision
referred to below, relating to the clandestine marriage of a girl of sixteen secured
by abduction.

make a similar order in case of a person of either sex whose age is alleged to exceed that just specified, but who is unable from any cause to produce an official record of his or her birth, to overcome the reasonable doubt of the town or city clerk or registrar. On receipt of a certified copy of this order such local officer is required to receive the notice of intention and issue a certificate, as in other cases.[1]

The statutes of all of these states contain a list of kindred by blood or affinity with whom marriage is prohibited. The restrictions, of course, invariably include all persons in the ascending or descending line; and also, as a rule, those related within the third degree of collateral consanguinity.[2] Only in New Hampshire are first cousins now forbidden to marry;[3] but throughout New England the inhibition extends to unions between aunts and nephews or uncles and nieces. In Connecticut for a time we find a survival of mediæval prejudice regarding affinity. Marriage with the daughter of a wife's sister or brother was there first permitted in 1750.[4] But it was not until 1793 that the prohibition of wedlock with a deceased wife's sister was dropped;[5] while, curiously enough, it was retained with respect to a deceased brother's wife until 1816.[6] By the existing law of all these states marriage with a step-parent is forbidden; and in them all, save Connecticut, a person may not, with impunity, wed a father-in-law or a mother-in-law. Marriage within the forbidden degrees is everywhere void;[7] the children illegiti-

[1] *Acts and Resolves of Mass.* (1899), 160; *cf. Revised Laws* (1902), II, 1347-49.

[2] SWIFT, *System of the Laws of Conn.* (1795), I, 186, 187.

[3] *Pub. Stat.* (1900), 588. *Cf.* WRIGHT, *Report*, 34.

[4] *Acts and Laws* (1750), 144.

[5] *Pub. Stat. Laws* (1808), I, 478, 479 n. 4.

[6] The law forbidding such unions was repealed in May, 1816: *Pub. Stat. Laws* (1816), 261.

[7] In Vermont, Connecticut, and Rhode Island such unions are void; in the other three states they are both void and incestuous; but in Vermont and Massachusetts they are void only when solemnized in the state; while in all the issue is illegiti-

mate, and the offenders liable to severe penalties.[1]   In
Connecticut until some years after the beginning of the last
century, just as in old colonial days, offenders against the
law of prohibited degrees were "set upon the gallows" and
condemned to wear the "scarlet letter."   The statute of that
state still required the adulterer to carry the halter round
his neck during life;[2] and similar penalties were yet prescribed in some other New England commonwealths.[3]

Marriages may also be void or voidable on grounds other
than the forbidden degrees.   Such grounds are want of lawful age of consent, in Maine, Vermont, and Massachusetts;[4]
insanity or idiocy, in those same states and in Rhode Island;[5]
physical incapacity, fraud, or violence, in Vermont;[6] and
bigamy everywhere except in Connecticut where the statute
is silent.[7]   In Maine[8]—as formerly in Rhode Island[9]—a

---

mate: *Pub. Stat. of N. H.* (1891), 493; *Pub. Stat. of Mass.* (1882), 808, 809, 1166; *Gen. Laws of R. I.* (1896), 621, 1000; *Vermont Stat.* (1894), 500, 505; *Gen. Stat. of Conn.* (1902), 1085; *Rev. Stat. of Maine* (1884), 520, 903.

[1] In Rhode Island marriage or carnal connection between persons so related is punishable by imprisonment of from five to twenty years: *Gen. Laws* (1896), 1001; in Connecticut, by two to five years' imprisonment: *Gen. Stat.* (1887), 343; in New Hampshire, by a fine of not exceeding $500 or imprisonment not exceeding three years: *Pub. Stat.* (1891), 728; in Massachusetts, by confinement in state's prison not exceeding twenty years, or in jail not exceeding three years: *Pub. Stat.* (1882), 1166; in Maine, one to ten years' imprisonment: *Rev. Stat.* (1884), 903; in Vermont, confinement in state's prison not more than five years or a fine of not more than one thousand dollars or both: *Vermont Stat.* (1894), 902, 903.

[2] *Pub. Stat. Laws* (1808), 478, 479 n. 4. See chap. xii, sec. iv.

[3] For adultery the Massachusetts statute prescribed the gallows, whipping, and the scarlet badge; Act of Feb. 17, 1785; *Laws of the Com. of Mass.*, *1780-1816*, I, 217; and the gallows with fine, whipping, or imprisonment appears in the early New Hampshire laws: *Laws of the State* (1794), 294, 295, 285.

[4] So by implication in Maine: WRIGHT, *Report*, 39 n. *k*. Cf. *Vermont Stat.* (1894), 506 (voidable); *Pub. Stat. of Mass.* (1882), 809.

[5] *Rev. Stat. of Maine* (1884), 515; *Vermont Stat.* (1894), 506 (voidable); *Pub. Stat. of Mass.* (1882), 809; *Gen. Laws of R. I.* (1896), 621.

[6] *Vermont Stat.* (1894), 506, 507 (voidable).

[7] *Pub. Stat. of N. H.* (1891), 495; *ibid.* (1900), 590; *Gen. Laws of R. I.* (1896), 621; *Vermont Stat.* (1894), 505; *Rev. Stat. of Me.* (1884), 515; *Pub. Stat. of Mass.* (1882), 809.

[8] Such unions were void without process in Maine: *Rev. Stat.* (1847), 364; *ibid.* (1857), 396. They are so now by implication: WRIGHT, *Report*, 39 n. *k*.

[9] So in Rhode Island as late, at any rate, as 1844: *Pub. Laws* (1844), 268.

marriage between a white person and a negro, Indian, or mulatto is void without legal process. Until 1843 Massachusetts had a similar law; and its repeal at that time seems to have been preceded for several years by much popular interest and discussion. Petitions for and against the repeal, numerously signed, were presented to the legislature. These were referred to committees, and several formal reports thereon were made. One of them, earnestly favoring the abrogation of the existing law, alleges that the petitions considered were in the aggregate signed by 3,674 men and 5,032 women. On the other hand, a House report in 1839 strongly opposes the proposed change and treats the petition of many good women of Lynn, Brookfield, Dorchester, and Plymouth with unseemly levity and ridicule.[1] In Connecticut a marriage attempted to be solemnized by an unauthorized person, whether the parties act in good faith or not, is likewise void without decree.[2] Furthermore, in Maine, Vermont, and Massachusetts marriages are void when residents, "intending to return, go into another state and have their marriage solemnized with intent to evade the prohibition against incestuous or bigamous marriages, or against marriage with an insane person or idiot, and afterwards return and reside in the home state."[3]

It should also be observed that unions which in some states are void or voidable, in others may be merely prohibited or placed under penalty. The laws of New England in this regard, like those of the other commonwealths, are sometimes confusing and far from uniform in their provisions;

[1] There are copies of three of these reports in the library of Harvard University, one marked "Mass. General Court, No. 46;" a second marked "No. 7, 1841;" and a House report marked "No. 28, 1839." For the repeal, see *Acts and Resolves* (1843), 40; *Supp. to Rev. Stat., 1836–1853*, 248.

[2] *Gen. Stat.* (1887), 609. The question of good faith is not raised in the statute. *Cf. Gen. Stat.* (1902), 1086.

[3] WRIGHT, *Report*, 28. *Cf. Vermont Stat.* (1894), 516; *Rev. Stat. of Mass.* (1836), 476; *ibid.* (1882), 809; *Rev. Laws of Mass.* (1902), II, 1346; *Rev. Stat. of Maine* (1884), 516; *ibid.* (1857), 391.

and, as Wright suggests, marriages which by the language of
the statute appear to be simply forbidden or punishable may
nevertheless be construed as void or voidable by the courts.[1]
For when the statute is silent the common law may be in force.
Bigamous marriages are so prohibited and punished in Connecticut;[2] the marriage of a female, procured by force,
menace, or duress, in Maine;[3] and the clandestine marriage
of a girl under sixteen years of age, in Massachusetts.[4] A
recent act of Connecticut has set up a bar to matrimony
which would be welcomed by the social reformer in other
states. Hereafter a couple, either of whom is epileptic,
imbecile, or feeble-minded, is forbidden to marry, when the
woman is under forty-five years of age; and any selectman
or other person aiding in procuring such a union or the
marriage of a pauper, when the woman is below that age, is
liable to a fine of not less than one thousand dollars or to
imprisonment for not less than one year, or to both penalties,
as the court may decide.[5] The laws of Maine also put some
check upon the propagation of paupers, the town clerk being
forbidden to issue marriage licenses to such persons when
the overseers deposit in his office a list of the paupers in
their charge.[6] A statute somewhat similar exists in Vermont.[7] On the other hand, the New England states afford
no example of direct statutory encouragement of wedlock

---

[1] WRIGHT, *Report*, 35.

[2] *Gen. Stat.* (1887), 343; *ibid.* (1902), 375.   [3] *Rev. Stat. of Me.* (1884), 883.

[4] In case of abduction. This offense is punishable by imprisonment for a term
of not more than one year or a fine of not exceeding $1,000: *Pub. Stat.* (1882), 1165.
This law originated in 1852: see the act of May 20, 1852 (*Supp. to Rev. Stat.*, *1836–1853*,
852), whose penalties are, however, not the same. *Cf. Rev. Laws* (1902), II, 1785.

[5] *Pub. Acts of Conn.* (1895), 667. This precedent has been followed by Minnesota
and Kansas: see p. 480, below.

[6] Under a penalty of $20 for each offense: *Rev. Stat.* (1884), 516; *ibid.* (1870), 484;
Acts and Resolves (1858), chap. xiv, secs. 2, 3, p. 12.

[7] In the case of paupers a license may not be issued without the written consent
of the selectmen or overseer of the poor of each of the towns where the parties reside,
or which are liable for their support: *Vermont Stat.* (1894), 501.

such as exists in a few instances elsewhere in this country; though in all of them, except Rhode Island, indirect encouragement is given through providing that illegitimate children may be legitimized by the marriage of their parents.[1] Agreements in consideration of marriage are generally void unless made in writing.[2]

c) Certificate and record.—With respect to the notice of intention required by law before a marriage may be solemnized, the century may be divided into two very nearly equal periods.   During the first half in all of the New England states proclamation by oral banns in the ancient ecclesiastical manner, or a written notice through posting by the town clerk, is left to the option of the persons; while during the second half the simple license or certificate of the clerk is deemed sufficient.   In Connecticut the institution of banns according to the form observed in colonial times was very tenacious.   By the statute of 1784 intentions of marriage must either be "sufficiently published in some public Meeting, or Congregation on the Lord's Day, or on some public Fast, Thanksgiving, or Lecture Day in the Town, Parish, or Society where the Parties, or either of them do ordinarily Reside;" or else be "set up in fair Writing upon some Door, or Post of their Meeting-House, or near the same in public View, there to stand, so as it may be read," eight days before the wedding.[3]   This provision—arising in a modification of the act of 1640 made in 1672[4]—appears in the revision of 1750 and each following edition of the laws until 1854, when

---

[1] In Maine such children are legitimized by marriage; in Connecticut, Massachusetts, New Hampshire, and Vermont, by marriage and acknowledgment of father: WRIGHT, *Report*, 26, 27.   *Cf. Pub. Stat. of N. H.* (1891), 495; *Vermont Stat.* (1894), 485; *Gen. Stat. of Conn.* (1887), 157; *Rev. Stat. of Me.* (1884), 611; *Pub. Stat. of Mass.* (1882), 743.

[2] *Gen. Laws of R. I.* (1896), 805, 806; *Rev. Stat. of Me.* (1884), 838, 839; *Vermont Stat.* (1894), 269, 270; *Pub. Stat. of N. H.* (1891), 596; *Gen. Stat. of Conn.* (1887), 318, 319.

[3] *Acts and Laws of Conn.* (1784), 135, 136.

[4] *Pub. Stat. Laws* (1808), I, 477 n. 1.

it gave place to the modern usage.[1] The New Hampshire plan is somewhat different. In that state there is a sort of blending in one of the ecclesiastical and lay notices. By the act of 1791 publication is to be made by the clerk; but at three "several public meeting days, or three sabbath days," in the respective towns of the bride and groom.[2] This plan was retained until 1854.[3] On the other hand, the Massachusetts law of 1786 is typical in this regard. Intentions must be announced in three public religious meetings, at intervals of three days' distance exclusively, or they must be posted by the town clerk during fourteen days. Should the banns be forbidden and the reasons therefor assigned in writing, the clerk is to "forbear issuing a certificate" until the matter has been examined by two justices of the county, *quorum unus.* But the person forbidding the banns must cause the question to be determined within seven days, unless the justices certify to the clerk that more time is needed. If the objections to the marriage are not sustained, the complainant must pay the costs of the proceedings, and the clerk shall issue the license. For pulling down or defacing a marriage notice a penalty of twenty shillings or of one hour in the stocks is imposed.[4] This dual system of notice, with little change in the trial of banns, appears in the statute-book until 1850.[5] The experience of the other three states is very similar: optional publication in church or by

---

[1] *Acts and Laws* (1750), 144. *Cf.* also *Acts and Laws* (1786), 135 ff.; *ibid.* (1805), 285, 286; *Pub. Stat. Laws* (1821), 316; *ibid.* (1835), 369, 370; *ibid.* (1839), 412, 413; *Rev. Stat.* (1849), 272; *Statutes* (1854), 374–78 (repeal of old law and enactment of a new registration system).

[2] *Laws of N. H.* (1797), 296.

[3] See *Const. and Laws* (1805), 296, 297; *Laws of the State* (1815), 350, 351; *ibid.* (1830), 172–74; *Rev. Stat.* (1843), 290–92; *Compiled Stat.* (1853), 375, 376; *Laws of N. H.* (1854), 1415, 1416 (new system introduced).

[4] *Laws of the Com. of Mass., 1780–1816,* I, 322, 323.

[5] *Laws of the Com. of Mass.* (1834), 251–57; *Rev. Stat.* (1836), 476; *Supp. to Rev. Stat., 1836–1853,* I, 597; *Acts and Resolves* (1850), 347 (act of March 28, establishing the modern license system).

posting being retained until the middle of the century, or in some cases even to a much later time.[1]

The various formalities to be observed in getting married and in registering the facts connected therewith, as required by the existing system, may now be briefly set forth. The first step is application to the town clerk or registrar for a license, or "certificate" as it is usually called. This takes the place of the certificate of publication issued by the minister, clerk, or other person asking the banns or posting the notice, provided for in the earlier laws. By the Massachusetts statute persons intending to be joined in marriage shall "cause notice of their intention to be entered in the office of the clerk or registrar of the city or town in which they respectively dwell, or, if they do not dwell within the commonwealth," then with the similar officer of the place "in which they purpose to have the marriage solemnized. If there is no such clerk or registrar in the place of their residence, the entry shall be made in an adjoining city or town." The certificate is issued at the time the notice is filed; but certificate to a minor[2] is forbidden except upon the application or consent in writing of the parent, master, or

---

[1] It was retained in Vermont until 1864: *Gen. Stat.* (2d ed., 1870), 856. *Cf.* the acts of 1779 and 1784 in SLADE, *State Papers*, 292, 484; and *Laws of the State* (1798), 330, 331; and in Maine until *after* 1858: compare *Laws of the State* (1821), I, 340 ff.; *Rev. Stat.* (1857), 390; *Acts and Resolves* (1858), 12 (new system introduced). A reactionary step was taken in the Rhode Island law of Jan., 1849. Hitherto the optional plan had prevailed; by this act, in all cases, solemnization is allowed only after at least one notice in a religious meeting: see *Public Laws, 1848-1851*, 757. The *Pub. Laws* (1844), 267, show the optional plan in force; but it does not appear in *Rev Stat.* (1857), 312, 313, a certificate of qualification presented by the parties to the person conducting the ceremony taking its place.

The following is the form of notice required to be posted for fourteen days, when application is made to a lay officer — justice, warden, and later a judge — as given in the *Pub. Laws of R. I.* (1798), 481, 482:

"KNOW all men by these presents, that A. B. of —— and C. D. of —— have declared unto me their intentions of marriage. . . . . I do therefore hereby make public the said intentions. If any person know any just cause or impediment why these persons shall not be joined together in marriage, they may declare the same as the law directs. Given under my hand and seal, at ——, this — day of ——."

[2] For the special case of a male under eighteen and a female under sixteen, see above, subsec. *b*.

guardian, if living in the state, under penalty of not to exceed one hundred dollars. To protect himself, the clerk or registrar "may require of an applicant for such certificate an affidavit setting forth the age of the parties;" which "affidavit shall be sworn to before a justice of the peace, and shall be sufficient proof of age to authorize the issuing of the certificate." For a false statement in the affidavit the penalty is not to exceed two hundred dollars.[1] In this state a town of more than two thousand inhabitants is allowed to choose a person other than the clerk to be registrar.[2]

The laws of Vermont and Maine differ but little in the leading points from those of Massachusetts; but in Maine the notice of intention must be recorded with the town clerk where each person resides, if both live in the state, at least five days before the marriage.[3] More elaborate are the provisions of the Rhode Island, New Hampshire, and Connecticut statutes, requiring the clerk to enter on the certificate the various facts gathered as statistics, to which reference will again be made.[4] In all cases a penalty, severe under some recent enactments, is imposed upon the minister, justice, or other officer who presumes to celebrate a marriage without first receiving the certificate signed as the law requires.[5]

---

[1] *Pub. Stat. of Mass.* (1882), 810; *Rev. Laws* (1902), II, 1347, 1348, 1352.

[2] *Pub. Stat. of Mass.* (1882), 258.

[3] *Rev. Stat. of Me.* (1884), 515, 516; *Vermont Stat.* (1894), 501.

[4] *Pub. Stat. of R. I.* (1882), 416, 417; *Gen. Laws* (1896), 622, 623, where the elaborate forms of the declarations of the "expectants" are given in full; and the act of 1898, *Acts and Resolves*, 47 ff. *Cf. Gen. Stat. of Conn.* (1887), 24, 608, 609; *Pub. Stat. of N. H.* (1891), 493, 494; *Gen. Laws of N. H.* (1878), 428; *Gen. Stat. of N. H.* (1867), 331; *Laws of N. H.* (1903), 79, requiring non-residents to file notice five days before issue of certificate.

[5] In Connecticut the fine for such illegal celebration was for a long time just $67: *Acts and Laws* (1805), 286; *Rev. Stat.* (1849), 273; but it is now $100: *Gen. Stat.* (1902), 1086. In Massachusetts the fine is not to exceed $500: *Acts and Resolves* (1896), 257; earlier it was $50 to $100: *Pub. Stat.* (1882), 811; in Rhode Island the penalty is $1,000, or not to exceed six months' imprisonment: *Gen. Laws* (1896), 625; *Acts and Resolves of R. I.* (1899), 51; in Maine, $100, one-third to the prosecutor and two-thirds to the county: *Rev. Stat.* (1884), 517; in Vermont, not less than $10: *Vermont Stat.* (1894), 502; in New Hampshire it is $60, to the parent, master, or guardian of either party, who may prosecute: *Pub. Stat.* (1891), 494; *Gen. Laws* (1878), 428.

Provision is everywhere made for a "return" or report by the persons or religious societies solemnizing marriages.[1] In Connecticut, Vermont, and Rhode Island the return is made by indorsement upon the certificate, which is then sent to the clerk or registrar of the city or town whence it was issued or in which the celebration took place.[2] By the Connecticut law of 1899 the return must be made before or during the first week of the month following the ceremony.[3] In Maine and Massachusetts the societies or persons authorized to celebrate marriages are required to keep a record, and from it make periodical return to the clerk or registrar of the town in which the license was issued. By the Maine law the return must be made by the fifteenth day of each month, and a similar report sent to the clerk of the town where the intention was entered.[4] The Massachusetts statute orders that between the first and tenth days of each month the certificate of each marriage celebrated shall be sent to the clerk or registrar of the city or town issuing the same, and if the marriage be solemnized in a city or town other than the place or places in which the persons reside, then a copy of the certificate, or of either certificate in case two were issued, must be returned to the proper officers of their respective places.[5] The Massachusetts laws provide also

---

[1] By the early laws of Rhode Island, after the wedding, the person solemnizing gave to the parties a certificate in the following form: "I hereby certify that A. B. of ——, son of ——, and C. D. of ——, daughter of ——, were lawfully joined together in marriage on the —— day of —— by me the subscriber."—*Pub. Laws* (1798), 486. At present the "indorsement" is in similar form: *Gen. Laws* (1896), 624.

[2] In Connecticut and Vermont the indorsed certificate is sent to the officer of the town whence it issued; in Rhode Island, to the officer of the town where the marriage was solemnized: *Gen. Stat. of Conn.* (1887), 609; *Vermont Stat.* (1894), 501, 502; *Acts and Resolves of R. I.* (1899), 49, 50; *Gen. Laws of R. I.* (1896), 624. The form of indorsement prescribed in Rhode Island is as follows: "I hereby certify that the herein described —— and —— were joined in marriage by me, in accordance with the law of the state of Rhode Island, in the —— of —— this —— day of ——, A. D., 189-." —*Ibid.*, 624. Earlier in Connecticut a separate certificate of the solemnization was sent to the clerk: *Pub. Stat. Laws* (1821), 317.

[3] *Pub. Acts of Conn.* (1899), 998.

[4] *Rev. Stat. of Me.* (1887), 517: FREEMAN, *Supp. to Rev. Stat.*, 368, 369.

[5] Act of May 17, 1892: *Acts and Resolves* (1892), 250-52.

that when marriages take place in another state between persons living in the commonwealth, such persons shall within seven days after their return file with the clerk or registrar of the town in which either lived at the time a certificate or declaration of the marriage, including the facts relating thereto required by law.[1] A like return of marriages celebrated outside the state is prescribed in Maine[2] and New Hampshire.[3] In Vermont a "male resident" so married must within sixty days thereafter deposit with the clerk of the town where he resides a certificate embracing the statistics required by law.[4] The statutes of Vermont also provide that the head of a family who moves into the state to become a permanent resident may cause a certificate of his marriage, including the same statistics, to be recorded in like manner.[5]

In recent years most of the New England states have made wiser provision than in the earlier period for the collection and preservation of statistics relating to marriage. The town clerk or registrar is required to keep a more complete record. The statutes prescribe a large number of details which must be entered by him, sometimes even as a condition of granting the license. An illustration is afforded by the Massachusetts act of 1897. Clerks are commanded in each case to enter and report the date of the record; the date and place of the marriage; the name, residence, and official station of the person solemnizing; the name, place of birth, residence, age, and color of each of the parties; the number of the marriage, and whether either party is widowed or divorced; the occupation of each; the names of the parents, with the maiden names of the mothers; and the maiden

---

[1] *Pub. Stat. of Mass.* (1882), 811.

[2] *Rev. Stat. of Me.* (1884), 516. But in Maine the certificate or declaration must be filed in the towns where the parties " respectively " dwell.

[3] *Pub. Stat. of N. H.* (1891), 494; *ibid.* (1900), 589; *Gen. Laws* (1878), 428.

[4] *Vermont Stat.* (1894), 540.   [5] *Ibid.*

name of the bride in case she be widowed or divorced.[1]   A similar list of facts is called for in New Hampshire;[2] while the recent enactments of Maine,[3] Connecticut,[4] and Rhode Island[5] on this subject are especially painstaking and elaborate.

Finally it may be noted, as a sign of the growing appreciation of the needs of social and statistical science, that throughout New England statutory provision has been made for state registration of marriages. The local clerks and registrars are required to make annual report of the facts collected and recorded by them to the general registrar, who is usually the secretary of the commonwealth or the secretary of the state board of health.[6] By the Rhode Island statutes the original indorsed certificates, returned to the town clerk and by him recorded, are to be sent to the secretary of the state board of health, who is to cause abstracts of them to be made and published. Thereafter they are to be deposited in the office of the secretary of state, where they shall be properly indexed and remain subject to inspection.[7] Connecticut is doing still better in this regard. By

[1] Acts and Resolves of Mass. (1897), 420, 421. For the earlier law as to the clerk's record see Pub. Stat. (1882), 256. In 1786 the town clerk is to report to the clerk of the general sessions of the peace in each county, who is to keep a record: Laws of the Com., 1780-1816, I, 323.

[2] Pub. Stat. of N. H. (1900), 588. Cf. Gen. Laws (1878), 428; Gen. Stat. (1867), 331; and the act of 1851, Laws of N. H. (1851), chap. 1103; Comp. Stat. (1853), 284, 285, which seem to have first introduced something like a modern provision for record.

[3] FREEMAN, Supp. to Rev. Stat., 1885-1895, 370-75; Laws (1891), chap. 118, 127, as amended by Laws (1893), chap. 233, 248, and Laws (1895), chap. 154, 169-73.

[4] Act of May 6, 1897: Pub. Acts, 850. Cf. for the earlier law Gen. Stat. (1887), 608.

[5] Gen. Laws of R. I. (1896), 331, 622, 623; superseded by act of May 6, 1898: Acts and Resolves, 47 ff.

[6] In Massachusetts report is made to the secretary of the commonwealth: Pub. Stat. (1882), 255-58; Acts and Resolves (1897), 421-29; in New Hampshire and Maine, to the state registrar of vital statistics, being the secretary of the state board of health: Pub. Stat. of N. H. (1891), 490-92; Laws (1899), 255, 256; FREEMAN, Supp. to Rev. Stat. of Me., 1885-1895, 370; in Connecticut, to the superintendent of registration of vital statistics, who is the secretary of the state board of health: Gen. Stat. (1887), 20 ff., 566; cf. Public Acts (1897), 850.

[7] Gen. Laws (1896), 624. See the act of 1899, Acts and Resolves, 19, providing for the registration of births, deaths, and marriages, knowledge of which may in any reliable way come to the recorder.

a series of acts, beginning in 1893, that state is making a
praiseworthy effort to complete her marriage records from
the date of the first incorporation of the various towns to
the present time;[1] and Maine has provided for the collection
and publication of the records of births, deaths, and marriages.[2] Vermont by an act of 1898 requires the secretary of the state board of health to prepare and furnish the
town and city clerks blank forms to be used as books of
records of "births, marriages, divorces, and deaths." Return
is to be made by the local officers, from which every second
year the secretary of the state board of health is to publish
a report.[3]

II.   THE SOUTHERN AND SOUTHWESTERN STATES[4]

Throughout this period in the South matrimonial legislation has moved more slowly than in New England and the
West, but toward the same goal. Sentiment has been more
conservative regarding innovation; and in general equal
progress has not been made in remodeling and improving
the details of administration or the safeguards of marriage
law. Originally, as elsewhere shown,[5] the English ecclesiastical forms were established in Virginia and nominally, in
a varying degree, in the neighboring colonies. Dissenters
were illiberally, often tyrannically, treated; and to satisfy
their consciences in this regard they were compelled to take
the law into their own hands. Still, at the Revolution, it

[1] By an act of 1893 the registrars of births, deaths, and marriages are directed,
so far as possible, to complete the records from Jan. 1, 1850: *Pub. Acts* (1893), 324.
This act has since been twice supplemented: *ibid.* (1895), 552; *ibid.* (1897), 836.

[2] *Acts and Resolves of Me.* (1903), 168.

[3] Act of Nov. 30, 1898: *Acts and Resolves of Vt.* (1898), 41–46, repealing the act of
1896 and all other acts in conflict. *Cf.* also *Vermont Stat.* (1894), 538–40.

[4] In this section the laws of marriage are traced for the following twenty-one
districts and commonwealths: the states of Alabama, Arkansas, Florida, Georgia,
Kentucky, Louisiana, Maryland, Mississippi, Missouri, North Carolina, South Carolina, Tennessee, Texas, Virginia, and West Virginia; Indian Territory, the territories
of Arizona, New Mexico, Oklahoma, Porto Rico, and the District of Columbia.

[5] See chap. xiii.

was apparent that the American type of matrimonial legislation, as in its essential features already existing in New England, must eventually triumph in the South.

a) Solemnization.—Old ideas were especially tenacious in Virginia. For the first time, in 1780, as already suggested,[1] the monopoly of the Anglican clergy was restricted through legislation. By the statute of that year, for the purpose of "encouraging marriages" and "removing doubts concerning the validity" of those heretofore celebrated by dissenting clergymen, not only are all such marriages declared "good and valid in law," but for the future ministers of "any society or congregation of Christians," as well as the Quakers and Menonists, are permitted to conduct the celebration according to their own rules and usages. License and banns are dispensed with in the case of Menonists and Quakers,[2] but the act limits the number of dissenting ministers who may take advantage of its provisions. On recommendation of the "elders of the several religious sects," the court of each county is authorized to license not more than four ministers of each dissenting society to solemnize marriages; and the licenses are to be "signed by the judge or elder magistrate under his hand and seal."[3] Four years later a new marriage act appears, by which the ordained ministers of all societies of Christians are placed on the same level. The provision for licensing a limited number is not retained. Any minister may celebrate marriages of "any persons" within the state, provided he first produce to the court of the county or borough in which he resides credentials of his ordination, and also of his being in regular communion with the society of which he is reputed a member, take the oath of allegiance to the commonwealth,

[1] See chap. xiii, sec. i.

[2] HENING, *Statutes*, X, 361-63; *cf.* JEFFERSON, *Notes on the State of Va.* (Brooklyn, 1794), 174.

[3] HENING, *op. cit.*, X, 363.

and enter into bond, with two or more sufficient securities, in the sum of five hundred pounds current money for the true and legal performance of his trust. A "testimonial" is then issued to him by the court.[1] "Itinerant" ministers, however, are not entitled to a testimonial. If any minister shall voluntarily decline, or be ejected from, his office, or "if any of his securities shall give him notice in writing that they desire to be released from their suretyship, in either of these cases," should he refuse or neglect "to give up his testimonials to the court from which they were obtained, any one of his securities, without instituting a suit, may proceed against him as if they were his special bail in an action of debt until he is thereunto compelled or gives them sufficient caution for their indemnification."[2] By this act also irregular marriages already contracted are made valid. Its provisions regarding solemnization are retained in the elaborate statute of 1792.[3]

Thus far the religious ceremony only had been acknowledged by law. A step toward civil marriage was taken in 1783. It is recited that, since "it hath been represented . . . . that many of the good people in the remote parts of this commonwealth are destitute of any persons, authorized by law, to solemnize marriages," therefore when it shall seem necessary, in the scarcity of clergymen, the court of any county "on the western waters" is empowered "to nominate so many sober and discreet laymen as will supply the deficiency." It is noticeable that such layman, "upon taking the oath of allegiance" to the state, is to receive a license to celebrate the rites of matrimony "according to

[1] The testimonial runs as follows: "This shall certify to all whom it may concern, that at a court held for ——, on the —— day of ——, one thousand seven hundred and ——, A. B. produced credentials of his ordination, and also of his being in regular communion with the —— church, took the oath of allegiance to the commonwealth, and entered into bond, as required . . . . , and that he is hereby authorized to celebrate the rites of matrimony," etc.—HENING, op. cit., XI, 503 (act of Oct., 1784).

[2] Ibid., 504.   [3] Act of Dec. 22, 1792: Acts of the Gen. Assembly (1794), 202–6.

the forms and customs of the church of which he is reputed
a member." It appears from this statute that magistrates
in such places had already been in the habit of celebrating
marriages; and these marriages are now legalized.[1] In
consequence of the scarcity of ministers, persons desiring
to be married were sometimes compelled to travel long dis-
tances across the mountains, exposed to danger from the
Indians. Hence in 1794 the courts of Lee and Randolph
counties were authorized to nominate two resident laymen
in each to perform the ceremony within the county where
they respectively resided. These commissioners[2] were to
take an oath of fidelity to the commonwealth; and each was
to "enter into bond for sufficient security in the sum of
fifteen hundred dollars" for the "true and faithful performance of his trust." This act differs from that of 1783 in
being silent as to the use of the religious ceremony; and so
marks a step in advance toward full civil marriage.[3]

The foundation of the law of Virginia regarding the marriage celebration, both civil and religious, as it still exists, was
thus laid more than a hundred years ago. A few changes,
most of them of minor importance, have been made in later
years. From time to time, by special law, the benefits of
the act of 1794 were extended to other counties;[4] and in
1830 this plan was adopted for the whole state. The court
of every county which should suffer "inconvenience" through
lack of ministers was then authorized to name one or two
persons to solemnize matrimony, on condition of giving
satisfactory bond, as required by earlier statutes.[5] As the

[1] Hening, *op. cit.*, XI, 281, 282. By the act of 1792, also, marriages celebrated by
magistrates before 1785 were legalized: *Acts of the Gen. Assem.*, 203.

[2] They are called "commissioners" in the act of 1830: *Acts* (1830-31), 103.

[3] *Acts of the Gen. Assem. of Va.* (1794), 331.

[4] So to Ohio and Brooke counties in 1796: *Acts of the Gen. Assem.* (1803), 371;
and to Bath county in 1830: *Acts* (1830-31), 103.

[5] Act of Dec. 20, 1830: *Acts* (1830-31), 103. Compare *Revised Code* (1819), I, 393-403;
and Tate, *Digest* (1823), 417, where the provisions of 1794 and 1792 as to lay commissioners and bond are retained and made general.

law now stands, "the court of every county which deems it expedient, may appoint one or more persons resident in such county to celebrate the rites of marriage within the same, or a particular district thereof, and upon any person so appointed giving such a bond as is required of an ordained minister, may make a like order" empowering him to act. But the court may rescind this order at pleasure.[1] It appears, therefore, contrary to the usual custom, that in Virginia the justice of the peace as such has no authority to perform the marriage ceremony. Regarding the religious celebration, the law remains very nearly as it was in 1784, except in one or two important provisions. At least since 1819 Jews have enjoyed the right of using their own marriage rites;[2] while already in 1812 ordained ministers in regular standing with any society of Christians, residing in any adjacent state, were authorized to solemnize wedlock in Virginia on filing credentials and giving bond in the court of the county where the marriage takes place, the oath of allegiance not being required.[3] The law was further liberalized in 1831. Any ordained minister in regular communion, as before, "who by the government and discipline of the church of which he is a member, has been assigned to a circuit, station, or district for the period of one year at the least," is allowed, on the same conditions as other ministers, to obtain a "testimonial" from any county or corporation court within such area authorizing him to perform the marriage rites.[4] With these changes the law of Virginia is complete, except that it is couched in more general phrase. "When a minister of any religious denomination shall, before the

---

[1] *Code of Va.* (1887), 555. *Cf. Code of Va.* (2d ed., 1860), 524, where this provision appears in the same terms.

[2] Laws of 1784 and 1792 as amended at the revision of 1819: *Revised Code* (1819), I, 396; TATE, *Digest*, 416.

[3] Act of Feb. 13, 1812, chap. 25: TATE, *Digest*, 416.

[4] Act of Feb. 16, 1831: *Acts* (1830-31), 102; also in *Supplement to Revised Code* (1833), 221.

court of any county or corporation in this state, produce
proof of his ordination, and of his being in regular communion with the religious society of which he is reputed a
member, and give bond in the penalty of five hundred
dollars, such court may make an order authorizing him to
celebrate the rites of marriage." No ceremony is prescribed;
but each religious body, though having no minister, may
use its own forms.[1]

West Virginia, made a separate state in 1863 by dismem-
berment of the Old Dominion, has taken a much more conservative course. In 1868 "any minister of the gospel," on
presenting the credentials of his ordination and of being in
regular communion, according to the plan of the mother-
commonwealth, is authorized to "celebrate the rites of marriage in all the counties of the state;" and no person other
than a minister who has thus "complied" with the law shall
hereafter be permitted to perform the ceremony.[2] No provision whatever is made for the lay celebration. This reactionary policy was, however, temporarily abandoned in 1873.
By a statute of that year the minister, otherwise to be qualified as under the act of 1868, is required in addition to give
bond in the sum of fifteen hundred dollars; and each county
court, as in Virginia, is authorized to appoint one or more
laymen with power to solemnize wedlock.[3] For four years
the lawmaker staid his hand; but in 1877 the illiberal principle of the act of 1868 was again enforced.[4] So to the
present hour only the religious celebration, either by a
clergyman or by the usages of a society having no officiating
minister, is legal in West Virginia. The lay ceremony is
not recognized there by statute.[5]

[1] *Code of Va.* (1878), 555.   [2] *Acts of the Legislature of W. Va.* (1868), 29.

[3] *Ibid.* (1872–73), 501.   [4] *Acts of the Legislature of W. Va.* (1877), 135.

[5] See the act of March 18, 1882: *Acts of the Leg.* (1882), 312, 313; which is retained
in *Code of W. Va.* (1897), 654, 655; and there has been no later legislation.

It is less surprising that Kentucky, whose territory until the admission of the state to the Union in 1792 was embraced in the jurisdiction of Virginia, should have retained the matrimonial law of the parent commonwealth. As regards solemnization, the act of 1798 in its substance is almost identical with the statutes of Virginia before that of 1794 appeared. It contains like provisions with respect to bond, credentials, testimonial, and oath of allegiance on the part of the minister; and Quakers, Menonists, and all societies of Christians are allowed to use their own rites.[1] In the next year the county courts of the state are authorized each to license one or more of their own magistrates to solemnize marriages, "where there shall not be a sufficient number of ministers of the gospel" for the purpose.[2] By the present law, which in all essential respects is identical with the act of 1851, marriages may be celebrated either by ministers of the gospel or priests of any denomination, in regular communion with a religious society; by judges of the county courts, and such justices of the peace as the county courts may authorize; or according to the usage of any religious society to which either person may belong.[3]

In Maryland no progress has been made regarding the marriage celebration since the Revolution. Ministers and priests still have a monopoly of the matrimonial business, as under the illiberal act of 1777, whose provisions have already been summarized.[4] Quakers are still allowed their own rites; but, as in West Virginia, the lay celebration is not

[1] Act of Feb. 3, 1798: *Stat. Law of Ky.* (ed. LITTELL), II, 65, 66. Provision was made in 1814 for revoking the testimonial whenever a minister shall be "suspended, deposed, or excommunicated, by and from the society to which he belongs, for any other cause than a difference in religious tenets."—*Ibid.*, V, 95, 96.

[2] Act of Dec. 12, 1799: *Stat. Law of Ky.*, II, 275, 276.

[3] *Kentucky Stat.* (1894), 764, 765; agreeing in essential provisions with the act of March 24, 1851, taking effect July 11, 852: in *Acts* (1850-51), 212-16. *Cf. Kentucky Stat.* (1899), 823.

[4] See chap. xiii, sec. ii, above.

authorized by the statute.[1] Until 1896, with slight modification, the marriage law of Maryland was in force in the District of Columbia. By a statute of that year the ceremony may be performed in the District by any justice of the peace; any judge of a court of record; or by any ordained or appointed minister residing anywhere in the United States, if authorized by a justice of the Supreme Court.[2]

Elsewhere the history of the matrimonial legislation of North Carolina has been traced to the act of 1766, the last statute adopted before the Revolution. The Quakers had practiced their own rites throughout the colonial era. By the act just mentioned the Presbyterians had been granted the same privilege, but on humiliating terms. With these exceptions, the clergy of the English church enjoyed a monopoly of the marriage celebration; for no other dissenting body save the Presbyterians was recognized by the law. All this was changed in 1778, after the establishment had been swept away. The "regular ministers of every denomination, having the cure of souls," and all justices of the peace in the state, are authorized to solemnize marriages; while the Quakers are to enjoy their ancient privileges.[3] So the law remains at the present time.[4]

Throughout the century the statutes of Tennessee governing the celebration of wedlock have been practically the same as those of North Carolina, the parent commonwealth, to whose jurisdiction the territory belonged until 1796.[5] At present "all regular ministers of the gospel of every denomination, and Jewish rabbis, having the cure of souls, and all

[1] POE, *Code of Md.* (1888), 975. Compare KILTY, *Laws*, 1777, chap. 12, sec. 3; and *Laws of Md.* (1787), 1777, chap. 12, sec. iii.

[2] Act of May 13: *U. S. Stat. at Large*, XXIX, 118-20; MOORE, *Code* (1902), 266.

[3] IREDELL-MARTIN, *Acts of the Gen. Assem., 1715–1803*, I, 253.

[4] *North Carolina Code*, I, 689, retaining the act in *Laws* (1871–72), chap. 193, sec. 3.

[5] For the early years see SCOTT, *Laws of the State of Tenn.* (1821), Index at "marriage;" *Statute Laws* (1831), 219, 220; CARUTHERS AND NICHOLSON, *Compilation* (1836), 449-52.

justices of the peace, judges, and chancellors in the state," as well as the governor and the speakers of the senate and house, are authorized to celebrate marriages.[1] No special ceremony is prescribed.

During the period under review South Carolina, like Pennsylvania, has made no legislative provision for the marriage celebration. The same usage prevails since the Revolution as before, except that in the colonial period usage prevailed in spite of the statutes. What Brevard said in 1814 is still true. "It is customary in this state," he declares, "to celebrate or publish the matrimonial contract, by or before a minister of the gospel—of any sect, and without regard to any *particular* form or ceremony—or by or before a justice of the peace, or other lawful civil magistrate."[2]

The optional civil or religious celebration before a minister or justice, existing by custom in Georgia from the foundation of the colony, was recognized by the act of 1785—the first legislation on the subject of matrimony after the organization of the state.[3] A few changes in details have brought the law into harmony with the prevailing practice of the country.[4] At present marriages may be solemnized by any judge, justice of the peace, minister of the

---

[1] *Code of Tenn.* (1884), 609. The judges were empowered by *Acts* (1846), chap. 145, pp. 220, 221; chancellors in 1842: *Statute Laws* (1846), 126; rabbis by *Acts* (1879) chap. 98; and the governor and speakers by *Acts* (1889), chap. 134, p. 272.

[2] Editorial note, BREVARD, *Alphabetical Digest* (1814), II, 438. *Cf.* on this point the remarks of EDITOR DESAUSSURE, in connection with the case of Vaigneur *et al., v.* Kirk (1808), in 2 *S. C. Equity Reports*, 644–46.

"In South Carolina the only reference to the parties by whom marriages may be solemnized is found in section 2034, General Statutes, 1882, which provides a penalty for the solemnization of marriage between white and colored persons by 'any clergyman, minister of the gospel, magistrate, or other person authorized by law to perform the marriage ceremony.'"—WRIGHT, *Report*, 50, 51.

[3] *Digest of the Laws of Georgia* (Philadelphia, 1801), 314. Contracts previously celebrated before any justice of the peace, minister, or preacher of the gospel are confirmed: and the same persons, if properly qualified or ordained, are in future authorized to perform the ceremony, in each case after due notice or license.

[4] Judges and justices of inferior courts are mentioned as having power to join persons in marriage in the act of 1799: *Digest of the Laws of Ga.*, 733.

gospel, Jewish minister, "or other person of any religious
society or sect" authorized by its rules to perform the ceremony.[1] By a unique provision "colored ministers of the
gospel, or ministers of the gospel of African descent," are
allowed to celebrate marriages "between freedmen and freed-
women, or persons of African descent, only."[2]

In all the other states and territories of the South and
Southwest the optional religious or civil celebration before a minister or judicial officer has been sanctioned by
statute from the beginning. Such is the case in Florida,
Arkansas, Indian Territory, Arizona, New Mexico, and Oklahoma; as also in Alabama, Mississippi,[3] and Missouri, where
in each case the typical optional plan was adopted under the
territorial legislation of 1805.[4]

[1] *Code of Ga.* (1882), 392, 393; *ibid.* (1896), 11, 223, 224.

[2] *Acts* (1866), 156, 157; *Code of Ga.* (1896), II, 5.

[3] An act of Feb. 19, 1836, validates marriages illegally solemnized by members of
the board of county police: *Code of Miss.* (1848), 496.

[4] In these states and territories marriage may be celebrated as follows:

(1) Florida: By "all ordained ministers of the gospel in communion with some
church, all judicial officers and notaries public": *Rev. Stat. of Florida* (1892), 679
(act of Feb. 8, 1861). For the earlier law see act of Nov. 2, 1829, in THOMPSON,
Manual or Digest (1847), 219; DUVAL, 88.

(2) Arkansas: By the governor of the state for the time being; any judge of the
courts of record; any justice of the peace of the county where the marriage is solemnized; any regularly ordained minister or priest of any religious sect or denomination, when he shall have caused to be recorded in the office of clerk and recorder
of some county in the state the license or credentials of his clerical character, and
shall have obtained from such clerk a certificate of the record thereof; religious
societies which reject formal ceremonies, to which the parties belong, using their
own rites: *Digest* (1894), 1126, 1127, being the same law as in *Rev. Stat.* (1838), 536–38.

(3) Arizona: By a regularly licensed or ordained minister of the gospel; any
judge of the courts of record; justices of the peace of the several counties: *Rev.
Stat.* (1887), 371; *ibid.* (1901), 808, 809.

(4) New Mexico: By any ordained clergyman, without regard to the sect to
which he may belong; any civil magistrate; any religious society by its own rites:
Compiled Laws (1897), 405, 406; see act of Feb. 2, 1860: *Laws* (1860), 120, or in *Rev.
Stat.* (1865), 534.

(5) Alabama: By any licensed minister of the gospel in regular communion with
the Christian church or society of which he is a member; pastor of any religious society, according to the rules ordained or customs established thereby; Quakers,
Menonists, and other Christian societies, according to their forms of consent published and declared before the congregation; all judges of supreme, circuit, or city
courts, or a chancelor, throughout the state; any judge of probate or justice of the
peace within his county: *Code of Alabama* (1897), I, 828. For the law of Jan. 5,

The laws of Louisiana have always shown ample evidence of their Latin origin. This is especially true of those governing marriage, divorce, and the family; except that the celebration was determined by statute, and was therefore soon brought into harmony with the practice prevailing in the southwestern states, the contemporary Virginia plan being at first adopted as a model. The vast region bearing the name of Louisiana was acquired from France in 1803.

1805, enacted by the "Legislative Council and House of Representatives of Mississippi Territory," see TOULMIN'S *Digest* (1823), 576, 577; or *Stat. of Miss. Territory* (1816), 328–30.

(6) Mississippi: By any minister of the gospel ordained according to the rules of his church or society, in good standing; judges of the supreme or circuit court; justices of the peace within their respective counties; members of the boards of supervisors within their respective counties; Quakers, Menonists, or any other Christian society, to which the parties belong, according to their own customs: *Annotated Code* (1892), 678. Compare the laws of Jan. 5 and July 20, 1805, revised and amended Feb. 10, 1807, in *Stat. of Miss. Territory* (1816), 328–30, already cited for Alabama, which was originally a part of the Mississippi Territory; also the act of June 29, 1822, in *Code of Miss.* (1848), 492, 493, being practically the same as the law of 1805 as modified by that of 1807.

(7) Missouri: By any judge of a court of record; any justice of the peace; or any licensed or ordained preacher of the gospel who is a citizen of the United States: act of March 1, 1897: *Laws*, 116; also in *Rev. Stat.* (1899), I, 1036. The statute of April 24, 1805, enacted by the "Governor and Judges of the Indiana Territory"—who were authorized and empowered by an act of Congress to make laws for the "District of Louisiana," of which Missouri was a part—allows judges of the general court, or of the county court of common pleas, in their respective jurisdictions, and ministers of any religious society or congregation within the districts in which they are settled, and Quakers in their public meetings to solemnize marriages: *Laws of a Pub. and Gen. Nature* (1842), I, 66. Compare the act of Feb. 20, 1835, in *Rev. Stat.* (1835), 401, 402; and *Rev. Stat.* (1845), 729–31.

(8) Indian Territory: By act of Congress, May 2, 1890, *U. S. Stat. at Large*, XXVI, 81, the marriage laws of Arkansas, except as expressly modified, are put in force. Thus, by federal enactment, marriages entered into by Indian customs are valid; and, in addition to the persons authorized in Arkansas, they may be solemnized by clerks, deputy clerks, and commissioners of the United States courts, *Annot. Stat. of Ind. Ter.* (1899), 12, 13, 507 ff.

(9) Oklahoma: By a justice of the supreme court, judge of the district or probate court, justice of the peace, a duly ordained, licensed, or authorized preacher or minister of the gospel or priest of any denomination; and previous to 1897, in case of Indians, by the peacemakers, their agents, or the superintendent of Indian affairs. Non-compliance with the statute does not invalidate a marriage: *Stat. of Oklahoma* (1893), 669; act of Feb. 26: *Session Laws* (1897), 210. By another act of 1897 Indian marriages hitherto celebrated by their own rites are validated, and for the future forbidden, the Indians having accepted land in severalty being subjected to the statute: *ibid.*, 212–15.

(10) Porto Rico: By any judge, or by any clergyman or minister of any religion or sect, whether a citizen of the Island or of the United States: *Rev. Stat. and Codes* (1902), 808, 811.

For the purpose of government it was presently divided into two parts, lying respectively north and south of the thirty-third parallel. The northern portion, called the "District of Louisiana," for law and administration was attached to Indiana Territory, while the southern portion, called the "Territory of Orleans"—having about fifty thousand inhabitants, French, Spanish, and English—in 1804 was provided with a separate government in which the lawmaking power was vested in a legislative council appointed by the president of the United States. In the next year this council was superseded by a representative assembly similar to that existing in the Mississippi Territory;[1] and at the same time the northern region, under the new name of the Territory of Louisiana, was given a centralized government in which the legislative authority was in the hands of the governor and three judges holding by presidential appointment.[2] A *Digest of the Civil Laws now in force in the Territory of Orleans* was later prepared. This contains minute provisions relating to marriage and divorce; but declares that, "besides the preceding general rules, there are divers formalities to be fulfilled for the publication and celebration of marriages, which are established by a special act of the legislature."[3] But "such marriages only are recognized by law as are contracted and solemnized according to the rules which *it* prescribes."[4]

On February 24, 1807, all contracts hitherto solemnized

---

[1] Compare the acts of March 26, 1804, and March 2, 1805: *U. S. Stat. at Large*, II, 283–89, 322, 323; also in POORE, *Charters*, I, 691–97.

[2] Act of March 3, 1805: *U. S. Stat. at Large*, II, 331, 332; also in POORE, *Charters*, I, 697, 698. This act places the appointment of the governor in the hands of the president; but the judges are merely to be "appointed" and hold their office for four years.

On the institution of government in the territory of Orleans see ADAMS, *U. S.*, II, chap. ii.

[3] *Digest of Civil Laws now in force in the Territory of Orleans* (1808), 26.

[4] *Ibid.*, 24.

by the judge of any county, a justice of the peace, minister of the gospel, or by any person legally discharging the duties of commandant, are validated so far as relates to the ceremony and the authority of the person officiating, provided they are in other respects according to law.[1] On April 6 of the same year appears a very elaborate statute—the "special act of the legislature" above mentioned—which in many of its provisions still constitutes the matrimonial law of Louisiana.[2] By this act "any priest or minister of the gospel, regularly ordained or admitted into any religious society, may obtain a licence to celebrate marriages within this territory." For this purpose he must produce the usual credentials "to the judge of the parish within which his domicile is situated, take the oath of allegiance, and the oath of affirmation to support the constitution of the United States, and give bond with security in the sum of two thousand dollars, for the faithful performance of his trust." Quakers and Menonists are allowed the use of their own rites; and "when any parish judge shall think that there is not a sufficient number" of qualified priests or ministers, he may grant licenses to justices of the peace to "celebrate marriages in the parish in which they reside," on their giving a legal bond. All marriages must be celebrated in the parish where one of the persons has his domicile and in the presence of three witnesses.[3]

The provisions of the act of 1807 requiring clergymen to procure license and give bond were repealed two years

---

[1] LISLET, *General Digest* (1828), II, 3.

[2] It is contained in LISLET, *op. cit.*, II, 3-13; also (in part) in the *Digest of the Civil Laws now in force in the Territory of Orleans*, 24 ff.; with the changes to date of publication in *Code civil de l'état de la Louisiane* (1825), 80 ff.; in the reprint of the last-named compilation in *Civil Code of La.* (1853). Compare the provisions of the present law in VOORHIES AND SAUNDERS, *Revised Civil Code* (1888), 60-68. See also *The Laws of Las Siete Partidas, which are still in force in the State of Louisiana*, translated from the Spanish (1820), I, 451-64.

[3] LISLET, *op. cit.*, II, 7-9, 10.

later.[1] In 1820 marriages irregularly celebrated by the parish justices were validated; and these magistrates were in future given power to act.[2] The law regarding the religious ceremony was made more flexible in 1826. "If there be no priest or minister of a religious sect domiciled in any one of the parishes of this state," it was then enacted, "the judge of that parish, if required by either of the parties, is authorized to send to any priest or minister residing in a neighboring parish a commission to come and celebrate marriages in the parish" where the judge has his jurisdiction.[3] "Regularly commissioned notaries of the state" for the parish of West Feliciana were authorized to act in 1850.[4] As the law now stands, the ceremony may be performed by these notaries; by justices of the peace and parish judges, within their respective parishes; by judges of the district courts; and by any minister or priest, "whether a citizen of the United States or not."[5]

The first matrimonial legislation of Texas coincides with the earliest experiment in organized rule by settlers from the United States in that Mexican province. By an ordinance of January 16, 1836, adopted by the provisional government, all "judges, alcades, commissarios, and regularly accredited ministers of the gospel of whatever denomination," are given "power to celebrate the rites of matrimony in their respective municipalities, which shall be done in the presence of not less than three disinterested witnesses." Certificates are to be made by the person officiating, attested by one or more witnesses, one of which is to be "given to the bride, and the other filed with the archives of the municipality." Marriages hitherto "celebrated by bond or

---

[1] Act of March 17, 1809: LISLET, *op. cit.*, II, 13.

[2] LISLET, *op. cit.*, II, 14.   [3] *Civil Code* (1853), 15.   [4] *Ibid.*

[5] *Revised Code* (1888), 62, 63. For the clause regarding citizenship see *Acts* (1855), 128. The present powers of justices and parish judges are determined by *Acts* (1864), 50. For the power of district judges see WRIGHT, *Report*, 53.

otherwise, under the heretofore existing laws," are declared valid; "provided that all officers who have attended to the same, shall on application of either party, or the friend of either party, file the bond or other evidence of such marriages with the archives and records of their respective municipalities." This must be done in ten days after the application, under penalty of one hundred dollars to the injured person, and the same fine from time to time every ten days till the papers are filed.[1]

The "Republic of Texas" was soon after set up by the settlers; and one of its first legislative measures was a general marriage law. "Whereas," runs this noteworthy act, which reveals the embarrassments of American pioneer life, "in many parts of Texas no person legally authorized to celebrate the rites of matrimony has existed; and whereas, from that cause many persons have resorted to the practice of marrying by bond, and others have been married by various officers of justice not authorized" to do so; "and whereas, public policy and the interests of families require some legislative action on the subject:" therefore it is enacted that "all persons who have so intermarried" are authorized to go before any of the persons provided for in this act, "and publicly solemnize the rites of matrimony; and all marriages so solemnized are . . . . declared of legal and binding effect, from the period the persons had previously intermarried agreeably to the custom of the times," and their issue is made legitimate. But the benefits of the act are conditioned on there being no legal bar to the marriage, and on celebration within six months from its passage.[2] For the future, all ordained ministers, judges of the

---

[1] *Ordinances and Decrees of the Consultation, Provisional Government of Texas, and the Convention Which Assembled at Washington March 1, 1836* (1838), 137, 138; also in DALLAM, *Digest of the Laws of Texas* (1845), 167.

[2] Act of June 5, 1837: *Laws of the Republic of Texas* (1838), 233.

"When persons have intermarried as aforesaid agreeably to the customs of the country and either the husband or wife has died previous to the passage of this law,"

district courts, justices of the county courts, and all justices of the peace of the several counties of the republic may perform the marriage ceremony.[1] The present law of the state is identical with the statute of the republic just cited, except that Jewish rabbis are also expressly empowered to join persons in wedlock.[2]

In only three instances, among the twenty-one commonwealths and territories under discussion, are witnesses required by statute at the celebration; although in Maryland, in the case of Quaker weddings, the contracting parties are to sign a "certificate to the effect that they have agreed to take each other for husband and wife," which certificate must be attested by twelve persons present, and within sixty days entered in the records of the society to which one of them belongs, or else in some court in the county or city where the marriage takes place.[3] But in Louisiana, by the act of 1807, all contracts are to be solemnized "in the presence of at least three witnesses, each of whom shall have attained the age of majority;"[4] and this provision is still retained in the law.[5] At least two adult competent witnesses are required in Oklahoma; and the same number in Porto Rico.[6]

Nowhere is any form of words prescribed for a legal

then such marriages are legal and binding and the issue are legitimized, provided the parties were living together as man and wife "at the said death of either party." —*Ibid.*, 233, 234.

[1] *Laws of the Rep. of Tex.*, 234; also DALLAM, *Digest*, 167, 168. An act of Feb. 5, 1841, validates marriages previously made by "bond": *Laws of Rep. of Tex.* (5th Cong.), 176.

[2] Act of April 13, 1891: *Gen. Laws of Tex.* (1891), 96; being the same except as to Jewish rabbis, as act of Nov. 1, 1866: *Laws* (1866), 72, and *Revised Civil Stat.* (1888), I, 877; *Ann. Civ. Stat. of Tex.* (1897), I, 1081.

[3] *Code of Md.* (1888), I, 975.

[4] LISLET, *General Digest* (1828), II, 8.

[5] VOORHIES AND SAUNDERS, *Revised Code of La.* (1888), 63; MERRICK, *Rev. Civil Code* (1900), 25.

[6] *Session Laws of Okla.* (1897), 210; WILSON, *Stat. of Okla.* (1903), I, 858. Earlier one witness was sufficient: *Stat. of Okla.* (1893), 669, 670. *Cf. Rev. Stat. and Codes of Porto Rico* (1902), 810.

celebration,[1] although in several cases the ceremony is negatively mentioned.   Thus, in Tennessee, it is expressly stated that no formula is requisite, except that the parties "shall respectively declare, in the presence of the minister or officer, that they accept each other as man and wife."[2]   The Oklahoma law requires marriage to be "contracted by a formal ceremony" in the presence of two witnesses.[3]   The consent of persons "who may be lawfully married," declares the North Carolina statute, "presently to take each other as husband and wife, freely, seriously, and plainly expressed by each in the presence of the other and in the presence" of a minister or justice, and the consequent declaration by him that they "are man and wife, shall be a valid and sufficient marriage."[4]   By the law of Arkansas and Indian Territory a marriage may be solemnized by a clergyman according to the forms and customs of his society; or by a civil officer in such a way as he "shall deem most appropriate."[5]   Mississippi has adopted a similar provision.[6]   In Arizona, by an act of 1887, "all persons who at any time heretofore have lived together as husband and wife, and who shall continue to live together" for one year after this law takes effect, or until one of the parties shall die, if within the year, "shall be considered as having been lawfully married and their children legitimate."[7]   Two years later the Arizona legislature produced the following extraordinary "blanket" provision.   It is most generously enacted that "every ceremony of marriage or in the nature of a marriage ceremony of any kind, in this Territory, whether either or both or more of the parties to such ceremony be

[1] It appears to be assumed in the earlier statutes of Georgia that the celebration before a minister or magistrate is to be according to the Anglican ritual: COBB, *Analysis of the Stat. of Ga.* (1846), 292, 293.

[2] *Code* (1884), 609; *ibid.* (1896), 1039.   [3] *Session Laws of Okla.* (1897), 210.

[4] *Code* (1883), I, 689; *Laws* (1871–72), chap. 193, sec. 3.

[5] *Digest* (1894), 1127; see *Rev. Stat.* (1838), 537; *Ann. Stat. of Ind. Ter.* (1899), 509.

[6] WRIGHT, *Report*, 57.   [7] *Rev. Stat. of Arizona* (1887), 372; *ibid.* (1901), 810.

lawfully competent to be the subjects of such marriage or ceremony or not, shall be certified by a certificate stating the fact and nature of such ceremony, the full name of each of the parties concerned, and the full name of every officer, priest, minister, and person by whatever style or designation called or known, in any way taking part in the performance of such ceremony, which certificate shall be drawn up and signed by the parties to such ceremony and by every officer, priest, minister, and person taking part" therein, and be filed for record within twenty days.[1]

The usual penalties are generally prescribed for unauthorized solemnization.[2] In most cases a marriage is not expressly declared void for neglect of legal formalities; but the Mississippi statute makes a license essential to a valid contract;[3] while, on the other hand, in Tennessee the validity of a marriage is not affected by the omission of the baptismal name of either person in the license and the use of a nickname instead, if the parties can be identified and have cohabited as man and wife.[4] Furthermore, it is provided in Virginia, West Virginia, Kentucky, and Georgia that celebration before an unauthorized person professing to have legal power shall not invalidate a contract entered into in good faith by the parties.[5] Marriages valid at common law are still good in Florida.[6] It is curious to find the statute of 32 Henry VIII., chap. 38, for marriages to stand notwith-

---

[1] Act of March 21, 1889: *Arizona Session Laws* (1889), 58. This provision seems not to be retained in the *Rev. Stat.* of 1901.

[2] In West Virginia the penalty is confinement in jail for not exceeding one year, or a fine of $500, or both: *Code* (1900), 972; in Virginia it is not exceeding one year in jail and a fine of not more than $500: *Code* (1887), 899; in Kentucky, not exceeding three years in the penitentiary, and the same penalty for falsely personating father, mother, or guardian: *Kentucky Stat.* (1894), 766; *ibid.* (1899), 824.

[3] *Miss. Ann. Code* (1892), 679.   [4] *Tenn. Code* (1884), 610, 611; *ibid.* (1896), 104.

[5] *Code of Va.* (1887), 555; *Code of W. Va.* (1900), 655; *Kentucky Stat.* (1894), 763, 764; *Code of Ga.* (1882), 393.

[6] See Daniel *v.* Sams, 17 *Florida Rep.*, 487, an interesting case involving a slave marriage.

standing pre-contracts—repealed for England under Edward
VI.—kept in full force by the laws of South Carolina at
least until 1873, and in those of Kentucky for some years
after the beginning of the century.[1]

After the Civil War the South found itself confronted by
a very serious problem—that of the social and legal status
of several millions of freedmen.   The unions of slave men
and women had existed, of course, only at the will of the
master.   They had no legal force at all.   It became necessary, therefore, to determine and to recognize the marriages
of the newly enfranchised negro population.   For this purpose in many of the southern states special statutes were
enacted.   In Virginia it was provided that when colored persons prior to February 27, 1866, agreed to occupy the
relation of husband and wife, and were then cohabiting as
such, "whether the rites of matrimony had been celebrated
or not," they shall be deemed husband and wife; and all
their children shall be legitimate, whether born before or
after that date; as were also the children of such parents
who had then ceased living together.[2]   Similar laws were
passed in West Virginia, Tennessee, South Carolina, Texas,
Florida, and Arkansas.[3]   There is a like provision for the
District of Columbia.[4]   By the Maryland act all reputed
marriages of colored persons before March 22, 1867, are
validated, if the parties establish before a justice of the
peace the fact of the marriage, of which then a certificate
is directed to be placed on record.[5]   The Georgia law is

---

[1] LITTELL, *Kentucky Stat.*, II (1810), 571, 572; COOPER, *Stat. at Large of S. C.*, II,
475, 476; BREVARD, *Alphabetical Digest*, II (1814), 41–44; *Rev. Stat.* (1873), 481.

[2] *Code of Va.* (1887), 556.

[3] Colored persons cohabiting as husband and wife before Feb. 28, 1867, were
recognized as such in West Virginia: *Code* (1900), 655; similarly in Tennessee: *Code*
(1884), 609, 610; before March 12, 1872, in South Carolina: *Rev. Stat.* (1894), I, 753;
when so living on Aug. 15, 1870, in Texas: *Rev. Civil Laws* (1888), I, 879; before Dec.
14, 1866, in Florida: *Acts and Resolves* (1866), 22, *Rev. Stat.* (1892), 681; before Dec.
20, 1866, in Arkansas: *Digest* (1894), 1128.

[4] MOORE, *Code of D. C.* (1902), 268.   [5] *Code of Md.* (1888), II, 977, 978.

unique.   Persons of color living together as husband and wife, March 9, 1866, are to sustain that legal relation to each other, unless a man then had two or more reputed wives, or a woman two or more reputed husbands.   In such event the man shall immediately select one of his reputed wives, with her consent, or the woman one of her reputed husbands, with his consent; and the ceremony of marriage between these two shall be performed, under severe penalty for refusal.[1]

b) Forbidden degrees: void and voidable marriages.—Everywhere in the region under discussion, except perhaps in Louisiana, according to the spirit, if not by the letter, of the laws, marriage appears as a relation of status as well as of contract.   Only in a few instances, however, is it actually defined or are its requirements formally laid down.   Thus, in Arkansas, Indian Territory, Oklahoma, Missouri, and New Mexico it is a civil contract to which the consent of parties capable in law of contracting is necessary.[2]   The same in substance is true of the statute of Louisiana, whose rhetorical Gallic phrases have not been essentially changed since 1807.   "The law considers marriage in no other view than as a civil contract. . . . . Such marriages only are recognized by law as are contracted and solemnized according to the rules which *it* prescribes."   Since they are thus considered by the law merely as civil contracts, "it sanctions all those marriages where the parties, at the time of making them, were (1) willing to contract; (2) able to contract;

---

[1] Subject to prosecution and punishment for fornication, or fornication and adultery, for refusal: *Code of Ga.* (1882), 356, 357. *Cf. Acts* (1865–66), 239, 240; *Acts* (1866), 156, 157; and also 61 *Georgia Reports*, 306, and 40 *Georgia Reports*, 244.

[2] *Digest of Ark.* (1894), 1125; *Ann. Stat. of Ind. Ter.* (1899), 507; the same in *Rev. Stat.* (1838), 553; *Rev. Stat. of Mo.* (1899), I, 1035: *Compiled Laws of N. M.* (1897), 405.

But the Oklahoma statute of 1893 adds: "Consent alone will not constitute a marriage; it must be followed by a solemnization, or by a mutual assumption of marital rights, duties, or obligations."—*Statutes* (1893), 668. By the act of 1897 for this passage is substituted: "and the marriage relation shall only be entered into, maintained, or abrogated as provided by law."—*Session Laws* (1897), 208.

(3) did contract pursuant to the forms and solemnities prescribed. . . . . No marriage is valid to which the parties
have not freely consented; consent is not free, (1) when
given to a ravisher, unless it has been given by the party
ravished, after she has been restored to the enjoyment of
liberty; (2) when it has been extorted by violence; (3) when
there is a mistake respecting the person whom one of the
parties intended to marry."[1]   By the Porto Rico code "marriage is a civil institution, originating in a civil contract
whereby a man and a woman mutually agree to become husband and wife and to discharge toward each other the duties
imposed by law.   It is valid only when contracted and solemnized in accordance with provisions of law."[2]   In Georgia,
"to constitute a valid marriage . . . . there must be (1)
parties able to contract; (2) an actual contract; (3) consummation according to law."   To constitute an actual contract
"the parties must be consenting thereto voluntarily, and
without any fraud practiced upon either.   Drunkenness at
the time of marriage, brought about by art or contrivance
to induce consent," is held to be a fraud.[3]

The age of consent to marriage is prescribed in fifteen of
these states and territories; and, as in other parts of the
country, it is often far too low, particularly in the case of
girls.   For males it is eighteen in Arizona, New Mexico,
Oklahoma, Porto Rico, and West Virginia; seventeen in
Alabama, Arkansas, Indian Territory, and Georgia; sixteen
in North Carolina, Texas, and the District of Columbia; and
fourteen in Kentucky, Louisiana, and Virginia.   For females
it is sixteen in Arizona, Porto Rico, and West Virginia; fifteen in New Mexico and Oklahoma; fourteen in Alabama,

---

[1] VOORHIES AND SAUNDERS, *Revised Code of La.* (1888), 60, 61; *cf.* the act of 1807,
in *Digest of Civil Laws Now in Force* (1808), 24; or LISLET, *Gen. Digest* (1828), 4; or
Code Civil (1825), 80-82.

[2] *Rev. Stat. and Codes of Porto Rico* (1902), 805.

[3] *Code of Ga.* (1882), 392. *Cf.* the law of North Carolina above cited: *Code of
N. C.* (1883), I, 689.

Arkansas, Indian Territory, Georgia, North Carolina, Texas, and the District of Columbia; and only twelve in Kentucky, Louisiana, and Virginia.[1]

Eighteen commonwealths of the group and the District of Columbia have fixed, for both sexes, the age below which the consent of parent or guardian is necessary to a legal contract. For males it is twenty-one in Alabama, Arizona, Arkansas, Florida, Indian Territory, Oklahoma, Kentucky, Louisiana, Maryland, Mississippi, Missouri, New Mexico, Porto Rico, Texas, Virginia, West Virginia, and the District of Columbia; eighteen in North Carolina; and but sixteen in Tennessee.[2]

For females, it is twenty-one in Florida, Kentucky, Louisiana, Porto Rico, Virginia, and West Virginia; eighteen in Alabama, Arkansas, Indian Territory, Mississippi, Missouri, New Mexico, North Carolina, Oklahoma, and Texas; and only sixteen in Arizona, Maryland, Tennessee, and the District of Columbia.[3] The age for females is eighteen in Georgia; but by the statutes of that state parental consent does not seem to be required for male minors, nor for females when publication is by banns.[4] In effect, the same appears

[1] For both sexes see *Code of Ala.* (1897), 829; *Digest of Ark.* (1894), 1125; also *Rev. Stat.* (1835), 535; *Ann. Stat. of Ind. Ter.* (1899), 507; *Rev. Stat. of Ariz.* (1887), 371; *Code of Ga.* (1896), II, 222; *Kentucky Stat.* (1899), 822; *Rev. Stat. and Codes of Porto Rico* (1902), 807; *Rev. Code of La.* (1888), 61; MERRICK, *Rev. Civ. Code of La.* (1900), 23; *Session Laws of Okla.* (1897), 208; WILSON, *Stat. of Okla.* (1903), I, 857; *Comp. Laws of N. M.* (1897), 407; *Code of N. C.* (1883), I, 688; *Rev. Civil Stat. of Tex.* (1888), I, 878 (law of 1837); *Ann. Civil Stat. of Texas* (1897), I, 1082; *Code of Va.* (1887), 560, 561; *Acts of W. Va.* (1897), chap. 34; *Code of W. Va.* (1900), 661; MOORE, *Code of D. C.*, 265. *Cf.* WRIGHT, *Report*, 29.

[2] By inference from the law below cited.

[3] For both sexes see *Code of Ala.* (1897), 828; *Rev. Stat. of Ariz.* (1887), 371; *ibid.* (1901), 810; *Digest of Ark.* (1894), 1129, 874; *Ann. Stat. of Ind. Ter.* (1899), 413, 510; *Rev. Stat. of Fla.* (1892), 679; *Stat. of Ky.* (1899), 824; *Session Laws of Okla.* (1897), 208, 209; *Rev. Code of La.* (1888), 61, and the same in 1807, LISLET'S *General Digest* (1828), II, 5; *Maryland Code* (1888), I, 976, or in *Laws* (1886), chap. 497; *Ann. Code of Miss.* (1892), 677; *Rev. Stat. of Mo.* (1899), I, 1037; *Compiled Laws of N. M.* (1897), 405, 406, 407; *Rev. Civil Stat. of Tex.* (1888), I, 378; *Ann. Civil Stat. of Tex.* (1897), I, 1082; *Code of Va.* (1887), 555; *Code of W. Va.* (1900), 654; *Compiled Laws of D. C.* (1894), 273; *Acts of Tenn.* (1899), 36.

[4] *Code of Ga.* (1882), 393; *ibid.* (1896), II, 223. *Cf.* WRIGHT, *Report*, 30.

to be the case in South Carolina, since a penalty is affixed
for marrying a female under sixteen without parental consent; while for male minors such consent is not prescribed.[1]
But in Alabama, Florida, Maryland, Virginia, West Virginia,
and the District of Columbia, it should be noted, parental
consent is not required, if the minor has been previously
married. In several cases the statutes contain important
special provisions regarding the marriage of minors which
modify the general rule laid down as to age and parental
consent. By the law of Alabama, before the issuance of a
license for the marriage of persons under the ages of twenty-
one and eighteen respectively, the judge of probate, in addition to parental consent, "must also require a bond to be
executed in the penal sum of two hundred dollars," payable
to the state, "with condition to be void if there is no lawful
cause why such marriage should not be celebrated."[2] In
Kentucky, if a female under sixteen marry without legal
consent, a court in her county having general equity jurisdiction may commit her estate to a receiver, who, under
direction of the court, may pay out the profits, after due
compensation, to her separate use during infancy. At the
age of twenty-one, the estate is to be delivered to her, unless
the court thinks fit to continue it longer in the receiver's
hands.[3] Under similar conditions, in West Virginia the
county court is empowered, "upon petition of her next
friend," to commit the estate of a girl between twelve and
fourteen years of age to a receiver, who is to give bond for
the faithful performance of his trust.[4] A Tennessee law of

---

[1] *Rev. Stat. of S. C.* (1894), II, 347, 348.

[2] *Code of Ala.* (1897), I, 828, 829; *cf.* WRIGHT, *Report*, 29.

[3] *Kentucky Stat.* (1899), 825. But the marriage of an infant without consent is
not for that reason void: Canon *v.* Alsbury, 1 A. K. MARSHALL, *Kentucky Reports*, 76.

[4] *Code of W. Va.* (1900), 656.
The *Rev. Code of S. C.* (1873), 441, contains the provision that if any "woman,
child or maiden, being above the age of twelve years, and under the age of sixteen
years, do at any time consent or agree to any contract of matrimony," against the

1899 prohibits the issue of a license to persons under sixteen years, without written consent of parent or guardian.[1] In Porto Rico marriage under the age of consent "shall, nevertheless, be valid *ipso facto* and without an express declaration, if one day after having arrived at the legal age of puberty the parties shall have lived together without the representative of either of them having brought suit against its validity, or if the woman shall have conceived before the legal age of puberty or before having established such suit."[2]

The Romano-French origin of the Louisiana laws is in no way more plainly revealed than in the elaborate provisions regarding the Family Council. This institution is given a prominent place in the regulation of domestic affairs; and, in the United States, it is peculiar to Louisiana. It has always exercised jurisdiction in approving the marriage of minors; and in appointing "tutors" or guardians; while at present its advice may be required in the disposal of children of divorced parents. By the act of 1807 consent of the parents is necessary to the marriage of minors of either sex under twenty-one years of age. In case of disagreement the father's approval is sufficient. If either parent be dead or incapable of consenting, the other is authorized to act, "although he or she may have contracted a second marriage." But if the parents are both dead or incapable, the grandfathers and grandmothers "shall supply their places as to this consent, and in case of difference of opinion, a majority shall prevail;[3] when they are equally divided in their opinions, the council of the family is invoked to decide." The council is likewise called in when parents and grand-

will or without the knowledge of parent or guardian, " by secret letters, messages, or otherwise," she shall forfeit her estate, including lands, tenements, and hereditaments, "to the next of kin who next would inherit, during the life of the offender, then to the one who would have inherited had there been no such child."

[1] *Acts* (1899), 36. [2] *Rev. Stat. and Codes of Porto Rico* (1902), 806.

[3] Probably the "majority" of the grandparents of the two persons is meant.

parents are all dead; but its decision must be made within one month after it is convoked and consent requested, otherwise the marriage may be celebrated. In all cases, whether by parents, grandparents, or council, approval is to be given or refused in presence of the parish judge. The consent must be drawn up in writing by that officer in presence of two witnesses and the persons consenting; and by all of these, including the magistrate, it must be signed. A certificate of consent is made out in duplicate: one copy being retained by the judge and the other given to the persons whose marriage is thus approved. In case of consent by the council the certificate "shall state the names of those of the family who assembled, their professions and places of residence, and which of them consented," together with "the names of the parties intending to marry."[1]

The regulation of consent is simplified under the present law, and the patriarchal features have in part disappeared. "The minor of either sex . . . . must have received the consent of his father and mother or of the survivor of them; and if they are both dead, the consent of his tutor." But the family council, or "meeting" as now called, still has important functions; and its composition and proceedings are carefully prescribed. In all cases the meeting is composed of "at least five relations, or in default of relations, friends of him in whose interests they are called upon to deliberate. These relations or friends must be selected from among those domiciled in the parish in which the meeting is held, or in a neighboring parish," provided it be at a distance of not more than thirty miles. "The relations shall be selected according to their proximity, beginning with the nearest;" and the "relation" shall be preferred to the "connection" of the same degree; while among relations of the

---

[1] LISLET, *General Digest* (1828), II, 5, 6; *Civil Laws Now in Force in the Territory* (1808), 62.

same degree the eldest shall be preferred. No person who has "interests conflicting with those of a minor" is competent to serve in the meeting, "although one of the nearest relations." Members of the meeting are appointed by the parish judge: and it must be held "before the recorder of the parish, a justice of the peace, or notary public appointed by the judge for the purpose." A meeting may be called for a fixed hour on three days' notice; and the members are to take oath to give advice according to their best knowledge.[1]

The laws of the southern and southwestern states regarding the forbidden degrees of lineal and collateral consanguinity are far from uniform in their details; but they are determined by the same general principles as those of New England already considered. Ascendants and descendants are, of course, always included.[2] In the side lines prohibition does not usually extend to first cousins. But in Arizona, Oklahoma, Indian Territory, Arkansas, Louisiana, and Missouri these may not legally marry;[3] and this restriction was also maintained in Georgia until 1865.[4] By the law of Porto Rico collaterals by consanguinity may not marry within the fourth degree; but the court may, for good cause, on petition of an interested person, waive this impediment.[5]

[1] *Rev. Civil Code of La.* (1888), 62, 91, 92; VOORHIES, *Rev. Laws* (1884), 236, 237; *Rev. Laws* (1897), 393. Since 1807 the council (or meeting) has been composed of at least five relatives or friends, summoned by the judge, and held before an officer, practically as required by the present law: see *Civil Laws Now in Force in the Territory* (1808), 62. For failure to attend a meeting, when cited, there is a fine of $20, in the discretion of the judge to be applied to the expenses of the meeting. In place of absentees "friends" may be appointed: *Rev. Civil Code* (1888), 92.

[2] *Rev. Stat. of Fla.* (1892), 820, for the first time expressly prohibiting marriage within "Levitical consanguinity;" but probably earlier the law intended the same restriction: MCCLELLAN, *Digest of the Laws of Fla.*, chap. 59, sec. 8; WRIGHT, *Report*, 32.

[3] *Rev. Stat. of Ariz.* (1887), 371; *ibid.* (1901), 809; *Digest of Ark.* (1894), 1125, 1126; *Rev. Stat. of Mo.* (1899), I, 1036; *Ann. Stat. of Ind. Ter.* (1899), 507; *Session Laws of Okla.* (1897), 208; *Acts of La.* (1900), 188.

[4] *Acts* (1865-66), 244, removing penalty for marriage of first cousins since Dec. 11, 1863, and repealing conflicting laws.

[5] *Rev. Stat. and Codes of Porto Rico* (1902), 806, 807.

Furthermore, in every place, except in Tennessee, either expressly or by implication, marriage between aunts and nephews or uncles and nieces is forbidden.[1] With respect to affinity it is not surprising to find still greater conservatism in communities where the influence of the English church had originally been so strong. Marriage with a brother's widow or a deceased wife's sister is forbidden by the Virginia statute of 1788.[2] The prohibition as to the latter does not seem to have been entirely removed until 1849;[3] while with regard to the former it lingered until 1860.[4] In Maryland the law containing these two restrictions and likewise prohibiting marriage with a deceased husband's brother or a deceased sister's husband was repealed as early as 1790.[5] A statute of Louisiana, in 1827, declares that, since the new civil code (1825) had abolished impediments on account of affinity existing "under the Spanish laws," and because even before the promulgation of that code "some doubts were entertained whether the Spanish laws on this subject were still in force," therefore to prevent litigation "all marriages between brothers-

---

[1] Assuming that this relationship is included in the restrictions of the Levitical law which is in force in Georgia, and probably also in Florida: see McCLELLAN, *Digest of the Laws of Fla.*, chap. 59, sec. 8; and compare WRIGHT, *Report*, 32.

[2] Act of Oct., 1788: HENING, *Statutes*, XII, 688, 689. Persons married contrary to the act shall be "separated by the definitive sentence or judgment of the high court of chancery."

[3] In 1827 the law forbidding marriage with a deceased wife's sister was considerably relaxed. The parties are no longer to be separated, but to be "deemed guilty of a misdemeanor, to be prosecuted by information, or indicted in the Superior Court of Law;" and on conviction they are to be punished by such fine or imprisonment or both, as the jury may determine: *Acts* (1826-27), 22. This law was still in force in 1841: TATE, *Digest* (2d ed.), 500, where the editor cites Vaughan's opinion in Hill *v.* Good, 2 *Virginia Cases*, 61. But the restriction does not appear in *Code of Va.* (1849), 470, 471 (degrees). *Cf.* LEIGH, 17.

[4] Act of March 15, 1860: *Acts of the Assembly* (1859-60), 188, 189. In West Virginia until later a man was not permitted to marry his brother's widow: see *Acts* (1872-73), chap. 161, p. 503, where the restriction is removed.

[5] *Laws of Md.* (1790), chap. xx, repealing the act of 1777, chap. 12, sec. 1, *Laws of Md., 1763-87* (1787), where these marriages are "void."

in-law and sisters-in-law contracted before the code went into
effect shall be held valid."[1]   The law of Georgia which for
many years forbade wedlock with a sister-in-law or a brother-
in-law seems also to have been abrogated.[2]   Finally it may be
noted that by the rule still existing in Alabama and Mississippi marriage with a step-mother or a step-father is
prohibited; and the same is true of Georgia, Kentucky,
Maryland, South Carolina, Tennessee, Texas, Virginia, West
Virginia, and the District of Columbia, where, in addition,
one is not permitted to contract matrimony with a father-in-
law or a mother-in-law.

According to the rule generally prevailing marriage
within the forbidden degrees is void or voidable;[3] the children are often declared illegitimate, either absolutely or
when born after annulment; and severe penalties are imposed for violation of the law.[4]   Likewise, as elsewhere in

---

[1] *Louisiana Acts* (1827), 4.

[2] This dual restriction appears in COBB'S *Analysis of Stat. of Ga.* (New York,
1846), 290, 291; but it does not seem to be retained in *Code of Ga.* (1861), 331 (prohibited degrees of affinity), and there is no later statute on the subject.

[3] In Alabama such marriages are incestuous and must be annulled by the court
on conviction; but the issue born before annulment is legitimate: *Code* (1897), 828;
in Arizona, Arkansas, Georgia, Indian Territory, Kentucky, Mississippi, and New
Mexico they are incestuous and void or voidable after decree: *Rev. Stat. of Ariz.*
(1887), 371; *Digest of Ark.* (1894), 1126; also *Rev. Stat. of Ark.* (1838), 536; *Code of Ga.*
(1896), II, 222; *Kentucky Stat.* (1894), 763; *Comp. Laws of N. M.* (1897), 406;
Ann. Code of Miss. (1892), 677.   In Maryland, District of Columbia, Missouri, and
North Carolina they are absolutely void or voidable after decree: *Code of Md.* (1888),
I, 973, 974; *Comp. Laws of D. C.* (1894), 271; *Rev. Stat. of Mo.* (1899), I, 1036; *Code of
N. C.* (1883), I, 688, 689.   But the laws of New Mexico, while declaring these marriages
"absolutely void," provides in sec. 1430 that they shall not be "declared void except
by decree of the district court;" and the North Carolina act has the condition that
no marriage followed by cohabitation and birth of issue shall be declared void after
the death of either of the parties for any of the causes stated, except in case of
unions of whites with negroes or Indians to the third generation.   In Virginia
prohibited marriages, if solemnized in the state, are void after decree, or when within
the forbidden degrees, from the time of conviction for incest; and the law of West
Virginia is similar: *Code of Va.* (1887), 560; *Code of W. Va.* (1891), 656, 661.   See also
Code of Tenn. (1884), 608; *Rev. Stat. of Fla.* (1892), 820; *Rev. Civil Code of La.* (1888),
61; *Rev. Stat. of S. C.* (1894), I, 751; and compare WRIGHT, *Report*, 35-45.

[4] For example, in Virginia the penalty for marriage within the forbidden degrees
is imprisonment not exceeding six months or a fine of not more than $500: *Code* (1887),
898; in West Virginia, one or both of these penalties: *Code* (1900), 972; in Georgia,

the country, marriages are declared void or voidable for a variety of reasons other than the forbidden degrees.   Here the greatest confusion and uncertainty exist; and there is most urgent need of a strong effort to bring the laws of the different states into harmony in this regard.   The evil is aggravated through the fact that transgressions which render a contract invalid in one state may in a neighboring community merely subject the offender to fine or imprisonment. Thus in Virginia, West Virginia, and apparently also in Georgia a marriage is void or voidable when celebrated out of the state by residents who seek to avoid the requirements of their own law.[1]   In Maryland under like conditions a fine is imposed[2] and in the District of Columbia such a marriage is illegal and may be declared void.[3]   On the other hand, in Kentucky, when persons there resident "shall marry in another state, such marriages shall be valid . . . . if valid . . . . where solemnized."[4]   The statutes of the other fifteen states and territories, except when the motive is union within the forbidden degrees,[5] appear to be entirely silent on the subject of clandestine marriage.

Bigamous marriages are invalid in Florida, Georgia, Kentucky, Louisiana, Maryland, District of Columbia, Missis-

imprisonment in the penitentiary from one to three years: *Code* (1896), III, 116; in Maryland incest is a felony punishable by one to ten years' imprisonment at the discretion of the court: *Code* (1888), I, 511; in Missouri the penalty for the same crime is not exceeding seven years in the penitentiary: *Rev. Stat.* (1889), II, 907; in the District of Columbia, for marriage within the "three degrees of lineal direct consanguinity, or within the first degree of collateral consanguinity," the penalty for each is "five hundred pounds current money ($1333.33⅓);" and within any of the other forbidden degrees of consanguinity or affinity, it is "two hundred pounds current money ($533.33⅓)": *Comp. Stat. of D. C.* (1894), 272.

[1] *Code of Va.* (1887), 560; *Code of W. Va.* (1891), 612, 918; *Code of Ga.* (1882), 287, 288.

[2] Formerly in Maryland any person marrying out of the state to evade the law was fined 500 pounds: KILTY, *Laws*, 1777, chap. 12, sec. 6.   Now each of the persons must pay $100: *Code* (1888), 523.

[3] MOORE, *Code of D. C.* (1902), 266.

[4] *Kentucky Stat.* (1894), 764; *ibid.* (1901), 823.

[5] In Mississippi marriages out of the state, to avoid penalties of forbidden degrees, are declared void: *Ann. Code of Miss.* (1892), 677.

sippi, Missouri, North Carolina, South Carolina, Tennessee, Virginia, and West Virginia; but in Alabama, Arizona, Arkansas, Indian Territory, and Texas they are only prohibited or made punishable; while the legislature of New Mexico attaches a penalty for the offense of two to seven years in the penitentiary.[1] Marriages obtained by fraud or by force, menace, or duress are dealt with in a similar spirit. They are prohibited or punishable in Alabama, Arizona, Mississippi, Missouri, Tennessee, and Texas;[2] void or voidable in District of Columbia, Arkansas, Indian Territory, Georgia, Kentucky, and Louisiana;[3] fraudulent contract is a ground of divorce in Oklahoma; while the statutes of the remaining states are either entirely silent, as in the case of Florida, Maryland, New Mexico, Virginia, and West Virginia; or such marriages are void at common law where no statute exists; or under general statutory provisions, as seems to be the case in North Carolina and South Carolina.[4] Various other grounds for invalidating a marriage are here and there assigned. Such

[1] See the lists in WRIGHT, Report, 35–45. On these marriages I have not found changes since 1887, the date of that compilation.

In Virginia bigamy was formerly punished by death: see the act of 1792, in Acts of Gen. Assem. (1794), 205; now the penalty is three to five years' imprisonment: Code (1887), 680; in West Virginia it is one to five years in the penitentiary: Code (1891), 918; in Florida, not exceeding five years in state's prison, or a fine of not more than $500: Rev. Stat. (1892), 820; in Missouri, not exceeding five years in the penitentiary, or less than six months in the county jail, or not less than $500, or by both a fine of not more than $100 and imprisonment in the county jail for not less than three months: Rev. Stat. (1899), I, 608, 609. Bigamy is prohibited in Rev. Civil Stat. of Tex. (1888), I, 877; WHITE, Penal Code (1901), 188; Digest of Ark. (1894), 1126.

[2] In Texas they are prohibited and punished "when the female is abducted or forced into marriage;" but they are voidable when the license has been fraudulently obtained: WRIGHT, Report, 43; Rev. Civil Stat. of Tex. (1888), I, 877, note; see Robertson v. Cole, 12 Texas, 356. Cf. WILSON, Supp. to Criminal Statutes (1900), 242, 243.

[3] See, for example, Kentucky Stat. (1894), 764; ibid. (1901), 822; Digest of Ark. (1894), 1126; MOORE, Code of D. C. (1902), 265.

[4] In North Carolina marriages are void when either person is "incapable of contracting from want of will or understanding": Code (1883), I, 688, 689; in South Carolina they are void or voidable when lacking consent of either party or for "any other cause going to show that at the time said supposed contract was made it was not a contract," provided not consummated by cohabitation: Rev. Stat. (1894), I, 752.

is lack of understanding, in North Carolina and Oklahoma; idiocy, in District of Columbia, Kentucky, and South Carolina; lunacy, insanity, or an unsound mind, in the two states last named, and also in Georgia, Virginia, West Virginia, and the District of Columbia; want of legal age of consent, in Alabama, Arkansas, Georgia, Kentucky, New Mexico, North Carolina, Oklahoma, Texas, and West Virginia; want of physical competence, in Arizona, Arkansas, Indian Territory, Georgia, North Carolina, Texas, Virginia, and West Virginia;[1] or lack of proper solemnization, in Kentucky.[2] But in these states as elsewhere, it must be remembered, the statutes are supplemented by the common law.

Very naturally, in the region where slavery existed before the Civil War a horror of intermarriage between whites and blacks is everywhere evinced by the statute-maker. Accordingly, every state and territory in the group under examination—except New Mexico, Porto Rico, and the District of Columbia—has enacted rigorous laws to prevent miscegenation. In Alabama and Tennessee such marriages are prohibited "to the third generation" under severe penalties ;[3] in all the other

[1] *Kentucky Stat.* (1894), 763; *Rev. Stat. of S. C.* (1894), I, 750-52; *Code of Ga.* (1896), II, 222; *Code of Va.* (1887), 560; *Code of W. Va.* (1891), 612; *Code of N. C.* (1883), I, 688, 689; *Digest of Ark.* (1894), 1126; *Code of Ala.* (1896), I, 828; *Comp. Laws of N. M.* (1897), 406, 407.

[2] In Kentucky marriages are void or voidable when not solemnized or contracted in the presence of an authorized person or society; but they are not so invalid if consummated with the belief of the parties or either of them that they have been lawfully married: WRIGHT, *Report*, 39.

The Louisiana act of 1807 makes one who is deaf and dumb from "nativity" incapable of marriage, "unless it be previously proved to the satisfaction of the judge . . . . that such person is capable of giving a rational consent." So also "criminals definitively sentenced to death" are incapable until pardoned; and "persons sentenced to whipping, imprisonment, pillory, or other infamous punishment" are prohibited from marrying, "until such punishment has been inflicted, or the offender pardoned."—LISLET, *Gen. Digest* (1828), II, 4, 5.

[3] By the statute of Tennessee marriage is prohibited between white persons and "negroes, mulattoes, or persons of mixed blood, descended from a negro to the third generation inclusive, or their living together as man and wife." Violation of the act is made a felony punishable by confinement in the penitentiary for a period of one to five years; though, on recommendation of the jury, the court may substitute a fine and imprisonment in the county jail: *Code* (1884), 608; *ibid.* (1896), 1038.

The law of Alabama is in substance the same; although to the clause prohibit-

states they are declared void or voidable, and usually the issue is absolutely illegitimate. Unfortunately, the statutes on this subject show a deplorable lack of uniformity. They are divergent in their most important provisions. Their language is not always clear, and even when it is technically exact, the occasional use of vulgar fractions to designate the degree of African blood interdicted must often put its certain interpretation far beyond the people whom it most vitally concerns. Thus in Arkansas, Indian Territory, and Kentucky[1] marriage is void between a white person and a negro or mulatto; in Georgia[2] it is so between a white person and a person of African descent; in Louisiana and Virginia, between white persons and persons of "color;" in West Virginia, between a white person and a negro; in Oklahoma, between persons of the white race and those of the negro race; in South Carolina, between a white person and an Indian, negro, mulatto, mestizo, or half-breed; in Florida between a white person and a colored person; in Maryland between a white person and a negro or a person of negro descent to the third generation inclusive; in North Carolina the interdiction is the same, except that Indians are included;[3] in Texas the prohibition is between persons of European blood and Africans or their descendants. Else-

ing intermarriage "to the third generation inclusive," the *Code*, sec. 4018, when affixing the penalty, adds the words, "though one ancestor of each generation was a white person": see *Code of Ala.* (1897), II, 381; WRIGHT, *Report*, 36.

[1] In 1810 the Virginia act of 1753, chap. 2, secs. 14, 15, for the prevention of that "abominable mixture and spurious issue," was still in force: *Stat. Law of Ky.* (1810), II, 572.

[2] In Georgia and Florida a person of color is one who has one-eighth negro or African blood in his veins: *Code of Ga.* (1882), 356; *cf. ibid.* (1896), II, 4, 224; *Rev. Stat. of Fla.* (1892), 681, 111.

[3] In North Carolina, furthermore, a negro may not marry a Croatan Indian: WRIGHT, *Report*, 42.

The code of this state is almost vindictive in its temper. The marriages between whites and negroes or Indians "shall be absolutely void to all intents and purposes, and shall be so held and declared by every court at all times, whether during the lives or after the deaths of the parties thereto; and it shall not be lawful for the issue of any such marriage to be legitimated to the supposed father."—*Code of N. C.* (1883), I, 514.

where the lawmaker resorts to arithmetic. Marriage is void in Mississippi[1] between a white person and a person having one-eighth or more negro or Mongolian blood; and in Missouri, where the negro blood amounts to one-eighth or more. Arizona, like Mississippi, objects strongly to the union of whites and Chinese; so a marriage is declared void between persons of "Caucasian" blood and Africans or "Mongolians," or with their descendants.[2]

But numerous and varied as are the legal restrictions put upon marriage in the southern and southwestern states, one regrets to discover that not even a beginning has yet been made in the effort to thus check the increase of paupers and vagrants, or to prevent the hereditary transmission of tendencies to vice, crime, or incurable disease.

In many cases indirect encouragement of matrimony is given in the usual way through legitimation of children or the suspension of penalty or prosecution.[3] Since 1856 the

[1] But see *Ann. Code of Miss.* (1892), 677: The marriage of a white person "with a negro, mulatto, or Mongolian or person who shall have one-eighth or more negro or Mongolian blood" is declared "unlawful and void."

[2] *Rev. Stat of Ariz.* (1887), 371; *ibid.* (1901), 809; *Ann. Code of Miss.* (1892), 677. In general, for the provisions regarding miscegenation, see also *Rev. Stat. of Fla.* (1892), 681; *Digest of Ark.* (1894), 1126; *Ann. Stat. of Ind. Ter.* (1899), 507; *Kentucky Stat.* (1894), 763; *Louisiana Acts* (1894), 105; *Rev. Stat. of Mo.* (1889), I, 908; *ibid.* (1899), I, 610; *Code of Va.* (1887), 560; *Code of W. Va.* (1900), 660, 661, 972 (void from decree); *Maryland Code* (1888), I, 523; *Code of N. C.* (1883), I, 514; *Rev. Stat. of S. C.* (1894), I, 753; *Gen. Laws of Tex.* (1891), I, 878; the same in 1837: *Laws of Republic of Tex.* (1838), 234, 235; *Sess. Laws of Okla.* (1897), 212.

[3] Illegitimate children are legitimized by the marriage of parents and acknowledgment of the father in Alabama, *Code* (1887), 530; *ibid.* (1897), sec. 364; Arizona, *Rev. Stat.* (1887), 371, 372; Florida, *Rev. Stat.* (1892), 686; Georgia, *Code* (1896), II, 254; Kentucky, *Stat.* (1894), 545; Maryland, *Code* (1888), II, 813; Mississippi, *Ann. Code* (1892), 172; Missouri, *Rev. Stat.* (1899), I, 740; Virginia, *Code* (1887), 620; West Virginia, *Code* (1891), 666.

Penalty or prosecution for seduction is suspended by marriage of parents in Arizona, *Rev. Stat.*, as cited; Kentucky, *Stat.*, as cited; Missouri, *Rev. Stat.* (1899), I, 548; New Mexico, *Comp. Laws* (1897), 344; Texas, Act of March 25, 1899: *Gen. Laws*, 66: and Virginia, *Code*, as cited. *Cf.* WRIGHT, *Report*, 27.

Prosecution for seduction is also suspended on marrying the woman in Arkansas; but it is specially provided that if at any time thereafter the accused shall wilfully and without such cause as now constitutes a legal ground of divorce desert and abandon the female, then the prosecution shall be continued and proceed as though no marriage had taken place. In such cases the female may be a witness: *Acts* (1899), 23, 24.

Statutes of New Mexico, in this connection, contain a somewhat novel clause.   It is "provided that when any persons
are found living together publicly as if they were married,
they shall be required immediately to contract marriage, if
there is no impediment to prevent their so doing; and if
they do not marry upon the first requirement of any justice,
they shall, upon accusation, be fined not less than twenty-
five nor more than eighty dollars for every time they shall
be so found."[1]   West Virginia favors wedlock in a different
way.   Not only may either person bring suit, in the manner
very commonly prescribed, to annul or validate a doubtful
marriage; but in that event and "in every other case where
the validity of a marriage is called in question, it shall be
presumed that the marriage is valid, unless the contrary be
clearly proven."[2]   Georgia, however, is the only state which
offers direct encouragment.   It is formally announced that
"marriage is encouraged by the law, and every effort to
restrain or discourage" it by "contract, condition, limitation, or otherwise is invalid and void."   Still, "prohibiting
marriage to a particular person or persons, or before a certain
seasonable age, or other prudential provision looking only to
the interest of the person to be benefitted, and not in general
restraint" of matrimony, will be allowed.[3]

    c) *Certificate and record.*—In the region whose laws are
under examination license from a county officer is now in most
cases essential before a marriage may be legally solemnized.
But originally in the older commonwealths there existed a
dual system of optional civil license or ecclesiastical banns,
which may be contrasted with the somewhat different system
by banns or posting so long preserved in the New England
states.   Indeed, in at least two instances it still survives.

---

[1] *Laws of N. M.* (1897), sec. 1346, pp. 391, 392. *Cf.* the law of Arizona, *Rev. Stat.* (1887), 371, 372.

[2] *Code of W. Va.* (1891), 612; *ibid.* (1900), 661.

[3] *Code of Ga.* (1882), 391; *ibid.* (1896), II, 221.

By the first legislation of Virginia after the Revolution the provisions of the act of 1748 on this subject are retained.[1] In 1780 it is provided that "no persons, except the people called Quakers and Menonists, shall hereafter be joined together as man and wife without lawful license first had, or thrice publication of banns in the respective parishes, or congregations," where such persons "severally" reside. Within three months a "certificate of solemnization" is to be filed with the clerk of the county where the marriage takes place. The fee for performing the ceremony is fixed at "twenty-five pounds of tobacco, and no more, to be paid in current money at the rate which shall be settled by the grand jury."[2] Under the elaborate statute of 1792 a license, or oral banns in case of members of the Protestant Episcopal church, is still requisite. On submitting an approved bond in the sum of one hundred and fifty dollars, license may be obtained from the clerk of the court of the county where the woman "usually resides." When either person is under twenty-one years of age, consent of parent or guardian, written or oral, is necessary before license may be issued. If written, the consent must be attested by two witnesses, one of whom, appearing in person, is to swear that the signature was made in his presence. Within twelve months—the time already fixed by the act of 1784—a certificate of the marriage must be returned to the clerk of the county or corporation in which it was solemnized.[3]

Thus, with slight change, the law of Virginia remained for over half a century.[4] But in 1848 oral banns were

---

[1] For the act of 1748, see *Acts of the Assem.* (1769), 246-48.

[2] Act of May, 1780, in HENING, *Statutes*, X, 361-63. Compare the acts of 1783 and 1784, where the system of banns or license is retained, *ibid.*, XI, 281, 282, 503-6. Later the fee was fixed at $1: TATE, *Digest* (1823), 417.

[3] Act of Dec. 22, 1792: *Acts of the Gen. Assem.* (1794), 204, 205.

[4] Compare the law of 1794: *Acts of Gen. Assem.* (1794), 331, 332; *Rev. Code* (1819), 393-403. But in 1803 the justice is no longer required to sign and direct the license: *Acts of Gen. Assem.*, 372 (act to take effect May 1, 1797). In 1832 the consent of the

abolished and the modern system by civil license only was established.[1]

In North Carolina a dual system of banns and license, similar to that of Virginia, was authorized by the act of 1778; and it did not yield to the modern plan until 1872, when banns were abolished and bond for license was no longer required.[2] Tennessee retained the system of the parent commonwealth, North Carolina, until, far down in the century, it gave way to the typical American plan.[3] Kentucky does not seem to have followed the example of Virginia; but civil license in all cases was there required from the origin of the state.[4] In Missouri, on the other hand, in 1805 a triple optional system of banns, posting, or license was established by the governor and judges of Indiana Territory. Notice of intention to marry is to be published for fifteen days at least, either orally on "three several Sundays, holy days, or other days of public worship, in the meeting in the towns where the parties respectively belong;" or by affixing a written notice signed by one of the judges or a justice of the peace in some public place where the persons respectively dwell. Otherwise a license under the governor's hand and seal, authorizing celebration without publication, must be obtained. By this law persons

mother is declared sufficient to authorize license to minors when there is no father or guardian: *Acts* (1831-32), 27; and in 1848 so much of the law of 1832 was repealed "as requires the consent of the mother of any infant desiring a marriage license to be certified under seal;" and henceforth in all cases the written consent of parents may be attested by one witness. When for any reason the clerk's office is vacant license may be issued by the "senior justice of the peace."—*Acts of the Assem.* (1847-48), 165.

[1] *Ibid.*

[2] IREDELL-MARTIN, *Public Acts, 1715-1803* (1804), act of 1778, chap. 7, I, 253. Compare *Laws of N. C.* (1821), I, 129; *Rev. Stat.* (1837), I, 386; and *Laws* (1871-72), 328-43. The register of deeds takes the place of the clerk of the county court as issuer of license in 1872. By the act of 1778 the bond necessary for license had been fixed at 500 pounds "lawful money."

[3] SCOTT, *Laws of Tenn.* (1821), Index at "Marriage": *Stat. Laws of Tenn.* (1831), 219, 220. But oral banns do not appear in *Code of Tenn.* (1858), 480-82.

[4] LITTELL, *Stat. Law of Ky.* II (1810), 64-69.

solemnizing marriages are to keep a record; and within three months, in each case, they are required to make a return to the registrar of the district.[1] Banns, however, do not seem ever to have been recognized after Missouri was admitted to the Union. The act of 1825 is entirely silent as to both banns and license. In place thereof it is provided that the marriage of a minor may not be celebrated unless parent or guardian be present and give consent; or else a written certificate of assent must be produced under the hand of such parent, guardian, or other person having legal control, attested by the oath or affirmation of a witness of full age.[2]

Maryland still clings to the system of license or ecclesiastical banns substantially as it appears in the act of 1777.[3] The same was formerly true of the District of Columbia, where the statute of Maryland was in force until 1896,[4] Georgia has been equally conservative. By the law of 1785 a magistrate or a clergyman may solemnize matrimony after eight days' "public notice" or on receiving a license from "his honor the governor, or register of probates."[5] This plan lasted only until 1799, when license or thrice publication of banns, in the usual way, was substituted.[6] So the law remained[7] until 1860, when a reactionary step was taken. In December of that year an act was passed by the legislature, to take effect January 1, 1862, containing a paragraph

[1] See act of April 24, 1805: *Acts of a Pub. and Gen. Nature* (1842), I, 66.

[2] Act of Jan. 4, 1825: *Laws of the State* (1825), I, 527. Persons or societies solemnizing marriages are required to keep a record; and a general record must also be made by the registrar of the county. The provision of 1825 is repeated in *Rev. Stat.* (1845), 730.

[3] Compare the act of 1777, chap. 12, secs. 5-12: see KILTY, *Laws;* or *Laws of Md.* (1787), at sections cited; and POE, *Code* (1888), I, 975.

[4] *Comp. Stat. of D. C.* (1894), 272.

[5] *Digest of Ga.* (1801), 314. But by the constitution of the state (1798), Art. III, sec. 6, *ibid.*, 40, the clerk of the inferior courts of the county, with powers of a court of ordinary or register of probates, shall issue marriage licenses.

[6] *Digest* (1801), 733.

[7] See HOTCHKISS, *Codification* (1845), 329; or COBB, *Digest* (1851), 282, 819.

which made either license or ecclesiastical banns essential to
a valid marriage.   However, on the repeal of this paragraph
in 1863, the old optional system by banns or license, without
declaring either essential to a valid contract, was restored;
and it has persisted to the present time.[1]

The peculiar procedure observed in Louisiana with
respect to parental consent or the consent of the family
council, in the case of the marriage of minors, has already
been described in the preceding section.   The act of 1807
contains also a general provision for notice and license.
Persons applying for license must satisfy the parish judge,
by two witnesses if necessary, that they are twenty-one
years of age; and the proof must be registered.   The intentions of the persons are then to be published by the judge
through "posting up a notice at the door of the nearest
church, [or] at the door of the court-house of the parish,
announcing a day on which a license would issue, unless
opposition should be made."   If no objection be raised
within fifteen days, the license may be issued, provided the
intended husband execute a bond, with sufficient security,
"in a sum proportioned to his fortune, at the discretion of
the judge," that there is no legal impediment to the marriage.   But there is an important exception to the general
rule.   In "certain cases," if minors are not concerned, "the
judge may dispense with the above mode of publishing marriages, by his special license to that effect, and under his
own responsibility."   Minors must apply to the judge of

[1]Paragraph 1658, pp. 331, 332, of the *Code of Ga.*, assented to Dec. 19, 1860, to take
effect Jan. 1, 1862, provides for obtaining license, and "publication of the banns of
marriage in a neighboring church, in the presence of the congregation, for at least
three Sabbath days prior to its solemnization," all other marriages being declared
invalid.   *Cf. Acts* (1863–64), 48, editorial note.   The change worked confusion.   The
preamble of the act of Dec. 14, 1863, declares that the "innovation" will "have the
effect of giving rise to perplexing questions of legitimacy of children, and rights of
property; and to domestic unhappiness."   Therefore the paragraph is repealed, and
marriages already solemnized under it are validated: *ibid.*, 48.

For the present law see *Code of Ga.* (1896), II, 223, 221.

the parish in which one of the persons has his domicile.
The application is then published, and "if no opposition be
made, the license shall be granted as directed in the case of
persons who have attained the age of twenty-one years."[1]
The wholesome provision requiring notice to be published
for a certain period before issuance of the license is no
longer in force.   Otherwise, though somewhat simplified,
the law of Louisiana remains today practically what it was
in 1807.   License is always requisite; it must be issued by
the proper officer in the parish where either the bride or
groom is domiciled; and the provision for the bond is expressed in exactly the same words as of old, except that the
duration of the security is limited to two years.   In the parish of Orleans licenses are granted by the board of health
and judges of the city courts; in the other parishes of the
state, by the clerks of the district courts, or by the district
judge when the clerk is himself a "party to the marriage."[2]

The general features of matrimonial administration in
the entire group of states may now be presented in rapid
outline.   Everywhere, except in Georgia and Maryland, as
already explained, and in New Mexico and South Carolina,
which have no legislation on the subject, license in every
case is required.   The present law of Virginia does not
differ materially from that of earlier years.   The marriage
license is issued by the clerk of the court of the county or
corporation in which the woman usually resides.   If the
office of clerk be vacant, then the judge of the county court
or the mayor of the corporation may act, making return to
the clerk "as soon as there may be one."   Before license is
granted for the marriage of a minor, there is requisite the
consent of the father or guardian, or, if none, of the mother,
given personally or in writing subscribed by a witness who

---

[1] Act of 1807: LISLET, *General Digest* (1828), II, 6-8.

[2] MERRICK, *Rev. Civil Code* (1900), I, 21-25.   But if objection be made on oath, the
marriage may be suspended for ten days by the judge.

must swear that the writing was signed in his presence. Similar functions are performed by the clerk of the county court in West Virginia,[1] Tennessee,[2] and Arkansas; the clerk of the circuit court, in Maryland, Texas, and Mississippi; the county register or recorder of deeds, in North Carolina and Missouri; the county ordinary or his deputy, in Georgia; the county judge, in Florida; the county judge of probate, in Alabama and Oklahoma; the clerk of the probate court, in Arizona; the county clerk, in Kentucky; the clerk of the district court, in Louisiana; the municipal judge, in Porto Rico; and by the clerk of the supreme court of the District of Columbia.[3] As in Virginia, license must be obtained from the proper officer of the county where the woman resides, in Alabama, Florida, Mississippi, and West Virginia. The same is true in Georgia, if the woman is "resident in the state;" and in Kentucky, unless she is of full age or a widow, and the license is issued on her personal or written application, when it may be granted by any county clerk. But in Maryland and North Carolina license must be obtained in the county where the marriage is expected to occur; in Tennessee, either in the county in which the bride resides or in that where the marriage is to be solemnized; while in Louisiana, as aleady seen, it may be issued in the county where either the bride or the groom is domiciled. The statutes of the remaining states appear to have no definite provisions on this subject. The law of Porto Rico is very careful in this regard. "Persons desiring to contract

[1] In West Virginia, where there is no lay celebration, the form of license is as follows: "To any person licensed to celebrate marriages: You are hereby authorized to join together in the holy state of matrimony, according to the rites and ceremonies of your church or religious denomination, and the laws of the state of West Virginia, —— —— and —— ——. Given under my hand, as clerk of the county court of ——, this —— day of ——."— *Code* (1891), 607.

[2] When either person is under sixteen, a license will not be issued without written consent of parent or guardian: *Acts of Tenn.* (1899), 36.

[3] In Baltimore city license is issued by the clerk of the court of common pleas: *Code* (1888), I, 975; in St. Louis, by the city recorder: WRIGHT, *Report*, 49 n. *cc.*

marriage shall first present themselves before the municipal
judge of their domicile if they shall have the same domicile,"
or before that officer in their respective places of abode if
they have different domiciles; "and first being duly sworn,
shall be examined as to their legal capacities and incapaci-
ties to enter into matrimony." They must also sign a sworn
declaration of their names, ages, and professions, with those
of their parents, which the judge is required to record in his
"marriage book." Not until ten days after the examination
may the judge issue the license, or refuse it if on proper trial
any objection to the marriage is sustained; nor may he issue
it in case the persons have different domiciles until the other
judge "has forwarded to him a copy of the record made by
the other contracting party."[1] In Arkansas, Indian Territory, Tennessee, and until recently in Mississippi,[2] a bond in
a definite sum, conditioned that the parties may lawfully
marry, must be given by the person applying for the license.
The same is true for Alabama in the case of minors; and
also for Kentucky when the persons are unknown to the
clerk. In the other states, if demanded by the official,
oath or affidavit usually takes the place of bond. For solemnizing a marriage without proper license presented the
offender is very generally subjected to severe penalties.[3]

[1] *Rev. Stat. and Codes of Porto Rico* (1902), 807–9.

[2] The *Ann. Code of Miss.* (1892), 677 ff., is silent as to bond.

[3] In Missouri, failure to keep a record or solemnization without license is a misdemeanor. The transgressor must pay a fine of not exceeding $500, and in addition
he is liable to a civil action by the parent or other person to whom "services" are
due, to recover not more than $500: *Laws* (1881), 161; *Rev. Stat.* (1889), II, 1606; *ibid.*
(1899), I, 1037. In Alabama the fine is $1,000, one-half to the state and one-half to the
person suing: *Code* (1896), I, 829; in North Carolina, solemnization without license
or failure to make return is a misdemeanor, subject to a fine of $200, payable to any-
one who sues: *Code* (1883), I, 691, 692; in Kentucky, a fine of not more than $1,000, or
imprisonment from one to twelve months, or both: *Stat.* (1894), 766; in Arkansas, a
high misdemeanor and a fine of not less than $100: *Digest* (1894), 1127; in Tennessee,
a misdemeanor and a fine of $500: *Code* (1896), 1040–41; in Georgia, a fine of $500: *Code*
(1896), II, 223; in Virginia and West Virginia, forfeiture of bond: *Code of Va.* (1887),
557; *Code of W. Va.* (1891), 608; in Maryland, a fine of $100 to $500: *Laws* (1894), 124;
in Texas, a misdemeanor and a fine of $50 to $500: Act of June 5, 1900: *Gen. Laws,*

In every commonwealth, except South Carolina, Arkansas, and Indian Territory,[1] it is the duty of the person or society conducting the celebration to make a "return" thereof to the proper official, either in the county where the woman dwells or in that of the marriage.[2] This report must be submitted within a fixed period, which is one month (or thirty days) in Alabama, Louisiana, and Maryland; two months (or sixty days) in Texas, Virginia, North Carolina, and Arkansas; three months (or ninety days) in Kentucky, Missouri, and Mississippi; six months in Tennessee; twenty days in Arizona; ten days in Florida and the District of Columbia; two days in Porto Rico; while in Oklahoma return must be made "without delay." The return to the clerk may be by a separate certificate, as in Alabama, Virginia,[3] Mississippi, Porto Rico, and Maryland; or by "endorsement" or "certificate appended," as in North Carolina, Oklahoma, Georgia, Tennessee,[4] West Virginia, Florida, Texas, and Arizona; or on a "coupon" issued with the license, as in the District of Columbia.[5] New Mexico requires two reports a year, on the first days of July and

307. In the District of Columbia for marriage without banns or license each of the parties and the person solemnizing are liable to a fine of 500 pounds current money: *Comp. Stat.* (1894), 272; Moore, *Code*, 266.

[1] Arkansas and Indian Territory have a peculiar provision. The person obtaining a license is required to report "the same to the office of the clerk of the county court within 60 days from the date of such license; and if the same be duly executed and officially signed by some person authorized by law to solemnize marriage," the bond of the person so applying for the license shall be null and void, otherwise of full force: *Digest* (1894), 1129; *Ann. Stat. of Ind. Ter.* (1899), 510.

[2] Return is made to the judge issuing the license in Porto Rico; to the proper officer in the county where the marriage is celebrated in Missouri, Mississippi, and New Mexico; in all other cases, in the county where the woman resides.

[3] The Virginia law requires the clerk to deliver to the person entitled the license and also a certificate containing the names of the parties, date of the proposed marriage, etc. The person solemnizing is to return the license and the clerk's certificate, together with his own certificate of the time and place of the marriage: *Code* (1887), 556.

[4] This is the form of indorsement required by the Tennessee law: "I solemnized the rite of matrimony between the above (or within) named parties, on the —— day of ——, 18——."—*Code* (1896), 1039.

[5] *Comp. Stat.* (1894), 274, 273; Moore, *Code*, 267.

January, or a report "at every regular term of the probate
court for each county." In the District of Columbia every
minister celebrating marriage by license must "annually, in
the month of November, return on oath a list of the names
of the persons, and the time when married," to the clerk of
the supreme court.[1] Mississippi has provided for bringing
delinquents to account. The clerk is directed "to examine
the records once a month, and if any . . . . person be found
in default, he shall institute inquiry," at the cost of the culprit, summoning him to make return of the certificate
according to law.[2] Similarly, in Missouri it is enacted that
the recorder of deeds "shall certify to the grand jury, at each
regular term of the court having criminal jurisdiction within
the county, a list of all marriage licenses issued by him,"
but not returned within the legal period of ninety days; the
negligent minister or officer being guilty of a misdemeanor
and liable to a fine of from five to twenty-five dollars.[3] Only
in two cases is there provision for report of the marriages of
residents celebrated without the state. By the statutes both
of Virginia and West Virginia a certificate or statement of
such contracts verified by any person present at the ceremony
"may be returned" to the clerk of the court of the county
where the husband resides, or if he be not a resident, then
where the wife dwells; and the usual abstract of it must be
recorded by the clerk.[4]

In a few instances the law directly provides for giving a
certificate to the newly wedded pair; although where the law
is silent the same may sometimes be done by custom when
request is made. Maryland, Porto Rico, Missouri, and the
District of Columbia have authorized such a certificate;[5]

---

[1] *Comp. Stat.* (1894), 273.   [2] *Ann. Code of Miss.* (1892), 678.

[3] *Rev. Stat. of Mo.* (1889), II, 1605: *ibid.* (1899), I, 1037.

[4] *Code of Va.* (1887), 557; *Code of W. Va.* (1891), 608; *ibid.* (1900), 656, 657.

[5] *Code of Md.* (1888), I, 975, 976: *Laws of Mo.* (1895), 222; MOORE, *Code of D. C.*
(1902), 267: *Rev. Stat. and Codes of Porto Rico* (1902), 810.

and Arkansas has enacted that after the license has been returned to the clerk, and by him duly recorded, he shall at once make out a certificate of such record, attach it to the license, and send it back to the person who presented the same.[1]

The southern and southwestern states have in general taken far less pains than those of New England to provide by law for a full record of marriages and for collecting, registering, and publishing the important social statistics connected with family life. In fact, there is much less completeness regarding essential details throughout the entire field of matrimonial legislation. New Mexico, Missouri, and Kentucky appear to be the only states or territories which require every person solemnizing marriages to keep a record; although the Quakers of Maryland, as already seen, must enter the contracts by them solemnized in their own records, or in the records of some court, city, or county where the wedding occurs; and both Alabama and Mississippi require marriages performed by the pastors of any religious society to be registered in a book kept for the purpose.[2]

Everywhere[3] the clerk or other officer must keep a register of the facts entered in the license, sometimes with other data; and usually the original license is placed on file. The laws of Virginia and West Virginia, being practically the same, are perhaps more complete and more wisely drawn as regards registration than those of any other state of this group. In Virginia the clerk is required to keep three books, to be called respectively the register of marriages, the register of births, and the register of deaths. At the time of issuing a license he is to ascertain, as nearly as may be, the date and place of the proposed marriage, the full names

---

[1] *Digest of Ark.* (1894), 1129.

[2] *Code of Ala.* (1897), I, 828; *Ann. Code of Miss.* (1892), 678.

[3] Except apparently in Tennessee.

of the parties, whether they are single, widowed, or divorced,[1] the place of their birth and residence, the names of their parents, and the husband's occupation. Within twenty days after return of the license and certificate by the person solemnizing, the clerk is to record a full abstract thereof in his marriage register, setting forth the facts in convenient tabular form.

These two states have also provided for the collection of statistics from coroners, heads of families, and physicians; and, like Kentucky and Arkansas, they have established state systems of registration. On or before the first of March annually the clerk or other official in every county is required to submit to the state auditor of public accounts a full report of the facts contained in his marriage register; and every year the auditor is to prepare an abstract of the county reports and submit it to the general assembly at each regular session.[2]

III.   THE MIDDLE AND WESTERN STATES[3]

a) *Solemnization.*—For half a century after the Declaration of Independence New York abstained from any legislation regarding the marriage celebration. The optional civil

[1] Act of Feb. 3, 1900: *Acts* (1899-1900), 283, 284.

[2] In West Virginia "the registration of births, marriages, and deaths of white and colored shall be kept separate and distinct."—*Code* (1900), 659. *Cf. Ky. Gen. Stat.* (1887), 204; *Digest of Ark.* (1894), 320, 321; *Code of Va.* (1887), 130, 558.

For the entire discussion of matrimonial administration in these states, as above given in subsec. *c*), compare *Code of Ala.* (1897), I, 827 ff.; *Rev. Stat. of Ariz.* (1887), 371, 372; *Digest of Ark.* (1894), 1126 ff.; *Rev. Stat. of Fla.* (1892), 679 ff.; *Code of Ga.* (1896), II, 221 ff.; *Kentucky Stat.* (1894), 765, 766; *Rev. Civil Code of La.* (1888), 60 ff.; *Code of Md.* (1888), I, 975 ff.; *Ann. Code of Miss.* (1892), 677, 678; *Rev. Stat. of Mo.* (1899), I, 1035 ff.; *Comp. Laws of N. M.* (1897), 403 ff.; *Code of N. C.* (1883), I, 690-92; *Code of Tenn.* (1884), 609-11; *Gen. Laws of Tex.* (1891), 96; *Rev. Civil Stat. of Tex.* (1888), I, 877, 878; *Code of Va.* (1887), 555-60; *Acts* (1900), 283, 284; *Code of W. Va.* (1900), 654 ff., 934; also *Acts of Leg.* (1887), chap. 64; *Ann. Stat. of Ind. Ter.* (1899), 507 ff.; *Session Laws of Oklahoma* (1897), 208 ff.; *Comp. Stat. of D. C.* (1894), 270-75.

[3] In this section the laws of the following twenty-five districts and states are considered: Alaska, California, Colorado, Delaware, Idaho, Illinois, Indiana, Iowa, Kansas, Michigan, Minnesota, Montana, Nebraska, Nevada, New Jersey, New York, North Dakota, Ohio, Oregon, Pennsylvania, South ¿Dakota, Utah, Washington, Wisconsin, and Wyoming.

or ecclesiastical ceremony was still allowed as in the provincial era. In the meantime acts were passed for the punishment of bigamous and other unlawful unions; and in 1813 the statute-maker felt himself called upon to deal with the same hard case of conscience which had long before troubled the people of Virginia and Massachusetts. It was decreed that "every negro, mulatto, or mestee within this state, who is now a slave for life, shall continue such . . . . unless manumitted according to law; and the . . . . baptizing of any slave shall not be deemed . . . . a manumission." All marriages contracted "wherein one or more of the parties was, were, or may be slaves, shall be considered equally valid" as if they were free; but here also it is carefully provided that nothing in the law shall be construed so as to cause the bondman to be manumitted.[1]

The revised statutes of 1827–28 contain a general "title" regulating matrimony which in many respects forms the basis of the existing law. "For the purpose of being registered and authenticated" marriage shall be solemnized only by the following persons: (1) ministers of the gospel and priests of every denomination; (2) mayors, recorders, and aldermen of cities; (3) judges of the county courts and justices of the peace. Quakers and Jews may "continue" to use their own rites. Record of marriage certificates is provided for; and in place of license or banns—neither of which is mentioned—the person performing the ceremony is authorized to identify the parties, if either is a stranger, by the oath of some person whom he knows.[2] The existing law contains a similar provision. Under like circumstances the minister or magistrate must ascertain from the applicants their right to contract marriage, and for that purpose he may examine one or both of them, or any other person under

[1] Act of April 9, 1813: *Laws of New York* (1813), II, 201, 202.
[2] *Rev. Stat., Passed 1827-28* (Albany, 1829), II, 139, 140.

oath, "which examination shall be reduced to writing and subscribed by the parties."[1]   Throughout the century the law regarding celebration has remained unchanged in general character, although authority to perform the ceremony has been extended to other officials and magistrates.[2] The state steadily maintained the validity of marriages entered into by simple agreement without any formal celebration.   It was enacted in 1887 that the provisions of the statute shall not be "construed to require the parties to any marriage, or any minister or magistrate to solemnize the same in the manner "therein prescribed;" but all lawful marriages contracted in the manner heretofore in use in this state, shall be as valid as if this article had not been passed."[3]

The usual evils followed: but an effective remedy seems at last to have been provided.   By an act of April 11, 1901, a marriage must be solemnized either (1) by a clergyman or minister of any religion, or the leader of the Society for Ethical Culture in the city of New York; (2) a mayor, recorder, alderman, police justice, or police magistrate of a city; (3) a justice or judge of a court of record or municipal court, or a justice of the peace; or (4) by "a written contract of marriage signed by both parties, and at least two witnesses who shall subscribe the same, stating the place of residence of each of the parties and witnesses and the date and place of marriage, and acknowledged by the parties and witnesses in the manner required for the acknowledgment of a conveyance of real estate to entitle the same to be recorded.   Such contract shall be filed within six months after its execution in the office of the clerk of the town or city in which the

---

[1] A false statement of either person is punishable as perjury: *Laws* (1873), chap. 25, pp. 19, 20; also in *Rev. Stat.* (1889), IV, 2597.

[2] To the leader of the Society for Ethical Culture in the city of New York and the justices and the judges of all courts of record: *Laws* (1888), chap. 78, pp. 122, 123, superseding an amendment to *Rev. Stat.* (1829) authorized by *Laws* (1887), chap. 77, pp. 89, 90, and *Laws* (1877), chap. 430; *Rev. Stat.* (1889), "supplement" in IV, 2596, 2597.

[3] *Laws* (1887), chap. 77, p. 90; also in *Rev. Stat.* (1889), IV, 2598.

marriage was solemnized." After the first day of January, 1902, no marriage claimed to have been contracted otherwise than in this article provided "shall be valid for any purpose whatever." The act, however, declares the validity of every lawful union formed "in the manner and pursuant to the regulations" of a religious society to which either person belongs.[1] Thus with the beginning of the new century the "common-law" marriage appears to have finished its long course in New York state.

The statutes of that commonwealth relating to contract or solemnization are extended to Indians residing in the state; although it is especially provided that those "who have heretofore or shall hereafter contract marriage according to the Indian custom or usage, and shall cohabit as husband and wife, shall be deemed lawfully married. Indian marriages may be solemnized by peace-makers within their jurisdiction with the same force and effect as by a justice of the peace."[2]

For New Jersey the first matrimonial law of the period under review is that of March 4, 1795, repealing an act of March 24, 1719. By this law every justice of the peace and "every stated and ordained minister" in the commonwealth is given power to perform the wedding ceremony; and, in addition, every religious society is permitted to employ its own usage in the marriage of its members; but such contracts are to be recorded in the same way as those before a minister or magistrate.[3] Amendments were made from time to time down to 1882, when an act appears which in nearly all of its leading provisions is still in force.[4] Marriage may now be solemnized in the state by every judge of a court of

---

[1] *Laws of N. Y.* (1901), II, 933-35.

[2] Act of May 18, 1892: *Rev. Stat.* (supplemental volume, 1892), V, 3742.

[3] *Laws of the State of N. J.* (1800), 158, 159.

[4] *Pub. Laws* (1882), 203; retained in *Gen. Stat. of N. J.* (1896), II, 2005. See for earlier acts amended *Pub. Laws* (1877), 168.

common pleas; any justice of the peace,[1] mayor, recorder, or police justice; and by every stated and ordained minister of the gospel. In addition, every religious society in the state may join together in wedlock persons one or both of whom are its members; and by a later enactment authority is conferred upon the chief justice and the associate justices of the supreme court, the chancellor and every vice-chancellor of the equity courts, in as full measure "as if the marriage were solemnized by a stated and ordained minister of the gospel."[2] The marriage of a minor may not be solemnized without certificate of parental consent, whose genuineness must be proved by the oath of at least one witness of full age and discretion.[3]

Pennsylvania has shown remarkable conservatism in her regulation of the marriage celebration. After two centuries, the act of 1701, taking its form in that of 1693, is with slight alteration still in force. It contains no precise designation of the persons who may perform the ceremony. Its spirit is revealed in the dictum of George Fox, elsewhere quoted: "We marry none, but are witnesses of it." Self-betrothal and self-*gifta*, as in early mediæval days, are still practiced by the Quaker descendants of the ancient Teutons. In 1885 a statute expressly authorizes a man and a woman to solemnize their own marriage.[4] This provision and a later requirement of license in all cases are the only legislative changes affecting the celebration since 1730, when certificate of parental consent was demanded. Now, as in 1701, the bride and groom, taking each other by the hand, are permitted to plight their vows in the presence of at least twelve witnesses, one of whom being a justice of the peace;

---

[1] A justice of the peace may solemnize a marriage out of the county for which he is commissioned: Pearson v. Howey, 6 HALSTED, *N. J. Reports*, 12.

[2] Act of June 13, 1890: *Pub. Laws* (1890), 439; *Gen. Stat.* (1896), II, 2006.

[3] *Pub. Laws* (1889), 139; *Rev. Stat.* (1896), II, 2005.

[4] *Laws* (1885), No. 115, sec. 1.

although the courts have decided, as indeed they could hardly fail to do, that this provision is merely "directory" and not mandatory;[1] for the original enactment declares that it shall not extend "to any that marry in their own society in the absence of a justice of the peace."[2] Such is the liberty permitted by the law; but the practice of the majority of the people probably does not differ much from the common usage elsewhere in the United States. From an act of 1849, still retained in the statute-book, one may perceive who are the officers usually called upon to perform or witness the wedding ceremony. "Every person in whose care or profession may be found the record kept by any minister of the gospel, judge, alderman, or justice of the peace, of any marriage contract solemnized" by or before the same shall on application, and the payment or tender of a fee of fifty cents, deliver to the applicant a full transcript of such record, with a proper certificate of its correctness.[3]

There is a sharp contrast between the broad liberalism of Pennsylvania and the narrow, even reactionary, policy of Delaware, whose territory also once formed a part of the proprietary domain of William Penn. The act of January 29, 1790, is decidedly retrogressive. Its keynote is pitched in the preamble, "Whereas," we are assured, "matrimony is an honorable institution of Almighty God, designed for the mutual convenience and happiness of mankind; and sober, discreet, and advised union of persons in matrimony is the duty of every good citizen, and the unadvised, clandestine, loose, and unseemly proceedings in marriage, tend to introduce a contempt and irreverent regard for that holy institu-

---

[1] Rodebaugh *v.* Sanks (1833), 2 Watts, 9; Fulkerson *v.* Day (1881), 15 *Phila. Reports*, 638. The provision of 1701 requiring the justice to subscribe the publication (or certificate) is not obsolete: Helffenstein *v.* Thomas (1835), 5 Rawle, *Reports*, 209.

[2] Above, chap. xii, sec. iii.

[3] Act of April 10: *Laws of the Gen. Assembly* (1849), 549; retained in Pepper and Lewis, *Digest* (1896), II, 2879.

tion, and a dissoluteness of manners among the thoughtless
part of the community;" furthermore, since evils may arise
"to persons secretly and improperly uniting themselves
. . . . without knowledge of their parents, guardians, or
friends; and the causes are now removed, which rendered it
convenient to have marriages celebrated by justices of the
peace": therefore, under penalty of one hundred pounds lawful money for disobedience, it is declared that marriages between white persons may be celebrated only by "ministers
or preachers of the gospel, appointed or ordained according
to the rites and ceremonies of their respective churches, or
by the religious society to which they belong" according to
its established mode and usage.[1] Civil marriage was thus
completely abrogated, to be grudgingly restored only after
more than fourscore years.   Since 1874 the mayor of Wil-
mington has had a share in the matrimonial business, otherwise the law of 1790 still governs the nuptial celebration.[2]

The foundation of Marietta in 1788, and the subsequent
organization of the first territory of the United States, under
the ordinance of 1787, constitutes an event scarcely second
in significance to any in the whole course of American history.   It marks the beginning of distinctively western institutions, although these, especially as regards the local
political organisms, are in many respects predetermined and
molded by those of the two old middle states, New York and
Pennsylvania.[3]   The laws adopted or enacted for the region
of Ohio, both before and after that state was admitted to the
Union in 1802, form in principle and often in detail the
models or prototypes on which rest the legal systems of the

---

[1] Act of Jan. 29, 1790: *Laws of the State of Del.* (1797), II, 972, 973.

[2] *Rev. Stat. of Del.* (1874), 473; also in *Rev. Stat.* (of 1852, as amended to 1893),
594. By the act of Feb. 25: *Laws of Del.* (1875), 260, the mayor of Newcastle was
granted the same power, but it seems not to be continued in the present law.

[3] On the significance of the settlement of Marietta, and the influence of the
middle states and provinces, see HOWARD, *Local Const. Hist.*, I, 408, 411, 387, *passim.*

numerous commonwealths filling the vast expanse of territory stretching from the Alleghanies to the Golden Gate. This is surely true in general of the laws of marriage; although Ohio, in still clinging to the optional plan of civil license or oral ecclesiastical banns, has retained an archaic feature which finds little imitation in the other western states.

By a law of the Northwestern Territory in 1788, after banns, license, or notice by posting, persons may be joined in wedlock before any judge of the general court, or of the courts of common pleas in their respective districts, or before a minister of any religious society or congregation where he is settled; and the Quakers are especially guaranteed the enjoyment of their peculiar rites.[1] Four years later the same authority is granted to all justices of the peace.[2] In 1803 a new act appears. Now justices of the peace may perform the ceremony in their proper counties; Quakers and Menonists may use their own rites; and every "ordained" minister of any society or congregation is given the same authority, on presenting his credentials to the county court of common pleas,[3] and receiving a license to that effect. But the function of such minister is no longer restricted to his own congregation; he may act anywhere in the state.[4] The law was thus practically complete. Under the present statute of Ohio[5] any ordained minister after obtaining a license from the county judge of probate; any justice of the peace in his county; any religious society "agreeably to the rules and regulations of their respective churches;" or the mayor of any city or incorporated village, in the county where it wholly or partly lies, is authorized to join persons

---

[1] Act of 1788: CHASE, *Stat. of Ohio and the Northwestern Ter.*, I, 101, 102.

[2] Act of Aug. 1, 1792: CHASE, *op. cit.*, I, 126.

[3] After 1810, at any rate, it is the county court of common pleas: CHASE, *op. cit.*, I, 672 (1810); II, 1211 (1822), 1407 (1824); SWAN, *Stat. of Ohio* (1853), 569–71.

[4] Act of April 4, 1803, repealing the two preceding laws: CHASE, *op. cit.*, I, 354, 355.

[5] *Ann. Rev. Stat. of Ohio* (1897), II, 3016.

in wedlock. A clergyman still has authority throughout the state; but since 1822, in each case, before he may legally act, it is necessary to exhibit his license to the court of the county where he intends to solemnize a marriage.[1] When the marriage is of a minor, without the authority of a license, the person solemnizing is required to satisfy himself that banns have been duly published, and that the consent of parent or guardian has been obtained.[2]

Indiana, admitted to the Union in 1816, Illinois in 1818, Michigan in 1837, and Wisconsin in 1848, were all included in the "Territory northwest of the Ohio," and, so far as they had inhabitants, were therefore originally affected by the laws and government established under the ordinance of 1787. Gradually, as each portion became a separate territory or an independent state, the early statutes, already considered in connection with Ohio, were retained, modified, or superseded. So far as the marriage celebration is concerned, the course of history in Indiana and Illinois need not here be dwelt upon. In the former commonwealth the ceremony may now be conducted by all ministers of the gospel and priests of every denomination, throughout the state; by judges of all courts of record, justices of the peace, and mayors of cities, within their respective counties; and by the Friends and German Baptists according to the rules of those societies. But no marriage, legal in other respects, is deemed void "on account of the incapacity of the person solemnizing the same."[3] The present law of Illinois shows several variations. The ceremony may be performed either

---

[1] The act of June 11, 1822: CHASE, *op. cit.*, II, 1211, requires the minister to produce his license to the clerk of the county court of common pleas, who shall "enter the name of such minister upon record as a minister of the gospel duly authorized to solemnize marriage within the state, and shall note the county from which said license" was issued. At present the license must be presented to the county court of probate.

[2] *Ann. Stat. of Ohio* (1897), II, 3017; *cf.* WRIGHT, *Report*, 56, 57.

[3] *Laws of the State of Ind.* (1897), 129 (act of March 4, 1897).

by a minister of the gospel in regular standing with the
church or society to which he belongs; by a judge of any
court of record; a justice of the peace; any superintendent
of a public institution for the education of the deaf and
dumb in the state; or, if either of the persons is a member
of the "religious society known as Friends or Quakers, they
may be lawfully married by making known their intention
. . . . to a standing committee of an official meeting, at
least one week before said marriage . . . . and by appearing
in a public meeting or private gathering, before official
witnesses of said body, with a certificate duly setting forth"
their names and residences, with those of the parents, if
living.   This certificate, duly signed by the contracting
persons and by the official witnesses, must be publicly read
by one of the witnesses, and afterward entered in the records
of an organized meeting of the society.   In addition, the
law guarantees every religious society the use of its own
rites.[1]

By the first marriage law of Michigan Territory, adopted
in 1805 from the statutes of Massachusetts, so "far as is necessary and suitable to the circumstances," the wedding ceremony may be performed by justices of the peace and regular
ministers of the gospel, when at least one of the persons
marrying is an "inhabitant" or "resident" of the district
where such clergyman or magistrate dwells; and there is the
usual clause securing to all religious societies their peculiar
usage or customs.[2]   In 1820 the contemporary law of Ohio
was adopted, authorizing celebration, after license, banns, or
posting, by justices of the peace in their own counties, or by
ministers of the gospel in regular communion with any
society of Christians according to the forms of the church to

---

[1] Act of May 30: *Laws* (1881), 112; retained in HURD, *Rev. Stat.* (1898), 1068; *cf.*
Rev. Stat. (1845), 343.

[2] Act of Aug. 2, 1805: *Laws of the Ter. of Mich.* (1871-84), I, 30 (from the "Wood-
ward Code"): repeated in the "Cass Code" (1816): *ibid.*, I, 202, 203.

which they respectively belong.[1] The same privilege is expressly ·reserved to Quakers and Menonists in 1827;[2] while in 1832 "ordained ministers" in regular communion with their societies, "but not otherwise," may perform the ceremony, provided their credentials are first entered "of record" with the county clerk.[3] The present statute is in substance nearly the same, except that the "ordained" minister, who "continues to preach the gospel" in the state, is not required to file his credentials as by the earlier acts. Non-resident clergymen are also authorized to perform the ceremony in the state, provided a proper record be kept and a return duly made according to law; but in all cases the person conducting the celebration is commanded first to examine at least one of the persons on oath as to the legality of the intended contract.[4]

Wisconsin, whose law on the subject has been but slightly altered since 1839, authorizes solemnization by justices of the peace or court commissioners in the counties where they are elected; and throughout the state by any judge of a court of record, or by a minister or priest in regular communion with any religious society, so long as he continues to preach the gospel. Since 1851 Minnesota has had a similar statute; except that court commissioners are not mentioned, and instead the superintendent of the department for the deaf and dumb in the Deaf, Dumb, and Blind Institute of the state is given authority. In both Minnesota and Wisconsin Quakers, on complying with the law as to return of certificate, are permitted to use their own forms;[5] a min-

---

[1] Act of 1820: *Laws of the Ter.*, I, 646, 647.

[2] Act of April 12, 1827: *Laws of the Ter.*, II, 412-14.

[3] Act of May 31, 1832: *Laws of the Ter.*, III, 914, 915.

[4] Act of July 31: *Laws* (1873), 20; also in HOWELL, *Gen. Stat.* (1882), II, 1619, 1620. It is expressly provided that marriage may be solemnized on Sunday: *ibid.*, I, sec. 2015; and in certain extreme cases the county judge of probate may perform the ceremony: see the acts of 1897 and 1899, referred to in subsec. *c*) below.

[5] But if the marriage among Quakers "does not take place in such meeting, such

ister, before being empowered to act, is required to file a copy of his credentials of ordination with the clerk of the court in some county, and receive from him a proper certificate thereof; and the magistrate or other person performing the ceremony may in all cases examine at least one of the parties on oath as to the legality of the intended marriage.[1]

In the remaining fifteen western states, not yet considered, there is relative uniformity regarding the law of celebration. Originating even as organized territories in recent years, these commonwealths have profited by the experience of the older communities whence their people have mainly come, and so there has been less reason for experimentation. The history of their marriage laws in general is therefore less eventful. Everywhere the optional civil or religious celebration is recognized. (1) In all cases justices of the peace are authorized to conduct the solemnization. Occasionally, as in Alaska, North Dakota, Oregon,[2] Nevada, and Washington, their power is expressly confined to their respective counties or districts; elsewhere no such restriction appears. (2) Everywhere without exception the judges or justices of the

---

certificate shall be signed by the parties, and at least six witnesses present, and filed for record " with the county clerk: *Gen. Stat. of Minn.* (1894), I, 1266; the same in *ibid.* (1866), 408; and nearly the same in *ibid.* (1851), 271, 272.

[1] The basis of the Wisconsin law of solemnization may be found in the *Stat.* (1838-39), 139, 140, giving authority to justices of the peace in their counties, to judges and commissioners of the supreme court, and to ordained ministers; and containing the provision regarding the filing of credentials with the clerk of the district court. See also *Rev. Stat.* (1849), 391-93, and *ibid.* (1858), 616-18; including the same provisions regarding celebration as *Ann. Stat.* (1889), I, 1354-56, except that the present authority for court commissioners in the counties is conferred by act of March 13, 1871: *Gen. Laws*, 99.

The Minnesota Law in *Rev. Stat. of the Ter.* (1851), 270-72, is practically the same regarding the celebration as in *Gen. Stat. of the State* (1866), 406, except the provisions in the latter regarding oath and credentials; and the law of 1866 is retained in WENZELL AND LANE, *Gen. Stat.* (1894), I, 1264-66, except that the provisions for solemnization by the superintendent of the deaf and dumb appear in *Laws* (1885), chap. 38, p. 47. Licentiates are also required to take out a certificate: *Gen. Laws* (1901), 285.

[2] The justice of the peace is not expressly given authority by the Oregon law; but in effect he is authorized by the general clause allowing " any judicial officer" to act within his proper jurisdiction: *Codes and Stat.* (1902), II, 1682.

higher courts of record are granted authority, although the particular courts named vary considerably from state to state. Thus, in Colorado, Kansas, Nebraska, and Wyoming the statute simply allows any "judge" to perform the ceremony; while in North Dakota the same power is bestowed upon every judge of a "court of record," and in Alaska and Oregon, on any "judicial officer" within his proper jurisdiction. It is granted to judges of the district courts, in their respective districts, in Nevada; to judges of the supreme and district courts, in Montana and Utah; to these same magistrates and to judges of probate, in Idaho; to the justices of the supreme court and the judges of superior courts, in California and Washington; to the justices of the supreme court and the judges of the circuit or county courts, in South Dakota; and to these same judges and to those of the district courts, in Iowa. (3) Throughout these states, in every instance, all ordained ministers, priests, or preachers of the gospel, duly authorized by the usages of their respective churches or societies, are allowed to celebrate matrimony; but there is wide diversity in the phraseology of the statutes. Their power is not limited to a particular place, but may be exercised anywhere in the state. Only in one case among these fifteen states, Nevada, is the clergyman required to exhibit his credentials and take out a formal license. Sometimes, as in Kansas, Nevada, and North Dakota, the Friends are expressly permitted to observe their own rites; or, as in California, Iowa, Nebraska, Montana, Washington, and the two Dakotas, there is a general clause in the law favoring all religious societies having peculiar methods of celebration. City mayors are allowed the same authority as magistrates and ministers in Iowa, Montana, Idaho, Utah, and South Dakota. By the law of the last-named state, as in New York, Indians are permitted to marry according to their own forms; and in the West, during the earlier stage of development, the governor has sometimes been granted authority to join persons in wedlock, such being the case formerly in Nevada and still in Idaho.

California, like New York, South Dakota, Wisconsin, Minnesota, and some other states, requires special precautions on the part of the person performing the ceremony, tending to prevent illegal or clandestine unions. He must first demand the "presentation of the marriage license; and if he has any reason to doubt the correctness of its statement of facts" as to identity of the persons, their names, ages, and places of residence, or the consent of their parents or guardians in case of minors, he must satisfy himself of the same; and "for that purpose he may administer oaths and examine the parties and witnesses in the like manner as the county clerk does before issuing the license." Idaho has a similar law; and that of Colorado allows the minister or magistrate, in case of minors having no parents or guardian, to perform the ceremony or not, according to his own judgment.[1]

The statutes of many of the middle and western states require the presence of witnesses at the celebration. One witness is sufficient in South Dakota,[2] as formerly in Dakota Territory; but two witnesses must attend in Alaska, Michigan, Montana, Minnesota since 1851, Idaho since 1864, Nebraska since 1867, Nevada since 1861, North Dakota since 1890, Oregon since 1854, Washington since 1866, Wisconsin since 1849, and Wyoming since 1869. New York requires one witness when the celebration takes place before a minister or a magistrate, and two witnesses when the marriage is by a written contract. The statutes sometimes contemplate the presence of witnesses when in terms it is not

---

[1] Deering, *Codes and Stat. of Cal.* (1886), II, 25, 26; *Rev. Stat. of Idaho* (1887), 302; Mills, *Ann. Stat. of Col.* (1891), II, 1681.

[2] The solemnizer is required to ascertain the "name and place of residence of the witness, or two witnesses, if more than one is present": *Ann. Stat. of S. D.* (1899), II, 1022.

prescribed.   Such is the case, for example, in New Jersey and California.[1]   In Pennsylvania the provision of 1701 requiring the attendance of twelve witnesses has not been expressly repealed; but, as already remarked, it is construed by the courts as being merely "directory," and "it has been ascertained that the requirement is no longer enforced. Two witnesses must be present" in that state "when any marriage is solemnized by the parties themselves."[2]

No definite formula for the celebration is anywhere pre-scribed.   Sometimes the statute contains a statement to that effect.   Thus in Alaska, California, Idaho, Michigan, Min-nesota, Nebraska, Nevada, North Dakota, South Dakota, Oregon, Pennsylvania, Washington, Wisconsin, and Wyo-ming it is expressly provided that no particular form for the ceremony is required, but the parties must solemnly declare in the presence of the person officiating, and usually of the attending witnesses, that they take each other as husband and wife.   The same is true of New York, if the ceremony is performed by a magistrate; but when a clergyman officiates, it may be "according to the forms and customs of the church or society to which he belongs."[3]   In the case of Quakers or religious societies having as such any peculiar mode of cele-brating marriage, the law usually provides, as already seen, that the ceremony or other mode of joining in wedlock shall be in accordance with their customs; and "where not so stated it is, of course, implied."[4]

[1] Witnesses are mentioned in the form of return to be made by the solemnizer: Gen. Stat. of N. J. (1896), II, 2006: DEERING, Codes and Stat. of Cal., II, 26, 27.

[2] WRIGHT, Report, 57.

[3] On witnesses and the form of ceremony see DEERING, Codes and Stat. of Cal. (1886), II, 26 (form); Rev. Stat. of Idaho (1887), 302; HOWELL, Gen. Stat. of Mich. (1882–90), II, 1619, 3602; Gen. Stat. of Minn. (1894), I, 1265; ibid. (1866), 407; Rev. Stat. of Minn. (1851), 271; Comp. Codes and Stat. of Mont. (1895), [477; Comp. Stat. of Neb. (1899), 757; Comp. Laws of Nev. (1900), 113; Rev. Stat. of N. Y. (1889), IV, 2597; same in ibid. (1827–28), 139, 140; Codes and Gen. Laws of Ore. (1892), II, 1319; same in Gen. Laws (1862), 86: Ann. Codes and Stat. of Wash. (1897), I, 1175, 1176; Rev. Stat. of Wyo. (1899), 791; Rev. Stat. of Wis. (1849), 392; also in Ann. Stat. of Wis. (1889), I, 1355.

[4] Cf. WRIGHT, Report, 56.

The laws of Montana, South Dakota, and formerly those of Idaho and California, contain a peculiar definition of matrimony and a provision for contract by "declaration," which, taken together, in effect allow persons to solemnize their own marriage, and to do so clandestinely, if they see fit. So by the California statute, as it stood from 1873 to 1895, marriage is defined as a "personal relation arising out of a civil contract, to which the consent of parties capable of making it is necessary. Consent alone will not constitute marriage; it must be followed by a solemnization, or by a mutual assumption of marital rights, duties, or obligations." Furthermore, "consent to and subsequent consummation of marriage may be manifested in any form, and may be proved under the same general rules of evidence as facts in other cases." "Persons married without the solemnization provided for" in the law "must jointly make a declaration of marriage substantially showing: 1. The names, ages and residences of the parties; 2. The fact of marriage; 3. That the marriage has not been solemnized. If no record of the solemnization of a marriage heretofore contracted be known to exist, the parties may join in a written declaration . . . . , substantially showing: 1. The names, ages, and residences of the parties; 2. The fact of marriage; 3. That no record of such marriage is known to exist." This declaration must be "subscribed by the parties and attested by at least three witnesses." These provisions are essentially vicious; and they gave rise to the so-called "contract" marriages, famous in California judicial history, the most notorious case being that of Sharon v. Sharon, which in its various phases was for years before the state and federal courts.[1] So great were

[1] Sharon v. Sharon, 67 Cal. (1885), 185 ff.; 75 Cal. (1888), 1-78; 79 Cal. (1889), 633-703; 84 Cal. (1890), 424 ff. For other cases of "contract" marriages under the code of 1873, see Kelly v. Murphy, 70 Cal. (1887), 560; Kilburn v. Kilburn, 89 Cal. (1891), 46; People v. Beevers, 99 Cal. (1893), 286; Toon v. Huberty, 104 Cal. (1894), 260; People v. Lehman, 104 Cal. (1894), 631; Hinckley v. Ayres, 105 Cal. (1895), 357. From 1849 to 1873 common-law marriages were good in California: see Graham v. Bennett, 2 Cal.

the evils of clandestine marriages, and the resulting conflicting and often false claims to property or inheritance
under this law, that in 1895 a tardy remedy was sought in
legislation.   Section 75 of the code, as above quoted, allowing a declaration of marriage, was repealed outright.   The
definition in sec. 55 was amended to read, "Consent alone
will not constitute marriage; it must be followed by a solemnization authorized by this Code;" and for the future sec. 57,
instead of its former dangerous terms, declares that "consent
to a marriage and solemnization thereof may be proved
under the same general rules of evidence as facts are
proved in other cases."[1]

Fourteen states of the middle and western group have
provided that when a marriage has been solemnized by a
person professing to be authorized, but not authorized by
law for that purpose, its validity is "not affected by such
lack of authority, if it is in other respects valid and consummated with the belief of the parties, or either of them,
that they have been lawfully married."[2]   These states are
Idaho, Indiana, Michigan, Minnesota, Montana, New York,
Nebraska, North Dakota, Nevada, Oregon, Utah, Washington, Wisconsin, and Wyoming.   In all cases the person
falsely representing himself to have authority is made liable

---

(1852), 503; Letters v. Cady, 10 Cal. (1858), 530; Case v. Case, 17 Cal. (1861), 598; People
v. Anderson, 26 Cal. (1864), 130; estate of Charles Beverson, 47 Cal. (1874), 621; estate
of McCausland, 52 Cal. (1878), 568; in re Briswalter, 72 Cal. (1887), 107; White v. White,
82 Cal. (1890), 427.   The facts in the four cases last mentioned arose before 1873.

[1] DEERING, Codes and Stat. of Cal. (1886), II, 18, 19, 20, 27; amended by act of
March 26, 1895: Stat. and Amendments to the Codes (1895), 121.   Compare the present
law of South Dakota: Ann. Stat. (1899), II, 1018, 1022; Rev. Codes of S. D. (1903), 596;
and that of Montana: Comp. Codes and Stat. (1895), 475, 477, 478, which in the definition delares that consent "must be followed by a solemnization, or by a mutual and
public assumption of the marital relation."   In the use of the word "public" the
present law of Montana differs from that of California previous to 1895.   Formerly
the laws of Idaho and California were identical; but now the provision for declaration is omitted from those of Idaho, although the prescribed celebration is not
essential to a valid marriage.   Cf. Comp. and Rev. Laws of Idaho (1875), 642, 645; Rev.
Stat. (1887), 301.

[2] Want of authority to solemnize does not avoid a marriage: State v. Brecht, 41
Minn., 50, 54; 42 N. W. Rep., 602; Martin v. Ryan, 2 PINNEY, Wis. Reports, 24.

to severe penalties.[1] California requires that "marriage must be licensed, solemnized, authenticated, and recorded;" but it is not invalidated by non-compliance with the law "by other than the parties" themselves.[2] Idaho, Montana, and South Dakota have similar statutes, although the act of the parties is not thus excepted.[3] In Iowa "marriages solemnized, with the consent of parties, in any other manner" than presented by the statute, "are valid; but the parties thereto, and all persons aiding or abetting them, shall forfeit to the school fund the sum of fifty dollars each; but this shall not apply to the person conducting the ceremony, if within ninety days thereafter he makes the required return to the clerk of the district court."[4] In Indiana "no marriage shall be void or voidable for want of license or

[1] For unauthorized solemnization and the penalty see *Rev. Stat. of Idaho* (1887), 303, 761: a misdemeanor punished by confinement in the county jail not exceeding six months, or a fine of not more than $300, or both; *Laws of Ind.* (1897), 129 (March 4); *Rev. Stat.* (1896), I, sec. 2148: a fine of $50 to $500, to which may be added imprisonment in the county jail for from ten days to three months; HOWELL, *Gen. Stat. of Mich.* (1883), II, 1620: a misdemeanor punishable by imprisonment in the county jail of not more than one year, or a fine of $50 to $500, or both; *Gen. Stat. of Minn.* (1894), I, 1266: a misdemeanor, with not over one year's imprisonment, or a fine of not exceeding $500, or both; *Comp. Codes and Stat. of Mont.* (1895), 477; *Comp. Stat. of Neb.* (1899), 757: a misdemeanor, with not more than one year in jail, or a fine not to exceed $500; *Comp. Laws of Nev.* (1900), 114: a fine of not more than $500, or imprisonment till paid; *Codes and Gen. Laws of Ore.* (1892), II, 1320–22; I, 967: not more than one year in jail, or a fine of $100 to $500; and the same penalty for illegal solemnization and for illegally issuing a license by the clerk; *Rev. Stat. of Utah* (1898), 331; *Laws* (1888), 90: not exceeding three years in the state prison, and the same penalty for false personation of parent or guardian, or for forging a certificate of consent; *Ann. Code of Wash.* (1897), I, 1175, 1178; *Ann. Stat. of Wis.* (1889), I, 1356: not exceeding one year in jail, or a fine of not more than $500, and the same for illegal solemnization, making false certificate, or for false personation; *Rev. Stat. of Wyo.* (1899), 791, 792: a misdemeanor, and the same penalty as in Wisconsin for unauthorized solemnization, which is prescribed also for false certificate or false record by the clerk; *Ann. Rev. Stat. of Ohio* (1897), II, 3017: imprisonment for six months, or a fine of $500, or both; *Laws of N. D.* (1890), 278: a misdemeanor with fine of $100 to $500 and costs, or imprisonment in the county jail for from three months to one year.

[2] *Amendments to the Civil Code* (1895), chap. 68.

[3] *Rev. Stat. of Idaho* (1887), 302; *Comp. Codes and Stat. of Mont.* (1895), 476; *Stat. of S. D.* (1899), II, 1020.

[4] *Code of Iowa* (1897), 1124; same in *ibid.* (1860), 428. *Cf. ibid.* (1851), secs. 1474, 1475. Thus the common-law contract is good: see Blanchard *v.* Lambert, 43 *Ia. Reports*, 228.

other formality required by law, if either of the parties thereto believed it to be legal marriage at the time."[1] The person solemnizing, in Colorado, is protected by the duly issued license, if he has no personal knowledge of the incompetency of the parties.[2] In Ohio, "when the person who solemnized the marriage had no license, it was held that it was to be inferred that the parties openly and mutually consented to a contract of present marriage;" and when they thereafter cohabited as husband and wife, "this consent constituted a legal marriage, and the man having then a wife living might properly be convicted of bigamy."[3]

b) *Forbidden degrees: void and voidable marriages.*— Nineteen out of the twenty-five middle and western states have each provided a statutory definition of marriage.[4] In Oregon, Indiana, and in Washington since 1854, it is defined briefly as a civil contract; in Alaska it is a civil contract which may be entered into by males of twenty-one and females of eighteen years, if otherwise capable; in Colorado and Kansas it is "considered in law" as a civil contract to which the consent of the parties is essential; in Iowa[5] since 1851, Nebraska since 1855, and Wyoming since 1869, it is

[1] HORNER, *Rev. Stat. of Ind.* (1896), II, sec. 5330; BURNS, *Ann. Stat.* (1901), III, 705.

[2] MILLS, *Ann. Stat. of Col.* (1891), II, 1680. The *Gen. Laws of Col.* (1877), 613, show the exigencies of pioneer life in the provision that "all marriages which have been solemnized in this state, whether by any president or judge of any mining district, elected under and acting by the laws thereof," shall be valid. So in Oregon by an act of Jan. 17, 1854 (*Stat. of Ore.*, 494), marriages contracted, with the consent of the parties, "when their residence is remote from any person duly authorized to solemnize such marriage, in any other manner than is prescribed, shall be valid; Provided that no legal impediment shall exist thereto; such contracts shall be made in writing duly attested, and shall be recorded in the office of the recorder of deeds of the proper county, within sixty days."

[3] Carmichael *v.* State, 12 *Ohio Reports*, 553.

[4] On the definition of marriage see Smith *v.* Smith, 17 *N. Y. Rep.*, 76; and on marriage as a question of status, Sewall *v.* Sewall, 122 *Mass.*, 156; Watkins *v.* Watkins, 135 *Mass.*, 84.

[5] "Marriage is a civil contract, requiring the consent of the parties capable of entering into other contracts, except as herein otherwise noted."—*Code of Iowa* (1897), 1123; *cf. ibid.* (1851), sec. 1464; *ibid.* (1873), sec. 2186.

a civil contract to which the consent of parties capable in law of contracting is necessary; in Michigan, Minnesota since 1866, Nevada since 1861, New York[1] since 1828, and Wisconsin since 1849, "so far as its validity in law is concerned," it is a civil contract under the same conditions as in the last-named group of states.   On the other hand, several commonwealths have sanctioned a definition which seems to imply the element of status in the marital relation.   Thus by the laws of Idaho, Montana, South Dakota, California, and North Dakota, marriage is a personal relation, arising out of a civil contract to which the consent of parties capable of making it is necessary.   In North Dakota, although marriage is a personal relation so arising, it must be "entered into, maintained, annulled, or dissolved" only as provided by law; and in California, since the reform of 1895, consent must be followed by a solemnization authorized by the code. Moreover, in South Dakota the consent to a marriage "must be to one commencing instantly, and not to an agreement to marry afterwards."   The law of Ohio is similar;[2] and in Idaho and California neither party to a nuptial contract is "bound by a promise made in ignorance of the other's want of personal chastity, and either is released therefrom by unchaste conduct" of the other, unless both participated therein.[3]

In all the states of the group under review, except in Colorado, New Jersey, and Pennsylvania, the age of consent to marriage is fixed by the law, or it may be inferred from its provisions.   For males it is twenty-one in Alaska and

[1] "Marriage, so far as its validity in law is concerned, shall continue in this state a civil contract, to which the consent of parties capable in law of contracting, shall be essential."— *Rev. Stat. of N. Y.* (1827–28), II, 138; *cf. ibid.* (1889), IV, 2595.

[2] "Mutual promises to marry in the future, though made by parties competent to contract, and followed by cohabitation as husband and wife, is not, in itself, a valid marriage."—Duncan *v.* Duncan, 10 *Ohio Reports*, 181.

[3] *Rev. Stat. of Idaho* (1887), 302; DEERING, *Codes and Stat. of Cal.* (1886), II, sec. 62, p. 24: act of March 30, 1874, *Amendments* (1873–74), 185.

Washington;[1] eighteen in California, Delaware,[2] Idaho,[3] Indiana, Michigan, Minnesota, Montana, Nebraska, Nevada, New York, Ohio, Oregon, South Dakota, Wisconsin, and Wyoming; seventeen in Illinois; sixteen in Iowa,[4] North Dakota,[5] and Utah;[6] and only fifteen in Kansas. For females it is eighteen in Alaska, Washington, Idaho, and New York; sixteen in Delaware, Indiana, Michigan, Montana, Nebraska, Nevada, Ohio, and Wyoming; fifteen in California, Minnesota, Oregon, South Dakota, and Wisconsin; fourteen in Illinois, Iowa, and Utah; thirteen in North Dakota; and only twelve in Kansas.

The age below which the consent of parent or guardian is required for the marriage of a minor is prescribed in all cases, except in Alaska, Kansas, New York, and Michigan.[7]

[1] The *Ann. Codes and Stat. of Wash.* (1897), I, 1174, fixes the age when marriage may be contracted at twenty-one for males and eighteen for females; but elsewhere provision is made for written consent of parent or guardian before license may be issued to persons below these ages respectively: *ibid.*, I, 1177.

[2] It is provided by the *Rev. Code of Del.* (1874), chap. 75, sec. 1, "that a divorce may be granted in case the parties were, when married, below the ages specified (eighteen and sixteen), and did not voluntarily ratify the marriage after arriving at those ages;" and this is retained in *Rev. Stat.* (1893), 596. *Cf.* WRIGHT, *Report*, 30.

[3] From 1864 to the act of Feb. 7, 1889, in Idaho, the ages of consent were respectively eighteen and sixteen for males and females; but in the last-named year eighteen was fixed as the age for both sexes: *Laws* (1863-64), 613: *Gen. Laws* (1889), 40.

[4] Below the ages of sixteen and fourteen in Iowa "marriage is a nullity or not, at the option of the minor, made known at any time before he or she is six months older than said ages."—WRIGHT, *Report*, 30; see *Code of Iowa* (1897), 1123; *ibid.* (1873), sec. 2186.

[5] North Dakota shows a retrogression. By the *Rev. Code* (1895), 608, the ages of consent to marriage are sixteen and thirteen: the same by the act of March 20, 1890: *Laws*, 276; which act had been superseded by that of March 9, 1891, *Laws*, 228, 229, which is in turn repealed by the act of 1895. Still earlier the laws of Dakota Territory had fixed the ages at eighteen and fifteen respectively: *Code of Dakota* (1883), sec. 36, p. 743; at sixteen and fourteen on May 7, 1862: *Gen. Laws* (1862), 390; and at fourteen and thirteen in 1866: *Civil Code* (1865-66), 11. By this last act the marriage of a woman under fourteen might be annulled, if contracted without consent of parent or guardian, and not followed by cohabitation, nor ratified after the girl attained that age.

[6] Formerly the ages in Utah were fourteen and twelve: *Laws* (1888), 88-91; they were fixed at sixteen and fourteen respectively for males and females by the act of March 11, 1897: *Laws*, 40.

[7] Solemnization against law as to age and parental consent does not invalidate: Parton *v.* Hervey, 1 *Gray*, 119, 122; Holtz *v.* Dick, 42 *Ohio Reports*, 791. In Kansas, 1859-67, the ages were twenty-one for males and eighteen for females: WEBB, *Gen. Stat.* (1897), II, 939, note.

Such consent must precede the granting of license; or, where the license system has not been adopted, it must be made known by certificate or otherwise to the person or society conducting the celebration before the ceremony may be performed.[1]   In all cases, save the three named, the age for males is twenty-one, except in Idaho, where it is eighteen. For females it is eighteen in all these states, except in Idaho, where it is sixteen; and in Pennsylvania and Wyoming, where it is twenty-one.   Formerly in Delaware indented servants could not lawfully marry without the master's consent; and for so doing such persons offending must "serve their respective masters or mistresses six months after the time of their servitude by indentures or engagements has expired; and if any person being free, shall marry with a servant without such consent . . . . he or she . . . . shall pay to the master or mistress of the servant, if a man, ten pounds, and if a woman, five pounds; and the servant so married shall abide with the master or mistress according to indenture or engagement six months as aforesaid."[2]   Later the penalty for a free person marrying a servant, if a man, was fixed at thirty dollars, of if a woman, at fifteen.[3]

All the states under consideration have legislated concerning forbidden degrees of consanguinity.   Relations in the direct line, with brothers and sisters, are, as elsewhere, always included; although many of the newer states and some of the older, have not thought it necessary to continue the solemn farce derived from ancient ecclesiastical usage of specifically interdicting wedlock with a grandparent or with a grandchild; and sometimes the connections by affinity are

[1] In Oregon a license may be issued for the marriage of a minor without such consent, when there is no parent or guardian resident in the state, if the female has lived in the county where the license is applied for during six months: *Codes and Gen. Laws* (1892), II, 1321; *Codes and Stat.* (1902), II, 1684.

[2] *Laws* (1797), II, 974.

[3] *Rev. Stat. of Del.* (1853), as amended (1893), 594.   This provision is now obsolete, though retained in the statutes.

not mentioned, or, as in Wyoming, they are expressly exempted from the inhibitions. Frequently, however, a man is denied the privilege of taking his step-mother or his mother-in-law to wife,[1] and in every state of the group, expressly or by implication,[2] marriage between aunts and nephews, or uncles and nieces, is forbidden. Minnesota since 1851, and Wisconsin since 1839, prohibit marriage between persons nearer of kin than first cousins, computing by the rules of the civil law; and in effect the same is true of Utah.[3] On the other hand, the statutes of Indiana, Ohio, Nevada, and Washington are more severe, allowing marriage only between persons "not nearer of kin than second cousins;" first cousins are likewise prohibited from intermarrying in Illinois, Kansas, Wyoming, the two Dakotas, Michigan, Pennsylvania, Oregon, and, apparently in Colorado;[4] while in Alaska marriages are prohibited within the fourth degree of the whole or the half-blood. But in no instance is a union between a sister-in-law or a brother-in-law interdicted. In all cases marriages within the prohibited degrees are both incestuous and void, except in Delaware, Minnesota, Oregon, Pennsylvania, Indiana, and South Dakota, where they are only void; in New Jersey, where they are only

---

[1] A marriage with a step-parent or parent-in-law is forbidden in Delaware, Iowa, Michigan, New Jersey, and Washington; apparently also in Pennsylvania. In the latter state marriages within the degrees of affinity, forbidden by the act of March 31, *Laws* (1860), 394, were legalized by the act of April 6, 1868; *Laws of the Gen. Assem.*, 67; or the same in PEPPER AND LEWIS, *Digest* (1896), II, 2884.

[2] Of course, such unions are included where marriage is expressly prohibited between persons nearer of kin than first or second cousins by the rules of the civil law.

[3] In Utah marriage is forbidden within, but not including, the fourth degree of collateral kinship according to the rules of the civil law. Originally Iowa had the same rule as Minnesota: *Code of Iowa* (1843), 434.

[4] First cousins are prohibited by act of March 10: *Session Laws of Col.* (1864), 108; the prohibition is retained in *Gen. Laws* (1877), 612; but omitted in *Gen. Stat.* (1883), 690, the change being made in *Session Laws* (1883), 243. But MILLS, *Ann. Stat.* (1891), sec. 1320, p. 931, declares the marriage of first cousins incestuous and void. See *Laws of Pa.* (1901), 597, for prohibition of marriage of first cousins; *Laws of Ore.* (1893), 41; *Codes and Stat. of Ore.* (1902), II, 1681.

voidable;[1] in Washington, where they are only incestuous; and in Ohio, where they are not expressly declared to be either incestuous or void. However, in the three states last named such unions are forbidden and punished; and in general for violation of the law by the persons contracting or the person solemnizing marriages declared void or voidable severe penalties are often imposed.[2] By exception, in Colorado, it is provided that nothing in the law regarding degrees "shall be so construed as to prevent the people living in that portion of the state acquired from Mexico from marrying according to the customs of that country."[3]

In these states the grounds for prohibiting wedlock other than kinship or affinity are as varied, confusing, and contradictory as in New England or the southern group. For the same cause a contract declared void in one state may be voidable or merely forbidden and punished in another. The statutes disclose a great diversity of conditional or qualifying clauses which render it almost hopeless to make any

[1] Such marriages are voidable in New Jersey, "and until dissolved by a court of competent jurisdiction must in all collateral proceedings, be treated as valid."— *Gen. Stat.* (1896), II, 2003. *Cf.* Boylan *v.* De Inzer, 18 STEWART, *N. J. Equity Reports*, 485.

[2] For example, in Colorado, knowingly contracting or solemnizing such a marriage is a misdemeanor subject to a fine of $50 to $500, or imprisonment from three months to two years, or both: MILLS, *Ann. Stat.* (1891), II, 1678; in Illinois incest is punished by imprisonment for not more than ten years, or twenty if the crime is that of father with daughter: HURD, *Rev. Stat.* (1898), 577; in Kansas, for contracting, solemnizing, or licensing a marriage within the forbidden degrees the offender is liable to a fine of from $100 to $1,000, or imprisonment for from three months to five years, or both: WEBB, *Gen. Stat.* (1897), II, 637; but elsewhere the law makes an incestuous marriage punishable by confinement and hard labor not exceeding seven years: *ibid.*, II, 301; in Ohio, persons nearer of kin than cousins committing fornication or adultery are liable to imprisonment for from one to seven years: BATES, *Ann. Stat.* (1897), III, 3220; in Utah, solemnizing a marriage within the forbidden degrees is punished by not exceeding three years in the penitentiary, or a fine of not more than $1,000, or both: *Rev. Stat.* (1898), 331; by *Laws* (1888), 91; in Washington the penalty for contracting is imprisonment in the penitentiary for from one to ten years: *Ann. Codes and Stat.* (1897), I, 1175; in North Dakota it is a misdemeanor, with imprisonment not more than six months, or a fine of not more than $500: *Laws* (1890), 276; but for incest the penalty is one to ten years in the penitentiary: *Rev. Codes* (1895), 1273; in Delaware, a fine of $100: *Rev. Stat.* (1893), 593.

[3] MILLS, *Ann. Stat. of Col.* (1891), II, 1678. On the Spanish laws and their effect see Smith *v.* Smith, 1 *Texas Reports*, 621; 46 *Am. Decis.*, 121, note, 130-34.

trustworthy generalizations.   Thus bigamous marriages are void or voidable by judicial decree in California, Delaware, Idaho, Indiana, Iowa, Kansas, Michigan, Minnesota, Montana, Nebraska, Nevada, New Jersey, New York, North Dakota, Oregon, Pennsylvania,[1] South Dakota, Utah, Wisconsin, and Wyoming; while in Colorado,[2] Illinois, Ohio, and Washington they are prohibited and made punishable.   In Michigan, Minnesota, Nevada, and Wisconsin the law applies only when the marriage was solemnized in the state; while in California, Idaho, Minnesota, North Dakota, New York, and South Dakota such unions are void or voidable unless, as expressed in the California statute, "the former husband or wife was absent, and not known to such person to be living for the space of five successive years immediately preceding such subsequent marriage, or was generally reputed or believed by such person to be dead" when the second marriage was contracted; "in either of which cases the subsequent marriage is valid until its nullity is adjudged by a competent tribunal."[3]   Illinois and Ohio have each a similar provision.[4]

On the abrogation of polygamy, Utah had a problem to

---

[1] Sec. 11 of the *Digest of the Laws of Pa.* (1883) provides that "in all cases where a supposed or alleged marriage shall have been contracted which is absolutely void by reason of one of the parties thereto having a husband or wife living at the time, the court of common pleas shall have power to decree the said supposed or alleged marriage to be null and void upon the application of the innocent or injured party;" and this provision is still in force: Pepper and Lewis, *Digest* (1896), I, 1634. Now, as in 1785, a bigamous marriage is a ground of divorce: *ibid.*, I, 1633. Myers, *Rev. Stat. of Ill.* (1895), 545, provides that "no divorce shall in any wise affect the legitimacy of children, except where the marriage shall be declared void on the ground of a prior marriage;" and Colorado has the same provision: Mills, *Ann. Stat.* (1891), I, 1035.

[2] A bigamous marriage is ground for divorce in Colorado: Mills, *Ann. Stat.*, III, 4341.

[3] See *Amendments to the Civil Code of Cal.* (1897), sec. 61. *Cf.* secs. 82-84 of Deering, *Codes and Stat.* (1886), II, 22, 28, 30. In New York the same exception is made when either spouse has been "finally sentenced to imprisonment for life": *Rev. Stat.* (1827-28), 139; *ibid.* (1889), IV, 2596.

[4] Bates, *Ann. Rev. Stat. of Ohio* (1897), III, 3220; Myers, *Rev. Stat. of Ill.* (1895), 445.

solve analogous to that of the southern states after the enfranchisement of the negroes. By an act of March 9, 1896, rights of inheritance were secured to the issue of bigamous and polygamous marriages; and a few days later, by general enactment, the children of such unions "heretofore contracted between members of the Church of Jesus Christ of Latter-day Saints, born on or prior to the fourth day of January," 1896, were legitimated.[1]

The laws of California, Idaho, Michigan, Minnesota, Nebraska, North Dakota, Oregon, South Dakota, Utah, Washington, Wisconsin, and Wyoming render a marriage void or voidable when entered into by either person through force or fraud;[2] those of New York,[3] when force, fraud, or duress has been practiced; and those of Nevada, when fraud has been proved.[4] In Colorado the marriage of a female obtained by force or fraud is prohibited and punished; in Iowa, Kansas, Montana, and Nevada, when obtained by force, menace, or duress; in Illinois, Montana, and New York, when the marriage of either person has been gained through false persuasion; while New Jersey, in more general phrase, treats as void the marriage of a female "against her will."

Marriages are also void or, usually, voidable when either person was of unsound mind, as in California, Idaho, or South Dakota; or insane or an idiot, as in Illinois, Indiana, Iowa, Kansas, Michigan, Nebraska, Utah, Wisconsin, and Wyoming;[5] or wanting in age or understanding, as in Indiana,

---

[1] *Laws* (1896), 128, 129, 271, 272.

[2] In Pennsylvania force or fraud in the marriage is a ground for divorce: PEPPER AND LEWIS, *Digest* (1896), I, 1635; *ibid.* (1902), II, 1830.

[3] STOVER, *Code of Civil Proced.* (1892), II, 1627.

[4] In Idaho, Michigan, Minnesota, Nebraska, New York, Oregon, Utah, Wisconsin, and Wyoming these marriages are not voidable when there has been subsequent voluntary cohabitation; in New York, Oregon, and Washington they are voidable only at the suit of the injured party; and in New York, only on a decree rendered during the lifetime of the parties.

[5] In Idaho a marriage is voidable for unsound mind, unless after the removal of the disability the parties freely cohabited; but in Iowa, when either party was

Kansas, Minnesota, Nevada, New Jersey, New York, Oregon, Washington, and Wisconsin;[1] or physically incompetent, as in California, Idaho, Iowa, Kansas, Montana, Nebraska, New Jersey, New York, Wyoming, and the two Dakotas;[2] or below age of legal consent, as in all the last-named states, and also in Michigan, Nevada, Ohio, Utah, Wisconsin, and Wyoming.[3]

Several states of this group, like those of the South, have attempted to check miscegenation by statute. Marriages between white persons and negroes or mulattoes are thus declared illegal and void in California,[4] Colorado, Dela-

impotent, insane, or an idiot, a marriage is not declared void by the statute, but provision is made for its annulment: McLAIN, *Ann. Code* (1888), I, 897. By the law of Michigan, such a marriage is voidable, if solemnized in the state; but there, as also in New York, Nebraska, and Wyoming, in case of lunacy, a marriage is not voidable when the parties have freely cohabited after the lunatic recovered.

[1] By the Indiana law such voidable marriages shall be declared void on application of the incapable party, and the children thereof shall be legitimate. The same is true in Kansas, but there cohabitation after incapacity ceases is a sufficient defense to the action for annulment. The law of Minnesota is similar. In Nevada and Nebraska a marriage is "not voidable for want of age, if after attaining the age of consent the parties for any time freely cohabited; nor for want of understanding, if after restoration to reason" they so cohabited. According to the New York statute a marriage is "not voidable on account of want of age at suit of the party who was of age of consent; nor where it appears that the parties after attaining such age freely cohabited; nor of a female under sixteen years of age if she had parental consent to the marriage," or when she ratified it after reaching that age. The law of Oregon is practically the same. In Michigan and Wyoming a marriage of persons below the age of consent is void if they separate during nonage and do not afterward cohabit.

[2] In Nebraska, New York, and Wyoming an action for annulment on the ground of impotence must be brought in two years; while for this cause in Colorado, Indiana, Illinois, Oregon, and some other states a "divorce" will be granted. Physical incapacity is cause for divorce in Michigan; and suit to "annul" a marriage on this ground must be brought within two years: MILLER, *Comp. Laws* (1899), III, 2664.

[3] By the Ohio law marriages "contracted by male persons under the age of eighteen and females under the age of fourteen [now sixteen] are invalid, unless confirmed by cohabitation after arriving at those ages respectively; and such marriage, not so confirmed, does not subject a person to punishment for bigamy for contracting a subsequent marriage while the first husband or wife is living": see Shafher *v.* State, 20 *Ohio Reports*, 1.

[4] California does not directly prohibit the intermarriage of whites and Chinese; but the county clerk is commanded not to "issue a license authorizing the marriage of a white person with a negro, mulatto, or Mongolian": DEERING, *Codes and Stat.* (1886), II, 25, sec. 69.

ware, and Idaho; and with negroes or Mongolians in Utah.
The prohibition of such unions in Nebraska extends to
persons having one-fourth, and in Indiana to those having
one-eighth, negro blood; while in Oregon since 1866 it has
been applied to those with one-half Indian or one-fourth
negro or Chinese blood in their veins.[1] In Nevada similar
unions, without specification of the degree of dark blood,
are forbidden and punished.   On the contrary, Michigan,
by an act of 1883, provides that "all marriages heretofore
contracted between white persons and those wholly or in
part of African descent are . . . . valid and effectual in
law for all purposes, and the issue" shall be deemed legitimate.[2]

Among the commonwealths of this group Delaware alone
has the honor of trying through legislation to put some limit
upon the increase of the indigent and incapable classes, the
marriage of paupers being forbidden under penalty.   Michigan has taken a still more important step in advance, setting
a worthy example of social legislation which ought to be
followed throughout the country.   By a stringent law of
1899, it is declared that no person afflicted with certain
syphilitic diseases "shall be capable of contracting marriage."
For so doing the transgressor shall be "deemed guilty of
felony and upon conviction thereof . . . . , shall be punished
by a fine of not less than five hundred dollars or more than
one thousand dollars, or by imprisonment in the state's
prison . . . . not more than five years, or by both such fine
and imprisonment in the discretion of the court."   Furthermore, it is especially provided that either husband or wife
may be examined as a witness; and in all cases arising under
the act a physician who has attended or prescribed for any

[1] Until *Laws of Ore.* (1893), 41, "Kanaka" blood was included in the prohibition.
Cf. Codes and Stat. (1902), II, 1681, 1682; I, 274.

[2] *Laws* (1883), 16; also in HOWELL, *Gen. Stat.* (1883), II, 1619; and retained in the
act of June 15: *Pub. Acts* (1899), 387.

person so affected "shall be compelled to testify to any facts found by him from such attendance."[1]

An enlightened policy in a parallel direction is revealed by a recent law of Minnesota, similar to that of Connecticut, prohibiting the marriage of persons either of whom is epileptic, imbecile, feeble-minded, or afflicted with insanity, when the woman is under forty-five years of age;[2] and Kansas has just enacted the same restraint.[3] On the other hand, in no instance, apparently, has any effort yet been made to prevent the clandestine marriage outside the state of residents who thus seek to evade the requirements of their own laws.[4]

Very generally, as elsewhere, indirect encouragement to matrimony is given by the suspension of prosecution or penalty, and through the legitimation of children. By the laws of Dakota and California, "every contract in restraint of the marriage of any person, other than a minor, is void;"[5] and the same is true in the latter state regarding conditions of ownership imposing like restraints; but this rule "does not affect limitations when the intent was not to forbid marriage, but only to give the use until marriage."[6]   In many

---

[1] *Pub. Acts of Mich.* (1899), 387, 388 (June 15). The law applies to "syphilis and gonorrhœa."

[2] "No woman under the age of forty-five (45) years or man of any age, except he marry a woman over the age of forty-five (45) years, either of whom is epileptic, imbecile, feeble minded, or afflicted with insanity, shall hereafter intermarry, or marry any other person within this state."—*Gen. Laws of Minn.* (1901), 334, 335.

[3] *Session Laws of Kan.* (1903), 373, 374.

[4] Except that in Delaware, if the parties to any marriage prohibited for consanguinity or affinity, or for miscegenation, "although the same may have been solemnized in another state, shall cohabit as husband and wife in this state, they shall each be deemed guilty of a misdemeanor and upon conviction thereof shall be fined $100."—*Rev. Stat.* (1893), 593.

[5] DEERING, *Codes and Statutes* (1886), II, sec. 1676, p. 311.

[6] *Ibid.*, sec. 710, p. 171; according to the amendment of March 30, 1874: *Amendments to Codes* (1873-74), 218. This provision "leaves no doubt but that the limitation of an estate to a widow so long as she remains unmarried is good;" and the "rules which govern a devise in restraint of a widow's marriage, apply to like devise in restraint of a widower's marriage: Bostwick v. Blades, 4 *Am. Law Rec.*, 729 (Md. Ct. of App.)." See EDITOR DEERING's valuable note in *Codes and Stat.*, II, 171, where cases are cited.

cases it is provided that marriages contracted out of the state are valid, if valid where they are formed; but Pennsylvania is the only commonwealth in the Union, except Georgia, directly promoting wedlock, her statute declaring that "all marriages not forbidden by the law of God shall be encouraged."[1]

c) Certificate and record.—The laws of the middle and western states have reached substantial harmony regarding the preliminaries of marriage. The provisions for license and the other leading features of matrimonial administration in their main features are much the same, except in a few of the older commonwealths, where the system of ecclesiastical

[1] The history of the various topics treated in this section *b*) for the several states may be traced as follows: (1) California: *Stat.* (1850), 424, 425; *Comp. Laws* (1853), 175–77; *Acts Amendatory of the Codes* (1873–74), 181 ff.; *Stat.* (1880), 121 ff.; DEERING, *Codes and Stat.* (1886), II, 18–37; *Amendments to Codes* (1895), 121; (2) Colorado: *Sess. Laws* (1861), 313; *ibid.* (1864), 108 ff.; *Gen. Laws* (1887), 611–13; *Gen. Stat.* (1883), 690–94; MILLS, *Ann. Stat.* (1891), II, 1675 ff.; (3) Delaware: *Rev. Stat.* (1893), 593, 594; (4) Idaho: *Laws* (1863–64), 613 ff.; *ibid.* (1864), 397; *ibid.* (1867), 71–73; *Comp. and Rev. Laws* (1875), 642–45; *Gen. Laws* (1889), 40, 278–80; *Rev. Stat.* (1887), 301–3; (5) Illinois: HURD, *Rev. Stat.* (1898), 630, 577, 1067–69; (6) Indiana: *Laws of the State* (1897), 129; *Indiana Stat.* (1896), II, secs. 5324 ff.; (7) Iowa: *Code* (1860), 747; *ibid.* (1873), 628; *ibid.* (1897), 1123–25, 1940; (8) Kansas: *Stat.* (1855), 488, 489; *Laws* (1857–58), 326; *Gen. Laws* (1859), 563, 564; *Laws* (1870), 157, 158; WEBB, *Gen. Stat.* (1897), II, 637 ff., 301, 339; (9) Michigan: *Laws of the Ter.* (1871–84), I, 30–32, 202, 203, 646–49; II, 412–14; III, 1191, 1192; HOWELL, *Gen. Stat.* (1882–90), II, 1618–20; *Comp. Laws of Mich.* (1899), III, 2645–52; (10) Minnesota: *Rev. Stat.* (1851), 270–72; *Gen. Stat.* (1866), 406–8; WENZELL AND LANE, *Gen. Stat.* (1894), I, 1264–66; (11) Montana: *Comp. Codes and Stat.* (1895), 474–78; (12) Nebraska: *Laws* (1855), 209–11; *ibid.* (1856), 150–52; *Stat.* (1867), 254–57; *Comp. Stat.* (1899), 756–58; (13) Nevada: *Laws* (1861), 93–96; *ibid.* (1867), 88, 89; *ibid.* (1881), 107, 108; *Comp. Laws* (1900), 112–15; (14) New Jersey: *Laws of the State* (1800), 158–60; *Gen. Stat.* (1896), II, 2003–6; I, 1064, 1066; (15) New York: *Rev. Stat.* (1829), II, 138–41; *ibid.* (1889), IV, 2596–98; STOVER, *Code of Civil Proced.* (1892), II, 1627, 1632 ff.; *ibid.* (1902), II, 1830–35; (16) North Dakota: *Laws* (1890), 276–79; *ibid.* (1891), 228, 229; *Rev. Codes* (1895), 608–11; *Revised Codes* (1899), 692–95, 1440, 1441, 1454, 1455; (17) Ohio: CHASE, *Stat. of Ohio and N. W. Ter.* (1833–35), I, 101, 102, 126, 354, 355, 672, 673; II, 1407, 1408; BATES, *Ann. Stat.* (1897), II, 3015–18, 2211; III, 3220; (18) Oregon: *Laws* (1843–49), 36, 80, 81; *Stat.* (1853–54), 492–94; *Code of Civil Proced. and Other Gen. Laws* (1862), 85–88; *Codes and Gen. Laws* (1892), II, 1317 ff.; I, 967; Act of Oct. 24, 1866: *Acts and Res.* (1866), 10, 11; (19) Pennsylvania: PEPPER AND LEWIS, *Digest* (1896), II, 2878–83; (20) South Dakota: *Stat.* (1899), II, 1018–25, 1917; *Rev. Codes* (1903), 596–99; (21) Utah: *Laws* (1888), 88–91; *Rev. Stat.* (1898), 329–31; (22) Washington: *Stat. of the Ter.* (1854), 404, 405; *ibid.* (1865–66), 80–85; *Ann. Codes and Stat.* (1897), I, 1174–78; II, 1952; (23) Wisconsin: *Stat. of the Ter.* (1838–39), 139, 140; *Rev. Stat.* (1849), 391–93; *Ann. Stat.* (1889), I, 1354–56; *Wis. Stat.* (1898), I, 1692–94; (24) Wyoming: *Rev. Laws* (1870), 458–61; *Rev. Stat.* (1887), 415–17; *ibid.* (1899), 790–92, 1213; (25) Alaska: *U. S. Statutes at Large*, XXXI, 494, 495. Laws since 1899 are cited in the previous footnotes.

banns and some other peculiar usages are still maintained. Thus in Delaware, by the act of 1790, no minister is allowed to conduct the ceremony without first receiving a license authorizing the persons to wed, or, instead, unless the banns shall "be published between such persons intending to marry, at some church, chapel, meetinghouse, or stationary place of public religious worship belonging to the district, or of the congregation wherein the woman so intending to be married shall be resident, or in the next adjacent congregation of the same society, on the two several Sundays before the celebration thereof, immediately after divine service." The license is granted by the president or commander-in-chief duly attested under his sign manual; and it is issued from the office of the secretary of state. "In order to avoid fraud and collusion in obtaining such license," the person applying is required to enter into bond with good security in such sum as the president shall judge proper.[1] All marriage licenses are to be lodged with the prothonotaries and justices of the peace of the respective counties, or with such of them as the secretary may think fit for convenience of the people, and these officers are required to submit a report every six months.[2] After a century the system thus outlined is still maintained in its essential features. License or banns, "published at some place of stated religious worship, within

[1] Following is the form of the marriage-license bond: "That if there shall not hereafter appear any lawful let or impediment, by reason of any precontract, consanguinity, affinity, or any other just cause whatsoever, but that (the parties) may lawfully marry; and that there is not any suit depending before any judge, ecclesiastical or civil, for or concerning such precontract, and also if the said parties, and each of them, are of the ages aforesaid, to wit, female of eighteen and male of twenty-one years, and are not under the tuition of his or her parents, or have the full consent of his or her parents or guardians, respectively, to the said marriage; and if they, or either of them, are not indented servants and do and shall save harmless, and keep indemnified the president and his successors, for and concerning the premises, and shall likewise save harmless and keep indemnified the minister or preacher of the gospel, who shall join the said parties in matrimony, for or by reason of his so doing; then the obligation to be void, else to remain in full force; which said bond shall be filed of record in the office of the secretary."—*Laws of Del.* (1797), II, 974, 975.

[2] By act of June 15, 1793: in *Laws of Del.* (1797), II, 1127, 1128.

the hundred of the woman's residence, on two Sabbaths immediately after divine service," is yet sanctioned. The requirement of bond is still retained.[1] It is the duty of the clerk of the peace to designate at least six justices of the peace in his county to dispense licenses; and the state derives a revenue of two dollars for each license issued. By a provision still appearing in the statute-book, though obsolete in practice, negroes or mulattoes may be married without license or publication of banns; provided "that each party (being free) shall produce the certificate of the justice of the peace of the county that such party has made before him satisfactory proof of freedom; or (being . . . . servant), shall produce the written consent of his master or mistress."[2]

The legislation of Ohio shows almost equal conservatism. For many years after the organization of the Northwest Territory a triple optional system of banns, license, or posting was there maintained. The law of 1788 requires that either on Sundays, holidays, or other days of public worship, in the towns where the bride and groom respectively dwell, the banns shall be thrice published; or that a written notice, under the hand and seal of a judge or a justice of the peace of the county, shall be affixed in some public place in such towns; or else a license shall be obtained from the governor authorizing the marriage without publication.[3] The details of the plan were changed in 1803. License is then to be obtained from the clerk of the court of common pleas for the county where the woman resides. Twice publication of banns, the first time ten days before the wedding; or notice by posting during fifteen days, is declared sufficient. In the case of minors a license may be issued only when consent of parent or guardian is personally given or certified to, attested by two witnesses, one of whom must personally appear and

---

[1] *Rev. Stat.* (1893), 103.   [2] *Ibid.*, 594; and *cf. ibid.* (1874), 473.

[3] CHASE, *Stat. of Ohio and the N. W. Ter.* (1833-35), I, 101.

make oath or affirmation that he saw the parent or guardian
subscribe or acknowledge the same.[1]   After 1824 provision
for public posting is no longer made,[2] thus reducing the
Ohio plan to the more familiar system of optional civil
license or ecclesiastical banns which still survives.   License
is now issued by the judge of probate in the county of the
female; and the law governing the consent of parent or
guardian in case of minors is identical with that of 1803,
except that since 1810 persons under age who have before
been married are not required to give evidence of such
approval.[3]

By the first matrimonial statute of Michigan in 1805 a
license system is not established; but evidence of parental
consent to the marriage of minors is to be presented to the
minister or magistrate performing the ceremony.   Within
one hundred days the latter is to return a certificate of the
celebration to a clerk of the court in the district where it
takes place, who is required to keep a record and report
annually to the clerk of the superior court of the territory.[4]
So the law remained until 1820, when the triple optional
system, as it then existed in Ohio, was introduced;[5] but this
is not found in the existing law, which requires license in
all cases according to the more common American usage.

Neither banns nor license has at any time been required
in New York during the century.   Instead, as already
pointed out, the person conducting the celebration is

[1] Act of April 4, 1803; CHASE, Stat., I, 354, 355.

[2] It is omitted in the act of Jan. 6, 1824: CHASE, Stat., II, 1407, 1408; nor does it
appear in SWAN, Stat. (1854), 569 ff.

[3] Ann. Rev. Stat. (1897), II, 3016.   Cf. the act of Feb. 16, 1810: CHASE, Stat., I, 672,
673.   See the act of April 25, 1898, requiring a statement under oath from persons
applying for license; also evidence of parental consent in case of minors; and allowing the parent or guardian, when non-resident, to appear before a judge of a court of
record in the county where he is domiciled, and give his consent in writing; such
written consent must be attested by two witnesses, certified to by the judge, and be
forwarded to the probate judge of the county where the license is to be issued: Laws
(1898), 309–11.

[4] Laws of the Ter. of Mich. (1871-84), I, 30–32.   [5] Ibid., I, 646–49.

authorized to identify the parties by examining them or any other persons under oath.[1] New Jersey has maintained a similar plan, except that non-residents are required to obtain a license from the county clerk five days before the wedding.[2] At present in case of minors the powers and procedure of the person solemnizing are substantially the same as those of the county clerk or other officer where the license system prevails.[3]

Pennsylvania has also followed methods peculiar to herself. From 1730 to 1885 certificate of parental consent seems to have been required for the marriage of minors; and such certificate was presented directly to the person or society conducting the celebration. By an act of the last-named year there was introduced a license system which in 1893 was modified so as to permit a license to be obtained from the clerk of the orphans' court, not only in the county where the marriage is to take place but also in the county of the residence of either the man or the woman.[4] The clerk is to keep a marriage-license docket, "in which he shall make a complete record of the issuing of said licenses, and all matters which he shall be required to ascertain, relative to the rights" of the persons to obtain a license, "together with their ages and residences." In getting a license the persons may proceed in one of two ways. "Either separately or together" they may apply directly to the clerk, who by oath or affirmation is authorized to inquire concerning the legality of the contemplated marriage, and if there be no legal objection, to issue the license; or in like manner, if they prefer, they may "appear before any magistrate, alderman, or

---

[1] *Cf. Rev. Stat. of N. Y.* (1827–28), 140: and *ibid.* (1889), IV, 2597.

[2] *Acts of N. J.* (1897), 378.

[3] See above, subsec. *a*) and *cf. Laws of N. J.* (1800), 158 (act of 1795) with *Gen. Stat.* (1896), II, 2005; *Pub. Laws* (1889), 139. The celebrant may administer an oath as to residence to either party; *Acts* (1900), 327, 328.

[4] See *in re* Marriage License Act, 15 *Pa. C. C.*, 345 (1894); and Pepper and Lewis, *Digest*, II, 2881, note.

justice of the peace of the township, ward or county, wherein
either . . . . resides, and in the county where the license
is desired, who may . . . . inquire of them touching the
legality of the contemplated marriage." These answers and
the replies, duly subscribed and sworn to before the officer,
may be forwarded to the clerk of the court, who if satisfied
therewith, and that no legal objection to the marriage exists,
may issue the license. But if either of the persons intending to marry is under the age of twenty-one, the consent of
parent or guardian, given personally or attested by witnesses
in the usual way, is necessary. The license shall have
appended to it two certificates, one marked "original" and
the other "duplicate." The certificate marked "original"
shall be given by the solemnizer to the persons married;
and the other must within thirty days be returned to the
clerk in the county of the celebration, to be filed of record.
It is, however, especially provided that in all cases where
the persons intend solemnizing their own marriage, the
clerk in "the proper county shall certify their right so to do
in a declaration in the following form": "Legal evidence
having been furnished to me, in accordance with the act of
assembly . . . . this certifies that I am satisfied that there
is no legal impediment to your joining yourselves together
in marriage." When self-*gifta* thus takes place, the persons contracting are required to make duplicate certificates
of their own wedding celebration, returning one of them to
the clerk, as in other cases provided by law.[1]

In the remaining nineteen states of this group not yet
considered, except Alaska, the simple license system has
been introduced. Save here and there in certain cases
specially provided for, a license is always required. Thus,
by the Minnesota law, "previous to persons being joined in

[1] *Laws* (1885), 146; *ibid.* (1893), 27; *ibid.* (1887), 170; PEPPER AND LEWIS, *Digest*
(1896), II, 2878-83.

marriage, a license shall be obtained from the clerk of the district court of the county in which the female resides," or, if she be not a resident of the state, then from the same officer "in the county where the marriage is to take place in the state;" but if there shall be no such clerk in either of the counties specified, no license is required. The clerk may inquire of the persons under oath as to the legality of the proposed marriage. If he "shall be satisfied that there is no legal impediment thereto," he shall grant a license and make a record thereof. Persons under age and not having had a former husband or wife must have the consent of the parents or guardians personally given or certified under their hands and seals, "attested by two witnesses, one of whom shall appear before said clerk, and make oath or affirmation that he saw said parent or guardian subscribe, or heard him or her acknowledge the same." If a "clerk shall in any other manner issue or sign any marriage license, he shall forfeit and pay a sum not exceeding one thousand dollars" to the persons aggrieved. The statute allows the clerk a fee of two dollars for each license issued.[1]

Similar powers and functions are exercised by the clerk of the district court in Iowa and Montana;[2] the county clerk, in California, Colorado, Illinois, Michigan,[3] Nevada, Oregon, Utah, Wisconsin, and Wyoming; the clerk of the

[1] *Gen. Stat. of Minn.* (1894), I, 1264, 1265.

Following is the form of license or "certificate" in Colorado: "Know all men by this Certificate, that any regular ordained minister of the Gospel authorized by the rules and usages of the Church or denomination of Christians, Hebrews, or religious body of which he may be a member, or any judge or justice of the peace to whom this may come, he not knowing of any lawful impediment thereto, is hereby authorized and empowered to solemnize the rites of matrimony between . . . . of . . . . of the county of . . . . Previously married ? . . . . Wife deceased ? . . . Divorced ? . . . . When ? . . . . Where ? . . . . On what grounds ? . . . . And . . . . of . . . . of the county of . . . . Previously married ? . . . . Husband deceased ? . . . . Divorced ? . . . . When ? . . . . Where ? . . . . On what grounds ? . . . . ."— MILLS, *Ann. Stat. of Col.* (1891), III, 828.

[2] Act of March 14, 1895: in *Comp. Codes and Stat.* (1895), 476.

[3] In Michigan a girl under eighteen must bring written consent of parent or guardian before license will be issued: *Pub. Acts* (1895), 536, 537.

circuit court, in Indiana and South Dakota; the probate judge, in Kansas and Ohio; the county judge, in Nebraska; the county auditor, in Washington; the county recorder, in Idaho; and by the judge of the county court, in North Dakota. The license is issued by such officer from the county of the woman's residence, in Indiana, Ohio, and Oregon; from the county where either the man or the woman resides, in Michigan; from the county where the marriage is to take place, in California, Idaho, Illinois, Iowa, Montana, Nebraska, North Dakota, South Dakota, and Wyoming; from the "proper" county, in Kansas; and from "any county," in Colorado; from "a county auditor" in Washington; the county where one or both of the persons dwell, or from any county when both are non-residents, in Nevada; from the county of the bride's residence, or, if she be a non-resident, from that of the proposed marriage, in Wisconsin and Minnesota; and in Utah, from the county where the female lives, provided that when she is a widow or of full age, and it is granted on her application, it may be issued from any county. In Kansas and Indiana a license is not required in the case of Friends marrying according to their own usage; and the same is true in Iowa, California, and South Dakota, for the members of "any particular denomination having, as such, any peculiar mode of entering the marriage relation." Wisconsin requires the license to be obtained not less than five days previous to the persons being joined in marriage; and has also provided for celebration without license in urgent cases. Upon the application of either party to a proposed marriage, any county judge, court of record, or presiding judge thereof, in his discretion, by order may authorize solemnization without license or the five days' notice. Such order must be delivered to the person performing the ceremony, who is to return it in place of or in connection with the license to the register of deeds or of vital statistics.[1] Michigan has likewise made provision for cases of emergency where social expediency seems to require exceptional rules. By a law of 1897, amended in 1899, entitled "an act to provide for the protection of the reputation and good name of certain persons," the judge of probate in each county is authorized to issue without publicity a license to any female who has lived with a man as his wife, or who for any other reason expressed in her application, deemed sufficient by the magistrate, "desires to keep the exact date of the marriage a secret, to protect the good name of herself and the reputation of her family."[2]

Generally throughout the region under discussion penalties by fine or imprisonment are prescribed for celebration without a license or for illegally issuing the same.

In every instance, except in Alaska, the person or society conducting the celebration is required to make a return to the officer authorized to receive it, either in the town or, usually, the county, where the license was issued, or in that of the marriage.[3] Such return is made either by separate

---

[1] Act of April 29: *Laws of Wis.* (1899), 529–31; *cf.* the act of 1903: *Laws*, 477, 478.

[2] The judge of probate must issue a license without publicity to a "female making application to him, under oath, containing a statement that she is with child, which if born alive before her marriage will become a bastard, or has lived with a man," etc. With consent of parent or guardian, such judge is empowered to marry persons under marriageable age, making such a statement, whenever he believes the marriage "would be a benefit to public morals." He is required to "file a complete set of all papers in each case in a private file, and shall within ten days after the marriage forward the duplicate thereof to the secretary of state, who shall file such duplicate in a private file and record the same in a private register." These private files of the probate judge and secretary of state "shall be open to inspection only upon the written order of the judge of any circuit or the supreme court of this state, and only for such use as is designated in such order. Such order shall be made only upon the written request of the person or persons who were so married, or when necessary to the protection of property rights arising from or affected by such marriage."—*Pub. Acts of Mich.* (1897), 230, 231; *ibid.* (1899), 363, 364.

[3] Return is made to the designated officer of the county (or town) where the license was issued, in Idaho (1899), Kansas, Michigan, Montana, Nebraska, Nevada (1899), and Utah; but where the marriage was solemnized, in California, Delaware, Illinois, Indiana, Minnesota, North Dakota, Washington, Wisconsin, Wyoming, and Iowa. The Pennsylvania act of 1893 requires the return to be made to the clerk of the orphans' court in the county where the marriage was solemnized; and this, doubtless, supersedes the law of 1885, which designates for this purpose the county from which license was issued, and which also appears in PEPPER AND LEWIS, *Digest*

certificate, by indorsement on the license, or by certificate
appended to it.   Several states, however, have enacted
special provisions.   In South Dakota, for example, the
marriage certificate must be "filed with the clerk of the
city or town where the marriage was solemnized, or where
either of the parties resides," or with the "register of deeds
of such county."   By the Colorado statute return is made
to the clerk issuing the license; and the solemnizer must
also send a report to the clerk of the county where the
marriage takes place.   In Iowa the person performing the
ceremony is to make return to the clerk of the district court;
and, "when the services of a clergyman or magistrate are
dispensed with, the husband must make the return."   California has enacted that "when unmarried persons, not
minors, have been living together as man and wife, they may,
without a license, be married by any clergyman.   A certificate of such marriage must be made and delivered by the
clergyman to the parties, and recorded upon the records of
the church of which the clergyman is a representative ;" and
"no other record need be made."   Furthermore, when
members of a religious society, having as such peculiar rites,
are married without a license, as the law permits, they must
join in a written declaration of the marriage, which shall be
signed by themselves and attested by at least three witnesses.
Within thirty days after the wedding this declaration must
be filed by the husband with the county recorder, who, after
it is duly acknowledged, shall record the same as in grants
of real property.[1]   New York requires that the certificate,

---

(1896), II, 2880, 2881, 2883. By the Ohio act of April 25, 1898, return is made to the
probate judge of the county where the license was issued, or where the congregation
in which publication of banns was made is located, or where the marriage was
celebrated: *Laws* (1898), 309-11. Of course, the county of issue of license and the
county of celebration are usually the same. In Oregon return is made both to the
county clerk issuing the license and to the clerk ₁of the county of the marriage:
General Laws (1903), 99, 100.

[1] *Statutes of S. D.* (1899), II, 1023; *Rev. Codes of S. D.* (1903), 598; MILLS, *Ann.
Stat. of Col.* (1891), II, 1679; *Code of Iowa* (1897), 1124, 1125; *Amendments to the Civil*

given to each of the married persons on request, signed by the officiating magistrate, shall be filed and recorded, if within six months it is presented to the clerk of the city or town where the marriage took place, or where either the bride or groom resided.   When it is a clergyman who conducts the celebration, his certificate thereof may in the same manner be filed and recorded, "if there be endorsed thereon or annexed thereto, a certificate of any magistrate residing within the same county with such clerk, setting forth that the minister is personally known to such magistrate, and has acknowledged the execution of the certificate in his presence;" or that the execution was proved to the magistrate by the oath of a witness known to him.[1]

By the rules prevailing in every state, save New Jersey, the official receiving the return must register or file the same of record.   The prescribed term within which the report of the celebration must be submitted is thirty days (or "one month") in California,[2] Colorado, Idaho, Illinois, Kansas, Minnesota, Montana, Nevada, New Jersey,[3] North Dakota, Ohio,[4] Oregon, Pennsylvania,[5] South Dakota, and Utah; ninety days (or "three months"), in Indiana, Iowa, Michigan, Nebraska, Washington, and Wyoming; and six months in New York.   South Dakota, in addition to the return by the solemnizer, provides that within six months after the

Code of Cal. (1873–74), 187; DEERING, Codes and Statutes (1886), II, 27, 28; Act of 1897: Amendments to the Civil Code, sec. 79½, p. 186.

[1] Rev. Stat. of N. Y. (1889), IV, 2598; the same in Rev. Stat. (1827–28), 140, 141.

[2] In California the original license, with the certificate of solemnization indorsed and attached must be filed with the county recorder in thirty days: DEERING, Codes and Stat. (1886), II, secs. 73, 74, pp. 26, 27; but, in addition, the state registration law requires every person solemnizing marriages to keep a "registry," and "quarterly" to submit to the county clerk a certified copy of it: ibid., I, secs. 3074, 3077, pp. 460, 461.

[3] So by the act of Feb. 15: Pub. Laws of N. J. (1888), 52 ff., as amended by that of March 29: Pub. Laws (1892), 351; both in Gen. Stat. (1896), II, 2011, 2012.

[4] The period within which the certificate must be returned to the probate judge was formerly ninety days: Ann. Stat. of Ohio (1897), II, 3017; but by the act of April 25, 1898, it is fixed at thirty days: Laws (1898), 309–11.

[5] By the act of March 1, 1893, amending that of June 23, 1885: PEPPER AND LEWIS, Digest (1896), II, 2880, 2881, 2883.

wedding the certificate given to the persons married may be
"filed" in the manner above described; and, when thus
filed, it must be entered in a book to be provided by the
clerk or register for the purpose.[1] By the Wisconsin law
the license, with a certificate of the marriage, must be
returned by the person conducting the celebration to the
register of deeds of the county where the license was issued,
provided that in cities of the first class the report shall be
sent to the registrar of vital statistics, who is to place it on
file.[2] In Delaware the person solemnizing must keep a
record and "annually, in March, deliver to the recorder of
deeds for the county, a true extract therefrom" of all entries
for the year preceding.[3]

Only in Wisconsin is there any provision for return when
the marriage of a resident takes place outside the state.

Provision for giving a certificate to the persons married,
on request or otherwise, is made by Alaska, California,
Idaho, Iowa, Michigan, Minnesota, Montana, Nebraska,
Nevada, New York, Oregon, Pennsylvania, South Dakota,
Washington, Wisconsin, and Wyoming. Creditable progress is also shown in a number of the states of this group
in providing for a proper record of marriages, and for the
collection, registration, and publication of social statistics.
Thus in California, Delaware, Idaho, Iowa, Michigan,
Nevada, New Jersey, New York, Ohio, South Dakota, and
Wisconsin the person conducting the celebration is required
to keep a record;[4] and everywhere, save in one instance, as
already seen, the clerk or other officer of the county or town
must register the facts contained in the license issued or the

---

[1] *Stat. of S. D.* (1899), II, 1021, 1023.

[2] A period within which the return is to be made does not seem to be fixed: Act
of April 29: *Laws of Wis.* (1899), 530.

[3] *Rev. Stat. of Del.* (1893), 594; practically the same in *ibid.* (1874), 472-74.

[4] The Pennsylvania act of 1849 requiring a transcript of the marriage record to
be given to the person applying therefor, on payment of the prescribed fee, still
appears to be in force: PEPPER AND LEWIS, *Digest* (1896), II, 2879.

certificate returned; and usually the original documents are filed for preservation.[1]   Moreover, a goodly number of commonwealths have wisely created systems of state registration which promise to be of great service in the future of American society.   Beginning in 1881, Delaware has established such a system.   The state board of health, composed of "seven physicians of skill," has general oversight, appointing one of its own number as secretary, who performs the duties of "superintendent of registration of vital statistics."   To him the recorders of the several counties are required to send information.[2]   An elaborate registration act was adopted in New Jersey in 1888; and this, as amended in 1892, is still in force.   Thirty days after the solemnization of any marriage a certificate thereof is to be sent to the proper officer, setting forth the "name, age, parentage, birthplace, occupation, and residence of each of the persons married, the time and place of the marriage, the condition of each of the persons married, whether single or widowed, the name of the minister, magistrate, or person by whom, or of the religious society before which the marriage was solemnized, and the names and residences of the witnesses."   The certificate is to be returned to the "registrar of vital statistics," or, if there be none, the clerk of any city, borough, town, or other municipal government, or to the assessor or clerk of a township.   These local officers are required each month to forward the certificates and the "special return" provided for by law to the state board of health, whose secretary is styled the "medical superintendent of vital statistics."[3]

[1] Both Oregon and Washington allow the solemnizer to keep the license, the clerk or auditor first recording the facts contained therein: *Codes and Stat. of Ore.* (1902), II, 1684; *Ann. Codes and Stat. of Wash.* (1897), I, 1177, 1178.

[2] See the act of April 7, 1881: *Laws*, XVI, chap. 381; act of March 13, 1879, amended and republished, April 11, 1893: *Rev. Stat.* (1893), 296–98, 405–8.

[3] Act of Feb. 15: *Pub. Laws of N. J.* (1888), 52 ff.; act of March 29: *ibid.* (1892), 351; *Gen. Stat.* (1896), II, 2006–12, 1634, 1635 (board of health); act of Feb. 27, 1901: *Acts of N. J.*, 36.

Ohio has a similar plan of local and state administration. The mayor of each of the smaller cities and villages, and six persons nominated by the council, including two medical practitioners, constitute a board of health which is authorized to appoint a health officer and "create a complete and accurate system of registration of births, marriages, deaths, and interments, for the purpose of legal and genealogical investigations, and to furnish facts for statistical, scientific, and sanitary inquiries." The secretary of state is required each year to prepare and submit to the general assembly a full and accurate report of the statistics of Ohio.[1] A system of state registration of births, marriages, deaths, and divorces has existed in Michigan since 1867. The secretary of state is required to furnish the clerks of the respective counties with suitable blank books for record and forms for reports. The reports of these local officials are to be properly bound and indexed under the direction of the secretary; "and with such assistance as may be voluntarily rendered by any authorized committee appointed by the medical faculty of the University of Michigan, or by any regularly authorized medical society . . . . , he shall prepare such tabular statements, results, and deductions therefrom as will render them of practical utility, and make report therof annually to the governor." But in reality this report, under the general direction of the secretary, is prepared and published by the secretary of the state board of health.[2]

As early as 1852 Wisconsin made provision for registration of births, marriages, and deaths; and the plan then adopted, with some modification, still exists. By a statute of 1897 the register of vital statistics in every city having

[1] The law does not apply to cities of the first class nor to those of the second class, Grades 1, 2, and 3a. Special provision is made for a board of health in Cincinnati (cities of the first grade of the first class) : BATES, Ann. Rev. Stat (1897), I, 97, 978, 979.

[2] Cf. act of 1867: Pub. Acts (1867), 266; that of 1869: ibid. (1869), 214; ibid. (1899), 67, 68; and HOWELL, Gen. Stat., 1, 96, 276-80, 464; Comp. Laws (1899), II, 1451 ff.

such an officer is required to keep a record of all marriages celebrated therein, in the same way as he does of births and deaths. To him the persons or societies conducting marriage celebrations are required to send certificates thereof; and every week these certificates must by him be forwarded to the register of deeds of the county or city. For the commonwealth the secretary of the state board of health, under the direction of the secretary of state, performs the same functions as discharged by that official in Michigan.[1]

Provision for similar registration, under authority of the state boards of health, is made by the laws of Indiana, Iowa, Kansas, Minnesota, and Pennsylvania. California has a similar statute. Careful provision is made for keeping registers of births by physicians and midwives; of deaths, by clergymen who officiate at funerals, coroners who hold inquests, sextons and undertakers who bury deceased persons; and by those who conduct marriage celebrations. Certified copies of all these registers are to be filed quarterly with the respective county recorders; and every three months these officials are required to transmit a "certified abstract" of their own registers to the secretary of the state board of health at Sacramento. This body consists of seven physicians appointed for four years by the governor; and at each biennial session of the legislature it is authorized to make a report, "with such suggestions as to legislative action" as it deems proper.[2]

The New York law is very careful and elaborate. There are local boards of health in towns, incorporated villages, and cities. In the town the board consists of the clerk and the justices of the peace, together with a "citizen" appointed by them; in the incorporated villages, of from three to seven

---

[1] *Cf. Acts* (1852), 763-69; *Rev. Stat.* (1858), 618-22; *Ann. Stat.* (1889), I, 648-52; *Laws* (1897), 373; *Wis. Stat.* (1898), I, 1055, 785 ff.

[2] DEERING, *Codes and Stat.* (1886), I, 442 ff., 460 ff.

members nominated by the village trustees. The village and town boards each hold office for one year, and each is authorized to appoint a "competent physician" to serve as "health officer," who, in the case of the village, may not be a member of the board. The city board is composed of six members, at least one of whom shall be a physician, all appointed by the common council. The board thus constituted is authorized to choose a president and to select a competent physician as health officer. The six members hold office for one, two, and three years, respectively, by pairs. It is made the duty of each of these local boards "to supervise and make complete the registration of all births, marriages, and deaths occurring within the limits of its jurisdiction in accordance with the methods and forms prescribed by the state board of health, and to secure the prompt forwarding of the certificates of birth, marriage, and death to the state bureau of vital statistics after local registration." To attain completeness in such registration, "it shall be the duty of the parents or custodians of every child, and the groom at every marriage, or the clergyman or magistrate performing the ceremony, to secure the return of the record of such birth or marriage to the board of health or person designated by them within thirty days from the date" of the same, "and each record shall be duly attested by the physician or midwife (if any) in attendance at such birth, or the clergyman officiating at such marriage." If in any place the state board of health ascertains that the registration is "not completely and well made," it may notify the delinquent local board that within one month such "defects and neglects in the records must be amended and prevented." If the abuses are not remedied within the period named, the state board is required to take control of the records, and to "enforce the rules and regulations" so as to make them complete.

The bureau of vital statistics has general charge of the

state system of registration, under direction of the state board of health. The latter body consists of three "state commissioners of health," appointed by the governor with the advice and consent of the senate, and six other members, three nominated by the governor, and three serving *ex officio*. It appoints a secretary who is "superintendent of registration of vital statistics;" and it makes an annual report to the governor regarding "vital statistics and the sanitary condition and prospects of the state."[1]

[1] *Cf.* the act for registration of births, marriages, and deaths: *Laws* (1847), chap. 152, repealed by *Laws* (1885), chap. 270; *Laws* (1880), chap. 322; and *Rev. Stat.* (1889), II, 1205, 1207, 1209, 1195-98 (state board), IV, 2610, 2611 (clauses relating to New York city).

In general, to trace the history of the topics treated in this subsec. *c*), consult the last note in subsec. *b*).